MANAGEMENT
CONCEPTS & PRACTICES

PEARSON
Education

We work with leading authors to develop the strongest
educational materials in business and management,
bringing cutting-edge thinking and best learning practice
to a global market.

Under a range of well-known imprints, including
Financial Times Prentice Hall, we craft high quality print
and electronic publications which help readers to understand
and apply their content, whether studying or at work.

To find out more about the complete range of our
publishing please visit us on the World Wide Web at:
www.pearsoned.co.uk

FOURTH EDITION

MANAGEMENT
CONCEPTS & PRACTICES

Tim Hannagan

With contributions from

ROGER BENNETT
RUTH BOADEN
LESLIE CHADWICK
DOMINIC COOPER
HELEN DAVIS
DAVID EDELSHAIN
LINDA GUNNELL
MIKE HARRY
LEN HOLDEN
KATE PRESCOTT
PETER A. STRACHAN
RICHARD WELFORD
MIK WISNIEWSKI

FT Prentice Hall
FINANCIAL TIMES

An imprint of **Pearson Education**
Harlow, England • London • New York • Boston • San Francisco • Toronto
Sydney • Tokyo • Singapore • Hong Kong • Seoul • Taipei • New Delhi
Cape Town • Madrid • Mexico City • Amsterdam • Munich • Paris • Milan

Pearson Education Limited

Edinburgh Gate
Harlow
Essex CM20 2JE

and Associated Companies throughout the world.

Visit us on the World Wide Web at:
www.pearsoned.co.uk

First published in Great Britain under the Pitman Publishing imprint in 1995
Second edition published 1998
Third edition published 2002
Fourth edition published 2005

ISBN 0 273 687689

British Library Cataloguing-in-Publication Data
A catalogue record for this book is available from the British Library

Library of Congress Cataloging-in-Publication Data

Hannagan, Tim.
    Management : concepts & practices / Tim Hannagan with contributions from Roger
Bennett ... [et al.].--34th ed.
        p. cm.
    ISBN 0-273-68768-9 (pbk.)
    1. Management. I. Bennett, Roger, 1944- II. Title.

    HD31.H316 2004
    658--dc22
                                                                    2004053296

10 9 8 7 6 5 4 3 2 1
09 08 07 06 05

Typeset by 30 in Stone Serif 9.5/12pt
Printed by Ashford Colour Press Ltd., Gosport

CONTENTS AT A GLANCE

CONTENTS

Section D

MANAGING THE ORGANISATION

Section E

MANAGEMENT ISSUES

Companion Website resources

Visit the Companion Website at **www.pearsoned.co.uk/hannagan**

For lecturers
- Complete, downloadable Instructor's Manual
- PowerPoint slides that can be downloaded and used as OHTs

LIST OF CONTRIBUTORS

Dr Roger Bennett, Reader, London Guildhall University (*Chapter 11*)

Dr Ruth Boaden, Senior Lecturer in Operations Management, Manchester School of Management, UMIST (*Chapter 14*)

Leslie Chadwick, Head of Work Experience Placements and Senior Lecturer in Accounting and Finance, Bradford University School of Management (*Chapter 16*)

Dominic Cooper, Chartered Psychologist and Professor of Safety at Indiana University, Bloomington, USA (*Chapter 12*)

Helen Davies, Senior Lecturer in Human Resource Strategies, London Guildhall University (*Chapter 11*)

David Edelshain, Senior Lecturer in International Business and Director of the Undergraduate Business Studies Degree programme at Cass Business School, London, and an Adjunct Professor at New York University in London (*Chapter 19*)

Linda Gunnell, Senior Lecturer in Human Resource Strategies, London Metropolitan University; and Private Consultant in Organisation and Senior Management Development (*Chapter 11*)

Dr Mike Harry, Senior Teaching Fellow in Management and Information Systems, University of Bradford Management Centre (*Chapter 15*)

Dr Len Holden, Principal Lecturer, Department of Human Resource Management, Leicester Business School, De Montfort University (*Chapter 10*)

Kate Prescott, former Lecturer in International Business, University of Bradford Management Centre (*Chapter 19*)

Dr Peter A. Strachan, Lecturer in Business Strategy and Environmental Management, The Robert Gordon University (*Chapters 17 and 18*)

Richard Welford, Professor of Business Economics, University of Huddersfield (*Chapters 17 and 18*)

Mik Wisniewski, Senior Research Fellow, Strathclyde Business School (*Chapter 13*)

PREFACE

Managers are facing increasingly rapid change in the technology, culture and environment in which they work. Rapid developments in the application of information technology are matched by equally rapid changes in the structure of organisations, in the role of managers and in the economy and society in which they operate. This puts pressure on management which helps to emphasise the importance of understanding both the concepts and practices involved. This new edition has been extensively rewritten and reorganised in order to reflect the latest changes in management thinking and practices.

The objective of this book is to analyse these management concepts and practices in all areas of management in order to provide an understanding of the way organisations are managed and an appreciation of the most recent developments in management theory and practice. This analysis, while being grounded in past experience, looks towards developments likely to take place in the future. A new chapter has been introduced in order to analyse the interface between private sector organisations and those in the public sector. This chapter highlights aspects of organisational culture, objectives and goals in both sectors and the differences in being a manager in the two sectors.

The book is intended for teachers and students on management and business studies programmes such as the Diploma in Management and MBA, first degree programmes, Higher National Programmes, and professional courses such as marketing, personnel and accounting. This general introduction to management is also important in engineering, building and construction, and project management as well as in many other areas of study and work.

This new edition brings the information in this book up to date and includes the very latest ideas on management development. For example, the chapter on information systems management includes a section on communications and the Internet and moves towards global computerisation, while the chapter on human resources management discusses recent legislation on equal opportunities and includes sections on sexual harassment in the workplace and on ageism.

The plan of the book provides an overview of its structure. All the chapters begin with a list of outcomes and give a summary of the main features covered in the chapter. Each chapter ends with questions for review and discussion. Case studies are included in the text and at the end of every chapter and provide a basis for further discussion and comment. A 'travel guide' or 'road map', which suggests routes through the book and different ways of using it, follows this preface, while this edition also includes new case studies. References to books, articles and websites are provided for each chapter in order to facilitate wider reading and research. The content of this book and the examples used in it are designed to provide both a European and international perspective. It has been produced to be user-friendly, and to appeal to undergraduates as well as graduates and post-experience managers on business, management and related professional programmes and courses. A *Lecturer's Guide* including questions on the case studies, answer points and additional materials is available free of charge to tutors and lecturers upon application to the publishers; this is also available on our website at **www.pearsoned.co.uk/hannagan**.

It is argued that the basic function of managers in the modern economy, and in the future, is the management of change. This is the underlying theme of the book. Chapters have been contributed by experts in their fields, while the whole book takes an integrated approach to management in order to establish the manager's role and a sense of direction for the organisation. In dealing with these issues, the book is divided into five main sections focusing on the major functions of management – which can be summarised as organising, controlling and planning – and on management at a time of change, looking forward also to those management issues which will be particularly important in the future.

The challenge of management is considered in terms of leadership, the importance of the customer, and in maintaining a competitive edge through marketing. Strategic management is considered from the viewpoint of both policy and implementation, combined with ensuring high-quality development and control both in the public as well as the private sector. The organising function is seen to involve working within a corporate culture to provide good communications and effective human resource management in order to motivate employees. In controlling the organisation, there is a focus on making management decisions, and on operations management, information management and financial management. Current issues in management which are given prominence include corporate responsibility and management ethics, environmental issues, multinational management and the role of the manager in the twenty-first century. The international dimension is a major theme and these issues help to highlight the importance of this wider perspective.

The importance of corporate culture is increasingly recognised as a factor in management and is strongly linked to business ethics and 'green' issues. Multinational factors play an essential part in the life of many managers with the opening up of the European market, developments in international trade and investment, and the use of the information superhighway. With all these developments taking place, the changes occurring for managers establishing a career path are recognised and the effect of those changes in the future are considered.

Organisational restructuring has meant that the career expectations of managers have changed dramatically. Managers now have to take control of their own careers to an extent unknown in the past. This provides a personal challenge as well as a challenge in working with other people. It is argued that this is a dynamic factor in a situation where, more than ever, effective and efficient management can make and is making a real difference in all types of organisation. Managers make a difference in private companies, in public sector institutions and in voluntary organisations, because of changes in technology, the pressure of competition, the problems of understanding customer needs, added to cultural developments and environmental challenges. The role of the manager has never been more rewarding or challenging and it has never been more important to understand this role.

Tim Hannagan

TRAVEL GUIDE FOR THE BOOK

Travel guides of countries provide information about visiting the country, suggest itineraries for travelling through it, the main tourist sites to visit and hints on its customs, language and other aspects of it. A travel guide of this book suggests different ways of using it, highlights the main themes to consider and provides hints on its main features and plans of action on reading it.

The major theme of this book is *management at a time of change*. This is to reflect the challenges facing managers with increasingly rapid changes in terms of technology, the culture and environment in which they work and the globalisation of ideas and of business activity. Organisations in the private and public sectors (and for that matter the voluntary sector) have to meet customer needs, however customers may be defined, and as these needs change, so too organisations have to change. According to the Chief Executive of Tesco, the 'secret' of successful retailing is 'never stop listening to customers and giving them what they want. It's that simple' (Chris Blackhurst, 'Sir Terry Leahy', *Management Today*, February 2004). Customers can be considered to be the 'end-users' of a product or service whether they are 'paying' customers in a supermarket or the recipients of a health service or an education service. At the same time, the context in which organisations are operating is altering in one way or another as a result of increased or reduced competition, or changes in the availability of resources, or changes in regulations or as a result of new technology.

This book is about what managers do now and what they will be expected to do in the future. For this reason, the historical perspective is left until the last chapter and is included there to emphasise the fact that ideas about how to manage change over periods of time build on and adapt the ideas of the past. As a result of globalisation and improved communications, management ideas move between countries and regions of the world even more easily than goods and services. This is not meant to suggest that there are no differences between the way people manage in different countries. Local customs vary, and legislation and management styles are not the same in different countries, or for that matter in different organisations.

The book often refers to 'organisations' as a way of suggesting that the same or at least similar concepts and practices can be applied in the public and voluntary sectors as in the private sector. There are important differences in the management of public sector corporations and services (such as the BBC, universities, hospital trusts), voluntary organisations (such as charities and societies) and private sector companies. In the private sector companies succeed or fail depending on whether they make profits or not; in the voluntary sector organisations depend on donations of one kind or another; and in the public sector corporations and trusts depend on government funding. However, many of the concepts and practices of management are the same or similar in these different sectors. They are all involved in **strategic management**, in **managing people**, in **managing operations** and in a range of **management issues**, and all need to face the **management challenge** involved in leadership, meeting the needs of their customers and coping with change. The contrasts between managing in the private and public sectors is analysed in a new chapter on strategic management in the public sector.

The changing face of management is illustrated by the rise of the e-commerce, 'dot-com' companies, which are well illustrated in Chapter 15 and in fact throughout the book. Although these companies are different from more traditional ones in some of the ways in which they operate, they still have to manage operations and people; they still require leadership and a focus on their customers. They need to market their services, they face multinational competition as well as ethical and environmental issues, they have to have a strategy in order to survive, and in the end they have to make a profit. All organisations – from the local football club to the multinational company with a turnover larger than the GDP of some countries – need good management if they are going to succeed in their purpose. The chapters of this book build up an understanding of the complexity of this process.

An itinerary or **route** through this book could suggest that it should be read from the first page through to the last page, although this is only one approach. Another approach would be to pick out topics of particular interest through referring to the list of **contents**, the **index** or the **glossary**. For example, if the main interest at the moment is 'financial management', then Chapter 16 is a starting point; if 'motivation in the workplace' is important, then Chapter 12 would be a better place to start. The **glossary** provides meanings of many of the terms used through the book, and can be used as a starting point in a similar way to the **index**. If there is a need to investigate a subject in more detail, the lists of references at the end of each chapter provide guidance on **further reading**. A different approach to the book would be to start each chapter by considering the **review and discussion questions** and then working through the chapter to compare the analysis in it with this consideration. For example: 'What is the function of organisational design?' Or: 'How does the span of management affect the role of a manager?' Such questions could be thought about individually or discussed in a group before reading Chapter 9 and comparing the analysis there with the ideas raised in the general discussion.

Websites are included at the end of every chapter in order to provide further information on the topics described and discussed in the chapter and to provide illustrations of the main issues that are raised. These can be used as initial research into these topics and as a basis for discussion and review of the issues. The websites are examples of the very many that are available in these areas, such as the large number of individual websites opened by companies. There is a range of 'search engines' which can be used to access information on particular topics and subjects, for example *Excite*: **http://www.excite.com/**, *Altavista*: **http://www.altavista.com/** and *Lycos*: **http://www.lycos.co.uk**.

The whole process of management is a complex one which is full of 'noise' and distraction and each chapter represents a facet of this complexity. Managers work in places where computers sometimes 'go down', where lifts break down, where transport systems to and from a particular location are unreliable and, above all, where people behave in unpredictable ways. In an ideal world, managers arrive at the office after a hassle-free journey, travel up to their floor in the lift, to find that their personal assistant has put the reports required later in the day on the desk with a list of the day's appointments. In practice, the train is late arriving or there has been a flood on the main road causing a time-consuming diversion; the lift does not work and the PA has telephoned in sick; the reports necessary for meetings later in the day have not arrived and have to be chased up; the computer is down and the list of appointments for the day has to be deduced from the PA's hastily scribbled notes from the previous day. This is the 'noise' – the forms of distraction – which surrounds a manager, and the skill of a manager is working through this to keep in focus the main objectives of the job.

Although there are a number of ways of working with this book, one obvious approach is to work through it from start to finish and the text is organised to build up a fully rounded picture of management. There is not one correct way to travel through the landscape and details of management, but this book provides a logical build-up of a complete picture. It moves from facing the **management challenge** to the consideration of **modern management issues**. At all levels, management involves **leadership** because it always involves other people, while at the same time managers have to focus on the objectives of the role which always involve, in one way or another, **meeting the needs of customers**. Managers need an understanding of **strategy** to appreciate the position and direction of their organisation and the context in which they are providing **organisation** and **control**. **Managing people** is what management is all about and an understanding of **culture**, **communications**, **motivation** and **human resource management** is an essential element of this. With this background it is possible to concentrate on particular **management operations** and **issues**.

What is the challenge of management? – *Dealing with continuous change – Providing leadership – Focusing on the consumer – Understanding the organisation through marketing.*

What is the organisational strategy? – *Strategic analysis and strategic options – Obtaining and retaining quality – Variations in strategic management caused by degree of 'publicness' and 'privateness'.*

How does one manage people? – *By organising and controlling with an understanding of organisational culture – The importance of communication – Personnel management – Motivation.*

How are operations managed? – *Management decision making – Managing operations – Information and finance.*

What are the issues that are important to managers? – *Ethical issues in management – Environmental issues – Multinational issues – A perspective on management and management careers.*

GUIDED TOUR

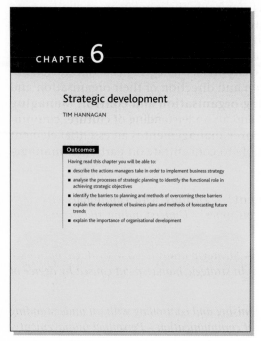

PRODUCTS AND SERVICES

'A product is anything that can be offered to a market for attention, acquisition, use or consumption that might satisfy a want or need. It includes physical objects, services, persons, places, organizations and ideas.'
(Kotler, 1986)

This definition includes services and it is useful to realise both that they are 'products' in the broadest sense and that there are differences between them and physical commodities (see the discussion in the case study on p 77). Whereas a commodity is tangible and its sale involves a change in ownership, a service is essentially intangible and does not result in the exchange of ownership. When a car is bought and sold, there is a change of ownership; when a holiday is bought and sold, ownership of the travel company, airbus or hotel remains unchanged.

Managers can view all commodities and services as solving consumer problems, and marketing as selling benefits rather than features, but, of course, features may be important if they help to provide benefits. For example, car salespeople may concentrate their sales drive on the special features their cars provide, while the ability of the cars to provide a reliable form of transport is taken for granted. The features help to differentiate one car from another, but they will not serve any purpose unless the benefit of transport can be guaranteed. In fact, competition is often not so much about the product as about the value added to it in the form of packaging, services, customer advice, financing, delivery arrangements and so on. For example, Exhibit 4.1 illustrates the importance of packaging.

Exhibit 4.1   Marketing: value added

In the run-up to Christmas 1993, Cadbury's decided to introduce a £5 million support package for 'Milk Tray'. This is one of the oldest and the best known mass-market brands and is the UK's biggest selling chocolate assortment brand. It had become squeezed by upmarket niche brands on one side and downmarket and own-label competitors on the other.

The support package was based on months of qualitative and quantitative research and was designed to increase the volume of sales by 20 per cent over 18 months. The revamp included the addition of two new flavours, truffle shell and praline fanfare – to reflect the company's view that consumers were being increasingly experimental in their tastes.

The big change was in the packaging for the chocolates, with a redesigned box to make it more upmarket with a cut-out lid, a separate choice card inside and a new tray design. The object was to make the product more 'feminine' and give it a more luxury feel.

In considering their target market, managers need to take account of all aspects of it. These can be summarised by considering basic questions about the market which can be divided into the six 'O's:

■ **Occupants** – which individuals constitute the market?
■ **Object** – what do consumers wish to buy?

Learning **Outcomes** clearly establish what is covered in each chapter and introduce important topics.

Exhibits illustrate theory with examples and bring the subject to life.

---

or managers take an optimistic view of the future
n they would choose the decision which gener-
ince they feel that the 'best' state of nature will
as the **maximax criterion** since we are searching
payoffs. In this problem the maximax decision
n Eastern Europe since this – potentially – gener-
00, compared with the best possible payoff of
n and £100 000 for the Scandinavian. In general
payoff for each decision is found and then the
oach has the advantage of focusing on the best
ive decisions under consideration.

■ **Monitoring the external envir**
firm operates is diverse and cor
reveal threats and opportunitie
nature of the firm's activities an
instability in the country of a ma

→ Ch. 4

■ **The internal environment.** A fir
the analysis of which should indi
relations, idle capacity, etc. Th
processes can be of prime import

→ Ch. 9

■ **Evaluation.** In addition to the
management must also take varic
ability of spare parts, flexibility, s

Key terms are highlighted for easy reference. Definitions for each key term can be found in the glossary at the back of the book.

Orientation arrows help you to find your way around the book and develop an understanding of the links between different management functions.

300 SECTION C · MANAGING PEOPLE

■ action taken to implement group decisions, to reinforce the view among the workforce that their contributions are well received;

■ the recognition that conflicting views have a place in developing initiatives.

Futurologists are already predicting that even this view will eventually diminish and even vanish as new technology increasingly impacts on communications in organisations. As Nick Land, a philosopher and researcher in the field of new technology, states:

'There is a similar pattern that you find in the structure of societies, in the structure of companies and in the structure of computers, and all three are moving in the same direction. That is, away from a top-down structure of a central command system giving the system instructions about how to behave, towards a system that is flat, which is a web, in which change moves from the bottom up. And this is going to happen across all institutions and technical devices. It's the way they work.'

(Quoted in Harrison, 1995)

In physical terms, office blocks, defined as the corporate ego trip of the 1980s, will be the social and economic dinosaurs of the next century. 'Businesses will concentrate on fewer, more efficient buildings, with all but management and key workers operating from home or satellite offices in the suburbs' (Brown, 1994). This vision of a cyberspace heaven in which the Internet and other technological developments will create a warm-home environment, has been contrasted with a societal hell in which those dispossessed of the new technology will languish in crumbling ghettos in the giant hulks of decaying cities (Handy, 1994; Harrison, 1995). Whatever the future holds, communication will still continue to be important, as will the skills needed to do it effectively.

SUMMARY

■ A review of various media channels was undertaken in the light of their classification into downward, upward and horizontal forms of organisational communication.

■ In this chapter an outline of communication models was undertaken, examining the mechanistic concepts of the Shannon and Weaver model and the feedback concept indicated in the Schramm model. Definitions of organisational communication were considered, including those of Krone, Jablin and Putnam, who view the communication process as being influenced by mechanistic, psychological, interpretive-symbolic and systems-interactive perspectives.

■ Clampitt identified three approaches to communication which he calls the arrow, circuit and dance models. The first two follow respectively the Shannon and Weaver mechanistic model, and the Schramm feedback model. The dance model he believes to be superior as it incorporates elements of organisational culture and other organic or human influences.

■ Trends in international communication were highlighted through the findings of a number of surveys, and a more detailed examination of Japanese communication and employee involvement practices was undertaken. Communications in an employee involvement context within the European Union were considered, with special attention given to the issue of the influence of the works council directive on the UK.

■ The chapter ended with some speculations and prognostications about the influence and direction of organisational communications in the future.

The chapter **Summary** recaps the issues covered to check you have achieved the learning outcomes and understood the chapter.

CHAPTER 13 · MANAGEMENT DECISION MAKING 421

those alternatives against the declared decision objectives, the use of a number of commonly used business models can be productive, although the output from such models must be seen as only part of the information-gathering process involved in decision making.

■ Such models are particularly valuable in decision situations where incomplete or inadequate information is available, where a number of alternatives are typically available and where uncertainty exists.

■ A number of these models have been introduced in this chapter, but it must also be said that the last two or three decades have seen a veritable explosion of such models being developed and used. The subject area known as management science has provided many of these model developments and a number of texts are detailed in the references for further reading which introduce additional models of potential use to the decision maker.

Review and discussion questions

1 From a management perspective what is the difference between decision making and problem solving?

2 Consider an organisation with which you are familiar. What is the organisation's attitude to risk? How does this affect its decision-making process?

3 As a manager facing some decision situation which has areas of uncertainty associated with it, is it possible to quantify such areas of uncertainty?

4 What are the key differences between management decision making and personal decision making?

5 Discuss how time affects the various stages of the decision-making process.

6 Consider the various decision support models introduced in this chapter. What factors would discourage managers from utilising the information derived from such models in the decision-making process?

7 'Decision making is the most important task for any manager.' Discuss this statement.

8 A manager in an organisation has been offered a considerable promotion. However, the promotion would involve moving to another part of the country.
  a Using the decision-making process model, consider how the manager would try to reach an appropriate decision.
  b Draw a decision tree representing the decision situation.
  c Assume the manager has decided to take the promotion. Draw a forcefield diagram to assess the critical factors which will affect the 'success' of the move.

9 When you have read the case study on Jaguar Cars, answer the following:
  a What are the main strategic and operational pressures affecting Jaguar Cars over the last few years in terms of the external business environment?
  b What are the key strategic and operational decisions facing Jaguar?
  c Which of the models introduced in this chapter do you think would help Jaguar's management?

Review and discussion questions can be used in class, or on your own at home, to test your understanding and help you to revise for exams.

---

422 SECTION D · MANAGING THE ORGANISATION

CASE STUDY

Jaguar Cars

*A Jaguar car
instantly recognisable almost anywhere in the world.*

Jaguar has had a chequered history over the last few decades. In the early 1980s the company came close to disappearing, with reducing market share, decreasing financial viability, outdated technology and working practices, and major product quality problems. With the introduction of new management it was able – painfully – to turn itself around and achieve improvements in efficiency, quality and profitability. Towards the end of the decade a worldwide recession emerged and the company again hit problems. In 1989 the company was bought by Ford Motor Company for around US$2.5 billion, with the new owner then having to find a further $700 million to help keep the company going in the short term.

Jaguar starkly illustrates the difficulties involved in decision making in today's environment. On the face of it, the company had tremendous potential. On the other hand, it faced a number of major short-term problems. These included:

■ the company was operating at a loss. It was estimated that in 1992 it actually lost $18 000 on each car sold;
■ in motor-industry terms it was very small, even when compared with its competitors in the luxury car market. Mercedes Benz, for example, has annual sales almost 20 times those of Jaguar;
■ it was operating at below breakeven output. Breakeven annual sales were estimated at 35 000. In 1993 Jaguar expected to produce and sell only 29 000 cars;
■ worldwide there had been a dramatic collapse in the market for luxury cars;
■ the company's cars had significant quality problems, particularly in relation to its major competitors, with, for example, a Jaguar car experiencing 75 per cent more defects than a Mercedes;
■ many of the company's cars were relatively old models. However, the development costs of a new model were likely to run into the hundreds of millions of £s. In addition, such development would take considerable time.

The new management of Jaguar faced an array of interlinked problems as well as considerable uncertainty about markets, demand, customer loyalty and competitors' strategy. It was also constrained by the desire to keep Jaguar as a unique product and not simply another variety of Ford car. A number of decisions were taken to try to move the company forward. These included:

■ immediate improvements in operating efficiency. Assembly man-hours per car, for example, were reduced by almost 40 per cent in a two-year period, with a further 50 per cent reduction planned;
■ significant quality improvements, with defects down by over 70 per cent on the XJ6 model alone;
■ a major cost-reduction programme leading to a reduction in the workforce of almost 50 per cent;
■ the introduction of, and development of, new models, but with decisions related to different timescales. In the short term the company decided to introduce a redesigned version of the XJ6 – which was a relatively quick and low-cost option – and longer term to invest in the design and the production of a totally new car aimed at the business executive market.

The decisions faced by the company's management were clearly a mixture of the strategic and the operational. At the operational level, decisions had to be taken about how best to improve the company's immediate position. These needed to be taken quickly and needed to have an immediate impact on the company's performance. While such decisions can be taken relatively easily – relating to quality, productivity and operating costs – implementing such decisions effectively can be more problematic given issues of staff morale and uncertainty, and there is clearly considerable scope for some of the problem-solving techniques introduced in this chapter.

At the same time, a number of key strategic decisions were needed to try to ensure the company's long-term future. Such decisions related to the size of the company's customer base, the range of models available, its pricing policy and the location of its production base. Over time a series of related decisions emerged, and the sequential decision models introduced in this chapter clearly have a lot of potential in such a situation. As a short-term measure the company launched a redesigned version of the XJ6. In 1996 the company launched the XK8 sports car. The X200 executive saloon was launched

---

Each chapter ends with a **Case Study** to show how the theory is applied in practice, and to help you relate your learning to real life management situations.

Lecturers can access a secure website with teaching resources such as an **Instructor's Manual**, including questions and answers to case studies, and down loadable **PowerPoint slides.**

www.pearsoned.co.uk/hannagan

ACKNOWLEDGEMENTS

Author's acknowledgements

A number of people have contributed to the production of this book. I would like to thank the contributors from a range of University Business Schools and Management Centres, who have used their expertise to provide chapters in their specialist fields; everybody at Pearson Education for their support; Yvonne, my wife, for providing me with the time to work on the book; and the many other people who have supported the project.

Publisher's acknowledgements

We are grateful to the following for permission to reproduce copyright material:

Figure 2.1 reprinted by permission of *Harvard Business Review*. From Blake, R. R., Mouton, J. S., Barnes, L. B., and Greiner, L. E. (1964) 'Breakthrough on Organizational development', *Harvard Business Review*, Nov–Dec. p. 136. Copyright © 1964 by Harvard Business School Publishing Corporation, all rights reserved; Figure 2.2 reprinted by permission of *Harvard Business Review*. From Tannenbaum, R., and Schmidt, W. H. 'How to choose a leadership pattern', *Harvard Business Review*, May–June 1973. Copyright © 1973 by Harvard Business School Publishing Corporation, all rights reserved; Figure 2.4 from Fiedler/Chemers, *Leadership and Effective Management*, first edition, © 1974. Reprinted by permission of Pearson Education, Inc., Upper Saddle River, NJ; Figure 2.5 reprinted from *Leadership and Decision Making*, by Victor H. Vroom and Philip W. Yetton, by permission of the University of Pittsburgh Press. © 1973 by University of Pittsburgh Press; Figure 5.1 reprinted with the permission of The Free Press, a division of Simon & Schuster Adult Publishing Group, from *The Rise and Fall of Strategic Planning* by Henry Mintzberg. Copyright © 1994 by Henry Mintzberg. All rights reserved; Figure 5.3 adapted with the permission of The Free Press, a division of Simon & Schuster Adult Publishing Group, from *Competitive Advantage: Techniques for Analysing Industries and Competitors* by Michael E. Porter. Copyright ©1980, 1998 by The Free Press; Table 10.3 from Krone, Jablin, Putnam (1987) in Jablin, F., Roberts, K., and Porter, L (eds.) *Handbook of Organizational Communication: An Interdisciplinary Perspective*, p. 33. ©1987 Sage Publications, Inc. Reprinted by permission of Sage Publications, Inc.; Table 10.4 from Clampitt, P. in *Communication for Managerial Effectiveness*, p. 3. © 1991 Sage Publications, Inc. Reprinted by permission of Sage Publications, Inc.; Table 10.5 from Clampitt, P. in *Communication for Managerial Effectiveness*, p.3. © 1991 Sage Publications, Inc. Reprinted by permission of Sage Publications, Inc.; Figure 12.1 from Bandura, Albert, *Social Foundations of Thought and Action: A Social Cognitive Theory*, first edition, © 1986. Reprinted by permission of Prentice Hall, Upper Saddle River, NJ; Table 12.1 from Caldwell and O'Reilly in the *Journal of Applied Psychology*, 75, 648–57. Copyright © 1990 the American Psychological Association. Adapted with permission; Figure 12.4 adapted from Cooper *et al.* 'Reducing accidents using goal-setting and feedback: a field study' in *Journal of Occupational and Organisational Psychology*, 67, pp. 219–40; Exhibit 12.4 from R. M. O'Brien, A. M. Dickson, M. P. Roscow, eds. *Industrial Behavior Modification: A Learning-Based Approach to Industrial Organizational Problems* © 1982. Published by Allyn and Bacon, Boston, MA. Copyright © 1982 Pearson Education; Figure 12.7 from Hackman and Oldman in the *Journal of Applied Psychology*, 60, 159–70. Copyright © 1975 the American Psychological Association. Adapted with permission; Figure 12.8 from Hackman and Oldman in the *Journal of Applied Psychology*, 60, 159-70. Copyright ©1975 by the American Psychological Association. Adapted with permission.; Figure 12.9 from Roe, R. A., Zinoieva, I. L., Dienes, E., and Ten Horn, L. A. (2000) 'A comparison of work motivation in Bulgaria, Hungary and The Netherlands: test of a model' in *Applied Psychology: An International Review*. 49, 658–87. Reprinted with permission of Blackwell Publishing; Figure 14.1 and Figure 14.4 from Lockyer et al. (1992) *Production and Operations Management, 6th edition*, Pearson Education Limited; Table 14.5 from Hill (1991) *Production Operations Management*, second edition. Reprinted with permission of the publishers, Pearson Education; Figure 14.5 adapted with permission of The Free Press, a division of Simon & Schuster Adult Publishing Group, from

Competitive Advantage: Creating and Sustaining Superior Performance by Michael E. Porter. Copyright © 1985, 1998 Michael E Porter. All rights reserved; Figure 14.6 from Slack and Lewis (2002) *Operations* Strategy, Pearson Education Limited; Exhibits 14.6, 14.7, 14.8, 14.9 and 14.11 from Slack *et al.* (2001) *Operations Management*, 3rd edition, Pearson Education Limited; Table 14.14 from Hill (1991) *Production Operations Management*, second edition. Reprinted with permission of the publishers, Pearson Education; Figure 16.3 from Chadwick (2001) *Essential Finance and Accounting for Managers*, Pearson Education Limited; Figure 18.4 Permission to reproduce this figure from BSI (1996) *Environmental Management Systems Handbook: A Guide to the BS EN ISO 14000 Series* is granted by BSI. British Standards can be obtained from BSI Customer Services, 389 Chiswick High Road, London W4 4AL. Tel: +44 (0) 20 8996 9001.email: cservices@bsi-global.com; Figure 18.5 from Welford (1998) 'The First Five Steps of ISO', *Corporate Environmental Management 1: Systems and Strategies*. Reprinted with permission of Earthscan, 8–12 Camden High Street, London NW1 0JH; Figure 19.5 from Freeman, C and Hagendoorn, J. (1992) *Globalisation of Technology*. Reprinted with kind permission of Professor J Hagedoorn and Professor C Freeman; Figures 20.2 and 20.3 from Coulson and Coe (1991) *The Flatter Organisation: Philosophy and Practice*. Reproduced with permission of the Chartered Management Institute (formerly the Institute of Management); Table 20.2 from Huczynski, A. A. (1993) in *Management Gurus*. Reprinted with kind permission of the author, Dr A. A. Huczynski; Exhibit 20.2 From *The Seasons of a Man's Life* by Daniel Levinson, Copyright © 1978 Daniel J. Levinson. Used by permission of Alfred A. Knopf, a division of Random House, Inc. and Sterling Lord Literistic Inc. Copyright © 1975 Daniel Levinson.

Haymarket Business Publications Ltd for extracts by John Major, November 1993 (Exhibit 2.5), Sir Graham Day, November 1993 (Exhibit 2.8), Chris Blackhurst, November 1993 (Tesco case study, p. 92) and Richard Bremner January 2004 (BMW and Fiat case study, pp. 123–6) published in *Management Today Magazine*; Ford Motor Company for 'Company mission, values and guiding principles' 1996 (Exhibit 5.5); The *Harvard Business Review* for an extract from 'Managers and leaders: are they different?' by Abraham Zaleznik (Managers and leaders case study, pp. 34–5) © 2004 Harvard Business School Publishing Corporation all rights reserved; Blackwell Publishing Ltd for extracts from 'Creativity, leadership and change' by Michael Bichard published in *Public Money and Management* April – June 2000 (Creativity, leadership and change case study, pp. 234–235) and 'On the globalization of Business' by Ray Hudson published in *British Journal of Management*, December 2002; People Management for extracts from 'Employee Consultation: Mind your own business' by Karen Higginbottom (Marks & Spencer case study, pp. 301–2), and 'Mergers and Acquisitions: Direct Line' by Jon Watkins (Merger at work communications case study, pp. 302–3), published in *People Management*, May 2003; Pearson Education Ltd for an extract from *Operations Management 2/e* by Nigel Slack et al 1998 (United Biscuits case study, p. 441); Guardian News Services Limited for an extract adapted from an interview with Alan Randall by John Hind published in *The Observer* 8th June 1997 (Operations management at a theme park case study, p. 441) © John Hind; Times Newspapers Ltd for extracts from 'Incentive plan 'used to falsify QMH profit'' published in *The Times* 7th October 1997 (part of case studies at end on Chapter 16, p. 544), 'Valuations 'altered to inflate QMH profit'' published in *The Times* 10th October 1997 (part of case studies at end of Chapter 16, p. 543), 'Queens Moat auditing under scrutiny' published in *The Times* 16 June 1998 (part of case studies at end of Chapter 16, p. 544), 'Judge orders former QMH directors to pay back £42m' published in *The Times* 24th September 1999 (part of case studies at end of Chapter 16, p. 545) by Dominic Walsh; and VNU Business Publications for an extract published in *Accountancy Age*, 15th October 1998 (part of case studies at end of Chapter 16, p. 545) by Phillip Inman © Accountancy Age.

We are grateful to the Financial Times Limited for permission to reprint the following material: Dare to be different, © *Financial Times*, 19 June 1997; In search of a modern structure, © *Financial Times*, 27 June 1997; Catalogue of mistakes at Queen's Moat, © *Financial Times*, 30 October 1993; Queen's moat plans to form core hotel chain, © *Financial Times*, 30 October 1993; Inside track law & business, © *Financial Times*, 23 September 2002; Shell to face shareholder vote on ethics, © *Financial Times*, 24 February 1997; BT's main overseas investments, from Company reports, © *Financial Times*, November 1991.

We are grateful to the following for permission to use copyright material:

Produced to price, from *The Financial Times Limited*, 13 June 1997, © John Kay; Know your place, from *The Financial Times Limited*, 27 June 1997, © John Kay; Loss of faith in managers, from *FT Mastering Management*, The Financial Times Limited, 6 June 1997, © Donald Sull and Sumantra Ghoshal.

In some instances we have been unable to trace the owners of copyright material, and we would appreciate any information that would enable us to do so.

SECTION A

THE MANAGEMENT CHALLENGE

What is the manager's role? What is the main focus of management today? What are the different levels of management responsibility? Why is it important for managers to be able to manage change? What part does leadership play in management? How do the different theories of leadership apply to management? What is the basis of the power of leaders? Is leadership necessary? Who is the customer? What are customer needs? How can organisations meet customer needs? Why is a marketing orientation so important for the success of organisations? What is the importance of marketing for the development of strategy in organisations?

This section sets the scene in terms of the manager's role in a time of change and the main focus of modern management. It considers levels of management responsibility and underlying theories of management. Leadership is seen as an essential element in management and different theories, style and sources of power and control are analysed. Every manager has to focus on the organisation's customers through flexible management structures and strategies, and this suggests that marketing is a fundamental aspect of an organisation in satisfying customers.

The challenge of management

TIM HANNAGAN

Outcomes

Having read this chapter, you will be able to:

- identify the manager's role in a time of change
- analyse different underlying theories of management
- consider the levels of management responsibility
- understand the management role and its responsibility in the management of change

THE MANAGEMENT CHALLENGE

The manager's role

It can be argued that, in the environment in which managers work, change is the natural order of things and the most important management skill is the management of change. This arises from the fact that the really skilful part of a manager's job is setting up the method of working in the first place, and then renewing and refreshing these methods again and again.

At first glance a manager's role is to organise, supervise and control people so that there is a productive outcome to work. Organisations of one type or another are essential for productive work because they bring people together with raw materials and equipment in order to achieve a variety of goals. By combining people's talents and energy with resources, very often more can be achieved than by individuals working on their own. Organisations, whether they are companies, educational institutions, hospitals or football teams, will all have objectives. They will all have a purpose for being in existence and for continuing their work. These objectives or goals may be expressed in terms of profits, market share, educational achievements, health or winning games. Every organisation will have a plan to achieve these objectives in order to make sure that they have the right people doing the right jobs with the best possible equipment at the right time.

Managers are the people responsible for helping organisations to achieve their objectives and for creating and implementing their plans. They are responsible for:

> *'the process of planning, organising, leading and controlling the efforts of organisation members and of using all organisational resources to achieve stated organisational goals.'*   (Mescon *et al.*,1985)

This definition helps to describe what managers do, while the skill of **management** can be described as:

> *'getting things done by other people.'*   (Parker Follett, 1941)

This definition emphasises the fact that managers achieve organisational objectives by arranging for other people to perform whatever tasks are required, and do not necessarily carry out these tasks themselves. This is obviously essential in a football team where even a player–manager must have other people to help the team to win. In industry one-person businesses can succeed by specialising in one aspect of the process, but major products and services are supplied by larger organisations because one-person businesses cannot produce a sufficient quantity of goods and services to meet consumer demand. It is a characteristic of developing economies that as the market for goods and services grows the importance of the one-person business declines relative to larger forms of organisation.

It can be argued that management is:

> *'the process of optimising human, material, and financial contributions for the achievement of organisational goals.'*   (Pearce and Robinson, 1989)

This definition begins to move the idea of the role of the manager into a more dynamic and up-to-date relationship with the organisation. The relatively 'old-fashioned' definitions emphasise the running of an organisation in terms of administration and control, which represents what can be described as an operational view of management. A more modern and dynamic view of management would suggest that management should be based on innovation, and satisfying the customer. This view suggests that people are imprisoned by their own experience and that in order to remain dynamic an organisation needs to change its structure frequently. The emphasis is not on running the organisation so much as planning, developing and changing it. In Figure 1.1 all managers may be involved with the operational aspects of management, but as they are promoted and develop, their role becomes increasingly one of planning, innovation and leadership.

When technological progress is slow and other aspects of organisations remain the same for many years, perhaps a major part of a working lifetime, the important skills are supervisory and administrative in order to make sure that the established process continues. Under these circumstances operating and controlling are paramount, but when working methods and processes change every few years or more or less constantly, managing change becomes the most important management attribute. As well as constant change in working methods, managers are now faced with increasingly complex organisations and a rapidly changing economic and social environment, which again makes the older definitions of management, in terms of running the business, inadequate and inappropriate descriptions of the role.

The challenge

The management challenge is to maintain control over the processes of an organisation while at the same time leading, inspiring, directing and making decisions on all sorts of matters. The challenge for modern managers is to deal with this tension between operating the present systems, structures and processes and the need to change in order to survive.

> '*Management as it has been systematised and professionalised, has developed many axioms over the past century. But in the past twenty years, the stable conditions (large scale mass-production) that led to the slow emergence of these universals have blown apart.*'
>
> (Peters, 1987)

If this was true in 1987, it has become even more obvious in the first decade of the twenty-first century. The 'knowledge revolution' has eventually caught up with past

Figure 1.1 **The management role**

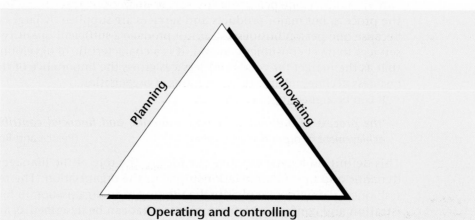

predictions. Electronic commerce, including sales via the Internet, has become an increasingly ordinary part of everyday life. For example, in the past, holiday planning has involved a situation where holiday-makers watch a travel agent look up flight times and availability and other aspects of the holiday on their computers with software packages not readily available to the booking public. Now anyone can access this information in the comfort of his or her own home. In the same way, instead of fighting the local Tesco car park and waiting in the check-out lines, shoppers can order their groceries via their PC screens. The 'dot-com' and e-commerce companies have arrived and managers and their organisations have to face this change.

Organisations, whether they are commercial companies or non-profit institutions, have to meet customer demands if they are to succeed. This is obvious with motor car companies and high street shops, but is now also true in the non-profit sector for organisations, such as schools, universities, hospitals and museums (*see* Chapter 8). As customer needs alter, so the business must change by anticipating customer wants, leading these where appropriate as well as responding to them. The emphasis today is on a focus on the customer, whether as a consumer of goods and services, a patient needing health services, a student seeking a university education or a visitor searching for information in a library or a museum. All managers are concerned with leading their organisation, section, unit or team to enable work to be carried out successfully in response to the needs of their market. As society and the economy develop and as managers are promoted from junior to middle and senior levels, the requirement to be flexible, creative, innovative and able to absorb and communicate new ideas becomes of increasing importance.

→ Ch. 8

This view of modern management suggests that it is about change, because in order to meet their objectives, organisations need to focus on their customers through a marketing culture. This is as true of a professional football team as of a multinational company, a hospital trust or a small business. Management of a kind is required in the smallest task; in a one-person business, that one person will have to combine all the qualities of management as well as working at an operational level. Above all, in one way or another, the individual running a one-person

Figure 1.2 **Levels of management**

business must satisfy the customers through the quality of the work and the service provided. The larger an organisation, the more specialised management can become with the separation of management functions, while at the highest level there will need again to be a convergence of specialised management skills, on a different plane, in order to develop organisational strategy (*see* Figure 1.2).

THE SCIENCE OF MANAGEMENT

➔ Ch. 20

The examples of approaches to management in the nineteenth century and the first half of the twentieth century discussed in Chapter 20 indicate that management problems have not particularly changed, while styles and approaches have. These are very much dependent on the circumstances of the time, so that although managers may feel they have a better approach than their predecessors, in fact it is a different approach which may be better or worse, according to the needs of the particular time. Operations research is a good example of this, developing out of the necessity in the UK to solve complex technical problems during the Second World War. At that time groups of mathematicians, scientists and engineers were brought together to solve such problems. The result was that significant technological and tactical breakthroughs were achieved by this approach, and after the war they were quickly applied to industry.

This management science approach has been characterised by solving problems through mixed teams of specialists from relevant disciplines who analyse the problem and suggest courses of action. Its main contribution to modern management has been in the development of models to help managers analyse complex statistical data in order to obtain a greater understanding of a problem. It has produced an emphasis on decision making, on the use of quantitative models in planning and the evaluation of the effectiveness of decisions which has been greatly encouraged in the second half of the twentieth century by the development of computers.

Managers' roles change as they move up an organisation, so that at the junior level they are more concerned with the detail than with the overall picture. For example, a junior sales manager may be heavily involved in selling or in supervising a small number of sales people. At a middle management level a sales manager may control an area or a department, unit or section, organising and controlling a number of junior sales managers and with an input into planning the sales function of the organisation, into innovation and perhaps into sales strategy. The sales director will be mainly responsible for ensuring that the sales strategy of the organisation assists in meeting its objectives. There may, of course, be a number of intermediate levels or layers of management and a whole range of titles, so that, for example, many sales people are now called 'account managers' or 'product specialists' or even 'advisers'.

Operations management is concerned with matters which are in the control of an organisation. Operationally an organisation performs a transformation or conversion process where it adds value to a commodity or service. This means that the value of the output of the organisation is greater than the costs of the inputs and the process involved, so that whatever an organisation starts with in terms of 'raw materials' to process, it applies added value to these. For example, bakers start with raw materials consisting of ingredients such as flour, and through their skill and with the correct equipment, such as an oven, they produce loaves of bread. At the end of the process, the price obtained for the bread exceeds the cost of the materials and the baking process. Similarly, in the service sector, a holiday company starts with a destination in mind, seats on airline flights, hotel room bookings and a variety of excursions organised by its representatives, and pulls these elements together into a package. This is sold to holiday-makers at a price which is greater than the cost of the various elements and the process of organising them. As a result, an airline seat is transformed from a 'raw material' into an important element in a holiday.

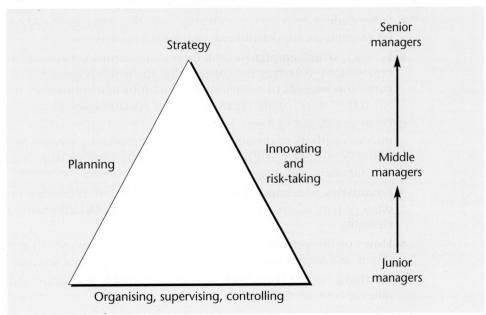

There is usually a linked set of transformations or conversion processes between the beginning of the process and the final product, which together constitute a value chain (*see* Chapter 5). Operational management is involved in the organising, supervising and controlling of these processes. It is about routine, and it is specific and relatively short-term, making sure that people know what to do and are doing it so that the objectives of the organisation are achieved. Although senior managers and middle managers are concerned with these processes, it is the junior managers who spend most of their time heavily involved in organising, supervising and controlling (*see* Figure 1.3). As managers are promoted, they become more involved in the strategy of the organisation, in innovating, risk-taking and planning. While strategic management provides a sense of purpose (*see* Chapter 5), operational management provides for the organisation, control and supervision that enables this sense of purpose to achieve a concrete form.

→ Ch. 5

→ Ch. 5

Management science

These approaches plus off-shoots and mixtures can be identified in modern management practice. John Harvey-Jones (1993) has written that:

> *'when I first started in industry in the fifties, attractions of work measurement and method study as a means of improving productivity seemed almost like a philosopher's stone.'*

Figure 1.3 **The management function**

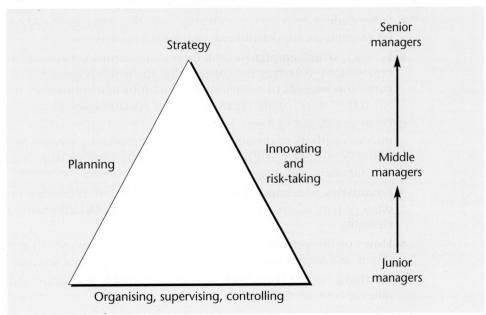

During the 1960s 'there seemed to be a common belief that everything could be measured', while the '1970s were the period when we discovered that concentrating on method and systems somehow didn't seem to make the expected breakthroughs' and 'social science came back in fashion'. He has noted the optimism of the 1980s in contrast to the pessimism of the 1990s, and has found it fascinating that 'management fashions seem to spread across the world with the speed of light, whereas transferring technology appears to be an extraordinarily difficult task to achieve'.

An example of the rapid spread of management fashions is the emphasis on quality management in the late 1980s and early 1990s, which can be seen as another way of dressing up old ideas in new clothing. It can be argued that like other management theories, quality management has been around a long time but it has to be discovered again by each new group of managers. In the same way, modern theories have included attempts to view the organisation as a single, integrated system, either through a systems approach or through a contingency approach, and these ideas are important in the understanding of modern management thinking and the role of managers.

The systems approach

The **systems approach** is based on the view that managers should focus on the role each part of an organisation plays in the whole organisation, rather than dealing separately with each part. It takes into account the different needs of various functional management areas, such as production, marketing and finance. For example, the marketing department might want to be able to sell a large variety of products, while the production unit would prefer to have long production runs of a few items, and financial managers might be mainly concerned with keeping costs as low as possible.

The systems approach means that managers have to discuss their various requirements in terms of the needs of the whole organisation. Production scheduling, for example, would only be completed once marketing and finance were in agreement with the plans. This interaction requires a high degree of communication and the breaking down of barriers between the various departments and functions of an organisation. The emphasis is on management awareness of:

- **Subsystems**, which are the individual parts that make up the whole organisation, for example a unit, department, company, industry.
- **Synergy**, which emphasises the interrelationships between all the parts of an organisation, reflecting the concept that the whole is greater than the sum of its parts. This suggests that departments and units in a business are more productive when they work together than when they operate separately.
- **Open and closed systems**, which reflect the extent to which an organisation interacts with its environment. Companies providing services to the public will normally be open systems, while those working within a larger organisation such as component part manufacturers will be more closed.
- **Boundaries**, which in a closed system will tend to be more rigid than those in an open system, where boundaries with the outside environments are constantly changing.
- **Flows** of information, materials and human energy which move through a system and are transformed in the process into goods and services.
- **Feedback**, which is the process of monitoring information about systems in order to evaluate their operation.

This approach implies that management at all levels needs to be sensitive to the complexity of the organisation and accept a system which enables the organisation to work efficiently.

The contingency approach

This can be described as the 'golf club approach'. Like picking out the right golf club for a particular shot at a specific time on a particular day, the contingency approach to management problems suggests that different problems and situations require different solutions. Much depends on managers' experience with this approach, and it is understood that what might work well in one situation may not work in another. The task of management is to identify which technique will work in particular circumstances. In one case the solution to creating greater productivity is to motivate employees by giving them greater responsibility; in another case, if the employees are relatively unskilled, for example, it may be better to provide extra training and supervision as at least a preliminary step.

The contingency approach has developed through attempts to apply concepts drawn from the major schools of management thought. In applying these to solve management problems, advocates of this approach take the pragmatic view that no one approach is universally applicable. For example, on the one hand techniques used in scientific management, such as time study, may be used to investigate a particular problem; on the other hand, the ideas of the behavioural school may be involved in an inquiry into workers' motivation, perhaps followed by a quantitative analysis of the results.

The pragmatic view

Like a golfer selecting a club with full regard to all the variables such as distance, obstacles to be avoided as well as wind direction and other conditions, so will a manager need to consider the objectives of a particular action, the people involved, the equipment available, and the internal and external conditions which prevail. The internal environment is the way the organisation works, its corporate culture, management structure and communication systems. Although golfers need to know their own capabilities and temperament in order to make a good start, they do not usually play as a team. A manager needs to take into account the abilities and temperament of his colleagues as well as his own. The external environment consists of the social, political and economic factors that affect an organisation, and a manager has to judge such matters as the movement of exchange rates and their effect on the international prices of company raw materials and finished products. Ethical considerations or green issues may play a part in the organisation's market and the manager will need to consider the effect of such issues when making decisions on products and their marketing.

Managers also need to be aware of the relationship between the internal and external environments. Green issues may cause problems for the design and production departments, but may be too important to ignore. For example, the move to unleaded petrol in the UK saw a major turnaround in the design of car engines and in the allocation of petrol pumps on service station forecourts.

At the same time there are internal constraints existing within every organisation that managers must take into account in making decisions. These include:

- **Technological constraints** which derive from the equipment required by a company in order to produce its goods and services. Steel plants, for example, require expensive capital equipment and it is difficult for them to change technology quickly to meet new demands. Car manufacturers need to have reasonable runs on their production lines in order to receive a profitable return on their investment. Small-scale engineering companies can use less specific capital equipment to produce special and individualised orders.

- **Task constraints** arise from the nature of the jobs performed and the skills of the workers involved. Assembly line workers may be able to move to a different assembly line with a minimum of training, while finding it more difficult to take on more varied work.

- **Human constraints** reflect the competence of the people employed by an organisation and their motivation. A competent, well-trained and motivated workforce will exert fewer constraints on a manager than a less competent and poorly motivated workforce.

- **Organisational performance**, in that the ability of an organisation to compete effectively in its external environment depends on the organisational performance, including designing, producing, marketing and supplying.

- **The resource base**, including physical resources (buildings and production and service facilities), human resources (including employee competence, skills and attitudes), and financial resources (such as financial assets, financial control and systems).

THE ART OF MANAGEMENT

A synthesis

The management challenge is to answer the questions: What are we doing?, How do we do it? and What do we do next? This is against the background of a rapidly changing external environment and has in the foreground an increasingly well-trained and educated workforce. The answer given by the contingency approach to these questions is, 'it all depends'. Each situation is examined to determine its unique attribute before a management decision is made. This contrasts with earlier approaches that tended to deal in universal principles which could be applied in every situation. The modern management approach is to analyse the situation and then to draw on the various schools of management thought in order to decide on the most appropriate combination. This contingency approach helps managers to be aware of the complexity in every situation and to take an active role in trying to determine what would work best in each case. It calls for a bringing together or synthesis of approaches, and this throws a strong element of responsibility on to management. On the one hand, managers are not encouraged to eliminate unpredictable circumstances; on the other hand, they are encouraged to consider all contingencies and to be sufficiently flexible to take all possibilities into account.

Managers are now encouraged to recognise the ability of the people they manage and to push decision making as near as possible to the point of action. This process can develop 'flexibility by **empowerment**' (Peters, 1987) and it carries the contingency approach to what might be considered its logical conclusion. This suggests that the people who have to implement a decision should make it, by analysing the situation and deciding on a course of action. Tom Peters believes that the empowering of people 'can most effectively be tapped when people are gathered in human scale groupings, that is, teams, or more precisely, self-managed teams'. This move to self-managed teams and decision making at the point of action makes it necessary for the integrative approach to management to come to terms with human-relations management. The integrated approach developed through systems management and contingency management, which between them view the organisation as a single integrated body, at the same time including the diversity of self-managed teams.

In the 1980s, William Ouchi (1981) observed that many of the most successful American companies displayed organisational behaviour similar to practices common in Japanese organisations. This included the emphasis on collective decision making and group responsibilities, on quality control based on periodic on-site meetings, and on the lifetime commitment to an organisation. On the other hand, he observed that the Japanese managerial style was borrowed from Western models of scientific management. He felt that an integration of these approaches would lead to management success. Scientific work methods could be incorporated into an integrative management theory and combined with human relations management. He felt that organisational goals could be achieved by making decision making a participatory activity for a greater number of employees, so that responsibility becomes a collaborative function as the product of group or team processes.

The corporate and national culture

If management can be seen as a synthesis of ideas, culminating in choices made in the end intuitively, then it can be described as an art. In golf, club selection may be based on scientific measurement, observation and experience, but there is also an intuitive element which can turn a good professional shot into a great one. In spite of all the information the golfer may have, the very skilful golfer may have an immediate insight into the club and shot required in the circumstances which overrules the rational information available. This is the skill or art of the professional golfer, and this skill or 'feel' for a situation plays a part in the work of the professional manager and is set against the background of management theories.

→ Ch. 20 Exhibit 1.1 summarises the management theories that have developed over the last two centuries (for further analysis, *see* Chapter 20). Modern management is essentially about managing people as well as processes, in a rapidly changing environment. There is a mass of information available to most managers in terms of costs, prices and market conditions, but in the end decisions may be based on 'hunch' or intuition. This is where experience and a 'feel' for the particular process and people involved becomes essential, and can be helped by the corporate culture of the organisation. Culture is an important factor in the art of management, because for any organisation to operate effectively it must, to some extent, have a generally accepted set of beliefs and assumptions. These will usually have evolved over time and represent a collective experience without which managers would have to start from scratch each time they made a decision. This collective experience will be influenced by wider cultural perspectives so that managers have to be aware of the social, economic and political context they are working in, whether it is a region of the UK or an organisation in another country.

Managers work in a national and social context and different national cultures and social norms produce different views on how management should be

Exhibit 1.1 Management theories

Scientific management:	
ADAM SMITH – BABBAGE – TOWNE – TAYLOR	1800–1914
Administrative management:	
FAYOL – WEBER	1900–1925
Behavioural theories:	
FOLLETT – BARNARD – MAYO	1900–1940
Management systems:	
OPERATIONS MANAGEMENT	
SYSTEMS MANAGEMENT	1940+
Contingency theories:	
PRAGMATIC MANAGEMENT – SITUATION THEORIES	1980+
Art of management:	
SYNTHESIS – INTEGRATION – ORGANISATIONAL CULTURE	1980+

→ Ch. 19 conducted (*see* Chapter 19). A generalised view of these differences suggests that Japanese management, for example, is based on collective responsibility for the success of the organisation and, at least in the 'ideal' Japanese organisations, is also based on training for a wide variety of roles, life-long careers and on trust and loyalty. In contrast, in the USA management is based on the use of systematic approaches to improving task performance, individualism, specific job roles and responsibilities, and the importance of market position. Other national business cultures challenge these models, so that the Arab style of management can be said to be based on strong social formalities where nepotism is expected and accepted and time constraints are not of primary importance.

The art of management can be characterised as reflection in action, so that managers' experience and understanding of the context in which they operate can be applied to the particular situations they face. They need to have a similar view to their colleagues of the nature of the organisation and the internal and external environment in which it operates. It is this organisational view of the world which helps interpret the changes facing the organisation and the individuals within it. Changes tend to develop incrementally, decisions building one upon another, so that past decisions mould future strategy. It is the management task to steer this process in the right direction, as well as being prepared to deal with the less frequent but more fundamental changes of direction that occur from time to time.

LEVELS OF MANAGEMENT

The art of management applies to all levels. Just as any job can be carried out well or badly, so can management at any level. While intuition is particularly important at the strategic level, applied experience is essential in the management of the most mundane task. An alert junior supervisor will quickly learn that there are various ways of achieving the same results from his or her subordinates. Although in any organisation managers can be distinguished by their functions and by their level of responsibility, the management skills they apply will depend on their actual role in the organisation. Attempts to produce flatter management structures may have reduced the number of stages in the hierarchy but have not greatly changed the underlying situation in most organisations. This remains a pyramid with a relatively small number of senior managers at the top, a larger number of middle managers at the centre, and an even larger group of junior managers supervising the majority of employees who are non-managerial (*see* Figure 1.4).

The 'typical' junior manager will be a supervisor of a unit or the senior member of a team. Junior managers are working at or very close to the operational level and may have titles such as foreman, team leader, co-ordinator, operational manager or, of course, supervisor. Their role is to co-ordinate the work of non-managerial employees and to have direct responsibility for machinery and materials. Junior managers are expected to be skilled at both overseeing work and doing it. They are able to supervise and to fill in when and where needed in order to maintain the smooth operation of the system. They are the non-commissioned officers of management who become immensely experienced in their area of work.

Figure 1.4 Management levels

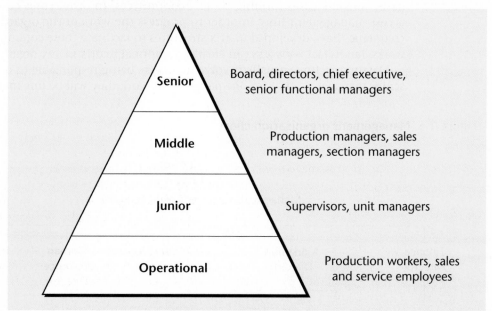

Middle managers are usually accountable for the work of junior managers and they in turn report to senior management. They will have a wider remit than the supervisors reporting to them and spend much more of their time on management functions rather than in an operational role. They may step into an operational role from time to time but they may be managing areas of expertise in which they have some knowledge but not at an operational level. The manager of a large store may be able to take over from sales, at the till or in filling shelves, but not necessarily in wordprocessing or in maintaining refrigerated units. At the same time, middle managers will have limits to their responsibilities, so that the store manager may not control pricing policy, advertising or training but may be involved in making sure that these policies are implemented.

Senior managers are the executives, at the highest level of the organisation, responsible for its overall direction and co-ordination and for directing its major activities. Senior managers are responsible for company-wide planning, organising, directing and controlling, and for providing strategic leadership to the company. They are also concerned with the demands imposed on the organisation by outside influences such as customers and suppliers. Above all, they are responsible for the overall direction and success or failure of the organisation.

Within these three layers of management there may be numerous intermediate stages, particularly in middle management. Figure 1.5 shows a simplified management organisation chart.

Line management and functional management

The chart in Figure 1.5 depicts the formal, line management relationship between members of an organisation, but does not attempt to show their functional relationship. In practice, there will be more or less formal networks of people on a functional basis, in some cases forming project committees, in other cases communicating across management lines in order to progress the work of the organisation. Some companies have developed matrix structures to facilitate these communication networks, but in fact networks can create an informal matrix in any organisation.

Matrix structures usually involve managers being responsible to more than one senior manager, so that for one part of their work they will be line managed by one

Figure 1.5 Management organisation chart

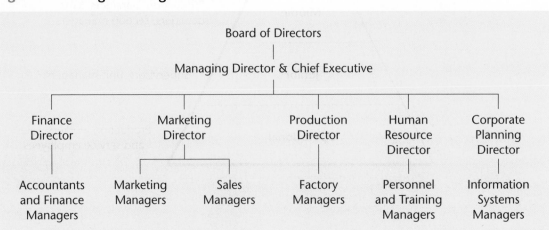

manager, and for another part by another. For example, the allocation of resources may be separated from the production process, so that a middle-ranking plant manager may be responsible to a marketing manager for the output and to a production manager for new materials. There may be responsibility to a third manager, say a human resource manager, for control of staff. It can be argued that this approach provides greater expertise in the various areas of work, but it lacks the simplicity and certainties of a hierarchical structure where the plant manager reports on all matters to, say, the production manager. As illustrated in Figure 1.6, matrix structures are usually based on a division between a functional management role, such as marketing, or a project role, such as the production of a particular commodity.

Flatter management structures aim at reducing the layers of control and approval or veto over decision making. Peter Drucker (1988) has suggested that the ultimate flat structure is the factory manager in Nebraska who has himself as manager and 120 operatives on the production line without any intermediate managers. In large and complex organisations this very simple approach may be difficult to implement while retaining control and co-ordination, but the move towards fewer layers of management can help speed up decision making and push the point of decision nearer the point of action. For example, companies can achieve one layer of senior management, one of middle and one of junior management, each with its own sphere of responsibility and decision making.

At every level, managers may have functional responsibilities or may be general managers responsible for a range of functions. Managers responsible for all the activities of the organisation or a complex part of it can be considered to be general managers. Most factory managers and shop/store managers are of this kind. They will line-manage people with a variety of skills and roles and will have some involvement in most of the organisational functions, such as finance, production, marketing and human relations. On the other hand, functional managers will be

Figure 1.6 Matrix structures

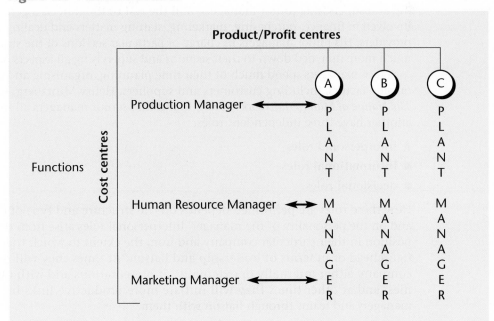

responsible for one activity within the organisation, such as marketing or finance. They will be responsible for line-managing staff within the same function. The marketing manager, for example, will be responsible for staff in sales, in promotions, advertising and public relations, and in market research. The market research manager will line-manage staff in data collection, statistics and information. In order to remain competitive, organisations have to find the structures which work best for them and reform these structures as necessary.

What managers do

It may be reasonably clear in an organisation who the managers are and the types and levels of responsibility they hold, but the question remains as to what they actually do. The theories of management provide some clues to what people in the past have considered to be the management job, while the level at which managers work also plays a part in what they do. Figure 1.1 indicated that managers move from a more operational role to one of planning and innovation as they move from junior to middle and senior management. Junior managers are likely to spend a large proportion of their time doing an operational job, whether it is production or sales. Depending on their exact role and the size of the unit they are managing, a greater or lesser proportion of their time will be spent on supervision, training and involvement with networks of other managers in the organisation. They may need to attend training sessions themselves in order to keep up to date, or they may be on a quality assurance committee or have regular briefing meetings with their line manager. A limited time will be spent planning and this will tend to be about specific projects.

The middle manager will have much less of an operational role and will spend most of the time on management. This will include much more co-ordination and monitoring than supervision, although this is likely to remain an important part of the job. Organising, controlling and some planning are likely to be the main elements of the work. The large branch store manager will spend some time planning and preparing for the next day or week or month, a large proportion of time monitoring and supervising junior managers, and the rest of the time as a general manager involved in finance, purchasing, marketing, staffing matters and dealing with outside providers. His junior managers in charge of particular sections of the store will spend much more time tied down to their sections and supervising all aspects of them.

Senior managers spend much of their time planning, organising and dealing with outside factors, including customers and suppliers. Henry Mintzberg, in a study on *The Nature of Managerial Work* (1980), found that senior managers all in one way or another have three independent roles:

- interpersonal roles
- informational roles
- decisional roles.

How these roles are performed depends on the structure and type of organisation and on the personality of the manager. Interpersonal roles arise from the managers' position in their particular company and from the extent to which they appear as a figurehead or in terms of leadership and liaison. At times they will represent the company either internally or externally, at presentations and with other companies, and at other times they will initiate more productive links between other managers and teams through liaison with them.

Senior managers will have an informational role because they become the focal point for receiving and sending information within the organisation and outside it. They monitor developments within the organisation, such as performance, as well as opportunities and threats outside the organisation, such as customer behaviour. They disseminate information in order to influence the actions of other people in the organisation, and they act as spokespeople and publicisers in representing the organisation to outside agencies. In decision making, managers strive to allocate resources in the most productive way, to encourage innovation and change, and to negotiate with other managers and groups within the organisation in order to develop it further. The way in which decisions are made in an organisation is an important indicator of the way it functions, whether it is relatively autocratic or democratic, and this in turn depends on the leadership role of senior managers and the resultant corporate culture (*see* Chapters 2 and 9).

→ Chs 2 & 9

How managers spend their time

As a clearer indication of what managers do, there have been surveys of how they spend their time. These show that at senior and middle levels, at least, time is spent in a range of activities, depending very much on the nature of the organisation and the character of the individual. Exhibit 1.2 is a list of these activities in rank order. It needs to be remembered, however, that because a particular function does not appear on the list does not necessarily mean that it does not happen. For example, management by walking about (MBWA) may not exist in some managers' time allocation, but was stressed by Tom Peters and Robert Waterman in *In Search of Excellence* (1982) as an essential element in managerial success. Any list will not represent the full range of activities of an individual manager.

Exhibit 1.2 **How managers spend their time**

- **Controlling**
- **Solving problems**
- **Planning**
- **Communicating informally and formally**
- **Communicating upwards**
- **Communicating downwards**
- **Attending meetings**
- **Reading**
- **Writing memos and letters**
- **Representing the company**

A 1997 survey of 258 chief executives carried out for the *Sunday Times* found that 79 per cent of those surveyed thought that the business, social and economic environment had created a culture in which cost cutting was the driving force for managers, instead of the development of the rounded skills needed to manage growth, expansion and innovation. Asked to name the most important management skills from a list of 11, the chief executives put leadership first, followed by vision, people management, communications and financial literacy. Although they said that a lack of management skills in their organisation had already prevented them from fully exploiting commercial opportunities, they were optimistic about the future because they thought that future managers would be better educated and trained and more aware of competition.

MANAGING CHANGE

Descriptions of what managers do and how they spend their time provide only a partial view of a manager's actual role. Almost by definition, managers are a small minority of people in the employment of any organisation and therefore most people do not have experience of being a manager. Whereas managers have usually been through the operational stage and can to some extent transfer this type of experience to any operational area, it is more difficult for operators who have never been managers to understand the management viewpoint. On the other hand, of course, most people have some understanding of management processes, because their work involves some of these processes, they have to manage their personal lives and their homes, and because they will experience the results of different management actions, approaches and styles. At a simple structural level there is often an understanding that work has to be managed, that someone has to make major decisions, and that the organisation and individual jobs within it depend on management functions being performed.

→ Ch. 20 The management of change in an organisation is an area of potential conflict because of these inherent issues of understanding and communication (*see* Chapter 20). Management actions to facilitate change can easily be misunderstood because the procedures and processes already in existence appear to be perfectly good. These days the management of change is the most important management skill because it can be seen as a constant process of setting up working methods to meet changing circumstances. These 'changing circumstances' need to be understood by everyone. John Harvey-Jones (1993) has stated that change is easier to manage when there is an element of danger present in an organisation and there is an obvious need for change:

> *'It is impossible to change organisations which do not accept the dangers of their present way of doing things.'*

Although the decision to implement change may be considered to be largely conceptual in nature, it takes effect in action and behaviour. Managing change is essentially about people and not concepts and ideas, while the results of change will be seen most clearly by most people in matters of detail. Faced with pressure for change, managers are likely to deal with the situation in ways which coincide with the culture of the organisation. This raises a particular challenge to management when the action required is outside the assumptions and beliefs of members of the organisation. Much change is incremental in that one change leads to another, and the main challenge to modern management is that the incremental steps are closer together than in the past. However, it is this increasing frequency of change which challenges the underlying culture of organisations: 'the way we do things around here'. For example, technological change may mean the gradual introduction of wordprocessors to replace typewriters, or the introduction of an automated assembly line with robots replacing the assembly line jobs all at the same time. In the first case, a few people will be left behind who are unable to make the change from typewriters to computers. In the second case, all or most jobs will disappear, with perhaps a few new ones appearing in the form of maintenance or quality control. As a result of technological and scientific development, 'the way we do things around here' may be altered overnight, but even in the most extreme cases the manager's role is to anticipate the change and prepare for it.

All change involves people and their working patterns and it can be argued that organisations can only change at the speed at which people in them are willing and able to change. Fundamental changes in attitudes take years rather than months, and the first part of the process is a clear understanding that the status quo is no longer possible. This may be through dissatisfaction with the present position or fear of the consequences of adhering to it. For example, if competitors are clearly affecting the viability of the company, the present position can be seen as a threat and the need for change will be easily appreciated.

Change and organisational culture

→ Ch. 8

An organisation's **culture** can be defined as 'the way we do things around here' (*see* Chapter 8). It can be considered as a complex mixture of tangible factors which can be seen and touched, assumptions about how people should behave in the organisation and people's actual behaviour. Culture can be the basis of competitive advantage in markets because it may prove difficult to imitate. On the other hand, it is also difficult to change and it can be argued that organisations are 'captured' by their own cultures in the sense of sharing more or less strongly a set of beliefs, customs, practices and ways of thinking and the development of ritual or accepted behaviour that they have come to share with each other through being and working together.

Tangible factors include the organisation's location, the buildings it inhabits, the decoration and layout of the workplaces. For example, so-called 'hot desking' has developed as a result of a particularly informal approach to work and stand-up discussion around a tall table has developed as a way of encouraging meetings to be short and businesslike. There may be assumptions about when people arrive at work and when they leave and how many breaks they take. Although working hours may be set out in an employment contract, employees may be expected to work longer hours than those written down. The actual behaviour of employees may mean that although they are at work for long hours, they take frequent breaks so that the actual hours they work are similar to those of employees who are at work for a shorter time.

The ritual behaviour, symbols, myths and stories in an organisation can be analysed in order to study its culture. The way the founder of the company behaved may create stories and myths which persist in the company long after the founder has gone and continue to affect people's behaviour. In the same way, the style and actions of the present chief executive may set the tone for the company even if some of the reported incidents are in fact stories or myths. A very formal approach to working relationships by a boss may establish the style for everyone else, while an informal manner may encourage different behaviour.

Figure 1.7 illustrates some of the influences on **organisational culture**. Stories and myths that people in an organisation tell about what has happened in the past can provide a view of what they think is important. These may revolve around successes and failures, particular individuals and so on, and can indicate whether innovation or stability is important or whether company loyalty is highly prized. Symbols can indicate power structures in an organisation through car-parking privileges, or the size of offices for different people or functions. For example, if the head of the marketing function is a junior manager, this may indicate the company's view of its importance.

The difficulty of managing cultural change in an organisation depends on the strength of the existing culture and the size of the proposed change. The NHS is an example of the attempt to impose a new culture on a strong existing one and expecting a large change. The existence of a number of subcultures within an organisation will make change even more difficult. Strategic managers need to be sure that strategy requires shifts in values and assumptions or whether changes can be achieved within the present culture. Successful organisations tend to have a way of doing things which support their strategy. In order to achieve this, managers can introduce a structure which encourages behaviours that do support organisational strategy. This includes the promotion and rewards structure and other policies which provide a clear message.

Organisations can perpetuate their cultures through a variety of **socialisation** mechanisms as well as more formal approaches (summarised in Exhibit 1.3). The **recruitment** process can be used to select people who will 'fit in' with the culture of the organisation and questions can be asked which help to create an awareness of

Figure 1.7 'Influences on 'the way we do things around here'

Exhibit 1.3 **Factors in the management of cultures**

- Socialisation

- Recruitment policies

- Induction processes

- Reward systems

- Promotion policy

- Leadership

- Training and development

what is important in the organisation. The **induction** process can be used in the same way to reinforce what is expected of the new recruit not only in terms of rules and regulations but also in terms of company policies and less formal expectations. Individuals will be at their most receptive to new ideas and ways of behaving at the early stages of their employment, and companies such as IBM have used this early stage to provide their new employees with something of their history and philosophy.

The **reward system** in an organisation sends a clear message to employees about what types of behaviour are expected and acclaimed by senior management. For example, if large bonuses are paid to teams rather than individuals, this will encourage team building and loyalty to the team. If bonuses are a small proportion of individuals' total remuneration, this may encourage a relatively cautious culture. At the same time if a company rewards the finance director to a much greater extent than the marketing director, this sends a message to everyone about the relative importance to the company of the two functions. Large corporations may have multiple reward systems reflecting the demands of different business situations or traditional differences between groups of employees. These systems may perpetuate multiple cultures, which means that managing cultures through reward systems may be difficult in large organisations.

Different salary systems can create or reinforce organisational cultures so that one way of managing the culture is to adjust the reward system. Where length of service is the most important criterion for salary increases, an organisation is likely to end up with large numbers of long-serving middle and senior managers, highly deferential to organisational norms and unlikely to show initiative or take risks. Where salary increases are determined by a rigid pay system, order and predictability will tend to become ingrained within the organisation; where pay increases are a matter of discretion on the part of senior managers, the formation of cliques and self-serving activity may develop; if pay is linked to measured performance, such as the level of completed sales, conflict and antagonism may be encouraged.

In a similar way to the reward system, the **promotion process** can also influence the culture of an organisation. A policy of internal promotion will encourage loyalty and consistency while basic assumptions about the 'way we do things' are unlikely to be questioned. On the other hand, a policy of looking for external appointees is more likely to result in cultural diversity and can more easily lead to cultural change.

The use of promotion to develop people and to indicate the organisation's commitment to its staff can contribute to an organisation with a common culture. In organisations with a highly competitive internal structure, promotions may be used to ensure that people with a particular viewpoint are in positions of influence.

Leadership is an important element in managing culture. Leaders can 'set a good example' in terms of their working habits. They can communicate important messages to employees, call meetings and shape agendas, and praise and reward members of staff who are considered to have worked well. Leaders can also act as barriers to culture change in that the leader may be the most resistant to change. For example, the founders of successful organisations may believe that they have a winning formula which they are very reluctant to change. The classic example is Henry Ford who had to be persuaded that the idea of 'a Model T car in any colour so long as it was black' was no longer a good idea when rival car companies began to produce cars of different colours.

Training and development may be used to try to introduce a change in the culture of an organisation. This approach involves explaining the reasons why a change is necessary, 'Why things need to be done differently around here,' and then trying to convince people so that this becomes part of their beliefs. This is particularly difficult unless all the other factors which can assist the management of culture are supporting the new approach. This means that, for example, the reward system, promotions and so on all point in the same direction in terms of cultural change. Above all, management leaders at all levels need to show by example the importance to them of the changes. Programmes of staff training, appraisal systems and coaching can combine to send a powerful message to everybody, but still may face the difficulty of overcoming basic beliefs and values. An example of the problems to be overcome is clearly seen where professionals are expected to start to run a business, in the way that doctors and consultants in the UK National Health Service and lecturers in the UK university system have done.

When faced with change in their organisation, it has been observed that people will often attempt to deal with the situation by searching for areas of change they can understand and cope with in terms of the existing culture. They will attempt to minimise the extent to which they are faced with uncertainty by looking for what is familiar. This will usually be as true of managers as of anybody else. Faced with change, managers will first seek a means of improving the implementation of existing strategy. They may start by tightening existing controls and making minor adjustments to the organisation. If this is not effective, they may move on to further changes in line with the existing procedures.

The problem with this approach is that it is backward-looking. For example, managers may consider price changes or attempt to reduce the costs of production. These may be the right policies arrived at almost by chance rather than by considering the fundamental reason for change, which may be, for example, alterations in the expectations of customers and the need to alter the products and services provided for them. It may be that changes in price and reduction in costs are the correct decisions, but it may be that the company is producing the wrong product range or has not concentrated sufficiently on staff training in order to provide high-quality customer service.

Change should be forward-looking, otherwise the organisation will gradually, perhaps imperceptibly, become more and more at odds with the environment in which it operates. Managers have to consider the type and quality of products or services that should be produced to meet the needs of their customers, and the level of service and back-up required to encourage customers to make use of them. At the strategic level at least, managers need to look forward towards the changes that are necessary for the success of the organisation and then start to prepare people in the organisation to meet these changes. Major changes in the marketplace may occur as a result of competitors altering their policies and practices in one way or another; there may be a change in fashion among consumers or there may be a sudden shortage of materials. Managers can make piecemeal modifications in the operations of the organisation to meet the changes if they can be predicted to some extent. These may be sufficient in the short term, but for more permanent change managers need to flag up situations in order to create a climate suited to more fundamental questioning of what is taken for granted. For example, this can be done by emphasising downturns in performance or putting a spotlight on external threats and, at the same time, the need for change can be signalled by making internal organisational changes.

Forces for change

Organisations have both influences encouraging change and other influences acting to keep the organisation in a state of equilibrium. Those forces which oppose change can also be seen to be supporting stability and the status quo. In **forcefield theory**, any behaviour can be seen as the result of an equilibrium between driving and restraining forces, with the driving forces pushing one way, the restraining forces the other. It can be argued that the performance that emerges is a reconciliation between these two sets of forces. For example, an increase in driving forces, say an autocratic style of management, may increase the level of active restraining forces, say distrust and resistance. This can mean that if managers attempt to initiate change by a series of orders and commands, this is likely to be met by either active resistance or more passive avoidance. It is not always easy entirely to avoid taking action which creates a strong counter-reaction. The extreme example is the closing down of a company, which can be accomplished while minimising disruption and hardship but particularly in times of recession may come very suddenly. Opposition to a sudden closure may take the form of some type of strike or legal action. However, these can be considered to be exceptional circumstances and most change within an organisation can be managed in such a way that restraining forces are minimised. This process has been highlighted by Kurt Lewin (1951) in his

→ Ch. 14

work on forcefield theory (*see also* Chapter 14). He has identified multiple causes of behaviour which are summarised in Figure 1.8. Programmes of planned change can have the objective of weakening the restraining forces and supporting the driving forces in order to create a high level of performance.

New technology, changes in raw materials supply and competition are among the factors which create a need for change, but these driving factors can also be seen in slightly different terms:

■ time
■ turbulence
■ interdependence
■ technology.

Figure 1.8 **Forcefield diagram**

These terms summarise the reasons for change, so that, for example, the **time span** for the communication of information has been radically reduced as the capability of IT has grown. Peter Drucker (1988) has referred to:

> *'a shift from the command and control organisation, to the information based organisation – the organisation of the knowledge specialists . . . it is the management challenge of the future.'*

The development of communication technologies and the power of the computer has enabled information-based tasks to be carried out more productively and more quickly and has necessitated considerable changes in business processes.

At the same time **turbulence** has been caused by rapid changes in politics, culture and society. Even in the most politically stable countries there are changes in policy, often as a result of economic pressures, necessitating considerable change in commercial and other organisations. Changes in exchange rates, trade regulations and educational and social policy will influence many organisations to a greater or lesser extent. At the same time there are cultural changes occurring, alternatives in tastes and fashions which can create forces for change. For example, the fluctuations in oil prices since 1974 have had an economic consequence on many companies, while government policies on interest rates have affected the cost of borrowing and the return on investment. The growing number of 'dependants' (such as students and old-age pensioners) as against productive workers in the UK has led to the consideration of major changes in social policy.

Interdependence has increased with growing specialisation and attempts to improve productivity. Many companies have moved away from the idea of controlling all the sources of supply or sale they require or all the services they might need. The 'outsourcing' of services has meant that a company may buy in functions such as training or legal advice and rely increasingly on consultants. The company can then specialise on what it can do best, leaving other specialists to provide raw materials or sales outlets. For example, many companies 'outsource' their cleaning and catering requirements as well as other specialist activities, such as information technology, premises management and aspects of personnel management.

Technology has altered whole areas of work, making some skills redundant while developing new areas. For example, automation has meant that some factories require more skills in terms of maintenance and quality control than in machine operation. The typing pool has been replaced by wordprocessors, photocopiers, fax machines and electronic mail. The need for quick responses, personally addressed correspondence and other forms of multiple or individual communication has been taken over by office machinery.

As a result of these forces, organisations require a dynamism which may be missing in the traditional culture, so that successful modern organisations do not simply respond to change, they see it coming and exploit the opportunities it creates. This requires a clearly articulated vision of the direction of the organisation and a strategy for change. It requires an ability to manage change and be able to intercept and respond to what is to come in the future. The challenge to management is to position an organisation so that it can move from its current state to its desired future state and be able to do this again and again.

The process of change

It is possible to recognise certain characteristics in the process of change. These include uncertainty about the causes and effects of change, unwillingness to give up existing practices, and awareness of problems in the change process. These characteristics arise from a natural reaction to deny that the change is necessary, to resist any change whatever its merits and, if necessary, to avoid changes when they are introduced.

Managers have to determine the actual causes of resistance to change and remain flexible enough in their approach to overcome them in an appropriate manner. There is a considerable degree of interaction between interdependent elements in any organisation, and this has to be recognised. The structure of the organisation, the technology which is applied and the people working in it are highly interdependent and all three have to be involved in the change process. The task of the manager is to direct energy away from feelings of powerlessness and looking backwards and towards seeing the opportunities for the future.

This is particularly important because in the process of change people feel that they are threatened by the future while they need to recognise the danger in the present position and the opportunity in the new one. The process may involve denial of the need to change and resistance to it, until the change is able to be explored when opportunities may be discussed and commitment created.

Figure 1.9 illustrates the transition that can take place in the change process, from denial and resistance to exploration and commitment. The challenge for managers is to help people through the process. People move from the familiar to the unknown and often experience a feeling of loss when they struggle to accept a new direction. This experience of loss can take a variety of forms:

■ **Security** – people feel unsure of their position in the organisation and how it will change; 'we don't know where we stand'.

■ **Competence** – they become worried about their ability to carry out new tasks; 'we don't know what to do'.

■ **Relationships** – they may feel that familiar contacts will be lost with other employees, with managers and teams and groups; 'we don't know to whom we report'.

Figure 1.9 Transition

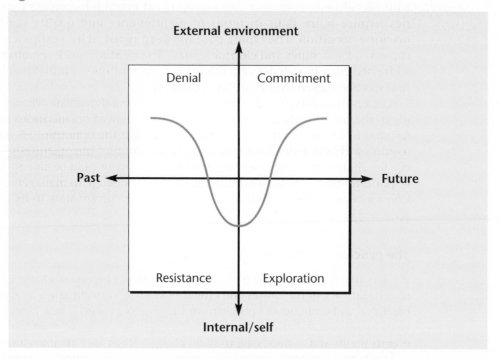

- **Territory** – they may feel uncertain about their work space or job responsibility; 'we don't know where we work or whether we can do this or not'.

- **Direction** – they lose a clear view of where they are going; 'why are we doing this?'

These feelings of loss are a normal part of the transition process. The management task is to acknowledge these feelings and attempt to allay them. This involves more than providing information because people in organisations will not necessarily alter their behaviour simply by being told. For example, many people have continued to smoke in spite of health warnings. People need support and encouragement and there is an important leadership role in the change process in creating a trusting and supportive relationship. This requires considerable management skill and can place managers in an exposed position.

Managing change

The purpose of change is to move an organisation from its present point to a different one which is more desirable in meeting its objectives. In managing this process the gap between the starting point and the desirable conclusion needs to be identified. The usual steps are:

- **Vision** – a process of reminding everybody and clarifying to everybody the direction of the organisation; 'where we are going'.

- **Strategy** – outlining how this is to be achieved through the development of objectives and goals; 'how we are going to get there'.

- **Monitoring change** – progress is measured in order to observe and encourage change; 'this is how far we are now'.

Different stages of changes require different strategies. At the denial stage, information has to be provided, and time given in order to explain this information and suggest action. At the resistance stage, managers have to have an acceptance of people's responses and encourage support. If people tell managers how they feel, the manager can be helped to respond effectively. In the exploration stage there can be a concentration on priorities, training can be provided and planning take place. There is then a commitment stage where long-term goals can be established with a concentration on team building.

The curve in Figure 1.10 can indicate the time taken by most people to move from one stage to the next. A deep curve can indicate a lengthy period of resistance and exploration before there is a commitment. At one extreme there may be an intense period of denial and resistance, with people becoming angry or anxious, depressed and frustrated, and a concentration on the impact the change will have on them personally.

Stress may appear during the exploration stage, with the expressed concern that the new system will be chaotic. Exploring new responsibilities and ways of doing things can mean that an understanding of a new system begins to emerge. Some people may experience what has been referred to as a 'Tarzan swing' in that they believe they have jumped to the final stage of commitment by swinging straight over resistance and exploration. This may be the result of a very persuasive manager or arise by concentrating on only one aspect of the change, perhaps particularly favourable to the individual. It may only be a short-term conversion which fades away over time and leaves long-term doubts. It may be better to work more slowly through the stages by developing a programme for change in order to establish long-term commitments.

Figure 1.10 Managing change

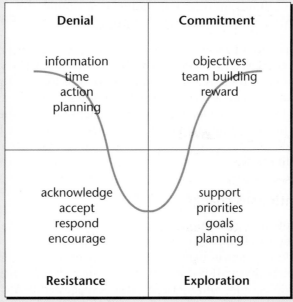

The programme for change will include:

- **leadership** – a person who provides a clear statement of the vision and objectives;
- **coherence** – agreement on the operational tasks and goals consistent with the strategic view;
- **communication** – the provision of clear and appropriate information to the relevant people about what is happening and why it is happening;
- **timing** – decisions on when to take action;
- **structure** – a structured approach which moves logically through an understanding of the forces for change to the agreement on the management of the change process.

This programme will inevitably contain traps for managers. Ignoring resistance to change or attempting to block it will tend to encourage resistance being felt more deeply and lasting longer. It can be argued that resistance should be sought out, taken seriously and the reasons for it should be discussed. Pushing too hard too soon on structural change or a change such as increasing productivity may prove to be counter-productive. Time to absorb the change needs to be provided in order to enable short-term responses, which may be emotional and negative, to fade and be overtaken by a more rational and positive approach.

This process is helped by involving people in planning for change and monitoring its progress. Active participation will help people to understand how the change will affect them and to come to terms with it. Employees need to be helped to say 'good goodbyes' to old practices, and resistance to change can be taken by managers as a sign that people have left the denial stage and are moving on. In this process it is essential that managers are clear about objectives, and that these are SMART:

- **Specific about what is to be accomplished**
- **Measurable differences must be identified**
- **Attainable targets should be established**
- **Result output oriented change is desirable**
- **Time limits should be established.**

There should also be a reward system for people attempting as well as accomplishing change. The rewards may be in the form of pay if this is appropriate, as for example if there is a change in contracts or job description, or in the form of status or recognition. A reward system can provide motivation, but that can also be developed through leadership and encouraging involvement. People need to be part of the process which makes change work, for example by being a member of a team which decides on the detail of the change and by participation in task forces and quality circles.

Continuous change

People in organisations are often unwilling or unable to alter long-established attitudes and behaviour. A change in management style or attitude or a change in working practices may be seen as a violation of people's self-image or an indication of inadequacy. It is difficult to introduce change without suggesting a criticism of previous styles and methods. If it is suggested to a work unit that they should do things in a different way, they will immediately wonder what is wrong with their present operating method. There is an implied criticism, however diplomatically the suggestion is worded. If change can be perceived as a continuous process, it may be possible to avoid this problem, because it will become part of working practices.

If change is seen to be a short-term process, after a brief period of doing things differently people may return to their earlier practices. In order to avoid this, a three-step model can be applied to the change process:

- **Unfreezing** – the need for change is made so obvious that individuals and teams can easily recognise and accept it.

- **Leadership** – managers foster new values, attitudes and behaviour through the process of identification and internalisation.

- **Refreezing** – the new practices are locked into place by supporting and reinforcing mechanisms so that they become the new norm.

This process can be used to improve an organisation's response to continuous change. This can be seen as:

> *'a top management-supported, long-range effort to improve an organisation's problem solving and renewal processes, particularly through a more effective and collaborative diagnosis and management of organisation culture.'*   (French and Ball, 1984)

This involves consultation right across the organisation, and one part of the change process is decentralising management by transferring ownership of the problem to the lowest possible level. Decentralisation, flatter management organisation and decisions taken at the point of action can increase both the ability to change and the speed with which change can be accomplished. Managers have to look at every way in which an organisation conducts itself in order to find the most productive and efficient processes.

Through this approach it is possible to institutionalise change so that it becomes a continuous process instead of a set piece every five years. This is the management view based on observation of Japanese management practices. For example, the concept of 'just-in-time' production involves close and flexible working between manufacturer, supplier and purchaser. Japanese car manufacturers can be seen as specifiers and assemblers rather than manufacturers in the old sense, whereas General Motors in the USA has aimed at a high degree of vertical integration, controlling the manufacturing process from raw material to final product and customers. The 'just-in-time' process recreates the producer/customer relationship at every stage so that there is an urgency at each point. This may be a difficult feeling to transfer to departments and sections of a large organisation.

The Japanese have been determined to have continuous incremental development and believe that this is most likely where there is a direct link with the customer. In an organisation which is managed vertically, that is with a chain of control running from the raw material to the retail outlet, there is a vast amount of capital invested before the person nearest to the ultimate customer is reached. However strong the links may be in this chain, the final and crucial link with the consumer may not be sufficiently strong to control the weight of expectations of the rest of the company. In large, vertically controlled companies, the people nearest to the ultimate customer may have difficulty in controlling everything that stands behind them. Rigidities tend to build up and pressures generate the wrong way. The 'just-in-time' philosophy may operate effectively in this type of organisation, but only if managers encourage close working between supplier and customer at every level and then leave them to resolve all the day-to-day problems, rather than pushing decisions up the line to others who will not feel the urgency of the situation.

THE MANAGEMENT CHALLENGE IN TIMES OF CHANGE

The management challenge is to fund, organise and control the efforts of an organisation to achieve particular goals, while at the same time identifying the need for change and implementing change though the development of an appropriate strategy. Changes in an organisation's environment may be reversible or irreversible. Irreversible changes are ones that are permanent or at least sufficiently long-term to require a fundamental change. The decline of the steel industry, for example, may in theory be reversible, but this is so unlikely that it can be considered permanent. Acts of Parliament, such as those to alter the structure of the railway industry, are able to be repealed and amended, but these are such long-term prospects that these alterations in structure can be considered fundamental. A reversible change may amount to seasonal or short-term alterations in conditions, which usually occur in the operating environment so that organisations can allow for them and alter their plans. Plans can be made for changes in the weather and particular events which will alter organisations' operational plans but may not result in fundamental change.

The Japanese approach is based on a need continuously to improve productivity faster than the competition. This can be seen as the challenge for all management in both the private and public sectors. In the public sector the challenge may be measured in different ways to those used in the private sector. Profit may not play a part, but measurement of activity against costs may replace monitoring of the return on capital invested. Income is now often linked to output and outcomes, while expenditure is firmly controlled and audited. Public sector managers are increasingly being asked to manage their organisations in a more commercial and effective way, exposed to competition and without any guarantee of survival. In many areas, public sector management is little different from that in the private sector, with the same urgencies and pressures. This is exemplified by the increasing frequency of movement of managers between the two sectors. The contrasts between the private and public sectors are analysed in Chapter 8.

→ Ch. 8

Managers in both sectors have to face changes in the environment which require changes not only in the organisation but also in the internal content within an organisation. The Pettigrew *et al.* (1992) model, which suggests that organisational change depends on the 'why', 'what' and 'how' of change, can be applied to organisations (companies, institutions, 'bodies') in both sectors. This model identifies an external and internal context of change for organisations. A major change in the external context, such as an economic, social or technological upheaval, requires a strategic response by managers if their organisations are to be successful. Marks & Spencer, for example, attempted for some years to ignore the trend among rival clothing retailers to use Far Eastern manufacturers as a relatively cheap source of supply, but competition from companies able to sell cheaper goods forced a change of policy.

In the Pettigrew *et al.* model, the internal context of organisations is seen as organisational structure, assets and resources, and organisational culture, which set the broad context in which change occurs and which could also offer reasons for the need for change to take place. The content of change is a question of 'what' needs to take place in the structure and culture of an organisation for it to adjust to changes in order to be successful. The 'how' of change is then the processes by which changes are made in relation to planning and development, communication and consultation, and environmental assessment in terms of market research and marketing. The leadership and management of these processes is a critical factor in the success of organisations which need to react positively to strategic change in order to create a fit between the operation of the organisation and its new internal and external contexts. At the same time the challenge for managers is to encourage environmental assessment in order for an organisation to learn to adapt to fresh developments and new strategic change.

SUMMARY

■ The manager's role is greater than the process of organising people in order to achieve particular outcomes. While it includes this process, the real challenge is to manage change by leading and inspiring people.

■ Change has become a central factor because in order to meet their objectives organisations need to focus on their customers and the changing requirements of these customers.

■ Past and present theories of management provide ideas about the practice and process of management in order to decide on questions of organisation, control and planning.

■ Management skills are required at a variety of different levels, in different organisational structures and functional responsibilities, and these skills are clearly necessary for dealing with the complexities involved in the management of change.

Review and discussion questions

1 *What other differences are there between managers and leaders apart from those discussed in the case study?*

2 *Are the main functions of managers involved with a reaction to change?*

3 *Is management a science or an art?*

4 *Are the same management skills required at different levels of management?*

5 *How far does forcefield theory help to explain the main influences for change in organisations?*

CASE STUDY

Managers and leaders

Manager versus leader personality

A managerial culture emphasizes rationality and control. Whether his or her energies are directed toward goals, resources, organization structures, or people, a manager is a problem solver. The manager asks: 'What problems have to be solved, and what are the best ways to achieve results so that people will continue to contribute to this organization?' From this perspective, leadership is simply a practical effort to direct affairs, and to fulfill his or her task, a manager requires that many people operate efficiently at different levels of status and responsibility. It takes neither genius nor heroism to be a manager, but rather persistence, toughmindedness, hard work, intelligence, analytical ability, and perhaps most important, tolerance and goodwill.

Another conception of leadership, however, attaches almost mystical beliefs to what a leader is and assumes that only great people are worthy of the drama of power and politics. Here leadership is a psychodrama in which a brilliant, lonely person must gain control of himself or herself as a precondition for controlling others. Such an expectation of leadership contrasts sharply with the mundane, practical, and yet important conception that leadership is really managing work that other people do.

Three questions come to mind. Is the leadership mystique merely a holdover from our childhood – from a sense of dependency and a longing for good and heroic parents? Or is it true that no matter how competent managers are, their leadership stagnates because of their limitations in visualizing purposes and generating value in work? Driven by narrow purposes, without an imaginative capacity and the ability to communicate, do managers then perpetuate group conflicts instead of reforming them into broader desires and goals?

If indeed problems demand greatness, then judging by past performance, the selection and development of leaders leave a great deal to chance. There are no known ways to train 'great' leaders. Further, beyond what we leave to chance, there is a deeper issue in the relationship between the need for competent managers and the longing for great leaders.

What it takes to ensure a supply of people who will assume practical responsibility may inhibit the development of great leaders. On the other hand, the presence of great leaders may undermine the development of managers who typically become very anxious in the relative disorder that leaders seem to generate.

It is easy enough to dismiss the dilemma of training managers, though we may need new leaders, or leaders at the expense of managers, by saying that the need is for people who can be both. But just as a managerial culture differs from the entrepreneurial culture that develops when leaders appear in organizations, managers and leaders are very different kinds of people. They differ in motivation, in personal history, and in how they think and act.

Attitudes toward goals

Managers tend to adopt impersonal, if not passive, attitudes toward goals. Managerial goals arise out of necessities rather than desires and, therefore, are deeply embedded in their organization's history and culture.

Frederic G. Donner, chairman and chief executive officer of General Motors from 1958 to 1967, expressed this kind of attitude toward goals in defining GM's position on product development:

'To meet the challenge of the marketplace, we must recognize changes in customer needs and desires far enough ahead to have the right products in the right places at the right time and in the right quantity.

'We must balance trends in preference against the many compromises that are necessary to make a final product that is both reliable and good looking, that performs well and that sells at a competitive price in the necessary volume. We must design not just the cars we would like to build but, more important, the cars that our customers want to buy.'

Nowhere in this statement is there a notion that consumer tastes and preferences arise in part as a result of what manufacturers do. In reality, through product design, advertising, and promotion, consumers learn to like what they then say they need. Few would argue that people who enjoy taking snapshots need a camera that also develops pictures. But in response to a need for novelty, convenience, and a shorter interval between acting (snapping the picture) and gaining pleasure (seeing the shot), the Polaroid camera succeeded in the marketplace. It is inconceivable that Edwin Land responded to impressions of consumer need. Instead, he translated a technology (polarization of light) into a product, which proliferated and stimulated consumers' desires.

The example of Polaroid and Land suggests how leaders think about goals. They are active instead of reactive, shaping ideas instead of responding to them. Leaders adopt a personal and active attitude toward goals. The influence a leader exerts in altering moods, in evoking images and expectations, and in establishing specific desires and objectives determines the direction a business takes. The net result of this influence changes the way people think about what is desirable, possible, and necessary

Source: 'Managers and Leaders: Are they different?' by Abraham Zaleznik (*Harvard Business Review*, January 2004, pp 74–81)

REFERENCES AND FURTHER READING

Argyris, Chris (2000) *Flawed Advice and the Management Trap*, Oxford: Oxford University Press.

Barnard, Chester I (1938) *The Functions of the Executive*, Cambridge, MA: Harvard University Press.

Beer, Michael and Nohria, Nitin (2000) 'Cracking the Code of Change', *Harvard Businesss Review*, May/June.

Christensen, Clayton M and Overdorf, Michael (2000) 'Meeting the Challenge of Disruptive Change', *Harvard Business Review*, March/April.

Drucker, Peter (1988) 'The coming of the new organization', *Harvard Business Review*, January/February.

Drucker, Peter F (1998) *Managing in a Time of Great Change*, New York: Plume.

Fayol, Henri (1930) *Industrial and General Administration*, Geneva: International Management Institute.

French, W L and Ball, C H (1984) *Organization Development: Behavioral Science Interventions for Organization Improvement*, Englewood Cliffs, NJ: Prentice-Hall.

Gilbreth, Lillian M (1914) *The Psychology of Management*, New York: Stangus & Walter.

Hamel, G and Prahalad, C K (1994) *Competing for the Future*, Boston, MA: Harvard Business School Press.

Harvey-Jones, John (1993) *Managing to Survive*, London: Heinemann.

Lewin, Kurt (1951) *Field Theory in Social Science*, New York: Harper & Brothers.

Mayo, Elton, Roethlisberger, F J and Dickson, W J (1939) *Management and the Worker*, Cambridge, MA: Harvard University Press.

Mescon, Michael H, Albert, Michael and Khedouri, Franklin (1985) *Management: Individual and Organizational Effectiveness*, New York: Harper & Row.

Mintzberg, Henry (1980) *The Nature of Managerial Work*, Englewood Cliffs, NJ: Prentice-Hall.

Ouchi, William (1981) *Theory Z: How American Business Can Meet the Japanese Challenge*, Reading, MA: Addison-Wesley.

Parker Follett, Mary (1941) *Collected Works*, New York: Harper & Brothers.

Pearce, John A and Robinson, Richard B Jr (1989) *Management*, New York: McGraw-Hill.

Peters, Tom (1987) *Thriving on Chaos*, London: Macmillan.

Peters, Tom and Waterman, Robert (1982) *In Search of Excellence*, New York: Harper & Row.

Pettigrew, A M (1988) *The Management of Strategic Change*, Oxford: Blackwell.

Pettigrew, A M, Ferlie, E and McKee, L (1992) *Shaping Strategic Change*, London: Sage.

Smith, Professor Sir Roland (1993) 'Windsor Business Forum', Cable Telecom.

Weber, Max (1947) *The Theory of Social and Economic Organizations*, New York: Free Press.

WEBSITES

http://cgl.pathfinder.com/fortune/careers/1999/01/11interview.html
This provides information about successful managers, such as Jack Welch, the CEO of General Electric.

http://www.FT.com
The *Financial Times*, the world's leading international business newspaper.

http://www.clickMT.com
Management Today and the *Professional Manager*, two of the leading British management magazines.

CHAPTER 2

Leadership in management

TIM HANNAGAN

Outcomes

Having read this chapter, you will be able to:

- describe leadership, consider its importance and identify the relationship between leadership and management

- analyse different theories of leadership as they apply to management

- examine styles of leadership and their impact on organisations

- understand leadership power and control

WHAT IS LEADERSHIP?

Definition

In all organisations, large or small, leadership is required in order for its objectives to be achieved. Good leadership can result in success, poor leadership can result in failure, and this leadership can be provided by one person or by a team of people. An important part of the management role is to provide leadership of one kind or another, because leadership is about providing direction for an organisation, making decisions on the methods and processes to achieve organisational objectives and helping to establish the 'style' and culture of an organisation – 'the way it operates'.

Leadership is the process of motivating other people to act in particular ways in order to achieve specific goals. The motivation of other people may be achieved in a variety of ways which affect leadership styles, and the way a person exercises leadership can be identified as a series of actions which are directed towards a particular objective. The emphasis is on action because, although leaders may exert influence through inspirational speeches, they are judged on what they do.

> *'Not the cry but the flight of the wild duck leads the flock to fly and to follow.'*
> (Chinese proverb quoted by Adair, 1989)

The word 'leader' derives from words meaning a path or road and suggests the importance of guidance on a journey. Both the word itself and the role of leader are about looking forward, identifying the way ahead or steering others towards agreed objectives. This process means that leaders need to have followers and to share common goals with their followers. People following leaders give up, temporarily at least, their ideas of the direction they should be going, in favour of the leader's ideas on this; they accede to the preferences of the leader in exchange for the rewards that they expect to receive as a result. The role of the leader is to convince them that this exchange is worthwhile; the greater the conviction, the higher the level of motivation there is likely to be and the more likely the common objectives will be attained.

Leadership involves other people, who by the degree of their willingness to accept direction help to define the leader's status. Leadership also involves authority and responsibility, in terms of deciding the way ahead and being held responsible for the success or failure of achieving the agreed objectives. Although leadership is most clearly seen at times of high drama, it can arise in all sorts of situations when an individual takes charge and decides what to do next. It can be argued that people can exhibit 'qualities of leadership' in a variety of circumstances. These qualities are usually seen to be in the taking of decisions and communicating them to other people in such a way that action is taken. At the same time people are sometimes referred to as 'born leaders', as though leadership is an inherent or even inherited quality. On the other hand, if leadership is seen as a process which can be analysed, and a series of actions which can be identified, then it can be learned, at least to some extent.

John Adair in *Great Leaders* (1989) suggests that:

> *'The common sense conclusion of this book is that leadership potential can be developed, but it does have to be there in the first place.'*

The delegation of decision making in organisations means that it is essential for many people at all levels of management to have and to develop some potential for leadership. Management implies leadership, and in fact the success or failure of managers can be judged on their leadership qualities. If the manager's role is to achieve organisational goals, then these are reached by showing people the way forward to find solutions and overcome obstacles. In a constantly changing social, economic and technological environment, leadership has become a more important attribute of management than in the past. In a more static environment, controlling and organising might be seen as more important than leadership for most managers, but this has changed. It is not just senior managers who need to look forward in order to foresee the changes which are coming and to act accordingly. Team managers and supervisors also have to implement change at their own level, to understand it and to take their working colleagues and subordinates along with them.

Leadership can be seen as a subset of management in the sense that management is broader in scope as it is concerned with behavioural as well as non-behavioural matters. It can be argued (*see* Massie and Douglas, 1977) that managers are concerned with bringing together resources, developing strategies, organising and controlling activities in order to achieve agreed objectives. At the same time managers, as leaders, have to select the goals and objectives of an organisation, decide what is to be done and motivate people to do it. Leadership can be seen as performing the influencing function of management, largely involved with establishing goals and motivating people to help achieve them. Looked at in this way, leaders decide 'where we are going' and influence people to take that particular direction, rather than describe 'how we are going to get there'. The debate on the role of the manager against that of the leader is perhaps more a question of definition than substance, although inspired leaders are not necessarily good organisers and excellent managers may appear to be rather mundane in terms of leadership. In practice, the most effective managers are also leaders, and the quality of leadership has become an increasingly important part of management ability. An organisation may be well organised and controlled, but without leadership it will be static and will not develop and progress.

THEORIES OF LEADERSHIP

There are a number of approaches to understanding leadership, ranging from the traditional view that leaders are born and not made, to the relatively recent view that leadership is more to do with the situation than to any universally desirable set of attributes.

Trait theories

The first systematic effort by researchers to understand leadership was the attempt to identify the personal characteristics of leaders. Their attempts can be termed as 'trait theories'. It can be argued that there is a predisposition to consider leaders as naturally braver, more aggressive, more decisive and more articulate than other people, so that they stand out in terms of physical characteristics, personality and intelligence. One popular myth is that natural leaders are tall and stand above the crowd like Charles de Gaulle or Abraham Lincoln.

Alexander the Great was of medium height at a time when physical height was associated with superiority. When he first sat on the throne of Cyrus the Great, it is reported that his servants had to replace the footstool with a low table. When he met some Persian emissaries they initially made their addresses to one of Alexander's staff who was the tallest man in the royal party. Alexander had other physical attributes which compensated for his lack of height, and above all he could inspire and motivate his soldiers.

The opposite popular view also exists, that natural leaders are below average height, like Napoleon Bonaparte or Mahatma Gandhi, and that they become leaders because they have to be more assertive than others. In fact, the results of studies on physical characteristics show that no physical traits clearly distinguish leaders from non-leaders. Some studies have shown that leaders as a group have been brighter, more extrovert and self-confident than non-leaders. However, although millions of people have these traits, few of them will attain positions of leadership. It is also possible that we are back again in the **self-fulfilling prophecy** situation, where individuals become more assertive and confident once they occupy a position of leadership, so that this trait may be the result rather than the cause of leadership ability.

Edwin Ghiselli researched the question of leadership personality traits for many years, while Fred Fiedler studied personality and intelligence traits. These researchers confirm the general conclusion that there are certain desirable traits in leaders, but the fact that an individual has some of them does not determine success. Ghiselli (1971) felt that the ability to supervise other people was important, along with intelligence and decisiveness. Fiedler (1971) concluded that successful leaders were more perceptive than their subordinates and more psychologically distant.

A complicating factor in this trait theory is the question of cultural bias. If there is a bias towards tall leaders, then most leaders will be tall because they are the ones who will be chosen. In the same way, the so-called 'glass ceiling' prevents women from becoming senior managers in some companies and therefore they do not emerge as leaders. When women do become senior managers, research shows that they can be just as effective leaders as men. Even though an increasing number of people believe in equality of ability and opportunity, persistent, often unconscious social stereotyping can still continue to be an obstacle in the recognition of women as leaders. Research has also shown that male and female managers are judged to be equally effective by their subordinates (Donnell and Hall, 1980).

The research into personality traits, or a set of qualities that can be used to discriminate leaders from non-leaders, has failed to produce any consistent position. It appears that no trait or combination of traits guarantees that a leader will be successful.

The behavioural approach to leadership

When it became evident that effective leaders did not apparently have any distinguishing traits or qualities, researchers tried to understand how successful and unsuccessful managers behave differently. Instead of trying to find out what effective leaders were, research turned to trying to determine what effective leaders did. The questions asked in these studies were about how leaders communicated to their subordinates, how they attempted to motivate them, how they made decisions and so on. It was felt that if the effective behaviours could be identified, then prospective managers who behaved in the more effective ways could be hired and current managers could be trained in such a way as to increase organisational productivity. The importance of arriving at this conclusion is that it meant the correct actions and behaviour could be learned and training could be provided for leadership.

Research by Ralph Stogdill (1957) and others at Ohio State University during the 1940s concluded that there were two principal dimensions to leader behaviour. On the one hand there was a concern for people, and on the other a concern for production:

- **A concern for people.** This behaviour involves a manager's concern for developing mutual trust with subordinates. This was seen as an employee-oriented approach characterised by managers' concern for their employees. The manager's behaviour encourages mutual trust and two-way communication.

- **A concern for the task.** This behaviour involves managers' concern for directing subordinates in order to achieve production targets. It is a task-oriented approach, where managers tend to be highly directive and emphasise completing a task according to plan.

The research discovered, as might be expected, that employee turnover rates were lowest and employee satisfaction highest under leaders who were rated high in consideration for people. Conversely, high grievance rates and high turnover were associated with leaders who were rated low in consideration for people and high in task orientation. However, it was not, of course, quite as simple as this. The researchers found that subordinates' ratings of their leaders' effectiveness depended not so much on the particular style of the leader as on the situation in which the style was used. For example, managers who worked in manufacturing and who exhibited high concern for task completion and low concern for people were rated by their supervisors as more proficient than more employee-centred managers. In service organisations, including hospitals and restaurants, the reverse was true, so that the most highly rated managers were those with a high concern for people and a lower concern for task completion.

The management grid

The research into leadership behaviour has shown that it is multidimensional. One approach to this has been the management grid (Blake and Mouton, 1985) which identifies a range of management behaviours based on various ways that task-oriented and employee-oriented styles can interact with each other (*see* Figure 2.1). There are 81 possible interactions, but to attempt to define every one would not be productive, so the researchers have described five extreme positions. Managers can then decide how close to any of these is their form of leadership.

- **Country club management** scores high on concern for people and low on concern for production. This management style may be based on a belief that the most important leadership activity is to secure the voluntary co-operation of group members in order to obtain high levels of productivity. Subordinates of these managers report generally high levels of satisfaction, but managers may be considered too easy-going and unable to make decisions.

- **Authoritarian management** scores a high concern for production and efficiency and a low concern for people. This management style is task-oriented and stresses the quality of the decision over the wishes of subordinates. Such managers believe that group-centred action may achieve mediocre results. They can be conscientious, loyal and personally capable, but can become alienated from their subordinates, who may do only enough to keep themselves out of trouble.

- **Impoverished management** scores a low concern for both people and production. This management style does not provide leadership in a positive sense but

Figure 2.1 **The management grid**

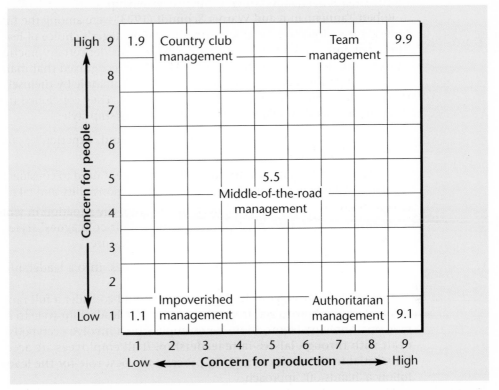

Source: Reprinted by permission of *Harvard Business Review*. R R Blake and J S Mouton (1985) *New Management Grid: The Key to Leadership Excellence*, Houston: Gulf Publishing Co. Adapted from Robert R Blake, Jane S Mouton, Louis B Barnes and Larry E Greiner (1964) 'Breakthrough in Organizational Development', *Harvard Business Review*, November–December, p 136. Copyright © 1964 by the Harvard Business School Publishing Corporation.

believes in a 'laissez-faire' approach, relying on previous practice to keep the organisation going.

■ **Middle-of-the-road management** scores a moderate amount of concern for both people and production. Managers applying this management style believe in compromise, so that decisions are taken but only if endorsed by subordinates. These managers may be dependable and support the status quo, but are not likely to be dynamic leaders and may have difficulty facing up to innovation and change.

■ **Team management** scores high on concern for both people and production. Blake and Mouton argue that this management style provides the most effective leadership. These managers believe that concern for people and for tasks are compatible. They believe that tasks need to be carefully explained and decisions agreed with subordinates to achieve a high level of commitment.

The contingency approach

Research into trait and behavioural approaches to effective leadership shows that it depends on many variables, in terms of individual personality, management style, corporate culture and the nature of the tasks to be performed. There is not one trait or approach which is effective in all situations. The contingency approach focuses on the situational factors which influence leadership.

Robert Tannenbaum and Warner Schmidt (1973) were among the first researchers to describe various factors which influenced a manager's choice of leadership style. They took into account the manager's need to consider certain practical considerations before deciding how to manage. Also they recognised that managers had to distinguish between types of problems they should handle by themselves and those they should resolve jointly with their subordinates. They concluded that there were three main 'forces' on managers in deciding a leadership style:

- **personal forces** – the managers' own background, experience, confidence and leadership inclinations;
- **the characteristics of subordinates** – the managers' need to consider subordinates' relative willingness or unwillingness to accept responsibility and take decisions;
- **the situation** – the managers' need to recognise the situation in which they find themselves, in terms of corporate culture, their colleagues' style of work, the nature of the tasks to be performed and time pressures.

Tannenbaum and Schmidt combined these 'forces' into a leadership continuum (Figure 2.2).

This continuum suggests that a manager should consider a full range of options before deciding how to act, from a very autocratic leadership style to a very democratic one. Some problems, those for example which involve everybody, may be best dealt with through laissez-faire leadership. If all employees are accountable and influential in the decision-making process, the best role for the leader may be to follow a 'hands-off' approach.

The discussion of management style demonstrates another **self-fulfilling prophecy**, in the sense that people will often react to a management style in such a way that managers will feel justified in their choice. For example, a leader may manage subordinates in an authoritarian style believing them to be low performers. This style may demotivate them, so that they do become low performers. A more democratic style may have encouraged greater initiative and high performance. This can affect the whole organisation because lower-level managers will model themselves on their superiors and attempt to manage in a similar way. E A Fleishman (1953) found that superiors who learned about new management styles in a human relations programme tended to change their actual behaviour if this was not consistent with their line manager's leadership style, and this was in spite of anything they learned on the programme.

Leadership and organisational culture

→ Ch. 8 The pressures to adopt a particular leadership style are also seen through the effects of corporate culture and peer expectations (*see* Chapter 8). Organisations have particular ways of doing things or place an emphasis on a particular measure of performance. For example, an advertising company may be fairly relaxed about working methods as long as the results are achieved. Leaders in this type of company may not be too concerned about how or when their employees work, provided that their outcomes and results are successful. On the other hand, a finance company may want to ensure strict accountability at every stage of its operation, so that there is close supervision of subordinates by senior managers. The

Figure 2.2 **Leadership continuum**

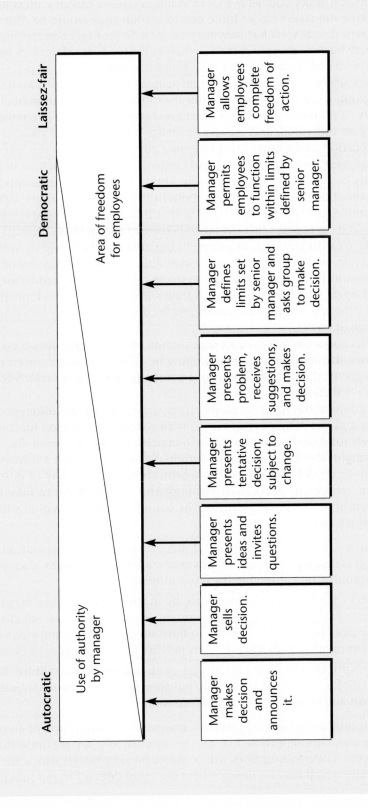

Autocratic	Democratic	Laissez-fair

Use of authority by manager

Area of freedom for employees

| Manager makes decision and announces it. | Manager sells decision. | Manager presents ideas and invites questions. | Manager presents tentative decision, subject to change. | Manager presents problem, receives suggestions, and makes decision. | Manager defines limits set by senior manager and asks group to make decision. | Manager permits employees to function within limits defined by senior manager. | Manager allows employees complete freedom of action. |

opinions, attitudes and behaviour of managers' peers can also affect leadership style in making managers either more cautious than they would be otherwise or more confident. If managers feel they may be criticised for an employee-based approach, they may become more autocratic, whereas if they know that their peers favour the employee-based approach, they may adopt this approach.

Power structures can influence how people behave in an organisation. The dominant group will usually be the senior management team, but marketing managers can have a powerful role in consumer goods companies and IT companies may rely heavily on individual and group knowledge. Organisational structures can also be an indication of dominant thinking in a company, with many layers of management suggesting a bureaucratic and controlled approach, while 'delayering' may not only be an attempt to cut costs but also to improve communications.

Organisational systems can be important in influencing culture. Control systems, for example, can be relatively 'hard' in that they have a financial implication, or relatively 'soft' in encouraging people to behave in certain ways. Reward systems often provide a 'carrot and stick' approach to organisational behaviour. At the same time, the way in which information is available to people may be of significance. Information systems and learning systems can indicate whether the organisation has an open structure which encourages learning and development, or a more closed structure where information and learning are held by individuals or groups as a form of power.

Stories about the leader of an organisation and his insistence on good timing will influence attitudes towards time keeping by all the employees, even if these stories are exaggerated. In practice, within a company different functions or departments may have different cultures which reflect both the people who work in it and expectations about it. For example, there may be a marked difference between the finance and the design departments, with the people working for finance dressing relatively formally and with a clearly hierarchical structure, while the design department employees dress much more informally and operate on a consensus basis.

It can be argued that **successful organisations have 'a way of doing things', or culture, which supports their strategy and leaders have to take into account different organisational cultures.** The culture of an organisation will tend to consist of three layers:

- **Values** – these may be written down as part of the organisation's mission or vision statement. They are often vague statements of intent, such as 'serving the community' or 'conserving the environment'.
- **Beliefs** – these tend to be more specific in the sense that they may be about such matters as which suppliers the company is prepared to use. For example, a company like The Body Shop wants to have suppliers with good environmental and human rights records because of its policies in these areas.
- **Assumptions** – these are at the core of an organisation's culture. They are often difficult for employees to explain, but they affect the day to day working of individuals and groups within the organisation.

The assumptions which are taken for granted are at the centre of an organisation's culture and, although these may not be articulated, they are understood by all the employees. These assumptions will be surrounded by beliefs which are more specific and values which may be strongly held but more difficult to put into practice.

In practice, the ability of leaders to organise, control and change their organ-isations will depend to a great extent on the culture that exists. There have been various studies which identify a range of cultures, none of which necessarily fit an organisation exactly but may provide an overall impression. For example, if an organisation is said to have a macho culture, it does provide an image of it even if it is not the whole story about the organisation. One way of describing cultures is to divide them into power, role, task and person cultures (Handy, 1993) (Exhibit 2.1).

A **power** culture is typically found in small entrepreneurial companies controlled by powerful figures. People in this culture share a belief in individuality and in taking risks, they believe that management should be an informal process with few rules and procedures. This type of culture suits people who thrive on political situa-tions and are confident about the use of power.

A **role** culture is associated with bureaucracies where people's functions are defined in a formal way and they specialise in particular roles. People here share a belief in the importance of security and predictability and they equate successful management with rules and regulations. In this culture people will tend to be slow to change and they value security and predictability. The civil service is an example and banking is another, certainly in the past if not today. A **task** culture is found where people focus on their job, or on a project, and share a belief in the impor-tance of teamwork, expertise and in being adaptable. This is often the culture preferred by middle and junior managers because they know what they have to do and they can build up teams. The **person** culture occurs where people believe that the organisation exists so that they can serve their own personal interests, for instance barristers and architects, and many other professionals.

Cultures tend to follow the life cycle of organisations, so that the power structure is often found in the early stages of a company's life when its structure is simple. At this stage there is a single source of power from which influence spreads throughout the organisation like a web. The internal organisation is highly dependent on trust, empathy and personal communications. Later the organisation will tend to change to the role culture as it grows and installs a functional structure, then it will develop a task culture to fit in with a structure based on sections and teams.

Another classification of cultures has been produced by Deal and Kennedy (1982) after the examination of hundreds of companies (Exhibit 2.2). They identified the **macho culture** which exists when an organisation is composed of individualists who are frequently called upon to take high risks and receive rapid feedback on the quality of their actions and decisions. These cultures were felt to focus on speed and the short term and place enormous pressures on individuals because they are risk-taking cultures in which those who succeed have to take a tough attitude towards

Exhibit 2.1 Handy's classification

- Power – individuality and powerful managers
- Role – bureaucratic and formal
- Task – focus on work and teamwork
- Person – serving personal interests

Exhibit 2.2 Deal and Kennedy's classification

- **Macho** – high risk, quick feedback
- **Work hard/play hard** – low risk, quick feedback
- **Bet-your-own-company** – high risk, long feedback
- **Process** – low risk, slow feedback

their work and their colleagues. Many sales organisations cultivate this type of culture which can be highly successful in high-risk quick-return environments but they are unable to benefit from co-operative activity and tend to have a high turnover.

The **work hard/play hard** culture is a low-risk, quick feedback culture which emphasises fun and action. Individual sales will not damage a member of staff and so production systems have many checks and balances built into them to neutralise the occurrence of big risks with rapid feedback on staff. These types of organisation are often customer-focused sales organisations or companies, like the fast-food chain McDonald's, which encourages competitions and systems of acknowledging good performance in order to maintain morale. These are often achievement cultures but they may displace volume for quality and concentrate heavily on the present rather than the future.

The **bet-your-own-company** culture exists in environments where the risks are high and the feedback on actions and decisions takes a long time. These companies invest in large-scale projects that take years to reach a conclusion. Decisions tend to be top-down, reflecting a hierarchical structure and a focus on the future. Employees are co-operative with colleagues and respect authority and technical competence. The **process** culture is relatively a low-risk and slow-feedback approach. Employees work with little feedback and so they focus on how they do something rather than on what they do. There is often a rigid hierarchy with a considerable emphasis on job titles and formality with relatively cautious employees who may be protective about their work and focused on technical perfection in the performance of their duties. Both of the bet-your-own-company and the process cultures are slow to respond to change.

Another classification (by Scholz, 1987) divides cultures into five primary types (Exhibit 2.3). These are **stable**, **reactive**, **anticipating**, **exploring** and **creative**. A **stable** culture is one that is averse to risk, backward-looking and 'introverted' and

Exhibit 2.3 Scholz's classification

- **Stable** – 'don't rock the boat'
- **Reactive** – 'roll on the punches'
- **Anticipating** – 'plan ahead'
- **Exploring** – 'be where the action is'
- **Creative** – 'invent the future'

does not accept change, while a **reactive** culture is one where risks are accepted, provided that they are small, and it is oriented to the present and accepts only minimal change. An **anticipating** culture accepts familiar risks, is still oriented to the present but accepts incremental change. An **exploring** culture is 'extroverted', oriented to the present and the future, operates on a risk against gain trade-off and accepts radical change. A **creative** structure is oriented to the future, and actually prefers unfamiliar risks and seeks novel change. These five culture types can be epitomised in terms of slogans such as 'don't rock the boat' (stable), 'roll with the punches' (reactive), 'plan ahead' (anticipating), 'be where the action is' (exploring), 'invent the future' (creative).

The problem with any classification of cultures is that organisations do not fit neatly into one or other type, although they may have dominant elements of one culture or another. Also within organisations there may be different cultures so that often the finance department of a business is thought of as being a 'stable' or a 'process' culture with a 'don't rock the boat' approach, the sales department may be considered to be more like an 'exploring' and perhaps 'macho' culture, with a 'be where the action is' approach. The classification of culture does encourage consideration of this aspect of an organisation in strategic management, while the actual effect may depend on the relative strength of the culture. For example, the introduction of professional managers into hospital trusts has often created a clash between the professional approach adopted by the medical staff and the business-like approach which the managers introduced.

Around the basic assumptions and values in an organisation, there are a number of views about such matters as attitudes to time and the working environment, innovation and learning, risks, power and control. For example, organisations need to be '**learning organisations**' so that the competencies of individuals, sections and the whole organisation are improved and maintained. This learning is in the sense that an organisation needs to learn faster than competitors so that it can meet customer needs better. It can be argued that this is not only a major strategic advantage, but perhaps the only sustainable long-term advantage. Working relationships are a feature of all organisations which can have a marked effect on the efficiency and effectiveness of their operations. In practice, companies try all sorts of approaches to create the desired culture in organisational relationships. Such approaches include team-building techniques such as 'outward bound' type courses, re-organising offices so that they are based on units of people working together, or are open plan, or where there is some form of 'hot-desking', and longer-term programmes to encourage a productive interaction between individuals and groups.

Where people need reassurance and certainty there may be a strong culture or the culture that exists may appear stronger. For example, the doctors and nurses in a hospital trust may close ranks and emphasise the importance of medical considerations as against those of business efficiency. Organisations with weak socialisation practices employing people on a part-time basis, such as supermarkets, will usually be weak in terms of both the degree of consensus and the degree of intensity in their culture.

Other organisations may evolve high consensus cultures which are not felt very deeply, so that a management is supported by all its employees but they would be likely to support another management if they were taken over. A high-intensity, low-consensus culture would be one in which the management was passionately supported by some employees, but by no means all of them. Japanese companies which have employed people for life in the past and provide a wide range of benefits and strong socialisation programmes are an example of companies with a high intensity and high consensus.

The main problem with thinking about the intensity of a culture or the degree of consensus in an organisation is that these are difficult factors to measure. However, when an organisation is subject to change for one reason or another, these factors do need to be considered. The change in the NHS over the last 20 years is a good example of this, with clear cultural differences between the medical staff and the professional managers, with both having strongly felt, but different, views of the culture in which they would like to work. In these circumstances adjustments may be required by both groups.

The approach that suggests various cultures require different leadership styles shifts the focus from the individual leader to the functions that leaders perform within an organisation. In order for any group to operate effectively, both tasks and problem-solving functions have to be performed and, at the same time, group-maintenance or 'social' functions. It can be argued that any group of people needs to have leadership in both functions, so that, on the one hand, decisions are made and, on the other hand, the ideas and feeling of the whole group are considered. The social functions can develop the cohesion of the group and may be carried out by encouragement and support, and by recognising the importance of all members of the group to its smooth operation.

The Situational Leadership® Model

Hersey and Blanchard (1982) developed the view that leadership approaches depended very much on the 'maturity' of their subordinates. They defined 'maturity' as a desire for achievement and willingness to accept responsibility. They developed the theory that the relationship between leaders and followers moves through phases as subordinates 'mature', and that managers need to vary their leadership style with each phase (*see* Figure 2.3).

Hersey (1998) considered that, in the initial phase, when employees first join an organisation, a high task orientation is most appropriate (Figure 2.3 (1)). New employees have to be instructed in their tasks and in the organisation's rules and procedures. At this stage a non-directive manager can cause anxiety in the new employee and confusion about what is to be done. As new employees become familiar with tasks and procedures, a more employee-oriented style can be introduced (2). As employees become familiar with the work and culture of the organisation they may seek greater responsibility and the leadership style can become participatory (3). A point may be reached when a high level of delegation can be achieved (4).

The idea that the situation plays an important part in leadership style provides a dynamic and flexible view of leadership rather than a static one, which suits the modern approach to management and corporate culture.

On the one hand, the manager can develop and encourage employees to take responsibility and become more 'mature'; on the other hand, the employees' willingness and ability to take decisions and manage themselves affect the leadership style a manager can adopt. The Situational Leadership® Model does depend on managers' ability to be flexible in their leadership style. If they can be flexible then they can be effective in a range of situations. If not, then they can only be effective in a situation which matches their particular style. This argument emphasises the importance of the 'followers' to leadership, and the fact that the employees are an important influence on

Figure 2.3 Selecting appropriate styles

Source: Paul Hersey (1998) *The Situational Leader*. Reprinted by permission of the Center for Leadership Studies, Escondido, California.

the style of leadership adopted in an organisation; they can be said to limit the power of a manager. The most effective followers or employees have characteristics which help the organisation to be successful. In a modern context this means that ideally they will be well behaved, responsible, energetic, committed and flexible. They will make sensible decisions in their sphere of control, and they will focus their energies. All this, of course, means that they may well succeed without strong leadership.

Research carried out by Fiedler (1971) was based on the view that managers have difficulty in altering the style which has helped them to achieve success, and that in fact they are not very flexible. It followed from this that trying to change a manager's style to fit the situation may be both useless and inefficient and, therefore, effective group performance could best be achieved by matching the manager to the situation or by changing the situation to match the manager. For example, an authoritarian manager can be selected to fill a post that requires directive leadership, or the job could be changed to give an authoritarian manager more formal authority over employees.

Fiedler argued that successful and effective leadership depended on three factors:

■ **Leader–member relations**. This is the most important factor in leader effectiveness. The degree to which leaders have the acceptance, confidence, support and loyalty of subordinates is an essential feature of leader effectiveness. When these relations are strong, the leader has a firm base from which to influence the behaviour of subordinates. When the leader–subordinate relation is weak, the influence of the leaders is only through the impersonal authority provided by their position in the organisation.

■ **Task structure**. This is measured by the complexity or simplicity of the job to be carried out in an organisation. Managers have considerable power where the work of employees is highly structured and routine, because it is possible in these circumstances to establish very specific criteria to enforce a desired level of performance. Managers will usually need to adopt a democratic, consultative leadership style if the work of an organisation is complex and employees have problem-solving responsibilities which are not routine.

■ **Leaders' position power**. The extent of formal or informal power which a manager is able to exert may be conferred on them by the organisation in which they work and the position they hold in it. The chief executives or managing directors of a company will have a great deal of authority because of their position in a commercial organisation. People in these positions can exert an autocratic style of leadership. Managers lower down the hierarchy of a company may have to be more democratic or laissez-faire.

The leadership styles contrasted by Fiedler are similar to the employee-centred and task-oriented approaches; Fiedler's model, however, uses a simple scale to measure leadership style to indicate 'the degree to which a man described favourably or unfavourably his least preferred co-worker'. This was the employee with whom the person could work least well. Fiedler's theory was that managers who described their least preferred co-worker (or LPC) in favourable terms were managers who had great concern for human relations. These are described as relationship-oriented leaders who are relatively permissive and considerate of the feelings of employees. On the other hand, it is argued that managers who describe their LPC in an unfavourable manner tend to be task-oriented leaders who are less concerned with human relations and are relatively autocratic in their leadership style. These low-LPC managers want to achieve the completion of a task, and the reaction of subordinates to their leadership style is of lower priority to them than the need to maintain production. This approach is a method of measuring the location of managers on the leadership style continuum.

In Figure 2.4 combinations 1, 2, 3 and 8 are most likely to prove successful for task-motivated leaders. The situation in combination 1 is very favourable to the leader, and followers will accept directives in order to maintain their good standing with the leader. Although the leader's organisation power is diminished in combination 2, the strength of the leader's personal power, combined with the limited discretion allowed by a structured task, provide considerable opportunities for the task-oriented manager. In combination 3, the strength of the leader's personal and organisational power makes forceful leadership possible. In combination 8, the situation facing the leader is so unfavourable that a forceful, directive approach offers the most promising option.

In the other four combinations (4, 5, 6 and 7) a relationship-oriented style is likely to be most effective. These situations require a wide variety of skills and knowledge that can only be provided by encouraging the abilities of a number of people.

Figure 2.4 **Situational determinants of effective leadership**

Source: F E Fiedler and M M Chemers (1974) *Leadership and Effective Management*, p. 80, Copyright © Pearson Education 1974. Reprinted by permission of Pearson Education, Inc. Upper Saddle River, NJ.

The path–goal theory of leadership

The **path–goal theory of leadership** was developed by Robert House (1971) and others as an approach to understanding and predicting leadership effectiveness in different situations. The theory focuses on the leader as a source of rewards and attempts to predict how different types of rewards and different leadership styles affect the performance of subordinates, based on the view that an individual's motivation depends both on the expectation and the attractiveness of the rewards available. The manager identifies the 'goals' and rewards which are available and the 'paths' to be taken to reach them.

In this process an effective leader:

■ identifies and communicates to subordinates the path they should follow in order to achieve personal and organisational objectives;

■ helps subordinates along this path;

■ helps to remove obstacles on the path that might prevent the achievement of these objectives.

The manager's leadership style will influence the perception of the rewards available and what has to be achieved to earn them. An employee-centred manager will offer a wide range of rewards and also be sensitive to individual needs. The rewards may be in terms of pay and promotion, but will also include support, encouragement and recognition. On the other hand, a task-oriented manager will offer a more limited set of rewards which will be less concerned with individual needs.

However, people working for this type of manager will know precisely what they have to do in order to obtain the particular rewards available. For example, extra pay may be obtained for a clearly defined increase in productivity. It follows from the expectancy model of motivation that the 'best' leadership style for particular employees depends on the type of rewards they want.

So the path–goal theory suggests that the most effective leadership style will depend on the personal characteristics of employees and on the situation in the workplace. For example:

- Employees who believe they have some control over their work situation and who are highly skilled may favour a participatory form of leadership which supports and encourages them and may resent an authoritarian approach.

- Employees who believe they have little control over 'how things are done' and who are less skilled may prefer more directive leadership, so that they can complete their tasks effectively and earn any bonus that is on offer.

This suggests that managers need to consider the characteristics of their employees and the work to be carried out, before deciding on their leadership style. Vroom and Jago (1988) have criticised the path–goal theory as incomplete because it fails to take into account the characteristics of the type of decision with which they are faced and the situation in which the decision is being made. This can be seen as a further theory of leadership based on the level of participation between managers and employees. (*See also* Chapter 12.)

→ Ch. 12

The participatory theory of leadership

Vroom and Yetton (1973) developed a model of situational leadership in order to help managers decide when and to what extent they should involve employees in solving a particular problem. They suggested that managers needed to ask themselves a number of questions before deciding on an appropriate leadership style:

- Is it necessary to make an objective decision with which employees may disagree?
- Do the managers have sufficient information or skill to solve the problem on their own?
- Is the problem structured?
- Is the acceptance of the employees critical for the success of the decision?
- If the decision was made by management, would it be accepted by the employees?
- Is there likely to be conflict among employees about the best solution?
- Do employees share the achievement of the same objectives in solving the problem?

Once these questions have been answered, it is then possible to select a leadership style, although there may be further choices to be made. Vroom and Yetton defined five leadership styles in terms of the degree of participation by subordinates in the decision-making process:

- **Autocratic I (AI)** – managers solve the problem or make the decisions themselves, using available information.
- **Autocratic II (AII)** – managers obtain information from subordinates before making a decision, and then decide on the solution to the problem themselves. The role of subordinates is to provide information for decision making, and they may or may not have been told what the information is for or what the problem is that needs to be solved.

- **Consultative I (CI)** – managers share the problem with the relevant subordinates individually and obtain their ideas and information. Managers then make the decision, which may or may not be influenced by the subordinates' opinions.
- **Consultative II (CII)** – managers share the problem with the relevant subordinates as a group and obtain their ideas and information. These may or may not be used in decision making.
- **Group Participation (G)** – managers share a problem with subordinates as a group. The managers and subordinates together analyse the problem and consider alternative solutions. Managers act as co-ordinators in order to enable the group to reach a consensus, which is then accepted and implemented.

Depending on the nature of the problem, more than one leadership style may be appropriate because, once managers have answered the questions they need to ask themselves, the quality of the decision and its acceptance have been taken into account. Vroom and Yetton developed a 'tree diagram' or flow chart (Figure 2.5) to provide a guide to the process of arriving at an appropriate leadership style. Their research has shown that decisions consistent with this model have tended to be

Figure 2.5 **Participative decision model**

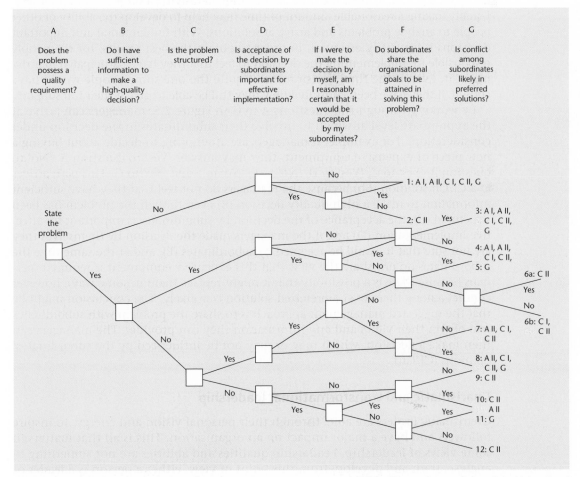

successful, while those that are inconsistent will tend to be unsuccessful. This research has been taken further to suggest that subordinates prefer their managers to make decisions consistent with this model.

When decisions have to be made quickly because of limited time and the managers have sufficient information to make a decision, an autocratic style may in fact satisfy everybody. On the other hand, if there are important problems to be solved in a situation where the subordinates have most of the information and it is important that they accept the choice of solution, then a participatory style of leadership is likely to be the most effective. In an emergency, a leader makes quick decisions often within an established framework or policy, while on long-term strategy the achievement of consensus may be more important, with the leader's role being concerned with maintaining a focus on the problem and co-ordination of the process of arriving at a solution.

It can be argued that the effectiveness of decisions may depend on:

- **the quality of the decisions**
- **the commitment made to the decision**
- **the time taken to make a decision.**

There is a cost factor, certainly in terms of time, in making effective decisions which has to be balanced against the time lag between identifying a problem and solving it. Equally, taking a reasonable amount of time may help to develop the ability of other people to analyse problems and arrive at solutions. With fundamental and important decisions it is usually essential, in order to obtain the best results, for the people responsible for implementing the decision to feel that they have participated in arriving at it. Even if the final decision is not quite the one some people would have chosen, if they have been consulted they may still be able to give it their full support.

By working through the questions A to G in Figure 2.5, managers can arrive at the appropriate level at which to involve their subordinates in the decision under consideration. For example, if managers are attempting to decide about buying a new piece of expensive equipment, they may answer 'Yes' to question A, 'No' to question B, 'Yes' to C, 'Yes' to D, 'No' to E, 'No' to F and 'No' to G. This path arrives at a CI/CII solution (6b) because the managers do not feel that they have sufficient information to make a high-quality decision (B) even though the problem has been structured (C), the acceptance of the decision by subordinates is important for effective implementation (D) and if the managers made the decision by themselves they are not sure that it would be accepted by subordinates (E), and at the same time the subordinates do not share the view that this expensive equipment is required (perhaps because there is a possibility that it might replace them in some way), however conflict among them over a preferred solution is unlikely. The conclusion might be that the suggested management approach is to share the problem with subordinates and obtain their views and any information they can provide. The managers can then make a decision, which may or may not be influenced by the subordinates' opinions (CI/CII).

Charismatic and transformational leadership

Charismatic leaders are able, through their personal vision and energy, to inspire followers and have a major impact on an organisation. This is all that matters in some views of leadership. Leadership qualities and abilities are not something to analyse, train and develop; from this point of view, either a person is a leader or not. This view of leadership suggests that it is a quality which is both mysterious and powerful and can act for either good or evil. **Charismatic leadership** can be identified in politics, war and industry, although whether leaders are charismatic or not is perhaps a matter of opinion. What Alexander the Great, Napoleon, Churchill, Hitler, Gandhi, John F Kennedy and Jim Jones had in common was their vision and their ability to persuade people to follow it. To their followers, charismatic leaders transform their lives in one way or another and they often do not want to ask too many questions about how this is achieved. More objective analysis of their achievements usually identifies that the leaders had 'clay feet' and that there was a variety of complex factors combining to help them shine brightly for a time. In spite of these arguments, the fact remains that some leaders are able to exert great charisma and considerable influence.

Max Weber, in the early part of the twentieth century, identified three forms of authority: traditional, charismatic and bureaucratic. According to Weber (1947), charisma is 'a certain quality of an individual personality by virtue of which he is considered extraordinary and treated as endowed with supernatural or exceptional forces or qualities'. In this sense, charisma is a quality which is generated from inside a person, and it derives from the capacity of particular people to arouse and maintain belief in themselves as the source of knowledge and authority. A tragic example of this was Jim Jones (Exhibit 2.4), who for a short time in the 1970s created a group of followers with blind faith in his leadership. A more recent example with some similarities to this was the leadership of David Koresh which led to hundreds of his followers dying at Waco in Texas in 1992.

Napoleon Bonaparte was considered to be a charismatic leader by the French nation of his day. Although the generals close to him recognised the mundane side of his character, they still considered that he possessed a magnetic attraction. Marshal Lannes was reported to have stated that 'I have always been the victim of my attachment to him', and Marshal Marmont wrote 'we marched surrounded by a kind of radiance whose warmth I can still feel as I did fifty years ago' (quoted in *Great Leaders* by John Adair, 1989).

The focus on leadership theory has moved from the attempt to identify the inborn traits of leaders, through the study of the roles and behaviour of leaders, to the analysis of the leadership situation, work tasks and followers. The concentration on the individual leader has shifted. Although some charismatic leaders have personal characteristics which do make a difference in their organisations, the fact is that exceptional leaders are rare, by definition. Not every organisation can have one, but where they do exist they can be a powerful amplifier of organisational energy and performance. These qualities are not fully taken into account in the

Exhibit 2.4 Jim Jones

In the early 1970s, Jim Jones, a pastor in the United States, created a devoted following in San Francisco called the People's Temple Sect. As a result of unwelcome interest in his activities in the USA, in 1974 Jones moved his sect to Guyana where he established a commune. Complaints of oppression within the commune led to a visit by a US congressman, who was shot along with his companions.

As the investigation into this shooting closed in on him, Jones gathered together his followers and invited them to participate in a mass suicide. Most of them obeyed him without question, including parents who administered cyanide to their children: 914 people died in this tragedy, including over 240 children.

theories that have been so far considered. Perhaps it is a question of 'place and time', as suggested by the former British Prime Minister in Exhibit 2.5.

In analysing the concept of **transformational leadership**, Bernard Bass (1985) contrasted two types of leadership: transactional and transformational. Transactional leaders determine what subordinates need to do to achieve their own and organisational objectives, then classify these requirements and help subordinates become confident that they can reach their objectives. In contrast, transformational leaders motivate people to do better than they would have expected by raising motivation and the importance of the value of people's tasks within the organisation. These leaders go beyond transactional leadership by using their personal vision and energy to inspire their followers.

Richard Boyd (1987) has proposed that there are new skills required of leaders:

- **anticipatory skills** in order to provide foresight into a constantly changing situation;
- **vision skills** in order to lead the organisation towards the leader's or the general objectives;
- **value skills** in order to be in touch with employees' needs, both physical and spiritual, so that shared values and goals can be encouraged;
- **empowerment skills**, so that power is shared;
- **self-understanding** in order for leaders to understand their own needs and those of their employees.

The question then arises of how far these skills can be taught. Peter Drucker (1992) has stated that:

'more leaders have been made by accidental circumstances, sheer grit, or will, than have been made by all the leadership courses put together.'

Exhibit 2.5 Leadership

'Great leadership comes in many different forms. From the steady determination and emotional appeal of a Winston Churchill to the gentler consensual style of a Stanley Baldwin. Both gave strong leadership, but they were leaders for different times and different circumstances. The British people needed a Churchill in War Years, but looked elsewhere when peace returned. As Carlyle observed, great leaders both lead and reflect the age in which they live.

It's the same in business. At one end of the scale is the colourful visionary with little taste for detail. At the other, the brilliant accountant, head full of figures, always looking at the costs and the fine point. Both have their place and their time.

But in my mind, there are two qualifications above all which I consider to be vital to good leadership. First, good leaders have the courage of their principles and clear, long-term objectives and goals. Second, good leaders never forget the people who work for them. The difference between passive obedience and active loyalty can make the difference between success and failure. From manager to messenger – they are all individuals with their own hopes, their own self-esteem and their own interest. A good leader remembers that and behaves accordingly.'

Source: John Major, British Prime Minister 1992–97, *Management Today*, November 1993. Reprinted with permission.

He suggests that heredity and early childhood experience may be the most important factors in leadership activity. Robert House (1971) considers that charismatic leaders communicate the imagination and energies of their followers. He suggests that they create an image of success and competence and set examples of the values they support through their own behaviour. They have high expectations of their followers and help to create the confidence that they can achieve high levels of performance.

Charismatic leaders of this kind provide for a need to find meaning in a common cause. This can be said to reflect a desire for certainty in a commercial world which has become more complex over the years.

Peter Drucker (1992) has written that leadership has little to do with leadership qualities and even less to do with charisma:

> *'Leadership is not by itself good or desirable. Leadership is a means. Leadership to what end is the crucial question. History knows no more charismatic leaders than this century's triad of Stalin, Hitler, and Mao – the misleaders who inflicted as much evil and suffering on humanity as have ever been recorded.'*

The feature which distinguishes what Drucker terms the misleaders from the leaders is their goals. In this, charisma can become the undoing of leaders. He argues that it makes them inflexible, convinced of their own infallibility and unable to change, so that charisma does not in itself guarantee effectiveness as a leader. Drucker gives the example of John F Kennedy as perhaps the most charismatic person ever to occupy the White House, but who in fact achieved very little.

THEORIES X AND Y

One of the greatest contributions to the understanding of leadership has been the work of Douglas McGregor (1960) in developing Theories X and Y. He described the potential for leadership in terms of two opposing sets of assumptions that managers might hold about their subordinates. For the sake of simplicity, these assumptions have been labelled **Theory X** and **Theory Y** to represent two extremes at opposite ends of a continuum.

Theory X managers tend to believe that people have an inherent dislike of work, regarding it as necessary for survival, and will avoid it wherever possible. Furthermore, these managers believe that people are lazy, prefer to be directed, want to avoid responsibility and are relatively unambitious. They have to be coerced, controlled and directed to make them work towards organisational goals. Above all, those managers who subscribe to Theory X believe that people want security. This means that these managers will be very directive in their approach to leadership and very strict and authoritarian with their subordinates. Organisational goals will not be agreed: they will be established, passed down from above and pushed through.

At the opposite end of the spectrum is Theory Y, which represents a much more optimistic view of human nature. Theory Y managers believe that people see work as a natural phenomenon, that they accept responsibility and in fact seek it. Furthermore, Theory Y managers believe that under the right circumstances people can derive satisfaction from their work and will work hard. They will help to achieve organisational objectives, provided that they both understand them and are rewarded for their efforts. This means that these managers will work co-operatively with subordinates in order to decide work objectives and the methods of achieving them. They will encourage the development of self-managed teams and the delegation of decisions towards the point of action. These managers believe in participative management and that the organisational structure as well as its culture can bring out the best in its employees by encouraging personal development and creativity.

Historically there has been a shift towards Theory Y approaches to leadership (see Exhibit 2.6). These developments remain patchy, with companies using different approaches in practice, sometimes at odds with their declared policy. Within an organisation there may be differences as well, so that attempts by the senior managers to lead in a participative way may be partly thwarted by middle or junior managers who implement this policy in an autocratic way. On the other hand, junior managers may attempt to encourage their subordinates to work as a self-managed team setting its own objectives and work schedules, while a dictatorial senior management may insist on particular objectives and work practices. In order to achieve a well-organised, efficient Theory Y working environment, subordinates need to become accustomed to this kind of leadership, so that they learn to take responsibility and make decisions.

It can be argued that in organisations where the workers are professionals, such as in teaching or in a science-based company, there is a good response to Theory Y leadership, while workers in unskilled jobs tend to work better under a more supervised Theory X approach. The reduction in unskilled work in recent years, added to the expansion of participation through self-managed teams and quality circles, belies this differentiation. There is now the view that many people have in the past left their creativity and responsibility at the factory or office door and leaders now want them to use these qualities and abilities as far as possible in the workplace.

The self-fulfilling prophecy

McGregor's research revealed that there was a **self-fulfilling prophecy** in leaders' views of their followers. His work showed that, to a large extent, subordinates behaved as their leaders and managers expected them to behave. This could mean that managers were good predictors of behaviour or that employees responded to their managers' expectations. His research illustrated that when managers believed their workers would perform well, objective controls showed that they did; and when workers were expected to perform poorly, they did. This situation arises because leaders themselves behave in accordance with their expectations about their subordinates. When they thought their subordinates would perform well, they supervised them, often without realising it, in a way that enhanced the likelihood of high performance. If leaders or managers have low expectations, they tend to behave in ways which inhibit the performance of subordinates and demotivate them.

Exhibit 2.6 **Management models**

	MODERN		TRADITIONAL	
Theory Y	Participation	Control		**Theory X**
	Co-operation	Direction		
Work is natural	Communication	Orders		*Work is a necessity*
	Creativity	Security		

This can be seen very clearly when a new leader takes over a situation. When General Montgomery assumed command of the British Eighth Army in North Africa in 1942 during the Second World War, he found a dispirited army and senior officers who had little confidence in a new commander, their fourth within a year. He had to change this situation quickly and decided to alter the way that the officers were thinking. Instead of considering the next position to which the army could fall back, he encouraged a positive attitude which did not allow for retreat:

'We will stand and fight here. If we can't stay here alive, then let us stay here dead.'
(General Montgomery, quoted in Adair, 1989)

This was an uncompromising position, but it worked. When a new chief executive takes over a company, he or she may be able to turn its fortunes around by an approach to leadership as much as by taking particular decisions. 'This is the way we will work' may be as important as 'this is what we will do'.

One of the most important tasks of a leader is to make decisions. Effective leadership requires the decisions to be both sound and practical, whether they are about the direction the organisation should take, or the means by which it will make its way there. Just as there are Theory X and Theory Y leaders, so there are relatively autocratic or relatively democratic ways of making decisions. Some leaders will not tolerate any opposition to their decisions or the process by which they arrive at them. Other leaders will reach a decision by a process of consultation and discussion so that a consensus opinion emerges (*see* Figure 2.2 on p 43).

To some extent these differences will depend on the personality and experience of the leader. Leaders' decision making will also depend on the confidence they have in their subordinates' development. Some leaders prefer to have absolute certainty about a decision, others can tolerate a degree of ambiguity. In delegating decision making to others a leader has to expect some uncertainty about how problems will be solved. In modern management situations, the role of managers as leaders will tend increasingly to be to encourage others to reach decisions on a wide range of issues.

The power of leaders

The power of managers over employees can be described as 'social power' because it is derived from the social interaction of leaders and their followers. This can be understood better by analysing this social power in more detail:

- **Coercive power** is a form of power that is often the main consideration in a general discussion on the subject. It is based on subordinates' fear of the leader and on punishment and threats, and is linked to the most extreme form of autocratic leadership.
- **Expert power** is based on the leader's possession of expertise, skill or knowledge, and the recognition of this by others provides the leader with the power to make decisions.
- **Legitimate power** is based on the hierarchy of the organisation and the perception of subordinates that they should obey the orders of senior managers. On this basis, the more senior the managers are, the more legitimate power they have.
- **Referent power** is based on the charismatic power of leaders. People will accede to these leaders because they admire them and want to increase identification with them.

- **Reward power** is based on the leader's ability to provide rewards for followers. Subordinates support these leaders because of positive rewards such as pay, promotion and recognition.

- **Connection power** is based on a leader's relationships with influential partners, both inside and outside the organisation. Followers may want to remain on good terms with this leader.

- **Information power** is based on the leader's access to information that is valuable to other people. Followers want to share this access or to be involved with somebody who has such access.

Studies by Pearce and Robinson (1987), for example, have shown that the most effective managers today rely more on expert, referent and connection power than on coercive, legitimate, reward or information power. Leaders now tend to use personal power rather than positional power as management structures have become flatter and management practice more open. Information is now more widely shared and management is seen as a form of partnership in order to achieve agreed objectives.

Above all, leaders have to act, they have to perform and show results. There may be many ways of doing this, but it can be argued that actions speak louder than words. When change becomes necessary in an organisation, the hardest problem may be to persuade people to agree on the causes of the difficulties. One way of doing this may be to emphasise the figures, another way may be to make an inspirational speech and try to cajole people to improve. Another way is to take action, in the sense of what Peters called 'Management By Walking About'. Another way of describing it is to break through the cognitive hurdle, the obstacle of what people know, what Kim and Mauborgne (2003) have called 'Tipping Point Leadership', the overcoming of political, resource, motivational and cognitive hurdles. Another way of describing this is to say that leaders need to be 'change agents', they need to put managers face to face with problems and customers.

The example used by Kim and Mauborgne was of William Bratton who among other jobs was Chief of Police of the New York Transit Police and then Commissioner of the New York Police Department (NYPD):

> *'When Bratton first went to New York to head the transit police in April 1990, he discovered that none of the senior officers rode the subway. They commuted to work and travelled around in cars provided by the city. Comfortably removed from the facts of underground life – and reassured by statistics showing that only 3% of the city's major crimes were committed in the subway – the senior managers had little sensitivity to riders' widespread concern about safety. In order to shatter the staff's complacency, Bratton began requiring that all transit police officials – beginning with himself – ride the subway to work, to meetings, and at night.'*   (Kim and Mauborgne, 2003)

As a result of this, many senior officers in the Transit Police experienced for the first time the problems of the subway, which included jammed turnstiles, aggressive beggars, gangs of youths jumping turnstiles and jostling people on the platforms and 5,000 people living in the subway system. When faced with the reality of fear and disorder in the New York subway, the senior managers could no longer deny the need for change in their policing methods. Bratton introduced 'zero-tolerance' policing and in two years robberies were down 40% in the subway, fare evasion was cut in half and more people used the system. There are still, of course, organisations which base their power on coercion and reward, and individual leaders who rely on these as the foundation of their power.

Leadership styles

The analysis of leadership suggests a range of styles, and research (Goleman, 2000) has shown that leaders who used styles that positively affected the climate in an organisation had decidedly better financial results than those who did not. Other factors were also found to be very important, such as economic conditions and competition, but the impact of leadership styles was felt to be much too important to ignore. The six styles identified were the coercive style, authoritative, affiliative, democratic, pacesetting and coaching (Exhibit 2.7).

The coercive leader requires immediate compliance in a drive for achievement. Decisions are taken at the top with little consideration for other people's ideas, so that initiative is stifled and people's sense of responsibility is eroded. Leaders with this style tend not to motivate people by showing them how their work fits into the organisational strategy so that they may wonder if their job matters. This style is felt to work best when a sudden major impact is needed to alter the direction of an organisation by shocking people into a new way of working but if it is used after the crisis has passed it will tend to have a negative impact on morale.

The authoritative style can mobilise people towards a new direction by having a clear vision for the organisation and by making it clear to people how their work fits into the organisational strategy. This means that people working for a leader of this type can understand why what they do matters and maximises commitment to the organisation's objectives. The standards for success are clear and the rewards transparent while initiative and innovation can be achieved within the umbrella of the leader's vision and strategy. This style of leadership can be effective in many business situations and particularly when an organisation lacks a sense of direction. It does not work when a manager becomes overbearing, or when a group of experts or peers are working together.

The affiliative style revolves around people to create harmony and keep employees happy. The objective is to create strong loyalty, improve communications and the sharing of ideas and initiatives. It allows for innovation and risk-taking and provides freedom for people to carry out their jobs in the way they think is most effective. This leadership style provides strong positive feedback and is highly motivating. It is particularly effective for team building and creating emotional links between team members by showing an interest in their personal lives and praising people at every opportunity. On the other hand, the focus on praise and support may mean that poor performance is tolerated and people may feel that they do not have a guiding sense of direction. On its own it can be seen as a relatively weak form of leadership which may be effective when a group of experts or a group of friends are working together but otherwise needs to be combined with another style. Linked to an authoritative style, for example, a leader can provide a sense of direction and also be caring and interested in people.

The democratic style tries to forge consensus through participation: the leader builds trust by listening to people's ideas and encouraging people to take responsibility by making or helping to make decisions. The main problem with this style of leadership is that crucial decisions may be put off while consensus is being built and people may feel that there is a lack of clear leadership. It works well to generate fresh ideas and where there are confident and competent employees and when it is combined with other styles. It can produce a very positive climate within an organisation, but may need to be combined with an authoritarian style, for example to provide a clear strategy and direction.

The pacesetting style sets high performance standards for everyone including the leader. This style requires good performance from everyone and does not tolerate poor performance and is obsessive about doing things better and faster. The problem with this style is that it can overwhelm employees so that they feel inadequate. They may become task oriented to an extent where initiatives are stifled as people try to do what they think the leader wants. The style works well when employees are self-motivated and highly competent and need little direction or organisation. Expert teams can work well with this leadership and it needs to be combined with other styles for wider success.

The coaching style helps employees to identify their strengths and weaknesses and encourages them to establish long-term development goals. Coaching leaders rely on delegation and agree with employees about their role and responsibilities. They give employees challenging assignments and encourage initiative. This style focuses on personal development rather than on immediate work-related tasks and may be considered to be time consuming. It has a positive effect on the climate of an organisation because employees know that their work is known about and that feedback will be rapid; they know what is expected of them and develop a strong sense of commitment. It works well when employees are prepared for it because they want to improve their performance and realise that if they develop themselves it will help them to advance. This leadership style does not work well when employees are resistant to learning or changing their ways, or when leaders lack the talent to help employees.

In fact, leaders need to use different styles at different times and situations. The most effective leaders switch between leadership styles as needed, especially the authoritative, democratic, affiliative and coaching styles. To do this leaders have to be sensitive to the impact they are having on others and adjust their style to achieve the best results. In order to develop a range of styles, leaders have to increase the strength of their emotional intelligence in terms of improving their empathy, in building relationships and in communication. The situational theory of leadership suggests that the situation plays an important part in the leadership style which will be most effective, while the contingency theories suggest a continuum from more autocratic to laissez-faire styles as a range of options.

Is leadership necessary?

It can be argued that leaders only emerge in response to a perceived need by followers. At the same time the development of participative management and self-managed work groups may have reduced the need for leadership in the old

Exhibit 2.7 Leadership styles in a phrase

- Coercive – 'Do what I tell you'
- Authoritative – 'Come with me'
- Affiliative – 'People come first'
- Democratic – 'What do you think?'
- Pacesetting – 'Do as I do, now'
- Coaching – 'Try this'

sense. Manz and Sims (1987) have suggested that, although organisations provide individual employees with certain attitudes and values, people have their own value systems. Organisational control systems direct the behaviour of individual employees, but the influence is indirect because it is on the self-control systems and values that individuals bring to an organisation. This is illustrated in Figure 2.6.

Manz and Sims argue that the new leadership roles that emerge with the development of self-managed groups are more effective than the more formal and traditional roles. They defined 'self-leadership' as the ability of workers to motivate themselves to perform tasks which are naturally appealing to them and those that are necessary but are not particularly attractive. They also suggest that this type of leadership encourages employee development and behaviour which does not deviate significantly from the organisation's behavioural standards. The creation of self-managed teams and groups requires the nurturing of a particular organisational culture which enables this process to work. It can be argued that leadership is still required to establish this situation and to provide the support necessary for this culture.

According to Charles Handy (1991), the modern organisation requires us:

> *'To learn new ways and new habits, to live with more uncertainty, but more trust, less control, but more creativity.'*

Figure 2.6 Organisational control system

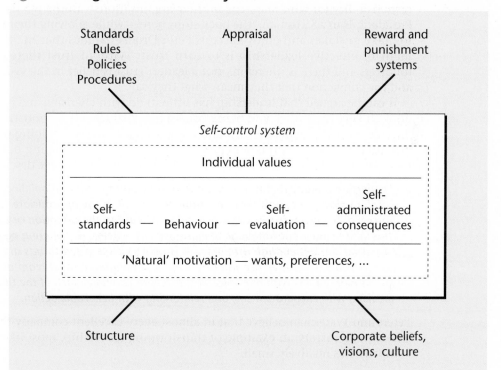

Source: Reprinted from *Academy of Management Review*. A figure from 'Self-leadership: Towards an expanded theory of self-influence processes in organizations', by Charles C Manz (Vol II, No 3, 1986). Copyright © 1986; all rights reserved.

He argues that leadership remains as difficult to pin down as ever, and it has to be seen in action to be recognised:

> *'The studies agree on very little but what they do agree on is probably at the heart of things. It is this: "A leader shapes and shares a vision which gives point to the work of others".'*

The conclusion is that leadership is necessary, but new organisations in new situations need to be run in new ways. Flatter organisations mean that the traditional idea of constant upward movement by promotion into leadership positions with ever-increasing responsibility is no longer valid. There are fewer promotional posts and ambitious managers have to look at the horizontal rather than the vertical fast track. This means that they have a succession of different jobs at the same level, which gives them a wide view of the organisation and an opportunity to test their skills in a wide variety of roles. This has to be based on the view that a horizontal career is a good thing and prepares people well for the few senior management posts which do exist.

The questioning of the need for leadership puts an emphasis on the argument that leadership is not by itself good or desirable; it is a means to an end, that is to achieving certain objectives. The foundation of effective leadership can be seen as thinking through an organisation's mission, defining it and establishing it. The role of the leader is to establish the goals and objectives and monitor progress towards achieving them. As Peter Drucker (1992) has written, 'The leader's first task is to be the trumpet that sounds a clear sound.' The second task of the leader is to accept that leadership is about responsibility rather than rank or privilege. Leaders accept responsibility for what happens in their organisations – in the words of a post US President, Harry S Truman, 'the buck stops here' – while allowing their subordinates to make mistakes and enjoy success. Peter Drucker argues that the third requirement of effective leadership is to earn trust. Without trust there are not any followers and there is, therefore, not a leader. Trust is belief in the vision of leaders and the conviction that they mean what they say.

It can be argued that leadership has little to do with charisma and much more to do with very hard work and being consistent. Real leaders demonstrate integrity, provide meaning, generate trust and communicate values. 'In doing so, they energise their followers, humanely push people to meet challenging business goals' (Bennis and O'Toole, 2000). As Peters and Waterman (1982) have described it:

> *'Leadership is many things. It is patient, usually boring coalition building. It is the purposeful seeking of cabals that one hopes will result in the appropriate ferment in the bowels of the organisation. It is meticulously shifting the attention of the institution through the mundane language of management systems. It is altering agendas so that new priorities get enough attention. It is being visible when things are going awry, and invisible when they are working well. It is building a loyal team at the top that speaks more or less with one voice. It is listening carefully much of the time, frequently speaking with encouragement, and reinforcing with believable action.'*

Peters and Waterman believe that in almost every excellent company there is somewhere in its history an example of transforming leadership, most likely when the company was relatively small.

> *'Ask any group of business people the question, "What do effective leaders do?" and you'll hear a sweep of answers. Leaders set strategy; they motivate; they create a mission; they build a culture. Then they ask, "What should leaders do?" If the group is seasoned, you'll likely hear one response: the leader's singular job is to get results.'*
>
> (Goleman, 2000)

Sir Graham Day has stated that a world-class firm will have a world-class leader (*see* Exhibit 2.8). He argues that leadership addresses the questions of motivation, the objectives of working and the improvement of organisations.

In *Thriving on Chaos* (1987), Tom Peters argues that the leader at any level in an organisation must become an empiricist:

> *'That is, the firm must become a hotbed of tests of the unconventional. It must become an experimenting (and learning), adaptive change-seeking organisation.'*

The organisation, it is argued, must ceaselessly send its people out to visit other interesting organisations of all kinds. The objective is for people to learn more and to learn faster so that they can deal proactively with change. 'The organisation learns from the past, swipes from the best, adapts, tests, risks, fails, and adjusts – over and over.' Peters suggests that the core paradox is that all leaders at all levels must contend with creating and fostering internal stability in order to encourage the pursuit of constant change. He argues that this dichotomous task has not been imposed on leaders before. They must on the one hand insist on a clear vision, a way forward, and on the other hand, insist upon the constant testing of this vision so that it is expanded, contracted and eventually destroyed and replaced with a new vision. In this sense, the role of the leader is simultaneously to promote stability and instability in the organisation.

So discussion and argument on leadership continue. Warren Bennis and Burt Nanus (1986) wrote that leadership remains the most studied and least understood topic in all the social sciences. They argue that, like beauty or love, we know it when we see it but we cannot easily define it or produce it on demand. They conclude that:

> *'Leaders articulate and define what has previously remained implicit or unsaid; they invent images, metaphors and models that provide a focus for new attention. By so doing, they consolidate a challenge provoking wisdom. In short, an essential factor in leadership is the capacity to influence and organise meaning for the members of the organisation.'*

Exhibit 2.8 World-class leaders

> *'I am very attracted by the words of Professor Abraham Zaleznik: "Leadership is made of substance, humanity and morality and we are painfully short of all three qualities in our collective lives."*
>
> *There's the John Wayne, gung ho, follow-me attitude – but if there is no perceived reality or no human touch then it is unlikely to touch the constituents you want to lead. And without morality you may as well be Adolf Hitler. Leadership is the ability to change compelled performers into willing participants. If you only have a mandatory leadership, you have three negatives: pressure without motivation; process without substance; organisation without improvement. True leadership addresses those negatives. The attributes which ultimately matter are the abilities to communicate and inspire.*
>
> *A world-class firm, regardless of size, will have a world-class leader. The CEO's ability and confidence in communicating his or her vision to all levels of the corporate hierarchy, and also to the community, will set him or her apart as an exceptional leader.'*

Source: Sir Graham Day, *Management Today*, November 1993. Reprinted with permission.

In looking at the relationship between management and leadership, Bennis and Nanus suggest that:

> *'Managers are people who do things right and leaders are people who do the right thing. The difference may be summarised as activities of vision and judgement – effectiveness versus activities of mastering routine efficiency.'*

It is difficult to avoid military metaphors when discussing leadership, because of the clear need for leadership in a military crisis. The link between the military and other spheres has been well summed up by General Sir Peter Inge in discussing his own views of the essential qualities of leadership (*see* the case study on pages 67–8). His list includes many of the qualities explored by other writers on the subject: personality, character, courage, willpower, knowledge and initiative.

SUMMARY

- It can be argued that management is largely concerned with leadership, because managers need to establish a sense of direction and to motivate people to move in that direction.

- The understanding of theories of leadership provides a basis for analysing leadership and management styles. This understanding is also a factor in the process of making decisions.

- The consideration of charismatic leadership helps to illustrate the power of leaders. Discussion of the need for leadership highlights the management tasks and objectives which are involved.

Review and discussion questions

1 *What is the connection between leadership and management?*

2 *How relevant are Theories X and Y to modern management?*

3 *Analyse the main considerations leaders need to take into account in making decisions.*

4 *Should the situation and the circumstances in which leadership is being exercised make a difference to the style of leadership?*

5 *What provides the power of leaders over their followers?*

6 *Is there a need for leadership?*

CASE STUDY

The qualities of leadership

The definition of a leader makes leadership sound simple: 'A person or thing that leads or a person followed by others.' In fact, the more one exercises leadership or is led, the more one realises that the fundamental nature of leadership is very personal and is not susceptible to clear scientific analysis. A study of great leaders shows an enormous diversity in their style of leadership, personalities and in their ethos. This variety of personality, character and style leads me to believe that leadership is an art and not a science.

We, of course, have to recognise that leadership is not always inherently good and, indeed, many evil men have been very effective leaders. I will concentrate on good leadership in a democracy and, in particular, leadership within armed forces.

In this context, good leadership is perhaps best described as getting others to do often difficult and sometimes dangerous tasks willingly. However, leadership is required in all walks of life and, although the way that leadership is exercised and emphasis given to particular qualities may vary, I believe many of the essentials are similar. It was Field Marshal The Viscount Slim who said, 'When talking about leadership, one always comes back to the same basic principles.' I have to declare my hand and admit that he is one of my military heroes and his analysis of leadership and the way he exercised it are second to none. I lean on him very heavily in the points which follow.

Before turning to some specific qualities in a successful leader I would like to make one general point. I believe that it is fundamentally important for a leader to have a credo or belief in what he stands for and in the organisation, formation or body in which he is a leader. I suspect everyone has his own list of the essential qualities necessary in a leader. Here are mine:

Personality and Character. Great leaders have the strength of character and personality to inspire confidence and to gain the trust of others. Clearly this is a personal thing but it can be developed by experience and training. I would emphasise that leaders do not have to be roaring extroverts to be successful. Some very charismatic leaders have been just quietly confident, although they had the ability to communicate.

Courage. Field Marshal Slim said, 'Courage is the greatest of all virtues for without it there are no other virtues.' Although he was talking about both physical and moral courage, it was moral courage on which he laid the greatest emphasis. Indeed, I believe that moral courage is the single most important quality for a successful leader. It is the courage to do what you believe to be right without bothering about the consequences for yourself. The funny thing is that the more you use your moral courage on small issues, the easier it becomes to use it on big issues. Physical courage is, of course, the reverse and is more like a bank account. The more you use it the more likely it is to become overdrawn.

Willpower. A leader has to learn to dominate events and never allow these events to get the better of him and this determination or willpower concerns not only rival organisations or, in the case of armed forces, the enemy, but equally colleagues and allies.

Knowledge. This means knowledge not only of your profession but equally knowledge of the men under your command. Knowing them well and being known to them is vital if you are to gain their confidence. As a newly-joined platoon commander, after every one of my first few muster parades, the company sergeant major always asked me about a particular soldier. I was never able to answer him satisfactorily. Eventually, I plucked up courage to ask him what he meant and why he was asking me these questions. He said, 'I watch you on muster parade, Sir, and you inspect the men very thoroughly, their belts, their boots and their weapons, but you don't look them in the eye. Every morning you must look your soldiers in the eye and that will tell you how they feel and if they have a problem.' It was outstanding advice and done in a way that made me never forget it. Quite a psychologist.

Initiative. This is, of course, a fundamentally important quality in any walk of life but nowhere more so than on the battlefield. I can do no better in this context than to quote Field Marshal Slim: 'Here one comes up against a conflict between determination, fixity of purpose and flexibility. There is always the danger that determination becomes plain obstinacy and flexibility, mere vacillation. If you can hold within yourself the balance between these two –

strength of will and flexibility of mind – you will be well on the road to becoming a leader in a big way.'

In conclusion, I would add two final qualities. They are unselfishness and showing that you enjoy being a leader. In summary, to quote General Sir John Hackett: 'Successful military leadership is impossible without the leader's total engagement in the task in hand and to the group committed to his care for its discharge.' For all I know, this may be so not only in the military but in other spheres as well.

Source: General Sir Peter Inge, *Management Today*, November 1993. Reprinted with permission.

REFERENCES AND FURTHER READING

Adair, John (1989) *Great Leaders*, Guildford: Talbot Adair Press.

Bass, Bernard M (1985) 'Leadership: Good, Better, Best', *Organizational Dynamics*, 3.

Bennis, Warren and Nanus, Burt (1986) *Leaders*, New York: Harper & Row.

Bennis, Warren and O'Toole, James (2000) 'Don't Hire the Wrong CEO', *Harvard Business Review*, May/June.

Blake, R R and Mouton, J S (1985) *New Management Grid III: The Key to Leadership Excellence*, Houston, TX: Gulf Publishing Co.

Boyd, Richard (1987) 'Corporate Leadership Skills: A New Synthesis', *Organizational Dynamics*, 1.

Deal, T and Kennedy, A D (1982) *Corporate Cultures: The Rites and Rituals of Corporate Life*, Reading, MA: Addison-Wesley.

Donnell, S and Hall, J (1980) 'Men and Women as Managers: A Significant Case of No Significant Difference', *Organizational Dynamics*, Spring.

Drucker, Peter (1992) *Managing for the Future*, Oxford: Butterworth-Heinemann.

Fiedler, Fred (1968) 'The Leader's Psychological Distance and Group Effectiveness', in D Cartwright and A Zander (eds), *Group Dynamics*, New York: Harper & Row.

Fiedler, Fred (1971) 'A Theory of Leadership Effectiveness', *Administrative Science Quarterly*, September.

Fiedler, Fred and Chemers, M M (1974) *Leadership and Effective Management*, Upper Saddle River, NJ: Pearson Education.

Fleishman, E A (1953) 'Leadership Climate, Human Relations Training Behaviour', *Personnel Psychology*, 2.

Ghiselli, Edwin (1971) *Explorations in Managerial Talents*, Santa Monica, CA: Goodyear.

Goleman, Daniel (2000) 'Leadership that Gets Results', *Harvard Business Review*, March/April.

Handy, Charles (1991) *The Age of Unreason*, London: Century.

Handy, Charles (1993) *Understanding Organisations* (4th edn), London: Penguin Books.

Hersey, Paul (1998) *The Situational Leader*, Escondido, CA: Center for Leadership Studies.

Hersey, P and Blanchard, K (1982) *Management of Organizational Behavior: Utilizing Human Resources*, Englewood Cliffs, NJ: Prentice-Hall.

House, R (1971) 'A Path Goal Theory of Leadership Effectiveness', *Administrative Science Quarterly*, September.

House, R and Mitchell, T (1974) 'Path–Goal Theory of Leadership', *Journal of Contemporary Business*, Autumn.

Kim, W Chan and Mauborgne, Reneé (2003) 'Tipping Point Leadership', *Harvard Business Review*, April.

McGregor, Douglas (1960) *The Human Side of Enterprise*, New York: McGraw-Hill.

Management Today (1993) 'Present Bearers of the Leadership Mantle . . .', November.

Manz, Charles (1986) 'Self-Leadership: Towards an Expanded Theory of Self-Influence Processes in Organizations', *Academy of Management Review*, 2(3).

Manz, Charles and Sims, Harry (1987) 'Leading Workers to Lead Themselves: The External Leadership of Self-Managing Work Teams', *Administrative Science Quarterly*, 32.

Massie, Joseph L and Douglas, John (1977) *Managing: A Contemporary Introduction*, Englewood Cliffs, NJ: Prentice-Hall.

Moore, James F (1997) *The Death of Competition: Leadership and Strategy in the Age of Business Ecosystems*, New York: Harper Business.

Nanus, Buit (1995) *Visionary Leadership*, San Francisco, CA: Jossey-Bass.

Pearce, J and Robinson, R (1987) 'A Measure of CEO Social Power in Strategic Decision Making', *Strategic Management Journal*, May/June.

Peters, Tom (1987) *Thriving on Chaos*, London: Macmillan.

Peters, Tom and Waterman, Robert Jr (1982) *In Search of Excellence*, New York: Harper & Row.

Ricie, R, Instone, D and Adams, J (1984) 'Leader Sex, Leader Success and Leadership Process: Two Field Studies', *Journal of Applied Psychology*, February.

Scholz, C (1987) 'Corporate Culture and Strategy – the Problem of Strategic Fit', *Long Range Planning*, 20(4).

Stogdill, R and Coons, A (1957) *Leader Behavior: Its Description and Measurement*, Columbus, OH: Ohio State University, Bureau of Business Research.

Tannenbaum, Robert and Schmidt, Warner (1973) 'How to Choose a Leadership Pattern', *Harvard Business Review*, May/June.

Vroom, V H and Jago, A G (1988) *The New Leadership: Managing Participation in Organizations*, Englewood Cliffs, NJ: Prentice-Hall.

Vroom, V H and Yetton, P W (1973) *Leadership and Decision Making*, Pittsburgh, PA: University of Pittsburgh Press.

Weber, Max (1947) *The Theory of Social and Economic Organizations*, New York: Free Press.

WEBSITES

http://www.leadership-development.com
This is concerned with leadership development.

http://www.mailbase.ac.uk/lists/critical management
This is a source of critical discussion, reflection and information on management.

CHAPTER 3

Managing a consumer focus

TIM HANNAGAN

Outcomes

Having read this chapter, you will be able to:

- appreciate the importance of customer service

- explain the importance of flexibility in management structures in order to be able to meet the needs of consumers

- analyse the strategies required to meet consumer needs and to maintain a competitive edge

- judge the effects of the focus on the customer on the qualities and skills required in management

- understand new forms of organisational structure designed to meet customer needs

THE CUSTOMER COMES FIRST

Organisations have changed and are changing as a result of a focus on the **customers**, and those which find themselves struggling to be successful often employ new managers to provide the organisation with a fresh focus on customer needs and to lead them in a successful direction. It is now recognised that meeting customer needs is the foundation of any successful organisation, and that the customers come first, second and third in organisational priorities. Customers have, of course, always been important; what has changed is the priority given to them and the urgency with which their needs are considered. It can be argued that customer service is now the only factor which distinguishes one organisation from another in the same business. At the same time, the customers have changed, they have become more demanding and they have more choice. It is these changes which have made imperative a change in the role of managers. For most organisations their customers' perceptions are formed by contact with people representing the organisation. In order to provide an excellent service, these representatives have to have the power to make decisions without constantly conferring with a line manager. Employees have become responsible for a range of decisions which would have previously required management approval.

→ Ch. 17

This change was heralded by the so-called 'death of bureaucracy' identified by Warren Bennis (1966), among others. He argued that every age develops the organisational form appropriate to its time and that bureaucracy was appropriate to the first two-thirds of the twentieth century but not beyond that (*see also* Chapter 17). His view was that the order, precision and impersonal nature of bureaucracy were a reaction to the personal and capricious nature of management in the nineteenth century, remnants of which survived well into the twentieth century. Bennis recognised that there were new conditions developing in the last third of the twentieth century which had major implications for management. There was rapid and unexpected change in the position of most organisations, with increasing diversity which created a need for flexibility and new and specialised skills. This changing world was predicted by Alan Toffler in *Future Shock* (1970), a book which produced as much interest in its time as *In Search of Excellence* more than a decade later. At the same time, the human relations approach to organisational management had emphasised the importance of leadership and communication, intrinsic job motivation, and practices which facilitated flexibility and involvement.

The changes recognised by Bennis and Toffler have encouraged the view that there is no one best way to manage an organisation and that the appropriate method depends on the particular situation. This contingency approach has developed and expanded since the 1960s in response to competition and technology. W R Scott (1987) pointed out:

> *'that previous definitions tend to view the organization as a closed system, separate from its environment and comprising a set of stable and easily identified participants. However, organizations are not closed systems, sealed off from their environments but are open to and dependent on flows of personnel and resources from outside.'*

Open organisations are characterised by uncertainty over the actions of others, such as customers, which leads them constantly to monitor these actions. They are also uncertain about the development of influences outside the organisation, for which they produce contingency plans. At the same time there are wide variations in the use of technology within organisations, even by those producing similar products or services, and in the speed of change and innovation. Organisations are also of different sizes and this has an effect on their management style. Some of the characteristics of open organisations and factors influencing their style are summarised in Exhibit 3.1.

Work at the University of Aston in the 1960s (Pugh and Hickson, 1976) found that size was the most important predictor of management style, so that the larger the organisation, the more likely it was to adopt bureaucratic structures, while the smaller the organisation the more likely it was to adopt flexible structures. The increasing emphasis on the customer now points to the need for all organisations, large or small, to have a high degree of flexibility.

Contingency theories have moved a long way towards suggesting that management needs to be flexible and to apply the appropriate techniques to factors such as the size and situation of an organisation. Even so, it can be argued that the contingency approach does not provide a convincing explanation of how organisations do and should operate. It may be considered that organisational culture is not sufficiently taken into account and that it has become increasingly important for members of an organisation to take control of their structure and decision-making

Exhibit 3.1 Open organisations

Uncertainty over matters and events outside the organisation including:

- the actions of others;
- the inability ever to understand and control events fully;
- the uncertainty of forecasts (such as economic forecasts);
- the dependence on outside events (such as the changes in the membership of the European Community);
- the uncertainty created by other people's forecasts (such as views about the depth and duration of the recession in the UK and other developed economies of the early 1990s, and in the Far Eastern economies in the late 1990s);
- the behaviour of customers and suppliers.

Development and innovations in technology:

- the use of different technologies by organisations producing different products and services;
- the use of different technologies by organisations producing similar products and services;
- the constant changes in technology owing to innovation.

Difference in size between organisations:

- it has become recognised that the structure and practices for the efficient organisation of large institutions may not be those most suitable for smaller ones;
- as organisations grow in size, more decentralised and impersonal structures may become appropriate.

processes. Peters and Waterman (1982), for example, attempted to predict the way companies would need to organise and operate in the future based on what the best companies were doing at the moment or planning to do in the future.

IN SEARCH OF EXCELLENCE

Peters and Waterman carried out a study for management consultants McKinsey and Company of the 62 most successful companies in the USA. They were able to identify eight key attributes which organisations needed to manifest in order to achieve excellence. It can be argued that every one of these attributes is about people, and most of them focus directly or indirectly on the customer. Peters and Waterman argue that these attributes are largely opposed to the rational theories of management which have been so popular in the past, whether they have been based on scientific management, bureaucratic control, human resource theories or a contingency approach. They argue that these rational approaches produced 'paralysis through analysis' to an extent where action stops and planning runs riot. Analysis may reach a point where it attempts to be precise about matters which are inherently uncertain, and at the same time the analysis of situations can become so complex that it becomes unwieldy. They suggest that a problem may arise where a 'correct' answer to a problem is identified irrespective of its application to the situation in question.

Peters and Waterman argue that past management techniques should be used as an aid to, but not a substitute for, human judgement. They suggest that it is the freedom given to managers and employees to innovate and experiment with different solutions which distinguishes excellent companies from the less successful ones. In their study, they identified the attributes which characterised most closely the distinct features of excellent, innovative companies, which are summarised in Exhibit 3.2.

In Peters and Waterman's view, these core values may be concerned with such matters as the quality of customer service, or the importance of reliability. For example, they quote the McDonald's food franchise slogan, QSCV: Quality, Service, Cleanliness and Value. Excellent companies really do get close to their customers, while others just talk about it. The best organisations take customer service to extreme lengths in order to achieve quality, service and reliability. They listen to their customers by observing the customer view on product, quantity, quality and service, and they claim to receive their best ideas for new products from listening intently and regularly to their customers. The excellent companies are:

'driven by their direct orientation to the customers rather than by technology or by a desire to be the low-cost producer. They seem to focus more on the revenue-generation side of their service.'

Rosabeth Moss Kanter (1989) has attempted to define what organisations need to be like in the future if they are to be successful. She believes that today's corporate elephants need to learn to dance as nimbly and speedily as mice if they are to survive in an increasingly competitive and rapidly changing world:

'If the main game of business is indeed like Alice in Wonderland croquet, then running it requires faster action, more creative manoeuvring, more flexibility and closer partnerships with employees and customers than was typical in the traditional corporate bureaucracy. It requires more agile, livelier management that pursues opportunity without being bogged down by cumbersome structures or weighty procedures that impede action. Corporate giants, in short, must learn how to dance.'

Exhibit 3.2 Excellent companies

■ A bias for action, rather than too much planning or waiting for something to happen

■ Keeping close to the customer by learning from the people they serve and providing a high quality and reliable service

■ Fostering autonomy and entrepreneurship through encouraging the development of leaders and innovators throughout the organisation and supporting creativity and risk taking

■ Developing productivity through people by recognising that the main productivity gains could be achieved by employees rather than through capital investment

■ Practising a hands-on, value-driven approach, by concentrating on achievements rather than technological or economic resources or organisational structure

■ 'Sticking to the knitting' by staying close to businesses that are already known and by following the approach that a company should never acquire a business it does not know how to run

■ Organising a 'simple form' and 'lean staff' structure, so that the organisation remains uncomplicated with relatively few top-level staff

■ Maintaining simultaneous loose–tight properties: both centralised and decentralised, with autonomy pushed down to the shop floor and product development team, and centralisation around the core values

Companies must be constantly alert and keep abreast of their competitors' intentions and their customers' needs, Kanter argues. Peters and Waterman (1982) have also illustrated the need for organisations to be alert and to be open to constant change. Although their ideas were very popular in the 1980s, some disenchantment has occurred since because a number of the companies they used in arriving at the eight attributes for excellence experienced strategic setbacks (*see* Chapter 4 for the example of IBM). However, it remains important for organisations to consider these attributes in their strategy, while recognising that achieving them is not a guarantee of continued success where both organisational environments and customer needs change.

→ Ch. 4

MANAGER 2000 PLUS

This theme of co-operation and collaboration has been developed by Robert Heller:

> *'Manager 2000 will practice co-operation and collaboration with everybody, inside and outside the firm, from colleagues and subordinates to customers and suppliers.'*
> (Heller, 1994b)

He argues that managers of the future have to be tolerant team players, putting the objectives of the team above the ambitions of an individual. This approach is encouraged by the devolution of power and delegation of decision making to self-managed teams at the point of production or customer service. Managers will work in organisations where the hierarchical pyramid is inverted, placing top management at the base and the customer at the summit (*see* Figure 3.1).

Figure 3.1 The inverted pyramid

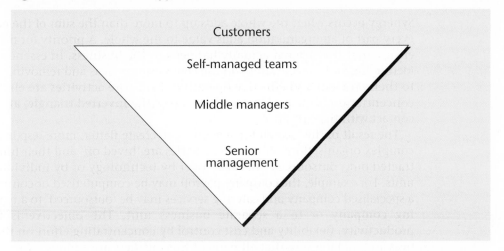

In this situation the manager's role is to support individuals and teams producing goods or supplying services directly to the customer. In placing the customer at the top of this pyramid, the objective is to provide the best in quality and service and through this process to find a competitive advantage. This in fact means 'keeping close to the customer' and finding out from them what they want in terms of quality and reliability.

'Managers 2000 plus', at all levels, will have to be involved in developing the potential of everybody around them. Hierarchical bureaucratic systems provided a framework for establishing and keeping the rules of an organisation, whether these were openly established or part of an accepted corporate culture. Heller argues that the horizontal principle is displacing the vertical principle in everything, from organisational structure to markets. The outcomes of business processes are all important and innovation has become a necessity. The development of self-managed teams is perhaps less about 'empowerment', which suggests giving people the ability to manage work more effectively, than about 'enablement' by ceasing to stop them from organising work effectively. In Rank Xerox, for example, the managing director is subjected to twice-yearly feedback from the 15 people who report directly to him, and the same applies to each of them and throughout the organisation. Everybody knows specifically what is expected of them and everybody is involved in deciding what they have to do.

It can be argued that organisations will be judged on their outcomes, and these will depend on looking at customer requirements with totally fresh eyes and reshaping the entire corporation in order to meet the redefined customer need:

> *'The "virtual corporation" seeks to meet customer needs in the shortest possible time by continual adaptation.'*   (Heller, 1994a)

As a result of this, managers 2000 plus will not expect their jobs to be static, because the business process will determine what is expected at any given time. They will advance in prestige and pay by moving from one successful assignment to the next, not by exchanging one title for another.

SYNERGY

Synergy occurs when the whole adds up to more than the sum of the parts, so that every part of an organisation adds value to the whole. A priority for managers is to ensure that this is what actually happens in the business. In essence this means identifying and concentrating on the core business areas and removing all obstacles to their efficient and effective operation. Non-core activities are eliminated and concentration is focused towards the top of the inverted triangle, at the point of contact with the customer.

The result of this 'search for synergy' is to create flatter, more responsive and less complex organisations. Non-core activities are 'hived off' and their functions contracted out, 'outsourced', or taken over by technology or by individual business units. For example, the company payroll may be computerised or contracted out to a specialised company and catering services may be 'outsourced' to a national catering company or to a separate business unit. The objective is to increase productivity, flexibility and cost control by concentrating effort on the core business and making sure that all parts of this business are adding value to the whole organisation. One of the results of this has been a change in employment patterns:

> *'The job for life is a thing of the past, part-time and flexible work patterns and fixed-term contracts are becoming the norm. Managers must recognise this. To keep their options open, they need to grasp every available training opportunity.'* (Young, 1993)

In a survey of long-term employment strategies carried out in 1993 by the Institute of Management and Manpower plc, a move towards flexible working was identified. Over the previous five years it was found that 90 per cent of the UK's largest organisations had restructured and for 86 per cent this had resulted in job losses at all levels. Nearly 40 per cent expected to restructure again in the following year and 66 per cent over the next four years. As well as shedding permanent jobs, it was noted that employers were introducing greater flexibility into the working patterns of the staff who remained: 75 per cent of the companies predicted an increase in contracting out over the next few years.

This process of change has led to a flattening of hierarchies and a shrinkage in chains of command. In most organisations the terms of employment and the business itself are no longer disconnected. There is not sufficient slack in the economy to allow this. The new reality draws a very close connection between a person's job and the success or failure of their organisation.

THE ECONOMIC FOCUS

At a basic level there are two agents involved in any transaction, a consumer and a producer. In economic terms the consumers attempt to maximise their 'utility' or 'satisfaction' by purchasing goods and services which give the greatest value relative to the price charged for them. On the other hand, the producer attempts to maximise profits by charging the highest price consumers will pay. In order to increase their profits, producers have two choices. Either they produce goods and services which deliver better value to customers than those offered by competitors and thereby expand volume and sales, or they can reduce their costs in order to enhance the margin for profit on each unit of a commodity or service sold. The competitive element will, in economic terms, keep the market in equilibrium. If the price is too high relative to the cost of producing particular goods and services, other producers will find it profitable to enter the market in order to take advantage of the high profit margin. This will have the effect of lowering prices, as the supply of the goods and services increases relative to the demand for them. If the price is too low, production will be reduced because profits are not high enough, and as supply falls below demand, prices will rise.

These basic economic laws of supply and demand mean that for companies to be successful they need to provide goods and services that customers want, and to do so better and/or at a lower cost than their competitors. Unless an organisation has some form of monopoly position, it will have to meet customer requirements better than its competitors in order to make a sale. Consumers will normally buy from a producer whose mix of product, price and service provides more value or satisfaction than that of its competitors. The only occasion when this will not be the case will be when consumers do not know what the competitors are offering or where there is no real choice. This lack of choice may be due to a monopoly position, where for example railways provide the only viable form of transport, or where there is a factor such as location, where for example there is only one major store within travelling distance, which in practice limits consumer choice.

CASE STUDY

Produced to price

I wrote an article in 1980 which explained why a contraction of manufacturing industry was an inevitable consequence of the growth of British North Sea oil production. This was my first encounter with manufacturing fetishists.

The article proved to be very controversial – it was, incidentally, right. Few critics focused on technical weaknesses in the argument. They said instead that what I was saying ought not to be true or, if true, ought not to be said.

I started to understand that for many people the role of manufacturing industry was an emotional issue rather than an economic one. 'Surely you don't think that an economy can survive on hairdressing and hamburger bars?' No, I did not, any more than I thought it could survive on steel and car production. But because I was not in favour of manufacturing industry, I was regarded as being against it.

It seems that it is impossible to be a disinterested observer of the share of manufacturing in national income – any more than it is possible to be a disinterested observer of Eric Cantona, or a test match between England and Australia.

The origins of manufacturing fetishism might be better explored by a psychologist or an anthropologist, but let me have a go.

Thousands of years ago people hunted, fished and made primitive implements. If a man was good at these things, his wife and children prospered; if not, they died. From this we have inherited the notion of a hierarchy of needs – food and shelter running ahead of chartered accountancy and cosmetic surgery. With it comes a notion of a hierarchy of importance for economic activities – agriculture and basic manufacturing running ahead of hairdressing and television programming.

All this ceased to have economic relevance, however, once technology advanced enough for it to be unnecessary to hunt and fish all day to get enough to eat – a state of affairs reached many years ago. Once primitive tribes achieved this, they started to add discretionary activities to the fulfilment of their basic needs.

The services that came into production then remain representative of the services we buy today. There was the priest, who warded off evil; the bureaucrat, who ruled over the tribe; the repair

▶

man, who sharpened the stones and the knives – and eventually the insurance agent, who organised a scheme of mutual support for unlucky villagers whose cow died or whose house burnt down.

With the rise of a market economy came Adam Smith's division of labour. Specialist tasks were assigned to those best qualified to fulfil them. As Smith noted, the division of labour was limited by the extent of the market, and the growth in the geographical scope of markets has steadily increased the division of labour. But even in the early stages of discretionary expenditure, rewards became divorced from the place activities enjoyed in the hierarchy of needs.

You got paid only for goods that people wanted, but it soon became apparent that insurance and priestly services were among the things they did want. Given that what you produced was wanted, earnings reflected the scarcity of the talents needed to produce them, and your position in the power structure of the tribe. The first explains why the insurance and repair men did well, and the second accounted for the prosperity of the bureaucrat and the priest.

Those who are lucky enough to have that power or these rare talents have often felt embarrassed by earning more than those who work to satisfy more basic elements in the hierarchy of needs. Often, they also enjoy occupations that are less arduous and more fun. The embarrassment is rarely very great, and does seem to have diminished recently, but

emphasising the importance we attach to these other supposedly more necessary, but less well-remunerated, activities is a means of assuaging it.

Whatever the truth of all this, none of it should provide a basis for economic policy or industrial strategy.

There is a slightly more persuasive version of the intellectual confusion that tends to the view that manufacturing is special. This suggests that manufacturing output is more important than services because manufacturing, unlike services, is sold to foreigners. Of course, many services are sold to foreigners and many manufactures are not, but there is some truth in the stereotype.

But the real weakness in this argument points the way to the correct answer to the valuation of different activities. If what matters is the tradeability of output, then why draw the line around the nation state? Why not draw it more broadly, or more narrowly? After all, neither the City of London nor a steelworks could survive on its own. You cannot drink derivatives or eat steel. They survive and are valuable because – and only because – they can persuade people outside their boundaries to value their output. The output is valuable, not because it can be sold to foreigners, but because it can be sold.

So the economic significance of an activity is not measured by its place in some objective hierarchy of needs. It is measured by what someone, other than the producer, thinks it is worth.

Source: Kay, J, *Financial Times*, 13 June 1997. Copyright John Kay, economist. Reprinted with permission.

→ Ch. 5

Strategic management can be said to be the understanding, planning and implementation of business policies based on these basic economic principles (*see* Chapter 5). It involves companies taking actions to direct their efforts towards the areas where customer value and competitive advantage can be achieved. It is in fact difficult for a company to decide how and where it should focus its efforts. Its marketing intelligence will help to do this, but this does involve answering complex questions about customer requirements, competitive response and relative cost position. Managers' decisions are likely to be based on a mixture of market research, forward planning, political and cultural forces and what can be referred to as 'hunch' or even as 'vision'. Managers need to understand the criteria by which their existing and potential customers choose to purchase their company's products or services, and how they decide from which company to make their purchases. Within a company different groups of people may have a variety of ideas about customer needs and may emphasise different factors in relation to their products, such as technical quality, lower prices, prompt delivery, packaging or advertising.

CUSTOMER STRATEGY

Managers need to understand their customers in order to meet those customers' needs better. From an economic point of view, customer demand will depend on a range of factors to do with costs, prices, preferences and **competitive advantage** (Exhibit 3.3).

Organisations need to know the specific requirements of each customer and whether these requirements can be segmented. If there are well-defined customer segments, this can have important implications for both product design and marketing. Companies will attempt to segment customer requirements in an attempt both to satisfy as many people as possible on the one hand, and on the other hand in order not to have to tailor-make every item for each individual customer. In the production of a tailor-made suit, for example, there is an attempt to make it fit an individual customer 'perfectly', while 'off-the-peg' suits are produced in large quantities to fit a range of people segmented by such means as height, waist and chest measurements.

'Getting to know the customer' also involves being aware of how many different people are involved in the purchasing decision and the different kinds of requirements they may have. Even in a family the purchase of a suit for one of their members may give rise to sharp differences of opinion. In a company, purchasing may be viewed very differently by the product, finance and marketing managers. The finance manager, for example, may be particularly concerned about costs in terms of cost saving, while the marketing manager may consider costs in a rather different way, perhaps largely by comparison with competitors.

At the same time, people will have different priorities in terms of the qualities they require in a product or service. These will include design, technical preferences, reliability and availability as well as price. The producers need to know how important these factors are to customers before they can decide which aspect to concentrate on improving. Without this knowledge it is very difficult for a manager to develop a strategy to obtain competitive advantage.

> *'The key element which distinguishes strategy from marketing is the explicit consideration of competitive advantage.'*   (Faulkner and Johnson, 1992)

Faulkner and Johnson, in their book in the Cranfield Management Research Series, argue that it is critical to know customer purchase criteria, and equally critical to understand how well a company meets these needs relative to those of its competitors. It is through an interaction of customer needs with competitor offering that determines who will make the sale, and it is the company which meets customer needs better than its competitors which is likely to grow and be successful.

Exhibit 3.3 Customer strategy

To meet customer needs better:

- **at lower cost**

- **at maximum customer satisfaction**

- **with competitive advantages**

In order to monitor this competitive success, a company's products and services have to be based on a fundamental advantage in cost or skills. It is critical for managers to understand what the company costs are and what skills it has compared to competing companies. The skills available to an organisation will depend very heavily on its structure and organisation, its recruitment and retention policy and on staff training and development. Cost differences may arise because of the level of investment in equipment linked to the skill and productivity of employees. The scale of the operation may influence costs and the efficiency of management. Any structural skills or cost differences which are difficult for a competitor to replicate can be the basis of a competitive advantage if they result in an organisation being able to service customer needs better and at a lower cost.

It follows from this that organisations, in order to be successful, need to concentrate their efforts or activities in areas in which they have or can develop and maintain a competitive advantage in terms of cost and skills. It can be argued, for example, that the British motorcycle industry collapsed in the 1960s and 1970s because it failed to keep up with competitor improvements in terms of costs and customer needs, and the success of the Japanese motorcycle industry was as a result of concentrating on both these factors.

As the economy develops, companies have to include consumer experience into their customer strategy. Largely as a result of increasing access to the Internet, consumers are able to learn about businesses on their own or through the collective knowledge of other customers. They now play an active role in creating and competing for value, they bring competence in the form of the knowledge and skills they possess and their willingness to learn and experiment. Prahalad and Ramaswamy (2000) have identified examples of this process in areas such as the software industry where 650,000 Microsoft customers were involved in testing a 'beta' version of Windows 2000™ and sharing with the company their ideas for changing some of the product's features.

Working with the 'beta' software not only provided a test bed for Microsoft; it also helped many of the customers understand how Windows 2000™ could create value for their own businesses. It has been estimated that the R&D investment by these customers in co-developing the product has been more than $500 million worth of time and effort. Other industries also involve their customers to a greater or lesser extent in the development of their products and services. For example, the availability of medical information on the Internet has meant that patients are able to increase their knowledge and shape their own health care. This has been recognised in the UK by the opening of the NHS Direct to provide an immediate source of information for patients. In the tourist industry people are increasingly accessing travel information for themselves so that customers have access to similar knowledge as that of the travel agents. Travel companies have therefore had to change their approaches and their products and services to take this into account.

Organisations have to learn to manage the variety of customer experiences in terms of the interface between a company and its customers, because the range of experience transcends the company's products and services. Managers have to develop products that shape themselves to the customer needs rather than the other way around. The product has to be developed so that future modifications and extensions are based on the customer's changing needs and the company's changing capabilities. A computer user may in practice use it for two or three main functions, for example as a wordprocessor and for e-mail, so these functions need to be easily accessible for that particular user. Another user may use it mainly for spreadsheets and to produce diagrams, charts and other illustrations, and for that user the priority is for this function to be easily accessible. These two users may change their needs over a period of time, for example to carry out research through the Internet, so the products they are using have to cope with these changing needs. Customers may find complicated menus annoying because they judge the product not by the number of functions it has but by the degree to which it provides the experiences they want.

Managers can help to shape customers' experiences by highlighting what is likely to be available next. This has to be a dialogue which makes sense to the consumer and is not so outside the consumer's experience that he or she ignores the developments. At the same time, because of the increasing access to information, customers are able to make greater demands on organisations. Managers can no longer assume that customers' knowledge of the product, prices and competing products is less than their own, so that in maintaining a competitive advantage for their organisation's products and services they have to take even more care than in the past to provide consumer benefits.

In the public sector there have also been attempts to meet 'customer' (public) needs. The UK Government has established an 'e-government' target to make all government services available electronically by the end of 2005. The ambitious objectives have been to reduce National Health Service waiting lists, to reduce benefits fraud, to control civil service costs, to introduce identity cards and to introduce a 'longitudinal' database of citizens. In 2004 volunteers were invited by the UK Passport Office to receive cards bearing electronically encoded biometric information. This trial was designed to test iris scans, fingerprints and electronic facial recognition. To complement the identity card, there has been work on a longitudinal database of work and benefits records by the Department for Work and Pensions in order to create a single record of every individual's history in employment, as benefit claimant and in retirement.

A national programme for information technology in the UK National Health Service has been designed to make an impact on frontline care with a national e-booking scheme that will allow doctors to reserve hospital appointments for their patients before they leave the doctor's surgery. While some of the public IT developments are controversial, this system is designed to be more patient-friendly than the present process. An Online Government Store has been established as a one-stop web shop to offer a variety of services to people, such as a system to provide easy access to car tax. This is a reflection of the explosion in online shopping which has removed the need to leave home to go to the local supermarket or travel agent, while computer search engines have replaced many of the functions of a reference library.

THE 'NEW' MANAGER

→ Ch. 2 In Chapter 2 McGregor's (1960) model in terms of Theory X and Theory Y was discussed in relation to leadership. It can be argued that Theory Y will dominate management in the twenty-first century as organisations attempt to gain competitive advantage through developing employees' own motivation. Theory Y is based on the optimistic view of human nature that employees will help to achieve organisational objectives. This theory views the manager's role as working co-operatively with other employees in order to decide work objectives and methods of achieving them. Managers will encourage the development of self-managed teams and the delegation of decisions towards the point of action, and they will seek to develop people's own motivation by involvement in the organisation. In this process the 'soft' values, such as shared corporate objectives, become more important than the 'hard' values of control and direction (*see* Exhibit 3.4).

The manager of the future has to 'live the vision' as well as being accountable for the performance of the organisation. The 'new' manager does less planning, organising and controlling and much more advising, enabling and encouraging. Jack Welch, the Chief Executive of General Electric in the USA, has been quoted as saying that the twenty-first century commercial wars are going to be won 'on our ideas, not by whips and chains'. Honeywell UK has developed self-managed manufacturing cells with full responsibility for product lines. The role of the manager in these circumstances is to advise self-managed groups, to ensure that they have the necessary resources and to encourage ideas and initiatives.

In an article entitled 'Survival Skills for a New Breed' (1993), Karen Clarke (the winner of a competition called 'Managing for Tomorrow') argues that:

> *'The manager as we know him or her – decision maker, expert, boss, director – is extinct. The 'new' manager has three roles – leader, coach and facilitator.'*

She argues that managerial success will be determined to an increasing extent by the ability to develop and position the organisation strategically and will be measured by staff performance. This means that managers have to accept the fact that they will no longer be the focus of attention but that they will be part of a team. It follows from this that rewards for managers will be based on the performance of the team. As leaders, managers will be looking at the wider picture, how the team fits into the plans for the whole organisation, and how well it is meeting customer needs.

In these circumstances managers are responsible for establishing the boundaries and the culture in which people can work successfully and creatively. One of the 'new' management roles is to act as 'coach'. In this role, managers help employees to be successful and creative by ensuring that they understand the boundaries of their responsibilities and the resources available to them. The 'coach' helps to build up confidence and trust and supports training and development to add to the skills of the team. Successful outcomes are then recorded, and as individuals and teams increase in expertise they are given more freedom to organise their own work.

Exhibit 3.4 British Telecom's 'soft' values

- **We put our customer first**

- **We are professional**

- **We respect each other**

- **We work as a team**

- **We are committed to continuous improvement**

The 'new' manager is also a facilitator in the sense of encouraging new ideas and helping to carry them forward. There can always be a gap between plans and initiatives and their implementation:

> *'If words were deeds, the remaining 1990s would be the Years of the Customer – and 2000 would usher in a whole century of customer worship. But management science is the study of the gap between verbiage and action: the more lip-service the customer receives, the wider the gap is liable to grow.'*   (Heller, 1994a)

The manager has to act as a facilitator in closing this gap, so that customers receive the benefits they want and come back for more. It has been estimated (by David Perkins of Loyalty Marketing Service) that typically it costs 80 per cent of the gross margin on an existing customer to obtain a new one. The manager has to make sure that the product or service is right first time and to research the scale and causes of customer loss. The manager as 'facilitator' has to recognise that although 'customers pay the bills, they do not pay the wages'. In other words, individuals and teams in organisations look inwards at colleagues as well as outwards at customers. Decisions on pay and promotion are made internally and it is essential that the correct organisational culture exists in order to enable confidence and trust to grow.

THE 'NEW' CULTURE

The rapid changes in the international marketplace have led to alterations in the corporate culture of even the organisations slowest to respond to culture change. Companies such as Delta Airlines and IBM, for example, had more or less official no-redundancy policies, but the increase in international competition and the worldwide recession changed this, so that in the early 1990s there were layoffs at Delta and considerable 'downsizing' at IBM. For managers as much as any other employees the idea of a 'job for life' has disappeared and the new contracts between many employers and their managers have become short term and based on mutual benefits. Apple Computers and General Electric, for example, have moved towards 'contractor charters' and away from the old-style long-term employment contracts (Egar, 1994).

These charters contract the services of a manager as long as the relationship is mutually beneficial. When forces outside the direct control of the company, such as the economy or competition, create difficulty for the company, then the future of the contract may become open to question. There is an emphasis on the employee as a 'contributor' rather than only a player, which means that the manager must find ways of adding value to the business, and grow and develop. The manager must become a 'learning person' within a 'learning organisation' which constantly changes, develops and grows. This form of 'contract' or 'charter' complements flatter organisational structures where promotions are scarce and movement is more likely to be horizontal than vertical. These horizontal moves are into positions which add value to the organisation and provide opportunity for the individual to develop. Rewards tend to be based on performance outcomes rather than on factors such as age or length of service. This type of charter is based on a view that the organisation provides opportunities for individuals to develop and be rewarded as long as this process is adding value to the organisation.

This approach to working life tends to appeal only to flexible, enterprising self-starters and not to managers and employees who are looking for a 'job for life'. The meaning of such words as 'commitment' and 'loyalty' is altered in these circumstances. People are committed to the organisation by adding value to its product and their loyalty is to the particular organisation which at a particular time provides them with the opportunity to develop and be rewarded for this. Under these conditions individuals have to take responsibility for their own development and career paths; they cannot expect this necessarily to be mapped out by the company for which they are working (*see* Chapter 20).

→ Ch. 20

> *'What people are increasingly working to acquire is the capital of their own individual reputation instead of the organisational capital that comes from learning one system well and meeting its idiosyncratic requirements. For many managers, it might be more important, for example, to acquire or demonstrate a talent that a future employer or financial advisor might value than to get to know the right people several layers above in the corporation where they currently work.'*
> (Kanter, 1989)

The 'new' culture promotes the idea of a 'shared destiny' that develops collaboration and 'alliances' and what could be described as 'enlightened self-interest'. In its most developed form this approach brings together all the 'stakeholders' in an area of activity in a mutually beneficial alliance. Competitors can prosper together by increasing the overall size of the market, while managers, employees, shareholders, suppliers and customers can collaborate in obtaining the required levels of service and value. The original Rover and Honda collaboration contained elements of this approach in the same way as did the alliance between IBM and Apple Computers. The takeover of Rover by BMW in 1994 could be seen as not only a commercial development, but also as the ending of the previous mutually beneficial alliance.

The obvious stakeholders in this form of alliance are shareholders, managers and employees who will share in the creation and distribution of wealth (*see* Exhibit 3.5). The customer can be a 'stakeholder' of such an alliance by being involved in the quality of the product or service. There is a need for two-way communication

Exhibit 3.5 Alliances

Stakeholders in an alliance need to:

■ create wealth and then distribute it

■ replace 'loyalty' with commitment to the creation of wealth

■ play an active part in wealth creation

■ invest in the future through technological and employee development

■ provide opportunities for managerial and employee development

■ take account of the realities of the marketplace

■ be prepared to accept change

■ help employees at a mutually beneficial time to return to the marketplace with transferable skills

■ encourage employees to accept responsibility for their development and their future through customer surveys, complaints procedures, open meetings and the development of a 'consumer charter' expressing the level of quality and service customers should be able to expect. It is the role of the 'Manager 2000' to ensure that there is a high level of co-operation and collaboration with customers so that the latter can be involved in product and service development.

NEW FORMS OF ORGANISATION

Charles Handy has argued in *The Age of Unreason* (1989) that there are fundamental changes taking place in organisational life. He suggests that companies are moving away from the labour-intensive organisations of the past to new knowledge-based structures. They will increasingly receive added value from their knowledge and creativity, and this is reflected in changing organisational structures. He acknowledges that companies are moving at different speeds and that the process is an evolutionary one, where they may take on some of the characteristics of a 'shamrock' organisation, which may or not be or become part of a 'federation' and will slowly evolve into a 'Triple I' type of organisation.

The shamrock organisation

Handy suggests that the **shamrock organisation**, like the plant after which it is named, has three interlocking leaves, in the sense that it is composed of three distinct groups of workers who are treated differently and have different expectations (*see* Figure 3.2).

A small group of specialist **'core' workers** form the first leaf. They are the nerve centre of the organisation in the sense that they are essential to its work and success. They are both specialists and generalists who run the organisation and control the technology which has replaced, to a large extent, much of the labour force. For example, a computer software or e-commerce company may have a small number of specialists at its centre providing the expertise on which the company is based.

The core workers are expected to be loyal to the organisation, and to be flexible in meeting the challenge of constant change in both competitors and customer requirements. Core workers operate as colleagues and partners in the organisation as opposed to superiors and subordinates. They are stakeholders in the company and in many ways they *are* the company. They expect to be rewarded for their

Figure 3.2 The shamrock organisation

achievements, rather than for any position they might occupy in the hierarchy. The role of the manager in this situation is one of coach, adviser and facilitator. There is considerable pressure on the core workers, 'a pressure which could be summed up by a new equation of half the people, paid twice as much, working three times as effectively' (Handy, 1989).

The shamrock organisation is small compared to its output. This is achieved by the use of technology on the one hand, and the contracting out, to individuals and other organisations, of work which was previously carried out by core employees.

> *'To get that three times improvement the smart organisation will equip their people with all the technological aids they need . . . It will also expect those people to be smart, to be dedicated to their work (none of the leisure age here) and to be prepared to invest enough time and energy to keep ahead of the game, to go on learning, in other words, in order that they can go on thinking.'* (Handy, 1989)

The second leaf, **the contractual fringe**, may or may not work exclusively for the company. Its constituents are contracted to carry out certain tasks for which they are paid a fee based on results, rather than based on the time taken. The advantages of this arrangement are that it is cost effective because companies only pay for what they receive, it makes management easier because fewer people are on the payroll, and when demand is reduced, it is the contractor who faces the problems rather than the company.

> *'Those organisations, although often smaller than the main organisation will have their own shamrocks, their own cores and their own subcontractors. It is a chinese box type of world. The individuals will be self-employed professionals or technicians, many of them past employees of the central organisation who ran out of roles in the core or who preferred the freedom of self-employment.'* (Handy, 1989)

For example, the maintenance and cleaning of the offices of a computer software company may be contracted out, or it may employ contracted workers in a special 'call centre' who may be paid on results, or there may be self-employed professionals who work from home for the company on contracted projects.

The third leaf of the shamrock organisation, **the flexible labour force**, comprises a pool of part-time workers who are available for use by the organisation. These are people with relevant skills who are not in need of, or who cannot obtain, full-time employment, but who are prepared to work on a part-time basis. They may be housewives who combine part-time work with raising a family, people who have retired early, or people who prefer to have a variety of part-time jobs. They do not have the commitment to the company that core workers do, but they enable the organisation to respond flexibly to changes in demand for their product or service. For example, a computer software company or e-commerce company may have a 'bank' of part-time specialists who can be called on when required.

The shamrock organisation can have a large output, while being small in terms of direct employees. It can be organised with little bureaucracy and modern management practices. It can be extremely flexible in order to react to or anticipate 'ups and downs' in customer demands. Core employees in particular can keep close to their customers and make sure that they satisfy their needs.

> *'The shamrock organisation, always there in embryo, has flourished because organisations have realised that you do not have to employ all the people all the time to get the work done.'* (Handy, 1989)

They are also going further and realising that they do not need necessarily to locate everybody in one place. The development of technology enables an increasing number of people to work at a distance so that 'the early morning crush in the commuter train will one day be a thing of the past or at least a twice weekly chore'.

There is another form of 'subcontracting', through the **customer**, which Handy suggests could be a 'fourth leaf' on the shamrock. This is the strong trend towards allowing the customer to do the work. This process is disguised as improving services whether it actually does so or not, while it creates a situation where the customer does work previously carried out by paid employees. Examples of this process include self-service in supermarkets, self-assembly furniture, cashpoints, carveries and buffet-style restaurants, self-service petrol stations which may include payment at the pump, and so on. These examples all have in common self-service by customers. This saves the organisations vast amounts of money in terms of wages for staff to provide these services. The services can then be provided at an extra charge so that it is no longer part of the core of the organisation but is part of the contractual fringe. Self-service is marketed as a benefit to customers when in fact its main advantage may be to the organisation.

The federal organisation

The federal organisation consists of a variety of individual organisations or groups of organisations allied together by a common approach and mutual interest. It provides a way for relatively small companies based on core workers to obtain the advantages of large companies:

> *'It allows individuals to work in organisation villages with the advantage of big city facilities.'*
> (Handy, 1989)

This enables organisations to enjoy the advantages of small, lean structures with the resources and power of big corporations. The drive and energy come from the parts of the federation rather than the centre:

> *'Federalism implies a variety of individual groups allied together under a common flag with some shared identity. Federalism seeks to make it big by keeping it small, or at least independent, by combining autocracy with co-operation. It is the method which businesses are slowly and powerfully evolving for getting the best of both worlds – the size which gives them clout in the market place and in the financial centres, as well as some economies of scale and the small unit size which gives them the flexibility which they need, as well as the sense of community for which individuals increasingly hanker.'*
> (Handy, 1989)

An example of this type of organisation is provided by Miles *et al.* (2000) in their description of Technical Computing and Graphics (TCG). This is an information technology company in Australia which is a federation of 13 small firms producing a wide range of technological products. They co-operate on searching for new product and service opportunities with the initiating firm acting as project leader for a new development.

Shamrock organisations will retain their own autonomy in this system, while the federation provides a common platform for the integration of their activities. The federal organisation will be concerned mainly with the future, in order to keep its members ahead of the competition. It seeks to maximise the innovative and creative potential of its members by specifying the central vision and quality standards and then encouraging innovation and initiative.

The management role in this situation is to provide an overall direction and then to develop opportunities for growth. At the same time the relatively small shamrock organisation members are able to maintain close links and alliances with their customers. Handy argues that:

> *'Organisational cities no longer work unless they are broken down into villages. In their big city mode they cannot cope with the variety needed in their products, their processes and their people. On the other hand, the villages on their own have not the resources nor the imagination to grow. Some villages, of course, will be content to survive, happy in their niche, but global markets need global products and large confederations to make them or do them.'*

The Triple I organisation

Both the idea of the shamrock organisation and the federation can develop into what Handy refers to as the **Triple I organisation**. This is one based on Intelligence, Information and Ideas which form the intellectual capital represented by the core workers. The three Is equal added value because as well as intelligence they need good information to work with and ideas to build on if value is to be made from knowledge. These core workers will be:

> *'expected to have not only the expertise appropriate to his or her particular role, but also be required to know and understand business, to have the technical skills of analysis and the human skills and the conceptual skills to keep them up-to-date.'*
>
> (Handy, 1989)

These are learning organisations, serving their customers as a result of their employees remaining at the leading edge of knowledge and skills. It is these types of organisations which require the changes in the role of the manager, concerned with performance more than formalities and acting as a coach, adviser and facilitator. There will still be mundane jobs in the organisation, but its heart will be a Triple I operation otherwise value will not be added to pay for the support services. The specialists and professionals involved cannot be managed in the old ways, they have to be managed by consent and not by command, and they are obsessed with the pursuit of learning in order to keep up with the pace of change of quality because that produces long-term success. This concentration on quality is based on the organisation's customers and on providing them with the benefits they require.

THE INTERNATIONAL DIMENSION

Organisational change and alterations in the role of the manager are taking place across the world. David Kilburn (1994) has noted changes in Japan, for example. In many ways the Japanese style of management presents a paradox. The obsession for focus on the customer is one side of the equation, while the other side is what appears to be at least paternalistic if not autocratic forms of management. Japanese companies have been characterised by a strong loyalty to the company by employees; many employees join a company until retirement so that when they work with colleagues they are doing so on the basis that they will be working together most of their lives. Japanese society has been described as more group-oriented than that of the USA or the UK, where the focus is more on individual achievement. The Japanese manager is essentially part of a team and will often not be able to hire or fire or restructure the team. The challenge to the Japanese manager is to motivate the team to achieve goals and to help them develop their abilities.

In the Japanese team many decisions are based on consensus and the manager's role is to lead the team towards this. This may take time, but once a decision has been made, everyone will be behind it so that implementation will be relatively smooth. Managers will tend to have paternalistic and deferential relationships with their superiors. Pay is related to the length of service rather than performance, with frequent on-the-job training in order to improve individual performance in achieving the strategic objectives of the company.

There are, however, signs that this traditional approach is changing. While it may still be true for the core workers, there is now greater mobility between jobs, more restructuring in companies, with a reduction in the workforce through voluntary retirement. Observers have noted that subsidiaries and affiliates are being used to a greater extent and that the softer corporate values are being emphasised now compared to the harder values, by concentrating more on staff training, developing skills and ensuring that all employees understand the organisation's values. Figure 3.3 illustrates the shift from the harder values of strategy, structure and systems to the softer ones of staff, skills and style.

At the same time, the paradox does continue in that the central selection of staff and control of training and development are still based on structure and systems. The slow growth in the 1990s has led to a need for flexibility and this is having an effect on Japanese companies as well as those in other countries. In comparison to Japanese culture it is argued that in the USA, management styles are too individualistic for the changes taking place. The individualists have to be moulded into teams and the specialists have either to become generalists or be prepared to work with a range of people in these teams.

As well as the theories of organisational change put forward by such management gurus as Charles Handy, there is also the view that many of the changes are pragmatic. Customer demands are changing and companies alter processes and services in order to meet these demands.

'Lofty strategic concepts are in the trash can of history. For example, the old idea that every corporation should have a "vision" has been shelved by Microsoft, IBM and Chrysler, to name a few, and in its place these companies are improving efficiency across a broad front.'   (Thakray, 1994)

Figure 3.3 **Corporate values**

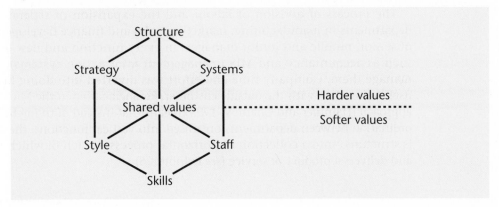

Peggy Salz-Trautman (1994) reports that it has been noted in Germany that tomorrow's manager will require broad-based skills and be able to work in teams. There are pressures on German companies to combine the solidity of industrial giants with the nimbleness of entrepreneurs. In other words, the giants have to 'learn to dance'. These pressures include cut-throat international competition, causing the restructuring of companies, and the expanding services sector based on meeting customer needs.

German managers have a long tradition of respect for technical expertise and attention to detail combined with a deep-seated respect for hierarchy and rank. Their managers of the future have to learn to be flexible and to embrace customer service in a wholehearted fashion. At the same time, companies such as Volkswagen AG recognise that the age of the charismatic individual leading the company is past and the role of the manager has shifted to one of being a coach, facilitator and team-worker. The technology-oriented German company based on 'hard' corporate values has had to shift towards the 'softer' values based on a customer focus.

The convergence of the world economy, brought about by vastly improved communication and seen in terms of both competition and co-operation, forces managers to adapt to new structures and fresh values or to see their organisations drown under a tidal wave of competition. In many companies, and large ones in particular, management teams are likely to include several nationalities. Just as American managers have top positions in European companies (such as Rank Xerox UK), so many European managers have top positions in US companies (such as General Motors). For the 'international' manager, boundaries between nations are no longer important. What is important is looking at customer requirements with fresh eyes and reshaping the organisation in order to meet customer need.

URGENCY

The objective of creating self-managed teams, concentrating on core workers and developing federations of relatively small companies is to keep an organisation close to its customers. The focus is an obsession with strategic innovation so that the company is different to its competitors and better fulfils customer needs. These processes help to create a sense of urgency throughout an organisation because most people can relate directly to customer needs. The flatter organisation means that there is not a hierarchy far removed from contact with customers and unable to relate to them.

The process of division of labour and the expansion of separate functional departments in manufacturing, marketing, sales and finance developed a structure of senior, middle and junior managers in every function and new departments, such as accountancy and MIS (**management information systems**), in order to manage them. Company time and effort was diverted into doing business with itself rather than with the outside customer. **Re-engineering** in the Michael Hammer approach (Hammer and Champy, 1993) means that instead of trying to improve co-ordination between departments organised into vertical functions, the organisation is structured into a collection of horizontal processes, each of which takes orders and delivers a product or service (*see* Exhibit 3.6).

Exhibit 3.6 Re-engineering

P	M	S	F		O	Dist/Mark/Sales/Fin	P	S
R	A	A	I		R		R	E
O	R	L	N		D		O	R
D	K	E	A	RE-ENGINEERED	E		D	V
U	E	S	N		R		U	I
C	T		C		S		C	C
T	I		E				T	E
I	N							
O	G							
N								

This 'horizontal' principle shifts the focus of attention onto activities which are necessary to meet customer needs rather than on efforts to develop co-operation between internal departments. For many employees it leads to multi-skilling and working in integrated teams which are 'empowered' to make a whole range of decisions about the way they work. Employers are 'involved' or experience 'job enrichment' so that their talents are used more effectively in order that the organisation becomes more competitive. Managers move away from the authoritarian image to one of leader, facilitator and coach.

At Forte's Harvester restaurants, for example, staff teams devise their own publicity, carry out their own recruitment and track their own sales targets. Supervisors have been eliminated and the branch manager's role has changed to one of facilitator. The company mission, menu and image remain central issues along with decor and uniforms. Rover, Lucas and Rank Xerox have all moved towards re-engineered self-managed teams. However, Hammer and Champy estimate that 70 per cent of all re-engineering efforts fail, because top managers do not, in the final analysis, support it, or middle managers subvert its implementation, or because the change is not communicated sufficiently well to employees.

This process of 're-engineering' develops a sense of urgency by promoting autonomy and entrepreneurship at the point of interface with the customer. It can be argued that in a fiercely competitive marketplace it is no longer enough simply to satisfy customers. It is now necessary to go beyond this in order to exceed customer expectations time and again. The organisation, it can be argued, has to become customer driven, so that the entire company is saturated by the 'voice' of the customer. In this situation, the customer is the driving force behind the corporate vision, and it is the customer who defines quality in products and services.

SUMMARY

- This chapter is concerned with the changes in organisational structure brought about by a focus on the customer. Customer service has become a major issue in managing and organising companies and institutions. This has been highlighted by *In Search of Exellence* and other studies of successful organisations.

- These developments have created the need for different qualities and skills in management. This has been emphasised by the 'search for synergy' in the move to flatter, less complex and more responsive organisations. The economic focus also emphasises the requirement to provide for customer needs.

- Customer strategy involves achieving a competitive advantage in terms of cost and skills. The 'new' manager has to develop new roles in order to achieve and maintain this advantage as leader, coach and facilitator. Corporate culture has altered and become much more flexible so that managers face new challenges in the workplace and in their own careers. New forms of organisation have developed to reflect the increases in flexibility and the greater emphasis on customer service.

Review and discussion questions

1 *Could the actions described in the case study be applied to other organisations?*

2 *How important are customer surveys in helping to meet their needs? Are there other ways of finding out what customers want?*

3 *How does this case study illustrate Management By Walking About (MBWA)? Can this approach be applied to other organisations?*

4 *Discuss the importance of knowing what competitors are doing and ways of checking on this.*

CASE STUDY

Tesco – Sir Terry Leahy

Starting as a shelf-stacker, Britain's most admired business leader has spent his whole career at Tesco, lifting it to fearsome market dominance. No charismatic general or smooth persuader, he bases his success on an ordinary man's extraordinary empathy with staff and customers.

In June, he went to a store in Royston and mucked in as a general assistant. Come on, this sort of thing – it's all for show, isn't it? 'Not at all, I enjoy it, I find it very satisfying. I'm learning as well. I want a better understanding of how these jobs are done.'

Leahy makes all his senior staff do it. Last year, 1,000 store managers worked in other stores and

1,000 staff from head office did the same. Top retailers will tell you how they visit stores and not just theirs but those of rivals, but Leahy takes trading places to a different level. Each week, he swoops on Tesco stores, wandering round, talking to staff and customers. And each week he tours a competitor. Does he ever go into the big Morrisons down the road? 'Every week. I talk to their staff. Some of them know me and show me round.'

Why can't he just put his feet up on his desk and bask in the glory of the soaring sales chart and the awards that adorn his office? 'I talk to people – I can smell how things are.' It's a party piece of his to tell you to brace yourself for the secret of successful retailing and then to say: 'It's this: never stop listening to customers and giving them what they want. It's that simple.'

On his way up the executive pole, he commissioned a survey of 250,000 Tesco customers, who said they wished Tesco would stop following Sainsbury and carve out its own identity. It was a pivotal point in Tesco's history, the moment when Tesco struck out on its own and left the rest of the industry trailing. It led to the Tesco Clubcard and Tesco Metro, the brand of smaller, high street stores, and to offering just about anything in the stores.

The sea change propelled Leahy to the top job. 'We've worked very hard over the years to organise ourselves from A to Z so we listen to customers.' Whether it's the Clubcard loyalty scheme or focus groups in stores or letters to him, Leahy puts them first. He answers every customer letter he gets personally. 'They really do matter. It's their values we live by.'

It's those values that tell him he's right to fight the farming and corner-shop lobbies, that Tesco customers vote with their feet. Some farmers who can't match the quality he demands and some corner shops that can't compete may go out of business, but so what? 'We're selling 50% more food than we did five years ago; we're the biggest customer of British farming there is and we've created 100,000 jobs in the last five years.'

Source: Extract from 'Sir Terry Leahy' by Chris Blackhurst, *Management Today*, February 2004, pp. 32–7.

REFERENCES AND FURTHER READING

Bennis, Warren (1966) 'The Coming Death of Bureaucracy', *Think*, November/December.

Bergman, Bo and Klefsjo, Bengt (1994) *Quality: From Customer Needs to Customer Satisfaction*, Maidenhead: McGraw-Hill.

Bhote, Keki R (1997) 'What Do Customers Want Anyway?', *American Management Association*, March.

Clarke, Karen (1993) 'Survival Skills for a New Breed', *Management Today*, December.

Egar, Gerard (1994) 'Hard Times Contracts', *Management Today*, January.

Faulkner, David and Johnson, Gerry (1992) *The Challenge of Strategic Management*, London: Kogan Page.

Hammer, Michael and Champy, James (1993) *Re-engineering the Corporate: A Manifesto for Business Revolution*, London: Nicholas Brealey.

Handy, Charles (1989) *The Age of Unreason*, London: Pan Books.

Heller, Robert (1994a) 'Customer Focus Means Commitment to Constant Change', *Management Today*, January.

Heller, Robert (1994b) 'The Manager's Dilemma', *Management Today*, January.

Heskett, James L, Sasser, W Earl and Schlesinger, Leonard A (1997) *The Service Profit Chain: How Leading Companies Link Profit and Growth to Loyalty, Satisfaction and Value*, New York: Free Press.

Kanter, Rosabeth Moss (1989) *When Giants Learn to Dance: Mastering the Challenges of Strategy, Management and Careers in the 1990s*, London: Unwin.

Kay, J (1997) 'Produced to Price', *Financial Times*, 13 June.

Kilburn, David (1994) 'Japanese Management', *Management Today*, January.

McGregor, Douglas (1960) *The Human Side of Enterprise*, New York: McGraw-Hill.

Miles, Raymond F, Snow, Charles C, Miles, Grant (2000) 'The Future Organisation', *Long Range Planning*, 33.

Peppers, Don and Rogers, Martha (1997) *The One to One Future: Building Relationships One Customer at a Time*, New York: Doubleday.

Peters, Tom and Waterman, Robert (1982) *In Search of Excellence: Lessons from America's Best Run Companies*, London: Harper & Row.

Porras, Jerry I and Collins, James C (1996) 'Building Your Company's Vision', *Harvard Business Review*, September/October.

Prahalad, CT and Ramaswamy, Venkatram (2000) 'Co-opting Customer Competence', *Harvard Business Review*, January/February.

Pugh, D S and Hickson, D J (1976) *Organisational Structure in its Context: The Aston Programme 1*, Farnborough: Saxon House.

Raynor, Michael A (1998) 'That Vision Thing: Do We Need It?', *Long Range Planning*, June.

▶

Reichleld, Frederick F (1996) *The Loyalty Effect: The Hidden Force Behind Growth, Profits and Lasting Value*, Boston, MA: Harvard Business School Press.

Salz-Trautman, Peggy (1994) 'The Manager's Dilemma: Germany', *Management Today*, January.

Scott, W R (1987) *Organizations: Rational, National and Open Systems*, Englewood Cliffs, NJ: Prentice-Hall.

Thakray, John (1994) 'Strategic Concepts', *Management Today*, January.

Toffler, Alan (1970) *Future Shock*, New York: Random House.

Young, Roger (1993) 'Jobs for Life', *Professional Manager*, Institute of Management, November.

WEBSITES

http://www.benchnet.com
This provides examples of benchmarking.

http://www.motel6.com
http://www.basshotel.com/holiday-inn
These describe the competitive strategies of two hotel chains, Motel 6 and Holiday Inn.

CHAPTER 4

Strategic marketing management

TIM HANNAGAN

Outcomes

Having read this chapter, you will be able to:

- analyse the importance of marketing for all managers
- discuss the fundamental relevance of marketing in all organisations
- describe the basic principles and theories of marketing and methods applied in marketing
- understand marketing concepts which can be applied to the formation of a marketing plan and strategy in all forms of organisation
- discuss the importance of market research

MARKETING ORIENTATION

Organisational objectives have moved on from an overriding concern with technical excellence, costs and price to a consideration of customer service, quality and employee development. The development of the customer-oriented organisation has made marketing a central activity in most companies and public sector institutions. The importance of the customer is recognised in the Chartered Institute of Marketing's definition:

'Marketing is the management process responsible for identifying, anticipating and satisfying customer requirements profitably.'

This consumer-centred view of economic activity can be traced back at least as far as Adam Smith's *Wealth of Nations*, published in 1776:

'Consumption is the role and purpose of all production; and the interest of the producer ought to be attended to only in so far as it may be necessary for promoting that of the consumer.'

Peter Drucker (1993) has defined marketing as:

'the whole business seen from the point of view of its final result, that is from the customer's point of view.'

This illustrates the shift of marketing as a management function from a relatively low position in the order of priorities to a central one. Marketing has moved from being at best a second-tier activity below production and finance, to being the integrating force represented at the top of organisational structures. Marketing is now a route to becoming a managing director or chief executive.

The position of the marketing function historically is often matched by the process by which companies raise the priority given to marketing. The nineteenth-century development of manufacturing industry was based on a product-orientation, with marketing hardly recognised as a separate activity. The early twentieth century saw the development of a sales-orientation based on the need to interest potential customers in the existing products and services which were increasingly threatened by competition. The second half of the twentieth century has seen the development of an increasing customer-orientation in all areas of the economy and society, based on determining the needs and wants of the customers and satisfying them.

This developing position in the overall economy has been reflected in particular sections of it and in particular organisations. The computer sales boom in the 1970s and 1980s was based on the development of products and programs, and it was only when computer companies met competition and found that selling their products became difficult that they turned to marketing in the 1980s and 1990s. Similarly, travel companies which had been successfully founded and expanded through selling cheap packaged holidays have had to adjust to customer demand for higher quality, more expensive holidays and those companies that have not paid attention to marketing have found it difficult to adjust. In the 1990s public sector institutions in the health service and education have been faced with the need to market their services as a result of changes to their corporate status and funding mechanisms, with the objective of making them more consumer, patient, client, pupil, student oriented.

MARKETING AND SELLING

A **marketing orientation** is not the same as a sales orientation; although the two overlap, they represent different approaches to management within a company. Marketing is the whole process directed at satisfying the needs and wants of people through exchange. Selling can be seen as the culmination of this process, the point at which an exchange is agreed between supplier and customer.

The marketing process comprises:

- **finding out what the customer wants**
- **developing products/services to satisfy those wants**
- **establishing a price consistent with the requirements of the supplier and the perceptions of the customer**
- **distributing products/services to the customer**
- **agreeing on the exchange – selling.**

At the point of sale, the objective is to persuade the customer to take the step from wanting a product or service to actually purchasing it. Some goods will 'sell themselves' and customers will actively seek them out, but in most circumstances this is not the case. The more closely the commodity or service matches the customer's needs, the easier it will be to close the sale. This is most likely to be the situation where the organisation is customer oriented.

The whole purpose of marketing is to provide a product/service that matches the customer's needs. In order to do this, managers have to understand that customers are not so much looking for particular products or services as for benefits. Consumers are looking for goods and services to satisfy their needs and there may be a variety of ways of doing this. A gardener who wants to remove a branch from a tree may immediately reach for a saw. If, however, the branch could be removed with a simple cut in the bark followed by an injection, the sale of saws could decline. Computer companies are well aware of this fact because many of them owe their development and success to having a solution to a particular business problem. When another company has found a cheaper or simpler solution to this problem, the demand for the original solution will decline sharply. In these examples the consumers' need is to remove the branch of a tree, not for a saw, and to solve a business problem, not for a particular computer program. In the same way, when a consumer buys a loaf of bread the basic need is not for bread but to satisfy hunger, and there are a variety of ways of doing this.

This view of consumer needs means that managers have to understand that they should be producing what can be sold rather than selling what can be made. This marketing concept changes the whole orientation of any organisation from one that produces what it is able to and then attempts to sell it, into one which produces what people want to buy. Managers have to determine the needs and wants of their target market and then deliver the desired satisfaction more effectively and efficiently than competitors. A selling orientation can easily concentrate on the needs of the seller, rather than the buyer, and the need to convert the company's product or service into cash. The selling concept starts with the company's existing product and looks for intense promotion to achieve profitable sales, while the marketing concept starts with the needs and wants of the company's target customers, and achieving profits through creating and maintaining customer satisfaction.

Figure 4.1 **The customer-oriented organisation**

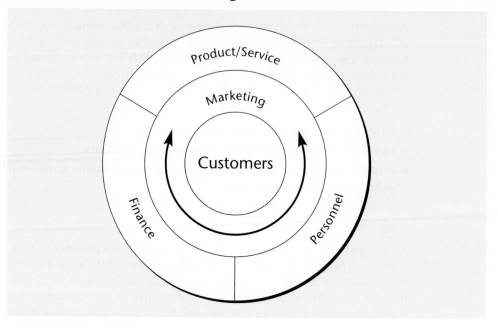

It can be argued that all managers are involved in marketing, even when they are far removed from the marketing function or where their organisation gives little attention to marketing. Product/service design, advertising and promotion or the provision of customer service are all aspects of marketing, just as all managers help to create and promote an image of their company in the way they carry out the job. The marketing-oriented manager will attempt to make selling as superfluous as possible by understanding the consumer so well that the product or service 'sells itself'. Ideally, marketing will result in a consumer who is ready to buy so that all that is needed to make a sale is for the product to be available (*see* Figure 4.1).

MANAGERS AND MARKETING

A fully integrated marketing orientation will permeate the whole structure of an organisation and will influence the thinking and the actions of every manager (*see* Figure 4.1). Managers need to realise that while profits continue to be fundamental to business survival, they depend on the organisation satisfying the customer. This is the approach that provides a competitive edge.

It is essential for any organisation to identify its customers if it is to improve its customer services and provide what the customer needs. The customer is usually identified as the person who pays for the product or service. Where there is not a direct payment, such as in the public sector, the customer can be identified as the person who receives the service. There are different 'types' or 'levels' of customer, because wholesalers can be considered to be customers of manufacturers and retailers customers of wholesalers. The 'final' customer is the person who eventually uses the product. It is this role which makes marketing an integrative function involving all areas of an organisation and everybody working in it. The marketing department is responsible for the technical aspects of a marketing policy, but everybody is involved to a greater or lesser extent so that the whole corporate culture is affected, the image of the organisation and its strategic plan.

One of the greatest challenges for managers is to change the words of mission statements, visions and corporate strategies into deeds. As the needs of customers change, so the means of satisfying them have to change in response and adjust at least as quickly and where possible in anticipation.

KNOWING THE CUSTOMER

Managers have to decide about two fundamental marketing questions: What business are we in? Who is our customer?

What business are we in?

The answer to this may appear obvious and straightforward, but the examples of the saw manufacturer and the computer company illustrate the importance of arriving at a more fundamental answer. The computer company may describe its business in terms of information technology or computing or a software package, when it is in fact in the business of solving business problems through the application of technology. Once this is understood, the opportunities for the company open up and the meaning of 'sticking to the knitting' becomes clear.

It can be argued that when a company begins to ask what 'line of business' it is actually in, it is beginning to identify marketing as an important management function. The next step is to appreciate the fact that marketing needs to permeate every area of the company. The question 'What is our business?' has to be defined in terms of the underlying consumer need that the organisation is trying to serve. A large retail store on the outskirts of a town may be trying to serve the shopping needs of a wide area, limited only by the ability to travel to it by car, while the corner shop situated in a residential location will be trying to serve the shopping needs of customers in an area defined by the ability to walk to it. In order to serve their customers they may both aim to carry a very wide variety of goods and to be open 'all hours', although the supermarket will be organised for regular but infrequent major shopping at relatively low prices, while the local shop will be organised for more irregular and more frequent shopping at relatively high prices. They will both survive while they are able to serve the needs of the consumers better than competitors. The local shop cannot hope to compete with the supermarket on price or variety, but it may do so on its proximity to a group of consumers and its relative convenience.

Who is the customer?

The straightforward and obvious answer is that the customer is the person who pays for the product or service, and it is possible to define the customer in these terms (*see* Figure 4.2). In fact, of course, the situation is more complicated than this. Some purchases are made for other people as gifts and although the person paying for the commodity is still the customer, receiving the benefit of purchasing a present, the final consumer is the person receiving the present. In the public sector there may not be a direct payment for a service, although payment may be indirect, through

Figure 4.2 The consumer

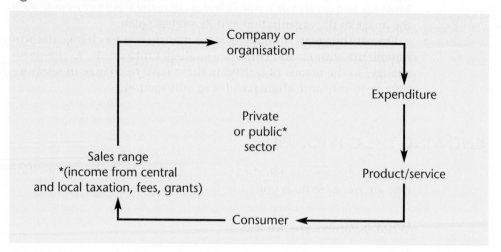

the taxation and national insurance system. In this case the customer can be described as the person who receives the service, whether it is health, education or leisure. Where children are involved in receiving a commodity or service, whether there is direct payment or not, the parents are also customers in that they may play a part in the payment and in the choices of their children, who may be considered the 'primary' consumers.

Every organisation needs to know its customers, not only who they are but also what influences their purchasing decisions, the extent of their disposable income, the way they live, where they live and so on. Marketing depends on a detailed knowledge of customers and their needs so that the company or institution can meet these needs in the right place, at the right time and at the right price, and also anticipate fluctuations and changes in needs.

MARKET RESEARCH

After the acquisition of Hilton International by Ladbroke in 1987 there was concern that the Hilton name was being devalued in customer perceptions because it had been transplanted to other hotels. In 1988 an international market research survey was instigated under the direction of National Opinion Poll. The results were reassuring to the company, because Hilton scored higher than its international competitors for both spontaneous and prompted awareness and as the first-choice chain of hotels. There were, however, some weaknesses identified by the research. The sub-brand Hilton National, created by Ladbroke from existing hotels, performed far less well in terms of awareness than the Hilton name; the Hilton International logo was the least well known of seven hotel logos tested; while although Hilton was noted number one in brand image, prestige, business orientation and efficiency, it was seen as unfriendly with a hint of traditionalism which was tinged with complacency.

This research was followed up by Ladbroke in a 'Take me to the Hilton' advertising campaign in 1989 which was translated into nine languages and seen by about 54 million people. Further research in 1991 showed that many of the problems remained, which led to the company reviewing its brand positioning so that the

Hilton International concentrated on international business travellers and wealthy tourists, while the Hilton National offered 'the Hilton experience' at affordable prices. Hotels have been reassessed and the Hilton National logo developed to emphasise the 'Hilton' connection. The company has recognised that:

> *'far-reaching decisions can be taken by senior management on what to the outsider may seem like pure instinct. Research can be the necessary counter-balance. It offers the means to monitor the consequences of decisions and, when appropriate, it provides a mechanism for reviewing and refining the course of action selected.'*
>
> (Marketing, 28 January 1993, p 26)

Market research is the planned, systematic collection, collation and analysis of data designed to help the management of an organisation to reach decisions about its operation and to monitor the results of these decisions. It can be said to provide, in the words of the British Market Research Society:

> *'information on people's preferences, attitudes, likes and needs, to help companies understand what consumers want.'*

Strictly speaking, market*ing* research is concerned with the marketing *process* while market research is concerned with the measurement and analysis of *markets*. In practice the two terms are often used synonymously, although facts about the market are 'neutral' and objective, while the attitudes and opinions of customers have to be interpreted in order to help managers to make decisions. Market analysis is undertaken to determine the opportunities existing in a particular market and is about defining the market, describing it and analysing it. In this sense, a market is the set of actual and potential consumers for particular goods and services. Managers are interested in:

- the size of the market for their products and services in terms of volume and value;
- the pattern of demand, including the economic, social, political and technical factors that might influence future demand and whether it is seasonal or cyclical;
- the market structure in terms of size and numbers of companies, income groups, sex and age distribution, and geographic location;
- the buying habits of people (both individuals as well as groups such as retailers and wholesalers) in the market;
- the market share of the company and how this compares with previous performance;
- past and future trends in areas such as population, national income;
- overseas markets that may present opportunities.

Managers need to be able to make predictions and decisions based on accurate information. While decisions can be made without very much information, a successful manager will want to have as many facts as possible before using judgement to make a decision. Market research enables decisions to be based on evidence and provides the basis for strategic planning and policy making.

The needs of customers in particular must be constantly monitored for managers to 'keep close to the customer'. It is important to know how satisfied customers are with products and services so that managers are able to introduce modifications or additions to satisfy customer needs more closely. The process will be a continuous one in order to keep up with or even ahead of changing needs (*see* Figure 4.3).

Figure 4.3 The research process

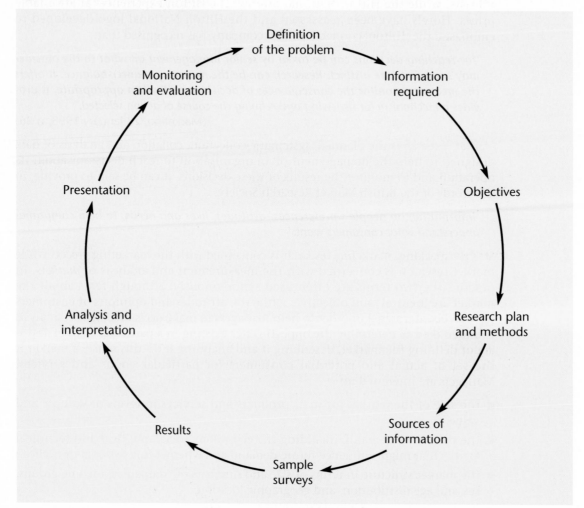

The questions to be answered to help managers make decisions have to be defined with as much clarity as possible about the information that is required. The objectives of the research need to be established so that there is agreement about the expected outcomes. If, for example, a company needs to know its customers' opinions of a new product, the objective of the market research will be to establish these opinions as clearly as possible so that the product can be modified to match them. A sample survey may be used for this research including a customer questionnaire and interviews. The results of this survey will be analysed and interpreted so that it can be presented to managers who will make decisions about the product. The research process will need to be monitored and as a result may be refined and the whole process will start again in order to see how well the modifications have been received by customers.

THE MARKETING PROCESS

Managers in any organisation must define the underlying need that it is trying to serve. This is reflected in the company mission statement or vision which describes the organisation's basic purpose. For example, a retail company may describe itself as offering customers a range of high quality, well designed and attractive merchandise at reasonable prices, while a computer company may want to emphasise the fact that it is not only about particular packages and products but that it concentrates on solving business problems. The corporate objectives will fill out the abstractions of the mission statements in more concrete terms, and lead to the operational detail that results in an action plan.

In a marketing-oriented company, much of this process is informed by marketing, on the grounds that there is no point in operating an organisation which is producing products or services which customers do not wish to buy. It can be argued that marketing analysis and planning begin and end with the customer. The starting point is to know about the organisation itself. This can be established through a marketing audit, which is a formal review of everything that has affected or may affect the organisation's marketing environment, internal marketing system and specific marketing activities.

The marketing audit

A company's marketing environment (as distinct from, although including, environmental issues) consists of all the factors that are external to its own marketing system and that impinge on a successful exchange process with its customers. These factors can be collected into categories, sometimes referred to as the STEP (social, technological, economic, political) or PESTLE factors, which are:

- Political
- Economic
- Social
- Technological
- Legal
- Environmental.

Companies need to keep up to date with **political** changes that are occurring not only in the countries in which they are operating but also across the world, because these will affect the work of the company in one way or another. For example, political disruption in the Middle East could result in reduced oil supplies and increases in the price of petrol and other fuel. This could have a knock-on effect for the cost of transport, which can affect the supply costs or distribution costs of even the smallest organisation. Changes in political parties and in governments can result in different policies being introduced, which can affect companies in one way or another. The more managers understand about the political situations in which they are working, the more they are able to foresee and make allowances for effects on their organisation.

In a similar way, managers need to keep up with **legislation** that affects their business. Health and safety regulations have to be met, European controls may have to be considered and pollution control may be the subject of new laws. There has been a growing interest in **environmental issues** and worldwide damage to the environment. The effects of different industrial sectors on the environment have been identified and vary considerably, so that, for example, it has been argued that oil companies can be environmentally damaging in their exploration for oil in the rainforests of the world, while the service sector has a less direct impact. Even in the service sector, of course, there are variations, so that tourism, for instance, can be polluting in environmentally sensitive areas of the world. This has encouraged the development of so-called 'eco-tourism', or environmentally friendly tourism.

Companies need to have a clear understanding of the **society** and the population to which their products and services are directed. As well as the size of the potential market, there are questions of age distribution, sex distribution, and income and education levels. As the population becomes wealthier or better educated, the range and quality of the goods demanded may change and companies have to keep up with these changes if they are to be successful. At the same time, **economic** factors, such as levels of disposable income, will greatly influence consumer demand. For example, if disposable income falls, consumers will continue to buy necessities but will reduce spending on luxuries. In a recession, house prices will fall and families may move house less often so that demand for household goods will be reduced.

Technological changes have a major impact on most companies and can have an effect on the competitive edge of a company and make it more or less cost-effective compared to its competitors. The rapidly expanding access to the Internet in the population has altered the amount of information available to organisations' customers. Travel agencies, for example, have had to take into account that tourists are now able to find out information on airline flights, hotels and excursions which is similar to the information they have in the agency; major stores, such as Tesco, have introduced 'Internet shopping' as a part of their service to customers; and there has been a huge expansion in the number of e-commerce 'dot-com' companies that have been established – often in competition with more traditional companies.

These external influences on an organisation's marketing environment do not, of course, fit neatly under these six headings. Environmental issues, such as pollution, are the subject of legislation and of social pressure; changes in taxation are political and have an economic impact; developments in technology can influence an organisation's costs and culture, and the whole way it works, and so on. All these 'external' influences on the market need to be understood by a successful company as well as information about its particular market and its own potential customers.

This gives rise to a further refinement of this consideration of the marketing environment which can be categorised as **Spectacles**:

- **Social**
- **Political**
- **Economic**
- **Cultural**
- **Technological**
- **Aesthetic**
- **Customers**
- **Legal**
- **Environmental**
- **Sectoral.**

As well as social, technological, economic, political, legal and environmental factors (covered in STEP, PEST and PESTLE), the influence of cultural, aesthetic, customer and sectoral factors in the environment of organisations is also taken into account.

Cultural factors can be defined as 'the way we do things around here', whether it is in an organisation, a particular society or region, or a country. The importance of culture within organisations is discussed in Chapters 1, 2 and 8 while external cultural influences on organisations are considered in both Chapters 2 and 19. Organisations cannot operate in exactly the same way in other countries as they do in the UK and although they may have a high level of standardisation (as, for example, with McDonald's restaurants), they have to take account of people's customs, expectations and behaviour. Some of the early problems at Disneyland Paris arose from an attempt to transfer a North American culture directly to France. Automobile companies (such as Ford) have taken differences between countries to heart by producing different cars for different countries in order to attempt to match customer requirements.

→ Chs 1, 2 and 8

→ Chs 2 and 19

Aesthetics can be thought of in terms of the appreciation of beauty or in terms of good taste; it can also be thought of in terms of image. There may be a difference between the image an organisation wants to project and the one it actually does project. The Body Shop, for example, attempts to project an environmentally friendly image, but people also realise that it is a commercial company that has to make a profit. Promotional campaigns are designed in order to project and influence the image of an organisation, but they do not always produce the expected result. Companies develop a reputation amongst consumers which they may find difficult to change. Marks & Spencer, for example, has attempted to alter its well established image in terms of its clothing products amongst consumers in order to compete with shops offering more trendy goods at cheaper prices.

→ Ch. 3

The importance of organisations understanding and reacting to **customer** requirements is analysed in Chapter 3. There has been a rise in 'consumerism' with an increase in the 'power' of customers, and organisations have to meet customer needs if they are to survive in the long run. **Sectoral** factors are an essential element of an organisation's competitive strategy. Managers have to analyse the position of their organisation in the sector or sectors in which they operate, as well as the position of any actual and potential rivals, so that they can maintain a competitive advantage.

→ Ch. 18

The growing interest in **environmental** factors is discussed in Chapter 18. Organisations and their industries have a varied impact on the environment, so that it can be argued that oil companies' very business is environmentally damaging, while the service sector has a less direct impact. However, the actual situation is complicated because, for example, the increasing demand for consumer goods has placed great pressures on resources and, as a result, on the environment. Managers face the challenge of meeting customer needs and integrating environmental considerations into their production and marketing plans.

SWOT analysis

Equally as important as this external business environment to a company's marketing plan is knowledge and understanding of its internal strengths and weaknesses. In marketing terms this process is known as a SWOT analysis:

- **Strengths**
- **Weaknesses**
- **Opportunities**
- **Threats.**

The SWOT analysis helps managers to focus their attention on the key areas within a company that need to be taken into account in producing a marketing plan. It highlights internal strengths and weaknesses from the customers' point of view as they relate to external opportunities and threats.

The strengths of an organisation may be in terms of proximity to its customers, its expertise, its ability to produce high-quality goods at low cost. Weaknesses will be the opposite of the strengths. A poor reputation, badly organised services and difficult communications may all be weaknesses of a company. The manager's role is to exploit the strengths of the company and to correct or compensate for the weaknesses.

The weaknesses of an organisation may give rise to opportunities, in the sense that the exposure of a weakness may be seen as an opportunity for development. A company that has been able to make a profit even though its customer care is poor can increase its profits and improve its position by taking the opportunity to improve its customer care. In terms of threats, competition is the most obvious for many companies and marketing is very much about maintaining a competitive edge. Other threats can be as a result of a fall in orders, increased import prices, changes in government regulations and changes in demand. The ability to meet and overcome these threats successfully is one of the strengths of a company and can separate those organisations which survive from those which do not.

THE MARKETING MIX

Once managers know the situation of their organisation in relation to its market, understand its internal and external position, and have an idea of what their customers need, they can develop a marketing strategy. Managers have four major variables that can be controlled in order to arrive at their marketing strategy. These are the product or service produced by the organisation, its price, the way it is promoted, and the place or places through which it is made available to the consumers. These are the **four 'Ps'** which constitute the **marketing mix**:

- **Product**
- **Price**
- **Place**
- **Promotion.**

The marketing mix is the appropriate combination, in a particular set of circumstances, of the four Ps. It consists of everything an organisation can do to influence the demand for its products and services. Management has to make sure that the balance between these four variables is maintained, or their marketing strategy will fail. What happens to one element in the marketing mix will have an effect on one or more of the others. For example, the quality of a product may be improved in order to meet customer demands, but this may increase the cost of production and the price. However, another possibility is that the improved quality increases demand so that sales rise, with the result that there are economies of scale and lower unit costs which can be reflected in the price.

An effective marketing strategy will bring the four variables together, in order to satisfy customer needs. To retain the competitive edge in a target market, managers have to develop and communicate the differences between their offering and those of competitors. The key to competitive positioning is to understand how members of the target market evaluate and choose between product brands. It may be on location, on price, or on the way the product is sold. Managers must choose a marketing mix that will support and reinforce their chosen competitive position at an expenditure level they can afford. By this process marketing managers seek to achieve the optimum marketing mix for their company, that is the least amount of money and effort required to make a profit. The process of achieving this optimum marketing mix can be summarised as APPEAL:

- **Assess the needs of consumers**
- **Produce the right commodity or service**
- **Price the commodity or service successfully**
- **Ensure a high quality product and service**
- **Advertise and promote the product/service effectively**
- **Launch an efficient distribution system.**

Managers can manipulate and vary this process and the four Ps in order to improve the effectiveness of the marketing programme.

In terms of service marketing, it is possible to add **three other Ps**:

- **People**
- **Process**
- **Physical evidence.**

Including **people** as a factor in the marketing mix emphasises the importance of all those involved in the transaction of a service, including the customer and the person (or people) providing the service. The success of the service will depend on the relationship between the customer and the provider. The customer will have certain expectations and, if these are not met by the provider, the service will not be a complete success. A holiday tour guide, for example, can provide minimal information to holiday-makers, or can suggest places to visit, arrange trips and provide support when problems arise. Some holiday-makers may be happy to be left alone, while others may want much more attention from the guide and be disappointed if they do not receive it.

The **process** is the interaction itself between all the people involved in the transaction. Training in service provision emphasises the importance of this interaction and the role of the provider in enabling the customer to receive the service in an efficient and effective way.

Physical evidence can range from the location in which the service takes place to the ticket or voucher with which the customer is provided. A flight ticket is the physical evidence that the traveller has purchased a seat on an aeroplane flight between two designated places, while a voucher may be the physical evidence that the holiday-maker has purchased a place on a guided tour.

The inclusion of these three extra Ps suggests that marketing must take them into account, particularly in the service sector. They emphasise that transactions are between people, that there is a process involved in each transaction and that consideration should be given to all the other aspects of the transaction.

PRODUCTS AND SERVICES

'A product is anything that can be offered to a market for attention, acquisition, use or consumption that might satisfy a want or need. It includes physical objects, services, persons, places, organizations and ideas.'   (Kotler, 1986)

This definition includes services and it is useful to realise both that they are 'products' in the broadest sense and that there are differences between them and physical commodities (see the discussion in the case study on p 77). Whereas a commodity is tangible and its sale involves a change in ownership, a service is essentially intangible and does not result in the exchange of ownership. When a car is bought and sold, there is a change of ownership; when a holiday is bought and sold, ownership of the travel company, airbus or hotel remains unchanged.

Managers can view all commodities and services as solving consumer problems, and marketing as selling benefits rather than features, but, of course, features may be important if they help to provide benefits. For example, car salespeople may concentrate their sales drive on the special features their cars provide, while the ability of the cars to provide a reliable form of transport is taken for granted. The features help to differentiate one car from another, but they will not serve any purpose unless the benefit of transport can be guaranteed. In fact, competition is often not so much about the product as about the value added to it in the form of packaging, services, customer advice, financing, delivery arrangements and so on. For example, Exhibit 4.1 illustrates the importance of packaging.

Exhibit 4.1 Marketing: value added

In the run-up to Christmas 1993, Cadbury's decided to introduce a £5 million support package for 'Milk Tray'. This is one of the oldest and the best known mass-market brands and is the UK's biggest selling chocolate assortment brand. It had become squeezed by upmarket niche brands on one side and downmarket and own-label competitors on the other.

The support package was based on months of qualitative and quantitative research and was designed to increase the volume of sales by 20 per cent over 18 months. The revamp included the addition of two new flavours, truffle shell and praline fanfare – to reflect the company's view that consumers were being increasingly experimental in their tastes.

The big change was in the packaging for the chocolates, with a redesigned box to make it more upmarket with a cut-out lid, a separate choice card inside and a new tray design. The object was to make the product more 'feminine' and give it a more luxury feel.

In considering their target market, managers need to take account of all aspects of it. These can be summarised by considering basic questions about the market which can be divided into the **six 'O's**:

- **Occupants** – which individuals constitute the market?
- **Object** – what do consumers wish to buy?

- **Occasions** – when do customers make purchases?
- **Organisations** – who is involved in the decision to purchase?
- **Objectives** – why do consumers buy particular commodities?
- **Operations** – how do consumers buy products and services?

Market research will help managers to understand their target markets so that their companies can produce the commodities and services wanted by the consumers in that particular market at a particular time. At the same time, managers need to base their decisions on who is involved in purchasing and how and where consumers make decisions on purchases.

Making sure that the product or service is right for the consumer can be described as the single most important activity of marketing. If managers do not produce a commodity or service consumers want, no amount of promotion or price incentives will encourage them to buy it, at least not more than once. In fact, managers will be aiming to satisfy the consumer so that demand is likely to be repeated and other products or services of the company are also demanded. An important element of marketing is about reputation and recommendation. Personal recommendation is one of the most important ways in which a company's reputation and image are developed.

Ideally, managers will extend the features of the product or service so that they provide unique benefits not found in the competition. The concept of the 'unique selling proposition' includes the quality of design, style and service, reliability and cost. The successful development of this concept will help enhance customer loyalty. Loyal customers tend to be worth more to a company than new customers. The extra cost of replacing an existing customer with a new one can be as high as tenfold. Loyal customers are believed to spend more and have a higher purchase frequency, and a satisfied customer is the best possible walking advertisement for any company.

The increase of competition in the 1990s has been matched by rising customer sophistication, combined with price sensitivity, and has given impetus to consideration of 'relationship marketing' and customer loyalty.

> *'This more competitive environment will focus greater attention on the potential of existing customers. This will take two forms: an assessment of lifetime value and therefore the value of promoting loyalty; the possibilities of increasing the value of given customers through cross selling/upgrading programmes.'*

(Henley Centre and Chartered Institute of Marketing, 1993)

The link between customer defections, or 'promiscuity', and profit offers an explanation for a move away from a culture where 'closing the sale' is of overriding importance, to one where encouraging customer loyalty is paramount. Customer retention (*see* Exhibit 4.2) can be defined as:

> *'the number of customers present at the beginning of a period who remain as customers at the end of the period, divided by the number of those present at the beginning.'*

Research from Bain and Company indicates that a business loses between 15 and 20 per cent of its customers each year (*Marketing*, 18 November 1993, p 24). In any business, the more satisfied the customer, the higher the retention rate.

Exhibit 4.2 **Customer retention rate**

1000 original customers, of which 800 are retained:

$$\frac{800}{1000} \times 100 = 80\% \text{ customer retention rate}$$

1000 original customers, of whom 200 are retained:

$$\frac{200}{1000} \times 100 = 20\% \text{ customer retention rate}$$

Long-term relationships with customers are more profitable because:

■ the cost of acquiring new customers can be substantial – a higher retention rate means that less marketing expenditure needs to be allocated to targeting potential customers;

■ loyal customers tend to spend more;

■ regular customers tend to place frequent, consistent orders, therefore usually cost less to serve;

■ satisfied customers are the best advertisement for any business and are likely to introduce new customers to the company through word-of-mouth recommendations;

■ satisfied customers are often willing to pay premium prices to a supplier they know and trust;

■ retaining customers makes gaining market entry or share gain difficult for competitors;

■ the information collated and held on loyal customers through database management allows the company to communicate regularly with them.

Sales can be increased by introducing tactical promotion and reactivating lapsed customers with specially targeted offers. The development of Air Miles to encourage customer loyalty has been spread across a number of products and is similar to long-term promotions such as petrol tokens. The objective of these promotions is the same: to encourage customers to buy products or services where they can obtain the petrol tokens or Air Miles.

For example, in 1989 Newey & Eyre became an Air Miles client when it launched a customer loyalty programme. The national marketing manager stated, 'We felt that travel was still one of the most powerful motivators. We were also attracted by its flexibility and the fact that the perceived reward is greater than the cost.' Newey & Eyre is the largest electrical wholesaler in the UK and in spite of the recession it measured a growth in sales of 24 per cent in 1992. The company targeted a core group of customers from its more than 100 000 accounts and also provided Air Miles as an incentive for its own salesforce. The promotion was risk free in the sense that it secured incremental revenue. If the target was not reached, the customer was not rewarded with Air Miles.

In 1993 the magazine *Marketing* noted an increasing range of customer-loyalty initiatives. Examples have included Vauxhall's GM card, Diners Club, Asda, American Express, Argos Premier Points, Sainsbury's Homebase and British Airways Air Miles.

LIFE-CYCLE ANALYSIS

Managers should understand the application of life-cycle analysis in terms of the products and services for which they are responsible. This analysis can also be applied to the general rise and fall of companies. All products and services have a life cycle in the sense that, after they are introduced, they often pass through periods of growth, then relative stability and finally decline. This process can be mirrored in the fate of companies who do not take or are unable to take sufficient notice of the life cycle. Many of the original 'excellent' companies from the early 1980s declined as their products and services were overtaken by others. IBM is an example of this (*see* Exhibit 4.3), although it has survived successfully.

Exhibit 4.3 The decline of IBM

In the early 1980s IBM controlled the newest and fastest growing technology and its name was synonymous with computing. By 1992 the company had experienced the largest ever loss recorded by any company anywhere.

IBM was one of Peters and Waterman's 'excellent' companies:

'With one act . . . IBM simultaneously reaffirmed its heroic dimension (satisfying the individual's need to be part of something great) and its concern for individual self-expression (the need to stick it out).'

In a period of 10 years the company moved from being held up as an example of the success of capitalism to an example of its failings. It could be said that it was within its major strengths that IBM's weakness appeared. Its strength was based on an almost monopolistic position in the market for automated information. It was first with punch-cards and then with the mainframe and minicomputer.

As long as computers were the preserve of major corporations the IBM strategy worked, but with the development of the desktop personal computer this changed. IBM decided not to launch the desktop computer because it did not believe that anyone would want such an item, and it was left to Apple Computers and other competitors to move into this market. IBM quickly followed, but without time to develop its own components it bought in chips from Intel and software from Microsoft. The launch of the IBM PC legitimised the desktop for corporations, but also meant that other companies could produce IBM PC clones and Intel and Microsoft could sell their components to these companies. By 1994 there were 3000 clone manufacturers in Taiwan alone, helped in their success by the ability to network PCs to do much of the work of mainframes and minis.

In his book, *The Fate of IBM*, Robert Heller comments that IBM played a difficult hand badly, but in the end the new market was simply too big and the pace of change too fast for one company to remain in control.

The performance of new products and services typically follows a pattern that includes four or five identifiable stages, each related to the passage of time and the levels of sales or demand (*see* Figure 4.4 below). The stages are:

- **Introduction** – a period of slow growth as the product/service is introduced;
- **Growth** – a period of rapid market acceptance;
- **Maturity** – a period of slower growth because the product/service has been accepted by most of the potential buyers;

Figure 4.4 Product life cycle

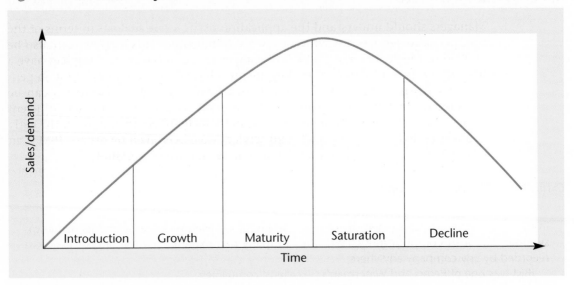

- **Saturation** – a period when there are many competitors in the market which itself is no longer growing. This period can be combined with maturity;
- **Decline** – a period when performance starts a strong downward drift.

Of course, not all products and services follow this exact pattern, and timescales can vary considerably, but careful analysis of the life cycle enables managers to focus on the appropriate marketing strategy for a particular stage in the life cycle of their products and service:

- **Introduction** – a new product or service may be a substitute for something else, either directly or indirectly. For a time, consumers may resist the new product while they consider that the old one still meets their needs. For this reason, and because the new product is not well known in the market, the demand will be slow in the introductory stage. The only exception to this is a fad or fashion which may make an immediate impact. The marketing strategy for most goods when they are introduced will be to target the groups of people who are likely to be most interested. Previous customers are an obvious target. Computer companies producing a new product or introducing a new service will send information to their previous customers in the first instance. They will also attempt to attract the attention of the 'innovators' who find out about new products without help and who do not need much persuasion.
- **Growth** – the benefit of the new product/service will have become accepted by this stage. Production difficulties will have been overcome and development costs covered, so that usually the price can be reduced. Marketing strategy will usually involve a wider promotion to target new customers. Competitors will begin to enter the market during this stage. They spend money on promoting their product, so the general awareness of it increases, helping to encourage further growth.
- **Maturity** – at this stage the product or service will have become widely accepted and competition will become the most important element for managers.

Marketing may be aimed at an attempt to retain or assume the position of market leader or at challenging the leader by emphasising the advantages of the company's particular product.

■ **Saturation** – sooner or later all the potential users of the product or service will have satisfied their demand for it, so that the market no longer grows. There will be plenty of suppliers competing in the market and this may lead to price wars. At the same time, managers will search for new products and services to replace the old ones.

■ **Decline** – as newer products and services are introduced, the demand for the old product or service will decline. Managers may decide to stop producing the commodity because it is felt to be better to invest in newer products. Advances in technology can cause the demand for a product to decline and changes in fashion or taste alter demand.

■ **Recovery** – it is possible for companies to recover, so that after a period of decline and heavy losses (IBM lost $16 billion between 1991 and 1993 – *see* Exhibit 4.4) a company may introduce changes which are sufficient to bring it back to an early stage of the life cycle. This company renewal may involve new products, internal restructuring or a fresh approach to marketing and sales which result in the company starting a new life cycle at the introduction or growth stage.

Life-cycle analysis is observed quite easily in the development and decline of a new model of a motor car. At introduction, the marketing strategy is likely to include heavy advertising to encourage early demand. As the growth of sales develops, promotion will be designed to establish market share. The reputation of the product will become more important than in the introduction stage when innovators and 'risk-takers' may be the main purchasers. Car manufacturers may emphasise matters such as reliability and security.

Exhibit 4.4 The recovery of IBM

Although IBM had experienced record losses by 1993, by 1997 the company had achieved a remarkable recovery. The appointment of a new chief executive, Lou Gerstner, in 1993 brought about one of the most remarkable corporate turnarounds in US history. In 1997, for the first time in 10 years, IBM's market value topped $100 billion and its shares were trading at record levels. Shipments of PCs rose 27 per cent in 1996 boosting IBM's market share from 8.1 to 8.9 per cent and the absorption of the software company, Lotus Development Corporation, in 1995 proved unexpectedly successful. One view was that the culture of the two companies would clash and that IBM's software division would not be revitalised, but Lotus sales rose 60 per cent in 1996 to $650 million.

It has been reported that Lou Gerstner had little knowledge of computers when he joined IBM, but he dismissed the idea that the company's problems were a lack of new products. His view was that the problem was in the company's management and one fundamental change he made was to instruct the company sales force to find out what customers really wanted, rather than believing that they knew best, and then giving it to them. At the same time the numbers of staff were being reduced from 300 000 to 215 000 and factories and research and development departments were closed. In 1997, two-thirds of IBM's revenue came from PCs and services and although the use of an IBM scoring system at the Atlanta Olympics ran into difficulties, the defeat of Gary Kasparov, the world chess champion, for the first time by IBM's 'Deep Blue' computer was a successful publicity stunt.

In maturity, the attempt will be made to retain market position against the competition, the emphasis may be on the quality of a well-established product and the features available in the car may play an important part in sales. Eventually the particular model of car will become relatively out of date compared with new models being introduced, and saturation will have been reached with a decline in sales. As demand declines, car manufacturers and showrooms may attempt to boost sales by producing 'special editions', or promotions which may involve price cuts. Some car manufacturers have followed a policy of replacing their models in a particular price range before a decline in demand is too obvious. This could be said, for example, of Ford's replacement of the Cortina by the Sierra and then the Mondeo.

MARKET SEGMENTATION

Where clear differences can be identified, it is possible to group customers into market segments for marketing and sales purposes. The reason for doing this is to find the most promising opportunities for a company's talents, so that its strengths are utilised and its weaknesses are not important. Car companies specialise in certain features or in producing, for example, off-road or commercial vehicles.

Market segmentation is based on the characteristics of customers, such as:

- **Income**
- **Age**
- **Geography**
- **Life style.**

This segmentation may lead to 'niche' marketing where a relatively small producer may find a particular segment of customer need which is not otherwise satisfied. A specialised car manufacturer such as Morgan is an example of this. One characteristic in the consideration of market segmentation is the 20/80 principle, sometimes described as the 'Pareto effect'. Managers may notice that, for example, 20 per cent of customers account for 80 per cent of demand. Some car producers sell 80 per cent of their cars to fleet or company buyers who may account for only 20 per cent of their individual customers, while for other producers it may be the other way around.

PRODUCT/SERVICE PORTFOLIO

Marketing is an essential factor in managers' decisions about the products and services a company will produce. As well as profits, managers are concerned with market share, because this is an indication of the extent to which a product can generate cash. In general terms, the larger the market share that a product obtains, the more cash it can generate. On the other hand, the greater the growth in the market, the more cash is used to support the expansion.

This situation can be summarised by a classification known as the Boston matrix. Figure 4.5 shows the main categories of products or services used in this classification, which are given distinctive names to indicate their prospects:

- **A star** has a high market share and a high market growth rate. It will tend to generate as much cash as it uses and will be self-financing. In periods of economic

Figure 4.5 The Boston matrix

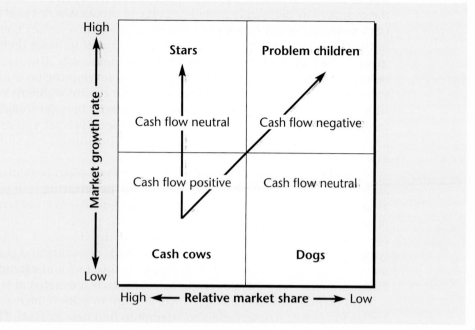

Source: Based on the Boston Consulting Group growth-share matrix

expansion there will be a large number of stars, products and services which are in a growing market and have a large share of that market. Particular models of motor cars may fall into this category, along with household goods, popular holidays and so on.

■ **A problem child** has a low market share but a high growth rate in a market that is itself growing. In order to increase market share, it may require investment and promotion and it will therefore use cash even though it is not generating very much. These products and services represent a problem because managers must decide whether to stop producing them or whether their potential growth makes an investment worthwhile. For example, a computer firm may decide that it is worth spending money on developing and promoting one of its software packages because, even though the sales are relatively small at the moment, there is considerable scope for expansion. It may be felt that the low sales are due to limited promotion and product development.

■ **The cash cow** has a high market share and a low market growth in a reasonably stable market. As a result of its established position this type of product or service does not require developing or promoting and therefore cash is generated. A well-known brand of processed food may need little advertising, for example, and may still hold a large share of the market.

■ **The dog** has a low market share and a low market growth, and in fact this type of product or service is likely to be a prime target for consideration for ending production. For example, a car model with poor and declining sales may cease to be manufactured, because the cost of the people and equipment employed in producing it may be considered a poor use of resources compared with the alternatives.

This analysis can provide managers with an indication of the type of policy they should follow for different products and services. The **product/service portfolio** of the company would ideally include a range of products/services at different stages. Cash generated by cash cows could, for example, be invested by company managers in the stars or in selected problem children in order to make them into stars (the 'rising stars') as indicated by the arrows in Figure 4.5. The stars in turn could become cash cows as the need to promote and develop the product declines. Even some dogs can be saved from extinction by identifying segments of the market on which to concentrate, or by improving productivity in order to reduce costs. A car, for example, may retain a niche market even though its sales have fallen and with low production costs it may still be profitable. The British Leyland/Rover Mini is an example of this.

In considering marketing strategies managers will often be concerned with other aspects of the market, such as how far they are **penetrating** it in terms of reaching as many potential customers as possible, and how they can **extend** it in terms of opening new markets by finding new uses for the products or entirely new markets. Managers may also be concerned with **product development**, which means modifying or adding to the product or service in terms of quality and performance. They may want to **diversify** by both developing the product and extending the market. These elements comprise the **Ansoff matrix** which is illustrated in Figure 4.6.

With existing products managers will attempt to achieve increased **market penetration** in existing markets and also attempt to find new markets. They will look for product development and help penetrate present markets, while aiming for new products or new uses for present products in order to diversify into new markets. Managers looking for market penetration and **market extension** in the computer industry began to look towards the so-called **SOHO** market in the middle 1990s. The 'small office, home office' developed as a potentially fast-growing area as the divide between work and leisure applications became blurred. Car manufacturers have

Figure 4.6 The Ansoff matrix

Source: Based on Ansoff (1989)

found it possible to extend their market for four-wheel-drive, off-road vehicles by developing more luxury products to sell as a fashionable vehicle to buyers who may never leave the tarmac road but who wish to enjoy a rugged, outdoor image.

Ideally, a company will produce a range of products which are at different stages of their life cycle, are stars and cash cows, and can be developed to further penetrate the market and extend it. It will do this by careful market research and developing new products to meet customer needs.

PRICE, PLACE AND PROMOTION

Price

An organisation will need to decide the price of its products and services based on marketing objectives. Price must be consistent with the total marketing strategy for a product. There is little point in charging a low price for a luxury item or a high price for a commodity to be sold in a mass market. In fact, price will depend very heavily on the supply and demand for the product (*see* Figure 4.7).

If supply is high and so is price (say, at point *a*), demand will be low (at *x*), while if supply is relatively low and so is the price (at point *b*), then demand will be high (at *y*). The equilibrium price (*e*) is where supply and demand are equal.

In practice, managers will want to maintain prices as low as possible in order to encourage demand, while still retaining a high enough price to provide a good margin of profit on the sale of the product. In the introductory stage of the product

Figure 4.7 Supply, demand and price

life cycle the demand may grow very quickly and supply may be limited. At the same time, price may not be a very important factor in consumers' decision making because they are anxious to be among the first to obtain the product. There is an opportunity for the organisation to charge relatively high prices to these 'innovators' and recover some of their research and development costs. The original personal computers, for example, were relatively expensive.

At the mature stage of the life cycle, the price of the product may be reduced in order to maintain or increase market share in what is likely to be an increasingly competitive market. At the saturation and decline stage, price will be manipulated depending on market share and sales volume. It may be raised in order to create a 'cash cow' within an established market, or lowered through sales 'promotions' in order to extend sales.

A company will often attempt to position itself in terms of the price of its products in one or other area of the market. A car manufacturer, for example, may see itself in the luxury area of the market and target products and prices accordingly, while another manufacturer may be aiming at wide coverage of the mass market and produce a range of cars to appeal to different segments. Although pricing policy may be a sophisticated process based on detailed market research and the consideration of a number of ratios, it is often based on a cost-plus process, on a consideration of competitors' prices, or on 'what the market will bear'. One factor in these approaches is that there is less uncertainty over costs than there is about demand, so that it is easy to arrive at a price by adding a percentage to costs. At the same time, it is not necessary to make frequent changes to price in response to changes in demand. 'Loss leaders' are often based on a price which covers fixed costs such as equipment, capital and overheads, while variable costs, such as labour, are subsidised for a limited time by other sources of income.

Prices may be fixed slightly above or below those of competitors. For example, petrol stations often follow this pattern. Or price may be based on what it is felt people will pay, 'what the market will bear'. In a relatively expensive area, where salaries are high, the price of food, petrol and other goods may be higher than the same goods bought in a cheaper area. However, the village shop may decide to charge high prices because it has a 'captive' market, while the city store may be cheaper because it is surrounded by competition. In practice, some products and services will have a far more price-sensitive market than others and managers need to take this into account in their pricing policy. At one extreme, a company may have a monopoly or near monopoly of the sale of a particular commodity. In these circumstances, the company can set whatever price it likes to match the desired level of demand. In more competitive markets, if a company puts a high price on its product, customers will not buy it because there are other suppliers. If an organisation lowers its price below that of other companies, competitors will lower their prices in order to compete.

Other things being equal, a high price will tend to reduce demand, while a low price will tend to increase demand. However, demand may be very responsive to changes in price (that is, elastic) or relatively unresponsive to changes in price (that is, inelastic). In a situation where managers have products which are not sensitive to price changes, they can use a price-skimming policy by charging a high initial price in order to recover development costs, and then lower prices as costs fall. When a product is more price sensitive, managers can introduce a low price to attract a large number of buyers and then raise prices to the normal level in the market, hoping to keep its market share. This will be helped by selling the product or service in the right place.

Place

In marketing terms, the '**place**' is where the final exchange occurs between the seller and customer. Managers have to make decisions about where this exchange takes place, and how, and channels of distribution. Bank services, for example, were at one time usually provided 'across the counter', but in recent years they have moved to cash points and increasingly telephone banking. A distribution channel is the process that brings together an organisation and its customers at a particular place and time for the purpose of exchange. This may be a shop, office, or via a computer link. Simple distribution channels between manufacturers, retailers and customers vary in length and breadth (*see* Figure 4.8).

Managers must decide how to organise their distribution channel, in terms of the number of outlets, whether to use middlemen and the preferences of their customers. Logistics management is about having the correct product or service in the right place at the right time. This has changed in recent years as consumers have become 'unfettered' in the sense that customers have become detached from the channels that used to claim them. They have become more 'adversarial' shoppers, in that they have been conditioned by discount stores and Internet offers to search for bargains more aggressively than in the past. Also, as customers have become more aware of how companies market to them, they have become more strategic, for example deciding when to book a holiday based on considerations of what time

Figure 4.8 Channel length and breadth

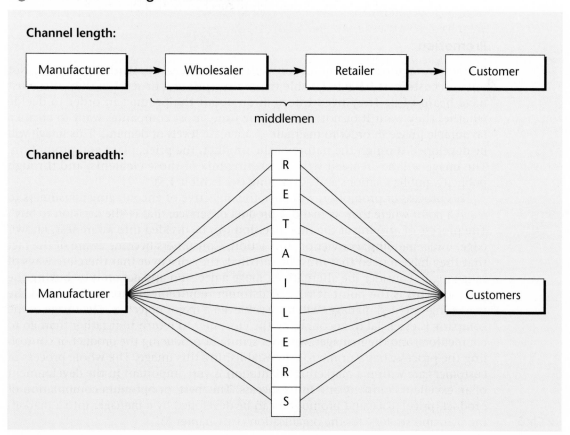

of the year the best deal will be available, or whether to book early or at the last minute. The consumer is now much better equipped with information and technology to make advantageous decisions, while on the other hand companies have discovered that their product quality, availability and pricing policy have become more transparent.

Meanwhile channels have proliferated with the expansion of such channels of distribution as websites, catalogues and factory outlets. Nunes and Cespedes (2003) identify key sets of customer shopping behaviours: **habitual shoppers** tend to purchase from the same place over and over again in the same manner; **high-value deal seekers** know their own needs and surf the channels before buying at the lowest possible price; **variety-loving shoppers** gather information in many channels and then buy in their favourite, regardless of whether the price is the lowest available; and **high-involvement shoppers** gather information in all channels, make their purchase in a low-cost channel and obtain customer support from the best source available.

Customers may behave one way for one purchase and in a different way for another purchase. They will typically progress through five predictable stages in the buying process. Potential buyers gain **awareness** of the product or service, then they **collect and consider** information about available alternatives, they evaluate the alternatives and arrive at a **preference**, they decide **where and how to purchase** and they consider what **after-sales service** may be required. In order to access customers, managers have to introduce a cross-channel selling strategy because the 'place' where the final exchange takes place has changed and managers have to make use of a variety of channels to meet consumer preferences.

Promotion

Promotion requires communication with customers and potential customers. Not only do customers have to be able to obtain a product or service, they also must have heard of it. They need information about the product in order to decide whether they want it or not. At the same time, most companies want to create a favourable image in order to maintain or increase levels of demand. This image will be developed through the nature of the product, the price, place and promotion. The image will be created by the marketing mix of those elements, and through publicity, public relations and advertising (*see* Exhibit 4.5).

This process of promotion will have the objective of encouraging consumers to reach a point where they 'demand' a product or service, that is 'the decision to buy'. The process of arriving at the final decision can be divided into awareness, knowledge, understanding, conviction and action. Consumers become aware of the fact that they have a need that must be satisfied, they discover that there are ways of satisfying it, consider the alternatives, make a decision and act on it by buying the product. This is the point at which customer requirements are satisfied and the marketing-oriented manager will have achieved a major objective. The image of the company is essential in encouraging the customer to return to it rather than go to competitors, and the manager, whether selling or producing the product or controlling the process, has a prime role in establishing this image. The whole process of customer care within a marketing orientation is very important in the development of an excellent company and in its success. The 'best' or optimum combination of product, price, place and promotion can be developed by a manager into a marketing plan and strategy for the organisation (*see* Chapter 5).

→ Ch. 5

Exhibit 4.5 Owners Abroad

In August 1994 the package-holiday company Owners Abroad decided to spend £5 million on a new image. This was widely reported in newspapers and marketing journals, and a change of name was proposed to First Choice Holidays.

The plan was to streamline overlapping brands and save cash by targeting three distinct sectors of the holiday market. Household names such as Enterprise, Falcon and Sunmed would give way to First Choice, Sovereign and Freespirit. The company was keen to boost its share of the £10 million UK holiday market in the summer of 1995.

It was expected that fierce competition between top tour operators Thomson and Airtours would launch a price war offering big discounts on 1995 packages. The company proposed to introduce a massive advertising campaign to make sunseekers more aware of Owners' brands. The main new brand name, First Choice, would cover family package holidays, while the successful Sovereign label would be kept to cover more expensive and exotic trips. But a special Freespirit grouping would offer holidays for the young, free and single, featuring adventure breaks. The company believed that up to £4 million worth of holidays a year could be booked under this brand. It would aim to provide informal packages to childless adults who wanted more than a Club 18–30 break.

It was reported that Owners' new management was determined to build on the strong foundations which helped the company to defend itself from Airtours' hostile £290 million takeover bid in the previous year.

Strategic marketing

Strategic management includes marketing at every stage, because unless the customers of an organisation are satisfied and there is a demand for the product and services that it produces, it will not be successful. Strategy involves positioning an organisation and giving it a sense of purpose, and this has to include the needs of the marketplace. The marketing process can be seen as the 'nuts and bolts' of strategy because it is about positioning the company's products and services in their markets. Market research and competitor analysis provide the information that managers require in order to decide where to position products and services. If the company's traditional customers are moving up-market because their disposable incomes are increasing, then the company's products will need to match this move.

Organisations need to anticipate demand and how customer benefits will be best satisfied in the future. In the years 1999 and 2000 Marks & Spencer began to lose market share in retail clothing because the company did not anticipate the importance of its competitors and the demands of its customers. In 1999 reports in the financial press described the company as 'struggling' as its profits were reduced and its share price fell. Christmas sales were down by 3 per cent compared with the previous year, while competitors, such as Next, had seen Christmas sales rise by 18 per cent. The company attempted to regain its customers in the year 2000 by revamping its products, reducing costs by changing suppliers and cutting prices, but by the end of the year there were reports of some stores closing.

The SWOT analysis provides a company with a picture of its particular strengths and the opportunities open to it, as well as its weaknesses and the threats to it. It can also provide a profile of the organisational competencies which can be compared to the marketing audit to analyse how far they match. In forecasting the required strategy for the future, technological changes have to be taken into account along with the social and economic trends, political and legal developments and environmental issues. In a similar way, the formulation of strategy about how and where products and services are offered is an essential element of marketing strategy. The rapidly developing access to the Internet, for example, has revolutionised the 'place' in which a whole range of goods and services are offered to customers and bought and sold. It has also extended the available means of promoting a company's offering so that a whole range of organisations now have their own websites providing information.

The strategic manager's role is to exploit the strengths of a company and to correct and compensate for weaknesses. A market-oriented company will have marketing at its centre, integrating the work of all the other functions in the organisation and providing the information and analysis required for developing strategy.

SUMMARY

- This chapter describes and analyses the importance of marketing in the management of organisations. The development of a focus on customer needs has created a position where marketing is a central and integrating activity in management.

- The difference between marketing and selling is considered, as is the importance of market research as a foundation for meeting customer needs. The marketing process is essential for organisations to understand their position in relation to competitors.

- The marketing mix is the combination of product or service, price, place and promotion which together can form a marketing strategy in order to meet customer needs and maintain a competitive edge.

Review and discussion questions

1 *Why is marketing such an important function for most organisations?*

2 *Is there any difference between marketing and selling, or are they the same activities described by different names?*

3 *What part can market research play in management decisions on product/service design?*

4 *How important is a marketing audit and SWOT analysis in the development of an organisation's marketing plan?*

5 *What is meant by a marketing strategy? Produce an outline strategy for a company, institution or club.*

6 *How is the price of a product or service determined? Is this an important element of an organisation's marketing strategy, or are promotion, advertising, location and product more important?*

CASE STUDY

BMW and Fiat

This is the decade for centennial party time across the car industry. The celebrations for the combination of four wheels and an internal combustion engine, however, have been muted. A business that began about 100 years ago in Europe as a cottage industry often run by families is now run by consolidated multinationals, most of which suffer from the problem of global oversupply. Yet two of Europe's major car manufacturers remain under family control: BMW, an athletic stripling of only 86, and Fiat, which is really feeling every one of its 104 years.

The Quandt and Agnelli clans control two middling producers on the world scene, punching out about a million (BMW) and two million (Fiat) cars respectively. In Europe, Fiat has about 7.4% of the car market and BMW 4.3%. Size is no guarantee of success, though. Whereas BMW, now with Rolls Royce on stream, may be at its zenith in terms of the success of its products, Fiat is in severe distress.

BMW posted its biggest ever profit of Eu3.3 billion in 2002 (and is on target for new record profits, and sales, in 2003), while Fiat recorded a loss of Eu4.3 billion in 2002, the year its patriarchal boss died. The broader picture in Turin is grim. Since 1990, Fiat's share of the European market has halved and, worse, its share of the vital home market has plummeted from well over 50% in its heyday to less than 30% last year. What has gone right and wrong for these two dynasties, and how have they ended up in such contrasting states?

When Fiat boss Giovanni Agnelli – the founder's grandson – died last January, more than 100 000 mourners paid their respects as his body lay in state. His coffin was applauded as it made its way to Turin cathedral, and Italy's leading newspaper *Corriere della Sera* devoted its first 19 pages to his life and times. The funeral was attended by prime minister Silvio Berlusconi who, not for the first time in his political career, put his foot in it by arriving in an Audi. The mourners booed.

Agnelli, *l'avoccato* (the lawyer), as he was known, was a wastrel in his youth, but he squared up to his responsibilities once in the driving seat at Fiat. He became Italy's leading businessman, a lifetime senator and, for many, the uncrowned king of Italy. Agnelli enjoyed trysts with film stars, was a friend to the Kennedys, Henry Kissinger, Richard Nixon and the Rockefellers, and turned the family firm into an international conglomerate.

By contrast, the BMW godmother, Johanna Quandt, 76, is silent to the point of secrecy over her family's £12 billion controlling interest in the German carmaker. She has reputedly never given an interview, and neither have her children, and fellow shareholders, Stefan and Susanne. Collectively, their stake amounts to 46.6%. Stefan, now the largest single shareholder, is said to be next in line for chairmanship of BMW's supervisory board. Susanne, who worked at the Regensberg plant, changed her surname to Cant to avoid recognition.

Although the Quandts appear to take a relatively passive role in BMW, they hold the key to the firm's continued independence. That independence was rumoured to be under threat during the late '90s when, after the Rover ownership debacle, Ford began to take a close interest in the company.

But if Fiat is in serious trouble today, its position is not as dire as BMW's was in 1959. The German company struggled to get back on its feet after the war, its factories having been dismantled for war reparations. But by the mid '50s, it had launched a trio of cars: these were a motley bunch – the 501 and 502 (a huge limousine known as the Baroque Angel) were far too thirsty for that fuel-starved era, and the beautiful 507 roadster was an expensive flop.

To compensate in the short term, BMW built the tiny Italian austerity-chic Isetta bubble car under licence, in a deal similar to the arrangement it had with Austin in 1929 to build the first BMW car, the Dixi. BMW knew it had to produce a car positioned between these extremes, but struggled to find the money to do so. In 1959, on the brink of being taken over by Mercedes, it was saved by the acquisition of a major stake by Herbert Quandt, who celebrated by marrying his secretary Johanna. (The family shareholding dated back to the '20s and the historic publicity-shyness of the Quandts may be connected to the fact that Herbert's stepfather was Joseph Goebbels.)

Quandt's backing enabled the Neue Klasse 1500 to be developed, a quality, compact car whose character set the die for every BMW since – sporty saloon motoring for the middle classes. BMW recovered sufficiently to launch the smaller 02 series in 1966, which developed into the famous 2002. This was replaced in 1975 by the first generation of the 3 series that we know so well today.

▶

Now a hugely successful model, the 3 series prompted accusations that BMW is a one-product company. It has long attempted to be more than that – its 2500 saloon, announced in the same year as the 02 series, was intended to take on the large Mercedes saloons – but it is only after several iterations of these big cars that it has got on level terms with Mercedes.

Today, BMW is fast filling all kinds of niches as the car market fragments to meet the demands of consumers who want their cars to be more individual. Besides the classic 3, 5 and 7 series, essentially the same saloon in different sizes, it offers coupé, estate and cabriolet versions of some of these cars, two four-wheel-drives, a sports car and a big coupé. It is a well-planned, coherent range with brand values so strong that sales have weathered the controversy surrounding BMW's new design language – see the new 7, 5 and Z4 – almost unaffected.

BMW has rarely been short of Teutonic confidence. As its chairman Dr Helmut Panke said recently: 'We operate in the most promising segment of our industry – worldwide, the premium segments will grow roughly twice as fast as the mass segments in the last decade. We do not build, and will never build, boring cars.'

Among the masses, the Fiat story is never boring, either. It, too, has enjoyed spectacular success at times. Fiat SpA – of which carmaker Fiat Auto is a part – is still Italy's biggest single conglomerate, with a turnover representing 4.8% of the country's GDP. It owns businesses ranging from newspapers to farm machinery.

The Fiat group has long been a diversified business – it was manufacturing commercial vehicles, marine engines and ball-bearings as long ago as 1902 – but for most of its history, car-making has been at the centre. Says Professor Garel Rhys of Cardiff Business School: 'Fiat had to create the industrial revolution in Italy.'

Where BMW's brand character is refined, aspirational, haughty and even arch, Fiat's brand character has its roots in the 1936 Topolino (little mouse), whose low price sped the motorisation of Italy. But the company's most famous car is the 1957 descendent of the Topolino, the Nuova 500, a cute, twin-cylinder bubble-like car of which more than 3.6 million were sold. It played a major role in the so-called 'economic miracle' in post-war Italy.

Fiat's failure to crack the market in bigger, more profitable cars goes some way to explaining why the company is in trouble. Whereas the margin on a BMW 3 series is a manufacturer's delight (and even more so on a 7 series), that on a Fiat Punto is tight. This failure has also led to an over-dependence by Fiat on one model. Today, that is the Punto, now in its second generation; before that it was the Uno – which rescued the company from another crisis in 1983. Before the Uno, it was the 127. Fiat also owns Lancia, which it bought for 10 lire in 1969, and Alfa Romeo, acquired in 1986, but its success with these brands has been inconsistent.

Fiat's car division was starved of money through the '70s, not least because the group was short of cash. At Agnelli's invitation, the Libyan government bought 10% of Fiat for $415 million, later adding another 4%, enough to win it two seats on the board. The arrangement persisted until 1986, when terrorist allegations surrounding Libya had the US blacklisting Fiat, and Agnelli had to raise $3.1 billion to buy the Libyans out. Investment was turned up again, but car design takes time and the new Uno did not appear until 1983. Fortunately for Agnelli, it was a great success.

Agnelli could not be accused of lacking vision. When he took control, many considered Fiat 'too big to be Italian, but too small to compete in Europe'. One of his greatest achievements was to make Fiat an international conglomerate, bringing together Case New Holland (the world's largest farm equipment manufacturer), Iveco trucks and the newspaper *La Stampa*. Yet a more committed approach to car exports might have proved a more valuable investment. Although Fiat had considerable success in Russia and central Europe, it had to withdraw from the US: unreliable products led to the joke: 'Fix It Again, Tony'.

But neither has BMW done everything right. In 1994, it embarked on a brand diversification strategy that was nothing short of startling – it bought Britain's troubled Rover Group. The objective was to provide the company with a portfolio of volume brands to complement its premium marque. So, it not only got the tarnished Rover badge, beloved only of the British pipe-and-slippers brigade, but also Land Rover, MG and Mini.

It knew it had bought a business in need of massive investment – which it provided on a scale not seen in decades – but it hadn't bargained on the infighting this provoked, both between BMW and Rover, and within BMW itself. At the Birmingham motor show launch of BMW's first Rover, the 75, boss Bernd Pischetsrieder heavily criticised the Longbridge plant with the intention of scaring the workforce into submission. It was a serious misjudgment.

Media analysts and workforce alike believed that BMW was giving up on the 'English Patient', and Pischetsrieder and his number two, Wolfgang Reitzle, were forced to resign from the company on the same day in February 1999. BMW then took direct control, flying in planeloads of executives from Munich to Birmingham to 'purge' the place, seriously damaging morale. Little more than a year later, BMW disposed of Rover and MG to the Phoenix Consortium, and sold Land Rover to Ford. It retained the Mini brand and produced a successful updated version of the legenday marque.

Since ditching Rover, BMW's margins, sales and profitability have blossomed. It recently announced plans to sell 1.4 million vehicles annually by 2008 – only 400,000 short of its target when Rover was still on board. Its share price is buoyant, and mutterings that the Quandt family want out have ceased. But growth will come in large part from the forthcoming BMW 1 series, which will compete at the premium end of the Ford Focus segment. It was this very car that Pischetsrieder, and many others at BMW, felt was a stretch too far for the brand and would compromise its premium character. It was the reason for buying Rover.

Meanwhile, Fiat, to the surprise of some analysts, is intent on pursuing a strategy closer to BMW's, by concentrating on the car business. Umberto Agnelli, Gianni's younger brother, is in charge after a series of family tragedies. First, the highly regarded Giovanni Alberto Agnelli, who turned Vespa-maker Piaggio around, died of a rare form of stomach cancer in 1997 aged 33. Then Edoardo, Agnelli's son, committed suicide in 2000 after an unhappy life that included heroin addiction.

'Crazy Eddie', as he was known in New York, had become increasingly unhappy at seeing his younger relatives given preferment. In an interview with the left-wing daily *Il Manifesto* in 1998, he complained that 'part of my family has been overtaken by a baroque and decadent logic. Meaning no offence to anyone, we are approaching the gesture of Caligula, who made his horse a senator'. This was thought to be a reference to his now 25-year-old cousin John Elkann, the hot tip to take over the reins when he is fully groomed.

Many thought that Umberto, now 69, was keen to sell Fiat Auto. But he and chief executive Giuseppe Morchio concluded that it was car-making and the industrial businesses that generated by far the biggest chunk of Fiat's Eu55 billion turnover. In a programme of disposals in 2003, the Toro insur-ance company was sold, along with Fiat Avio and 51% of Fidis, Fiat's retail finance arm. The Agnelli family invested Eu250 million as part of a recapitalisation plan that has yielded Eu1 billion in total.

Shareholder GM did not subscribe to the recapitalisation, with the result that its 20% share has halved. Fiat's link with GM was forged in 2000, amid the possibility that Fiat might be sold to DaimlerChrysler in a $13 billion deal that would have given the Agnellis a 26% share in the German company. Umberto favoured the deal but Gianni did not, and Fiat remained in their hands. But it gave rise to the idea that Umberto wanted out of the car business; not so, says a Fiat insider – he just thought it a good deal.

The GM deal famously included a put option that could have forced the American giant to buy Fiat during 2004, but GM now argues that Fiat's restructuring invalidates the put. Fiat, which has sold its 6% holding in GM, argues otherwise, but the two have postponed the discussion for a year, not least because they have a highly successful joint venture covering purchasing and powertrain development.

Fiat claims it will recover without GM's money, with break-even during 2004, positive cashflow in 2005 and a 4% return on sales by 2006. The group also plans to launch 24 new models by 2010. This despite the failure to make redundancies on anything like the necessary scale and a shrinking European market pressured by discounting. Morchio also values Ferrari – part of Fiat SpA rather than Fiat Auto – as an R&D centre; although Fiat sold 34% of the company, it retains more than 50%.

If that suggests a Fiat wealthier than it appears, bear in mind that this company has many assets beyond car brands. With Iveco trucks, Comau – the global number one in automation systems for the auto industry – and Magneti Marelli, a car components supplier, Fiat has a turnover of Eu55 billion, Eu23 billion of which is accounted for by Fiat Auto. Despite being owned by Fiat, Italy's second-largest power producer Edison is not consolidated into the accounts. It's valuable and could also be sold.

Just as Fiat is more than cars, the Agnellis are more than Fiat. The family owns the supermarket chain La Rinascente, Juventus football club and even paper manufacturer Arjowiggins. The constitutional rules of these companies state that shares can be sold only to other family members, thus protecting the business. So, although Fiat has been in deep trouble, and has not left it behind, it has a substantial safety net.

But there's a lot of ground to be made up. Alfa Romeo is a great brand name, which during the 1960s was a model for BMW to emulate. Fiat saved it from the near-terminal effects of a cash drought during its state ownership, but poor after-sales service and a model range based on Fiat platforms has held it back.

Lancia was once great too, but has been allowed to atrophy and retreat to its home market. As to Fiat itself, there has been recent good news with the new Panda, which has just won the European Car of the Year award and has a fat order book. But if Fiat cannot make a success of small cars, it is doomed.

So both families have problems to address. *MT*'s contributing editor and car observer Stephen Bayley has watched both companies for years: 'Family ownership of Fiat and BMW is only one contributor to their distinctive personalities. For good or bad, they reflect national characteristics: Fiat's strength and weakness was a distribution system based on village blacksmiths selling to customers with loyalties as fierce as *arrabiata*. BMW is a classic German Mittelstand business selling increasingly irrelevant technological *Bratwürst* to the image-conscious. Fierce competition threatens the first, changing taste the second. In future, it will be "family hold back" and let new products do the work.'

Source: Bremner, R. (2004) *Management Today*, January.

REFERENCES AND FURTHER READING

Ansoff, I (1989) *Corporate Strategy*, Harmondsworth: Penguin.

Drucker, Peter (1993) *Managing for the Future*, Oxford: Butterworth-Heinemann.

Grant, Alan W H and Schlesinger, Leonard A (1995) 'Realise Your Customers' Full Profit Potential', *Harvard Business Review*, September/October.

Hamel, G and Prahalad, CK (1994) *Competing for the Future*, Boston, MA: Harvard Business School Press.

Hannagan, Tim (1992) *Marketing for the Non-Profit Sector*, London: Macmillan.

Hannagan, Tim (1999) *The Effective Use of Statistics: A Practical Guide for Managers*, London: Kogan Page.

Heller, Robert (1994) *The Fate of IBM*, New York: Little, Brown.

Henley Centre and Chartered Institute of Marketing (1993) *Customer Loyalty*.

Kay, John (1995) *Why Firms Succeed: Choosing Markets and Challenging Competitors to Add Value*, Oxford: Oxford University Press.

Kotler, Philip (1986) *Principles of Marketing* (3rd edn), Englewood Cliffs, NJ: Prentice-Hall.

Kotler, Philip (1996) *Marketing Management: Analysis, Planning, Implementation and Control*, Englewood Cliffs, NJ: Prentice-Hall.

Myers, James H (1996) *Segmentation and Positioning for Strategic Marketing Decisions*, New York: American Marketing Association.

Nunes, Paul F and Cespedes, Frank V (2003) 'The Customer Has Escaped', *Harvard Business Review*, November.

Porras, Jerry I and Collins, James C (1996) *Building Your Company's Vision*, Boston, MA: Harvard Business School, September/October.

Raynor, Michael A (1998) 'That Vision Thing: Do We Need It?', *Long Range Planning*, June.

Slywotzky, Adrian J (1996) *Value Migration: How to Think Several Moves Ahead of the Competition*, Boston, MA: Harvard Business School.

Smith, Adam (1776) *An Inquiry into the Nature and Causes of the Wealth of Nations*, London: A Strahn and T Caddell.

Zimmerman, John with Tregee, Benjamin (1997) *The Culture of Success: Building a Sustained Competitive Advantage by Living Your Corporate Beliefs*, New York: McGraw-Hill.

WEBSITES

http://www.benetton.com
This provides information on the importance of marketing and a knowledge of Benetton's wider strategy.

http://www.nestle.com
This profiles 'the world food company', Nestlé, and puts the company's wider operation in context.

http://www.statistics.gov.uk/statbase/mainmenu.asp
Information on UK statistics which can be used for market research.

SECTION B

STRATEGIC MANAGEMENT

What is strategy? Why is strategic management important to managers at all levels? What is the difference between strategy and planning? What are the competitive forces affecting corporate strategy? How is corporate strategy implemented? What are the barriers to organisational planning and how can these be overcome? What is the importance of organisational development? How are business plans developed? What does quality mean in terms of industry and commerce? How are quality systems introduced and managed in organisations? Why is quality control important in terms of strategic management? What are the differences between strategic management in the public sector and in the private sector? How important is organisational culture in relation to management in the two sectors?

Strategic management is concerned with the overall positioning and direction of an organisation and can be seen as a vital management activity of concern to managers at all levels. Modern management practices provide more opportunities than in the past for managers to be involved with the strategy of their organisations. Strategy can be developed through a process and through planning, although there is a difference between strategy and planning. A strategy to ensure total quality management is an important factor in meeting customer needs. There are similarities in strategic management in the public sector and in the private sector as well as differences. Organisational culture is an important factor in management in both sectors.

Strategic management

TIM HANNAGAN

Outcomes

Having read this chapter, you will be able to:

- analyse the importance of strategic management
- explain the role of planning in management
- apply strategic management and planning to the process of developing corporate strategy
- identify the factors influencing the corporate portfolio
- analyse the competitive forces affecting corporate strategy

WHAT IS STRATEGIC MANAGEMENT?

Strategic management consists of decisions and actions used to formulate and implement strategies that will provide a competitively superior fit between the organisation and its environment to enable it to achieve organisational objectives. It is not the same as strategic planning, although it may involve it, in that planning is associated with an activity carried out a little apart from the line management of an organisation and reviewed at periodic well-defined intervals. Strategic planning tends to be associated with medium or long-term planning trends which are extrapolated for the key business variables and assumes a future point at which the organisation will arrive. Strategic management is concerned with establishing a competitive advantage, sustainable over time, not simply by tactical manoeuvring, but by taking an overall long-term perspective.

Strategic management is about enabling an organisation to move from its present position to one it wants to be in, in order to align it with its objectives and with the environment in which it is working. It can be considered to be the most complex task facing a manager because a strategic direction has to be established in an unknown future in the face of a range of choices, in a volatile and dynamic environment and involving everybody in the organisation. While strategic management is involved in all areas of management and the working of an organisation, it is not the same as day-to-day management because strategic management is concerned with issues affecting the fundamentals of an organisation.

Operational management provides for organisation, control and supervision, while strategic management provides a sense of purpose. Companies of all sizes, schools, universities, hospitals, charities and all other organisations, will have a purpose, whether it is to make profits, maintain market share, promote educational achievement, provide good health or support particular groups of people. Operational management is essential because in order to achieve these purposes a variety of management functions has to be carried out. Strategic management emphasises the challenge to modern managers in maintaining dynamic roles in organisations, which requires great management skill given the speed of change in their environment.

→ Ch. 4   The PESTLE, STEP or SPECTACLES factors (described in Chapter 4) are the environment of an organisation: that is everything that influences its success or failure. These factors may include competition from other companies, uncertainty about raw material supplies, price fluctuations, government legislation and even natural disasters. The speed of change means that managers have to be prepared to constantly redevelop and reconstruct their company, so that as well as being operational they have to provide strategic leadership. They have to 'look ahead' in a way which is more complicated than simply planning a journey in order to travel, or even just to arrive at a destination, because it involves taking into account constant changes in the organisation's working environment as well as changes in the organisation's personnel and competencies.

Strategic management is ambiguous and complex because the objective of a company may be very clearly defined, but the way to achieve it may not be obvious. A company may have as its objective 'to increase market share' and this may be more closely defined by identifying a target percentage which the company hopes to achieve. The way to realise this objective may be obvious to start with but the reaction to these early moves and other changes in the environment may provide obstacles to its achievement. It is at this point that an underlying strategy is required, an approach that will enable the organisation to survive and prosper even after temporary setbacks.

In military terms, *strategos* is Greek for 'general', who is the strategist who plans the whole campaign, while the lower ranks of the army are the people who operationally make sure that troops and equipment are in the right places at the right time. Drucker (1961) has described strategy as:

> *'the pattern of major objectives, purposes or goals and essential policies or plans for achieving these goals, stated in such a way as to define what business the company is in or is to be in and the kind of company it is or is to be.'*

Strategic issues are attempts to answer such questions as: Who are our customers? Who are our competitors? What products and services should we offer? How can we offer these products and services most efficiently? These questions help to focus the attention of managers on how to position their organisation in relation to rival organisations. These decisions affect the long-term direction of the company and are usually concerned with gaining some advantage for the company.

Strategic decisions can be thought of as the search for an effective 'position' for an organisation in relation to competitors in order to achieve an advantage. The 'position' or '**positioning**' is where the business sees itself in its market, which may be in terms of total market share but also involves the 'positioning' of each of the company products and services. Strategy is also concerned with the 'scope' of an organisation's activities in terms of whether it concentrates on one area of activity or whether it is concerned with many. This is an indication of the organisation's boundaries, the number and range of its products and services (*see also* Chapter 6). Tesco may be mainly a food retailer but it also sells clothes and other goods, and it has moved into financial services.

→ Ch. 6

Strategy is also about 'fit', which is the match between the resources and capabilities of the organisation and the opportunities open to it, and 'stretch', which is the process of innovation and development involved in finding new opportunities and creating a competitive advantage from the organisation's resources and competencies. Strategy involves matching the activities of an organisation to the environment in which it operates so that there is a 'strategic fit'. It is an attempt to identify the opportunities available and to tailor the strategy of the organisation to capitalise on them. There will also be an attempt to 'stretch' resources and apply 'leverage' to them in order to create opportunities and to be in a position to exploit them.

Exhibit 5.1 **Characteristics of strategic management**

■ Fundamental	■ Long term
■ A sense of direction	■ Looking ahead
■ A sense of purpose	■ A search for competitive advantage
■ Positioning	■ Scope of activities
■ Strategic fit	■ Stretching and leverage

Strategy involves identifying the 'core competencies' that an organisation requires in order to optimise its ability to meet the opportunities and challenges it faces. The 'core competencies' are those capabilities and skills which are necessary to underpin the organisation's competitive advantage. This is not only a question of making sure that the correct resources and competencies are available, but of identifying existing ones which can be used for creating new opportunities in the future.

Of course, managers may have a strategy without realising it. They may work on the basis that they do not have a strategy; they simply continue to do what they are doing now. This is, of course, in its own way a plan. The problem with a 'passive' strategy based on continuing to work as at present is that however successful this may have been in the past and is now, it may not be successful in the future. 'Other things' will not remain 'equal'. On the one hand, the external environment will change in terms of economic factors and political policies as well as technological development; on the other hand, competitors will be searching for ways to expand their share of the market.

This was a problem in the 1930s, for example, when the Ford Motor Company continued to produce its Model T in 'any colour the customer required as long as it was black', while their competitors produced more varied models which met customer requirements more closely. In the same way, in the 1980s many computer companies experienced similar problems when what they had always produced was superseded. For example, the computer games company Nintendo took an early lead in the video games market when it expanded in the late 1980s. The company developed its Gameboy hand-held 8-bit games console which made it a major force in this developing market. It was then beaten into the 16-bit market by Sega which introduced its Mega Drive. Market share of the UK's video games in 1994 was 55 per cent to Nintendo and 34 per cent to Sega, but Sega claimed 70 per cent of the 16-bit market and, at this time, Sega and other companies were developing 32-bit video games. Nintendo has struggled to keep up with these developments; rather than concentrate on the 32-bit market it decided to move on to develop a 64-bit machine, Project Reality, and to 'leapfrog' into a technological lead.

Given the pitfalls of not having a strategy or having a 'passive' one, managers need to have an 'active' strategy, a way forward on which to base their decisions. A past chief executive of Sears, the largest retailer of drug and soft goods in the USA, has stated that:

> *'Business is like a war in one respect: if its ground strategy is correct, any number of tactical errors can be made and yet the enterprise proves successful.'*
> (General Robert E Wood, quoted in Pearce and Robinson, 1989)

In this statement, it is being suggested that even if the detailed actions are wrong, they can be overcome where the overall strategy is effective. In other words, if travellers are on the correct road to their destination, a few diversions or stops may hold them up, but will not prevent them from arriving where they want to be. If they do not know their destination, or they are on the wrong road, their chances of arriving in the right place are very limited and in fact are a matter of chance. In this sense, strategy is a plan, a direction or a future course of action. It can also be seen as a pattern of behaviour over time, and it can be described as an organisation's way of doing things or, for that matter, what it actually does. However, even this idea of aiming at a particular place or achieving particular objectives does not adequately describe strategy in terms of management. When organisations achieve a particular 'destination' it may be found that now they need to be in a slightly different place because they have moved on since the 'journey' started. A company may achieve the objectives it set itself two years earlier only to find that it arrives at a position it needed to be in a year earlier and now it needs to move forward again to keep up with the competition.

STRATEGIC OPTIONS

Strategic management is a method of defining the 'position' of an organisation, its objectives and how it expects to achieve them. In this process, organisations have to choose between broad strategies and the actions to be taken to achieve long-term objectives. These include options of retrenchment, growth or stability.

A company may decide to reduce its size in terms of employees, production, assets and other factors. This decision may arise from a decline in demand for its products, changes in competition, the introduction of new technology, or for some other reason. The **retrenchment** usually involves reducing business units, selling off parts of the business, or in the final analysis the liquidation of the entire organisation.

In the recession of the early 1990s, many companies reduced the size of their operations by using all these methods. '**Outsourcing**' areas of activity was a common process, and enabled a company to relinquish ownership while retaining the service. 'Re-engineering' involves reducing the size of the labour force in order to reduce costs. Selling off parts of a company enables it to concentrate on what it considers to be its main core business. During this period Thorn-EMI, for example, reduced its training programme, sold off parts of its business and outsourced other areas. Rank Xerox UK decided to concentrate on its main business, photocopying and office documentation, and outsourced such areas as its information technology needs.

Stability involves a company attempting to remain the same size or grow in a very slow, controlled way. This 'pause strategy' often follows a period of rapid growth, when it is felt that time is needed to consolidate this expansion to make sure that it does not disappear.

On the other hand, **growth** is often considered to be a company policy which will provide motivation and incentives to its employees and ensure its position in its markets. Increasing investment, product development, diversification into new markets and the acquisition of competitors are all processes for encouraging expansion.

In order to grow, a company may decide to follow a **multinational** policy by expanding into foreign markets. Developments such as those in Europe with the dropping of customs barriers in 1992 have helped to encourage this type of growth, as has the development of information technology and improved communications in the 1990s and 2000s. Car manufacturers such as Ford have on the one hand tried to produce models for particular markets such as North America and Europe, and on the other produced models for a worldwide market with models such as the Focus and the Mondeo.

When organisations become complex and diversified, such as is the case with major national and multinational companies, **strategy** is very much the role of top management because co-ordination of the organisation's functional areas becomes crucial. Strategy at lower levels can be described as 'operational' strategy. While overall strategy concentrates on effectiveness, that is 'doing the right things', operational strategy concentrates on efficiency, that is 'doing things right'. Strategic plans can provide guidance and boundaries for operational management and the

Exhibit 5.2 Characteristics of operation management

- **Organising**

- **Supervising and controlling**

- **Routine**

- **Short-term implications**

- **Operationally specific**

two overlap in providing organisational strategy and the operational activity to achieve it. The grand plan represents the top-management view of the direction the organisation needs to take at any particular time. It provides a sense of direction which has to be implemented at all levels in the organisation if it is to succeed. This implementation requires a more 'operational' strategy which ultimately arrives at a series of actions which need to be carried out in order to achieve it (Exhibit 5.2).

This 'operational' strategy increasingly coincides with the organisation's marketing strategy, because of the recognition that marketing provides the integration of organisational functions and that without customers to demand its products and services an organisation does not have a *raison d'être*. Meeting the needs of customers is the first priority for any organisation, whether it is in the private or the public sector. Therefore the overall strategy in practice coincides with the marketing strategy. It is both informed by market research, in determining what should be done, and focuses on customer needs, in deciding how it is to be done. This is reflected in an organisation's formal, written strategic plan, which usually involves a series of stages moving from the relatively abstract to the very concrete, as outlined in Exhibit 5.3.

Exhibit 5.3 Corporate strategy

■ **Mission statement or vision**	*What business are we in?*
■ **Corporate objectives, goals and aims**	*Where do we want to go and how do we get there?*
■ **Market research**	*Who are our customers and what are their needs?*
■ **Audit of external environment**	*What are the threats and opportunities we face?*
■ **Analysis of resources**	*What are our strengths and weaknesses?*
■ **Marketing objectives**	*How do we achieve our objectives in marketing terms?*
■ **Strategic plan**	*How do we match our objectives with our resources?*
■ **Action plan**	*What do we have to do to achieve our objectives?*

(A further stage can be added looping back to the beginning of the process in terms of monitoring and review.)

THE STRATEGIC PLAN

The strategic plan of an organisation provides an idea of the overall direction of a company, the way it is planning to develop if it is able to control matters. This may be particularly difficult with growth and multinationalism. However, even retrenchment and stability may be difficult to achieve in practice. In a recession, stability may prove to be an optimistic aim, while attempts to sell off part of the business may prove difficult in practice. The actual strategy and the strategic intent of an organisation may be, in practice, different from the strategic plan, because the written plan is produced at particular intervals of time and for a purpose, such as satisfying major stakeholders. Actual strategy is constantly adjusted to circumstances and may be more or less focused than suggested in the written plan.

Increasingly, organisations have attempted to encapsulate the purpose of their activity, as much as the direction they wish to take, in a single short vision or mission statement. This statement represents the 'vision' or 'mission' of the organisation, or 'what it is about'. See, for example, the Ford Motor Company's Statement of Mission, Values and Guiding Principles, in Exhibit 5.5 (p 138).

The mission statements are changed by companies from time to time in order to reflect adjustments by the company to markets and competition. The examples of mission or vision statements in this chapter are provided to illustrate the form they take and may not be the ones in use by the companies now. The 'mission' might include the general direction the company is to take, but this may be expressed more clearly in the organisation's aims and objectives. In 1993 the airline British Midland described its mission in terms of improving service to meet customers' needs, 'allowing us to expand our business throughout Europe and, in doing so, generate the necessary profit to develop our company'.

The mission statement describes an organisation's basic purpose. A computer company, for example, may describe itself as providing low-cost, high-quality solutions to business problems. A record company may describe itself as being in the entertainment business, a retail company may describe itself as offering customers a range of high-quality, well-designed and attractive merchandise at reasonable prices. Cadbury Schweppes has described its task as building on its tradition of quality and value to provide brands, products, financial results and management performance that meet the interest of its shareholders, consumers, employees, customers, suppliers and the communities in which it operates.

A characteristic of mission statements is that they are succinct, distinctive and wide in scope; they are 'short in numbers and long in rhetoric' in the sense that they identify the organisation without providing a very specific approach to dealing with a target market. The mission statement outlines the present view of the organisation's purpose without restricting future possible development (*see* Exhibit 5.4). The computer company may wish to emphasise its width of possible work: it is not simply concerned with computer hardware or solving problems in information technology, it is concerned with using computers to solve business problems. The retail company may want to emphasise that it offers high quality goods of all types at reasonable prices.

The mission statement of any organisation should answer the question: What business are we in? The National Children's Bureau, for example, has stated that it 'exists to promote and protect the welfare, interests and rights of all children in the UK, on the basis of research and knowledge'. An engineering consultancy has

Exhibit 5.4 Mission statements

Mission statements focus on:

■ **What business are we in?**

■ **Who is to be served?**

■ **What benefits are to be delivered?**

■ **How are consumers to be satisfied?**

described its purpose to be 'a leading engineering consultancy engaged in the management and execution of projects requiring the effective application of engineering technologies and physical sciences'. There can be little doubt about what these two organisations do and what business they are in. The National Children's Bureau's purpose is to look after the interests of children, specifically in the UK, based on high-quality information. The Bureau is not concerned with the education or the health of children unless their welfare or rights need protecting in these areas. The management consultancy is clearly in engineering and not other areas of consultancy and the application of engineering technology. In the same way, British Airways has attempted to produce a mission statement that supports its slogan of 'The world's favourite airline' and has in the past declared its mission to be 'the best and most successful company in the airline business'. In support of this statement British Airways has emphasised the importance of safety and security, of financial strength, of the need to provide services and value, to anticipate and quickly respond to customer needs, to be a good employer and to be a good neighbour concerned for the community and the environment.

Once an organisation identifies what type of business it is in, it needs to answer the question: What benefits do our customers seek? Customers may be seeking the benefit of a solution to business problems which they want solved in the most cost-effective way possible. Whether this involves computers and information technology may not be important, provided that the solutions are effective. The question – What is our business? – has to be defined in terms of the underlying need that the organisation is trying to serve. The engineering consultancy is offering the effective application of engineering technologies and the customers it serves will be looking for benefits in terms of these applications. The Ford Motor Company has made the quality of its products and services the number one priority in order to meet customer needs, to prosper and to provide a reasonable return to those who have invested in it. The statement reproduced in Exhibit 5.5 emphasises the importance of company employees, the quality of its products and the company's willingness to be judged on its profits. In order to achieve these profits, guiding principles are set out with quality and a customer focus at the top of the list. This was a statement for the company to live up to, and it indicates its support for its major stakeholders in the form of its owners, its employees, its customers and its business partners. The statement provides an indication of the scope of the company's activities, automotive and financial products and services, and desired company approach to its work through social responsibility and equal opportunities.

Exhibit 5.5 Ford Motor Company's statement of mission, values and guiding principles

Ford Motor Company
Company mission, values and guiding principles

Mission

Ford Motor Company is a worldwide leader in automotive and financial products and services. Our mission is to improve continually our products and services to meet our customers' needs, allowing us to prosper as a business and to provide a reasonable return for our stockholders, the owners of our business.

Values

How we accomplish our mission is as important as the mission itself. Fundamental to success for the Company are these basic values:

► **People** – Our people are the source of our strength. They provide our corporate intelligence and determine our reputation and vitality. Involvement and teamwork are our core human values.

► **Products** – Our products are the end result of our efforts, and they should be the best in serving customers worldwide. As our products are viewed, so are we viewed.

► **Profits** – Profits are the ultimate measure of how efficiently we provide customers with the best products for their needs. Profits are required to survive and grow.

Guiding principles

► **Quality comes first** – To achieve customer satisfaction, the quality of our products and services must be our number one priority.

► **Customers are the focus of everything we do** – Our work must be done with our customers in mind, providing better products and services than our competition.

► **Continuous improvement is essential to our success** – We must strive for excellence in everything we do: in our products, in their safety and value – and in our services, our human relations, our competitiveness, and our profitability.

► **Employee involvement in our way of life** – We are a team. We must treat each other with trust and respect.

► **Dealers and suppliers are our partners** – The Company must maintain mutually beneficial relationships with dealers, suppliers and our other business associates.

► **Integrity is never compromised** – The conduct of our Company worldwide must be pursued in a manner that is socially responsible and commands respect for its integrity and for its positive contributions to society. Our doors are open to men and women alike without discrimination and without regard to ethnic origin or personal beliefs.

GOALS, AIMS AND OBJECTIVES

Once an organisation has decided on the business it is in, it can focus very clearly on its goals, aims and objectives. The corporate objectives of an organisation emphasise its direct aims, and in contrast to vision or mission statements, these are precise statements of intent. They must be capable of measurement, by one method or another, in order to confirm whether or not objectives have been achieved. It is possible to distinguish between objectives, which fill out the abstractions of the mission statement in more concrete terms, and corporate goals and aims, which provide the operational detail that can lead to an action plan. Organisational goals and aims are objectives restated in an operational and measurable form, and most of the time very little distinction is made in the use of these three terms. While the objectives may be expressed in terms of the grand plan, combined with the goals and aims they will provide a concrete idea of the direction of the organisation and how it will get there.

The computer company with a mission statement concerned with solving business problems may have corporate objectives which state that it aims at a particular level of profitability and that it intends to obtain a particular percentage share of its market. Objectives are often expressed in terms of profit, market share, growth, or all three. Therefore, while the mission statement is a relatively abstract statement of the organisation's purpose, the corporate objectives, aims and goals are a combination of the grand plan (Where do we want to go?) and an idea of how to achieve it (How do we get there?). The objectives will not only express the fact that the organisation intends to grow but also by how much and perhaps the main market or markets to be penetrated. For example DHL Worldwide Express has specified the aim to 'become the acknowledged global leader in the express delivery of documents and packages'. DHL has also declared that leadership would be achieved by establishing industry standards of excellence for quality service and by monitoring the lowest cost position relative to the company service commitment in all markets of the world. These can be seen as specific market aims, leadership position and costing policy. The corporate objective is for DHL to become the global leader in its field. This objective would be achieved by establishing standards of excellence for quality services and by monitoring the cost position in all world markets, and provides a statement of what the company wants to achieve and an indication of how it will do this.

Corporate objectives can be seen either as primary or secondary objectives. **Primary objectives** are those which must be achieved if the organisation is to survive and succeed. These are often expressed in terms of profit, sales or market share, so that if a certain level of profit is not achieved the company will collapse. If certain levels of sales or market share are not attained, the company will not succeed and again may be faced with the ultimate problem of survival. **Secondary objectives** are a measure of the efficiency of an organisation. They are critical for success, but may not affect survival for some time. They may be to do with customer care, product development, administrative efficiency, new office buildings and so on. In recent years many organisations, both in the private and public sectors, have raised the standing of such objectives as improving customer care from a secondary objective which is only considered to affect survival over a long period, to a primary objective which will have a much more direct effect on levels of activity, profits and therefore survival. Whatever the priority given to particular objectives, it is important that they are clearly expressed, measurable in one way or another and therefore realistic, with an assigned responsibility and a deadline for completion (*see* Exhibit 5.6).

Exhibit 5.6 **SMART objectives**

Specific:	clearly and precisely expressed
Measurable:	so that there is confirmation of whether or not they are achieved
Agreed:	with those responsible for achieving them
Realistic:	so that they can be achieved
Timed:	with a deadline for achievement

An organisation needs to base its objectives on market research which should enable it to understand the customer's needs. The information arising from market research helps the organisation to be customer oriented and to produce goods and services which meet customer needs. Market research will help to decide:

- **customer needs at present**
- **customer location and characteristics**
- **customer perceptions of the organisation's products and services**
- **customer needs in the future**
- **levels of customer satisfaction.**

Managers have to ensure that the entire organisation is customer oriented, otherwise one part of it may pull in a different direction. The mission statement, corporate objectives, goals and aims, and the marketing strategy need to interact so that they are all directed one way. At the same time, managers have to carry out an audit of the external environment. This 'environmental analysis' provides a systematic assessment of information about an organisation's strategic opportunities, as well as threats and problems which might prove to be obstacles to its development. This analysis enables managers to shape and evaluate strategic options and develop corporate strategy. In marketing terms, this is part of the SWOT (strengths, weaknesses, opportunities and threats) analysis. Opportunities may be discovered by revealing a part of the potential market that is relatively untouched. For example, a computer company may discover that while it has been concentrating on finding solutions to business problems in terms of products and finance there is a gap in terms of personnel and training functions. Clive Sinclair has invented products to fill perceived opportunities in the market such as portable computers, electric cars and powered bicycles, with more or less success.

Competition is the most obvious threat for most organisations. Market research identifies rival producers of goods and services. Most organisations are concerned with their market share and profitability and competing firms will have similar objectives. For example, McDonald's UK has described its purpose to be 'the United Kingdom's number one favourite quick service restaurant', led by the needs of its customers, committed to the welfare and development of its staff, with the provision of great tasting food in a relaxed, safe and consistent restaurant environment.

Matters such as competitors' product development and pricing policy will be taken into account in determining an organisation's own policies. For example, from time to time newspapers have entered into strong price competition. In 1994 *The Times,* in the UK, reduced its price to 20 pence while its rivals were priced at more than twice that level. This had a particular effect on the *Independent*, which attempted to counteract this pricing policy by reducing its own price to 30 pence. In 2003 the *Independent* produced a 'tabloid' version of the paper as an alternative to its usual layout. This smaller issue was designed to be easier to read on commuter trains and in other crowded places and to compete on design rather than price with other broadsheet newspapers. Later in the year *The Times* followed this development with its own tabloid version.

Threats may also take the form of political, social, economic and technological changes. These may also represent opportunities, depending on how they affect the environment of the organisation. Tax changes, for example, may adversely affect a company or an industry. The changes in taxation on company cars in the UK, for example, have reduced their importance as a perk for managers and have altered the demand for particular cars. One change which illustrates this point was introduced in 1994. Instead of taxation being based on the cubic capacity of the car, it was based on its retail price. This enabled, on the one hand, larger-engined cars to be more widely sold to company car buyers, and, on the other hand, car companies had to look very carefully at their prices and margins and those of their competitors.

Changes in government regulation and European Union laws may affect companies, particularly in matters such as environmental control and human resource legislation. At the same time, the introduction of training grants and industrial development areas has provided opportunities for many companies. Social changes, such as the increase in leisure activities or the shifting age structure of the population, create opportunities for companies in the leisure business or for those who provide goods and services to pensioners, while presenting threats to companies producing goods for children. The development of technology presents opportunities to computer companies while representing a threat to companies whose technology cannot keep pace with that of competitors.

The marketing strategy of an organisation will depend on the analysis of its market position, and an evaluation of its external threats and opportunities and its internal strengths and weaknesses. The strengths of organisations may include location, product development, internal organisation, a skilled and dedicated labour force, good communications and image. Weaknesses may include the lack of financial resources, a small market share, a limited range of products and dilapidated premises. Of course many of the weaknesses represent opportunities for improvement and could therefore be turned into strengths. It will then hope to build on its strengths and opportunities so that it can meet its strategic objectives and achieve its vision. An example of this was IBM in the 1980s which considered its main strengths to be in the corporate market with the development of mainframes. It believed that its lack of direct retail experience with individual buyers constituted a weakness in terms of the new PC market. In comparing itself through market research with its competitors, it decided to enter the PC market by selling to business and corporate customers and gradually overcoming its weakness by licensing the sale of IBM PCs. At the time this appeared to be a sensible strategic marketing

➔ Ch. 4   plan (see Exhibit 4.3 in Chapter 4).

STRATEGY

The **strategy** of an organisation involves matching its corporate objectives and its available resources. In this development of strategy, managers are concerned with reconciling the business the organisation is in with the allocation of resources. The use of resources has to support the aims and goals agreed in the organisation and these in turn will determine the priorities in terms of resource use. If growth is a major element in the grand plan, then resources are likely to be allocated to marketing and product development, while if contraction or 'retrenchment' is the goal, then more resources may be given to paying for the costs of redundancy payments, early retirement and the negotiations and consultations involved. This allocation process is concerned with the general purposes of an organisation, whether it is part of a grand plan, the overall objectives or a 'strategy' designed to keep the organisation in business.

While the overall strategy may be determined at a senior level, the detail may be better left to those as close as possible to the organisation's customers. This view is supported by Tom Peters (1992) in terms of strategy:

> *'I don't believe top management should be in the business of strategy setting at all, except as creators of a general business mission. Strategies must be set from below. (No, not "from" below. Set "in" below – i.e. by the autonomous business units, for the autonomous business units.)'*

Strategy involves senior managers in establishing the overall purpose of the organisation and the objectives, aims and goals, while the question of tactics and approach to customers is decided at the level of individual business units. The strategic plan is the process of allocating resources in an organisation in order to achieve its strategic aims. This allocation will again be carried out at different levels, so that while resources may be allocated in a general way, detailed allocation will be left to business units or work teams. Of course, in many 'autonomous' business units the whole unit may prosper or fail depending on its relative success, and this will depend on its own strategic plan and the success of its implementation. However, it remains the situation that the overall purpose of an organisation, its vision and values remain the responsibility of senior management. Changing this vision and these values is a slow process which requires the allocation of resources over a period of years.

Large companies, such as British Airways, have introduced staff training sessions, quality initiatives or corporate change programmes over many years in order to create different behavioural approaches in the company and to reinforce company values. Resources are allocated centrally to these programmes in order to promote developments which match the mission and corporate objectives of the company. For example, in the 1980s British Airways developed its 'Putting People First' and 'Managing People First' programmes in order to improve its service. It then evolved its mission statement ('to be the best and most successful company in the airline business') out of the purpose and success of its training programme (Exhibit 5.7).

It is possible to distinguish at least three levels of strategy: corporate, business and functional. **Corporate strategy** applies to large companies which are divided into a number of discrete and fairly autonomous units. Holding companies are typical of this type of organisation in which a number of companies are grouped together, usually for financial reasons such as the efficient allocation of capital and

Exhibit 5.7 British Airways

In November 1983 British Airways introduced a training programme called 'Putting People First'. The aim was to put 12 000 customer contact people through a two-day course to improve their customer service skills. The programme consisted of a mixture of presentations, exercises and group discussions in which staff reviewed their personal experience as customers of other service organisations. They also examined the implications for British Airways and were pressed to identify what they would do about these implications. The response to the training programme was mixed – some were sceptical, some saw it as a harmonising exercise, some dropped out, and others were enthusiastic. But top management continued to support the programme, demonstrating their commitment to customer service. The non-front-line staff began asking to be included and gradually the level of cynicism faded away. Staff began identifying the obstacles, confronting their managers with the fact that resources were insufficient to deliver the levels of customer care called for. The management responded to these issues and so encouraged staff to identify others.

Then in 1984, a programme for managers called 'Managing People First' was launched to change management styles. At the time, management style was perceived to be dominated by sales and procedures and the aim of the training programme was to replace this with something more open and dynamic.

Other changes were made to reinforce the training programmes. For example, quality assurance and performance related reward systems were introduced. The services being offered by the airline were also improved, demonstrating to staff that they would get the resources required to deliver better service.

It was only once the changes in behaviour were starting to show up as better service and greater customer satisfaction that mission statements were formulated in 1986.

Source: Campbell, *et al.* (1990).

investment. Corporate strategy is the responsibility of the corporate head office, with the fundamental issue being the reason for the different businesses being collected together.

Companies may be bought or sold by the holding company as their strategy changes, so at one time it may decide to extend its operations into new fields by buying companies outside its usual area of operation, at another time it may decide that the correct strategy is to consolidate on one industry or area of industry and sell companies that do not fit in with this strategy. Strategy may be based around investment, the economies of scale or the sharing of core competencies, and in particular, decisions about the portfolio of businesses. In practice, the corporation may adopt a hands-off approach to the individual companies or units under its control as long as they fulfil the corporate objectives.

At the level of **business strategy**, the critical issues will be in terms of markets, critical success factors, the organisation of the business and overall competitive strategy. At the **functional level**, the focus will be on departments or divisions of organisations. Most companies have some elements in their organisation of a functional structure in which people concentrate on a particular specialism, such as finance, information systems, manufacturing and so on, and the overall business strategy has to be reflected and linked with the functional level strategies. This means that financial strategy, marketing strategy and human resource strategy have to reflect the overall company approach and may inform it as well as being shaped by it. The structure of a business needs to assist the business level strategy in one way or another, otherwise responsibilities for parts of the strategy may not be picked up by the functional units. At the same time, it is possible for the functional units to interpret the business strategy in ways that suit them rather than reflecting the needs of the whole business.

At all levels, strategic managers will be aiming to achieve a **sustainable competitive advantage**. A competitive advantage arises when a company receives a return on investment that is greater than the norm for its competitors for a period long enough to alter the relative standing of the company amongst its rivals. The product or service has to be sufficiently durable in terms of its life cycle to achieve the required return on investment and to enhance the reputation of the company. In due course competitors will succeed in imitating it and technological advances and social change can shorten product life, and an enhanced reputation can offset this to some extent.

A sustainable competitive advantage also depends on how easy or difficult it is for rivals to imitate or emulate the company offerings. A potential competitor will have to acquire the resources necessary to replicate the processes in order to develop a similar or better product so that if this is difficult the advantage can be more easily sustained. The development of strategy involves the identification of those factors which are critical in achieving an advantage. These critical success factors are those components of strategy where the organisation must excel to outperform competition. Managers have to assess the resources and competencies which have been built up through the delivery of the company's current and previous strategy, but a danger is that they may then favour new strategies that use these factors without taking account of the threats and the opportunities which may arise.

Exhibit 5.8 Types of strategy

- **Planned strategy**   a company decides a way of proceeding or on a strategic plan

- **Intended strategy**   a company decides to execute a pattern of decision making

- **Deliberate strategy**   a company intends a particular strategy and it is accomplished

- **Imposed strategy**   a company has strategy imposed by an outside agency

- **Realised strategy**   a company strategy that has been accomplished

- **Unrealised strategy**   an intended or deliberate company strategy which is not accomplished

- **Emergent strategy**   where a company strategy is not intended but emerges over time

→ Ch. 6

If there is too much reliance on factors which have produced success in the past, there can be strategic drift in an organisation where the actual strategy drifts further and further away from the strategy which is required for success (*see* Chapter 6). It may be possible for a company to exploit its unique critical success factors by taking advantage of new opportunities and 'stretching' its resources and competencies in ways which rivals find difficult to match. A company that has a good reputation in one area may move into new areas where its reputation will 'carry over'. For example, Tesco has moved into areas such as clothing and finance based on its reputation for value in food retailing, the location of its stores and its ability to provide what people want.

TYPES OF STRATEGY

Strategic management is concerned with ensuring that there are sufficient core competencies to secure a competitive advantage. Strategy can be directed at improving and developing such areas as customer service, location, design and advertising skills, if these are felt to be core competencies which can provide an advantage. In practice strategy is not always carefully **planned**, although (as in Exhibit 5.7) it may be. Strategy may be **'intended'** so that it does indicate the desired processes and direction for the business, deliberately formulated by strategic managers. This **'deliberate'** strategy will then be a systematic process of development and implementation.

'Realised' strategy is the strategy that a business is actually following in practice, which may be different from intended or deliberate strategy because although these may be planned, they may not be implemented. However good the intended strategy might appear to be, it may be decided by managers that it will not be put into effect; the organisational culture may be in opposition to it so that for one reason or another it is not realised. The culture of the organisation may be opposed to it, stakeholders may block it, or there may be power bases within the structure of a company which prevent the favoured form of strategy from being followed. Strategy can also be **'imposed'** on a business, for example as a result of overall corporate strategy, or as a result of government legislation or regulation or in some other way. Anti-monopoly legislation, for example, may limit a merger policy, or environmental regulations may place obstacles in the favoured strategy of a company.

The development of strategy is most clearly seen in the distinction between deliberate and emergent strategy with the view that strategy can be formulated through complicated plans in a deliberate manner, or it emerges over time, step by step, in an incremental approach. Figure 5.1 illustrates the link between the various perspectives on strategy.

Incremental strategy is a process of carrying out actions and gradually blending initiatives together into a coherent pattern. It is much more similar to the unstructured and unpredictable processes of exploration and invention than the orderly processes of design and production. This view of strategy sees planning as useful for routine tasks that need to be efficiently organised but less suitable for non-routine activities and innovation. Although 'planning' can mean simply 'a way of proceeding', it is often expected to involve preparing a written report, or a drawing or a tabulated statement.

Figure 5.1 Forms of strategy

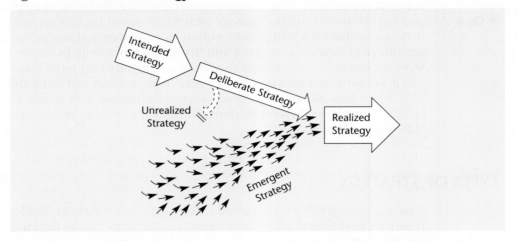

Source: Mintzberg, H (2000) *The Rise and Fall of Strategic Planning*, Simon & Schuster. Reproduced with permission.

TRANSFORMATION AND VALUE

Operationally a business performs a conversion or transformation process through which it adds value to a commodity or service, in the sense that the value of the output of the organisation is greater than the cost of the inputs and the process involved. Whatever the business, it starts with 'raw materials', whether these are goods or services, and, at whatever stage of production it is, the processes it applies to them add value. For example, a car assembly plant may start with raw materials of car body parts, engines, tyres, window glass, electrical components and so on, and by using the skill and competencies of the people working in the plant and its machinery and technology, finished motor cars are assembled which are of greater value than the sum of all the components. Another example is provided by travel agents, who start with the raw materials of access to flights, hotel rooms, excursions and so on, and put these into a package which they are able to sell to tourists at a price which is greater than the cost of the various elements and the process of bringing them together for the consumer.

The 'value' of a product or service consists of the price plus the consumer surplus, which is a concept used by economists to distinguish between the price a consumer is prepared to pay for a product and the price the consumer does pay. Provided that the price of the product or service is below the value to the consumer, it is likely to sell; if it is not, a sale is unlikely. This means that the package holiday is likely to sell to tourists if they feel that it is good 'value', that is if the cost to them is less than the price they are prepared to pay. Similarly, a motor car retailer will buy a car from an assembly plant to sell on to a consumer, if it is thought that the price they can sell it for is greater than the cost of buying it, advertising it and so on.

The conversion or transformation process usually consists of a linked set of stages of 'production' from basic raw materials to the final consumer. In the production of a motor car, the basic raw materials are such goods as steel and rubber, which are converted into car panels and tyres and passed on to car assemblers, from them to distributors and retailers until the finished new car is bought by the consumer. The 'value chain' passes through steel foundries, panel makers, car assemblers, distributors, retailers and consumers. This is a simple value chain because each link will in practice be involved with other value chains. For example, panel makers may receive their steel from a number of foundries and may pass on their finished panels to a number of assembly plants. They will also be involved in value chains which provide them with power, lighting and machinery.

Car assembly companies are in the same situation where even in the simplest view of a value chain they are receiving parts from a range of suppliers and passing on their finished cars to a number of distributors. All the value chains considered together can be said to form an 'industry', the motor car industry. A company in this industry will be in competition with other companies in the industry, as well as in a wider sense be in competition with other forms of transport and consumer spending in general. Businesses use a range of strategies to gain a competitive advantage over their rivals. They may try to make their product different from their competitors' products, with more features which add value to it. They may focus on a particular segment of the market in an attempt to provide exactly what it wants or they may form alliances of various types with competing companies or with businesses further down or up the value chain. The actual environment in which strategy is developed will depend on the value chains of a business and the level of competition.

In deciding on a strategy, managers have to consider the 'risks' involved in the sense of 'uncertainty', in that a particular course of action can lead to a number of possible outcomes. In this sense all courses of action carry risks including doing nothing, because rivals will also be formulating strategies and there can be no guarantee that they are doing nothing. There are, of course, financial implications in alternative strategies and this is why 'doing nothing' is often appealing. Innovation and change imply investment in design, testing, training, new plant and technology and usually increase the gearing ratio of the business, that is the ratio of the debt

→ Ch. 16 finance to shareholders' funds (*see* Chapter 16). Any alteration in strategy has to be accepted in one way or another by the business stakeholders, such as shareholders.

STAKEHOLDER STRATEGY

Stakeholders can be described as individuals and groups who are affected by the activities of an organisation. The most important stakeholders can be seen as those with the most to lose from the organisation's actions, but this does not always reflect their relative power. For example, the employees of a company may have most to lose from the success or failure of the strategies employed, but financial backers may be the most powerful in actual decisions because they are in a stronger position to make or break the company. Strategies have to be developed taking into account the interests of stakeholders and their relative power.

All these stakeholders (Exhibit 5.9) have an interest in the company and may want to influence its future strategy. Managers have to reconcile the variety of interests that individuals and groups represent. Shareholders may be mainly interested in large dividends and a rise in the value of their shares, so they may be in favour of a strategy which maximises profits rather than the long-term development and growth of the company. Employees may be mainly concerned about the stability of their employment and the level of pay and other benefits, while the customers may be more concerned with the price of the goods the company produces, their quality and where they are available.

Exhibit 5.9 **Typical business stakeholders**

■ **Shareholders**	own the company and receive dividends
■ **Financial bodies**	fund companies and receive interest
■ **Employees**	provide labour and skills, and receive pay
■ **Managers**	provide organisation and control, and receive pay
■ **Government**	legislates, regulates and receives taxation
■ **Customers**	consume the product and receive benefits
■ **Suppliers**	provide 'raw materials' and receive costs

'Stakeholder mapping' is a process of analysing their influence on a company and how interested each group is to impress its expectations on the organisation's choice of strategies. Strong unions may be able and be interested in exerting considerable pressure on the choice of strategy while where the unions are weak, employees' interests may not be such an important pressure on the company. However, if particular employees are in short supply, perhaps because they have essential skills and competencies, their influence on strategic choice will be greater. Managers are faced with these and many other considerations when they choose strategies for their organisation. Strategic options are the broad choices open to a business and those that are selected are its 'strategic pathway'.

A strategic pathway consists of all the goods and services a company decides to offer and the quantities in which they are offered and their quality. Strategy is involved in the positioning of each product and service within its particular market and implies considerations of access to the resources and competencies required, sources of funds and the expectations of returns. Positioning is itself linked to questions of quality, price and design and such considerations as whether the commodity will be targeted at the luxury end of the market or the economy end or somewhere in the middle. A company will have a portfolio of offers of goods and services and strategic choices have to be made about each of these as well as the overall portfolio.

THE ACTION PLAN

Once the strategy has been agreed, managers need to decide on particular courses of action in order to achieve corporate objectives with the resources available. Detailed guidelines have to be developed in order to initiate and control action. The purpose of an action plan is to ensure that people responsible for accomplishing short-term and long-term objectives have clear guidance on what they need to do and how they are to achieve these objectives. Action plans also provide a mechanism by which top managers can satisfy themselves that what is being implemented is consistent with the intention of organisational strategy.

Action plans are concerned with turning priorities and organisational strategy into reality, and they are linked to the use of resources in the form of both physical and human resources. They may show how many people are to be involved with a particular activity, the numbers of people and their skills and qualifications. Action plans also take into account how much money is available for a particular activity and the amount and type of equipment and premises required. In reflecting the organisation's strategic plan, action plans have a major impact on the successful implementation of these strategies in showing what actions are required and the timescale for completion.

At their simplest, action plans are lists of actions to be carried out by particular managers or operatives in order to achieve the requirements of the business unit. They are often the responsibility of operating managers in order to ensure that those responsible for implementing a strategy are also involved in developing it. They are usually accompanied by detailed budgets, which may act as a means of control as well as a means of communicating an action plan.

- **Functional plans** are produced to guide decisions and actions in the various functional areas of an organisation.
- **Project plans** are produced on a one-off basis in order to control specific programmes of work.
- **Long-term plans**, **policies** or **procedures** are used to establish guidelines for recurring activities.

These action plans can then be translated into detailed plans for individual employees or relatively small working units or teams. Corporate planning can mean that functional plans and policies become clear guidelines for individual action. In a sense, the working position can be seen as a series of projects, each planned in order to control specific programmes of work and operating within policy guidelines. These project actions may be agreed by the self-managed team and the individuals within it, keeping within the policies established by corporate managers in order to achieve corporate objectives. For example, at its simplest the action plan of a salesperson may set out very clear actions and objectives in terms of the number of customers to be contacted, or the value of sales to be made in a particular period. The action plan may go further in establishing how the salesperson should function in terms of customer care, following up complaints and so on.

MONITORING AND REVIEW

The strategic planning process involves agreeing on a mission statement, deciding on corporate objectives, analysing markets and resources, auditing the internal and external environment, and arriving at an action plan. It is not, of course, a static process, and once the framework is in place and is working, it needs to be frequently reviewed in the light of any changes. Managers should review all aspects of the strategy constantly. At one extreme the action plan requires constant monitoring and adjustment, while at the other, the mission statement may need to be altered only rarely. This should reflect the fact that while the direction of the organisation should not be changing too frequently, the actions required to maintain that direction will entail frequent adjustment.

In reviewing the 'closeness of fit' between corporate actions and corporate direction and values alternative strategies may be considered. Managers look at existing strategies and can perform what is called 'gap analysis'. Here they simply attempt to determine whether a performance gap exists between what their existing strategy can realistically be expected to accomplish and the objectives that have been established. This can be in areas such as sales, productivity and profitability and also in areas such as staff training and development, customer care and in environmental issues. Where there is not a gap, managers can assume that the current strategy is probably the appropriate one. Where serious gaps are found to exist, managers will need to investigate these and look for alternative strategies. In extreme cases there may be a need for a significant change in the firm's strategy.

The monitoring and review process provides the loop back to all stages of organisational strategy and should provide a reminder that change and improvement are constant features of organisational life. The planning objective in general terms is an upward spiral of improved market information, better systems for competitor analysis, and more efficient and effective use of resources. In monitoring the strategy and the strategic plan, they can be matched against the corporate values and the guiding principles of the organisation. The review process can help to answer the question of how far the organisation's policies and actions coincide with and are supportive of its perceived values.

The values and guiding principles of an organisation are concerned with 'how it goes about its business'. As well as deciding what business it is in, what objectives it has and how it will achieve them, an organisation has to decide on its underlying values. These may be explicitly expressed (as in the case of the Ford Motor Company in Exhibit 5.5) or implied in the way in which business is conducted in an organisation. Usually this is expressed in terms of quality factors, customer care and employee development rather than in terms of corporate ethics, but social responsibility, equal opportunities and environmental issues may form an explicit part of the company 'philosophy'.

THE STRATEGIC PORTFOLIO

→ Ch. 6

Every organisation consists of at least one and usually many more products and services. Between them, these represent the 'business portfolio' (*see also* Chapter 6). For example, in the case of automobile companies, there are different models of car and various services provided in relation to cars. With travel agents, their portfolio consists of a range of travel services which may include a number of different holidays. A company can be viewed as a 'portfolio' of business investments which managers must balance by expanding investment in some, while reducing investment in others. Decisions have to be made by managers on the investment of resources in the various areas of the portfolio and their contribution to the business in order to provide the company with a competitive advantage. Most companies like to have a balanced mix of business units which are at various points in their respective life cycles.

→ Ch. 4

One approach found to be useful in this process has been the **Boston matrix** (sometimes referred to as the Boston Consulting Group, or BCG, matrix or the growth–share matrix – *see* Chapter 4). The use of this for business units or product/service teams can help the corporation to define the questions of: What business should we be in? What is our basic mission? How should we allocate corporate resources across the units and teams? The matrix analyses businesses along two dimensions, business growth and market share. Business growth measures how rapidly the whole industry is increasing in size, while market share measures the share a business unit has of this market compared to competitors.

Once it has been decided what the growth rate is in a market and the particular product/service market share, it is possible to allocate each unit to one of four quadrants in the matrix (*see* Figure 5.2). The arrangement of business units that emerges within the matrix can provide managers with a means of establishing and describing corporate strategy. In terms of balance, the desired grouping may be to have a number of units in each quadrant, because there would then be a number of products and services producing a cash flow, with others requiring an injection of cash to move them from being problems to stars and with other units on their way out. This means that units in the lower part of the matrix, the so-called '**cash cows**' and 'dogs', could be used as a source of excess cash for investment in the 'problem children' (also referred to as 'question marks') and the 'stars' which represent the best opportunities for future growth and survival.

The allocation of individual business units to a particular position on the matrix helps managers to define strategic plans for the business with levels of activity consistent with corporate strategy. For example, 'cash cow' managers may be expected to produce relatively short-term profits, 'dog' managers may be expected to minimise expenditure and to reduce part of their operations to allow any available resources to be invested elsewhere, 'star' unit managers may be expected to increase market share with the help of investment in equipment and marketing, 'problem children' managers may be expected to review and evaluate the future potential of their business unit and to justify its continuation. It is, of course, crucial that a particular business unit is described accurately. For example, if a product or service has

Figure 5.2 The Boston matrix: cash flows

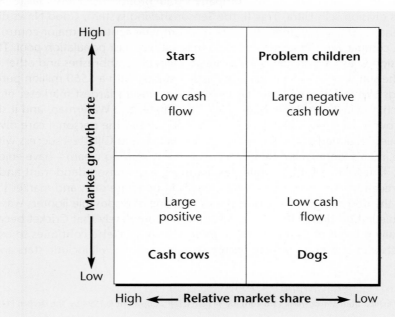

a low relative market share in a market with low growth, then it should be described as a 'dog' and therefore as a likely candidate for 'divestment' by the company so that its resources can be reinvested in another product or service.

The growth-share matrix approach has been criticised because of the difficulty of describing some products/services and business units sufficiently accurately. At the margin, the difference between a subject for 'divesting' and a 'problem child' with potential for growth and development into a 'star' may be very small. It may be based on an estimation of market growth and the potential for future growth. It can be argued that the approach oversimplifies the situation in many organisations and that the terminology used in the matrix encourages this oversimplification. It does, however, provide an excellent starting point for analysing the position of business units, and it would be an unwise corporation that did not use the portfolio approach in one way or another (see Exhibit 5.10). A range of variations on the Boston matrix have been developed, such as dividing the matrix into nine sections in order to define market share and market growth in more detail, but the basis of the process remains the same.

One of the frameworks used by managers in terms of portfolio strategy is life-cycle analysis. In this process business units' products/services are analysed and placed on a point against one of the four or five stages of the life cycle – introduction, growth, maturity (and saturation) and decline (see Figure 4.4). The typical situation is that managers are investing money in a product or service at the introductory stage, while expecting products at the mature stage to be cash cows and producing money for investment. Stars are likely to be seen in the growth stage, where the market is still

Exhibit 5.10 Portfolio analyses

Gillette Company

Gillette has several cash cows in its corporate portfolio. The most famous is the shaving division, which accounts for two-thirds of the company's total profits and holds a large share of a stable market. This division sells Ultra, Trac II, the Sensor shaving system, Good News disposable razor and new Sensor razor for women. In 1992 the company captured major control of the largest major blade company in China and access to that nation's vast population pool. The Oral-B laboratories division is also a cash cow with its steady sales of toothbrushes and other dental hygiene products. The stationery products division has star status. With a $560 million purchase of Parker Pen Holdings Limited, this division has become the world's largest marketer of writing instruments, which also includes Paper Mate, Flair, Erasemate, and Waterman, and it shows potential for rapid growth overseas. Gillette's question marks are in the personal care division. A line of women's toiletries aimed at the European market failed, and Gillette's success with other lines – for example, men's Right Guard deodorant and Foamy shaving cream – have enjoyed only cyclical success. A new line of men's toiletries featuring a gel-based deodorant and a gel shaving cream was recently launched. If this new line fails to generate sales and market share, it may be assigned to the dog category, to which the Cricket line of disposable lighters was relegated. The Bic disposable lighter dominated the Cricket line so completely that Cricket became a dog and was eventually put out of its misery through liquidation. Gillette continues to experiment with new products and question marks to ensure that its portfolio will include stars and cash cows in the future.

Source: Excerpt and Exhibit from *Management* (3rd edn), by Richard L Daft. Copyright © 1994 by The Dryden Press. Reprinted by permission of the publisher.

growing and there is an expectation that the product will achieve an increased share of the market. Dogs will usually be in the decline stage, although they may be at another stage, such as introductory, but in fact be unsuccessful in terms of market share, or as a result of a lower than expected market growth.

Introductory stage strategies focus on confirming that market growth and market share do exist and that the product or service is meeting customer needs. At the same time, managers have to arrange for the financial support of the product at a time when investment significantly exceeds revenue. Growth stage strategy will focus on the size and potential of the market and opportunities to broaden the customer base. Managers need to strengthen the product/service's appeal by developing such areas as brand identification, distribution outlets and price. At the maturity stage, managers are faced with increasing competition and more resources may need to be invested in marketing, and searching for new sales opportunities. In the decline stage, managers will attempt either to monitor the business unit through a refocus of the customer base and cost cutting, or employ strategies to enable the organisation to move out of that particular product/service while retaining resources to reinvest elsewhere.

Competitive forces strategy

Michael Porter, a professor of economics and business strategy at Harvard Business School, has identified 'forces' that can be seen as the main factors which an organisation needs to take into account in order to exploit opportunities in its environment and to protect itself against competition. This has been referred to as the **competitive forces strategy**. He argued that five competitive forces exist in an organisation's environment (*see* Figure 5.3):

- Potential new entrants have more difficulty in setting up in a high capital-intensive industry (such as motor cars) than in a service industry (such as an estate agency). Capital requirements and the scale are both potential barriers to entry.

- The bargaining power of buyers increases as advertising and consumer information create a situation where customers know about the full range of price and product options available. This is especially true when a company sells mainly to a few customers, such as is the case where manufacturers are supplying one or two retailers.

- The bargaining power of suppliers depends on the availability of substitute suppliers. A sole supplier will have great power.

- The threat of substitute products is most powerful where there are alternatives and substitutes for a company's product. Changes in opinions about the environment, costs and so on may influence the demand for these products.

- Rivalry among competitors may appear in terms of advertising, price and product differentiation, such as appeared in the 'cola wars' between Pepsi-Cola and Coca-Cola.

Porter suggested that a company could find a competitive advantage against these competitive forces either through differentiation or cost leadership, or by combining policies focused on a particular strategic target. For example, the **differentiation strategy** involves an attempt to distinguish the company's products and services from others in the industry. Product differentiation may involve product branding, adding distinct features or providing extra services. If a product is felt by consumers

Figure 5.3 Competitive forces

Source: Adapted and reprinted with permission of The Free Press, a Division of Simon & Schuster from *Competitive Strategy: Techniques for Analyzing Industries and Competitors* by Michael E Porter. Copyright © 1980, 1988 by The Free Press.

to be different from its competitors they may be prepared to pay high prices. Chanel No. 5 perfume, Mercedes-Benz cars and Rolex watches are all examples of this approach.

A **cost leadership strategy** involves reducing costs in order to undercut competitors' prices while providing a similar quality product. Companies such as Tesco and Kwik-Fit have followed this policy, while the John Lewis stores chain claims not to be undercut on price. These companies are in a good position to withstand a price war: customers have difficulty in finding lower prices and buyers will have little scope for price negotiations with suppliers. The low price acts as a barrier against new entrants and substitute products. A **combined strategy** involves the company using a differentiation or low-cost approach concentrated on a narrow target market. For example, some companies, such as Sun Alliance, have introduced low-cost insurance for the over-fifties.

Porter (1996) has argued (*see* the Case Study at the end of this chapter) that a sustainable strategic position requires trade-offs. Choosing a unique position is not enough to guarantee a sustainable advantage, because a valuable position will attract imitation either by matching the superior performance or by 'straddling'. The 'straddler' attempts to match the benefit of a successful position while maintaining its existing position, but a strategic position is not sustainable unless there are trade-offs with other positions. Trade-offs create the need for choice and a purposeful limitation on what a company offers. They deter straddling or repositioning because competitors that engage in these approaches undermine their strategies and degrade the value of their existing activities, and positions built on systems of activities are generally far more sustainable than those built on individual activities.

The managers' role is to create fit among a company's activities and to integrate them so that the company does many things well. This requires trade-offs in competing in order to achieve a sustainable advantage, so that managers have to decide what not to do as well as what to do.

STRATEGIC MANAGEMENT

In practice, many organisations apply a range of strategies depending on changes in circumstances. In order to remain competitive and survive managers need to be creative and innovative as well as using all the strategies available to them. Companies attempt to expand their markets by attracting new customers, and by moving into national or international markets. Organisations develop their products by adding features or modifying the design to remain ahead of the competition. This is a process adapted by car companies in updating their models by relatively small changes, adding features or producing special editions.

Organisations also use a number of other strategies in order to remain ahead of the competition. **Vertical integration** is a strategy with the aim of controlling channels of both supply and distribution. The company seeks to control its suppliers so that its supplies can be guaranteed at the lowest possible cost and at the quality it requires, and its distributors so that it is able to work closely with the final consumers. **Horizontal integration** is a strategy aimed at controlling competitors at the same level of production. A company may take over or merge with another company in order to acquire economies of scale, increased buying power and access to a wider range of consumers.

→ Ch. 2

Diversification involves a strategy of spreading an organisation's activity beyond its main business. The main problem with this is that managers may find themselves working in areas where they do not have any expertise. Tom Peters has suggested that in fact managers should 'stick to the knitting' (*see* Chapter 2), in the sense of diversifying only into areas where managers do have expertise. This needs to be an area to which they can transfer an already acquired skill. Manufacturers may move increasingly into a related service area in which they have already been working on a small scale. For example, motor companies have moved into car leasing and car hire services. Restructuring strategy can include a range of approaches designed to reorganise the company in order to meet new challenges. Periods of recession cause retrenchment and possibly liquidation when a company is sold for its tangible assets, not as a going concern. On the other hand 'retrenchment' and 're-engineering' are often approaches designed to concentrate on the main business of an organisation by 'outsourcing' or putting out to contract all those products or services which are not an essential part of the main business. Cleaning and catering services are among the most obvious of these, but others include car leasing, information technology and advertising.

Strategic management can be seen as actions concerned with what an organisation should do in order to survive. Ralph Stacey (1999) has argued that the process is a highly complex one, involving, as it does, a whole range of networks and control systems within an organisation of any size, and given the many unpredictable elements with which managers have to contend. He suggests that 'one approach to strategy is based on the idea that successful organisations are pulled to an identified future point'. In this case the task of management is to maintain the status quo until the future point is reached. Stacey argues that this is an impossible approach in practice and if it is applied it will fail.

> *'To succeed managers must practise the other approach, the one based on the idea that successful organisations are driven from where they are now to a destination that they create and discover.'*

Hamel and Prahalad (1989) have questioned the idea of 'fit' and the view that successful organisations adapt to their environment. In their study of successful companies in the late 1980s (such as Honda, Komatsu and Canon) as against the less successful ones (General Motors, Caterpillar and Xerox), they found that a distinguishing factor was the different mental models of strategy guiding their respective actions. They observed that less successful companies followed the conventional approach to maintaining strategic fit, leading to a trimming of ambitions to those that could be met by available resources. Such companies were concerned mainly with product-market units rather than core competencies. Consistency was preserved through requiring conformity in behaviour and a focus on achieving financial objectives. On the other hand, the focus of successful companies was on leveraging resources, that is using what they had in new and innovative ways in order to reach new goals. The main concern of these companies was to use their resources in challenging and stretching ways to build up a number of core competencies. Consistency was maintained by all sharing a central strategic intent.

Hamel and Prahalad (1993) have supported the idea that organisational success arises from organisation-wide intention or strategic intent which is based on a challenging shared vision of the future leadership of the organisation. This is based on organisational learning, an obsession for winning, an understanding that competitive advantages are not inherently sustainable and that an organisation succeeds not by long-term planning but by achieving a broad, stretching and challenging intention to build core competencies. They argue that what distinguishes a small developing company from a larger developing one is not the smaller resource base, but the greater gap that exists between the resource base and the aspiration of the company. This gap they refer to as 'stretch', so that the problem of large, established companies is not a lack of resource but insufficient ambition, a lack of stretch in their aspirations. They suggest that companies such as NEC, CNN, Sony, Glaxo and Honda are more united by the unreasonableness of their ambitions and their creativity in obtaining the most from the least than from any cultural or institutional heritage. They suggest that creating stretch is the single most important task of senior management.

The strategic role of managers therefore is not so much to stake out the future of an organisation but to help to accelerate the acquisition of market and industry knowledge. Managers use the resources they have to create requirements of the environment which they can meet, they push to achieve stretching goals and they aim to continually renew and transform their organisation. The creation of a 'learning organisation' is an essential element in modern management in both the private and the public sectors because, with improvments in the availability of information, competition has become more fierce rather than less so and in order to cope with this successful organisations have to embrace new technology and new ideas. There is a sense of creative tension in strategic management because the development of a new direction and the concentration on stretch and leverage destroys the old certainties, and it is, therefore, at the forefront of the process of continuous change.

SUMMARY

■ Strategic management is concerned with providing a purpose in order to establish the way forward for an organisation. It involves creating a sustainable competitive advantage for the organisation.

■ The purpose of strategy is to enable an organisation to achieve its objectives in a well organised and co-ordinated way. This is based on an effective understanding of customer needs and the integration of the marketing strategy into the organisational strategy in order to achieve the desired objectives.

■ Organisational strategy is the process by which the vision or mission of an organisation is converted into an action plan. The purpose of the action plan is to ensure that everybody in an organisation understands the objectives of the organisation, their responsibilities in relation to them, the achievement of stretch and leverage, and how to put these factors into action in order to achieve the desired results.

■ The action plan will include the formation of a corporate portfolio of products and services taking into account competitive forces. The whole process will need to be reviewed and monitored at regular intervals and then adjusted as necessary.

Review and discussion questions

1 *What is likely to be the result for an organisation of not developing a strategy?*

2 *Is the management of change an inevitable aspect of strategic management?*

3 *What processes can be used in developing organisational strategy from mission statement to action plan?*

4 *How important is competition as a factor in developing an organisation's product/service portfolio?*

5 *How should an organisation carry out the monitoring and review of its organisational strategy?*

CASE STUDY

Dare to be different

If the theory of corporate strategy is a rising market, Michael Porter's stock has not quite kept pace. His reputation in the field, although immense, is based mainly on books published in the early 1980s. His best-known book, *The Competitive Advantage of Nations* (1990), is not primarily about corporations at all. But as professor of business administration at Harvard Business School, Porter is hardly out of touch. Nor, at 50, is he resting on his laurels. Much of his work lately has been on corporate strategy, and as he sees it, the discipline has taken some serious wrong turnings in the past decade. First, he says, the idea has grown up in some quarters that strategy is the same as operational efficiency. Companies need only employ modern techniques, such as total quality management or time-based competition, and the future will take care of itself. In reality, strategy and efficiency are fundamentally distinct. 'Operational improvement is doing the same thing better,' Porter says. Strategy, by contrast, involves choosing. 'Choice arises from doing things differently from the rival. And strategy is about trade-offs, where you decide to do this and not that.'

The essence of strategy, in fact, lies in deciding what not to do.

'That is the manifestation that you have a strategy. It also collides with many messages that managers have been assimilating for some time: be close to your customer, and be customer-responsive. Strategy is the deliberate choice not to respond to some customers, or choosing which customer needs you are going to respond to.'

At this point, Porter introduces the second part of his thesis. If strategy does not consist of operational improvement, neither does it consist of focusing on a few core competencies. Real sustainable advantage comes rather from the way the activities of a company fit together.

'Any individual thing that a company does can usually be imitated. The whole notion that you should rest your success on a few core competencies is an idea that invites destructive competition. Successful companies don't compete that way. They fit together the things they do in a way which is very hard to replicate. You have to match everything, or you've basically matched nothing.'

An example he gives is the car rental business.

'The companies your readers will be familiar with are Hertz and Avis, and National and Budget. Those will be seen as the "successful" companies because they have strong brand images, and people see them at the airport when they're travelling around. It turns out that none of those companies has been very profitable, ever. They are all locked into an operational effectiveness competition, offering the same kind of cars at the same kind of airports with the same kind of technology.'

Compare that with Enterprise, a family-run company. 'They do very little consumer advertising, and have no on-airport locations. Their whole strategy is to provide cars for people whose car is stuck in the repair shop, or who have wrecked their car and are waiting for a replacement.' Enterprise has a lot of smaller locations, and will often deliver the car to the customer. The cars are older and kept in the fleet longer. It hires more educated staff, who sell to car-service companies or insurance agents. 'They've chosen not just to try harder, like Avis, but to do almost everything differently. They've made clear trade-offs. They've walked away from the business travel market at airports, and from meeting a lot of needs that rental customers have,' says Porter.

For most companies, Porter argues, this kind of thinking presents immense problems. 'To put it simply, managers don't like to choose. There are tremendous organisational pressures towards imitation and matching what the competitor does. Over time, this slowly but surely undermines the uniqueness of the competitive position.' In part, he says, this comes from a curious notion which has grown up over the past decade: that there are no trade-offs any more. 'People have come to think that you can achieve low cost and the highest quality, or high service and the lowest cost. They confuse moving to the frontier with where you are on the frontier.' This is because when a company has been badly managed, it is often possible to improve quality and cost simultaneously. 'But once you get to good process designs, you have to make choices again. This notion that quality is free has caused many managers to believe not only that they don't have to make choices, but that they shouldn't.'

All this leads many companies to destroy their own strategies. 'They start out with a clear position, and over time they're drawn into a competitive convergence where they and their rivals are all basically doing the same thing. Those kind of competitions become stalemates.'

Porter used to believe, he says, that the hard thing about strategy was understanding the external environment.

'I've now become convinced an equally hard part is coping with the internal forces which work against making clear trade-offs and strategic choices. This has led me to a new interest in the role of leadership in strategy. Most often, it's to make the choices. Strategy can't be delegated. Nobody in the organisation will appreciate these trade-offs except the leader. Once a strategy has been established, most of what leaders do is essentially to say "no": to screen the constant barrage of ideas and opportunities against the strategy, and see if they fit.'

In some industries, he argues, the competitors are clones – companies so similar they cannot even conceive of a different way of competing. The task then is to decide whether the economics of the industry are such that there are no opportunities for trade-offs.

'That's usually the key question. What if I only did that; could I do it better? What if I chose this technology and not that, or this customer group and no others? If you can do terrifically well at X by giving up Y, that gives you the basis for a distinctive position. If there's basically only one dominant way of competing, then you're the hamster running around on the wheel. If you're in that kind of industry, you have to configure your organisation for that kind of world. You're just going to keep trying harder. I argue those industries are worth avoiding.'

Some would argue that in an era of global competition, all industries will come to look like that. Porter disagrees.

'I don't think we're moving towards a hyper-competitive world in which there are no trade-offs. We're probably moving in the other direction. There are more customer segments than ever before, more technological options, more distribution channels. That ought to create lots of opportunities for unique positions.'

Source: Financial Times, 19 June 1997. Reprinted with permission.

REFERENCES AND FURTHER READING

Argyris, Chris (2000) *Flawed Advice and the Management Trap*, Oxford: Oxford University Press.

Campbell, Andrew, Devine, Marion and Young, David (1990) *A Sense of Mission*, London: Hutchinson.

Daft, Richard L (1994) *Management*, Orlando, FL: Dryden Press.

Drucker, Peter (1961) *The Practice of Management*, London: Mercury Books.

Evans, Philip and Wursten, Thomas S (1997) 'Strategy and the New Economics of Information', *Harvard Business Review*, September/October.

Foster, Timothy R V (1993) *101 Great Mission Statements*, London: Kogan Page.

Goold, Michael, Campbell, Andrew and Alexander, Marcus (1994) *Corporate-Level Strategy: Creating Value in the Multibusiness Company*, New York: John Wiley.

Hamel, Gary (1996) 'Strategy as Revolution', *Harvard Business Review*, July/August.

Hamel, Gary (1997) 'Killer Strategies that Make Shareholders Rich', *Fortune*, 23 June.

Hamel, Gary and Prahalad, C K (1989) 'Do You Really Have a Global Strategy?', *Harvard Business Review*, July/August.

Hamel, Gary and Prahalad, C K (1993) 'Strategy as Stretch and Leverage', *Harvard Business Review*, March/April.

Hannagan, Tim (2001) *Mastering Strategic Management*, Basingstoke: Palgrave/Macmillan.

Harris, Ira C and Ruefli, Timothy (2000) 'The Strategy/Structure Debate: An Examination of the Performance Implications', *Journal of Management Studies*, June.

Joyce, Paul (1999) *Strategic Management for the Public Services*, Buckingham: Open University Press

Joyce, Paul (2000) *Strategy in the Public Sector*, New York: John Wiley.

Kelly, James (2000) 'Every Little Helps', *Long Range Planning*, 33.

Mintzberg, Henry (2000) *The Rise and Fall of Strategic Planning*, Harlow: FT Prentice Hall.

Mintzberg, H and Waters, JH (1985) 'Of Strategies Deliberate and Emergent', *Strategic Management Journal*, 6.

Ohmae, Kenichi (1996) *The Mind of the Strategist: The Art of Japanese Business*, New York: McGraw-Hill.

Orit, Gadiesh and Gilbert, James L (1998) 'Profit Pools: A Fresh Look at Strategy', *Harvard Business Review*, May/June.

Pearce, John A and Robinson, Richard B Jr (1989) *Management*, New York: McGraw-Hill.

Peterof M A (1993) 'The Cornerstone of Competitive Advantage: A Resource-based View', *Strategic Management Journal*, 14.

Peters, Tom (1992) *Liberation Management*, Basingstoke: Macmillan.

Porter, Michael E (1980) *Competitive Strategy: Techniques for Analyzing Industries and Competitors*, New York: Free Press.

Porter, Micheal E (1990) *The Competitive Advantage of Nations*, New York: Free Press.

Porter, Michael E (1996) 'What is Strategy?', *Harvard Business Review*, November/December

Porter, Michael E (1998) *Competitive Advantage: Creating and Sustaining Superior Performance*, New York: Free Press.

Prahalad C K and Hamel, Gary (1990) 'The Core Competence of the Corporation', *Harvard Business Review*, May/June.

Rappaport, Alfred (1997) *Creating Shareholder Value: A Guide for Managers and Investors*, New York: Free Press

Ringland, Gill (1998) *Scenario Planning: Managing for the Future*, New York: John Wiley.

Schwartz, Peter (1996) *The Art of Long View: Planning for the Future in an Uncertain World*, New York: Doubleday.

Segal-Hom, Susan (1998) *The Strategy Reader,* Buckingham: The Open University/Blackwell.

Stacey, Ralph D (1999) *Strategic Management and Organisational Dynamics* (3rd edn), Harlow: FT Prentice Hall.

Zimmerman, John, with Tregee, Benjamin (1997) *The Culture of Success: Building a Sustained Competitive Advantage by Living Your Corporate Beliefs*, Maidenhead: McGraw-Hill.

WEBSITES

http://www.tdindustries.com/
Provides information on organisational mission statements.

http://www.the–body–shop.com
Information about The Body Shop and its policies.

CHAPTER 6

Strategic development

TIM HANNAGAN

Outcomes

Having read this chapter, you will be able to:

- describe the actions managers take in order to implement business strategy

- analyse the processes of strategic planning to identify the functional role in achieving strategic objectives

- identify the barriers to planning and methods of overcoming these barriers

- explain the development of business plans and methods of forecasting future trends

- explain the importance of organisational development

FORMULATING A STRATEGIC PLAN

Modern managers are faced with a situation in which change is the only 'constant' on which they can 'rely'. One certainty in their lives is that things will not be the same in a year, three years or five years from now. The difficulty is to decide what these changes will be, and it can be argued that it is only by planning that the nature of the changes taking place can be fully charted and understood. In fact, managers take into account possible changes in deciding a course of action, in the form of contingency plans. This is part of the process of turning business strategy into detailed plans of action. While the strategy sets the expected, proposed and desired direction and the objectives to be achieved, this has to be translated into activity which can be implemented and controlled. Exhibit 6.1 illustrates the importance a company can put on the meeting of objectives, while behind this success lies detailed activity in meeting its 'tough objectives' to satisfy its 'customers, shareholders and employees'.

Strategy has to be operationalised into small action plans to be carried out by employees so that taken together these actions should achieve the objectives established by the business strategy. Much of this process is aimed at institutionalising the strategy so that it becomes part of the day-to-day work of the organisation; it has to become part of the culture of the organisation, 'the way we do things around here'. This process becomes overt and perhaps even obvious when an organisation is introducing major strategic change. For example, the British Airways customer service 'campaign' of the 1980s was designed to change the behaviour of its

Exhibit 6.1   TRW Inc of Cleveland, Ohio

Automotive, Aerospace, Information, Innovation

Tomorrow is here: We used to say 'Tomorrow is Taking Shape at a Company called TRW'. While TRW has been helping to shape our world, we have also been working hard to streamline and strengthen our company.

We have set a course that aims to delight our three key constituent groups – customers, shareholders and employees – by providing each with superior performance. The facts demonstrate we are doing just that.

Several years ago, we set ourselves some tough objectives. We are meeting these objectives. Today, we are number one in our key markets. We are the world leader in occupant restraints, in steering systems, in certain automotive electronics markets, in advanced spacecraft technology, in defense communications and in consumer credit information, among others. We are also the world leader in complex systems integration.

Our businesses are in segments of industries that are outgrowing the markets themselves, and we are managing that growth for profit. Cost structures have been improved dramatically, and we are beginning to experience the benefits of our strategic investments over the past five years.

Further technology leadership, always a core TRW strength, is now helping to make us more competitive in all our businesses. Management is also stronger. Supporting a seasoned group of top managers, we have a highly qualified, energetic and experienced team around the globe.

What are our priorities? Delivering on our commitments to customers, shareholders and employees. We are positioned for sustainable, significant increases in both sales and earnings. We are doing what we say we will do, and we will continue to deliver our promises.

Source: TRW Annual Report, 1994.

→ Ch. 5 employees, so that in all their operations they put the customer first (*see* Exhibit 5.7 in Chapter 5). This plan had the objective of creating major changes in behaviour. Many plans simply build on structures and accepted methods that already exist and are ingrained in the systems of the organisation.

Strategy, as applied to planning, is concerned with looking ahead.

> *'The maxim "managing means looking ahead" gives some idea of the importance attached to planning in the business world, and it is true that if foresight is not the whole of management at least it is an essential part of it.'* (Fayol, 1949)

Strategic management is certainly about decision making, and action based on plans, and it is clear that this process needs to be managed so that plans can be seen as a drawing together of a set of independent decisions.

> *'Planning, of course, is not a separate, recognisable act . . . every management act, mental or physical is inexorably intertwined with planning. It is as much a part of every managerial act as breathing is to the living human.'* (George, 1972)

→ Ch. 5 In this way, planning can be seen as integrated decision making, in the sense of bringing together a series of decisions so that they relate to each other and form a rational whole to establish the action to be taken (*see also* p 13 and Chapter 5).

One of the major changes in organisations in the 2000s has been the need for flexibility in the workforce, which means an ability to change as circumstances alter and not to expect that present working patterns will last for ever or even for very long. Technology has been a major factor in the pace of change and in the revolution in working methods and conditions for many people, and as a result of computerisation and information technology the working lives of many people have been completely altered. Managers often have difficulty in knowing how quickly these changes will take place and they may prove quicker or slower than expected. The demise of the manual and electric typewriter was predicted for many years until quite suddenly wordprocessors made a clean sweep in a matter of a year or two.

Where an organisation is on course in terms of its strategic plans, the manager's role may be to fine tune the situation by making relatively small decisions on a routine basis in response to problems that arise or in an attempt to improve a business unit's performance. Minor problems can be solved immediately by management intervention while ignoring the effect of the decisions being made on other parts of the organisation. In contrast to these small decisions and minor problems, serious problems may demand planned management interventions in more than one area of the organisation. Managers have to recognise the effect on the various parts of the organisation and arrange for appropriate actions to be taken to satisfy the various areas affected and to monitor progress on the strategic plan.

WHAT IS THE PURPOSE OF PLANNING?

The major argument in favour of planning is in the co-ordination of decision making so that an organisation is moving in a well-focused direction. Without planning the efforts of the organisation may not be well co-ordinated and managers and staff may be heading in different directions. Planning, whether this consists of an elaborate written document or a series of reports on agreed procedures, actions and understandings, also helps to ensure that the future is taken into account, so that the organisation can control the situation it finds itself in as far as possible and prepare for unexpected eventualities. Daily routines can lead to the future being forgotten if everybody is too busy to consider medium- or long-term problems. It can be argued also that planning is a rational form of management which enables organisations to acquire greater control over their future development.

In the past, scientific management, by emphasising the codification of routine tasks, encouraged the planning of operations. Mariann Jelinek (1979) argued that the equivalent of Taylor's work-study methods (*see* Chapter 20) in terms of strategy is a system of planning and control to establish a pattern which is not overwhelmed by operational details. Corporate strategy has:

→ Ch. 20

> *'made possible for the first time concerted co-ordination . . . and true policy for such organisations. So long as management is overwhelmed by the details of task performance, planning and policy will not occur . . . that is, until what is routine is systematised and performance replicable without extensive management attention, management attention will necessarily focus on the routine. By the time of Du Pont and General Motors, the specification of task had moved from codifying workers' routine activities to codifying managers' routine activities.'* (Jelinek, 1979)

The argument used here is that planning is seen as the key to the formulation of strategy. As organisations have become more complex, the need for plans and systems has grown. At its extreme this argument suggests that it is not people so much as systems that create the strategies, because systems are reliable and consistent while people are relatively unreliable.

> *'It is the responsibility of planning to make sure that the entire organisation knows very well what its customers' requirements are, what is the direction in which customer needs and customer expectations are changing, how technology is moving and how competitors serve their customers.'* (Marquanett, 1990)

This quotation by the head of planning for Bell & Howell states that responsibility is held by planning, rather than by planners. In his book on *The Rise and Fall of Strategic Planning* (2000), Henry Mintzberg seeks to demonstrate the fallaciousness of this approach. He argues that approaches based on formalisation, detachment and predetermination are not correct. The idea that a strategic plan can be translated into a system which accurately predicts the future is called into question. Forecasting is generally recognised as an uncertain science because all types of assumptions have to be made and a range of unpredictable forces may influence the outcomes. He quotes an earlier work in suggesting that:

> *'The pressure of the managerial environment does not encourage the development of reflective planners, the classical literature notwithstanding. The job breeds adaptive information-manipulators who prefer the live, concrete situation. The manager works in an environment of stimulus-response, and he develops in his work a clear preference for live action.'* (Mintzberg, 1973)

It is also the case that the less 'closed' the system, the more difficult accurate forecasting becomes. The Soviet Union attempted to create a closed and planned system under communism. This was of very limited success. Most managers work in much more 'open' systems where they are faced with the uncertainties of economic, social, political, technological and other change. Mintzberg concludes that too much planning may lead to chaos, but too little planning may also lead to chaos and more directly:

'Several decades of experience with strategic planning has taught us about the need to loosen up the process of strategy formation rather than try to seal it off through arbitrary formalisation.'
(Mintzberg, 2000)

It is, of course, an unwise organisation that insists on keeping to its strategic plans in spite of changing circumstances. It can be argued that insistence on maintaining what had previously been a successful plan was the major cause of the collapse of the British motorcycle industry in the face of Japanese competition. This does not invalidate the whole planning process, but does illustrate its dangers. Planning may have benefits even where plans have to be changed from time to time, and these changes themselves may be able to be made against a background of relative 'planned' stability.

It is possible to identify behavioural benefits in organisations where strategic planning is encouraged:

- managers are in a position to detect problems and how best to resolve them;
- alternative strategies can be considered in making decisions;
- employees gain a better understanding of their organisation's strategies and may become more committed to them;
- strategic planning can help clarify everyone's responsibilities;
- lower uncertainty about the future consequences of decisions can reduce resistance to change.

However, the dangers of a rigid adherence to planning need to be recognised. The plan may become inappropriate as factors such as competition and technology change, and a well-established plan may become so well accepted that it creates opposition to change.

THE PLANNING PROCESS

Operational managers have to develop plans of one kind or another at the appropriate level in order to produce the actions required on a day-to-day basis to implement organisational strategy and the strategic plan, assuming this accurately reflects it. Each functional area of the organisation will need a plan, whether it is a written document or an agreed set of procedures and actions, to guide its decisions and actions. If the strategic plan has the objective of growth in a particular market, then the sales and marketing division will have to decide how they are going to penetrate that market or expand in it if they are already present. This may involve market research into customer needs, pilot promotions to test customer response, and establishing outlets and channels of distribution. At the same time, the production or service department will have to ensure that the product or service is adapted for the market and that suppliers will be available for the expected customer demand. The finance department will have to make sure that money is available to support an increase in output and increases in the marketing and sales expenditure. The personnel department will be involved in the appropriate recruitment of staff and the relocation of employees as necessary.

All the functional departmental plans have to be drawn together so that they operate smoothly in supporting each other. If the finance is not available at the right time or if the production department cannot meet sales orders, then all the functional plans and the overall strategic plan will have to be reviewed to avoid chaos. In large organisations the importance of this co-ordination is taken to the point of establishing a separate corporate planning unit whose role is to make sure that all the various plans do fit together and support each other both in operation and in time. Where there is not such a unit, corporate planning will usually be the responsibility of a senior manager.

It is in the operation of these functional plans that marketing has its integrating function in matching customer requirements to the product or service. The marketing department will be close to the point of sale and customer service on the one hand, and on the other hand close to the design and production department. In Exhibit 6.2 the strategic plan is translated into functional plans for marketing, sales, production, personnel and finance.

Other functional departments and divisions, such as sites and buildings, transport, purchasing and supplies, and administration will all need to have action plans which relate to the strategic plan and to the other functional plans. The sites and buildings department, for example, will need to discuss capital expenditure on new outlets for the company's products with the finance department. The finance department will be considering the financial control systems required by the new developments over purchasing and supplies, and any expansion in transport and distribution requirements.

Functional plans are usually developed to last for a relatively short period and they are then updated and possibly changed dramatically. However, they are designed over time. They can be distinguished in this way from project plans which are characterised by being designed for a one-off occasion which will not be

Exhibit 6.2 Functional plans

STRATEGIC PLAN: growth in a new regional market

FUNCTIONAL PLANS:

Marketing	■ research into customer needs ■ establishing possible outlets ■ establishing channels of distribution ■ carrying out pilot studies
Sales	■ establishing contacts ■ preliminary advertising and sales promotion
Production	■ redesigning products as appropriate ■ organising expansion of production ■ arranging for increased supply of new materials ■ co-ordinating transport and distribution requirements
Personnel	■ recruiting new salespeople and administrators ■ relocating employees to the new regional staff
Finance	■ considering capital outlay ■ supporting investment in design and production ■ establishing cashflow plans ■ paying wages for staff in new region

repeated. This type of plan can be divided into programme plans and project plans, on the grounds that the programme plans are of greater complexity; however, it is often difficult to distinguish between these two types of activity. Whenever there is the need to plan for a one-off activity, whether it is to do with, say, health and safety training or building a new office block, it can be described as a project plan.

Project plans can be distinguished from functional plans in that they are established for a particular timeframe and they include more detail than is usually found in a functional plan. Once the plan has been implemented and the project is completed, the plans will be of little further use. Typical project plans are to build a new office block, design a one-off advertising campaign, or develop an employee sickness policy. Once the block is completed, the advertising campaign has taken place or the sickness policy has been established, these plans have achieved their objective and they are of little further direct use.

A plan to build a new office block will often be produced by a project team consisting of people seconded temporarily and on a part-time basis from the various functional departments. There will be representatives from sites and buildings, finance, personnel and administration. They will produce draft plans to be considered by senior management and from these they will produce a brief for the architects and surveyors to translate into the detail of drawings and specifications. They will produce a schedule of activities to be completed by certain dates and a flowchart to show the sequence of events that should lead to the completion of the project. All of this has to be set within the context of the capital funds available and also within the context of the company's strategic views on the appearance of the office and the way it should function (Figure 6.1). The retail company, Tesco for example, builds its stores to an established design both externally and internally, so that the project plans for the building of a new store have to include these designs whatever the shape or location of the site.

Managers will also produce policies and procedures which establish the boundary lines for making recurring decisions. These policies provide a framework for action, a reference point for employees in their actions. Design policy in an organisation may influence plans, while plans concerned with factors such as employee training may become policies to be applied in all cases. For example, it may become company policy for all staff to receive training in customer care. Policies are created in order to meet the objectives of the organisation and should, with other plans, help in the implementation of the strategic plan and company strategy.

Figure 6.1 Project plans: simple scheduling and flowcharts

BARRIERS TO STRATEGY

Strategy can be obstructed both by individuals establishing barriers to its success and as a result of the structure of the organisation.

There may be individual barriers because managers are more concerned with problem solving than long-term strategy, and their focus is on day-to-day matters. This is more likely to be the case the closer managers are to the operations of an organisation, because their daily tasks involve an action-oriented approach, moving from one problem to the next. From their point of view, strategic planning may be seen as an unnecessary luxury taking up valuable time which could be used to solve more problems and make more decisions. Individuals may also view strategy as a threat in that it may 'put ideas into people's heads' by encouraging them to think ahead. Managers may feel that the process of developing stratagey raises the prospect of changing established methods and may raise more worries and concerns than it allays.

Strategic planning also requires a commitment to specific objectives and results, which may be commitments managers are reluctant to make. This may be magnified by a lack of understanding about the purpose and process of planning by managers who have been promoted from the operational level without training in planning.

Organisational barriers may arise when there is little top-management support for strategy, or where there is support for strategic planning at senior management level but little support for this process being carried down to middle managers and the operational level. Even if there is support, the strategy and strategic plan may be too abstract or too statistical to be translated into operational terms. There is a danger that too much emphasis on planning will lead to very well produced plans, expertly drafted but not in fact leading to implementation, so that operational activities ignore the plan and are based on the requirements of solving problems. Strategy needs to involve everybody concerned in both the process and in agreeing the objectives and the approach to implementation. Top-management support is essential if middle management and operational teams are to allocate time and effort to strategy and its implementation.

Environmental barriers may become important when complex and rapidly changing circumstances surrounding an organisation discourage strategic planning, because any plans will have to be hedged around with contingencies. Strategy is produced provided that the economy remains stable, exchange rates do not change to any extent, supplies of new materials can be guaranteed, government policy does not drastically alter, and so on. Managers may feel that these factors, combined with increasing competition from rivals, make strategic planning a useless activity and that they should concentrate on counteracting the threats and challenges the organisation faces. This is a 'passive' approach, or at best 'reactive' approach, to the work of any organisation, allowing other rival organisations and events to dictate its activity. Against this approach, strategic planning can be seen as a 'positive' and 'active' setting of unique objectives and directions for the organisation to follow and to be defended as far as possible from outside interference.

This is not to ignore the importance of external forces on an organisation. There is a danger of 'overplanning', that is spending too long on the strategic planning process and sticking to strategies and plans that are no longer either viable or wise. Organisations at all levels require a sense of purpose and require strategies in order to keep up the momentum of moving in that direction, but they do not keep moving in a direction that proves to be a dead end (Exhibit 6.3).

Exhibit 6.3 **Effects of strategic planning**

Strategic plans can:

- promote the uniform handling of similar issues;

- establish control over independent action by establishing clear policies;

- ensure quicker decisions by establishing a framework for decision making;

- offer a predetermined answer to routine problems;

- counteract further resistance to change once the plan has been agreed;

- avoid the making of hasty and ill-conceived decisions;

- establish a time horizon for monitoring progress on developments;

- establish long-term, medium-term and short-term patterns of activity.

Overcoming barriers to strategy

Strategic planning is part of every manager's role. Before managers can lead, organise or control a work situation, they must decide what needs to be done, when and how it needs to be done, and who will do it. Overcoming barriers to this type of planning is an important part of this process.

Top-management support is crucial to the success of strategic planning. Senior managers must not only support strategy but must be involved in it and be seen to be involved. Only then will middle managers and operational teams treat strategic planning as a priority by allocating time to it.

The need for strategic planning exists at all levels in an organisation, and this need is greatest at the top where it has the greatest potential impact on the organisation's success. Senior managers usually devote a majority of their time to strategy and their skill in doing this and in making sure strategies are implemented is how they earn their salaries. Even a small organisation needs to have a senior manager who plans and has a strategy, otherwise although day-to-day problems may be solved effectively events will catch up on the organisation for which it is not prepared.

Many barriers to strategic planning can be overcome by senior manager support and any organisation which does not have this support is facing great difficulty. The solution to this is through management training, as managers are promoted through the organisation, in order to provide time to consider the role and guidance on it.

Allocation of responsibility is an essential element of the planning process. Someone has to be responsible for the successful completion of the strategic plan, otherwise it will not be anybody's top priority to achieve it. The chief executive of an organisation will be responsible for the success of the strategic plan and the success or failure of the organisation, while other managers, at the appropriate level, need to be identified as responsible for specific plans designed to meet the overall objectives. Reporting and appraisal systems, management by objectives and other organisation and control systems are all designed to support this process.

Consultation and communication procedures in this area help to reduce barriers to planning by involving a wide range of people in the process. If managers and other employees have been consulted in the development of strategic plans, they will feel some responsibility for their success and 'ownership' of their implementation. At the least people in an organisation need to be able to obtain and understand information relevant to planning and any plan with which they are concerned.

Training in planning skills and the implementation of the details of strategic plans encourage people to plan and use plans effectively. Individual barriers can be lowered by this process, particularly those associated with a lack of confidence in strategy and planning, fear of failure, and unwillingness to relinquish established systems.

Self-managed teams as a form of organisational structure can encourage planning at the operational level. Managers and teams can feel committed to plans they have produced themselves or have helped to shape. Teams will often be able to contribute to wider plans so that a two-way process can be developed, with strategic plans coming downwards and more detailed plans for implementation arising from the expertise and information of the self-managed teams. Their proximity to the organisation's customers and clients means that they are a valuable source of information in the development of a strategic plan, in monitoring it and in making adjustments to it.

Reward and encouragement for individuals and teams can be attached to the outcome of plans. This may be by a system of managing by objectives or by a performance-related pay structure where individual and team rewards are linked to the accomplishment of objectives established in the strategic planning process. These systems will increase the attention paid to planning and the commitment to it. Many reward systems have been organised more or less formally in this way, with a bonus, productivity pay or performance-related pay system attached to meeting planned objectives (*see* Chapters 9 and 12).

➜ Chs 9 and 12

Contingency strategy consists of preparing an alternative course of action in case the preferred course either becomes impossible or no longer desirable. Contingency planning has become of increased importance as change and innovation have become a usual part of many organisations' environment. These plans provide a 'safety-valve' for individuals or groups of people who have doubts about the ability of plans to 'work'. They may be more prepared to try the plan when they see that there are alternative planned courses of action available.

The so-called 'worst-case' scenario is an extreme example of this process and can be based on taking 'what ifs' to their logical conclusion. For example, posing the question 'What if competitors reduce their prices significantly?' may lead to careful consideration of how costs could be contained, how long the organisation could sustain a price war, the importance of producing a quality product so that the price war could be ignored, and other possible courses of action. This approach can help to emphasise the importance of producing plans which are realistic and which clearly help to provide a competitive edge.

BUSINESS PLANS

As well as strategic planning being 'a good idea' essential for the development of an organisation and for judging its progress, it is also a necessity in many circumstances, essential in order that an organisation can obtain financial support. In this more narrow sense, 'business plans' have developed over many years as a major component of investment decisions. A company seeking a loan or investment will be required by potential customers to produce a business plan in support of its application. This will be used to convince outsiders that managers have carefully thought out the direction the business will follow in the future, that given their present resources, and the proposed new investment, the company will be able to achieve its plans. Business plans may also be required in large organisations before a business unit can convince the 'parent' organisation to invest in it.

Many small organisations will have little more than a business plan with which to convince the bank manager that the banks should lend them enough money to start up or expand their business. The plan has to enable the bank manager or other investor to assess the degree of risk and the quality of the people involved. This plan can convert a 'bright idea' into a well-structured plan of action. A business plan can be seen simply as a more focused form of corporate plan:

'A Business Plan is a written statement setting out how the organisation making it intends to organise itself to satisfy the demands of its clients and thereby develop its business.'

(Chartered Institute of Public Finance and Accountancy, 1992)

As well as a mission or vision, a statement of objectives and a clear view of strengths and weaknesses, opportunities and threats, a business plan must convince prospective investors that the planners have considered exactly who their customers are and what finance and resources are required in order to implement the plan. Customer needs can be ascertained by interviews and surveys which can determine the type of product or service they want and their views on the products or services available. This involves the production of qualitative information on customer views, expectations and perceptions, as much as quantitative information on how many customers buy a product or use a service. In terms of financial and resource planning, there will need to be an attempt to forecast the future budget and trading position and an analysis of the effects of inflation, taxation and other factors. This includes a risk analysis to consider how 'risky' the assumptions are that have been made in the plan, and a sensitivity analysis assessing how sensitive the plan is to change. This process involves the 'what if' approach – what if the assumptions prove wrong, or the environment changes – and will also need to assess how great will be the impact of the 'what if' factors on the plan.

A new business may assume a growth in sales of 20 per cent a year, based on their customer surveys, pilot sales schemes and the general growth of the market. What happens if the sales grow by only 10 per cent a year? Can the company survive on this or not? Similar questions can be asked about assumptions made on labour costs, raw material prices, changes in taxation, market growth rate, competitor activities and so on. While the usual barriers to planning exist with business plans, the fact that they are necessary in order to receive financial support removes the most obvious obstacles in terms of the purpose of planning. In large organisations there will be a number of planning levels (Figure 6.2), with each unit, cost centre or self-managed team producing its own business plan, both to convince senior managers of their viability and also to help inform functional and corporate planning. In small organisations, the business plan may serve similar functions to the corporate and strategic plans of a large organisation.

Figure 6.2 **Planning levels in large organisations**

STRATEGIC PLANNING TECHNIQUES

Forecasting is involved in all plans because, like strategy formulation, there will be an attempt to predict what will happen in the future. The fact that forecasts are sometimes proved wrong does not mean that they are useless. Perhaps the most obvious and notorious use of forecasting is weather forecasting. In the UK people may plan to have a barbecue at the weekend because dry, warm weather is forecast, but they will have as a contingency plan the possibility of moving the barbecue inside if necessary. If it does rain on the night, this does not prove the uselessness of listening to weather forecasts, simply that not too much reliance should be put on them in a country with a volatile weather system. If the forecast had been for continuous heavy rain, it would have been unwise to plan for a barbecue in the first place.

In fact, most daily actions are based on some type of forecast which needs to be sufficiently accurate, sufficiently often to guide present actions in a valid and purposeful way. While not too much reliance is placed on weather forecasts in the UK, in countries with a more stable weather structure considerable reliance can be placed on forecasts. In fact, the most important use of forecasts is in order to arrive at the basic assumptions or premises on which the plan is based. The reliance that can be placed on any particular forecast is a matter of managerial judgement, and this is an area where a manager's experience can play an important part in business success. Forecasting is used, for example, in estimating market trends and then making business decisions based on them. A simple example is that if industrial and consumer surveys show that the market will grow in the next year, how does the organisation take advantage of this?

Forecasting is often based on **quantitative** data, for example that the market for packaged holidays will be 10 million holidaymakers next year. A common development of such data is to look at growth trends by taking past data and extrapolating it into the future. Not only can the general growth of packaged holidays be charted in this way, but also the growth or decline in the popularity of particular holiday destinations and the relative changes in different types of market, such as the family market and the singles market.

The extrapolating of past data is always open to variation and change as a result of altered circumstances and events. Where established data is not available or is unreliable, **qualitative** forecasting may be appropriate. This involves surveys, questionnaires and interviews asking for people's opinions and making judgements on the basis of the available information. Rating scales of various types can be used, for example asking consumers to note their views on a service on a scale between one and ten. Qualitative techniques are often used with new products because sales figures are unavailable and therefore potential consumers' opinions are particularly relevant. For example, once there are sales figures about the most popular colours for a product, marketing can be based on them, but with a new product a consumer survey can be used asking potential customers to note colours in order of preference. Other qualitative forecasting techniques include the so-called Delphi technique, where panels of experts are asked their opinions on a new product and the average of these groups of opinions are then used as a base for arriving at a judgement of the future of the product. Salesforce estimates are used by some organisations to predict the likely sales in each sales area and then to aggregate these for overall product forecasts. These and similar techniques all have the disadvantage of relying on subjective views, but they are usually very much better than not doing anything.

Quantitative techniques are statistical techniques which are usually considered to provide more reliable information on future trends than can be arrived at by subjective methods. Many statistics are already available to most organisations in terms of sales, turnover, marketing expenditure and so on. These can be analysed to produce ratios and trends which are very useful for planning.

Time-series analysis involves charting a variable, such as sales, over a period. The assumption is that the analysis of the past is a good predictor of the future. For example, if sales figures have risen over a series of months, then it may be assumed that this growth will continue. Trends such as seasonal variation in sales and the rate of growth can be analysed in order to plan production and marketing as well as cash flow for the company (Figure 6.3).

Figure 6.3 Moving average

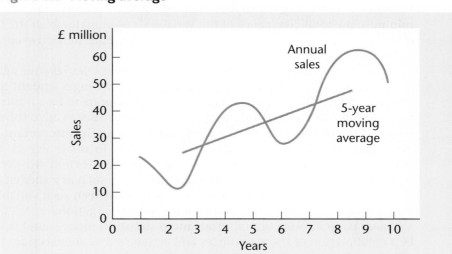

Figure 6.3 shows a five-year moving average of sales against the annual sales figure. The moving average shows a trend of rising sales over a 10-year period with regular fluctuations between the troughs and peaks of sales occurring approximately every three years. At the end of the 10-year period sales are beginning to fall again, and past trends would suggest that they will fall for a year or so before beginning to rise again. Past trends also suggest that the troughs will not be as deep as in years 2 and 6. In this extrapolation of the information, managers have to be very careful that they allow for the possibility that past trends will not be a good guide to the future, and do not become complacent in expecting these trends to occur in spite of any action they might take. In practice, managers need to try to prevent the downturn in years 9 and 10 and start to plan for this during the years of growth. For example, it may be possible to develop new products or to penetrate new markets in order to prevent what may appear to be an 'inevitable' fall in sales. A less optimistic strategy would be to prepare for the 'inevitable', by, for example, cutting costs so that the organisation could weather the period of relatively low sales and wait for the next period of growth.

Correlation and regression modelling may be used to consider the effects of different variables on each other. For example, organisations want to know the results of a marketing campaign on sales. **Regression analysis** is designed to estimate one variable (such as the sales volume) on the basis of one or more other variables (such as marketing expenditure) which are assumed to have some causal link with it. Correlation analysis compares two variables which are assumed to have an association with each other, so that a change in one will affect a change in the other. For example, an increase in advertising may be assumed to increase sales. While correlation shows whether there is an association between the two variables, the strength of this association and its direction, regression indicates the rate of change in one variable against the other. Between them it is possible to estimate, for example, whether increases in expenditure on advertising increase or decrease sales (i.e. the direction of association), as well as an indication of the amount of change in sales caused by a particular increase in advertising expenditure.

Linear trends can be shown by a straight line if there is in fact a linear relationship between the variables. A 'line of best fit' can be calculated, which is the line closest to the two variables. A simple method for producing this is illustrated in Figure 6.4, while more complex methods include regression lines which aim to minimise the total divergence of the variables' co-ordinates from the line. This is an objective mathematical approach rather than the more subjective approach used in the scatter diagram in Figure 6.4.

The scatter diagram is a simple matter of plotting sales revenue against advertising expenditure over a period of time and then drawing a straight line as close to the co-ordinates as possible. In Figure 6.4 there appears to be a positive correlation between sales and advertising, so that sales revenue rises as advertising expenditure rises and the relationship can be described as 'linear'. It is important to note, however, that correlation does not prove causality. In other words, the increased advertising expenditure may not have caused rising sales and vice versa. There may be a third ingredient which was of equal influence, such as a sudden growth in the market. The fact that there is a linear association between such variables does, however, provide a useful starting point for further investigation.

Linear programming is a more advanced statistical process used to determine the best combination of those resources and activities that are necessary to optimise an objective. For example, if the objective is to reduce costs, then the constraints in

Figure 6.4 Line of best fit

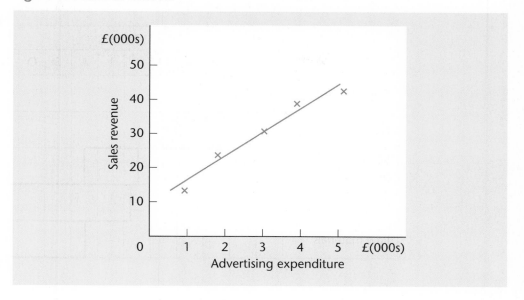

doing this have to be identified. These may be resources, capacity or the time available to accomplish the objective. Both the costs and the items that represent constraints then need to be expressed in linear terms either algebraically or in a graphical form, in order to provide a means for the manager to reach a 'solution'. The manager in this case will usually be the operations manager (*see* Chapter 14).

→ Ch. 14

Scheduling techniques are designed to assist in the process of co-ordinating the activities of people and business units and the use of resources in order to achieve the completion of a specific task. For example, in the introduction of a new product the marketing manager needs to know exactly what customers want and the production manager needs to translate these demands into a design or a product. A schedule of a logical sequence of actions, and the co-ordination of people and resources are required to start the production of a successful product. A range of computer models are available as techniques to assist in the successful flow of activity to reach the desired aim. Operations management has developed into an important part of any large organisation's functions.

The basis of scheduling techniques is the ability to plan activities to achieve a desired end and to reveal discrepancies between planned and actual achievement as the project progresses. If a gap appears between planned progress and actual achievement, managers can provide extra people and resources to fill this gap. For example, Gantt charts have been used for many years as a means of control, with time charted on the horizontal axis and actions and tasks on the vertical axis (see Figure 6.5). Horizontal bars represent planned schedules and the time required for each task. In Figure 6.5 the filled bars show the actual progress against the outline bar which shows the time allotted (while the customer survey and design have been completed, production staff have only just begun to be employed). The use of colour coding can add to the complexity and the visual impact of such charts.

PERT (program evaluation review technique) is a long-standing technique which helps managers schedule large-scale projects. It enables managers to create an accurate estimate of the time required to complete a project. All the activities necessary

Figure 6.5 Gantt chart

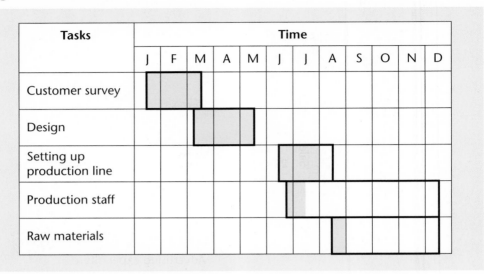

Tasks	Time											
	J	F	M	A	M	J	J	A	S	O	N	D
Customer survey												
Design												
Setting up production line												
Production staff												
Raw materials												

for completion are identified, with the events that indicate completion and the time required for each activity. This information is used to create a network diagram, which displays all the activities, events and times that are involved from the start to the end of the project. The PERT diagram is then used as a control and monitoring device. For example, in the building of a new office block, managers need to identify all the actions necessary to complete the project and construct a diagram to show the relationship between the different activities and events. A time is allocated for the completion of each activity and the sequence of activities is then tracked through to the completion of the project. Critical path analysis (CPA) is then applied to track the sequence of events which have to occur in a particular order, within a given time for the completion of the project on the due date. In the case of a new office block, the concept and design will be the first stage, along with the identification of finance and planning provision. Only when these factors have been identified and agreed can the building process actually start (*see* Figure 6.6).

The critical path represents the least amount of time that a project can take from start to finish. This will be determined by such matters as the length of time required to obtain planning consent, the time required to lay foundations and so

Figure 6.6 PERT

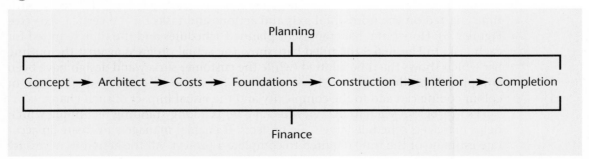

on. If an event on the critical path is delayed, this will hold up the entire project. Both PERT and CPA are designed to save time and therefore save costs. They are based on actual time constraints as well as judgements about how long it takes to lay the foundations for a new office block, for example. They form the basis of a range of computer modelling techniques designed to assist managers in the planning process.

ORGANISATIONAL DEVELOPMENT

→ Chs 1, 2 and 8

Managing an organisation's strategy is easier when it is consistent with the organisation's culture, that is the shared values, beliefs and attitudes that shape the behaviour of each member of the organisation (*see* Chapters 1, 2 and 8). The priorities and attitudes of the strategy and culture need to coincide, and if this is not the case it becomes very difficult to implement the strategic plan. For example, where public sector organisations have been privatised, one of the main problems they have met is the market culture with which they are faced and the service culture to which the employees and consumers are accustomed. In these circumstances, managers have to seek to change the organisation's culture. This is a slow process because it does involve attitudes and 'how we do things around here'. British Airways did this

→ Ch. 5

in the 1980s with their 'Putting People First' programme (*see* Chapter 5).

Both the move to privatise UK public sector organisations and the effects of recession in the 1980s and 1990s have led to considerable discontinuities between strategy and culture in many areas. The old, cautious, traditional culture, based on 'jobs for life' and an established approach to clients and customers, has had to be replaced by a more aggressive competitive culture that promotes risk taking. Examples include British Airways, gas and electricity companies and hospital trusts in the public sector, and companies such as IBM in the private sector. In the 1990s IBM had to change their culture of a 'job for life' based on a strong organisational cultural identity, to a less certain job situation for employees and a more aggressive approach to meet competition.

In order to bring organisational strategy and culture closer together, managers responsible for the change process will have to concentrate on people and their attitudes, perceptions, behaviour and expectations. Organisational development (OD) is the skilled application of behavioural science to bringing about organisational change through people. It is a planned change, usually of the whole organisation, supported by senior managers. In large organisations it is an ongoing process which may be implemented through an OD manager and an OD department designed to improve internal relationships and to improve problem solving and with the ability to deal with environmental changes.

Organisational development can help managers to address a range of organisational problems. The most obvious of these are when two companies merge or one company is the subject of a takeover by another. In the process of merging the two companies, managers may concentrate on how well the products will fit together, or the marketing and management information systems, but fail to consider how closely they fit in terms of values, beliefs and practices. They may have quite different ways of 'doing things around here' which can greatly affect performance if it creates internal tensions. At the time of mergers and acquisitions managers may focus on finance rather than cultural differences, while in order to be sure of a smooth transition and integration, organisational development techniques need to be applied.

Another obvious source of potential behavioural problems in organisations is during a period of recession and decline. If the performance of the organisation leads to redundancies and reorganisation, tensions can develop which produce a lack of trust and also stress. The same may be true during a period of rapid change when people are asked to work in different ways or to increase their productivity. Although the strategy may be clear, its implementation may be held up by conflicts created by the speed of change. In fact conflicts may be a managerial problem at any time within a successful organisation. For example, there may be a conflict between the product designers and the marketing team, both perhaps believing that they know what the customer wants.

There are a range of activities which can be used in organisational development to help to solve the problem:

- **Training** is the most frequently used technique to bring about change. In the British Airways case, the whole organisation was involved because this was an attempt to change behaviour and not simply skills.
- **Team building** can enhance the cohesiveness of both units and the whole organisation. For example, cross-organisational teams can help employees from different departments and units to understand each other's problems and to co-operate with each other.
- **Communication** can be improved between various parts of the organisation and regarding strategic plans and their implementation. Understanding the reasons for changes in working practices and values can help employees come to terms with the changes. Consultation about the changes and their implementation can help both managers and other employees to understand and acquire ownership of the changes, particularly when they are as deep rooted as values and practices.
- **Survey-Feedback-Action (SFA)** techniques can be applied in order to encourage consultation and feedback. A questionnaire can be distributed to employees on such matters as working practices, values and organisation culture. After the survey is completed, an OD consultant can meet with groups of employees to provide feedback about their responses and the problems that have been identified, and to discuss the way forward. For example, British Airways used the slogan 'The World's Favourite Airline' to show the standards to which they aspired.

→ Ch. 1 The process of achieving behavioural and attitudinal change involves unfreezing the situation, changing it and then refreezing it into the new mould (*see* Chapter 1). The unfreezing process requires a high level of communication and consultation in order to convince people that the changes are necessary. The immediate reaction of many people will be: How does this affect me? The so-called SARAH process will come into effect, with shock at the changes being proposed and anger at the apparent rejection of the present, well-tried and apparently successful working practices (Exhibit 6.4).

Why do we need to change? What is wrong with the present system? Why are THEY proposing these changes? These are the kind of questions produced by shock and anger. This period of change is often associated with a diagnosis of the present situation and why a new one needs to be developed. A 'change agent' can be involved at this stage, which may be an OD specialist who performs a systematic diagnosis of the organisation and identifies work-related problems. The role of the specialist is to gather and analyse information through personal interviews, questionnaires and by observing meetings. The diagnosis helps to determine the extent of organisational problems and helps managers to unfreeze by making them aware of problems in their behaviour. The 'change agent' may be an outsider who comes in as a consultant, or the OD unit within an organisation can perform this task.

Exhibit 6.4 The change process

- **Shock**
- **Anger**
- **Rejection**
- **Acceptance**
- **Help**

As an ongoing process the survey–feedback–action technique can be used for 'upward feedback' by which managers assess the senior manager to whom they report. The managers complete a questionnaire and the overall results are then discussed by the OD specialist with the senior manager. A meeting is chaired by the OD specialist with the senior manager and the reporting managers in order for them to express their views about their boss. This process can produce surprises for senior managers about how they are viewed by the people who work directly for them. This process of 'reverse appraisal' can be applied throughout the organisation, starting at the top and working down to self-managed teams. In today's fast-changing work environment, managers need to update their diagnosis of the situation on a continual basis, rather than only when 'major change' is taking place. It does, of course, have particular importance at sensitive times, such as when mergers, contraction or, for that matter, rapid expansion is taking place.

The changing stage occurs when people begin to experiment with new behaviour and learn new skills in the workforce. This process is assisted by the intervention of OD specialists and others, with specific plans for training and development of managers and employees. Training programmes will emphasise the new values and approaches, such as customer-first programmes, quality developments and 'investors in people'. Team building is encouraged, consultation on work practices and symbolic leadership activities introduced. The rejection of change may be particularly vehement at the beginning of this stage, followed later by acceptance. Gradually, the people who have most strongly rejected the changes may be the ones who most wholeheartedly come to accept them.

The refreezing stage occurs when individuals acquire new attitudes, values and behaviours and are rewarded for them by the organisation. The OD specialist will provide help for everybody to change and an increasing number of people will look for help to adjust to the new values and approaches. The impact of new behaviours will be evaluated and reinforced. The reinforcement will be through training programmes, team meetings and the reward system.

The organisational development process suggests techniques which managers should apply continuously in organisations so that change is the accepted 'norm' rather than an occasional and rare phenomenon. In this sense, the use of terms such as unfreezing and refreezing suggests an end to the process before it starts again. In the altering of attitudes and behaviours it can be argued that in fact this is what often happens. While strategic change can be incremental, a step at a time, it is not always like this. The theory is that managers sense the changes required in the environment in which their organisations are working and gradually adapt to these changes through adjustment to the strategic plan and its implementation.

However, studies in the 1980s have suggested that managers resist change until a crisis occurs:

> *'Here managers resist changes that conflict with their predominant way of understanding their organisation and its environment, until some crisis makes it impossible to continue to do so.'*　　　　　　　　　　　　　　　　　　　(Stacey, 1999)

This leads to **strategic drift** (Figure 6.7), because the organisation is carried forward by its own momentum, becoming more and more out of line with its environment. When this gap becomes too great, the organisation makes sudden adjustments.

Greiner (1972) has argued that strategic drift is virtually endemic in organisations in that they pass through a number of stages in order to sustain acceptable levels of performance. At each level they have to introduce major changes to the 'way they do things':

- **Growth through creativity** – the organisation grows through the creativity of a small group of people who manage in a highly personal style.
- **Growth through direction** – the organisation reaches a stage where it has to develop professional, functional management. This is often centrally directed and can develop into a restrictive hierarchy.
- **Growth through delegation** – **delegation** and decentralisation help to resolve the crisis of a rigid hierarchy, but may create divisions within the organisation.
- **Growth through co-ordination** – systems may be introduced to encourage co-ordination and co-operation, but this may produce a crisis of bureaucracy.
- **Growth through collaboration** – cultural change produces collaboration which is supported by teamwork.

Figure 6.7 Strategic drift

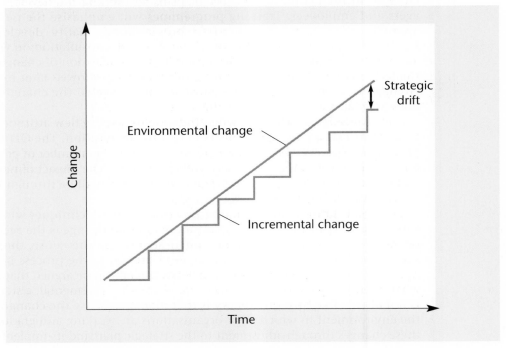

Organisations may, of course, become stuck at one of these stages and not change their plans to grow further. The inability to change may stunt growth, and the processes of corporate planning and organisational development are essential to assist this process through encouraging consultation, communication, training and the constant re-evaluation of strategic planning.

ORGANISATIONAL OBJECTIVES

Central to the implementation of the strategic plan is the setting of annual objectives. They are important because they establish precisely what must be accomplished each year in order to achieve an organisation's plan. In the process they establish the targets and objectives for managers, units and teams throughout the organisation. The annual objectives help to clarify managers' tasks and their role in the process of achieving the strategy and plans, and they can provide a sense of purpose and motivation. They also provide a means of monitoring performance, and to do this they should be measurable.

The development of annual objectives can reflect shifts in the strategic plan and can provide for incremental growth. If an organisation is skilled in corporate planning and organisational development, it can perhaps avoid a 'crisis' change with dramatic alterations in direction or values. However, if external factors outside the control of the organisation alter dramatically, then it is difficult to avoid quite fundamental shifts in the corporate plan. The annual objectives can reflect this shift of position.

For example, government policy on the funding and governance of public sector institutions during the 1980s and 1990s has caused major changes in these institutions' ways of doing things and approach to the future. UK government policy encouraged the rapid expansion of higher education in the early years of the 1990s and then suddenly cut back on this expansion in 1994. In the same way, further education was encouraged to expand by 25 per cent in the period 1993–96 through the funding mechanism. Furthermore, the recession of the late 1980s and early 1990s caused private sector companies to re-evaluate their structures and organisation. Outsourcing of many services became common and there was a major shift to a group of core workers responsible for the core business of the company.

In order to implement annual objectives, managers have to develop a process to carry them through business units and to individuals. Management by objectives (MBO) was first proposed by Peter Drucker in *The Practice of Management* in 1955, and was very popular as a method of implementing strategic objectives in the 1960s and 1970s. Although it has fallen out of fashion as a system, many present-day methods are very similar to MBO in their approach and results.

MBO describes a set of procedures that begins with objective setting and continues through performance review. Each person's major areas of responsibility are clearly defined in terms of measurable results, so that they can be used by the employee in planning his/her work, and by both employees and managers in monitoring progress. Performance reviews are conducted jointly over time and fresh objectives are established at appropriate intervals. The objectives identify the individual actions needed to fulfil the organisation's or business unit's strategy and annual objectives. Through this process, MBO provides a method of integrating and focusing the work of all the members of an organisation on the strategic plan.

While this process involves objective setting by managers in line with the corporate objectives, Drucker emphasised from the start the importance of participation by all employees. He supported the ideas and principles of Douglas McGregor's 'Theory Y' (*see* Chapter 2) and felt that unless people were actually involved in their own objective setting, they could be half-hearted about the process. In more recent terminology, they need to feel 'ownership' of the objectives and the plans to meet them. This is of particular importance because of the autonomy usually provided in implementing plans. While it may be difficult to provide this autonomy for everybody in an organisation, managers, supervisors and team leaders are usually able to decide on the actions they need to carry out to achieve their objectives and those of the members of their team.

→ Ch. 2

The essential elements of MBO have been carried forward into a range of company- and institution-based schemes of appraisal and performance review and evaluation, which have been developed under a variety of names to match particular organisational needs. The development of increasing autonomy in business units and self-managed teams encouraged the setting of objectives at these levels, with a feedback mechanism within the unit and team as well as on an organisation-wide basis. The advantages are seen in terms of improvements on past performance, particularly when individuals determine their own objectives and when there is feedback on performance.

In the 1980s and 1990s and into the twenty-first century the process of relating performance against objectives to the reward system has been extended through performance-related pay. However these systems have developed, the fundamental elements of MBO remain the focus on individual objectives and the feedback on their achievement. This focus has been considered to be a major motivator for many people in knowing what is expected of them and in their positive feeling of success when objectives are met. The participation of individuals in the process is essential in ensuring that the objectives which are established are realistic.

Strategic management involves making decisions which will enable an organisation to achieve its organisational objectives. These decisions have to be translated into action in one way or another. In turning strategic policy into action managers have to identify what is needed to realise strategic objectives, as well as recognising barriers to action that may arise and methods of overcoming these barriers. While forecasting and planning may be seen as activities which stand apart from operational management, plans have to be translated into actions. Business plans may be useful in describing how an organisation will be organised and how it will satisfy the needs of its customers, but the success of these plans will be judged by how they are put into action, that is the way the organisation operates. Action plans need not only to show how objectives will be achieved but they need to be followed by employees at all levels in an organisation, in the way that a builder follows building plans. Action plans are concerned with turning objectives and priorities into reality and provide a mechanism by which senior managers can satisfy themselves that what is being implemented is consistent with the intentions of organisational strategy.

SUMMARY

■ Once an organisation has decided on a strategy, the managers have then to decide how to implement it. Overall action plans have to be operationalised into smaller plans and tasks for employees to carry out. The role of management is to make relatively small decisions in order to fine tune the situation to achieve the organisation's objectives. These may be drawn together by reference to an overall strategic plan.

- The strategic planning process includes the development of plans at appropriate levels to produce the actions required to implement the strategic plan. The plans and actions of functional departments need to be drawn together so that the organisation operates smoothly. Marketing is the integrating function in matching customer requirements to the final product or service.

- There are individual, organisational and environmental barriers to strategic planning which experienced management can overcome. Business plans establish how organisations intend to organise themselves to satisfy the demands of customers. This process is supported by forecasting techniques, both qualitative and quantitative.

- Organisational development can help managers to deal with changes through staff training and development, team building and internal communication. If managers resist change or attempt to avoid implementing it, strategic drift can occur.

- Strategic objectives can be implemented by processes such as appraisal, review and performance-related pay. These systems focus on individual objectives and feedback on their achievement.

Review and discussion questions

1 *What are the main problems of implementing an organisation's strategy?*

2 *How are an organisation's strategic plans translated into detailed actions?*

3 *When is it appropriate to establish a project team? How will its operation differ from a more functional approach?*

4 *Outline the main barriers to planning. How can managers overcome these barriers?*

5 *What techniques are used in the development of business plans?*

6 *How important are performance measures in attaining an organisation's strategic objectives?*

CASE STUDY

Know your place

Standard Life and National Westminster are two businesses in the news. Each is an organisation with a great past behind it. Each of them has a name which commands envy and respect. Each of them has well-publicised problems. And, although the businesses and problems are very different, there is an important sense in which the issues they face are the same.

The banks, which were central to the British economy in the twentieth century, are products of the nineteenth century. They came into existence in order to mobilise the small savings of individuals and lend them on to growing companies. Their effectiveness rested on the local knowledge of their managers. These managers were traditionally key figures in the local community. Their local knowledge gave confidence to depositors and allowed shrewd and informed assessments of the viability of the businesses the banks supported. There were some advantages to scale in banking. National coverage gave depositors confidence in the stability of the institutions which they trusted with their sav-

▶

ings. An institution with branches from Carlisle to Camborne seemed likely still to be there when savers wanted their money back. The marble banking halls and grandiose head offices reinforced the sense of permanence.

And bigger banks were needed to handle bigger borrowers. By the 1920s the number of leading clearing banks in Britain was reduced to five. Midland, its roots in Britain's manufacturing heartland, was not just the largest bank in Britain; it was the largest bank in the world. Its rivals – Barclays, Lloyds, National Provincial and Westminster – were not too far behind. But around this time, the rationale for the banks' traditional collection of functions disappeared. Securities markets developed. That meant that you did not need to be a big financial services retailer to lend money to large corporations. And the skills involved in the two activities of retail deposit taking and business lending, once rather similar, had become quite distinct.

Nobody really noticed. As competitive pressures increased, the British banks followed the usual strategies of companies which do not really know what to do. They sought greater size by merger and internal expansion, and engaged in unfocused diversification into new businesses and new areas of the world. All of that was irrelevant, or worse. One final mega-merger created the National Westminster Bank, but the government blocked further concentration. Banks discovered that it is easy to meet targets for growing your balance sheet so long as you are not too bothered about getting your money back. And they lost a packet buying stockbrokers and American banks.

Standard Life, too, had a golden era of success. It pioneered the retailing of equities to a mass market. That was not what the business said it was doing; in fact, if it had, it would probably have been stopped. But by packaging equities as a life insurance product, it avoided restrictive regulation and secured effective distribution. There was not a long-term business there. It became easier, both legally and operationally, to sell shares more directly to individuals. And once that happened, there ceased to be a rationale for linking the three main things which Standard Life did: financial services retailing, investment management and the underwriting of risks.

Standard Life's response has been another standard recourse for those with no easy strategic options: if you are not doing well enough at what you are doing already, try something else. Become a bank, or an investment management house. But there do seem to be quite a lot of well capitalised banks and successful investment management houses around already. What National Westminster and Standard Life have in common is that each embraces a range of functions which were sensibly undertaken together at a particular point in history, but for which the rationale of combination has now disappeared.

And each business has found that when you unpick the individual things they do, most of them are performed better by someone else. The banks found that their retail deposit services were upstaged by building societies, that their merchant banking arms found it difficult to match the resources and professionalism of specialist investment banks, and that lending to very large corporate and sovereign borrowers was so competitive that no one has made any money out of it, or is ever likely to.

British insurers learnt that their retailing capabilities were very limited in competition with people who had branch networks – or a red telephone; that their investment skills were inferior to those of specialist fund managers; and that their underwriting was outstripped in professionalism by continental reinsurers.

So what should businesses faced with these kinds of strategic dilemmas do? The main requirement is to identify which of the many activities such a business will be engaged in are ones in which it has an ongoing competitive advantage. What can you do that others cannot readily do as well? Lloyds did this in the 1980s when it understood that its strengths were in retail financial services and lending to small businesses, and quit the more glamorous but less profitable activities which required it to compete with every other bank in the world.

But sometimes strategic dilemmas have no solution. This is difficult for executives to accept, but not all questions have answers. Sometimes the proper job of managers is to preside over an orderly transfer of the activities they control to other businesses. This does not often happen quickly or without the costs and uncertainties associated with the takeover process. Perhaps it should.

Source: Kay, J, *Financial Times*, 27 June 1997. Copyright John Kay, economist. Reprinted with permission.

REFERENCES AND FURTHER READING

Chartered Institute of Public Finance and Accountancy (1992) *Business Plans: A Move in the Right Direction,* London: CIPFA.

Drucker, Peter (1955) *The Practice of Management,* London: Heinemann.

Drucker, Peter (1988) 'The Coming of the New Organization', *Harvard Business Review,* January/February.

Evans, Philip and Wurster, Thomas S (1997) 'Strategy and the New Economics of Information', *Harvard Business Review,* September/October.

Faulkner, David and Johnson, Gerry (1992) *The Challenge of Strategic Management,* London: Kogan Page.

Fayol, Henri (1949) *General and Industrial Management,* London: Pitman Publishing

Finlay, Paul (2000) *Strategic Management,* Harlow: FT Prentice Hall.

George, C (1972) *The History of Management Thought,* London: Prentice Hall.

Goold, Michael, Campbell, Andrew and Alexander, Marcus (1994) *Corporate-Level Strategy: Creating Value in the Multibusiness Company,* New York: John Wiley.

Greiner, L E (1972) 'Evolution and Devolution as Organizations Grow', *Harvard Business Review,* July/August.

Grundy, Tony (1992) *Corporate Strategy and Financial Decisions,* London: Kogan Page.

Grundy, Tony (1993) *Implementing Strategic Change,* London: Kogan Page.

Hamel, Gary (1996) 'Strategy as Revolution', *Harvard Business Review,* June/August.

Hamel, Gary and Prahalad, C K (1994) *Competing for the Future,* Boston, MA: Harvard Business School Press.

Hannagan, Tim (2001) *Mastering Strategic Management,* Basingstoke: Palgrave/Macmillan.

Harris, Ian C and Ruefli, Timothy W (2000) 'The Strategy/Structure Debate: An Examination of Performance Implications', *Journal of Management Studies,* June.

Jelinek, Mariann (1979) *Institutional Innovation,* New York: Praeger.

Kaplan, Richard S and Norton, David P (1996) *The Balanced Scorecard: Translating Strategy into Action,* Boston, MA: Harvard Business Press.

Kay, J (1997) 'Know your Place', *Financial Times,* 27 June.

McDonald, Malcolm (1992) *Strategic Marketing Planning,* London: Kogan Page.

Marquanett, I A (1990) 'Corporate Planning Challenges', *Journal of Business Strategy,* June.

Mintzberg, Henry (1973) *The Nature of Managerial Work,* New York: Harper & Row.

Mintzberg, Henry (2000) *The Rise and Fall of Strategic Planning,* Harlow: FT Prentice Hall.

Nutt, Paul C (2000) 'Decision-Making in Public, Private and Third Sector Organisations: Finding Sector Dependent Best Practice', *Journal of Management Studies,* January.

Ohmae, Kenichi (1996) *The Mind of the Strategist: The Art of Japanese Business,* London: McGraw-Hill.

Porter, Michael E (1996) 'What is Strategy?', *Harvard Business Review,* November/December.

Porter, Michael E (1998) *Competitive Advantages: Creating and Sustaining Superior Performance,* New York: Free Press.

Stacey, Ralph D (1999) *Strategic Management and Organisational Dynamics* (3rd edn), Harlow: FT Prentice Hall.

WEBSITES

http://learning.mit.edu/res/kv/index.html
Discusses the idea of the learning organisation.

http://www.carol.co.uk
Provides access to company reports.

http://www.nissan-na.com/smyrna/ind.html
Information about the Nissan company organisation.

CHAPTER 7

Quality management strategy

TIM HANNAGAN

Outcomes

Having read this chapter, you will be able to understand:

- the concept of 'quality' applied to commerce and industry
- the application of this concept to all types of organisation
- how a quality system can be introduced and managed within an organisation
- the importance of focusing on the customer
- the link between total quality and the management of change
- the strategic importance of corporate objectives
- the use of performance management
- the differences between quality control and quality assurance
- techniques such as 'right-first-time', 'just-in-time', and zero defects
- the way in which quality can inform the whole approach to management

WHAT IS 'QUALITY'?

'In today's competitive environment, ignoring the quality issue is tantamount to corporate suicide.'   (President of Hewlett-Packard, *Fortune*, October 1985)

In business and management terms there is an attempt to focus on a measurable concept of **quality** by concentrating on 'fitness for purpose'. A specification is supplied by the customer and the quality of the product is measured by how closely it conforms to this specification. It is based on the customer's perception of quality. In these terms quality can be defined as:

'continually meeting agreed customer needs' or 'what it takes to satisfy the customer', or simply 'fitness for purpose'.

In more general terms, quality is an elusive concept and the usual dictionary definition does not help to make it less so: 'That which makes a thing what it is, its attributes, its characteristics'. The 'quality' of a person may be measured by certain characteristics, such as honesty and courage.

This approach involves values and judgements, while a statement such as 'the quality of a strawberry plant is that it bears strawberries' is value and judgement free – it is a statement of what the plant is. However, the fruit from different plants will be compared in size, colour and flavour and then may be graded into strawberries of different 'quality' in the more limited commercial sense.

Quality can be seen as an attribute of a product or service which ensures that it is attractive in the eyes of the customer. It is a relative property rather than an absolute one, in that a given product or service will be attractive to customers if it fulfils their expectations more fully than any other product or service under consideration. It means delivering the right product or service, which is fit for the purposes required by the customer, at the right price, and at the right time and place. A company that produces and delivers a beautiful-looking car to a customer will not be considered to produce quality goods if the car does not work well. Whatever the costs involved, the materials used, or the care taken in manufacture, the quality of the car will be considered poor if it is unreliable. A lawnmower that does not cut the lawn effectively is of no use to the customer whatever its price or however firmly the manufacturer describes it as a 'quality' or 'excellent' product.

WHY IS THE MANAGEMENT OF QUALITY IMPORTANT?

→ Ch. 3

The management of quality is important because of the need to focus on the customer and because meeting customer needs is the foundation of any successful organisation (*see* Chapter 3). Products and services have to be of a quality to meet customer requirements, as the quality of a product or service may be the distinguishing factor between the offerings of competing companies from which the consumer has to choose. Two products may serve the same purpose, but if they sell for the same price and one is well designed and constructed from high-standard materials and the other is not, consumer demand is likely to be for the well-made product. This is even more likely to be the case if this product is more reliable and the company offers good after-sales service. If two restaurants in the same street charge similar prices for meals, but one provides slapdash service and the other looks after its customers, it is the one that provides a good service which is likely to be more successful.

'You get what you pay for' is a saying which suggests that the more you pay the better the quality of a product or service. Of course this does not always follow, but in consumer surveys there may be a distinction between the best product on offer in terms of quality and the best in relation to a balance between quality and price or what may be called 'value for money'. The very highest quality may be expensive to achieve in relation to the material costs in the use of the very best materials and labour costs because of the time involved in ensuring high quality. However, whatever the costs and the price, the quality has to be sufficient to meet the requirements of enough customers to make the sale of the product or service successful.

In organisational terms, a lack of quality is likely to be a waste of resources through scrapped materials and wasted time as well as through rejection by consumers. Market research can help to identify what customers want (*see* Chapter 4), their purchasing behaviour and the requirements that organisations need to meet if they are to be successful. Quality improvement programmes in organisations combine product improvement, the more closer matching of customer needs, and process improvement. They not only result in a focus on quality matters, but they can also create a demand for ever-higher standards, therefore making quality improvement an ongoing process.

→ Ch. 4

FOCUS ON THE CUSTOMER

If it is accepted that high quality is a measure of excellence taken from the customer's point of view, then although producers may grade their goods in terms of quality, whether the producers' view of the grading is upheld will depend on customer perception. If customers like their strawberries to be large, firm, red and sweet, then fruit with those characteristics will be considered to be of the highest quality, and the producer of smaller, paler strawberries may not be able to convince customers of the high quality of their output, however sweet they may taste.

The focus on the customer means that quality is conceptualised in terms of the customer's perceptions. The organisation's objective is to identify customer requirements so that both the customer's and the organisation's needs are met. It is also the intention to meet these requirements first time and thus avoid the cost of sorting out problems. The process involves:

■ **research**
■ **specification and planning**
■ **delivery**
■ **review**.

→ Chs 5 and 6

This process focuses on the customer at key points and returns constantly to research (*see* Chapters 5 and 6) into changing customer needs (*see* Figure 7.1). When customer needs are identified, planning can take place into exactly what has to be delivered. The specifications and standards are determined so priorities can be established to ensure that the product or service delivered is what the customer needs and that it meets customer perceptions. Although costs and price play an important part in this, most customers will pay what is necessary in order to receive what in their view is good quality. This in turn will generate profits as customers demand this product or service above others.

Figure 7.1 Focus on the customer

A customer can be defined as anyone who receives a product or service. This approach has been extended by many companies beyond the satisfaction of the external consumer in order also to include the internal customer. One department in an organisation receives products or services from another department and passes these on to a third group. On an assembly line a commodity is passed along the line from one individual or team to another, each dependent on the other for the receipt of the commodity at the correct quality at the correct time, and aiming to pass it on with the correct added value and, again, on time.

The concept of the internal customer means that each process is viewed as a product so that evaluation takes place at once by the immediate customer or by the processor. This system will help to eliminate waste and reduce cost, while the overall objective will remain the satisfaction of the external customer. The product or service will be 'right first time' so that errors will be prevented through the need to satisfy the internal customer at each stage rather than through a final inspection.

TOTAL QUALITY MANAGEMENT

As companies have made a conscious effort to 'focus on the customer', **total quality management** (TQM) and other methods have been introduced to implement this. Total quality management is known by other names such as total quality improvement (TQI) or total quality control (TQC), or simply as total quality or as strategic quality management (SQM), and so on (*see also* Chapters 10 and 14).

→ Chs 10 and 14

It is possible to identify differences between total quality management and titles such as strategic quality management. How important these are remains a matter of opinion. Total quality management is often described as a 'value-based' approach to quality management; it may be seen either as a goal which an organisation aims to achieve, or the idea of a goal of *total* quality may be considered unattainable. On the other hand, strategic quality management can be described as both systematic and value based. It can be seen to suggest that the reason for improving quality is that it will have maximum strategic impact on the future of the organisation. Strategic quality management is designed as a practical and pragmatic framework in which the drive towards quality improvement can be sustained while not making claims on *total* quality. A counter-argument to this is to consider the word 'total' in the context of total quality management to mean that every part of an organisation is involved.

The approach can be recognised, whatever its title, by its objectives. Total (or strategic) quality management can be defined as:

'an intensive, long-term effort to transform all parts of the organisation in order to produce the best product and service possible to meet customer needs.'

In some Japanese companies there is no such thing as total or strategic quality management; it is simply the way they operate and it does not need a title, although it could be described as 'right first time', in order to make sure that it happens (*see also* Chapter 19). The management at the Toyota plant in Japan has stated that:

→ Ch. 19

'We estimate it will take you twenty years to be where we are now, and by that time we will have progressed further. We have moved from quality philosophy to measuring defects on an acceptable quality level basis to reducing our defect rate to below five to six parts per billion. Our last product recall was 1969 when we first started introducing what you know as Total Quality Management.' (Atkinson, 1990)

Total quality management can be seen as a metaphor for the process and management of change, designed to realign the culture and working practices of an organisation for the pursuit of continued quality improvement. Initially the concept of quality tended to be considered in terms of narrow and specific techniques, such as quality circles (*see* p 196) or statistical process (or quality) control (*see* pp 203–206). The concept has developed into a pervasive one (*see* p 205, the Taguchi method), touching every aspect of the organisation, including suppliers and customers.

In an organisation that practises total quality management, quality becomes the standard operating procedure and part of the culture (*see* p 192 for a description of benchmarking). It is not simply a programme or project, but a way of life. It is proved by the quality of materials purchased from suppliers, the approach to defect control on the production line, the appearance of the building, the way problems are solved for customers, the way employees are organised and the organisation's internal communication system (*see* Chapter 10 for an analysis of organisational communication and TQM). This approach is founded on the premise that quality depends on individual effort and attitude. It is a rigorous, highly disciplined and skilled process which may challenge present practice and depends on a training programme throughout the organisation. Total quality management is predicated on a commitment to customer interests, needs, requirements and expectations, and on the commitment of everyone to the constant improvement of the quality of everything that the organisation does and provides for its customers (*see* pp 204, 461 and 638 for a description of 'just-in-time' techniques).

→ Ch. 10

→ Ch. 14

→ Ch. 19

TQM is a strategic approach within an organisation which can provide an 'umbrella' under which a number of quality initiatives can be managed (*see* Figure 7.2). These are all part of a quality culture. The philosophy that supported this culture and the practical application of it originated through the ideas of Dr W Edwards Deming (1982, 1986), an American who provided the intellectual and practical drive behind Japan's post-war reconstruction. He encouraged Japanese companies to introduce total quality, and in particular to involve and consult with customers in an attempt to bring about continuous improvement of the product. J M Juran (1992) worked with Deming and concentrated on people-based management. He argued that in a normal situation, the general attitude was that maintaining and perpetuating current standards or levels of performance was good enough. He insisted that present performance in any function, at any level, can and

Figure 7.2 **Total quality**

should be improved, and that to achieve this improvement an organisation begins with identifying the internal obstacles that prevent people doing the best they can and then eliminates them.

Philip Crosby (1978) has been another important influence on total quality, again with a focus on the people responsible for improving quality. Peters and Waterman expanded on these approaches in their book *In Search of Excellence* (1982). They found that many of the foremost 'excellent' companies were equally obsessed by quality and punctuality. They describe how the Caterpillar Tractor Company offers customers a 48-hour guaranteed parts delivery service anywhere in the world. If this guarantee is not met, the customer receives the part free.

An article in *Fortune* magazine is quoted as stating:

> *'The company's operating principles are excellence of quality, reliability of performance, and loyalty in dealer relationships. Caterpillar has zealously pursued the goal of building a better, more efficient crawler tractor than anybody else in the world.'*
>
> (Peters and Waterman, 1982)

Another company highlighted by Peters and Waterman is McDonald's, whose theme is 'Quality, Service, Cleanliness and Value'. Founder Ray Kroc says, 'If I had a brick for every time I've repeated the phrase QSCV, I think I'd probably be able to bridge the Atlantic Ocean with them.' Quality is the priority because that is what McDonald's wants customers to enjoy every time they visit a McDonald's restaurant. All establishments are regularly monitored for QSCV and the results are linked to the manager's pay, while consistent failure to meet the McDonald's standards can lead to managers being sacked or the termination of the franchise. QSCV is not only applied to customer service but to all aspects of the business. The best ingredients are used in the food, and cleanliness is insisted upon. Peters and Waterman quote a former griddle tender as saying:

'There was never an idle moment, whenever there was a slack time in the store, we were cleaning something.'

The computer company Hewlett-Packard has the same approach to quality. Routine systems in the company are made to reinforce the quality objectives. These are built into the management-by-objectives programme so that everyone receives the latest quality information as well as data on orders, sales and profits. There is a quality 'web' throughout the company, appropriately called the LACE (Lab Awareness of Customer Environment) programme, in which Hewlett-Packard customers make presentations to company engineers on their own needs and reactions to the products and services they receive.

'A Quality focus is ubiquitous in Hewlett-Packard because the employees don't seem to be able to separate it from anything else they are doing. If you ask them about personnel, they talk quality. If you ask them about field sales, they talk quality. If you ask them about management-by-objectives, they talk about quality-by-objectives.'

(Peters and Waterman, 1982)

Peters and Waterman found that quality and reliability were preferred by many leading companies to innovation, to being first in the field. Hewlett-Packard is quoted again:

'The company is seldom first into the market with its new products. The company's marketing strategy is normally that of a counterpuncher. A competitor's new product comes on the market and Hewlett-Packard engineers, when making service calls on Hewlett-Packard equipment ask the customers what they like or dislike about the new product, what features the customers would like to have . . . and pretty soon the Hewlett-Packard salesmen are calling on customers again with a new product that answers their needs and wants. The result: happy and loyal customers.'

In these examples, and during the period of development of quality as the top priority for an organisation, it is apparent that total quality management involves the creation of an appropriate company culture, a climate based on 'never being satisfied' with the current quality of product and service in meeting customers' identified needs, requirements, interests and expectations. This search for opportunities for improvements can be referred to as total quality improvement. Not being satisfied with current inputs, processes, practices and outcomes encourages a system to be established covering research, analysis of needs, measurement of results, consideration of efficiency and effectiveness, in order to improve what is produced and how it is produced.

Benchmarking is a process whereby a business compares its operations with those of similar organisations and, if it is able to, the best of its competitors. Companies have always benchmarked themselves with other companies in an informal way, although it is relatively recently that a formal and rigorous process has been introduced. The objective is to create and sustain excellence. The usual method is to select a business process to improve and to select a project team with the person responsible for the process in the business as team leader. The team develops a set of key process measures to compare with other companies' processes.

Comparisons are then made with companies within the same corporation, competitors and the best companies in other industries. Although some processes cannot easily be compared across industries, areas such as customer service can be compared. It is then a question of obtaining collaboration from the target companies and investigating their processes. Whereas some of this investigation can be carried out at a 'distance' through documents and looking at delivery systems, benchmarking really requires visits to the target company. Without these visits, it is likely to be of little value. The investigation should reveal gaps between the company's processes and best practices. The team then develops an action plan to implement the improved process. It is at this stage that having the person responsible for the process as team leader or as a member of the team can prove a critical success factor for implementation.

The main areas to be benchmarked are usually those processes known to be inefficient or where there is some evidence that competitors or companies in other industries have better processes. The main advantages of benchmarking are the overcoming of a natural disbelief in the feasibility of improvements, making sure that improvement targets are high enough and helping to create a learning and outward-looking culture in the company.

In Figure 7.3 a competitive edge is achieved by encouraging the best possible utilisation of resources by a highly adaptable workforce in order to achieve corporate quality objectives. Competitive advantage is achieved and maintained within a framework of efficiency and effectiveness and acceptance of a process of continuous improvement. TQM as a 'metaphor for the management of change' is a process for encouraging the attitude that change is the usual situation, because through this come quality improvement and success.

The keys to total quality management can be summarised as:

- **measuring quality**
- **incorporating quality objectives into strategic planning**
- **obtaining commitment of top management**
- **forming teams in a structure of participative management**
- **using resources efficiently and effectively**

Figure 7.3 **Total quality improvement**

- including suppliers and customers in quality improvement
- building skills through training (*see* pp 325–8)
- developing an attitude which welcomes change.

This is perhaps summed up in Japanese management by *kaizen*, which is a continuous striving for perfection, and in quality terms constant, continuous improvement. This includes all aspects of the organisation, such as staff training and development, product improvement, production and output improvement and attention to administration. At its best, this results in the output of high volumes of high-quality products supported by adaption and innovation.

IMPLICATIONS FOR MANAGEMENT

Total quality management impinges on every function in an organisation and will include marketing, product design, human resource development, financial resourcing, sites and buildings and estates management, and so on. The cultural change required in most organisations in order to introduce and maintain TQM has to be led by senior managers. They need to be aware of and understand the principles and practices of total quality and be prepared to support it at every level. Particularly important is the need to ensure monitoring, measurement and evaluation of progress in all functions, against identified and if possible quantified needs and specifications. Managers can use this evaluation in order to plan developments in TQM, as well as measuring the extent to which quality has been improved. The process can be applied inside an organisation as well as outside it, in the sense that everyone has a 'customer' and is a 'customer' inside the organisation, relying on others' work and service and passing on work and service to others. Factual evidence can be obtained by monitoring progress against agreed objectives, and this can inform the plans of each team in meeting its particular targets or objectives, which will in turn depend on other teams or individuals providing support in the form of high-quality goods or services.

TQM is implemented at the top of an organisation first because it is at this level that change can be initiated. Top managers require skills to enable them to change the way they work, so they can practise and promote quality management and then help others to acquire the necessary techniques and understanding.

The introduction of TQM through the whole organisation is a long-term strategy requiring a variety of approaches. For most organisations it is about the management of change and involves all aspects of human resource management, including leadership, problem solving, coaching, counselling, communication and team building. Training will be required at all levels, usually starting with those with a co-ordinating, supervisory or management role, but also concentrating on teams. Although TQM encourages consideration of factual information, it also encourages 'people-based' management.

This style of management is participative, designed to enable people at every level to share in management decisions and in responsibility for them. This means in one way or another devolving decision making to the closest possible point to where the effects of the decisions are felt. Decision making may be delegated to an individual or a team. People are encouraged to identify and 'own' problems and their solutions, rather than passing them up or around the organisation. At an early stage, teamwork becomes essential if problems are to be identified and addressed and not hidden away. This approach focuses on corporate goals, and teams identify with problems of specific relevance to their functions.

Teams need to know how their work relates to corporate goals and objectives so that they can understand the direction in which they are moving and can look for improvement opportunities. They need to have a clear idea of the resources at their disposal in order to achieve their particular objectives. It is then possible for the team to decide which members will carry out particular tasks, the methods to be employed, materials and equipment to use, and how and when to work. All of this puts great pressure on teamwork and on the team's responsibility for their own results (*see* Figure 7.4).

In the 1970s the Saab motor company broke away from the assembly-line system customarily used in car manufacturing and organised its workforce into teams working around each car. Teams could decide to rotate jobs and introduce other flexibilities into the way they worked, so long as they achieved their target output at the requisite cost and quality levels.

Black & Decker adopted a total quality plan in 1980 to include every aspect of the business. A 'People Plan' was formed in order to 'free the people for their fullest contribution to business success'. To implement total quality the company formed quality circles, and after four years there were 35 successful circles in operation. In 1984 this development was reviewed and considered to require rejuvenation. A new total customer service initiative was introduced which encompassed quality circles while focusing on 'excellence in everything we do'.

The Ciba Corning company also believes in total quality as a complete way of life affecting attitudes and commitments, 'a framework for bringing out the best in all employees'. The four principles underlying its approach are:

■ **meeting the requirements of customers**
■ **error-free work**

Figure 7.4 Introducing total quality management

Introduction
- Senior management
- Vision statement
- Corporate objectives
- Management of change

Implementation
- Reorganise and train to support TQM
- Form teams
- Train: awareness, participative management, team management skills

Customer focus
- Work with customers and suppliers to improve quality
- Monitor
- Review
- Evaluate
- Redesign

Build Total Quality Management objectives into the organisation's strategic and operational plans and objectives

■ **managing by preventing errors rather than inspecting for error**

■ **measuring by cost of quality.**

These principles are delivered through a ten-point action plan which includes commitment from the top, communication, education and involvement for all employees. One approach to obtaining this involvement is the organisation of quality circles.

TEAM PROBLEM SOLVING AND QUALITY CIRCLES

Team problem solving has been a major workplace innovation aimed at improving the variety and reliability of products and services. Issue handling in large organisations is an interactive process, because the issues are complex they require a range of informational inputs and they have widespread repercussions, while implementation is difficult. Using a group of people in order to solve these problems has the advantage that the group has more information and knowledge than an individual and implementation is easier if the implementors are involved in the issue discussions. The problem with group discussions is that they can take longer to reach conclusions than an individual and the result may be a compromise rather than a clear-cut decision.

Quality circles and similar approaches are long standing examples of team problem solving which have been developed over the years.

A quality circle can be described as

'a group who meet voluntarily and regularly to identify and solve their own work related problems and implement their solutions with management approval.'

(Industrial Society)

Small groups of employees, usually from the same workplace and under the same supervisor, volunteer to meet to identify problems and find solutions. They look at the problems that occur in their work area and that affect their own job. The group itself applies the solutions if it has the authority; otherwise, management is presented with recommendations and decides on implementation.

Membership of quality circles is usually voluntary, with a welcome for anyone who wishes to join and no official pressure for anyone to become a member. If the circle is successful, active and enthusiastic, it is expected that people will want to join. The supervisor of a work area will usually lead the circle. His or her role is to encourage volunteers to establish a group which he or she will chair because of previous experience and training in organising and running quality circles. The supervisor guides the circle in order to help it develop into a cohesive team and to focus on solving problems and improving quality. The circle will usually consist of between six and twelve members, large enough to generate a variety of ideas; small enough for everybody to be involved and have their say. If there are too many volunteers, either membership can be rotated or subgroups can be formed to consider particular tasks.

Management has to follow a 'hands-off' policy up to the point of implementation of a decision. Success depends on members of a quality circle being assured that it 'belongs to them' and has not been formed by management. Management can be supportive and may suggest topics for consideration by the circle, but if it is more 'heavy handed' the role of members will be restricted. The most important consideration for management is to ensure that actions do follow any ideas or decisions reached by a quality circle, or to provide good reasons for not following up such ideas or decisions.

Quality circles were originally an American idea but were first practised on a wide scale in Japan. In order to compete with other industrial nations, Japanese industry realised in the late 1940s and 1950s that old ideas of management had to be discarded and the initiative and skills of everybody on the workforce had to be harnessed. Emphasis was placed on training at shopfloor level and every effort was made to pass as much responsibility as possible to supervisors and operators. There was a particular emphasis on identifying quality problems at all levels and in all areas of companies.

In the late 1950s and through the 1960s Japanese companies introduced quality circles extensively, so that by 1980 it was estimated that over one million quality circles and 10 million workers were involved. It is significant that the literal translation of the Japanese term for quality circles is:

'The gathering of the wisdom of the people.'

The concept of the quality circle coincides with the culture of Japanese companies and builds on loyalty to the company. The 'family company' approach of duty to the company by employees and responsibility by the company for the welfare of its employees is well developed, while there is also a well-nurtured culture of it being in everyone's interest for the company to succeed, combined with peer pressure to encourage the success of a voluntary approach. Professor Ishikawa has suggested (1984) that quality circles act as a 'focus of perception' to identify personal pride and self-esteem with corporate achievement (*see* Chapter 14).

→ Ch. 14

Quality circles have been used across the world to draw on the expertise and knowledge of workers on the shopfloor in order to improve quality. They have been adapted by such companies as General Motors, Honeywell and Lockheed in the USA, and by Philips, Ford, Rolls-Royce and Marks & Spencer in the UK.

In many British companies, however, the culture has not been conducive to the development of quality circles. Where there is a strongly defended hierarchical structure, or sections and departments based on specialised expertise, the view that ideas from the shopfloor should be given priority is difficult to foster. At the same time, the attitude that it is up to 'them' to solve problems may be strong at an operational level. Management/union dissension in the past has certainly discouraged the effective development of this kind of initiative.

It is clear that successful quality circles are not concerned with grumbles or complaints or irrelevant discussion of non-related subjects such as pay, personality conflicts or other grievances. The stress is on solving problems and producing action plans. For this approach to be understood and successful, the culture of the company has to be one which encourages participative management. If the culture has bred suspicion and secrecy, grumbles and complaints may be at the top of the agenda. Quality circles are encouraged to discuss practicalities and not theories, so that positive results are produced rather than simply argument. One approach is to list problem areas and then to establish priorities and seek solutions by drawing on the skill and knowledge of the group. When problems are beyond solution by the group, specialists may be asked to join the circle for a number of meetings, or a sub-group may be established to investigate the problem in more detail.

Where the members of the quality circle have discretion to make a decision they will carry it out, while on matters where they do not have authority, they will make a presentation to the managers involved in the proposed change (*see* Figure 7.5). This may be a technical problem to do with the operation of machinery or equipment, it may be a staffing problem to do with skills or working times, it may be a question of the supply of materials, the purchase of spare parts, or it may be to do with costs and finance. The managers must then decide to take action or explain in detail the reasons for not taking action at this time. Managers also have to make sure that people do not identify too strongly with their particular circle, when total quality has to be identified with the aims and objectives of the organisation as a whole. At the same time, some problems need to be solved on the spot, rather than waiting for a quality circle meeting to sort them out.

An enterprising quality circle will, of course, anticipate as many problems as possible and solve them.

ITT has provided an example of a solution discovered by a quality circle:

> *'It was standard practice to completely remove capacitors from the metal handling equipment to check for correct nominal capacitance. After this operation the capacitors were discarded. By purchasing hand held capacitance meters it is possible to take the equipment to the work and simply applying one terminal lead, measure the nominal capacitance while the remaining terminal lead is retained on the handling strip. This enables the capacitor to continue with the batch through the finishing operations. This change will result in a saving of more than $10,000 when it is fully implemented.'*

(ITT Circle News, March 1981)

Managers play an important part in the success of quality circles. There has to be a commitment to the system throughout the organisation, and one or two unsympathetic managers can ruin the whole process. Managers have to allow time and money for the circle meetings and for the preliminary training; they must be ready to attend presentations, to listen with an open mind to the proposals and to decide on their value on merit. Unions need also to be involved in the process so that their representatives understand what is happening. Unions will usually be supportive of the process because it involves the workforce more closely in the organisation and has the objective of improving job satisfaction. After all, quality circles have been described as 'a structured way of making management listen' by the Industrial Society.

Figure 7.5 **Quality circles**

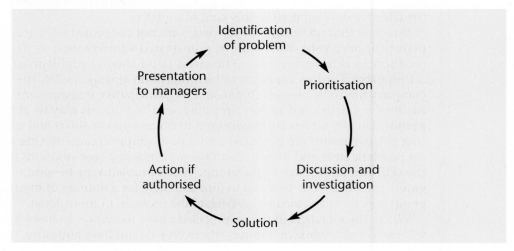

FOCUS ON TOTAL QUALITY

Whether it is quality circles or another method of providing a focus on quality, the pursuit of total quality must be led from the front, by the chief executive, otherwise it may be considered an afterthought. Deming put this another way:

> *'There is so much talk about involvement of employees, quality of work life, communications and other poetic words. What is needed is involvement of management: get the management involved. Employees will become involved, the quality of life will improve, once management takes on the job of restoring dignity to the hourly worker.'*
>
> (Deming, 1982)

Combined with competitive pressures and the higher priority given to human resource management, the focus on quality has encouraged reorganisation in many companies in the 1980s and 1990s. These developments have been away from the single, giant pyramid structures consisting of many different layers of management and grades of operative, towards flatter structures often based on a total quality concept. Whole functions and levels have been eliminated in order to produce an organisation which is more flexible and speedier in response to market needs.

Waterman (1988) cites the Dana Company in the USA, which in the mid-1970s had 14 layers of management between the chief executive and the staff floor. By the mid-1980s these layers had been reduced to five:

> *'At the extreme the company has one plant in Nebraska that employs 120 people – the organisation structure there is simple: 120 people, one plant manager, nothing in between.'*

The key to this approach is often greater delegation. Many areas of decision making and accountability have been pushed down the organisation to be nearer the point where the decision takes effect. Senior management will adopt a more strategic role, setting broad objectives as a framework to ensure that all units are functioning effectively and working towards the corporate goals. The operational units are the closest group to their markets and they know best the requirements of the consumer. It is impossible for this level of delegation to work unless the practice and beliefs of management adapt to the new circumstances. There is a decline in supervision throughout the organisation as employees take on greater responsibility. The role of the manager is to initiate new ideas and policies, to facilitate the work of the operational units and to monitor their progress.

In order to introduce this level of involvement, there has to be a clear recognition that the purpose of this strategy is to increase mutual understanding and to improve the individual's contribution. This is a policy of openness, of encouraging individual creativity and initiative in the interests of the organisation.

In order to achieve this level of delegation it is necessary to:

■ make certain that each individual understands what is expected from them in terms of their time at work;

■ set the limits of delegation so that everyone knows the extent of their responsibility;

■ train individuals so that they understand the aims and objectives of the delegated system and are technically able to cope with it;

■ communicate effectively the corporate business goals so that everyone understands how these relate to them;

■ enable a reverse flow of information to take place, from the shopfloor upwards, so that each manager knows the attitudes and aspirations of each person reporting to him or her.

At the same time as this focus on the individual, there has to be a clear understanding of teamwork. In the introduction of total quality, teams are not the same as quality circles. The quality-circle approach is based on voluntary groups of employees considering particular tasks. Total quality management teams include everybody working in a particular area or function or in a cross-functional role. Individuals cannot opt out of this team or of meetings to consider the working of the group, or fail to take responsibility for their work. The team will be responsible for making sure that everybody contributes to its success, and for discussing and implementing ways in which the whole team can improve performance. These teams may coincide with quality circles or the latter may form a separate system for considering quality – an alternative, perhaps task-oriented group. The usual process is for the functional team itself to become a type of quality circle on its own.

This process of delegating decision and responsibility to teams at the 'salt face' or 'firing line' is again not quite the same as a process popular in the 1980s known as 'team briefing'. These are meetings at regular intervals when leaders bring their teams together to communicate what is happening at the workplace. In the team briefing system, the priority is to achieve understanding of what people need to know because it affects their job; it is a systematic way of telling all employees about progress, policy, decisions, performance and future plans. It is not necessarily consultative and is not usually a method of encouraging two-way communication. Team briefing is a useful method of communication for management, but it should not be confused with the purposes behind setting up teams in a TQM system.

The same is true of consultative committees, which are structured meetings of management and employee representatives, with the purpose of discussing management matters of common interest. They are a way of seeking the views of employees before management decisions are finally made or before they are implemented. They may be used whenever decisions affect employees, but they are not about negotiation on such matters as pay, which requires once again a separate format of meetings. Consultative committees can play an important part in, for example, the management of change, and can be a way of informing discussion on quality teams when managers are considering the initiation of new policies.

The Confederation of British Industry in *The Will to Win* (1980) stated that 'the system of giving the line employee more responsibility increases his/her job satisfaction and involvement'. In contrast, the division of labour and scientific management or 'Taylorism' have encouraged the analysis of work into constituent activities and given particular tasks to individual workers. The close definition of the worker's specialist role has meant that at its extreme, workers respond by living up to the limited expectations of them by carrying out the tasks they have been given and no more or less.

Some organisations may have been paternalistic in their approach by not treating employees as adults; at the same time, other organisations do not regard their employees as the prime source of their prosperity. With a limited view of their job, employees substitute habit for understanding, and every change can, in Drucker's view, represent to the employee 'a challenge of the incomprehensible and . . .

threatens his psychological security'. Drucker attacks scientific management for confusing analysis with action, for divorcing planning from doing. The successful companies 'hire a whole man or woman' and realise that 'with every pair of hands a mind comes free'. Ignoring the ideas of employees is epitomised by a General Motors' car worker in the USA whom Drucker (1968) quotes as saying:

'I guess I got laid off because I made poor quality cars. In 16 years not once was I ever asked for a suggestion as to how to do my job better. Not once.'

In response to this, many successful companies have introduced suggestion schemes. In the USA, IBM has said that its suggestion plan yielded ideas from 30 000 employees during 1985 which resulted in savings of more than $125 million. The company was happy to pay the employees $18 million in cash awards for these suggestions. While these schemes can be very effective, they have to fit into the overall company policy because it may be difficult to run financial inducements for ideas alongside voluntary consultation and a delegated team approach. If the company ethos encourages everybody to think in terms of constant improvement and enables people to communicate ideas, a suggestion box may not be necessary (*see* Figure 7.6).

Strategies designed to maximise the potential and actual contribution of every employee have to give considerable emphasis to communication and involvement policies. The move away from an organisation based on command and authority from the top, with limited and routine tasks at the bottom, has created a re-evaluation of the way companies communicate internally. It is no longer a question of ensuring that instructions are passed to the relevant people and then monitoring what happens. Communication is now seen as a means of improving understanding, of securing involvement through a free flow of information in order to create cohesion and mutual commitment on the part of all members of the organisation.

Managers rely on the capabilities of those carrying out the various tasks allotted to them. Managers have to ensure effective teamwork and co-operation and are responsible for co-ordinating, planning and monitoring to make sure that more flexible and less authoritarian structures nevertheless meet their objectives. This requires the listening skills of a facilitator able to anticipate and solve problems, to

Figure 7.6 Focus on quality

treat individuals sympathetically and with respect, and to identify the relative strengths and weaknesses of everyone involved.

Managers need to communicate the corporate business goals effectively to every team or group so that they are understood in sufficient depth and related to the team and the individuals in it. This understanding must also include an appreciation of the external influences on the organisation, such as the nature of the competition, the impact of new technologies, the influence of government policy, and the importance of markets and customers. Managers have to assess the level of understanding of these matters by teams and individuals. Surveys, meetings and discussions can help to do this, and many organisations have found the most effective means of 'upward' communication to be a system of appraisal and performance review (*see* Chapters 6 and 8).

→ Chs 6 and 9

MEASURING QUALITY

The measurement of quality should not be thought of as a single and simple process, although in fact it can be if the one measurement that is used is profit. A simple indication such as profit growth, market share or the return on capital invested can be used to judge how well a quality management system has worked, and these certainly should be among the measures used. The problem is that taken on their own they do not indicate how they were achieved and, if successful, how they can be maintained. For this an analysis of the organisation is required with measurement taken at various levels.

At a strategic level, for example, in order to decide whether or not a performance management system has helped to put quality management into effect, it may be sensible to seek the answers to a number of questions:

■ Is there a strategic plan supported by senior managers which establishes the organisation's direction?

■ Is there a well-defined structure to support and develop a quality approach by managers, including a performance management system?

■ Are skills and techniques for quality improvement part of the training for managers and supervisors?

■ Are employees held accountable for on-the-job performance (*see* pp 261–5 and 329–32)?

At the same time, there has to be a decision about what is to be evaluated. This can be achieved by a clear statement of overall objectives, plus objectives for every unit and team as well as individuals. At the operational level this will mean detailed production or service targets. At a more strategic level managers may prefer non-routine activities and those of short duration; they may prefer to be problem solvers rather than planners (*see* Table 7.1). This tendency can be offset by a participative process for establishing objectives and forms of evaluation, so that managers can see the importance of longer-term objectives in establishing the context for detailed targets.

A manager needs to be both a problem solver and a planner and to be able to communicate the importance of medium- and long-term objectives to employees at all levels so as to support the attainment of objectives and targets and measure performance against these.

Table 7.1 **Planners and problem solvers**

PROBLEM SOLVERS	PLANNERS
Short-duration activities	Advance planning
Non-routine tasks	Agreed systems
Emphasis on decisive action	Systems and schedules
Informal interaction	Formal, regular sessions
Effectiveness through authority	Roles of coach and counsellor
Low priority given to personnel task	Human resource management

In *Thriving on Chaos* (1987) Tom Peters identifies 12 attributes of a quality system, which in themselves represent a checklist against which an organisation's management can assess the stage it has reached in the development of such a system:

- management is obsessed with quality;
- the company has a guiding system or ideology;
- quality is measured;
- quality is rewarded;
- everyone is trained in techniques for assessing quality;
- there is a shift of managerial philosophy from adversarial to co-operative;
- it is recognised that there is no such thing as an insignificant improvement;
- there is constant stimulation to improve quality;
- there is a structure within the company dedicated to quality improvement;
- everybody is involved in quality management, including suppliers, distributors, customers;
- it is understood that costs decline as quality increases;
- it is recognised that quality is relative and improvement is never ending.

QUALITY CONTROL AND QUALITY ASSURANCE

One of the 12 items on Peters' checklist suggests that quality improvement is never ending. It is a relative value compared with the competition as perceived through the customer's eyes. It is an elusive concept because customer perception is itself difficult to predict. Peters argues that if you own a car in which some major part goes wrong, you may have a better view of its quality than if a number of small things go wrong. If the carburettor stops working or the gear box collapses, you take the car to the garage and have the component repaired or replaced. If the service is efficient and problems do not recur, then you can forget about the problem.

If the radio crackles, the door squeaks, the window sticks and there are a number of other small problems, they may not, even cumulatively, be worth the trouble of taking the car to the garage until the next service. Meanwhile they remain a constant reminder of the poor quality of the car. All these problems can be seen as a problem of quality control, which can be defined as being:

'concerned with checking for errors during and after the process of manufacture.'

Quality control often occurs at the end of the manufacturing process as a check to see if the commodity works. If it does not, it is rejected and either scrapped or reworked. The problem with this approach is that there is heavy dependence on inspectors. This is expensive and obviously it is much better to identify the error at an earlier stage. **Statistical process control** (SPC) is a method of monitoring the conformity of a product to agreed specifications. By sampling units of the product, deviations from these specifications can be identified and adjustments made during the production process (*see* p 638).

→ Ch. 19

Modern control techniques are based on the idea of an 'error-free' or 'zero-defect' approach, or 'doing it right first time'. This concept arises because of the costs involved in correcting errors and the fact that the costs are usually greater the later they are identified. Under the TQM approach the team is made responsible for quality control, for reducing wastage and for ensuring that adjustments are made as soon as they are identified.

At a strategic level, quality can be built into the planning of the product or service. Juran and Deming worked extensively with the Japanese to enhance product quality through statistical methods. The first stage is to ensure that the product conforms to design specifications. The next stage is the use of SQC (statistical quality control) or process-control procedures in order to monitor quality during the production of the commodity or rendering of the service. Work teams or quality circles can decide and be delegated the power to decide how to reduce errors and 'do it right first time', while management has to support this process at every stage.

The Ford Motor Company in the 1980s introduced a slogan, 'At Ford, Quality is Job One.' A programme of quality control was introduced along with a new policy of participative management. The emphasis on achieving quotas was changed so that the quality of the product came first. Employee groups were made an important element in the quality control process rather than relying on a separate team of inspectors. Ford's President Donald Peterson stated his commitment to quality:

'The principles by which we will live and die, is that once we can do something well, we have to figure out how to do it even better.'

(Quoted by Stoner and Freeman, 1989)

A concept which builds on quality control is the 'just-in-time' (JIT) principle. This is concerned with improving production efficiency and reducing waste. It is a technique for minimising storage through careful planning and purchasing to meet the exact requirements of the customer, internal or external, and this is only possible if the product does in fact meet agreed specifications and suppliers co-operate fully.

It is at the strategic management level that decisions are made about total quality management and systems of quality control. The strategic approach includes:

- analysis of current position;
- choice of an appropriate starting point;
- implementation of policy, deciding what will be done, how, by whom and by when.

Quality assurance (QA) provides a framework for quality control and quality improvement. Quality assurance supports teams of employees with systems, resources and discretion appropriate to their unique contribution to the organisation, to keep them in tune with progress of quality management and improvement. This aspect of management can help teams:

- understand quality characteristics;
- be realistic about the standards to be attained;
- undertake quality control through a measurement process, interpret the results and make or propose changes.

This process may be supported by a number of techniques such as QUEST (Quality in Every Single Task). This is the idea that everybody in an organisation is a 'customer' and 'supplier' and receives products and services from colleagues within the organisation.

The idea of service within the organisation enables each individual or group to undertake a **QUEST analysis**:

- Who are my customers?
- What do they demand from me?
- In what way do I meet these demands?
- How can I improve my service?

And

- Who are my suppliers?
- What service do I demand of them?
- In what way do they meet these demands?
- How can they improve their service?

KRA (key result areas) is a technique aimed at focusing on realistic outcomes for each team or individual. This may be by:

- identifying a range of quality characteristics for the team which are consistent with the company's strategy;
- agreeing realistic standards for each of these quality characteristics;
- devising a system which can be measured and monitored.

The **Taguchi method** is based on the ideas of Dr Genichi Taguchi (1986) who developed his approach to improve quality engineering at a low cost. It helps to quantify the loss due to lack of quality of a performance characteristic, with the objective of identifying the real cause of a problem. It concentrates on the design of products, reducing variation of performance against the target specification. The Taguchi method depends on a management culture committed to TQM and it has, therefore, developed most successfully in Japan and the USA.

The concentration on customer specification has produced approaches such as the British Standard 5750 registration mark and its international counterpart ISO 9000. These do not establish a level of excellence for a product or service, but they do provide:

'a way of describing the capability of a system to produce goods or services to a specification.'

Customers and potential customers should not expect BS 5750 to make a product the best available, and the registration mark is not a necessary prerequisite to total quality management. Quality is as much about 'doing the right thing' as 'doing things right', while BS 5750 is about 'doing things right'. It arises from the need in quality assurance to supply evidence to other organisations about a particular organisation's effectiveness.

These other organisations may be other companies, which are being supplied with the product or service, government agencies, consumer organisations or any other group which perceives, rightly or wrongly, that the possession of BS 5750 or ISO 9000 is a kitemark of effectiveness, efficiency or quality. The UK has been the leader in this process of certification since a Government White Paper in 1982 required BS 5750 registration for nationalised industries and for public sector procurement generally.

BS 5750 places great emphasis on written evidence, documented systems and procedures. It is based on the status quo rather than on continual improvement, which is the main goal of TQM. The British Standard is a procedural system for companies to follow in order to set up and document an organisation's operational systems. The approach is designed to control each step in a process so that products or services match the specification. This type of process originally developed in industries where safety was a critical factor, such as aerospace, nuclear power and defence. This background is what has provided its particular approach: a very careful, closely audited step-by-step control for procedures. The procedures are established to meet a particular specification and then audited to ensure they are being adhered to in detail. In the 1960s and 1970s the Ministry of Defence and the Central Electricity Board used their inspectors to visit potential suppliers to check that they could produce goods uniformly.

This is still the most important type of use for BS 5750, although some large companies (such as Ford and Marks & Spencer) 'inspect' potential suppliers and set their own operational and product quality standards which suppliers must meet. Some firms conduct their own auditing system in order to standardise procedures. None of these approaches should be confused with TQM.

INVESTING IN PEOPLE

For many organisations people represent their largest cost, often 70 or 80 per cent of the total. In the UK, an initiative which recognises this fact and has the goal of attaining quality in organisations has been 'Investors in People' (IIP). This rested on the premise that companies which have developed, or are developing, an awareness of quality acknowledge that people are the real key to achieving improvements. In a 'quality' culture, people take ownership of their work and responsibility for the quality of their work. This arises from 'gap analysis', such as the gap identified by the Confederation of British Industry:

> *'The crucial importance of people to business success is now almost universally recognised by companies. But there is a huge gap between recognising this, and knowing exactly what to do about it.'*

(Department of Employment, 1990c)

'Investing in people' is concerned with the contribution people can make to business success. By learning from the actions of those organisations which are already developing and using their people successfully, other organisations can adopt, and benefit from, an 'investing in people' (IIP) approach.

IIP arose from the 1988 UK Government White Paper *Employment for the 1990s* which launched a partnership between business and government. The National Training Task Force was established and the Training and Enterprise Councils (TECs) and Local Enterprise Councils (in Scotland) were launched. A major priority of this initiative was to raise employer commitment to training by listening to businesses' ideas and needs, and looking at the people factors which made one organisation more successful than another.

Organisations' own agendas are centred around:

- **productivity**
- **quality**
- **focus on the customer**
- **flexibility.**

These priorities have given rise to operational and management practices such as TQM, and include customer care programmes, 'just-in-time' manufacturing and workplace teams. In all these practices, people are understood to be the key to achieving total quality, and there is an emphasis on teams and seeing colleagues as internal customers, while being genuinely motivated to develop existing skills, develop new ones, accept the devolution of responsibility, make the best use of current or new resources, and if required, acquire new managerial skills.

The investing in people approach aims to help organisations improve performance through a planned approach to:

- **setting and communicating business goals**
- **developing people to meet these goals**

so that:

- **what people can do and are motivated to do**
- **matches what the organisation needs them to do.**

This can be seen diagrammatically in Figure 7.7.

Figure 7.7 Investing in people

The objective is to encourage organisations to think consistently of their people as an investment, not a cost, and act in a way which reflects this perspective. Organisations need to recognise people as a valuable business resource, which can be used to create, protect or waste assets; that there are investment costs as well as benefits in this process; that the benefits will be greater than the costs; and that organisations will only benefit fully from investing in people if they start with clearly defined objectives and actions.

The actions required to improve quality through the investing in people approach can be summarised in a form based on the UK IIP programme:

- Every employer should have a written but flexible plan which sets out business goals and targets, considers how employees will contribute to achieving the plan and specifies how development needs in particular will be assessed and met.

- Management should develop and communicate to all employees a vision of where the organisation is going and the contribution employees will make to its success, involving employee representatives as appropriate.

- The resources for training and developing employees should be clearly identified in the business plan.

- Managers should be responsible for regularly agreeing training and development needs with each employee in the context of business objectives, setting targets and standards linked, where appropriate, to the achievement of National Vocational Qualifications (or relevant units) and, in Scotland, Scottish Vocational Qualifications.

- Action should focus on the training needs of all new recruits and continually developing and improving the skills of existing employees.

- All employees should be encouraged to contribute to identifying and meeting their own job-related development needs.

- The investment, the competence and commitment of employees, and the use made of skills learned, should be reviewed at all levels against business goals and targets.

- The effectiveness of training and development should be reviewed at the top level and lead to renewed commitment and target setting.

In 1999 the UK Government introduced a White Paper, *Learning to Succeed*, which heralded another change in vocational education and training by establishing a 'Learning and Skills Council' in 2001 to replace the previous funding arrangement and the Training and Enterprise Councils. The objective of the new skills body was to 'drive forward improvements in standards and bring together coherence and response' (HMSO, 1999) by putting the whole of vocational training under the Council so that the standards of skills and the lifelong learning required by the country in the twenty-first century could be achieved. Whatever the result of government initiatives may be, and whatever the techniques that may be applied, the importance of the contribution of people to organisational success remains a crucial factor in quality management strategy.

CONCLUSION

Improving **productivity** and effectiveness means not only raising the quantity of output per unit, it also involves improving quality. A key to understanding the importance of quality management is the conviction that costs decline as quality increases. The opposite point of view is well rehearsed in all sorts of organisations and situations. A frequent approach centres on the point of view that 'of course we could improve the quality if we had more money and resources', and the idea that 'you get what you pay for', based on the premise that the more you pay the better the quality.

There is, of course, some truth in these ideas, and they may in fact describe the position very accurately in some situations. On the other hand, very often this is not the case. The increase in Japanese car sales in the 1980s and 1990s has been based on producing cars which are 'fit for the purpose'; they are designed to fulfil customer requirements, they are reliable and they are relatively cheap. Their success has been based on providing what people want at a price they can afford. At the extreme, it can be argued that a Rolls-Royce is a more carefully made car, which is reliable and of very high 'quality' or excellence, but the price puts it out of the reach of most people so that its quality will be compared with other 'hand-made' cars and not with the family saloon. Volvo has based the success of its cars on such factors as safety, reliability and longevity rather than price, because it believes that these are the qualities potential customers want. In fact the important feature of its cars is that they are different, and it is the difference in quality which the company relies on for its sales and profit.

If a company concentrates mainly on price, as for example cars produced by organisations in some eastern European countries, then here there is a chance the relatively cheap car may not sell well because it does not have other qualities which customers require. The essential point is to produce goods which customers want at a price they can afford in a particular market, and the key to producing goods at a competitive price and with good quality is high productivity. The difference between the productivity of car manufacturers in Britain is considerable, with the most productive British worker employed by Japanese companies able to produce twice as many cars a year as the least productive British worker employed by British/American companies.

Differences between companies in terms of productivity arise as a result of greater investment in new equipment and technology, but as important as this are differences in management. The emphasis on quality, focusing of people's jobs, participative management, gaining the co-operation of unions, encouraging teamwork, setting clearly understood performance targets – these are all part of the difference. The lack of these aspects of management encourages expensive situations such as the rejection of products at the point of inspection or eventually by the customer, the waste of materials, unnecessary expense on 'troubleshooters', wasteful hold-ups on supply lines and the maintenance of large and costly inventories to replace rejected products or parts. At the same time, if too much energy is expended on fighting internal battles within the organisation, either between management and unions or between different sections and departments, there is a dissipation of the effort required to fight the real external competition. The competitive edge is achieved by creating a positive and productive internal organisation while focusing on beating external competitors.

A 'quality first', 'right first time' approach means that customers are satisfied and stocks of spare parts and replacements can be kept to a minimum. If performance targets are the responsibility of the individual and team and the internal customer approach is prevalent, there is little need for inspection of the end product, supervision can be reduced to a minimum and a comparatively 'flat' hierarchy can manage the company. All of this will save costs.

The TQM approach is based on the idea that managers are sure of their objectives within a broad vision, for everybody in the organisation to have both a clear focus on their aims and goals and an understanding of the context in which they are working, as well as taking responsibility for work over which they have control. Accountability then becomes a question of peer pressure for most people within the 'internal customer' framework. Quality improvement within an organisation structured in this way is not delegated or subcontracted, it is a responsibility that everyone actively shares.

Management has a responsibility for leading this approach by providing the structural framework and by presenting an example of hard, productive and effective work. The Japanese suggest that management is a way of life which is a progression towards self-enlightenment. They perceive the human skills of imagination, personality, leadership and creativity as just as important as management skills, so that managers are engaged in creating a vision or mission to motivate the workforce. Quality management is concerned with how managers see themselves, what standards they set for themselves and how they motivate others. Out of this analysis should arise the appropriate structure for the organisation.

TQM is a business management philosophy which recognises that customer needs and business goals are inseparable. It pervades an organisation's culture, inspires commitment and encourages communication in all directions, based on work teams and quality systems which utilise resources effectively (see Figure 7.8). At its best, TQM can release a dynamic factor within an organisation which encourages success and profitability.

Figure 7.8 TQM

SUMMARY

■ The management of quality is an essential feature in any organisation for maintaining a competitive advantage. It has always been a feature of industry and commerce in one way or another, but since the 1940s it has become a priority interest of managers because of fierce competition in world markets. The Japanese needed to catch up and compete with the major industrial countries in the 1940s and 1950s, and by the 1960s they were doing this based on a total quality concept. UK managers in the 1980s, 1990s and into the twenty-first century have been in a similar position, finding themselves outcompeted in world markets, so that total quality has become an essential feature of their fightback.

■ Underlying the quest for quality is the need to increase productivity by raising investment levels in high technology and by making the most of the workforce. This involves the delegation of decision making and responsibility in the process of achieving quality objectives. It also involves a concentration on training and development based on high expectations and increasing people's ability to deal with modern technology and participative management.

■ Actions to achieve quality include the introduction of TQM programmes, focus on the customer and the development of techniques such as 'right first time' and 'just in time'. Performance management programmes and the investing in people approach are other ways of concentrating the attention of managers and everybody else in an organisation on the quality of their work and ultimately on the quality of products or services.

Review and discussion questions

1 *What is meant by strategic management? Is there an important difference between strategic and total quality management?*

2 *Consider an organisation that has a quality management programme. Summarise it. How does it compare with the examples outlined in this chapter?*

3 *How important is participative management for a total quality programme?*

4 *How do vision, mission statement and corporate objectives link to TQM?*

5 *What are the advantages and drawbacks of quality circles? What part can management play in quality circles?*

6 *What are the implications of total quality for the management structure of an organisation? How do your conclusions compare to the situation in your own organisation or one that you know?*

7 *How important is a performance management and appraisal system as a prerequisite for a total quality programme?*

8 *What are the differences between strategic quality management, quality assurance and quality control?*

CASE STUDY

British Aerospace

The Airbus Division is part of British Aerospace commercial division which handles work arising from the company's 20 per cent stake in Airbus Industries. Approximately two-thirds of the Airbus Division's payroll of 9000 is engaged in producing Airbus wingsets, while the other activities include a maintenance contract for the US Air Force.

Quality assurance has been developed in the Airbus Division over the last 22 years. Quality managers have progressively been introduced to replace inspectors whose numbers have gradually fallen. A different philosophy of product quality has accompanied this change. Formerly, the aim was to produce 'engineering excellence' but now the goal is 'excellent engineering', a concept requiring a broader view of an item's function and with a higher priority for costs and the complexities of production. Essentially, the need is for excellent engineering at an affordable cost.

This has led to fresh approaches to all activities, from design onwards. Statistical quality control methods still have some applications, but not as many as in mass-production flowline operations. Training has been a high priority from apprentices through to management. Stress is placed on topics such as customer orientation, the awareness of suppliers and what constitutes an affordable cost. There is an approved list of suppliers, with inspections every two years. This has been found to work well with large suppliers but not so well with smaller suppliers, and those with a proven record of high quality have come to be valued.

It has been found that growth at British Aerospace has enhanced quality rather than caused a decline in it. This has been put down to the scale of investment, the long production lines with increased volume, and the concentration on quality as the top priority. Where amendments are made to production, a rule has been introduced that quality has to stay constant or improve. As a result, the larger the production lines, the more changes are made and the greater the number of quality improvements. This has been reinforced by the introduction of a total quality programme.

REFERENCES AND FURTHER READING

Atkinson, P E (1990) *Creating Culture Change: The Key to Successful Total Quality Management*, London: FS Publications.

Bergman, Bo and Klefsjo, Bengt (1994) *Quality from Customer Needs to Customer Satisfaction*, Maidenhead: McGraw-Hill.

Camison, Cesar (1998) 'Total Quality Management and Cultural Change: A Model of Organisational Development', *International Journal of Technology Management*.

Collard, R (1989) *Total Quality Success Through People*, London: IPM.

Confederation of British Industry (1980) *The Will to Win*, CBI.

Confederation of British Industry (1990a) *Investors in People*, London: CBI.

Confederation of British Industry (1990b) *Working for Customers*, London: CBI.

Creech, Bill (1995) *The Five Pillars of TQM: How to Make TQM Work for You*, New York: Plume.

Crosby, P B (1978) *Quality is Free*, Maidenhead: McGraw-Hill.

Deming, W Edwards (1982) *Quality, Productivity and Competitive Position*, Cambridge, MA: MIT Press.

Deming, W Edwards (1986) *Out of the Crisis*, Cambridge, MA: MIT Press.

Department of Employment (1988) *Employment for the 1990s*, cm 540, London, HMSO.

Department of Employment (1990a) *Managing Quality*, London: DoE.

Department of Employment (1990b) *Investors in People: The Context*, November, DoE.

Department of Employment (1990c) Investors in People *Briefing Document 1*, London: DoE, November.

Drucker, P F (1968) *The Practice of Management*, London: Pan.

Harrington, H James (1996) *The Complete Benchmarking Implementation Guide: Total Benchmarking Management*, Maidenhead: McGraw-Hill.

Harris, Ian C and Ruefli, Timothy W (2000) 'The Strategy/Structure Debate: An Examination of Performance Implications', *Journal of Management Studies*, June.

Heikman, Robinson Gill and Creighton-Zoller, Ann (1998) 'Diverse Self Directed Work Teams: Developing Strategic Initiatives for 21st Century Organisations', *Public Personnel Management*, Summer.

HMSO (1999) *Learning to Succeed: A New Framework for Post-16 Learning*, HMSO, CM 4392, June.

Imai, Masaaki (1997) *Gemba Kaizen: A Common Sense, Low-Cost Approach to Management*, Maidenhead: McGraw-Hill.

Ishikawa, K (1984) *What is Total Quality Control the Japanese Way?*, Englewood Cliffs, NJ: Prentice-Hall.

Juran, J (1970) *Quality Planning and Analysis*, Maidenhead: McGraw-Hill.

Juran, J M (1992) *Juran on Quality by Design: The Next Steps for Planning Quality into Goods and Services*, New York: Free Press.

Martiboye, R J (1989) *Leadership and Quality Management: A Guide for Chief Executives*, London: Department of Trade and Industry.

Mohamed, Zairi (1998) *Benchmarking for Best Practice: Continuous Learning through Sustainable Innovation*, Oxford: Butterworth-Heinemann.

Morland, J (1981) *Quality Circles*, London: The Industrial Society.

Oakland, J S (1986) *Total Quality Management*, London: Heinemann.

Peters, T J (1987) *Thriving on Chaos*, Basingstoke: Macmillan.

Peters, T J and Waterman, R H (1982) *In Search of Excellence*, New York: Harper & Row.

Schneier, C E, Beatty, R W and Baird, L S (1987) *The Performance Management Sourcebook*, New York: Human Resource Development Press.

Stoner, J A F and Freeman, R E (1989) *Management*, Englewood Cliffs, NJ: Prentice-Hall.

Taguchi, G (1986) *Introduction to Quality Engineering*, OECD, Paris: Asian Productivity Organisation.

Waterman, R H (1988) *The Renewal Factor*, New York: Barton.

Webb, I (1991) *Quest for Quality*, London: The Industrial Society.

WEBSITES

http://www.severn-trent.co.uk
Provides information on how the Severn-Trent Water Company measures water quality.

http://www.tesco.co.uk
Information about the Tesco Internet Superstore.

CHAPTER 8

Strategic management in the public sector

TIM HANNAGAN

Outcomes

Having read this chapter, you will be able to:

- explain the similarities and differences between management in the private and public sectors

- expand on the consideration of organisational culture raised in earlier chapters

- analyse the 'privatisation' of the public sector

- discuss the importance of accountability, stakeholders and marketing in the public sector

- comment on the movement of managers between the private and public sectors

PRIVATE AND PUBLIC SECTOR MANAGEMENT

Opinions are divided between those who argue that the public sector is unique and operates under different conditions from the private sector and those who suggest that increasingly any differences between the two sectors have become blurred. There is no doubt that there are some differences between the two sectors and that any manager moving from an organisation in one sector to an organisation in the other sector has to take these differences into account and to adapt to the different cultures of the two sectors. In management terms there is a question of how great these differences are, how far the approaches to management adopted in one sector can be applied to the management of the other, and how far there is a body of people with special skills in managing public sector organisations. In considering this question it should be noted that different countries have varying views as to the extent to which the public sector is seen as needing to learn from the private sector. It has been argued (Saint-Martin, 2000) that while in the UK there has been one-way traffic in ideas and techniques from the private sector into the public sector, in France this has been much weaker because of the social prestige of sections of the central state (such as the '*grand corps*') which has retained control over valued technical knowledge, in particular accounting knowledge.

The starting point can be provided by consideration of the views of Socrates, who argued that:

'whatever a man controls, if he knows what he wants and can get it he will be a good controller, whether he controls a chorus, an estate, a city or an army'.   (Adair, 1989)

Socrates did not see a difference between managing one kind of organisation and another kind; he did not believe that expertise in a particular area was a necessary requirement for management. He argued that the most experienced soldier was not necessarily the best person to lead an army. Rather, it was more important that the general leading the army had shown the ability to find the best experts in any field of activity, knew what he wanted to achieve and how to achieve it, and had an eagerness to avoid defeat, to engage the enemy at the right time and to understand the importance of succeeding.

These arguments find modern expression in the headhunting of managers across industries so that a chief executive may be sought who is not an expert in a particular industry but who has already proved the ability to be successful. It is seen in the appointment of generals and admirals to run charities or the appointment of majors and captains to be secretaries of golf clubs. These transitions do not always work, because they do depend on the ability of the manager to adapt to the culture and requirements of the new industry. A person who is successful in the disciplined world of the military services may find it difficult to adapt to a situation where control has to be achieved through different means. Similarly, a manager who has been successful in the private sector may find it difficult to adapt to the accepted norms of the public sector and vice versa. On the other hand, there are many examples of managers who have worked their way up through one industry or particular company, and hands-on 'insider' experience may be felt to be of prime importance. Organisations are usually managed by people with experience in the industry if not in the particular company. Large, long-standing companies such as Shell Petroleum tend to promote their senior managers from within, banks are usually headed by managers with long experience in banking, football clubs tend to be managed by ex-footballers, schools are managed by people who have been teachers.

Public sector organisations have, in the past, usually been managed by practitioners, for example local authority chief executives have tended to be people whose whole career has been in local government, university vice-chancellors are usually people who have worked in the sector for many years, head teachers have usually been promoted from the classroom. 'Permeability' has increased between the private and public sectors, partly because of privatisation over the years, but intersector movement of managers does not happen as much as in the USA and there is still a tendency for 'each breed to stay in its own silo' (Cook, 2004). Since the 1980s in the UK, changes have occurred in parts of the public sector, for example in the National Health Service where hospital trusts have had specialist, non-practitioner managers appointed to run them. This has caused its own problems because the practitioners may feel that the 'non-practitioner' managers do not understand their problems. There are different views as to how far managers can be 'parachuted' into an organisation in an industry where they have little or no expertise because of their expertise in management in another sector. Socrates' viewpoint was that:

> *'the management of private concerns differs only in point of number from that of public affairs. In other respects they are much alike, and particularly in this, that neither can be carried on without men, and the men employed in public and private transactions are the same.'*   (Adair, 1989) (*See also* page 32)

SIMILARITIES BETWEEN THE PUBLIC AND PRIVATE SECTORS

The process of management is concerned with the management of people and similar basic problems are raised whatever the form of organisation being managed. Rewards and punishments may be different, organisational cultures may vary but in the end people have to be organised and controlled. This view is based on the argument that management is a clear and distinct function, a science or an art, which is distinct from what is being managed. The opposite argument is that a knowledge of what is being managed is essential for good management, so that only people who have worked their way up through an industry should be a manager in an organisation within it – only university lecturers should become university managers, only medical practitioners should manage hospital trusts. It is argued that only in this way can the manager understand the intricacies of the organisation being managed and the difficulties of the people working in it (Exhibit 8.1).

Exhibit 8.1 **Similarities between private and public sector management**

- ■ **The control of people**
- ■ **Knowledge of purpose**
- ■ **Achievement of an objective**
- ■ **Practitioner experience**
- ■ **Need for adaptation to new organisational cultures**

In fact of course, a manager is unable to have experience of all aspects of an organisation. Senior managers may have been promoted through the finance route, or the production route or marketing or sales or human resources. At some point in the promotion ladder the specialist becomes a generalist, having to understand the working of the whole section, department or company. In practice, a manager who has moved from managing a specialist function will only have expertise in that one function and will have to develop the ability to manage wider areas of responsibility. It can be argued that working through an organisation in one capacity or another gives a 'feel' for it which somebody from outside will not have acquired. This 'feel' involves an understanding of how the industry works, its customs and norms, the products and services it provides, its organisational culture.

The increasingly volatile careers of people in management has encouraged the view that management is a transferable skill, so that if you can manage in one area of activity you can manage in another. In practice, most people do become managers in the areas in which they have expertise and movement between industries and movement between the private and public sector tend to be largely in specialist functions. Accountants, information technology specialists and human resource experts may move relatively freely between sectors, but there has not been evidence of a free flow of more general managers. In terms of the private and public sectors, this is partly explained by differences in pay and benefits but is also based on fundamental differences between the two sectors.

DIFFERENCES BETWEEN THE PUBLIC AND THE PRIVATE SECTORS

The environment of public organisations is littered with considerations of accountability. Public opinion, interest groups, lobbying and interventions by elected officials and contractors are attempts at influence and control which have to be dealt with in public organisations by negotiation and bargaining. These attempts at influencing public organisations lead them to build buffers in the form of coalitions, advisory groups and bringing members of key groups into aspects of the management or governance of the organisation. Private organisations have fewer needs for these buffers and tend to have simpler, more traceable organisational arrangements. Public sector organisations are susceptible to greater and more open accountability than those in the private sector. Politicians, pressure groups, taxpayers and voters all have an interest in the performance of public sector organisations, they are all stakeholders and feel that they have a right to question performance. Private sector organisations also have stakeholders who have rights to question performance, but they will tend to be more circumscribed than in the public sector (Table 8.1).

Strategic management in public settings must identify the beliefs and demands of key stakeholders because the organisation is influenced by the views of opinion leaders, the manipulation of legislators and interest groups and opposition to the activities of the organisation which can swamp the economic issues which are crucial for private organisations. How things are viewed and understood by **stakeholders** is important to any organisation, whether in the public or the private sector, but while in the private sector the views of the public may make themselves known largely through the market and through **shareholder** value, in the public sector these views may be applied directly to the organisation through representation on governing bodies or the boards of public corporations, or through advisory groups and other pressure groups. This means that decisions such as

Table 8.1 Differences between private and public sector management

PRIVATE SECTOR	PUBLIC SECTOR
Profit motive	Service motive
Shareholder accountability	Stakeholder accountability
Market forces	Public value
Customer sovereignty	Patient, student, public needs
Goals	Ideals
Efficiency	Equity
'Bottom line'	Multiple goals
'Private' goods and services	'Public' goods and services

whether to offer new products or services or to modify existing ones have to pay particular attention to implementation as much as the apparent soundness of the proposed changes.

Whereas private organisations can test their efficiency and effectiveness by comparison with competitors or through the market and **customer** reaction, the beliefs of key stakeholders may override these tests in public organisations. Public organisations have less freedom to add or delete services or to carry out other actions thought to be desirable and there may be constraints that limit spheres of action. In the past, schools and colleges have had geographical 'catchment' areas from which they could draw their **pupils** and **students** and hospital trusts have geographical areas of responsibility for **patients**, which have precluded marketing to find new customers. Public organisations may also have a stipulated set of services that they are expected to provide. Schools are expected to provide learning opportunities for particular age groups, hospitals are expected to provide health services, libraries to act as media resource centres. If these organisations move too far outside their specified area of activity, they will have to satisfy their stakeholders that their new activities are legitimate and they face both public and political opposition. This could be true, for example, if public sector hospitals became agents for pharmaceutical companies or schools became involved in the marketing of children's toys.

Private organisations can undertake proactive strategies which include divestiture or horizontal and vertical integration and acquisition. They can decide on the activities they carry out and they can decide not to be involved in particular activities. On the other hand, public organisations are expected to provide particular services for reasons other than those indicated by the market. They may be expected to provide services as a result of tradition or because they are the only suppliers in an area or because there is felt to be a need. They have to make changes on a more proactive basis, usually involving an incremental move that balances opportunity and threat. However, if they are too proactive, opposition may be crystallised, providing obstacles to action which may absorb efforts which could have been used to provide the new development.

OBJECTIVES IN THE PUBLIC SECTOR

Public organisations often have **multiple goals** that are both vague and conflicting. There is not a '**bottom line**' that can be used as a proxy measure of success. Instead, the demands of interest groups and manipulation by important stakeholders and third parties create a complex and confusing set of expectations that are frequently conflicting. Hospitals are judged using one set of standards by patients, another by medical staff and a third by their funding bodies. Funding bodies want efficiency targets to be achieved, patients want personalised care, medical staff demand improved resources. Goal ambiguity in public organisations makes performance expectations difficult to specify. Vague performance expectations mean that success cannot be easily recognised so that it is often difficult to identify and reward key contributors, while failure cannot be detected and corrected in a timely manner. There is often less urgency in public organisations than in private sector organisations, as periodic elections, political changes and changes in rules and regulations interrupt public organisations' plans and projects.

Inertia can be encouraged in public sector organisations by having to 'bring up to speed' newly appointed individuals in **stakeholder** positions and to find out their agendas. A new minister in charge of prisons, for example, may have strong views on the penal system and may not understand the practical problems of the service. There may be disruption to the normal flow of activity and uncertainty about demands for the future which make it easy to rationalise inaction and can lead to cautiousness, inflexibility and low rates of innovation. Hospitals are expected to produce quality performance in all their services, but there are problems in measuring 'quality' because the meaning of the term is both elusive and disputed. Consultants may be very concerned with procedure and results, patients with levels of care, hospital managers with the throughput of patients.

In the public sector strategic managers can use **ideals** in the place of **goals**. Ideals provide a picture of the desired future state of the organisation, giving concrete cues on which to build action. Ideals indicate best- and worst-case situations, with the worst case providing a floor on which to build and the best case a target towards which to plan. Ideals provide targets and offer ways to seek compromise among competing views that dictate what the organisation is (or is not) about. Strategic objectives in the public sector may be ill-defined and expressed in vague and abstract terms, such as 'serving the public', 'maintaining law and order', 'reducing inequality' or 'improving health'. Ideals may take the form of, for example, providing first-class health services for everybody. The introduction of targets, often linked to funding, has made some objectives more precise, for example waiting list targets for hospital operations or pupil and student number targets for schools, colleges and universities. Attempts to measure levels of service and service quality have led to targets based on the 'outcomes' of educational services. It is a matter of opinion as to whether these targets go any way to measuring quality.

MARKETS

The extent to which an organisation is in the public sector or the private sector can be measured by the extent to which it is open to **market forces** (Figure 8.1). The less market forces are allowed to affect an organisation, the more clearly it can be

Figure 8.1 Market forces and public goods and services

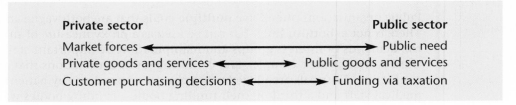

said to be in the public sector. It can be argued that some goods and particularly services have to be provided by the state because they are in some way a collective need that private sector organisations cannot adequately provide. Defence and law and order are both examples of these services. While it is possible to have private sector armies and private law enforcement agencies, examples of them are usually found in countries where the rule of law is weak or non-existent. In these circumstances, the private armies carry out the wishes of particular warlords rather than the wishes of an established government. The same is true of private police forces. In practice, there has been an increase even in democracies of privately employed bodyguards and security teams, but they are still subject to the requirements of the law and the national police force.

Other '**public goods and services**' include waste and refuse collection, street lighting, the provision of clean air, noise abatement, customs and excise services, immigration services and so on. The provision of these services cannot be left to the vagaries of the market, although parts of them have been 'privatised' by providing contracts to private companies to carry out particular functions. Parts of waste disposal and refuse collection have been contracted to private companies, prison management has in some cases been taken over by private security companies, the supply of public utilities has been contracted out to private providers. These contracted services are all contracted out by government agencies and come under government scrutiny and monitoring.

Public service organisations are established in such a way that whatever product or service they provide, their purpose is to be of **service to the public**, rather than to produce a **profit** for their owners. Views on what can and cannot be provided by the public and private sectors have changed over the years, so that more and more of the activities which used to be provided by the public sector have been privatised in one way or another. While some products and services have been considered to be national assets, because they included a strong element of natural monopoly they needed to be under the direct control of the government. This view has changed so that contracts have been offered to private companies for particular services, public/private partnerships have been formed and public sector organisations have been increasingly exposed to market forces. While in the 1940s and 1950s areas such as steel production, coal mining and railway services were nationalised to bring them under public ownership, since the 1980s denationalisation has placed most parts of these industries under private ownership.

However, the debate since the 1980s has shifted towards questions of how these products and services can be provided with greater **efficiency**, and developments such as the European Community have raised questions about national subsidies for particular industries. Both steel and coal production have been exposed to market forces and elements of the market have also been introduced into the provision of railways. Transport is an area which cuts across the private/public divide and is a rich area of debate. Roads are built and maintained by the use of public money, while there have been attempts to privatise the provision of railway lines At the same time the production of cars and petrol comes under the private sector and the provision of railway services has been privatised under strict public scrutiny and government targets. Increasingly, private sector investment has been encouraged by governments in areas which have been provided by the public sector, with arrangements made for the private sector to receive profits from their activities. The national lottery has been a government-controlled initiative organised by a private profit-making company.

This blurring of the divide between the two sectors has meant that even areas of the public sector largely funded by taxation have been exposed to market forces. This has been the case with education and health services, with hospital trusts competing for funds, and colleges and universities competing for students and the funds they attract. This has meant that whereas many of the public organisations involved in these areas were protected from market forces by regulations to ensure demand for their services, the removal of the so-called 'catchment' areas for schools and colleges, for example, has introduced an element of competition to these organisations.

Public organisations lack an economic market that provides them with resources in the form of revenues. In the private sector, the buying behaviour of people is the primary source of information, indicating which products and services are or are not effective. Public sector organisations are dependent on oversight bodies for resources or reimbursement for services based on funding formulas. These formulas may be based to some extent on market forces, or they may be based on public policies or other considerations. They may allow public organisations to avoid efficiency and effectiveness considerations until these are raised by the oversight bodies, and budget allocations from these bodies may follow historical precedents, creating incentives for organisations to spend at previous levels whether or not spending has produced useful outcomes. These 'oversight' or funding bodies make up the 'market' for many public sector organisations. Universities and colleges are funded on the basis of student numbers and other factors, such as staying-on rates for students and student success, which are established by the funding body and may be changed over time. This means that colleges and universities have to change their offerings to meet the demands of the funding bodies in order to maximise funding The degree of 'publicness' as against 'privateness' of an organisation is illustrated in Figure 8.2.

Publicness, in the sense of how far an organisation is in the public sector, declines if direct charges can be made, just as privateness increases as direct market dealing develops. The extent to which an organisation is in the public or private sector is indicated by the strength of market signals, the extent of competition,

Figure 8.2 Degrees of 'publicness'

'Publicness'		'Privateness'
Lack of market signals	⟵⟶	Market signals
Lack of competition	⟵⟶	Competition
Indirect charging for goods and services	⟵⟶	Direct charging

financial arrangements and the availability of data to provide information about potential customers. Competition for customers can be limited in public sector organisations because they may be expected to collaborate with other organisations offering similar services. Competing for customers would be seen as creating a duplication of services which may be felt to be undesirable, and new competitors may be discouraged by regulatory bodies.

STRATEGIC MANAGEMENT IN THE PUBLIC SECTOR

It can be argued that strategic models that are competitive models are of little use in organisations with a significant degree of publicness because in the public sector strategy should be sought that enhances co-operation and collaboration. Strategic leaders in the public sector have to identify and appraise the historical context in which their organisations must operate. This is because issues arise from the tensions created by claims and counter-claims that characterise the beliefs of people who control public sector organisations and the demands of clients, politicians, professional and other stakeholders. Cumbersome mechanisms are needed in the public sector to deal with the logistics of consulting stakeholders and the public. Devices including governing bodies, advisory committees, task forces, public meetings and public announcements are used in order to determine expectations and refine understandings about what the organisation should do and how it should act.

Equity in dealing with clients and providing services may be more important than **efficiency** in the public sector, while efficiency dominates the concerns of the private sector. As publicness increases, efficiency and its comparatively clear cost-related goal become less useful and equity becomes more important. This means that an emphasis on efficiency may cause problems in the public sector. For example, libraries may find that the most efficient process is to keep books on the shelves, cut hours and limit the range of services, whereas most people want libraries to be open for long hours and want wide information services and encouraged book use. In these circumstances, goals other than efficiency have to be established.

While **strategic management in the public sector** is undertaken to prompt action and discover agendas of activities that fit within political timeframes and respond to consensual demands for change, private sector organisations use strategic management to provide an overview of activities and to slow activity rather than to prompt action. The concentration on efficiency means that strategic management in private organisations will be concerned with matters such as product viability. At the same time strategic planning in the public sector has to take into account the short-term considerations of politicians, who will tend to be looking for quick returns so that they can point to successes and achievements – they need to be confident about their ability to win the next election before they will look to the longer term. Public organisations may have a broader impact than private organisations in the sense that schools, for example, may be thought to be important in dealing with poverty, racism, child abuse, juvenile crime and other social problems as well as their educational responsibilities. Everyone may feel they have an ownership stake in public organisations, so they are expected to show integrity, fairness, responsiveness, honesty and accountability to the public, while private organisations will have fewer implied obligations and people place fewer demands on them. The different priorities in strategic management in the public and private sectors is summarised in Table 8.2.

Table 8.2 The different priorities of strategic management in the public and private sectors

PUBLIC SECTOR	PRIVATE SECTOR
Discover agendas	Product viability
Prompt action	Overview of activities
Equity	Efficiency
Meeting political/social obligations	Profit

In the public sector, strategy may have to be developed with little support data. There may be limited information about markets and an unwillingness to divert funds into the collection of this information. At the same time it is difficult for public organisations to keep strategy and information secret. Outsiders may have a right to review and interpret information. Floating ideas to see what happens can be a problem in public settings, while strategy has to be devised in the face of public scrutiny. Demonstrations of involvement may be as important as good ideas and politics involves the managing of many stakeholders external to the organisation who control or influence sources of money and whose support is essential. In private organisations, politics seldom goes far beyond coping with resistance to change.

Public sector managers have weaker power bases and less authority to alter or reshape the system they manage than do private sector managers. Autonomy and flexibility are generally lower in public organisations, making authority limits a key ingredient in defining publicness. For example, hospitals cannot promote service changes without the advice and consent of their medical staff, a group who may have limited commitment to the organisation. Consensus has to be established to accompany strategy formation. Encouraging effective performance by using incentives is much more difficult in public organisations than it is in private ones. It is generally more difficult to provide incentives in pay or other ways in order to enhance performance. In private organisations individuals' contributions to profit can be rewarded monetarily. Public sector employees may prefer job security, important tasks or power and recognition over financial rewards. Job security and promotion can only be given once and may not be available when a reward is needed, and linking people's performance to these rewards is more difficult than with financial rewards. Financial rewards can be tied to measurable performance in the private sector. Other means are needed to encourage productive behaviour in these circumstances, and this calls for creativity in strategy formulation.

MANAGEMENT IN THE PUBLIC SECTOR

It was reported in 2003 that the Ministry of Health was to appoint headhunters to:

'seek high-powered managers to bring a harder hitting entrepreneurial culture to the boardrooms of the NHS in England.'

(John Carvel, Social Affairs Editor, *The Guardian*, 3 March 2003, p 2)

It wanted young managers from the private sector to join the boards of hospitals and primary care trusts. At the same time the Ministry announced a revolution to convert the National Health Service from a nationalised service into a network of competing providers, striving to give patients the best free health care. The start of this process was the establishment of so-called 'foundation hospitals' that are no longer under direct NHS ownership. The objective of moving private sector managers into the NHS and moving high-achieving hospitals out of the NHS was to bring a decisive change in the culture of the NHS, which the Health Secretary believed was still locked in the attitudes of the 1940s.

The problems of private sector managers moving into the public sector has been highlighted by these initiatives. The Chief Executive of the NHS (Sir Nigel Crisp) was recruited from a private company and rose to become director of the London region of the NHS before promotion to the top job. He was understood to have known other private sector managers who took jobs in the NHS but found the management style so alien that they left. In order to overcome this problem in this government initiative, recruits would be supported and mentored to help them in the new culture. Private sector managers have already been recruited or seconded to run central NHS facilities, including information technology and diagnostic and treatment centres. Also, a scheme has been introduced to build up a cohort of talented managers who could be placed in senior leadership roles in the NHS whenever they became available. The aim was to extend this approach into hospitals and primary care trusts which were the local bodies controlling most of the health budget in England.

A ministerial source was quoted as saying about the Health Secretary that:

'he knows we have got to get out of the mindset that the only people who can be good managers are those who have come through the NHS route'

(*The Guardian*, March 2003)

but *The Guardian* Social Affairs Editor recognised that this attitude was unlikely to win friends among public service professionals who had experienced the failure of successive governments in their attempts to recruit from industry and the armed forces. It is likely that the most successful movement of managers from one sector to the other is in technical services such as information technology and accountancy, where the same or similar skills are required in both sectors. This may also apply to facilities management and human resource management, but the major obstacle remains the different mindset or culture of the two sectors. Changing mindsets is a notoriously difficult process and the problems arise in moving from the private sector into the public sector. The private sector manager arrives with one mindset into a situation where other mindsets are prevalent and of course the mindset of managers from the armed forces will be different again.

An accountant who moved from working for 30 years in private companies to become the Financial Director of a further education corporation felt that in this corporation, in contrast to the companies in which he had worked, managers did not have the on-the-job management training and development that they needed. He thought that in general, although the corporation had been independent of local authority control for some years,:

'the mindset is still in local authority mode so that if there is any money left in the capital budgets bids are put in for it.' (Hannagan, 2003)

He was used to managers working out what they needed to deliver a product or service and then asking for it. He had found that entering the public sector after a long career in the private sector had been a

'cultural shock. In general people are better educated than in manufacturing industry, but everything becomes a debate, there is little discipline, everything is a debating society.'

(Hannagan, 2003)

He also felt that there were limited sanctions in the public sector, so that while in the private sector, *'if you do well you will earn a bonus and share options, if you do badly you are fired'*. In contrast, he quoted the example of a senior member of his present staff who had made a serious mistake and had received a verbal warning.

Mindsets can be seen as ways of working and expected ways of working so that an officer in the armed forces may expect people to obey a command and will not expect very much discussion. In the private sector senior managers will expect their orders and requests to be obeyed but will understand that these will have to fall within the job description of the employee. In the public sector an order or request may lead to a discussion about the reasons for it and its effects on the service. These differences arise because of the different organisational cultures that exist in various sectors of the economy. These so-called mindsets arise through exposure to particular organisational cultures and help to perpetuate them in the sense that a general view may be held that this is the way we do things around here and this is the way we have always done things and should always do things (*see* Chapters 1 and 2).

→ Chs 1 and 2

ORGANISATIONAL CULTURE AND THE PUBLIC SECTOR

Meek (1988) thought that the concept of organisational culture could be

'a powerful analytical tool in the analysis and interpretation of human action within complex organisations.'

He argued that those intent upon creating a healthy and successful corporate climate might concentrate on 'what is' in the pursuit of 'what should be', while corporate success could be more dependent upon external influences of the marketplace than on internal interpersonal dynamics. He concluded that:

'the assumption that a corporate culture can be created so as to unite members for the effective and efficient attainment of corporate goals flies in the face of almost everyone's experience of organisational life.'   (Meek 1988)

His argument suggests that organisations were not one homogeneous culture, but they were multicultural. Although this can be seen in private sector companies, particular examples of this can be seen in public sector organisations such as tertiary education institutions and health services. For example, academics may have a greater allegiance to their profession than their institution and this could produce a conflict between the interests of the individual and the management of the institution. However, Meek did argue that there was a successful 'feel' about a successful organisation and the difference between them and not so successful organisations went beyond explanations based on superior technology, efficient management and an advantageous position in the market. **Organisational culture** has been defined by Schein (1992) as:

> *'a pattern of shared basic assumptions that a group learned as it solved its problems of external adaptation and internal integration, that have worked well enough to be considered valid and, therefore, to be taught to new members as the correct way to perceive, think and feel in relation to those problems.'*

It is a complex mixture of tangible factors which can be seen and touched, such as an office space and its fixtures and fittings, assumptions about how people should behave in the organisation and people's actual behaviour.

> *'The culture of any group of people is that set of beliefs, customs, practices and ways of thinking that they have come to share with each other through being and working together. At the visible level the culture of a group takes the form of ritual behaviour, symbols, myths, stories, sounds and artefacts.'* (Stacey, 1999)

→ Chs 1 and 2

An organisation's culture is 'the way we do things around here' (*see* Chapter 1, pp 13–14 and 21–5, and Chapter 2, pp 42–8) and it may vary from office to office and department to department. In some offices the custom is to arrive at a particular time in the morning and leave at a particular time in the evening, in others the starting time is treated more casually and people feel they need to stay on as long as possible in the evenings to show how hard they are working. Some offices have traditional offices and desks, others are open plan with shared space and equipment, while others may have lounge areas, kitchens and mini-gyms. The factors which make up the culture of a group can be described as the TAB factors (Exhibit 8.2).

Group and organisational values and assumptions may be based on what has happened in the past, on leadership, on organisational structures and systems, on routine and ritual and power structures. The **assumptions** which are taken for granted are at the centre of an organisation's culture and are surrounded by **beliefs** which are more specific and **values** which may be strongly held but more difficult to put into practice (Figure 8.3). Peters and Waterman (1982) considered that organisations that were value-driven were likely to be most successful, while Deal and Kennedy (1982) thought that organisations which shared strong and cohesive cultures were more likely to be flexible and co-operative and that transformation leadership could be a source of 'culture busting' to bring about strategic change. However, Pettigrew (1990) questioned to what extent cultures were in fact manageable because they were so embedded in organisations, and Newman (1994) suggested that culture prefigures the way in which strategy is made in a particular organisation. She thought that existing organisational culture would influence strategies that were developed in organisations and could blinker the perception of important strategic issues. She thought that change in the public sector involved radical changes to roles and boundaries within and between organisations so that fixed identities based on a profession, function or role were eroded and a sense of social purpose might clash with notions of progress.

Exhibit 8.2 Organisational culture – the TAB factors

- Tangible factors – physical conditions

- Assumptions – expected attitudes and behaviour

- Behaviour – how people actually behave

Figure 8.3 **Layers of culture within an organisation**

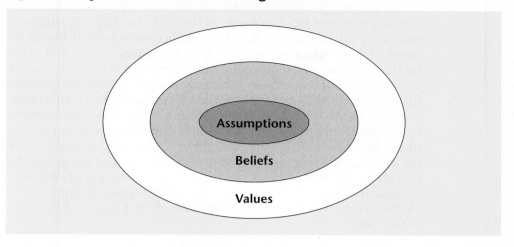

Bryson (1995) argued that strategies were tailored to fit an organisation's culture even if the purpose of the strategy was to change that culture in some way, and that the organisation's culture becomes more important during strategy formation because whatever patterns exist are typically manifestations of its culture. He argued that every organisation had an existing strategy, whether or not it was any good, which provided the pattern that supported its policies, decisions, resource allocations and other actions. This pattern, which was typically a manifestation of its culture, would need to be refined or sharpened or (less frequently) changed altogether for it to provide an effective bridge between the organisation and its environment. In the UK this environment began to change in the 1980s as public sector organisations had to become customer-oriented, entrepreneurial, innovative, flexible and responsive. Newman (1994) suggested that it was at this time that the public sector discovered 'culture' as a key dimension of change.

Newman argued that although there were elements of shared values in the public sector, in many cases cultures divided along departmental, functional or professional lines, with different sets of values and practices. Consensus could be difficult in the public sector where conflict might arise between professional and old public sector values as against newly encouraged business and market-based values. She felt that assumptions based on the idea that culture was generated by, and centred on, the leader, took little account of the complex dynamics in the public sector. She suggested that culture could not be separated from strategic change because the process of change was intimately intertwined with cultural norms and values. She argued that in the past those working in the public sector were able to operate within a framework of meanings about their role as public servants, with a sense of purpose based on doing good or benefiting society, and this was in exchange for a certain status and security. Strategic change produced conflicts over meanings, exposed conflicting values, created shifts in power bases and realigned groups. Individuals learned the rhetoric of new values and adopted new cultural symbols in order to defend or expand their power base.

Although organisational culture is an important element for the leadership of a public sector organisation to consider in the process of change, in extreme situations it may be swept aside because of an overriding priority. Accountability to the dominant stakeholder may be so important for a public sector organisation that the existing culture may be overridden in the need for change, in spite of the opposition of professionals. As a result of the 1992 Further and Higher Education Act, colleges of further education in England became corporate bodies limited by guarantee. Most of their funding came from a funding council and in order to achieve this funding they had to reach a number of targets in terms of student numbers and unit costs. In order to achieve these targets some colleges were prepared to put aside the organisational culture that existed (Hannagan 2003). This raises questions on the views of Meek (1988) that culture was not an independent variable to be altered by the efforts of managers, it was something an organisation *is* rather than something an organisation *has*, although it supports Bryson's (1995) view that sometimes, although rarely, culture could be changed altogether in order for it to provide an effective bridge between the organisation and its environment.

Organisational culture in the public sector is often strongly held but it has been challenged by developments in the last 20 or 30 years. A director of personnel stated that:

> *'cultural change has been slow although it is easier with new staff, but staff who come to the College from industry soon become indoctrinated with the old culture.'*

(Hannagan, 2003)

In the report on their research in the UK National Health Service, McNulty and Whittington (1992) quoted a doctor as saying:

> *'as a doctor I have three distinct priorities of loyalty. My first loyalty must always be to my individual patients. My second loyalty must be to my profession's standards and my third loyalty, and putting it third does not mean it is rubbish, is to whoever employs me at a particular time.'*

They identified conflicts between the organisation and the professional working in it in disputes over professional freedom and the preservation and development of professional standards so that cultural homogeneity (a feature of excellent organisations identified by Peters and Waterman, 1982) was difficult to achieve in public sector organisations. Public sector organisations have conflicting obligations which make it difficult to develop the homogeneous culture which may be possible in private organisations. Public sector values can be described as 'pluralistic' in the sense that there are a range of loyalties and stakeholders.

A major difference between the two sectors is that the public sector has an obligation to provide a public service whether it is in terms of health, learning or law and order. Public sector organisations have a responsibility to satisfy social obligations in providing jobs, making 'good citizens' and ensuring publicly responsible behaviour, and they may also be seen to have an economic obligation in encouraging economic growth and providing economic leverage effects on the economy. At the same time public sector organisations are not profit-making and they cannot redefine themselves. They may be allowed to retain surpluses but they do not have an overriding objective to provide returns for their shareholders. They are not established in order to make profits and therefore their approach is more 'soft-edged' than a private sector organisation. Also they cannot change the whole nature of their operation in the way that is open to private sector organisations. They are established for a particular purpose, such as providing education or health services, and they have to continue to do this. They can diversify within this brief to some extent but they cannot change the main thrust of their activities. James Strachan, who has been Managing Director of Merrill Lynch and Chairman of the Audit Commission, has been quoted (in Cook, 2004) as arguing that calculated risk can be a route to success in the public sector:

> *'It's important to change the culture, to alter the gross imbalance between the reward for success and the punishment for failure, which prevents people in the public sector putting their heads above the parapet.'*   (Cook, 2004, p 55)

These are fundamental differences between the two sectors, which is reflected in their cultures. The private sector culture is a profit-driven one, where competition has to be met and the disciplines of the market apply. Organisational objectives are based around profit margins, share of the market and product and service viability, and these concerns are passed down to individual managers and operatives. Jobs and remuneration depend on the success of the organisation. Individuals can be rewarded for the contribution they make to this success and they will lose their jobs if the organisation or their part of it is not successful. The public sector culture is a service-driven one where the needs of the people receiving the service have to be met and the disciplines implied by this apply. Organisational objectives are based around the successful provision of this service and the satisfying of various stakeholders which include the public, and these concerns are passed down to individual managers and operatives. Jobs depend on stakeholder support for the provision of this service, while remuneration depends on historical precedents, bargaining power and by a concept of 'worth' based on public or other perceptions. Individuals may not be rewarded in a tangible form for their contribution to the success of the organisation, the reward may be in the form of satisfaction. There may be a concept of people following a 'vocation' used in the sense of a 'calling', in which matters of remuneration are secondary to the provision of the service.

THE 'PRIVATISATION' OF THE PUBLIC SECTOR

Since the 1980s governments in the UK have tried to introduce elements of private sector culture into the public sector. The reason for this approach has been the increasing awareness of the cost of providing public services, pressures on national budgets and attempts to increase efficiency in the provision of public services. The actual situation of every service varies depending on the service they provide and the recipients of that service. For example, the ageing population of the country has put pressure on the National Health Service as the demand for services for older people has increased and the rise in the number of retired people means that fewer people are contributing to the national insurance which pays for the service. At the same time medical advances have meant that more and more expensive procedures are now available at a cost, and there is simultaneously an increase in people's expectations of what they are entitled to receive. The cost of the NHS has risen, and one way of meeting this rise has been to charge directly for an increasing range of services. The increased 'privatisation' of the public sector has been reflected in the increasing use of management consultants in the sector and the use of temporary management experts or 'interim managers'. The public sector provided 13 per cent of overall revenue for the largest consultancy firms in 2002 compared with 9 per cent in 2000, along with an increase in the use of 'interims' to bridge gaps and improve quality. The increasing use of consultants in the UK was closely linked to the provision of accounting advice and associated information technology advice, and, as was noted at the beginning of this chapter, accounting knowledge remained concentrated in one of the governmental *grand corps*.

Exhibit 8.3 provides an example of the 'privatisation' of the public sector, the degree of free enterprise introduced, along with the controls imposed by a government-established and controlled body. These controls included organisational objectives and the types of service which were to be provided.

Newman (1994) suggested that the public sector discovered 'culture' in the late 1980s as a key dimension of change, as public sector organisations had to become customer-oriented, entrepreneurial, innovative, flexible and responsive. She argued that while there were elements of shared values in the public sector, in many cases cultures divided along departmental, functional or professional lines, with different sets of values and practices. Consensus was difficult because conflict arose between the old public sector and professional values and the new business and market-based values. In the past, those working in the public service were able to operate within a framework of meanings about their role as public servants with a sense of purpose based on doing good or benefiting society, and this was in exchange for a certain status and security. Changes brought about by moves towards privatisation produced conflicts over meanings, exposed conflicting values, created shifts in power bases and realigned groups. Individuals learned the rhetoric of new values and adopted new cultural symbols in order to defend or expand their power base.

Exhibit 8.3 The 'privatisation' of further education in England

In further education in England, the Further and Higher Education Act (1992) established further education colleges as public sector corporations with the power to employ people, earn and borrow money and decide how to spend their budgets. The dictionary definition of a corporation is '*a body or society authorised by law to act as one individual unit … such as a company*' (*Chambers Maxi Dictionary*, 1992, p 230). Further education corporations were like private companies in that they could employ people, borrow money, decide how to spend the money they received, decide how to use their assets, including their buildings, and decide how they achieved their strategic objectives. However, they did not have complete freedom to choose these objectives because they were established to a large extent by their stakeholders.

The chief stakeholder was the Further Education Funding Council (FEFC), which was superseded by the Learning and Skills Council in 2001. The Council was the conduit for funds to flow from the government to the college corporations. In return for these funds, colleges had to provide part-time and full-time education for people over compulsory school age. At the same time the government established targets to be met by the corporation, including an expansion of 25 per cent in student numbers in three years, increased efficiency and an ability for the colleges to demonstrate that they were contributing to the economic success of the locality and the nation. Providing colleges met these objectives they could earn money in other ways and spend their money in any way they wished. The clear mission of colleges was in terms of providing education and training services to people over the age of 16, mainly but not exclusively from their locality. Most of the funds they received were in practice tied to the provision of particular services required by the stakeholders. At the same time the governing body of each college became the corporation board while the principal became the chief executive.

Newman argued that strategy, culture and change interacted to produce tensions and ambiguities.

In further education colleges the pressure was to become more 'business-like' after incorporation because they were working in a more competitive market and had to become more productive and efficient in order to prosper. The gap between managers and their need to meet efficiency targets and practitioners and their professionalism was emphasised by these changes. Dunleavy and Hood (1994) suggested that traditionally the public sector was built on the idea of a highly distinctive public sector group and a dense grid of general procedural rules governing the conduct of its activities. The changes that occurred made the public sector less distinctive from the private sector in areas such as personnel policies, reward structure and methods of doing business, and also reduced the extent to which discretionary power was limited by uniform and general rules of procedure, particularly over staff, contracts and money. The direction of change was in terms of the reworking of budgets to make them more transparent in accounting terms and viewing public sector organisations as a chain of principal–agent relationships, with a network of contracts linking incentives to performance and disaggregating separable functions into quasi-contractual or quasi-market forms.

It can be argued (Dunleavy and Hood, 1994) that corporatisation falls short of full privatisation and is an unsatisfactory halfway house between the traditional structure of public administration and a system based on enforceable contracts and individual legal rights. As the central government planning role is eroded, there could be a failure of guidance, administrative advice and outside expertise, while a narrow range of performance targets might cause managers to push through cost-minimising changes. There was also a risk of public services reflecting the interests of senior public servants rather that those of the service users, and public sector organisations might be reshaped in the format that suited the personal interests of senior managers. At the same time the service could be less accountable and accessible to the public, even if services were reformed with contrary aims and objectives. Big differences in pay levels between public and private sectors limited the degree to which really capable private sector managers with a strong track record could be brought into public bodies, so that a *de facto* public sector corps of managers remained in place.

There is evidence (Hannagan, 2003) that the incorporation model applied to further education did release pent-up forces of dynamism and entrepreneurship, ended ossified structures and encouraged innovation and competition. Structures were reformed, innovation was encouraged and competition had to be faced. However, Dopson and Stewart (1990) considered that public sector managers were cautious because accomplishments often went unrecognised, while mistakes were widely publicised and ridiculed. They questioned whether private sector management concepts could be transferred to the public sector and argued that public sector managers were likely to be less positive about new managerial practices than their counterparts in the private sector because of reduced public spending, the demands of central government for economies and low pay. Change created a demand for greater leadership at all levels while traditional public sector managers were looked upon more as administrators. At the same time private sector managers were more in control of the resources they needed to achieve their objectives than managers in the public sector.

CONCLUSION

The differences between the two sectors can be seen particularly in such areas as marketing. The marketing function is critical to the private sector, leading to an emphasis on the relation of the company to its customers. Public sector organisations have many relationships with the public as customers, clients and citizens, so that as well as being concerned with market demand, a public sector organisation also has to be concerned with public need. Whereas the private sector organisation is accountable to the market, the public sector is accountable to a range of people and bodies and to the public at large. The public sector has to explain and justify its actions to a wider stakeholder interest than the private sector and pressure groups have a particularly significant influence because resources are both finite and limited, and distributed as an act of political will. This creates an immediate dilemma for the application of consumer principles. The public domain may be used to reconcile interests that may not be reconcilable and to meet aspirations that may not be capable of attainment, while the private sector organisation resolves such dilemmas by defining them out of its area of organisation concern. The fundamental dilemma of the public sector can be illustrated by reference to the British health services where the demand for health care always outstrips the supply of it. The level of demand has risen almost exponentially, while the willingness to pay has not. The developments in science and technology, social changes such as the ageing population, changing lifestyles such as those causing obesity, patterns of disease with a decline in some but an increase in others such as cancer and Aids, and changes in the economy, including levels of employment, all place pressures on the health services and the managers in the service.

Marketing is essential for the private sector because profits can only be achieved by meeting customer needs. Producing goods and services in the hope that people will want them is not a recipe for success in a competitive market. The 'privatisation' of the public sector has introduced competition into the market for some public sector organisations. In the research carried out by the author in the further education sector, this was seen as one of the main causes of change in nearly 90 per cent of the colleges surveyed (Hannagan, 2003). The attitude to competition was a distinguishing feature of the colleges in this research, with the more successful colleges recognising the increased competition they faced after the barriers to it were removed at incorporation, while the less successful colleges wanted either to ignore it or believe that they could not do anything about it. The more successful colleges responded to competition by reacting to it either in an instinctive and unstructured way or through a structured approach to marketing. The evidence suggested that while the instinctive approach could be successful in the short run, long-term and steady success depended on well-organised market research and customer care. Exhibit 8.4 illustrates the use of market research in the public sector.

In some areas of the public sector the importance of marketing has been recognised after 'privatisation', so that in the public utilities, for example, competition has encouraged organisations such as British Telecommunications, British Gas and the electricity boards to greatly enhance their marketing and customer care programmes. These are organisations that have been almost completely privatised, with share capital and profits replacing their public sector requirements. As in any organisation, whether in the public or private sector, the actual functioning of marketing and other aspects of management have to be adapted to the needs of the organisation and its market.

Exhibit 8.4 Marketing in the public sector

One view of marketing in a college of further education was that '*marketing is sticking adverts in the paper*', another view was '*we know what we want, we provide the right courses and they can come and do them*' and '*we provide what they [students] want, because they don't know themselves*'. In contrast to these approaches in another college of further education, a director of marketing was appointed at a senior management level. She carried out detailed market research so that the college knew its customers in the form of students and potential students. She also carried out market research into the schools that provided the main supply of students as well as into employers in the locality of the college and other organisations which could supply college customers or clients. She had segmented the college market and developed a brand for each segment and she had developed a 'customer service' unit that staffed the college reception service and provided information and promotional materials. She had produced a detailed marketing plan and she had attempted to integrate marketing into the activities of the college, so that the marketing plan was felt in this college to be an essential element in its strategic management.

The main differences between management in the private sector and the public sector are in terms of accountability, taken in a wide sense of the term, in the need to make profits and in the ability to decide on the nature of the business. Private organisations are accountable to their shareholders and owners, and to their customers. Public organisations are accountable to the government or a government agency and to the public as well as to their customers. While they need to remain financially viable they do not need to make profits and they have to provide the service for which they were established. They have to meet public need and add 'public value' (Moore, 1995), so that the particular problem for public sector managers is in satisfying both the need for accountability and the need to provide a public service which requires particular skill in the leadership of public sector organisations. Heymann (1987) explained that while public management was like business management in many respects, in one very important respect it was different, and that was that public managers were politically accountable. While Moore (1995) argued that the justification for managerial action in the public sector was the preferences that arose from representative processes, the aim of managerial work in the public sector is to create **public value**, just as the aim of managerial work in the private sector is to create private value.

If the privatisation of public sector organisations is taken to its logical conclusion, the organisation is moved into the private sector and has shares, but many organisations remain in the public sector with varying degrees of 'privatisation'. The degree to which this process impinges on the work and success of the organisation helps to determine the amount of private sector management function that it needs to acquire. The Institute of Public Policy Research has suggested that some public services could be improved by setting up public interest companies on the model of the NHS foundation trusts and housing associations. The distinctive feature of these companies is that while they deliver a public service, they are independent of the state and do not have shareholders, thus avoiding the difficulties of delivering complex public services through shareholder-owned companies in which public needs may conflict with those of the shareholders. In general, in terms of management, the differences between the two sectors suggests that the managers working in them need to approach their tasks differently, although they are essentially carrying out similar functions.

SUMMARY

■ There are important differences between management in the public sector and in the private sector as well as similarities. The process of management in both sectors is concerned with managing people and similar problems arise.

■ The major distinguishing factors in the public sector are stakeholder accountability, a service rather than a profit motive and the concept of public value rather than market forces.

■ As market forces and competition increase in the public sector, the degree of 'publicness' in public sector organisations decreases.

■ Managers in the public sector have to take more account of political and social obligations than their counterparts in the private sector.

■ Organisational culture is important in strategic management in both sectors, although there are differences because public sector culture tends to be service-driven, while private sector culture is profit-driven.

Review and discussion questions

1 *What are the differences between management in the public sector and in the private sector?*

2 *Why is stakeholder accountability so important in the public sector?*

3 *There has been a trend towards more 'privateness' in the public sector organisations in the UK in the last two decades. What does this mean and what is its importance?*

4 *What is meant by the concept of 'public value'? How does the concept of a 'customer' apply in public sector organisations?*

5 *Discuss the importance of organisational culture in public and private sector organisations and the differences between organisational culture in the two sectors.*

CASE STUDY

Creativity, leadership and change

When I arrived in the civil service nearly a decade ago one of my Benefits Agency directors said to me in my first week: 'You need to understand that the civil service is the culture of the written word.' I have often reflected just how right he was – and, of course local government was not that different. The trouble is that words are of limited value. 'What I hear I forget, what I see I remember, what I do I know', which roughly translated, means that no-one was ever inspired by a memo. No-one's life was ever changed by a carefully crafted paper to Ministers. No-one ever made a major creative breakthrough writing a report. Words can stultify creativity, slowing things down and encouraging the search for theoretical perfection at a time when you should be more concerned with momentum and action. Too much paper isn't just a costly frustration, it strangles creativity.

There is no better time to look forward with optimism than the start of a new millennium. To think afresh about how we want to modernise this country's public services. But it is time to look back too, and to ask ourselves what lessons have been drawn from the recent past. Just what have the past twenty years meant for the public services? Are there lessons as we turn to the future? . . . Looking back, I am . . . struck by the way in which we seem increasingly to have assumed that the success of our economy, and indeed the success of our society and our public services, depends primarily on the success and profitability of the private wealth-creating sector. Certainly a strong dynamic private sector is vitally important; but success depends on coupling that with a vibrant creative public sector capable of anticipating and planning for change and facilitating economic success. . . .

Creativity is, by definition, an act of courage because it requires making connections which are out of the ordinary. This exposes you to potential ridicule and to above-average levels of risk. In the public sector, this is an additional problem because the prevailing climate is so risk-averse – partly because of an innate conservatism, partly because politicians tend not to relish unpleasant surprises and partly because the accountability frameworks are unsympathetic to risks which go wrong. In addition, my experience has been that telling public servants that they should take risks can open the floodgates to abdication and anarchy.

On the other hand, we have to face up to the risk issue, because it is the reason given by many public servants for eschewing innovation and creativity. Merely to exhort people to take risks is to leave them dangerously exposed. We need to help people to manage risk, which means helping to identify it, to develop a nose for it; it means helping them to develop the skills to define risk – is it financial, political or more to do with personal/individual credibility; and to assess the scale of the risk, whether in crude terms it is acceptable or unacceptable; it means ensuring people take reasonable steps to minimise risk. All of which may well take the form of getting alongside staff who are involved in creative activities and sharing the risk with them.

Finally, we, the leaders in the public sector, have a responsibility to help change the accountability frameworks so that they not only say they will look kindly on a well-managed risk which goes wrong, but that they actually do it. Whether or not someone is prepared to take a risk will depend upon the level of trust they are feeling. So certain organisations are likely to be organisations with high levels of trust, and creative teams are likely to trust their leader . . . this suggests to me that organisations which will find creativity most difficult are organisations which are:

- Hierarchical
- Centralist
- Prescriptive
- Analytical/judgemental
- Introspective/exclusive
- Deferential
- Risk-averse
- Word bound
- Controlling (people and resources)
- Status-conscious
- Poor listeners
- Conflictual

Regrettably, these words seem to me to have a pretty good match with the traditional public sector culture. Or to put it more positively – the kind of organisations most likely to be creative have fewer organisational levels, high management trust, active flow of ideas, effective idea management processes, routine future envisioning, managers who challenge, a balanced view of risk-takers, managers who delegate, and managers who involve outsiders.

Source: Excerpts from Michael Bichard (2000) 'Creativity, Leadership and Change', *Public Money and Management,* April/June. Michael Bichard is Permanent Secretary at the Department of Education and Employment (DfEE).

REFERENCES AND FURTHER READING

Adair, J (1989) *Great Leaders*, Guildford: Talbot Adair Press.

Bichard, Michael (2000) 'Creativity, Leadership and Change', *Public Money and Management*, April/June.

Bryson, J M (1995) *Strategic Planning for Public and Nonprofit Organisations*, San Francisco, CA: Jossey-Bass.

Cook, Stephen (2004) 'Public Attraction', *Management Today*, January.

Deal, T and Kennedy, A D (1982) *Corporate Cultures: The Rites and Rituals of Corporate Life*, Reading, MA: Addison-Wesley.

Dopson, S and Stewart, R (1990) 'Public and Private Sector Management: The Case for a Wider Debate', *Public Money and Management*, Spring: 37–9.

Dunleavy, P and Hood, C (1994) 'From Old Public Administration to New Public Management', *Public Money and Management*, Summer: 9–16.

Hannagan, T (2003) 'Strategic Change in Further Education', Doctoral Thesis, Open University, Milton Keynes

Heymann, P B (1987) *The Politics of Public Management*, New Haven, CT and London: Yale University Press.

McNulty, T and Whittington, R (1992) *Managing Strategic Change in Public and Private Sectors*, The Local Government Centre, University of Warwick, Coventry.

Meek, V L (1988) 'Organisational Culture: Origins and Weaknesses', *Organisation Studies*, 9 (4): 453–73.

Moore, M H (1995) *Creating Public Value: Strategic Management in Government*, Cambridge, MA and London: Harvard University Press.

Newman, J (1994) 'Beyond the Vision: Cultural Change in the Public Sector', *Public Money and Management*, April–June, 59–64.

Peters, T J and Waterman, R H (1982) *In Search of Excellence*, New York: Harper & Row.

Pettigrew, A M (1990) 'Is Corporate Culture Manageable?', in Wilson, D and Rosenfeld, R (eds), *Managing Organisations: Text, Readings and Cases*, London: McGraw-Hill.

Saint-Martin, D (2000) *Building the New Managerialist State*, Oxford: Oxford University Press.

Schein, E H (1992) *Organisational Culture and Leadership*, San Francisco, CA: Jossey-Bass.

Stacey, R D (1999) *Strategic Management and Organisational Dynamics* (3rd edn), London: Pitman.

WEBSITES

www.meb.co.uk/ijpsm.htm
Website of the *International Journal of Public Sector Management*.

www.publicnet.co.uk
For everybody interested in the public sector and its management.

www.blackwellpublishing.com
Website of the *Journal of Public Money and Management*.

www.cipfa-org-uk/
Website of the Chartered Institute of Public Finance and Accountancy (CIPFA).

www.statistics-gov.uk
National statistics online.

SECTION C

MANAGING PEOPLE

What is the structure of organisations? How are they organised and controlled? How is the work of organisations monitored? Why is organisational communication an important part of management? What are the different types of communication? What will communications be like in the future? What is involved in human resource management? What are the differences between personnel management and human resource management? What are the current trends in the techniques for managing human resources? What is the importance of human resource management for the efficiency and effectiveness of an organisation? What motivates people at work?

Good communication between people in all organisations is essential for success and there is a variety of types and models. The developments of recent years have been described as a 'communication revolution'. There is a difference between personnel management and human resource management. Human resource planning and good management are essential for efficient and effective organisations. There is a variety of factors influencing motivation at work for managers to appreciate in organising people.

CHAPTER 9

Organisational management

TIM HANNAGAN

Outcomes

Having read this chapter, you will be able to:

- describe the process of organising
- analyse the structure of organisations
- discuss organisational functions and co-ordination
- explain the importance of division of work, delegation and authority
- analyse performance management and management control

ORGANISING

The work of all organisations has to be organised and controlled. The strategy and corporate objectives describe the purpose and direction to be taken, and the targets and the aims if the organisation is to be a success. Once the process of implementation and the action plan are agreed, managers have to organise the activities involved. **Organising** is the process of defining the tasks and activities to be carried out by a number of people to achieve particular objectives, while **management control** is the process of monitoring and adjusting these activities in order to achieve the greatest efficiency and effectiveness in meeting those objectives. In other words, organising is deciding what is to be done and who is to do it, while control is making sure that it is done and done well. These are fundamental areas of the manager's role at all levels, because it is through the process of organising and directing people and resources that the work of the organisation is accomplished. The control function loops back to the planning function as a review mechanism (see Figure 9.1).

Organising and controlling include all management functions because of the need to organise all of them, allocate resources and integrate everybody's work. Organisation lies at the heart of all activities; without it, very little can be accomplished. It is, of course, possible to organise matters badly, so that people and resources do not work together effectively; the management role is to organise activities in such a way that the efficiency and quality of an organisation's output and work are improved. When this is achieved people working together can accomplish more than the sum of their individual efforts, just as a football team can play far better with a high level of teamwork than it can if team members play as individuals. The process of organisation involves the allocation of responsibilities so that everyone knows what their task is and what resources they have at their disposal in order to accomplish this within a particular timeframe. This promotes accountability so that employees know to whom they are responsible for the completion of tasks, and the structure of the organisation will establish these lines of responsibility.

The structure also establishes the formal communication system, but it must be recognised that informal networks may create quite different patterns. The communication system should be efficient vertically, up and down, as well as horizontally across it, and the organisation structure can assist this process. It should also reflect

Figure 9.1 **The control loop**

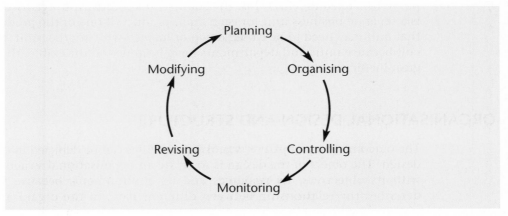

Table 9.1 **Stages in organising**

STAGES	ORGANISATION OF
Determine essential actions and tasks	Division of work
Divide action and tasks between teams and units	Structure
Divide actions and tasks into assignments for each individual	Action plans
Decide who is responsible for the completion of actions and tasks	Delegation
Arrange the co-ordination of the work of each team and department	Co-ordination

the needs of the organisation in terms of accountability and control. The management of an organisation can be seen as a series of stages moving from original concepts to actual practice, so that managers at different levels have to:

■ determine the essential actions and tasks required to achieve the organisation's aims;

■ divide these actions and tasks into assignments which can be carried out by departments, units or teams;

■ divide these actions into assignments for each individual person;

■ decide who is responsible for each action and task;

■ organise the co-ordination of the work of each team or group.

The second and third stages may be reversed, depending on whether the activities and tasks are grouped together before being subdivided into individual actions or afterwards. These stages describe the division of work within an organisation and the distribution of responsibility and authority (Table 9.1). Their operation may be determined by the structure of an established organisation, or may help to determine the structure for a new organisation. In practice, companies should alter their structures to meet the needs of their customers, and if the gap widens between tasks and activities and the organisation's structure, tensions and inefficiencies are likely to arise. Therefore, if the work of a company changes to any extent, the structure has to be altered to reflect this. For example, if a company is organised so that there is a separate business unit for each main product, if one of the products declines, that unit may need to be closed down or merged with another unit. If this is difficult because units and departments have become too inflexible, this can lead to great inefficiencies.

ORGANISATIONAL DESIGN AND STRUCTURE

The outcome of a company's organising activities can be depicted in organisational design. The object of the design is to create an organisational structure which fits with its objectives, its resources and its environment, because the structure describes the relationship between different parts of the organisation and the people in it. It specifies the division of work, the hierarchy and authority structure, and the formal links that exist between people within the organisation. In practice, of course, there are cross-functional relationships, networks and informal links which are not described by a formal structure but may be of equal importance. A management or organisation chart is a diagram of an organisation's formal structure describing the functions, departments and position of people within the organisation and how they are related.

→ Ch. 1

An organisation chart usually consists of a 'line' diagram showing the chain of command and official channels of communication (*see* Chapter 1, pp 16–17). A hierarchical structure will usually be described in terms of the organisation of line management and reporting, while a matrix structure will be described more in terms of relationships between units and people and processes of co-ordination. In order both to describe company structure and reflect the company priorities other forms of diagram may be designed, or more than one diagram may be felt to be appropriate. For example, in order to focus on the importance of customers, a diagram such as an inverted triangle (*see* Figure 9.2) may be felt to be appropriate.

→ Ch. 3

In Figure 9.2 the teams and employees closest to the organisation's customers are at the top of the triangle in order to emphasise the supporting role of functional departments and senior management (*see also* Figure 3.1 in Chapter 3, p 75). Of course, much greater detail can be included in this type of diagram and it can simply consist of an inverted management chart. Figure 9.3 shows a more traditional chart with senior managers at the top, middle managers below them and operational staff at the bottom. At the same time, the chart is divided into functional groupings with line management and responsibility flowing down the functions. It is difficult in this type of diagram to show functional links, co-ordination of projects and informal relationships. Some attempt can be made to do this by using dotted lines.

Figure 9.2 Inverted triangle

Functional structure

The functional structure illustrated in Figure 9.3 brings together all those engaged in related activities into one department. The production director and the production department are responsible for all the products manufactured by the company and the sales managers are responsible for all the sales of these products. This 'traditional' structure is often seen as the most 'logical' method for dividing up the work of the organisation. It is used in small and medium organisations and in an adapted form it may be used in large organisations. However, the disadvantage of this structure becomes more obvious as an organisation grows in size (Table 9.2 summarises advantages and disadvantages).

This functional structure can bring together specialists and specialist equipment in order to develop high-quality products and services from their particular department. The staff in these departments can provide support for each other and their teamwork can help innovation develop within their relatively narrow area. Line management control, leadership and authority are all very easily understood within this structure, and employees can develop considerable loyalty towards their department which may be more difficult to create for the whole company. This loyalty may develop into some suspicion and even antagonism towards other departments. Other departments may be blamed when things go wrong, or they may appear to be favoured by senior management and to receive more than their fair share of resources.

The advantages for managers and employees of a functional structure are that they can develop their expertise, they have a clear promotion path within the

Figure 9.3 Organisation chart

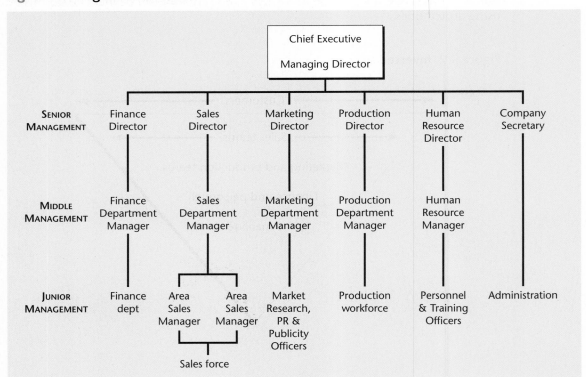

Table 9.2 **Functional organisation**

ADVANTAGES	DISADVANTAGES
Efficient use of specialised resources	Empire building and bureaucracy
Responsibility, authority and control are clear	Slow response to customer needs
Encourages specialised management expertise	Narrow perspective and limited innovation
Promotes employee loyalty to small unit	Obscures responsibility for overall tasks
Clear promotion path	Limits scope for development of general managers and employees to move into new areas
Good 'vertical' communication	Poor networks and 'horizontal' communication

department, and they can communicate easily with other people with similar backgrounds and working on similar tasks. These departments can develop a paternalistic form of leadership and management which may favour some people at the expense of others. At the same time, the differences between the 'home' department and the others may be manifested in a variety of ways. Particular jargon may develop which makes it difficult for people from other departments to understand what is being said, stereotypes may be used to describe people working in other departments, company policies may be interpreted and put into practice differently in the various departments, and jealousies may develop over working space, equipment levels and so on.

Functional departments can encourage bureaucracy and empire building. The department may feel it is more important the greater resources it uses and the larger its staff. Managers and other staff may become reluctant to pass specialised information to people not in their department. There may be slow responses to changes in customer needs, particularly from those departments which have little contact with the final customer. Tasks which cut across departments may take a long time because they have to move sequentially from one department to another. This can be exacerbated by a lack of clear responsibility for such tasks, with each department able to lay blame for any delay on another department. For example, all employees may be taken on through the personnel department and if it is slow in this process, other departments may have a long wait for salespeople or production workers. Genuine conflicts may develop over priorities, so that, for example, new designs and innovation may not be seen as particularly important by the production department, whereas the marketing department considers that new designs are essential to meet customer needs.

As organisations grow in size, either by broadening their products and services or by expanding geographically, the disadvantages of a functional structure become apparent. It becomes more difficult to obtain quick decisions on actions because functional managers have to report to the central headquarters in order to have their decision endorsed. At the same time, control over the departments becomes more difficult, and co-ordination may not be able to create a situation where the organisation's objectives can be achieved. These developments cause large organisations to consider other forms of structure to reflect their new requirements. The most extreme of these is the matrix structure.

Matrix structure

The usual matrix structure is designed to answer the main problems of the functional structure. It combines a vertical chain of command, through functions and departments or units, with a horizontal 'project', 'business unit' or 'product' team. The purpose of the matrix structure is to promote across the company groupings of people and skills to provide a team in order to produce a product or service. This lateral structure is led by a project or group manager who is expert in the team's assigned area of specialisation. The individual therefore has two bosses, a functional manager and a project or group manager. This is the basis for the use of the term 'matrix' which in mathematics applies to an array of vertical columns and horizontal rows.

→ Ch. 1   An example of a matrix structure is shown in Figure 9.4 (*see also* Figure 1.6 on p 17). Staff from production, marketing, sales, human resource and administration are divided into four project (or product/service) teams which consist of staff from all five functions under project managers who report to the chief executive. An individual employee in production, for instance, will be in a project team manufacturing a product and reporting to a project manager. The project manager is

Figure 9.4 **Matrix structure**

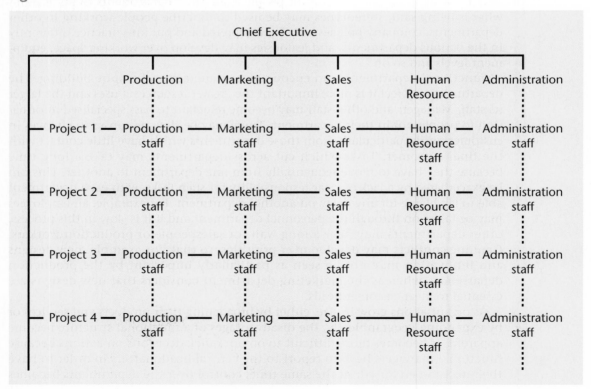

responsible for making sure that the team not only makes the product as specified but also markets it and sells it. Personnel, training or administrative staff may also be allocated to the team. The production employee will also report to the production manager of the company, who will be responsible for initially allocating the employee to this specific project and for the career of the employee in the organisation. The production manager is in fact the employee's line and functional manager, while the project manager is the task or activity manager.

In a similar way members of teams or units may have separate functional managers on a vertical scale, while the whole team moves together from one project to the next. Research teams in science and engineering will often work in this way, because the skills of the team may be complementary and essential for the completion of the task. At the same time, the functional managers provide the specialist support and career path which may not be available through the team. In this way the matrix structure is intended to combine the advantages of functional specialisation with product or project specialisation. The matrix team work on relatively narrowly defined projects, while individuals retain the link with the functional structure of the organisation.

In some organisations a particular unit or section has a matrix structure, while the rest of the organisation has a functional structure. It has proved quite difficult in fact to organise on a full matrix in a large organisation, while small consultancies, research teams, advertising agencies and so on are able to work within this structure very easily. This is because an effective matrix structure requires a high degree of co-operation and flexibility from everybody at all levels. There need to be open and direct lines of communication horizontally and vertically and a high level of confidence between managers and between employees. For these reasons matrix structures can work well where staff members have similar qualifications and share common goals, and where teamwork is more important than authority. Consultancies and research teams are good examples of this situation, and organisations such as advertising agencies may also operate in this way because everybody is working together on a variety of accounts.

The matrix structure can be an effective means of bringing together people with the diverse skills required to solve a complex problem, such as in research teams and consultancies. It throws the focus on the project to be completed. This provides a common purpose with a well-defined objective for which the whole team or group can be responsible, while the functional structure can too easily fragment the clarity of this aim. By working together, people from various functions can understand the demands placed on other people from different areas of work. For example, preconceptions by marketing personnel about engineers can be overcome in this way and vice versa. This understanding can produce a more realistic approach to each other's work. If the structure is sufficiently flexible and has not become rigid, it can help to keep down the costs of an organisation, because managers need only assign the number of people needed to complete a particular project (*see* Table 9.3).

Although the matrix structure may be easy to design and appears to have great advantages over the functional structure, it may be difficult to implement. Problems can arise over shared responsibility, the use of resources in common and the question of priorities. One manager may be played off against another by employees, so that the project manager, for example, is told that the functional manager has decided to pull an individual out of the team to work elsewhere. If this happens without proper consultation it can cause great problems for the project team.

Table 9.3 **Advantages and disadvantages of a matrix structure**

ADVANTAGES	DISADVANTAGES
Focuses on end product	Requires excellent communications
Stimulates creativity	Encourages power struggles
Provides challenges	Risks duplication of effort
Enables flexibility in an organisation	Confuses lines of responsibility
Improves communication and understanding	Requires high levels of interpersonal skills
	May lead to more discussion than action

Product, market and geographical structures

As a company diversifies so that its **products** and **services** penetrate a range of markets and expands to cover broad geographical areas, its structure needs to reflect these changes. The functional structure is usually felt to be inadequate for these circumstances. Functional managers can find themselves responsible for the production or marketing of numerous and vastly different products and services, and senior managers can become responsible for co-ordinating areas which it is beyond their capacity to monitor and control. At the same time the matrix structure may not be suitable because it does not provide the necessary control over wide-ranging areas of work, and too many people of different qualifications, experiences and backgrounds will be involved.

There are a number of different approaches to the problem of finding a structure to match the requirements of a company in this situation, but the usual approach is to develop divisions or units which, unlike a functional department, resemble a separate business. There is a divisional head who is responsible for the operation of the division and may be accountable for its profitability; however, unlike a separate business, the division has to conform to the company requirements and is accountable to it.

The company may establish the rules and policies for its divisions in connection with such areas as finance, training, personnel, advertising and so on. Some 'divisions' are given a high degree of autonomy in, say, a geographical area, so that they become 'satellite companies' run as almost separate entities but owned by the parent company and responsible to it. For example, Rank Xerox UK plc is owned by the parent North American company, but enjoys a high degree of autonomy within the UK and Europe. The creation of a divisional structure has been advantageous in a geographically distinct area. The local company can produce products for its geographically local markets, it can develop marketing and sales techniques which are tailor-made for the local area, and it can develop a culture which is sympathetic to the locality. For example, Ford UK produces motor cars aimed specifically at the UK and European markets and adapts its marketing and sales techniques to the requirements of these markets. Through this process the UK can be treated as a distinct market requiring clear focus in the approach to it.

Of course, these factors are true also where there are clearly different markets for the same product or service, or where a company is producing clearly different

Table 9.4 **Divisional structure**

ADVANTAGES	DISADVANTAGES
Focus on a product/service/market	May develop a conflict of interests
Clearly defines responsibilities and accountability	Possibility of a drift in meeting corporate objectives
Provides autonomy to managers	May produce neglect of long-term priorities
Provides supporting services from the centre to divisions	Central control may stifle local innovation

products or services for the same market. For example, many publishers have an education division for publishing educational and training books and a general or fiction division for publishing novels. This may be subdivided by age group, so that a children's book division concentrates on that market. Some books will cross the divisional lines and may be sold as a children's book by one division, as an educational reader by another and as a general work of fiction by a third.

A divisional type structure (*see* Table 9.4) has the advantage of combining all the activities, skills and expertise required to produce and market particular products or a product in a particular marketplace. The whole process can be easily co-ordinated and the speed of decision making can be increased, because divisional decisions are made relatively close to the point of implementation. Divisions are able to focus on the needs of their particular customers and managers have a degree of autonomy in meeting these needs. On the other hand, of course, there may be disadvantages to this structure. The interests of the division can be placed above those of the whole organisation. The division may not place organisational objectives in quite the same order of priority as the central organisation, and may place its short-term interests above the longer-term interests of the whole company.

Divisional structures can lead to a conflict of interest between divisions which develop different objectives and priorities, and it is the role of the central organisation to be responsible for co-ordinating the work of divisions. This is not the same → Ch. 3 as the federal organisation described in Chapter 3 (pp 87–8), where a number of separate organisations or companies come together out of mutual interest, although one of their objectives is to gain some of the advantages of a division of a large → Ch. 3 organisation in terms of support. Chapter 3 describes changes to organisational structure brought about by greater flexibility in the labour force, and this flexibility needs to be reflected in whichever management structure is chosen.

CO-ORDINATION

Co-ordination is the integration of the activities of individuals and units into a concerted effort that works towards a common objective. In order to achieve this managers have to make sure that people, teams, units and divisions all work together towards a common aim. This requires a well-understood chain of command and span of management. It has been considered an essential feature of a chain of command for there to be 'unity of command', that is, one person in charge. For example, Henri Fayol wrote in 1916 that:

> *'a body with two heads in the social as in the animal sphere is a monster and has diffi-culty surviving.'* (Quoted in Fayol, 1949)

One of the major weaknesses of a matrix structure is that each employee will have two bosses and strong co-ordination will be required to prevent conflict. On the other hand, it can be argued that strong command systems can be too rigid for the constant changes faced by organisations, and that managers require flexibility and excellent horizontal communication as well as the vertical communication promoted by a functional structure. The conflict arises, therefore, between unity of command on the one hand and the necessity to communicate between functions and other areas of expertise on the other. This has led to companies developing a variety of organisational designs, particularly in large and complex corporations.

As well as a clear 'boss', co-ordination requires a clear 'chain of command' in which authority is seen to start at the top and is scaled down through an organisation in an unbroken chain. In the traditional organisation chart (Figure 9.3) this means that most authority resides at the top of the pyramid and at successively lower levels it is dispensed among more people. This type of organisational design defines the formal lines of communication between subordinates and immediate superiors, and because there is absolute clarity about this it helps to reinforce the unity of command. For example, in Figure 9.3 a salesperson knows that his or her approach to the managing director will be through the area sales manager, the sales department manager and the sales director and, at the same time, directives will be passed down through this chain of command. It is of course essential that the salesperson can communicate with people in other functional areas without having to send a message up the sales chain of command and down the other functional chain of command. Discussion with, for example, a market researcher should be possible directly without involving the sales and marketing directors. This is the informal network that can be developed into cross-organisational project teams.

The span of command or **span of management** or span of control is the number of people or units for whom a manager is responsible. Choosing the correct span of control is important if an organisation's activities are to be successfully co-ordinated. If a manager is given too many subordinates to co-ordinate and control, the management of them may not be effective, while too few may not utilise the manager's abilities or may create a situation where there is very limited co-ordination. Attempts have been made to find an optimum span of management in terms of an ideal number of employees for a manager to control. The number recommended in recent times has often been around six, on the grounds that many more than this would mean the manager could not spend sufficient time with each subordinate to provide effective monitoring and control. However, it has become recognised that in practice the appropriate span of management depends on the work to be carried out.

It is now argued that the organisation's need to co-ordinate should dictate the most productive span of management. For example, a narrowly defined role in financial management may require an equally narrow span of management because the need to co-ordinate the work of the function is small, while a widely defined role in marketing may require an equally wide span of management to include area marketing and sales managers, market research staff, advertising, public relations and communications staff. Much will in fact depend on the work to be co-ordinated and controlled. Where the work is routine and procedures are standardised, it

Table 9.5 **Span of management**

FACTORS INFLUENCING THE WIDTH OF CONTROL	RELATIONSHIP TO SPAN OF MANAGEMENT
Complexity of work activities	The more complex, the narrower the span
Variety of work activities	The greater the variety, the narrower the span
Quality of manager	The more talented the manager, the wider the span
Quality of subordinates	The more responsible and able, the wider the span

may be possible for a manager to have a very wide span of management. For example, store managers tend to control a fairly large number of people because their work is largely routine, while management information systems (MIS) managers may have a narrow span of management because this is a capital-intensive area of work with the need for innovative solutions to company requirements. Once these solutions become routine, the span of control of the MIS manager can be extended.

At the same time, managers vary in their ability to manage a number of people. Some managers are better at controlling a small team with a focus on a particular area of work, while others are able to cope with a general management role dealing with a variety of people and controlling a wide area of work. The amount of time a manager requires to co-ordinate the activities of workers is a factor in this, while the nature of the marketing situation will also be an important influence. Some managers are given a range of tasks to complete, while others have a fairly simple list of objectives. At the same time, the role of subordinates, their competence and ability to work on their own will have an effect on the optimum span of management. The proximity of employees to the manager and the effectiveness of communication can also be factors in the span of management. A manager will usually have more difficulty in co-ordinating workers in different locations than in a single location, but much will depend on the efficiency of internal communications (Table 9.5).

Frequently, as managers are promoted, their span of control widens. They will take responsibility for more areas of work with more variety and complexity. In order to be effective in these areas, many of which might usually call for a narrow span of management, managers need to be of a high quality.

ORGANISATIONAL DESIGN IN PRACTICE

Organisational design is the process of fitting the way an organisation works to its strategy in order to achieve the most successful possible performance. The way an organisation works includes a 'formal' structure, its informal attitudes and culture, the way decisions are made and the reward systems. These are not static factors and they change in organisations all the time. Organisational design has to change with them if discontinuity is to be avoided. The effect of not changing is strategic drift

→ Ch. 6 (*see* Chapter 6, pp 180–1), with an increasing gap appearing between the way the organisation works and its strategy. This can create tensions which will adversely affect performance. It is, therefore, important that:

- as an organisation grows in size, the design is increasingly decentralised and managers delegate decision making to those parts of the organisation best placed to make these particular decisions;
- as an organisation changes its strategy, the organisational design remains consistent with this change;
- as the priorities as well as the products and services of an organisation change over time, organisational design reflects these changes;
- as technology changes, so organisational design changes because of alterations to information requirements and decision making.

Large organisations develop divisional and unit structures, while the move to focus on the customer has given rise to the development of self-managed teams whose role is to meet customer needs. The structure behind these teams is designed to be supportive (see the inverted triangle in Figure 9.2). Grouping of staff in teams or units may change as a result of alterations to the product/service portfolio, so that departmental barriers to people's or team's mobility have to be discouraged in order to retain flexibility. The introduction of new technology such as robotics, for example, has developed the need to consider the best form of structure in factories with fewer and perhaps more specialised staff.

Tension and discontinuity can arise because different parts of an organisation disagree over the purpose or direction of the organisation. The teams close to the customer, such as the sales teams, may be convinced that there is a need for a change in the design and packaging of the product, while the production team is convinced that the product is well made and to the specification required by consumers. Perhaps the salespeople view the company mission as being to 'serve the customer', while the production staff place much more emphasis on quality control and view the company mission in terms of 'producing a reliable, high-quality product'. In an organisation in which people are unsure of their mission and objectives, there is a communication problem which may be to do with organisational design. The design may need to be more sharply defined, with direction, purpose and responsibilities established very clearly.

The organisational design should set out the decision-making process so that a senior manager does not have to make decisions lower down the organisation except in a crisis. It should establish levels of responsibility and spheres of control. It should define the division of work, areas of responsibility and delegation. These should not be matters of conjecture and doubt if an organisation is to work smoothly. This definition may be on relatively 'mechanistic' lines so that the activities of the organisation are broken down into separate specialised tasks, with the objectives and authority for each individual unit precisely defined by senior managers. Or it may be more 'organic' in the sense that individuals work in groups, there is less emphasis on authority coming down the levels of management and more emphasis on communication across all levels of the organisation. In the constantly changing environment of modern management there is often an attempt to have a mixture of systems. The changes require flexibility and the ability of teams to react, while a feeling of stability may be promoted by a strong central system of delegation and overall objective setting.

DIVISION OF WORK

The **division of work** is the breaking down of tasks into component parts so that individuals are responsible for an activity or a limited set of activities instead of the whole task. The division of labour and specialisation have been recognised for a long time as an essential process in improving the productivity of an organisation.

For example, Adam Smith in *The Wealth of Nations*, published in 1776, described the vast increases in output which could be achieved by a division of work or division of labour. The illustration he used was in pin manufacturing. This relatively simple operation could be carried out by one person completing each individual pin or by a number of people working on parts of the production. He showed that 10 people working on their own produced 200 pins a day (20 each), while by dividing up the work they were able to produce 48 000 pins a day (4800 pins each). This remarkable difference was due to specialisation, according to Adam Smith. The task of producing pins was divided into drawing the wire, straightening it, cutting it, grinding the point and so on. Each person specialised in one of these operations and, because of this, became expert in that particular operation. This enabled them to work much faster and more efficiently. They did not have to move from one operation to another and their skill in carrying out a single operation greatly increased.

→ Chs 1 and 20

This approach to the division of work was supported by Frederick Taylor and the supporters of scientific management (*see* Chapters 1 and 20). In practice, it was applied to the work of textile factories in the late eighteenth and nineteenth centuries and to other manufacturing processes during the Industrial Revolution of the nineteenth century. In the twentieth century the application has spread to service organisations such as McDonald's restaurants, which have broken down the process of producing food into small steps. This process has considerable advantages, particularly in relation to efficiency and productivity:

- less skilled workers can be used, because the task has been simplified to a single operation or a few simple operations;
- training can be quick and relatively easy because each person can be trained on a particular task without the need to develop a wide range of skills;
- proficiency is gained very rapidly, because the specialised task is repetitive and the worker has a great deal of practice at it;
- there is an increase in efficiency because workers do not waste time moving between tasks;
- this increases the speed of operation;
- workers can choose or be assigned to the operation which best suits their aptitudes and preferences.

These advantages led to the assembly line based factories which have characterised manufacturing from early in the industrial revolution to the present. Specialisation and the breaking down of tasks into simple component parts have enabled the development of mechanisation and the use of robots to replace people in many operations. Machines have been invented to take over the work of assembly-line workers so that labour-intensive industries have become increasingly capital intensive. Computers have been developed to control the manufacturing process so that monitoring progress and quality has also become mechanised. A similar process has been taking place in service industries and in management itself with the development of information technology.

At the same time, this division of work and specialisation have given rise to problems and disadvantages as well as advantages:

- workers become skilled in only one operation and when that skill is no longer needed they have to be retrained;

- the mechanisation of many industrial operations has greatly reduced the demand for workers with limited skills and it is difficult to retrain workers to higher levels of skill if they do not have relatively high basic levels of education and training in the first place;

- constant repetition of a single operation is very boring and demotivating for many people;

- teamwork and creative innovation are not encouraged by this process;

- workers have to rely on a constant supply of products on which to carry out their particular operation and this may cause bottlenecks in production;

- workers are not motivated by a pride in the finished product or in the organisation because they perform such a small part of the overall production process.

In an attempt to overcome these disadvantages there has been a variety of schemes to establish different working systems to promote teamwork, pride in the product and quality. For example, the Saab Motor Company developed a system of producing its cars by teams of workers in the 1970s while other automobile manufacturers were using assembly-line processes. Each car was produced by a team working around an 'island' workstation, with the component parts being supplied to the island for the team to assemble the car. In this system, if any faults were detected the whole team was responsible for their correction. Teamwork was encouraged in order to raise productivity, the team assembled a finished product in which they could take pride, and they could carry out different tasks from day to day or week to week on the agreement of the team.

The traditional division of labour gave rise to the need for supervisors, progress chasers, foremen and quality control inspectors. The team process requires a team leader and the ability to access specialists such as maintenance engineers. Progress and quality will be controlled by the teams, particularly if rewards are linked to output. This structure does require flexibility and wide skills in that an individual may be called upon to carry out various tasks by the team. This can be described as 'job enlargement', where a number of routine jobs are within the worker's scope. The team approach also provides for job enrichment in that the team and each individual in it are given responsibility for deciding how the work is to be completed and how well it is carried out.

A central issue for managers is to determine the degree of specialisation appropriate to the effective completion of work. The 'narrower' the scope of the job and the 'shallower' it is, the greater the level of specialisation but the lower the employee's satisfaction may be. Work which is 'narrow' in scope will consist of one or a very limited number of operations. If it is also lacking 'depth', that is the worker has little control over it, it may be very boring. However, some people do prefer to have a limited, very predictable job which they can carry out without much thought. They know 'where they are' each day and do not have to face frequent changes. It can be argued that most people find this type of work boring and look for 'job enlargement' in terms of an increased number of activities related to their work, and job enrichment in terms of more autonomy over how they work.

Exhibit 9.1 provides a list of some of the characteristics of work which can help managers to decide on the content of individual tasks and to match the ability of individuals to particular areas of work. Work can be analysed in terms of the skill required to complete it, whether it can be divided into separate tasks or not, the degree to which an individual can decide on the job schedule, the extent to which the other people depend on the completion of the task, and the type of feedback to be given.

A highly specialised job on an assembly line, for example, may require limited skill, no autonomy, be a small part of the whole process and receive direct feedback in terms of the number of operations completed. Attaching an item such as door handles on a motor car assembly line could have these work characteristics. The task would be very dependent on the supply of car bodies at the correct stage of readiness to work on and would in turn need to be carried out before the car is completed. On the other hand, a job such as product design requires a range of skills in matching the design to customer needs and company specifications, may have a high degree of autonomy in that the designer can schedule the work provided that deadlines are met, may at least involve seeing a product design through to completion, and be very significant in terms of the dependency of many people on the final design. Feedback would come in terms of the relative success of the design, perhaps measured by customer satisfaction.

Once the manager has decided on the nature of the work to be completed and has as far as possible matched this and the skills of the available workforce, he or she then has to group the operations and the work in such a way that they can be effectively managed. One way of doing this is to form teams of people with complementary talents so that a whole task can be completed. The team may have a high degree of autonomy and may only be dependent on others at the beginning and end of its process. Individuals and teams will normally be grouped into departments, divisions or units.

Exhibit 9.1   Work characteristics

Skill	The variety of talents required to complete a task; work that requires initiative and creativity tends to be more skilled than work which is operational and repetitive.
Autonomy	The extent to which the individual who performs a task has the freedom to plan and schedule the work programme.
Dimension	The work which involves completing a product may provide greater satisfaction and create a clearer job identity than that which is a small part of the overall process.
Significance	The extent to which work affects other people, either in terms of health and safety, or in terms of the dependence of other people on the completion of the tasks involved.
Feedback	The extent to which an individual receives information about the effectiveness of completed work.

DEPARTMENTALISATION

Whatever the unit of management is called, the process of departmentalisation is the grouping of jobs, tasks, processes and resources into logical units to perform an operation within an organisation. The term 'operation' is to some extent appropriate here, because in managing a medical operation a group of individuals is brought together to complete a particular task. They form a team dependent on each other while the operation is being performed. It is possible for managers to organise the people in these teams into a department, responsible for carrying out particular types of operation, or they can be organised into more specialised departments and brought together for a particular project. Departments can be function-, product- or market-based.

The functional approach is the grouping of jobs and resources within an organisation so that employees performing similar tasks are in the same department. In most organisations there are functional departments which will include production, finance, human resources, marketing.

The purpose of this arrangement is to bring experts and specialists together so that they can further develop their expertise, while the departmental manager has to understand and co-ordinate only a relatively narrow range of skills. However, it is possible that members of the department may lose sight of the organisation's overall business because they are concentrating on their own department and expertise. A functional departmental structure may cause bottlenecks when work has to flow from one to another and when each functional area has to make its own separate decisions.

The product approach is the grouping of jobs and resources around the products and services offered by an organisation. Products or services may be grouped together in relation to their particular needs. This may be based on geographical location, on marketing or on some other division which is considered advantageous.

The product or products can become the central focus of the department and functions can adapt their roles to support it. Decision making can be facilitated by this focus and responsibilities can be clearly defined. However, each department will need its own functional specialists, which can be expensive, and the departments may concentrate on their own products or services at the expense of others produced in the organisation.

The market approach is the grouping of jobs and resources around the markets and customer groups identified by the organisation. The success of this form of departmentalisation depends on the ability to identify unique categories of customers and to focus on their particular requirements. One example of this exists in banks and other financial companies, which are able to distinguish between individual customers, small businesses and large corporations.

Departments based on markets are able to focus on the customers and to adjust rapidly to their needs. However, a high degree of co-ordination is required in order to make sure that this approach meets corporate objectives.

AUTHORITY AND DELEGATION

Authority is the power related to each position within the organisation. It involves the right to give orders, make decisions and spend resources. In an organisation authority provides a right to do these things supported by the structure of the organisation and understood by every employee when they join. The contract or job description will usually describe to whom the employees are responsible and for whom they are responsible. This means that employees accept orders and decisions and expect these to be carried out if they are agreed through the established structure.

Power is the ability to carry out an action, whereas authority can be seen as the right to do this. **Delegation** is the distribution of authority from a manager to a subordinate. **Responsibility** is an obligation to be liable for a task, decision or action. While authority can be delegated, responsibility cannot, so that a manager can provide a subordinate with the power to make a decision but still retains responsibility for it in the sense of being liable for the result. If the subordinate makes a decision which leads to a success, the manager can accept some of the praise; but if the decision leads to a problem, the manager is obliged to accept the blame. The managers are unable to simply pass all blame onto the subordinates, because they have been responsible for the delegation of authority and if this has led to a problem this can be traced back to their decision to delegate.

Delegation of authority can only be successful when the subordinate has the ability, information and willingness to perform a task or take a decision. This can be supported by the organisational structure where clear lines of management and communication can enable the process to operate without difficulty. The position of an individual in the organisation endows that person with a particular type of power, sometimes referred to as legitimate power. Both power and authority can be different to this, in that authority may arise, for example, out of respect for a person's expertise rather than their position, while power can arise from control over resources. An accountant, for example, may have the power to accumulate large amounts of clients' money without having the authority to do so. Managers may have the authority to make decisions in an organisation, but may not have the power to carry them out because their subordinates do not respect their decisions and find ways of ignoring them.

The classical theory of authority is based on the hierarchical principle that authority flows down from the top of an organisation and is also dependent on the position held. When removed from this position the individual no longer has the authority associated with it. The opposite to this view is the 'acceptance' theory proposed by Mary Parker Follett (1941) and Chester Barnard (1938) (*see* Chapter 20). In this theory managers' authority depends on their subordinates and whether these do or do not choose to accept the managers' orders. Subordinates have the power to deny authority or to accept it. A different approach to this suggests that circumstances decide who is in authority and this person will be different in different circumstances. For example, in an accident the first person on the scene may assume authority until the emergency services arrive, when the senior officer may take over. It follows on from this that it may be the most knowledgeable person in a given situation who has authority, so that, for example, the managing director of a company may exert authority over a senior management meeting, but will defer to the company accountant when there is a meeting on the financial accounts of the company or a meeting with the external auditors.

In practice, authority is often a mixture of these theories in that, while managers' positions in an organisation will greatly affect their range and depth of authority, these can only be exerted where they will be accepted. This acceptance may arise out of line management control, because subordinates will depend on their senior line managers for reports and promotion, or out of respect for the judgement and experience of a more senior manager or as a result of a consensus. It is important to

→ Ch. 20

be aware how authority is exerted so that instructions are not confused, and so that as organisations become more democratic decisions increasingly arise from a consensus of what needs to be done.

Delegation arises because one manager cannot do all the work of the organisation. By delegating, the managers are able to extend their capability and capacity. They can take on new tasks while monitoring others delegated to subordinates. These more junior managers gain from the experience of taking on new tasks knowing that they can turn to the senior manager for help, and they can build up specialised knowledge and expertise. While responsibility for a task is given to subordinates, the ultimate responsibility remains with the manager; this cannot be delegated. Authority to make decisions and use resources can be delegated and will be necessary for a task to be accomplished. If a task is delegated without the necessary authority the subordinate will not be able to complete it. The subordinate will be accountable for the outcome of a delegated task to the manager who will be accountable to a more senior manager and so on. To an extent, authority flows upwards through an organisation.

→ Chs 1 and 2

Obstacles to delegation arise from managers' attitudes towards it or subordinates' reluctance to accept it, or because of factors related to the organisation and its culture (*see* Chapters 1 and 2). Managers may not want to relinquish authority to a subordinate, or they may feel that 'if you want a job done properly, do it yourself'. They may have a concern either that to delegate may indicate they cannot carry out the job themselves, or that if it is carried out very well by the subordinates they will themselves appear to be less competent. Managers may feel that it is too time consuming to teach a subordinate how to carry out a task. Subordinates may lack confidence in their ability to complete a task and they may be afraid of failing in it. They may view delegation as simply giving them extra work, and they may not want to find out how to complete the task because it is easier to ask the manager. Some organisations are too small to provide much scope for delegation and in some it is not the 'corporate culture'. People may be assigned tasks which they are expected to carry out without recourse to delegation. The more centralised an organisation is the less delegation there is, because authority will not be widely distributed. In decentralised organisations, authority is widely delegated between business units, departments and teams, or between people.

CONSULTATION AND NEGOTIATION

Sound human resource management policies help to foster good industrial relations. The culture of an organisation will be reflected in its industrial relations policy. This policy defines the relationship between management and employees over such matters as pay and working conditions, selection and recruitment, health and safety. Personnel managers and industrial relations officers are specialists in consultation and negotiation and may take a lead in the communications involved in the process. All managers, however, have a role in consultation and negotiation (*see* Chapter 12), because of the importance of pay, working conditions, recruitment and redundancy in the process of change (*see* Chapter 1). Communication is an essential element of management and industrial relations, and consultation and negotiation are an important part of the work of all managers, because of the manager's authority, credibility, access to information and responsibility for the allocation of resources.

→ Ch. 12

→ Ch. 1

Negotiation means that two or more parties meet in an attempt to reach a solution systematically. It is a structural attempt at logical problem solving to identify and resolve a conflict or a potential conflict. Consultation is the process by which managers discuss matters of mutual interest with employees in an organisation. The actual purpose and process of consultation will depend on the culture of an organisation and the communication structures which have been developed in it. Levels of consultation will depend essentially on the prevailing management style (*see* Chapter 2). The 'leadership continuum' may tend to be autocratic, where managers rely on their authority, or democratic or laissez-faire, where there is much more freedom for employees' points of view. Consultation may provide:

→ Ch. 2

- a communications channel in which management, having made a decision, simply informs employee representatives of the decision which has been made;
- a forum in which management seeks the views, feelings and ideas of employees prior to making a decision, while retaining the right to make that decision;
- a structure by which employees' views are made a part of a joint decision process.

In small organisations the process of consultation and/or negotiation can be on an informal basis between individuals and managers, with each person effectively carrying out their own pay and conditions bargaining. In large organisations, individual bargaining becomes impractical and systems are developed for classifying groups of employees into categories for pay and conditions purposes. Changes in levels of pay or in working conditions within categories or grades are negotiated by representatives drawn from employees or by representatives of a trade union. In many medium-sized and large organisations the usual process of consultation and negotiation is between management and unions.

The development of unions has meant that conflict over pay and conditions can be guided into agreed channels with a process of discussion, consultation and negotiation. Basic pay and working conditions may be negotiated at a national level, while the details are negotiated at a local level. While the system may be a familiar process for both unions and management, the expectations of the two 'sides' may differ considerably. Management will have priorities in relation to minimising costs and maintaining competitiveness or keeping within spending limits. Unions will be attempting to obtain the best pay and working conditions for their members. What is involved in the process of negotiation and the eventual arrival at an acceptable compromise is the 'structuring' or 'conditioning' of such contrasting expectations to meet on common ground (*see* Figure 9.5).

In this negotiating process, both management and unions will start with an initial position which may be more extreme than they expect the other side to accept. At the same time, each side has a fall-back position which is the absolute limit to which it would consider being pushed by the other side. In between these two position it is necessary to establish common ground. This is an area within which each side will receive something of what it wants, and will be prepared to make concessions in order to achieve it. Somewhere in this common ground there is a realistic position where agreement can be reached. Where agreements are not reached, strikes and lock-outs may occur, but in the end, if the organisation is to continue to operate, agreement has to be reached.

In this process managers need negotiating skills, patience and a clear view of their objectives. The goal of negotiation is to arrive at a position where both sides feel that they have won something, a 'win–win' situation. If one side feels it has lost heavily (a 'win–lose' outcome), the resulting agreement may be difficult to manage

Figure 9.5 The process of negotiation

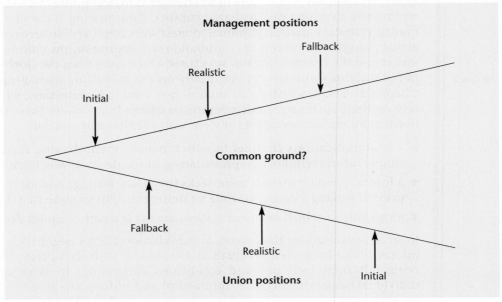

in the future because one side will be attempting to make up for its 'loss' and dis-agreements may become frequent. Negotiating skills involve:

- testing and summarising what is being agreed to make sure that everybody inter-prets the substance of the agreement in the same way – an agreement has to work and ignoring even small points of dispute will make this very difficult;
- understanding the other side's need in order to discover and explore the common ground;
- communicating the reasons for a particular suggestion or action so that the other side knows what the motives are for a particular policy;
- assessing the process of negotiation to see if it could be improved.

Organisational culture will have a marked effect on the context in which these negotiations will take place. Open communication within an organisation can reduce the possibility of conflict arising and can develop trust and confidence between all employees. Where changes are being proposed, they need to be dis-cussed in detail with all employees, explaining the need for them and consulting on alternative methods of implementation. Managers need to show that they under-stand the employees' concerns and to involve them in the process of change.

The history of industrial relations has seen rises and falls in the relative power of unions, reflected in their membership. In the UK, unions were strong in the 1960s and 1970s. In the 1990s the membership of many unions in the UK declined as a result of high unemployment, reductions in the labour force of many organisations and legislation controlling union activities. At the same time investment in the UK by overseas companies, such as Japanese-owned corporations, has been based on 'no-strike' deals, with firm structures and systems for agreeing pay and conditions. The process for 'delayering' and 'restructuring' in many companies has often been accompanied by the development of self-managed teams at various levels, with the objective of placing more decision making in the hands of employees. In some organisations, particularly in Germany, employee and/or union representatives are members of the highest decision-making bodies.

The way that managers consult and negotiate in an organisation provides a clear indication of its culture. If senior management believes in and supports a process of open consultation with all employees, and promotes a situation where self-managed teams can make decisions about matters important to them, then the possibility of conflict within the organisation can be reduced. Where there is a co-operative approach, the role of unions and negotiation can be viewed by managers as essential for the future success of the organisation.

PERFORMANCE MANAGEMENT

The process of managing organisations and control eventually comes down to the individual employee working in an organisation. Whatever the structure, the division of work, the level of co-ordination and the system of authority and delegation, the individuals have to know what they are to do and this has to be monitored. **Performance management** systems are designed to establish individual objectives which assist the achievement of corporate objectives and monitor progress on accomplishing them. The term 'performance management' means different practices to different managers, but usually includes the following elements:

- the organisation has a shared vision of its objectives, or a mission statement or corporate objectives, which it communicates to its employees;
- individual performance management targets are set which are related to the organisational objectives;
- a regular, formal review is carried out to monitor progress toward these objectives;
- the review process is used to identify training needs, career development and possible rewards;
- the effectiveness of the whole process is evaluated against the overall performance of the organisation.

There is usually a strong emphasis on objective setting and formal appraisal and there is often a sequence of steps in the performance management cycle. Although these steps may be called by different names they include:

- **agreement on the job description**
- **establishing priorities**
- **arriving at objectives**
- **setting a time horizon**
- **reviewing and monitoring.**

This process results in the assessment of the individual's performance, and in 'coaching' in the sense of identifying means of improving performance through training and development and establishing career progression. Performance management can be defined as a method of improving business performance by focusing on key areas of activity.

Performance management can be thought of as an extension of management by objectives (*see* Chapter 6). This system establishes objectives for an individual or a

→ Ch. 6

group and then judges performance on how well they have been achieved. The main problems with this approach are that sometimes the objectives are established by more senior managers for their subordinates without any agreement, and that the 'coaching' and 'counselling' elements, felt to be so important in recent approaches, are left out. Although the objectives are supported by senior management, they are in some cases seen to be imposed with little help forthcoming from above. In a well-organised process, managers will be helped to appreciate the value of their personal efforts and the way these efforts are expected to fit into the contributions to be made by those above and below. This approach can lead to a fully integrated appreciation of the links to corporate objectives (Figure 9.6).

Modern performance management places a very high emphasis on participation and on 'coaching' at all levels. The emphasis is on progression and development rather than measurement and control. Increasingly, it is seen as a fundamental support for total quality management. Drucker (1955) outlines the story of the three stone-cutters to illustrate the point. When asked what they were doing:

'The first replied, "I am making a living."

'The second said, "I am doing the best job of stone-cutting in the entire country."

'The third looked up and said, "I am building a cathedral."'

It can be argued that the first man knows what he wants from a day's work. He will give 'a fair day's work for a day's pay'. He will carry out his task but leave everything else to managers and supervisors. The second is a craftsman with his concentration on carrying out the best work possible within the limits of his craft. He will believe that he is accomplishing something useful by cutting and polishing stones expertly, but if, in fact, his work does not fit in with what is required for the building, then it is useless. Managers may often find themselves in this position, working with great expertise on a particular function and developing habits which concentrate on the performance of the function rather than the objective of the whole business. Managers, may for example, appraise their subordinates according to their craftsmanship and promote and reward them accordingly. The third stone-cutter does

Figure 9.6 Performance management

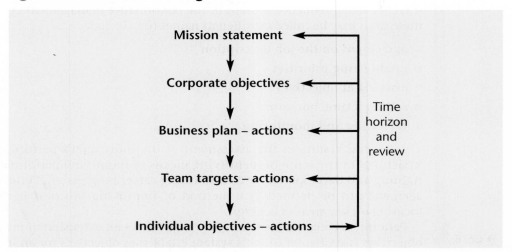

have a vision of the objectives of his work, of how his contribution fits in. He will not be content to carry out work which does not help to make progress in the building of the cathedral. He may suggest ways of improving the effectiveness of his work to ensure the objective is reached. For Drucker, the definition of a manager is that 'in what he does he takes responsibility for the whole – that in cutting stone, he builds the whole cathedral'.

This situation cannot be achieved by maintaining occasional drives or campaigns on particular issues. An economy drive, for example, will usually not lead to efficiencies across the company, but may lead to a cutback on staff and consumables where possible, which may not be in the most effective places for the company in the medium or long term. Managers need to take responsibility for their own work and to set objectives for themselves and their teams. They will take responsibility for their subordinates' performance in the same way that their line managers take responsibility for them.

In this form the MBO approach differs very little from modern performance management ideas: they both help to put into effect corporate objectives by directing attention to key areas of activity. One way or another managers need to assess their subordinates and to be assessed themselves by their supervisors (Figure 9.7). The appraisal process can judge people on:

- **what they achieve**
- **what they do**
- **what they are.**

→ Ch. 11 In operating a performance management system, managers will start by appraising themselves (*see also* pp 329–32). This process begins with outlining the main tasks of the post and from this establishing a description of the job. This job description can then be agreed with a manager's immediate boss, that is the line manager. The next stage is to agree on the main priorities of the job in particular time periods, say three months, six months and a year. The line manager will need to make sure that this fits in with company objectives. Then the manager's objectives can be arrived at, again by agreement, which is essential if the manager is to feel responsible for achieving the objectives. At the same time line managers will want to help to achieve these objectives in any way possible because they reflect their own objectives (Figure 9.8).

Figure 9.7 **Management appraisal**

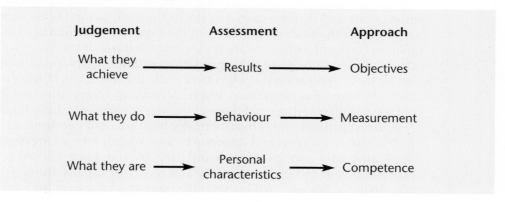

Judgement	Assessment	Approach
What they achieve	→ Results	→ Objectives
What they do	→ Behaviour	→ Measurement
What they are	→ Personal characteristics	→ Competence

Figure 9.8   **Performance management cycle**

The objectives agreed by managers will take the form of actions to be completed within a certain period. They will be reviewed from time to time and may be altered in the light of changing circumstances by agreement between the manager and line manager. The process is not one of appraising for weakness, but analysing the situation. If the manager and his or her boss can agree on an area for improvement, then this may be able to be helped through training. Alternatively, it may be possible to focus the job on the manager's strengths so that personal characteristics and behavioural patterns can assist in arriving at achievements.

The whole emphasis of this approach is on the future, not on the past. It is all about performance and help, or 'coaching' to achieve good performance. The personality of the manager is less of an issue in this system, while the company can provide financial support and time for training if problems are identified or it is considered important to develop particular management techniques. Many companies provide training in such subjects as time management, assertiveness and report writing. The performance management system provides leverage points for integration with total quality management by encouraging policies, procedures and values which promote performance and ongoing activities based on a set of skills which facilitate high performance.

This process may or may not be attached to a salary review and performance pay. It may be thought to be more effective if it is linked to a reward system; however, performance is not the only criterion used in determining salary increases and promotions, and in many cases may not be the main factor. The accountability of one manager for the work of another and the focus on particular activities in order to achieve corporate objectives are the essential features of this process. The approach can be applied throughout the organisation, with managers and supervisors responsible for their teams achieving objectives while the teams are, in turn, accountable to them. At a very operational level, where members of a team share or even interchange tasks, the team objectives and those of the individual may be indistinguishable.

A well-organised and sympathetically implemented performance management system can build trust and improve communication in all areas of an organisation, and this can promote similarity in the high level of performance expectations; it can promote equity and recognise quality through financial and non-financial rewards. While executive support is necessary for total quality management, executive action is critical and performance management can provide the focus for this action down to the most operational level. The strategic plan emphasises the direction a company must follow to take advantage of opportunities and to reach medium- and long-term objectives, while action plans make this a reality.

MANAGEMENT CONTROL

→ Ch. 14

Management control is necessary in order to monitor what people are doing, how they are doing it and what they accomplish. **Operational** control is at the level where managers are concerned with using physical, financial and human resources to accomplish organisational objectives (*see also* Chapter 14). **Strategic** control is at the level of factors which may affect the strategy of the organisation. This involves monitoring customers, competitors, suppliers, government policies, changes in technology and developments in the community. Managers face constant changes, and this dynamic factor in the internal and external environment of organisations emphasises the importance of the link between planning and control. The time factor is important in this process because in the period between establishing objectives and accomplishing them changes can occur and will have to be taken on board. Well-designed controls enable managers to predict, monitor and adjust to changes. **Management** control can be seen as the process of monitoring and adjusting organisational activities in order to facilitate the accomplishment of organisational objectives. It is making something happen the way it was planned to happen.

The process of establishing objectives for individuals, teams and units through performance management helps to provide control, sometimes referred to as '**feedforward** control'. Performance management establishes what people are going to do and how they are going to do it. The attempt is made to predict problems and to consider ways of overcoming them in developing an action plan. '**Concurrent** control' is the process of controlling actions while they are being taken. The primary role of supervisors and foremen is to provide day-to-day, minute-to-minute control, making adjustments as a process is taking place. Team leaders, operational and junior managers control tasks and activities as they take place, watching daily, weekly and monthly results, making decisions, fine-tuning the process so that the objectives can be achieved. As a new office block or factory is built, the plans will need to be adjusted and adapted while sight is not lost of the overall objective. The plans are agreed, drawings of the completed building are presented and the actions required to reach this point are established. When the foundations are dug out it may be that an unexpected layer of rock is discovered and decisions will have to be made to adjust the plans to deal with this problem. '**Feedback** control' concentrates on the outcomes of action. It is at this point that judgements are made about the original plans and the actions taken to turn them into reality. Feedback is a process of evaluating the success of the tasks and activities, the work of individuals and teams, and plans made for future development. For example, questions can be asked and answered regarding how well the building was planned, how well it was built, what problems arose during the construction, and how well it is in fact suited to its purpose.

The process of control starts with establishing standards of desired outcomes. These may be in numerical terms, for example an assembly line will produce a thousand units a day, or in financial terms, such as a retail store being expected to

Figure 9.9 Control process

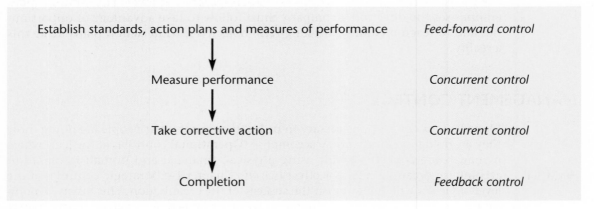

create sales of £10 000 a day, or in quality terms, that a unit of production or a building has to be fit for the purpose for which it is to be used and meets expectations. Standards may include a time factor and may be measured by customer satisfaction or by some other qualitative method.

Once standards have been established, the next stage is to monitor progress through quality control and observation. Points of reference may be fixed in order to check on progress. The manager has to compare outcomes to the established standards, decide how much deviation is acceptable and sort out any problems that may arise. This process of comparing performance to standards is followed by corrective action. Functional managers will have their own monitoring and control systems. Financial control will be provided by the organisation's financial management to ensure that any project remains within the planned limits. Production and premises managers will control physical plant and premises, supplies and energy. Human resource managers use performance appraisal systems to monitor people's work. Operations management, management information systems, the process of decision making and financial management are all aspects of this control process (see Figure 9.9).

These systems do not, of course, decide the performance of an organisation; they are an essential element in this performance and monitor and control it. Performance is as much to do with people as with the physical assets on which they work. In the division of labour between capital, labour, raw materials and enterprise, all four have to be present and working together for anything to be produced. What is produced and how it is produced will depend on the materials and investment available and very heavily on the ability of the people who are available, their attitudes, creativity and competencies, and on how well the whole process is managed.

SUMMARY

■ The role of management is to organise and control the tasks and activities to be carried out in order to achieve the strategic objectives of a company or institution. Without organisation, actions will not be taken in order to achieve these objectives and to ensure the quality of products and services produced.

- There is a variety of organisational structures which help to achieve these actions and companies need to adapt their structures in order to support and facilitate their operations. In the process of deciding on the structure of an organisation, managers need to consider questions of co-ordination, delegation and authority.

- Managers will have a particular span of control depending on the complexity of activities undertaken, the variety of work and the quality of managers and employees. Organisational design is the process of fitting the way an organisation works to its strategy in order to achieve the best possible performance.

- Work has to be divided between people, and jobs and tasks grouped into units in order to perform operations. In the end, individuals in an organisation have to know their roles, and managers design performance measures in order both to establish individual objectives and monitor progress on accomplishing them. An appraisal process will assist this and enable management control to be focused at an individual level.

Review and discussion questions

1 *Why is management control important in any form of work? What purpose does it perform?*

2 *What is the function of organisational design?*

3 *What are the problems of a matrix structure as against a more functional design?*

4 *How does the span of management affect the role of a manager?*

5 *Is delegation an essential element of management or is it possible to manage without it?*

6 *Discuss the importance of management control and performance management.*

CASE STUDY

In search of a modern structure

Bertelsmann, the third largest media company in the world, is often held up as a model of corporate management in Germany. In spite of its size, however, it has always played up its origins as a small-town publisher and has maintained a decentralised structure.

The company has been one of the most noticeable examples of *Mittelstand* – small and medium-sized business – success. But now, principally as a result of sweeping change in the media sector, Bertelsmann is having to rethink its management structures, including the way in which its prized decentralisation works.

Possible changes include the flotation of some of the group's businesses – a significant move for the privately owned company. Originally a printer of hymnals and bibles based in the Westphalian town of Gutersloh, the company was rebuilt after 1945 by Reinhard Mohn, who expanded successfully into book clubs and general publishing. The money earned from these activities financed the acquisition of the majority of Gruner & Jahr, the magazine and newspaper publisher. Other acquisitions, in the 1980s, included the US companies Doubleday, the publisher, and record label RCA.

▶

While the company has long outgrown the *Mittelstand* and Gutersloh – last year it had sales of DM21.5 bn (£7.5 bn) and net profits of DM905 m – Mohn sought to keep Bertelsmann, in spirit at least, close to its roots. Rather than opting for a monolithic structure, a web of *Mittelstand*-like entities was created in which managers are encouraged to behave as if they were running their own companies.

While Mohn, who stood down as chief executive in the 1980s, sought to retain the vigour of *Mittelstand* culture, he also tried to resolve the issues of ownership and generational change which often plague Mittelstand companies. He created a charitable foundation which owns the majority of the shares in the company, creating a structure which appeared to offer the best of all worlds. While retaining *Mittelstand* character in the group's subsidiaries, it eliminated some of the risks that go with family ownership and avoided the pitfalls of going public.

Recently, however, the decentralised structure has been called into question. Mark Wossner, chief executive, engaged consultants to canvass the most senior managers. The results gave him a shock: rather than basking in the independence, the managers complained about the lack of synergies across the group. Says Wossner, who joined Bertelsmann nearly 30 years ago: 'Decentralisation brought all of us into this company. I would not have come here if I hadn't known I had the chance to run a company (profit centre) at a young age.' Wossner says the goal now is to create more 'cross-sections' in areas such as information technology within the group – without undermining the autonomy of managers. 'Back-office and infrastructure processes can be centralised. But the operational autonomy and the cultural and national approach in the different countries will be maintained,' he says.

For Wossner, the implementation of reforms also has a personal dimension, for he is due to stand down as chief executive next year. Before he goes he would like to leave his successor – thought most likely to be Thomas Middelhof, the board member responsible for the group's new media activities – with a reinvigorated structure

Source: Studeman, F, *Financial Times*, 27 June 1997. Reprinted with permission.

REFERENCES AND FURTHER READING

Barnard, Chester (1938) *The Functions of the Executive*, Cambridge, MA: Harvard University Press.

Chinges, Peter T (1997) *Paying for Performance: A Guide to Compensation Management*, New York: John Wiley.

Davidow, W H and Malone, M S (1992) The *Virtual Corporations: Structuring and Revitalizing the Corporation for the 21st Century*, New York: Harper Business.

Drucker, Peter (1955) *The Practice of Management*, London: Heinemann.

Fayol, Henri (1949) *General and Industrial Administration*, London: Pitman Publishing.

Harris, Ira C and Ruefli, Timothy W (2000) 'The Strategy/ Structure Debate: An Examination of the Performance Implications, *Journal of Management Studies*, June.

Harvey-Jones, John (1993) *Managing to Survive*, London: Heinemann.

Joyce, W F (1999) *Mega Change: How Today's Leading Companies Have Transformed Their Workforces*, New York: Free Press.

Kaplan, Robert S and Norton, David P (1996) *The Balanced Scorecard: Translating Strategy into Action*, Boston, MA: Harvard Business School Press.

Kerr, Steven (1997) *Ultimate Rewards: What Really Motivates People to Achieve*, Boston, MA: Harvard Business School Press.

Lipnock, J and Stamps, J (1997) *Virtual Teams: Reaching Across Space, Time and Organizations in the Technology*, New York: John Wiley.

Miles, Raymond E, Snow, Charles C and Miles, Grant (2000) 'The Future.Org', *Long Range Planning*, 33.

Mullin, Rick (1996) 'Knowledge Management: A Cultural Revolution', *Journal of Business Strategy*, September/ October.

Nonaka, I and Takeuchi, H (1995) *The Knowledge-Creating Company: How Japanese Companies Create the Dynamics of Innovation*, Oxford: Oxford University Press.

Parker Follett, Mary (1941), *Collected Works*, New York: Harper and Brothers.

Smith, Adam (1776) *An Inquiry into the Nature and Causes of the Wealth of Nations*, London: A Strahn and T Caddell.

Studeman, Frederick (1997) 'In Search of a Modern Structure', *Financial Times*, 27 June.

Wenger, Elienne C and Snyder, William M (2000) 'Communities of Practice: The Organizational Frontier', *Harvard Business Review*, January/February.

WEBSITES

http://www.hmso.gov.uk
The HMSO website with information about Acts of Parliament and other government publications.

http://www.pepsico.com
A description of the Pepsi-Cola Company structure.

http://www.business.managementarena.com
Information about a range of business and management journals.

CHAPTER 10

Organisational communication

LEN HOLDEN

Outcomes

Having read this chapter, you will be able to understand:

- the definitions of organisational communication and communication media
- downward, upward and horizontal types of communication
- models of communication: the Krone, Jablin and Putnam typology of communication and Clampitt's models of communication
- international aspects of communication
- communications and the future

ORGANISATIONAL COMMUNICATION: DEFINITIONS

Communication, whether in the form of writing, talking or listening, is an inherent part of a manager's role and takes up a considerable amount of a manager's time. Mintzberg (1973) found that most managers spend between 50 and 90 per cent of their time talking to people.

Communication is pervasive, continually in operation and covers an enormous range of activities. For example, some of the more obvious modes of communication with which most people would readily identify are:

- sending a memo to an employee as a reminder to do a task;
- telephoning an order for new stock;
- posting a notice of a forthcoming meeting on the noticeboard;
- sending an e-mail message or a fax to an overseas subsidiary;
- writing a letter to placate an angry customer.

From these examples the Advisory, Conciliation and Arbitration Service (ACAS) definition would suffice in describing organisational communications as:

'the provision and passing of information and instructions which enable a company or any employing organisation to function efficiently and employees to be properly informed about developments. It covers information of all kinds which can be provided; the channels along which it passes; and the means of passing it.'

(ACAS, 1982, p 2)

However, communication is also a very complex series of processes operating at all levels within organisations, ranging from the 'grapevine' heavily laden with rumour, to formalised systems such as **joint consultative committees** (JCCs) or **works councils**. They can operate at the localised level of the shopfloor or office between supervisor and staff and the staff themselves, or at a distance by means of representatives such as union officials or messages from the boardroom or the chief executive to various branches or subsidiaries of large and complex organisations. They can be one-way or two-way, top-down or down-up as well as across the organisation.

Communication can operate at a personal level and informal level as well as through formal channels such as those cited above. Thus, the following examples can equally be categorised as organisational communications and can contribute as much to the efficiency or inefficiency of the organisation:

- an unsympathetic supervisor ignoring the explanations of lateness by an employee;
- an angry discussion in the canteen between employees about a low pay-rise;
- an employee sitting with crossed arms and legs while a line manager attempts to broach a delicate subject about lack of commitment to work;
- a rumour that large-scale redundancies will be made by the company shortly.

These examples embrace informal channels of communication, such as gossip or the grapevine, body language and interpersonal behaviour. They are based in organic or human interactive processes and can be as important as mechanistic and formal channels of communication in conveying positive or negative messages. It is only relatively recently that these informal processes have come to be recognised as being as important as the formal processes.

What can also be added to the ACAS definition is that communication is a two-way process. What is being increasingly recognised is that messages to and, equally important, from the workforce have considerable significance. Thus communication is important for conveying the organisation's mission, business aims and objectives, and its general ethos or culture. It is also needed to enable the thoughts and feelings of the workforce to be expressed and, of equal significance, heeded and acted upon. Such policies are being heavily influenced and underscored by human resource management practices.

Communication systems also carry implicit messages about the mediation of power within organisations. Employee-involvement communication systems (which are examined more closely below) are processes which enable the workforce to have a greater say in decision making to varying degrees, with the concomitant loss of managerial prerogatives, an issue which can create, as well as attempting to allay, conflict. Communication systems are also influenced by political, social and economic trends within society, which change and evolve over time and in turn influence the perceptions of those engaged in the employment relationship. In addition, the nature of the communication channel can affect the message as does the culture(s) existing within and outside the organisation (Clampitt, 1991; Jablin *et al.*, 1987).

Thus even the simplest message can be misunderstood or misconstrued because of the complex influences which act on the communication process. Equally important and potentially disastrous is that communication channels can send conflicting messages. An oft-cited case is the company which encouraged employees to take up share options entitling them to attend the annual shareholders' meeting, where they were told how successfully the company had performed over the previous year. Many of these same employees were also in the trade union to which management communicated later that, because of the poor performance of the company over the previous year, the pay increases requested could not be met!

COMMUNICATION MEDIA

The number and types of channels of communication have increased at a phenomenal rate since 1945 and with even greater acceleration and facilitation since the 1980s, transforming organisations and the way they operate. Within a 50-year time-frame most organisations have moved from pencil and typewriter-dominated environments, with the telephone as the main medium of distant communication, to computer terminal-oriented environments with the increasing predominance of voice mail, fax, e-mail, modem systems and the Internet. In addition, we have moved towards teleconferencing as well as computer conferencing. Indeed, in the world of the telecommuter in his or her telecottage, he or she may do a job but never leave home. This is the world of work made possible by increasingly advanced channels of communication.

Despite these developments, face-to-face communication is probably what most people prefer and what still predominates in most organisations. It enables instant feedback, allows re-explanation and there is no substitute, as yet anyway, to meeting someone in the flesh. Recent studies of why telecommuting has not been as popular as predicted is that 'loneliness' is an important factor in its unpopularity. Meeting people and hearing the office gossip is part of the social communication process which people enjoy about work.

Table 10.1 attempts to categorise multifarious communication mechanisms in accordance with their feedback potential and how quickly (immediacy) the feedback can operate in organisations.

Table 10.1 Communication channels and feedback

TYPE	CHANNEL	FEEDBACK POTENTIAL	FEEDBACK IMMEDIACY
Written/printed	Memos	low	low
	Post – internal/external	low	low
	Company newspaper/journal	low	low
	Newsletters	low	low
	Company reports	low	low
	Bulletins	low	low
	Noticeboard	low	low
	Suggestion scheme	med/high	low
	Attitude survey	high	low
Speech	Formal presentations	low	low
	Mass meetings	low	low
	Departmental meetings	medium	high
	Team briefing groups	medium	high
	Quality circles	high	high
	Grapevine	high	high
	Face-to-face/one-to-one	high	high
	Appraisal	high	high
Non-verbal	Body language	high	high
Mechanical	Audio tape	low	low
	Video tape	low	low
	Television	low	low
	Voice mail	low	low
	Fax	medium	medium
	E-mail	medium	medium
	Telephone and mobile phone	high	high
	Teleconferencing	high	high
	Internet and Intranet	high	high

(Please note this is not an exhaustive list)

DOWNWARD, UPWARD AND HORIZONTAL TYPES OF COMMUNICATION

Another way of categorising communications is by their route through organisations, the most common being downward and upward. More recently emphasis has been on the horizontal channels in organisations, particularly in quality, customer service (internal and external) and similar schemes. Delayering, downsizing, empowerment and devolvement have led to flatter organisational structures in which the team unit has become the operational pivot. Thus communications within the team and with other teams (departments or internal customers) is seen to have considerable significance.

- **Downwards communication (top-down)**, e.g. from managers to other employees. This includes channels such as house journals, company newspapers, employee reports and regular briefing sessions, often with videos.
- **Upwards communication** is designed to tap into employees' knowledge and opinions, either at an individual level or through the mechanism of small groups. This includes practices such as suggestion schemes and attitude surveys.
- **Horizontal communication** takes place between individuals and teams, and within and between departments or work groups, such as operate in quality circles, total quality management and customer care programmes.

In many organisations a combination of these forms of communication will exist, hopefully supporting and complementing each other.

In a book of this nature it would be impossible to examine all of these approaches in detail, but a closer study of some of the more popular and recent schemes in each category may serve to illustrate current trends.

Downward communication

The company magazine or newspaper

One of the most common methods of downward communication which has witnessed a considerable increase since the mid-1970s is the proliferation of company newspapers or magazines (CBI, 1989). Reviewing methods of communications in six surveys of organisations conducted between 1975 and 1983, Townley (1989) indicated that most put the company newspaper or house journal either as the most popular or second most popular form of communication. The problem is that they can vary in quality from amateur desktop-published affairs produced by employees in their 'spare' time, to lavish glossy productions, which have been part of the communications systems of many large companies for a number of years.

There is also the question of editorial control which may restrict the messages that are conveyed to the workforce. Continual, glowing reports of the company successes or anodyne and meaningless information may have negative results in the long run. Genuine expressions of employee feelings via letters pages or forthright quotes from employee representatives, even of a negative nature, may show the desire of management to achieve fairness. Of course, the judgement of the editor will come into play in deciding the content of the newspaper or journal, which in turn will be affected by the organisational culture and management views.

For example, a militant shop steward during a dispute called the managing director a 'fascist' which the personnel director urged the editor to expunge as being insulting. The editor defended the decision to retain the quote on the grounds that he had sought one from the shop steward and not to print it would look like corporate censorship. In addition, such a quote was so patently absurd that it would have a negative effect. In the event the quote was left to stand and the prediction of the editor proved true when the shop steward was spurned by his fellow employees and the union felt moved to publicly apologise for the comment (Wilkinson, 1989).

Team briefings

Team briefings have witnessed a considerable increase in the past five years, although they have been in existence in some organisations for longer (Marchington *et al.*, 1992). They are often used to cascade information or managerial messages throughout the organisation. The teams are usually based round a common production or service area, rather than an occupation, and usually comprise between four and 15 people. The leader of the team is usually the manager or supervisor of the section, and should be trained in the principles and skills of how to brief. The meetings last for no more than 30 minutes, and time should be left for questions from employees. Meetings should be held at least monthly or on a regular pre-arranged basis.

Surveys often reveal considerable satisfaction with team briefings by both employers and management (e.g. CBI, 1989) as they are effective in reinforcing company aims and objectives at the personal face-to-face level. Ramsay (1992a, p 223), however, urges caution in accepting this rosy picture because success depends on context 'to a significant extent'. For example, they might be postponed or cancelled in times when business is brisk, which may undermine commitment to holding them at all in the long run. If the intention is to undermine union messages, the success will very much depend on the strength of the union and the conviction of management. A sceptical and undertrained management and supervisory force can do much to undermine the effectiveness of team briefings.

Upward communication

These schemes can also be described as two-way communication and are most associated with managerial concepts such as human resource management (HRM). They are clearly aimed at increasing employee motivation and 'influence' within the organisation. They also aim to improve employee morale, loyalty and commitment, with a view to improving service and efficiency. Another facet of these types of scheme is to facilitate acceptance of changes in work practices, functional flexibility and new technology, as well as engender an atmosphere conducive to co-operation and team building (Ramsay, 1992a).

Attitude surveys

Although not a new concept, attitude surveys have witnessed a considerable increase in vogue in recent years. They are often conducted by personnel or HR departments and sometimes consultants are hired to carry them out. They most often take the form of questionnaires, but can also involve face-to-face or telephone interviews. Employee responses are often marked with the intention of eliciting the feelings of numbers of employees on a range of issues, for example feelings of involvement in various organisational issues and procedures, and what employees think of various schemes. This is not only seen as useful in that employees have a chance to air their views, but it also helps to monitor the success or failure of initiatives, enabling management to decide whether to retain, remove or improve them.

Employees can come to view them with an air of cynicism as time-wasting exercises if there is little or no feedback. It is important to communicate to employees how surveys have been used and how they have affected the organisation and its policies. Publication of the results can be made in the company newspaper, journal or news sheet.

Suggestion schemes

Suggestion schemes have had a long history and many organisations still retain them, although many have abandoned them in favour of feedback and new ideas emanating from problem-solving sessions such as quality circles. Suggestion schemes have come into and gone out of fashion many times over the years, and the suggestion box limply hanging off the wall with a solitary yellowing note upon which is written an anonymous rude message to the managing director is a familiar joke. When operated seriously, these schemes can be very effective. Suggestions on how to improve work and improve the working environment have saved companies enormous amounts of money, and in the best schemes the originator of the idea is justly rewarded with a cash bonus or other perquisites, and often with a picture and story in the company newspaper. Publicising the event is important because it shows that the scheme is working, that employees are listened to and their ideas are valued, and it will encourage others to do the same. These days the suggestion box itself is no longer necessary as suggestions can be channelled through the company newspaper or magazine, or some other point of collection, such as through team briefing.

Horizontal communication

These schemes are often associated with attempts at culture change and restructuring within organisations, and emphasise employee ownership and empowerment, in the hope of increasing employee commitment, and consequently giving greater productivity and better service.

Quality circles

One of the first methods identified with the 'new', involved approach to management was the quality circle (QC) (*see also* Chapter 7). It first arrived in the UK via the USA from Japan, as has been noted in Chapter 7, although QCs were implanted in Japan in the post-war years by two American consultants, W Edwards Deming and J M Duran (Clutterbuck and Grainer, 1990).

→ Ch. 7

QCs are made up of six to ten employees holding regular meetings weekly or fortnightly during working time. The principal aim is to:

> *'identify problems from their own area and, using data collection methods and statistical techniques acquired during circle training, analyse these problems and devise possible solutions; the proposed solutions are then presented formally to the manager of the section who may decide to implement the circle's proposal.'*   (Brennan, 1991)

There was tremendous interest shown in QCs by British managers in the early 1980s, but within a few years they began to decline in popularity. A number of reasons have been identified for this decline but principal among them was the attitude of middle managers. For example, it is crucial that a manager or supervisor with the requisite qualities and training leads the circle. Technical competence alone is not enough to guide the circle and studies began to highlight the necessity for interpersonal skills. Some managers also felt that their power and authority was undermined by the QC, and others just lacked commitment in the initial stages, which had the effect of making QCs difficult to develop effectively. There were also difficulties from the over-enthusiastic facilitator who deliberately gave an overtly positive but false impression of the circle's operation, possibly for career progression reasons. This makes it difficult to identify problems within the circle to improve its effectiveness (Brennan, 1991).

Suspicion of circles could be engendered if they were seen as a way of undermining trade union functions. Non-consultation with the union, particularly when setting up QCs, often bred suspicions that this was another anti-union management ploy, and the QC was, therefore, effectively undermined by non-co-operative attitudes.

Other circles failed because suggestions by the workforce were not actually applied or even considered, thus rendering them a waste of time in the minds of the participants. Finally, many circles simply 'ran out of steam' after the initial burst of enthusiasm. The need for continual reinforcement of their function and purpose was evident (Collard and Dale, 1989; Ramsay, 1992a).

Teamworking

Teamworking is an initiative in employee involvement (EI) and like QCs originated in Japan. It emphasises problem solving in a teamworking situation and in order to function effectively it must be bound up with policies of task flexibility and job rotation (Price, 1989). Teams vary in size from seven to ten people or even more, and large elements of training are necessary to ensure that workers, team leaders, supervisors and managers have the requisite skills to enable the team to function efficiently. A large part of such training is of a managerial or interpersonal skill and communicational nature, as well as of a technical nature.

Total quality management

Whether employee involvement works or not depends on the aims and objectives of the EI scheme. In addition, there are times when certain schemes will work successfully and times when they will be unsuccessful, and this is why EI, like many other HRM policies, goes through changes in fashion. The economic, political and social context influences the type and success of the scheme which organisations adopt (Ramsay, 1992a). A further factor is the type, size and sector of the organisation. What may work in a small firm, for example, may not work so well in a large bureaucratic organisation. What may work in a democratic organisational culture will probably be unsuccessful in a more authoritarian one (Wilkinson, 1989).

Even schemes such as **total quality managerment** (TQM), which begin life for the most positive reasons, such as the enhancement of employee commitment, motivation and empowerment, may become distorted. Factors, both internal and external, may turn them into something unworkable and, from the employee point of view, they may be seen as a sinister attempt to gain more commitment, work and productivity, without the concomitant reward, control or empowerment.

TQM in practice

Total quality management has witnessed a rise in popularity in many organisations in recent years and is often bound up with culture changes and other HRM and managerial initiatives, such as customer service programmes (see also Chapter 7).

→ Ch. 7

TQM operates at both a local and establishment-wide level and is pervasive throughout the whole organisation. It is concerned with concepts such as culture change, which in turn engender attitudinal changes in the workforce. At workplace level emphasis can be placed purely on improving the quality of product or service. Like customer service schemes, this can also be the implementation of more efficiency between internal departments (which can be seen as internal customers) and external customers themselves. Like quality circles, the idea stems from the writings of Deming, Juran and, more recently, Crosby (1979, 1984). They have also been linked to British Standard BS 5750 and ISO 9000 approaches, although many claim that this is more suitable for production-oriented rather than service sector work.

Wilkinson *et al.* (1992) point out clearly the differences (and therefore the implications) between QCs and TQM (*see* Table 10.2).

Table 10.2 **Ideal types**

	QUALITY CIRCLES	TQM
Choice	voluntary	compulsory
Structure	bolt-on	integrated quality system
Direction	bottom-up	top-down
Scope	within departments or units	company-wide
Aims	employee relations improvements	quality improvements

The compulsory nature of TQM with its top-down overtones suggests a system whereby worker empowerment is restricted very much within the boundaries set by management. In its operation in production companies, Sewell and Wilkinson (1992) also propose that it has an air of surveillance, whereby the performance of individual workers is monitored by electronic devices which control their work to conform to the group norm – a norm set by management. They describe how in an electronic components factory the teams – especially the team leader – which make the components 'have a great deal of discretion in the way labour resources are deployed across the cell (the unit of manufacture)' (Sewell and Wilkinson, 1992). Multi-skilling is encouraged and work rotation allocated by the team and team leader. Within the team individuals are encouraged to improve personal performance and innovations should be made to improve productivity and product quality. Team meetings provide the forum where such issues are debated and information shared.

Quality is controlled by a visual inspection and electronic tests, which also trace the individual responsible for the fault. This information, together with data on absenteeism, conformity to standard times and production planning targets, is prominently displayed for all the team to see. Naturally, the information forms the basis of much discussion between team members. In turn this creates a situation where the team will 'discipline' those that it feels are not conforming to the norms. This is a form of what Friedman (1977, quoted in Sewell and Wilkinson, 1992) called 'responsible autonomy', a situation where the group acts as the controller of the individual and therefore the team. Thus managers can clearly claim that the workforce is being 'empowered'. This delegation of power, however, has a dual nature which, according to Muetzfeldt (quoted in Sewell and Wilkinson, 1992), 'can actually increase the power of the delegating agency, so long as it can legitimate and retain its authority, and undermine it if the obedience of the delegated agents cannot be assured'.

Sewell and Wilkinson see this system of TQM as an analogy of the work of Foucault, who stressed the importance of tracing the loci of power in organisations in order to understand its importance and how it is used.

Wilkinson *et al.* (1992), in their research into EI for the Department of Employment (*see* Marchington *et al.*, 1992), visited 25 organisations, of which the majority had TQM programmes in operation. In examining these practices it was evident that TQM operated in a wide variety of forms and, like HRM, was open to a variety of definitions and interpretations. In a close examination of TQM in three typical UK companies in engineering, finance and marketing, they discovered several problems in its implementation and operation. All of the schemes were difficult to sustain for four basic reasons:

1 The schemes were narrow in conception and 'bolted-on to, rather than integrated into, key management policies' (Wilkinson *et al.*, 1992). As a result, some schemes looked very similar to quality circles and thus had many of their faults. Companies tended to look for immediate gains rather than look to long-term cultural changes. 'If these are not forthcoming TQM is short-lived' (Wilkinson *et al.*, 1992). In turn, this created an obsession with 'the cost of quality and immediacy of return, concepts which are totally different from Japanese thinking' (Wilkinson *et al.*, 1992).

2 The role of middle managers became unclear and confused, and was looked upon as one group of managers imposing itself on another. This had the effect of creating conflicts. Because TQM was carried out in a highly centralised framework in most organisations, teams were reliant on the services of other departments, with which they were competing for resources, and each department was often in ignorance of how they were affected by each other. The competition thus militated against mutually co-operative solutions.

3 Industrial relations, while impacting on TQM programmes, are rarely considered by employers. Thus there was usually neglect in obtaining union agreement or establishing a positive working climate before implementing TQM schemes, a situation almost guaranteed to create suspicions either in the unions or the workforce. TQM affects strongly such issues as job control, working practices and reward, all of which can, if not handled sensitively, create problems, as unions and workers may place obstacles in the way of the system's operation.

4 Aspects of employee involvement in TQM schemes can have contradictory elements. Similarly to the findings of Sewell and Wilkinson (1992), it was discovered that there was a contradiction in the language of employee involvement (empowerment of the workforce, etc.) and the actuality of the work situation in which power very much rested in the hands of management.

These studies point to a number of problems in the implementation of TQM. Ramsay (1992a) has noted, with some laconic interest, the rise and fall of fads and fashions in employee involvement and speculates what might be next on the agenda if TQM does not succeed! What is certain is that easy solutions do not exist and the implementation of new systems has to be viewed in a long-term framework and reviewed constantly with the full consent and approval of the workforce.

COMMUNICATION AND 'NEW' TECHNOLOGY

E-mail: benefit or curse?

E-mail has become ubiquitous in modern organisations and, like computers and previous technological advances, we now wonder how we managed without it. It has undoubtedly brought great benefits in terms of modern communications, and managers and employees can be sent messages at any time of the day or night from virtually anywhere in the world. It can be used for sending bulletins and lengthy documents by attachments as well as sending pithy and often ungrammatical messages when in haste. And, like text messaging, it has even been used to sack people – a flagrant misuse of such a medium in terms of poor management and unethical practices.

Another problem with the use of e-mail is the communicational overload. If a manager has been away or is unable to access his or her computer for several days or longer, the dreaded 'in-box' e-mail problem rears its ugly head. The manager can not only be swamped with copious amounts of 'spam' but the normal flow of messages, which are managed on a daily basis, becomes a torrent once one finally 'logs on'. It can take hours to deal with so many messages. This problem has reached such proportions that some employees are becoming stressed in trying to keep up with the flow of messages. Up to two hours a day (often more) can be spent in just reading and answering e-mails. A recent survey found that '82 per cent of managers in the UK believe that the volume of information they have to handle has greatly increased over the past three years. And 54 per cent claim to suffer information overload' (Russell, 2001, p 38). Some US firms now have an e-mail-free day each week where employees are encouraged not to look at their e-mail in-boxes, and courses are now becoming popular in how to deal with email overload.

The real problem is getting information that is important and relevant to the right person but this can have 'political' implications. Managers, as the creators and interpreters of policy, have the power to withhold key information. HRM advocates believe that a 'high trust' and open organisational culture can help resolve many of these problems, but it would be naïve to presuppose that the problem would vanish entirely.

Internet and intranet

The Internet is a useful way of publicising a company's activities and allows potential customers and other interested parties to communicate more easily. A good web page can be an impressive introduction to a company and can bolster its image considerably.

Many companies have adapted the Internet for internal company usage. The resulting intranets can be used for a variety of purposes. They can contain company directives, the company mission statement, vision, values, strategies, rules and regulations and even employee attitude surveys can be posted on them. A number of organisations have electronic recruitment, selection and training software programes on them (*see* Exhibit 10.1).

Some writers have alluded to Internet use in organisations as the creation of a virtual representation of the organisation with built-in surveillance and controls (Lewis, 2002). For example in many organisations there are automatic checks on whether e-mails have been opened. Whether electronic forms of communication are considered to be utopian or distopian, good or bad, they will remain and increasingly become a central part of organisational functions.

Exhibit 10.1 IT in a time share call centre

A number of organisations that operate call centres use IT to save on the cost of resourcing. For example, in one call centre in a time share company much of the recruitment and selection process is carried out electronically. Candidates enter a room full of computers and are asked to complete a battery of electronic tests for a call centre position. The company knows that these positions have a high turnover and it wants a quick and easy-to-administer selection process. These tests include a personality test, an aptitude test and a customer-response simulation program. This last is set up with several levels of simulation, ranging from a customer ringing to make a simple request for information up to the top level whereby the candidate has to deal with a very awkward and angry customer. How the candidate deals with these 'imaginary' customers is then assessed and graded. Those candidates scoring below a certain grade are eliminated from the recruitment process. The remaining candidates then go on for an interview. The company claims that this is a quick and easy process to administer and saves time and staff in the selection process.

MODELS OF COMMUNICATION

It would be apposite at this point to examine some models of communication before proposing more sophisticated definitions of organisational communication and examining other forms of communication.

The first model of communication to emerge was conceived by Shannon and Weaver (1949) and initially had a mathematical basis (*see* Figure 10.1). It was devised to help Bell Telephone Company engineers understand how to transmit electrical impulses most efficiently from one place to another. Although created for mechanistic reasons, it is applicable to organisational and other communication processes.

Figure 10.1 The Shannon and Weaver model of communication

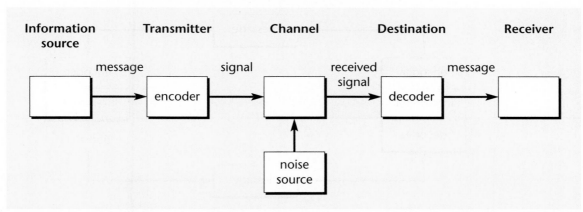

Source: C Shannon and W Weaver, *The Mathematical Theory of Communication*. Copyright 1949 by the Board of Trustees of the University of Illinois. Used with permission of the authors and the University of Illinois Press.

The message is encoded, i.e. turned from an idea into a verbal or written message; the message is then sent from the information source to the receiver, travelling via a channel, and is then decoded by the receiver, either by hearing or reading the message. The problem is that the message can get distorted by noise sources or interference. In the mechanistic version of the telephone this might be interference on the telephone line, thus making the communication difficult and unclear. In the case of a manager speaking to an employee, it could be more subtle. The noise source which distorts the message could be personal. For example, the employee may dislike the manager, or be unhappy with the situation in which he or she works, or have a headache or personal problems at home.

One criticism of the Shannon and Weaver model is that communication is seen as only a one-way process. Observers in the field of human behaviour have stated that this is not so, even in communications between the most seemingly compliant employee and manager. The employee may communicate dissatisfaction through body language or through another source, such as his or her work group. Later communication model builders therefore added the element of 'feedback' to the communication model (Schramm, 1954; DeFleur, 1966).

Thus while the Shannon and Weaver model concentrates on the channels between sender and receiver, the Schramm model devotes its discussion to the main actors in the communication process, allowing both to send and receive messages (*see* Figure 10.2).

While these communication models have been refined and elaborated (McQuail and Windahl, 1981), they nevertheless contain the essence of the communication process as represented in most organisations.

The medium is the message

The communication models clearly show that messages, whether one-way or two-way, can be influenced by a variety of distorting influences (noise), which may be part of a contextual influence of the communication medium. Indeed, McLuhan (1964) has gone so far as to suggest that 'the medium is the message', that the mes-

Figure 10.2 **The Osgood Schramm model of communication**

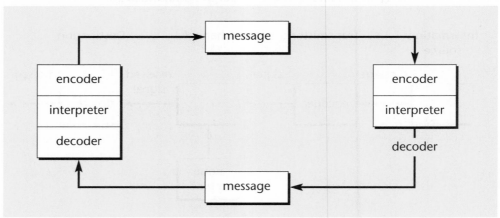

Source: W Schramm, 'How Communication Works', from *The Process and Effects of Mass Communication*. Copyright 1954 by the Board of Trustees of the University of Illinois. Used with permission of the author and the University of Illinois Press.

sage is influenced by the kind and type of channel or medium used. A well-known example was the live US presidential debate between Kennedy and Nixon in 1960. Listeners on the radio thought Nixon won the debate with a convincing set of arguments, whereas viewers of the television broadcast gave the debate to Kennedy. Analysts later pointed to the visual power of the television medium which showed a young, handsome Kennedy opposing a seedy-looking Nixon who was sweating, had 'five-o'clock shadow' and was wearing a suit which did not allow him to stand out from his background. The visual imagery acted as a powerful influence on the message.

THE KRONE, JABLIN AND PUTNAM DEFINITION

With these diverse influences on communication in mind, Krone, Jablin and Putnam in 1987 posed a more complex series of definitions. While they acknowledged that empirical research exploring organisational communication processes had burgeoned over the last two decades, they also recognised the necessity of developing a theoretical base, the starting point from which attempts should be made at a more rigorous definition of organisational communication.

They focused on four 'fairly comprehensive yet parsimonious' perspectives: mechanistic, psychological, interpretive-symbolic and systems-interaction (Jablin *et al.*, 1987).

The mechanistic perspective

This concentrates on the channel of communication and the transmission of the message. It follows very much the model posed by Shannon and Weaver. Thus the mechanistic perspective views communication as a linear connection between communicators in which A causes B. The clarity of the message is thus affected by the degree of interference or 'noise' in transmission. An example of this type of organisational communication exists very strongly in military structures where officers pass orders down through various communication channels which are understood by the recipients and acted upon. As we are all aware, this image of communicational efficiency is not always lived up to in the heat of battle, as Tolstoy (in *War and Peace*) and many other writers have attested.

The psychological perspective

The psychological perspective focuses specifically on how characteristics of individuals (personality, mood, ideology, etc.) impact on the reception and interpretation of communications. As a result: *'the conceptual filters of individuals become the locus of communication. These filters consist of the communicators' attitudes, cognitions and perceptions'* (Krone *et al.*, 1987). These filters thus become vital in the encoding and decoding process. From this perspective organisational communication is seen very much as an interpersonal activity, and individuals as information processors influenced by conceptual filters – for example, how individuals view themselves, perceptions of power and control in the organisation, work expectations and other factors.

One psychological barrier to communication pointed to by many surveys is the gulf between hierarchical levels in the organisation. Consistent studies in the USA and the UK since the 1950s have shown that superiors think they adequately communicate with their subordinates, whereas subordinates think the opposite – that they send more messages upwards but receive less feedback from their bosses. Psychological explanations of this phenomenon regard the prime cause as perceptual differences of the same processes, and how each relates to those processes and the people who carry them out.

Vicki Smith, in studying a Californian bank, clearly shows how the strategy conceived at boardroom level becomes increasingly distorted as it travels down the line to workplace level. Each level in the hierarchy perceives the strategy slightly differently, and sometimes very differently. The implementers of strategy have their own personal and psychological agendas. For example, if the implementation of strategy means taking painful decisions which would upset subordinates, line managers would distort the messages to fit in with their perceptions of creating less distress but conforming to what they perceive to be the received strategy (Smith, 1990).

The interpretive-symbolic perspective

This perspective extends the psychological perspective into the realms of socially shared meanings of what constitutes the organisation.

> *'Thus, rather than passively submitting to some organisationally determined view of the workplace, the interpretive symbolic perspective posits that by virtue of their ability to communicate, individuals are capable of creating and shaping their own social reality.'*
> (Krone *et al.*, 1987)

Within this perspective shared meanings of common events and actions become important.

> *'Thus behaviour is not simply the response of conceptual filters to information stimuli; rather, it develops through social interaction and it changes as the social context changes.'*
> (Krone *et al.*, 1987)

In essence, the interpretive-symbolic perspective emphasises how culture has an impact on the interpretive processes, and how interpretive processes through shared meanings impact on and create organisational culture.

In illustrating this, most people entering a new organisational environment quickly become aware of the 'ways of doing things' and how the organisation is constituted, constructed and perceived by their fellow workers. If a newcomer, for example, proposes a different way of carrying out a work function, this can be received in a hostile manner if it is perceived that this does not fit into or threatens the previous ways of doing things or the perceptions of the existing work culture.

The Challenger space shuttle disaster

Perhaps the most startling example of this operating in a dysfunctional way was the Challenger space shuttle disaster in the 1980s, in which all the members of the crew were killed. Concerns about the shuttle's safety had not been adequately relayed back from the engineers at the launch base to top management at control. This was not a simple breakdown in communication but the subconscious misreading of messages, influenced heavily by organisational culture. The overriding shared cultural meaning of the event was that the shuttle launch had to be a success in every way as the future programme budgets from Congress hinged upon it. The launch thus had to be publicly seen as successful in all respects, including a punctual lift-off for the waiting world media. These concerns overrode the safety messages and the resulting disaster ironically put an effective end to those original objectives of the programme.

Pace and Boren (1973) sum up this situation well by stating that:

'messages in serial production, like water in a great river, change through losses, gains, absorptions and combinations along the route from the headwaters to their final destinations'.

A well-known example is the famous First World War communication in which an officer in a trench asks the soldier next to him to pass on down the line of soldiers the following message for headquarters:

'We're going to advance. Send reinforcements.'

By the time the message has passed along the line, it has become distorted to:

'We're going to a dance. Send three and fourpence!'

The systems-interactive perspective

The systems-interactive perspective has similarities with the mechanistic approach, in concentrating on external behaviours of groups and individuals, and examining how and with what frequency communication systems are used. The emphasis is thus on **patterned sequential behaviour** which examines the categories, forms and sequential patterns of message behaviour. However, this systems-interactive perspective is different from the mechanistic perspective in the sense that an individual does not 'do' communication, but becomes 'part' of communication.

This approach has been used to look at superior–subordinate communication and conflictual relations in industrial relations by examining responses to communication acts and tracing their processes. For example, Fairhurst *et al.* (1987) examined dominance patterns of manager–subordinate interactions. Their findings indicated that managers who displayed a high number of dominant attitudes in their communications perceived that their subordinates had less interest in decision involvement and rated them as being lower in performance than managers who used fewer controlling patterns. Putnam and Jones (1982), in examining labour–management communication, found that labour (trade unions) specialised in using offensive manoeuvres such as attacking arguments and threats, while management relied on defensive tactics such as commitments and self-supporting arguments. Thus, reversing this pattern, the unions providing information to an enquiring management seems to have the tendency to prevent or lower conflict. If each side tries to match the other in a one-upmanship pattern, it tends to lead to higher conflict and a bargaining impasse.

These four communication perspectives are summarised in Table 10.3 (*see* page 286).

CLAMPITT'S MODELS OF COMMUNICATION

Other writers, most notably Clampitt (1991), have also developed models of communication. He identifies three main approaches to communication: the arrow, the circuit and the dance.

Table 10.3 **Alternative perspectives to organisational communication**

PERSPECTIVE	LOCUS OF COMMUNICATION	CHARACTERISTICS/ IMPLICATIONS
Mechanistic	Channel and message transmission	Focus on conveying information and accuracy of message reception
		Message sending/receiving considered as linear process
		Somewhat dehumanising; little attention to receiver and role of meaning in communication
		Tendency to oversimplify and re-identify the communication process
Psychological	Conceptual filters	Receiver as active message interpreter
		Emphasises intentions and human aspects of communications
Interpretive-symbolic	Role taking	Considers role of self and group – cultural context of communication
		Emphasis on symbols and 'shared' meaning
Systems-interaction	Sequences of communication behaviour	Feedback patterns; conflict management, work group development
		Treats communication as an evolving system
		Focuses on types of message sequence functions and behaviours

Source: Adapted from Krone *et al.* (1987, p 33), in F Jablin, L Putnam, K Roberts and L Porter (eds) (1987) *Handbook of Organizational Communication: An Interdisciplinary Perspective.* Copyright © 1987 by Sage Publications, Inc. Reprinted by permission of Sage Publications, Inc.

The arrow approach

The 'arrow' is closely identified with the mechanistic view and the Shannon and Weaver communication model and is concerned with the conveyance of clear messages unhindered by 'noise'. For example, when a manager gives instructions to an employee, the manager 'A' conceives instructions which are sent by a medium (face-to-face, telephone, memo, etc.) to 'B', an employee. The arrow metaphor is the direction of the communication from A to B. Clampitt believes that within each form of communication a number of assumptions are made. The arrow manager's assumptions are illustrated in Table 10.4.

As can be imagined, there could be enormous differences between the perceived communication effectiveness and the underlying assumptions, and the actual communication reception by the receiver, i.e. the employee. For example, it is possible that the employee may not share the assumptions of the manager either consciously or subconsciously, thus causing a communication breakdown.

Table 10.4 **Evaluation of arrow manager's assumptions**

COMMUNICATION EFFECTIVENESS	UNDERLYING ASSUMPTIONS
Being able clearly and precisely to put my thoughts into words.	What is clear and precise to one person is clear and precise to another.
Speaking with credibility and authority.	Credibility is something the speaker possesses and not something given to the speaker by the audience.
Getting the results I want by talking to my people.	Communication is primarily a one-way activity.

Source: P Clampitt (1991) *Communicating for Managerial Effectiveness*, p 3. Copyright © 1991 by Sage Publications, Inc. Reprinted by permission of Sage Publications, Inc.

Managers who hold dear to this view of the communication process are liable to blame the employee:

> *'Why didn't they just follow my instructions?'*

Or

> *'Why can't they get it right? If I've told them once, I've told them a thousand times.'*

The circuit approach

> *'The circuit approach represents an evolution from the arrow to the circle. Circuit managers stress feedback over response, relationship over content, connotation over denotations, understanding over compliance. Communication is seen as a two-way process involving the dynamic interplay of an active sender and receiver.'*

> (Clampitt, 1991)

This approach conforms much more to the Osgood Schramm Model (*see* Figure 10.2), which emphasises that communication is a two-way process. This is also congruent with recent trends towards employee participation styles of management as embodied in total quality management (TQM), business process re-engineering, and customer service schemes. As with the arrow manager, the circuit manager holds a set of assumptions, as shown in Table 10.5.

The circuit manager recognises that there will be communication breakdowns and the oft-cited reasons are as follows:

- People just 'don't connect' in the sense that their values, emotions and ideas are too dissimilar.
- Poor listening skills often mar and distort the communication.
- There may be 'hidden agendas' or unarticulated goals which may cause friction when revealed at a later time or in another context.
- Communicational relationships can only operate under certain conditions. For example, if a proper climate for the exchange of information and ideas does not exist, then this will hamper attempts at communication.

Table 10.5 **Evaluation of circuit manager's assumptions**

COMMUNICATION EFFECTIVENESS	UNDERLYING ASSUMPTIONS
Listening to employees, in order to make them happy.	Job satisfaction is the goal of organisational communication.
Being sensitive to employees, in order to adapt messages to each individual.	Messages are exclusively interpreted in the context of interpersonal relationships.
Being open and understanding.	Openness is useful in all circumstances. Understanding is always more acceptable than ambiguity.

Source: P Clampitt (1991), *Communicating for Managerial Effectiveness*, p 3. Copyright © 1991 by Sage Publications, Inc. Reprinted by permission of Sage Publications, Inc.

Despite these potential weaknesses, the circuit approach to communication is much more empathetic and more likely to succeed in work environments of high trust. Problems arise when these approaches are inadvertently applied to environments of low trust in the belief that they can act as an agent for change.

The dance approach

Clampitt finally describes what he sees as a superior approach to communication by using the metaphor of dance. Comparing communication to dance may seem odd but Clampitt justifies it by suggesting that:

> *'Dance involves patterns, movements and creativity. It can be enjoyed by participants as well as observers. There are as many styles as people. Tastes vary. Standards differ. Styles change. Trends come and go. But dance has been and always will be part of the human community. Once a dance is performed it can never be recaptured in the same way again. . . . It may be one of the highest and unique forms of human expression. So, too, is communication.'*   (Clampitt, 1991)

The dance metaphor is used by Clampitt to illustrate the complexity and diversity of communication and the communication process, and that simple explanations can be misleading. For example, the purpose of communication is not always clear, and communicators may have multiple goals for a single message.

> *'Effectiveness can only be determined in the light of the communicators' goals – whatever they may be – including obfuscation, confusion, or deception . . . hence, there is no single measure of communication effectiveness.'*   (Clampitt, 1991)

For example, politicians can be very effective communicators in hard-hitting election campaigns, using slogans, simplifying complex ideas and relating party policy to the average voter; but in times of adversity they can use those same skills to obfuscate, fudge and mislead their audiences. Similarly, hidden agendas and multiplicity of purpose can pervade the communication process in organisations, be it the managing director making reassuring noises to shareholders about profits or to the workforce about redundancy at a time when market share and sales are falling. This means recognising that communication is used for multiple purposes and, importantly, requires the co-ordination of meanings – so that the diversity of meanings are implicitly and explicitly guided towards the same objectives within the organisational culture.

Communication, like dance, tends to be rule-governed. Thus, just as in dance certain steps and movements are acceptable, so too in communication there are implicit and explicit rules. For example, effective listeners may use the following rules (Clampitt, 1991):

- **Initiate conversations with questions about unrisky topics**
- **If a person's comments are unclear, then ask for clarification**
- **If a person appears defensive, nod head**
- **Terminate conversations by summarising the conversation.**

Communicators develop a repertoire of skills. Just as the dancer no longer thinks about the execution of certain steps and movements, so too does the communication process become a subconscious and automatic process to the experienced communicator.

Communication can also be viewed as a pattern activity in which certain exchanges can become inured into positive and, more worryingly, negative patterns of communication, just as dancers can develop 'bad' habits in the execution of movements. For example, Clampitt uses the following conversation to explain these communicational difficulties caused by negative patterns of reinforcement.

> *A manager may jokingly insult an employee:*
>
> *'Hey, Pat! Has your golf game improved yet?'*
>
> **The manager interprets this as a greeting; the employee as an insult. The employee replies, however, with what she sees as a placatory response – a factual reply to the question:**
>
> *'I haven't been golfing lately.'*
>
> **The manager interprets this as meaning that the employee is ignoring him, and tries to re-establish the conversation with another 'playful' question:**
>
> *'Well how's that old banger of a car going?'*
>
> **The employee regards this as another insult and mentally asks 'What kind of a game is he playing?' She again responds to the 'insult' with a placatory and factual answer:**
>
> *'I sold it.'*
>
> **The manager thinks, 'She's catching on, but still takes the conversation too seriously.' He continues the conversation with another 'jokey' insult:**
>
> *'I hope you didn't buy another heap of rubbish.'*
>
> **The employee sees this as another insult and that he is now questioning her decision-making ability. This time she is not placatory:**
>
> *'Why don't you just get off my back and mind your own business!'*
>
> **The manager interprets this: 'Why is she so upset? I'm just trying to build some rapport. The employee has no sense of humour.'**
>
> **The employee interprets this: 'If placating doesn't work then stand up for yourself. My only alternative is to be assertive. He's insensitive and unprofessional.'**

Neither the manager nor the employee sees the overall pattern resulting from their personal rules of interaction. In a group situation, the margin for error multiplies considerably. Recognising these negative patterns and changing them therefore becomes an important aspect of communication.

Organisations where communications flow in a positive way are those where the rules and patterns, together with the subconscious understandings, create a culture of commitment and congruence, as Clampitt would suggest, like the most beautiful and creative dance partners performing a work of magnificence with elegant ease.

Criticism can be levelled at these perspectives in that they do not fully consider external influences on the organisation such as social, economic and political trends. Investigators into employee involvement (EI) operations have attempted to take these factors into consideration, most notable Poole (1986) and Ramsay (1977).

INTERNATIONAL ASPECTS OF COMMUNICATION

Communications are extremely important in the conduct of international business and the increase in telecommunications, forms of IT communications such as the Internet, intranet and e-mail and international travel have considerably improved the ways that organisations can send and receive messages from their subsidiaries and overseas partners. In the nineteenth- and early twentieth-century company overseas subsidiaries often enjoyed considerable autonomy due to the fact that it may have taken several months for messages to be carried and received via the postal system and sailing ships. The increasing speed of communication and travel in the present day can only lead us to agree with Marshall McLuhan (1964) that the world is becoming a 'global village'. In addition, increases in forms of communication have enabled multinational corporations to co-ordinate and control their businesses much more effiectively.

Paradoxically, while it would appear that communication is on the increase between parent and affiliate companies, it would be foolish to believe that the increase in speed of communications has solved most of our communicational problems. Indeed, it can be argued that it has made the world of management a more complex place. Despite the increase in communicational channels, there are still considerable barriers to communication between people from different countries. The most obvious are language and cultural differences, and it has become increasingly recognised that managers need training in these areas if they are to be successful in coping with an international assignment. The conversation in Table 10.6 between an American expatriate manager and a Greek host country employee illustrates this well.

This example of communication breakdown is typical of the misunderstanding that expatriate managers and their host country staff could experience. The cause of this communication failure is initially language. Both are speaking in English but through their own cultural filters. The boss's spoken English is informed by American values, and his employee's by Greek values. These values are in turn formed by their respective cultures. Before returning to analyse this dialogue, another example will serve to support the 'we speak the same language but with different understandings' thesis.

Table 10.6 Cultural misunderstanding in international communication

BEHAVIOUR	ATTRIBUTION
American: 'How long will it take you to finish this report?'	**American:** I asked him to participate. **Greek:** His behaviour makes no sense. He is the boss. Why doesn't he tell me?
Greek: 'I don't know. How long should it take?'	**American:** He refuses to take responsibility for his actions. **Greek:** I asked him for an order.
American: 'You are in the best position to analyse time requirements.'	**American:** I press him to take responsibility for his actions. **Greek:** What nonsense! I'd better give him an answer.
Greek: 'Ten days.'	**American:** He lacks the ability to estimate time; this time estimate is totally inadequate.
American: 'Take 15. Is it agreed? You will do it within 15 days?'	**American:** I offer a contract. **Greek:** These are my orders: 15 days.

In fact, the report needed 30 days of work. So the Greek worked night and day, but at the end of the fifteenth day, he still needed to do one more day's work.

American: 'Where is the report?'	**American:** I'm making sure he fulfils his contract. **Greek:** He is asking for the report.
Greek: 'It will be ready tomorrow.'	(Both attribute that it is not ready.)
American: 'But we agreed it would be ready today.'	**American:** I must teach him to fulfil a contract. **Greek:** The stupid, incompetent boss! Not only did he give me the wrong orders, but he didn't even appreciate that I did a 30-day job in 16 days.

The Greek hands in his resignation notice. The American is surprised.

	Greek: I can't work for such a man.

Source: Adapted from Triandis (1977).

What went wrong?

We see in Exhibit 10.2 (on the next page) what Hall and Hall (1990) would describe as high-context culture meeting low-context culture. In high-context cultures meanings are conveyed not only with words but in the context of body language and levels of meaning. In low-context cultures the meanings are conveyed much more with words only. So in this conversation when the English managers say 'interesting' it has to be listened to in context, i.e how it is said, with an edge of hesitation and doubt. Other English people would pick this up as a criticism and interpret 'interesting' in this context as meaning a doubtful proposition or even a very poor proposal. The Swedish manager only hears the words 'interesting' and

Exhibit 10.2 Different levels of context

A Swedish HR manager was transferred to England to run a subsidiary's HR system. She gathered her team of English HR managers about her and gave them a written HR strategy to read. She then asked them what they thought of it. The English managers did not think it was very good, but in English culture direct judgement is often avoided, so they said it was 'interesting'. She interpreted this as approval, so she then said: 'Shall I go ahead with it?' The English managers were now in a quandary, so they gave a non-committal reply: 'If you like.' She went ahead with it and it did not work very well. She was furious with the English managers whom she believed had misled her.

misses the English cultural context. Similarly, when the English reply, 'if you like', to her question to go ahead with the proposal, the contextual interpretation for the English is 'on your head be it'.

The Swedish manager's interpretation is that they said my proposal was 'interesting', meaning that it may be a good proposal. If it is a good proposal and the English manager's reply to my question, 'Shall I go ahead with it?' is: 'If you like', then I should go ahead with it. The way that even a common language is spoken can thus provide pitfalls. Even native English speakers like Americans, British and Canadians can misunderstand one another. Many British and Americans fall into the trap that because we speak the same language we have the same meanings. As George Bernard Shaw said, 'The British and the Americans are separated by a common language.'

What went wrong in the American–Greek dialogue?

Returning to our dialogue between the American and Greek, we can see that other cultural differences have come into play. What Hofstede (1980) has defined as four cultural dimensions: power distance, uncertainty avoidance, individualism and masculinity (*see also* Chapters 2 and 19) helps us to understand the difficulties that the American expatriate manager and his Greek employee have in understanding one another.

→ Chs 2
and 19

Power distance index (PDI)

By **power distance** Hofstede means:

'the extent to which the less powerful members of institutions and organisations within a country expect and accept that power is distributed unequally.'

(Hofstede, 1991, p 28)

For example, in democratic societies the distance between the government and the governed is narrower than in authoritarian states. In other words, a worker in the Philippines will have far less chance of influencing the decisions of the government than would a worker in Sweden; and the same applies in the workplace. Greeks have a higher PDI than Americans. In the context of the dialogue, the Greek employee would expect the American manager, who is higher in authority, to give him directions and even orders, rather than to work out things for himself. The American would be more likely to expect the reverse.

Uncertainty avoidance index (UAI)

The definition of uncertainty avoidance involves,

inter alia, the creation of rules and structures to eliminate ambiguity in organisations and support beliefs promising certainty and protecting conformity.

In simple terms, this means that human beings try in various ways to avoid uncertainty in their lives by controlling their environment through predictable ways of working. For example, France and Germany are much higher in uncertainty avoidance than Britain and Sweden. In other words, the Germans and French feel a much greater need to adhere to rules and regulations than do the Swedes and British.

In UAI country scores the Greeks come out the highest and the Americans below the norm. There would thus be a high expectation of difficulty between Greeks and Americans on this dimension. We can see this clearly in the dialogue where the Greek wants certainty as to the number of days the assignment will take. The American lets the Greek judge that for himself. To the Greek, the American manager is operating without any firm rules and is shirking his responsibility as a manager. To the American, the Greek is unable to do things for himself and is too reliant on direction.

Individualism index (IDV)

Individualism describes the

relationship between the individual and the group to which he or she belongs or the preference for living and working in collectivist or individual ways.

Not surprisingly, the USA and Britain score high on the individual index and South American and Asian countries score low. In the latter, there is much more reliance on the extended family and the subsuming of the individual identity within the group, whereas in countries with high individual indexes, like the USA and northern European countries, there is a tendency to revere individual achievement. The Greeks score low on the individualism index and, as we have already noted, the Americans score high. The Greek will thus be looking forward for support from the American manager, as a father looks after the family. The American would, by contrast, value individual endeavour and initiative. In addition, the American is much more task-oriented and is looking for results. While the Greek will also seek successful completion of the project, with Greek culture being more collectivist, there is an expectation of a more personal relationship based on trust.

In collectivist cultures, business is done with people; in individualist cultures, business is about product and service targets, and how an individual performs in relation to these criteria.

Masculinity index

Hofstede's last and perhaps most controversial index of culture is that of masculinity. This pertains to societies in which social gender roles are clearly distinct, i.e. men are supposed to be assertive, tough and focused on material success. Femininity pertains to societies in which women are supposed to be more modest, tender and concerned with the quality of life (Hofstede, 1991, p 82). In Hofstede's index masculine and feminine values can apply to both men and women. Thus, we find that in Sweden, the least masculine country in the index, feminine values apply also to men. However, in the most masculine country, Japan, women seem to retain their feminine values. On this dimension Greeks and Americans are very close and so this would seem not to pose a great cultural problem.

Universalism and particularism

Trompenaars (1993) also has used dimensions of culture to analyse behaviours of business people in international contexts. Although space prohibits a close examination of his work, it would be worth mentioning that his dimension 'universalism–particularism' can also help us understand the difficulties that the American and Greek experienced. In universalist cultures, like the USA, managers focus more on rules than relationships. In particularist cultures, like Greece, there is more of a focus on relationships than rules. The less reliance on relationships in universalist cultures means that legal contracts are more readily drawn up. In particularist cultures legal contracts are readily modified in the light of evolving relationships.

In analysing our dialogue we can see that the American was keen to ensure that his Greek employee was fulfilling his contract. To the Greek this ignores their relationship and sends the message that his American manager does not trust him.

Culture and time

Time orientation is also important in understanding other cultures. In Western cultures like the USA acts and functions are usually carried out in **sequential** time, i.e. doing only one activity at a time. In sequential time cultures, time is measurable, appointments are strictly kept, and there is a strong preference for the initial plan. In **synchronic** time cultures, like Greece, people will do more than one activity at a time and schedules are generally subordinate to relationships.

In analysing our dialogue once more we can see that the American's need to have a specific time schedule is very important, and the failure to fulfil the assignment on time is a reflection of the person's ability to work hard or plan carefully. The Greek is trying to please the American manager by attempting to keep to the schedule agreed, even though this was impossible. When the American manager reminds him of the agreed time for completion, the Greek believes he is more concerned about the task than about his employee's welfare and their working relationship. He thus resigns in disgust.

This example of communication breakdown illustrates the importance of understanding a variety of cultures. Neither the Greek nor the American was necessarily wrong. There was just a number of communication barriers to overcome caused by cultural misunderstandings. There was an inability to comprehend and appreciate each other's ways of doing things and perceiving the world.

COMPARATIVE INTERNATIONAL COMMUNICATION

In examining communications in a comparative context, compared with the international organisational context above, we can see how national institutional factors affect the operation of communications. Trade unions and other employee voice mechanisms will tend to vary in importance and function depending on the laws, political and social climate and economic institutions and performance of different nations and regions.

Trade unions and communications

In many countries in Europe and the rest of the world, trade unions still act as one of the most important communication channels, despite the fact that there has been a decline in membership worldwide over the past 20 years. Their importance is still central in Scandinavian countries, especially Sweden, and they still carry considerable weight in Germany and Britain, despite the decline in the old staple industries like shipbuilding, coal, iron and steel and engineering, where unionism had a strong traditional base.

The Price Waterhouse Cranfield Surveys into International Strategic HRM (Price Waterhouse Cranfield Project, 1990, 1991, 1995; CRANEFE, 1999) investigating European countries found consistent increases in verbal and written communications such as forms of teamworking, suggestion schemes, employee attitude surveys, company newspapers and magazines, etc. While these trends are to be welcomed, companies do not implement such arrangements for purely altruistic and democratic reasons. Empowerment schemes and other employee involvement schemes are a powerful way of presenting the company case in times of dispute and therefore the aims and objectives of an increase in the number and intensity of communication channels may have specific 'political' reasons. In the past many companies found themselves at a comparative disadvantage in disputes as the unions virtually had monopoly of the informational channels to the workforce. This was no fault of the unions but more a reflection of the incompetence of management, incapable of creating effective communication channels, which they suspected could be used at other times for what might be perceived as more negative purposes (Monks, 1989). In other words, management can itself suffer from its own ideology of operating 'mushroom systems' (keeping the workforce in the dark and piling 'manure' on them), which maintains a climate of distrust and attitudes of 'us and them'.

Fortunately, other surveys supported the findings from the Price Waterhouse Cranfield survey and indicated that in many organisations such ideas were becoming less popular (CBI, 1989; Marchington *et al.*, 1992). These obviously show a greater desire by employers to increase communication, inspired by HRM trends that have become popular since the 1980s.

While communication between workforce and management is increasing at workplace level, the more established forms of communication and forms of EI at a company level, such as unions, works councils and JCCs, are still important. Nevertheless, these surveys do not indicate the degree of participation by employees in organisations. Research by Fröhlich and Krieger (1990), Cressey and Williams (1990), Boreham (1992) and Gill (1993) has tried to address this issue in comparative contexts. Fröhlich and Krieger (1990) examined the extent of employee participation in technological change in five EC countries: UK, France, Germany, Italy and Denmark. They discovered that in the four phases of introducing new technology (planning, selection, implementation and subsequent evaluation) workers were more likely to be involved in the latter stages and that full participation, particularly in decision making, remained relatively low for all countries and for all stages. Cressey and Williams (1990) in a similar survey, but covering all 12 EC countries, found comparable results and posed a 'paradox of participation'. As the scope for influence by employees over the processes of technological change decreased, so the intensity of participation increased. In other words, there was more scope for participation in the implementation stage (the later stage) when participative influence concerning fundamental decisions was reduced, and less participation in the crucial earlier planning stages in the introduction of new technology.

Boreham (1992) investigated the degree of employee control over labour processes in seven countries (Australia, Britain, Canada, Germany, Japan, Sweden and USA). He was particularly interested to know whether employee control was enhanced by the introduction of new practices associated with post-Fordist systems, such as flexible working linked to quality improvement and greater response to market conditions. The assumption here was that efficiency was improved by decentralisation and democratised decision-making practices. The findings clearly indicated that 'the nearer one approaches the core of status and power in the enterprise the more likely it is that one be allowed discretion over one's work arrangements' (Boreham, 1992, p 18). He also found that there was little evidence 'to support the view that management will cede its decision making prerogatives in the interests of more rational production methods' (Boreham, 1992, p 21). This pattern was generally true of Japanese and Swedish organisations which are associated with employee-involvement styles of management.

These surveys clearly indicate a contradiction in managers' perceptions that employee involvement is an effective way of increasing work efficiency, but is outweighed by the challenge to their prerogatives over decision making. Thus, employee involvement is very limited and is more likely to take the form of information dissemination to, and consultation with, the workforce, which is not the same as 'empowerment', to which many HRM textbooks allude.

Boreham (1992) also stresses the significance of flexible employment patterns and involvement. In a world where increases in part-time, fixed-contract and short-term working is becoming more pronounced, he shows that these employees have even less involvement in workplace decisions, and that core groups, particularly in management categories, still hold far greater sway over the organisation and control of work. Such evidence casts huge question marks over growing trends, for example 'zero hours contracts' alongside involvement schemes aimed at motivating workers.

Employee involvement and the European Union

One of the most controversial issues surrounding the European social dimension has been the issue of employee involvement. The refusal to adopt the Social Charter and the works council directive of 1991 by the UK Conservative government is also reflective of some employer attitudes throughout Europe in which legislation is viewed as a threat to managerial prerogatives. Nevertheless, most European countries have *in situ* laws supporting works councils and other employee rights to consultation.

The works council directive was adopted by the European Union (EU) in 1994 and allows formal employee information and consultation procedures into companies and groups with more than 1000 employees and with at least 150 employees in two different countries. It requires employers to disclose to employee representatives a considerable amount of information concerning its activities, for example company structures, financial position, employment situation and probable trends concerning production, sales and future developments. The directive also requires parent companies to establish formal consultative procedures to take place on any decision 'liable to have serious consequences for the interests of employees of its subsidiaries in the community'. It was also agreed that information was to be furnished and consultation was to be carried out in the implementation of new technologies.

Most of these provisions were adopted into the Social Charter, particularly for the following cases:

- when technological changes, which from the point of view of working conditions and work organisation have major implications for the workforce, are introduced into undertakings;
- in connection with restructuring operations in undertakings or in cases of mergers having an impact on the employment of workers;
- in cases of collective redundancy procedures;
- when transfrontier workers, in particular, are affected by the employment policies pursued by the undertaking where they are employed.

While previous British Conservative governments were implacably opposed to the works council directive and the directives on participation embodied in the Social Charter, Tony Blair's Labour government immediately signed up to the Social Charter on being elected in 1997, and subsequently adopted the works council directive in December 1999.

Despite the fact that all EU countries now subscribe to the directive, the presence of works councils does not guarantee a voice in managerial policy making. In 1998 Renault closed its Vilvoorde plant in Belgium without adequately consulting and informing its employees. Union protests led to a French court ruling that Renault did not act in accordance with the EU legislation in closing the plant. Obviously, this retrospective censure has not returned those Renault jobs to Belgian workers, and the European trade union movement (ETUC) has demanded amendments tightening the European works council (EWC) legislation, so far without success.

In addition the European Union passed a directive in 2001 that requires employers to give relevant information to, and allow consultation with, employees. This will come into effect in 2005 and will apply to all organisations with 150 or more employees. In 2007 it will apply to all businesses of more than 100 employees and in 2008 to those with 50 or more.

Japanese employee involvement

Japan is often cited as an exemplar of excellent organisational communication, particularly through employee participatory practices, most notably in giant corporations such as Komatsu, Hitachi, Nissan, Honda, Mitsubishi and Toyota. The most commonly emulated participatory technique has been quality circles (QCs), implanted in Japanese organisations in the 1950s. Since then employee involvement techniques such as QCs and teamworking have been part and parcel of the working practices of Japanese subsidiaries such as Nissan in Sunderland and Toyota in Derby. Many studies have been made of Japanese organisations in order to discover the secrets of their economic success, and teamworking techniques have received much attention as a perceived key to efficient work practices.

Pascale and Athos (1982, p 125) emphasise that the work group is the basic building block of Japanese organisations:

> *'Owing to the central importance of group efforts in their thinking, the Japanese are extremely sensitive to and concerned about group interactions and relationships.'*

They liken the Japanese worker's view of the group to that of a marriage which rests on commitment, trust, sharing and loyalty and, while power ultimately rests with management, the group leader handles the interaction within the group carefully. This 'participation assumption' is also related to a lifetime employment assumption, which ensures that the worker has a strong stake in the firm and its success. Finally, and perhaps most importantly, participation is backed up by training of both group leaders and workers in the skills of group participation (Dore and Sako, 1989). Employee involvement, like training, is thus embedded in Japanese organisations.

A number of observers have pointed out that employee involvement should not be confused with decision making, particularly at the higher levels within the organisation:

> *'The reality is that not all employees wield real power . . . [and] when it comes to making the decision, workers feel under great pressure to agree with supervisors and unpopular decisions are simply ignored.'*
>
> (Klauss and Bass, 1974; Naoi and Schooler, 1985, quoted in Briggs, 1991, p 40)

Briggs sees this paradox of employee involvement and emasculation of power as being explained by the split between opinion and behaviour. In a number of surveys Japanese workers have rated themselves low on job satisfaction and yet they work far more hours for less reward than their American and British counterparts. This cannot be explained by coercive methods alone, and Briggs points to the extent of unionisation, albeit organised around large corporations, and finds this view untenable. Her explanation is based on cultural factors in that the Japanese have 'a deep felt desire to keep the realm of duty separate from the realm of personal feeling . . . duty must come first and must exist totally separate from the domain of personal feelings' (Briggs, 1991).

If this is the case, then this has ramifications for the export of such EI practices to other countries, most notably Britain, which has received enormous amounts of Japanese investment. Wickens (1987), in his exposition of how Nissan implanted Japanese practices into its Sunderland factory, strongly believes that people are capable of change and the institution of Japanese-style working practices was partly effected by a watering-down process to meet British attitudes, combined with a process of education and training to enable newly hired (often novice) workers in car manufacturing to be imbued with Japanese-style practices. This was reinforced by a 'greenfield' culture, with workers who had predominantly been recruited from regions where high unemployment meant an eagerness to gain and retain employment.

A number of observers have pointed out that control and the mechanisms of employee involvement in Japanese-owned British organisations still resides firmly in the hands of management. Lewis (1989), in his study of employee participation in a Japanese-owned electronics factory, found that, while a board was set up (a kind of JCC) to represent employee interests, employees were not quite sure what was meant by involvement. Most of the issues raised were not about the overall running of the operation but more parochial shopfloor concerns, and the real aim in setting up the board was to introduce unitarist principles in the company, such as single-status terms and conditions, no-strike arrangements and flexible working practices. All were reinforced with powerful symbols of unitarism, such as brightly coloured jackets which everyone wore, replete with the owner's forename. This sent messages of egalitarianism and that the organisation was one happy family. The single-status restaurants and toilets were also part of this symbolic reinforcement of unitarism. Oliver and Lowe (1991) endorse this unitarist view of Japanese-style management. In comparing styles of HRM in Japanese, American and British computer companies based in the UK, they found the Japanese emphasised consensus and collectivism with 'a thin dividing line between the public and the private and a strong sense of mutual support and awareness'.

In essence, the implementation of EI, even in Japanese organisations which have strong commitments to such systems, are not in existence as decision-making instruments *per se* or even conduits of employee criticism, but as mechanisms which reinforce common aims and goals within the unitarist organisational context.

Ramsay (1992b) has also pointed out that few non-Japanese-owned British organisations have adopted Japanese EI measures in the long term. Quality circles, after an initial flurry of interest, dropped from 63 per cent in 1980 to 10 per cent in 1989 in British organisations, and by the late 1980s only a few companies were still experimenting with teamworking. He concludes: 'no matter what the degree of genuine autonomy or control in Swedish or Japanese work group experiments, the greater constraints on the prospect for worker influence came from the institutional settings and – even more critically – the broader social and cultural contexts' (Ramsay, 1992b).

COMMUNICATIONS AND THE FUTURE

The 'communications revolution', as some people have dubbed recent developments in new technology, will have a profound effect on the way companies and workplaces are organised. However, the process of radical restructuring of communicational modes and channels had already begun to get under way in the late 1980s with the introduction of managerial policies such as 'delayering', which were partly devised to shorten communicational lines in the vertical organisational structure. In the 1990s these were increasingly being combined with management-driven policies which embody ideas of 'empowerment' and 'employee influence' at workplace level and are justified as ultimately increasing the efficiency of the organisation. In these delayered and downsized organisations the core workforce will increasingly be composed of highly educated personnel, empowered and willing to take decisions. The teams of which they will be part will be democratic units. These future workers will expect consultation, information and involvement.

Studies have already indicated that the transition to such 'ideal' workplaces will not be smooth. Management will be posed with the dilemma of how much power to extend to the workforce while harnessing their creative energies, while at the same time not undermining managerial prerogatives. However, a number of suggestions can be made which may well enable these new EI and communicational mechanisms to function more efficiently. There must be:

- a willingness by management to concede some of their prerogatives;
- recognition of the necessity to train managers in EI initiatives such as teamworking;
- a clear policy regarding the role and prerogatives of line managers in relation to senior management and the workforce under their supervision;
- recognition of the necessity to train workers in group working skills such as presentation, leadership, assertiveness, problem solving, etc.;
- recognition of the necessity of providing proper feedback mechanisms which clearly indicate that the workforce is being listened to and not purely in a 'lip-service fashion';

- action taken to implement group decisions, to reinforce the view among the workforce that their contributions are well received;
- the recognition that conflicting views have a place in developing initiatives.

Futurologists are already predicting that even this view will eventually diminish and even vanish as new technology increasingly impacts on communications in organisations. As Nick Land, a philosopher and researcher in the field of new technology, states:

> *'There is a similar pattern that you find in the structure of societies, in the structure of companies and in the structure of computers, and all three are moving in the same direction. That is, away from a top-down structure of a central command system giving the system instructions about how to behave, towards a system that is flat, which is a web, in which change moves from the bottom up. And this is going to happen across all institutions and technical devices. It's the way they work.'*

(Quoted in Harrison, 1995)

In physical terms, office blocks, defined as the corporate ego trip of the 1980s, will be the social and economic dinosaurs of the next century. 'Businesses will concentrate on fewer, more efficient buildings, with all but management and key workers operating from home or satellite offices in the suburbs' (Brown, 1994). This vision of a cyberspace heaven in which the Internet and other technological developments will create a work–home environment, has been contrasted with a societal hell in which those dispossessed of the new technology will languish in crumbling ghettos in the giant hulks of decaying cities (Handy, 1994; Harrison, 1995). Whatever the future holds, communication will still continue to be important, as will the skills needed to do it effectively.

SUMMARY

- A review of various media channels was undertaken in the light of their classification into downward, upward and horizontal forms of organisational communication.
- In this chapter an outline of communication models was undertaken, examining the mechanistic concepts of the Shannon and Weaver model and the feedback concept indicated in the Schramm model. Definitions of organisational communication were considered, including those of Krone, Jablin and Putnam, who view the communication process as being influenced by mechanistic, psychological, interpretive-symbolic and systems-interactive perspectives.
- Clampitt identified three approaches to communication which he calls the arrow, circuit and dance models. The first two follow respectively the Shannon and Weaver mechanistic model, and the Schramm feedback model. The dance model he believes to be superior as it incorporates elements of organisational culture and other organic or human influences.
- Trends in international communication were highlighted through the findings of a number of surveys, and a more detailed examination of Japanese communication and employee involvement practices was undertaken. Communications in an employee involvement context within the European Union were considered, with special attention given to the issue of the influence of the works council directive on the UK.
- The chapter ended with some speculations and prognostications about the influence and direction of organisational communications in the future.

Review and discussion questions

1 *What informal ways are there to communicate information in organisations? Why can these be often more effective than formal channels?*

2 *What lessons can be learned from Japanese communication and employee involvement practices?*

3 *What editorial policies would you decide to adopt in creating a company newspaper? What difficulties could you foresee in their implementation?*

4 *What are the common pitfalls in implementing a total quality management (TQM) scheme, and how can they be avoided?*

5 *Have you sent an e-mail that was interpreted entirely differently from the way it was intended? Why did it go wrong? What could you do to improve things if that situation occurred again?*

6 *What are the benefits in carrying out employee attitude surveys for management and for employees? What kinds of question would you include in a survey questionnaire? Think carefully about the sort of information you would want from it. To what uses could the survey be put?*

CASE STUDY 10.1

Marks & Spencer and 'Big'

Setting up a works council

In compliance with and in anticipation of European Union law (which comes into effect in March 2005) Marks & Spencer has set up a works council. It has called this body 'Big', short for National Business Involvement Group. Its role is to debate business decisions and HR policies face to face with its chief executive, Roger Holmes. This is built on, and in addition to, already existing employee forums that have been in existence in M&S for a number of years, and the body is the culmination of a series of measures aimed at improving employee communications. The works council concept itself is not new to M&S and in 1995 it established a European Council although this was confined to the continent.

So how will the new forum work? Under the revised employee involvement framework, 13 representatives will be drawn from 43 area Bigs to sit on the national Big. Eight of those representatives will come from the 40 area Bigs for stores, and two from head office, one from the distribution centre, one from the financial services and one from Burnley

Print (M&S's print and reprographic company). This forum will also include the remnants of the European Council, now confined to the Irish Republic, since the closure of its European branches.

To run as a representative for the national Big, staff have to be members of one of the area Bigs and their application has to be seconded by a fellow member. A list of candidates is drawn up by an election co-ordinator for each division, which can encompass up to ten area Bigs. The members of the area Bigs within a division then vote for the list of candidates and the national representative is the candidate with most votes.

Holmes will chair the council and states that it is:

'a critical part of managing business and going forward. What is tremendously powerful about the new structure is there is an opportunity to listen to the whole organisation. That is why I am taking up the role of being chair of the national Big group. The national Big will provide a two-way communication channel across the whole workforce.'

▶

He defines the role of a Big representative as making sure that he or she helps colleagues understand important work issues. Having a CEO chair the Big forum indicates the seriousness with which the organisation regards this body and the issues which it discusses. The employment standards team has issued a trainee toolkit called 'Big place' which explains how Bigs work and their role within the organisation. Despite this excellent practice by M&S there are potential pitfalls in running a works council.

Questions

1 *What potential pitfalls do you envisage may occur in setting up this works council and its operation? (Hints: M&S is a non-unionised company; developing staff; feedback; locations.)*

2 *What possible solutions could you put forward to avoid these pitfalls and sort out potential problems?*

Source: Karen Higginbottom (2003) 'Employee Consultation: Mind Your Own Business', *People Management*, 1 May, pp 32–5.

CASE STUDY 10.2

Merger at Work Communications

Communications are key

A highly sensitive area among employees is when a company merges with, or is taken over by another company. The situation produces an air of insecurity and at best uncertainty. Will staff become surplus to requirements? Will they have to move? Who will their immediate line manager be? Will their job disappear in a restructuring exercise? These are just some of the questions that will immediately spring to mind for most staff. So when Work Communications acquired Park HR, a rival recruitment advertising firm with a workforce of 115 spread around the country, Work Communications knew it had to get the process of keeping everyone informed absolutely right. Staff at Park were sceptical about promises made by Work Communications to retain the previous structure.

Work Communications decided to make a concerted effort via an internal communications offensive to inform them of any moves it might make after the takeover and calm any fears of 'wholesale changes'. Work Communications decided not to use a PR agency for this process as Simon Howard, co-founder, stated:

'When these deals are announced, a lot of companies spend shed-loads of money on PR, but often the staff get no more than a note on their desk. There's a sense of "start as you mean to go on".'

Employees at Park were initially informed of the takeover via e-mail – a method that Howard and his team used carefully:

'We had to have a degree of caution. What we did was say that we'd put a paper pack on everyone's desk by the following morning in which we may say things that we wouldn't necessarily want outsiders to read. Although using e-mail was never going to be perfect, it did let us tell our people and competitors the bare facts of what was happening, so that they didn't find out through Chinese whispers.'

As well as e-mail, staff received details of a specially designed website containing information about Work Communications, biographies of the company's employees and a list of answers to frequently asked questions (FAQs). The website allowed employees to e-mail in their own questions anonymously, and queries received from them reflected the fact that many employees were still worried about their jobs. From the answers they received Howard said that they were better able to gauge the general mood among Park employees during the takeover. One employee wrote in:

'It's clear that we are all very worried about losing our jobs. More importantly, I would like to know how you are going to make your decisions. In the past Park has based a lot of decisions on who likes whom – not on how capable you are or how good you are at the job.'

This open questioning was encouraged and in many instances these questions were forwarded to all employees with the Board's response.

The communications team also reviewed the kind of language being used in the programme. For example, the use of informal and relaxed language encouraged employees to raise their concerns and also helped to convey the company's culture.

Once the takeover situation had been clarified, Work Communication's directors set about meeting as many staff as they could. With offices spread across the UK, this was a hard task that took longer than the week they had planned to achieve this, but eventually everyone was seen by the following Tuesday. This was one thing they wanted to do better. Nevertheless the chance to meet new people was really valuable. Watson stated:

'The communications programme showed us that there's a sense of openness and accessibility. It's very reassuring for the future.'

Questions

1 *What could be the danger of using only e-mail in this situation?*

2 *Why do you think language was an important concern in communications with staff?*

3 *How could the face-to-face meeting of Park staff have been more efficient?*

4 *Are there any other questions and concerns regarding the use of a company website as a communications media in this situation?*

Source: Jon Watkins (2003) 'Mergers and Acquisitions: Direct Line', *People Management*, 15 May, pp 42–3.

REFERENCES AND FURTHER READING

Adler, N (1997) *International Dimensions of Organizational Behavior* (3rd edn), Cincinnati, OH: ITP; South-Western College Publishing.

Advisory, Conciliation and Arbitration Service (ACAS) (1982) *Workplace Communications*, Advisory Booklet No. 8, London: ACAS.

Booth, A (1988) *The Communications Audit: A Guide for Managers*, Aldershot: Gower.

Boreham, P (1992) 'The Myth of Post-Fordist Management: Work Organisation and Employee Discretion in Seven Countries', *Employee Relations*, 14 (2): 13–24.

Brennan, B (1991) 'Mismanagement and Quality Circles: How Middle Managers Influence Direct Participation', *Employee Relations*, 13 (5).

Briggs, P (1991) 'Organisational Commitment: The Key to Japanese Success?, in Brewster, C and Tyson, S (eds), *International Comparisons in Human Resource Management*, London: Pitman Publishing.

Brown, P. (1994) 'Dinosaur Offices Heading for Extinction', *The Guardian*, 14 November.

CBI (Confederation of British Industry) (1989) *Employee Involvement: Shaping the Future Business*, London: CBI.

Chaney, L and Martin, J (1995) *Intercultural Business Communications*, Englewood Cliffs, NJ: Prentice-Hall.

Clampitt, P (1991) *Communicating for Managerial Effectiveness*, Newbury Park, CA: Sage.

Clutterbuck, D and Grainer, S (1990) *Makers of Management: Men and Women Who Changed the Business World*, London: Macmillan.

Collard, R and Dale, B (1989) 'Quality Circles', in Sisson, K (ed.), *Personnel Management in Britain*, Oxford: Blackwell.

CRANEFE (Cranfield Network for European Human Resource Management) (1999) *International Executive Report*, Cranfield: Cranfield School of Management.

Cressey, P and Williams, R (1990) *Participation in Change: New Technology and the Role of Employee Involvement*, Dublin: European Foundation for the Improvement of Living and Working Conditions.

Crosby, P (1979) *Quality is Free*, New York: McGraw-Hill.

Crosby, P (1984) *Quality Without Tears*, New York: McGraw-Hill.

DeFleur, M (1966) *Theories of Mass Communication*, New York: David Mckay.

Dore, R and Sako, M (1989) *How the Japanese Learn to Work*, London: Routledge.

Fairhurst, G, Rogers, L and Saar, R (1987) 'Manager–Subordinate Control Patterns and Judgement about Relationship', in McLaughlin, M (ed.), *Communication Yearbook 10*, Newbury Park, CA: Sage, pp 395–415.

Foy, N (1994) *Empowering People at Work*, Aldershot: Gower.

Fröhlich, D and Krieger, H (1990) 'Technological Change and Worker Participation in Europe', *New Technology, Work and Employment*, 5 (2), Autumn.

Gill, C (1993) 'Technological Change and Participation in Work Organisation: Recent Results from a European Survey', *The International Journal of Human Resource Management*, 4 (2), May.

Hall, E and Hall, M (1990) *Understanding Cultural Differences*, Yarmouth: Intercultural Press.

Handy, C (1994) *The Empty Raincoat: Making Sense of the Future*, London: Hutchinson.

Harrison, M (1995) *Visions of Heaven and Hell*, London: Channel 4 Television.

Hofstede, G (1980) *Culture's Consequences: International Differences in Work Related Values*, Beverly Hills, CA: Sage.

Hofstede, G (1991) *Cultures and Organisations: Software of the Mind*, London: McGraw-Hill.

Hurst, B (1991) *The Handbook of Communication Skills*, London: Kogan Page.

Jablin, F, Putnam, L, Roberts, K and Porter, L (eds) (1987) *Handbook of Organizational Communication: An Interdisciplinary Perspective*, Newbury Park, CA: Sage.

Klauss, R and Bass, B (1974) 'Group Influence on Individual Behaviour Across Cultures', *Journal of Cross Cultural Psychology*, 5, pp 236–46.

Krone, K, Jablin, F and Putnam, L (1987) 'Communication Theory and Organizational Behavior: Multiple Perspectives', in Jablin *et al.* (eds), *Handbook of Organizational Communication: An Interdisciplinary Perspective*, Newbury Park, CA: Sage, pp 18–40.

Lawler, E (1986) *High-Involvement Management*, San Francisco, CA: Jossey-Bass.

Lewis, B (1989) 'Quality in the Service Sector: A Review', *International Journal of Bank Marketing*, 7 (5): pp 4–12.

Lewis, J (2002) 'The Culture of New Communications Technology', in Lewis, J, *Cultural Studies*, London: Sage, pp 379-418.

McLuhan, M (1964) *Understanding Media*, London: Routledge & Kegan Paul.

McQuail, D and Windahl, S (1981) *Communication Models*, Hemel Hempstead: Prentice Hall.

Marchington, M (1992) *Managing the Team: A Guide to Successful Employee Involvement*, Oxford: Blackwell.

Marchington, M, Goodman, J, Wilkinson, A and Ackers, P (1992) *New Developments in Employee Involvement*, Manchester: Manchester School of Management, Employment Department Research Series No. 2.

Mintzberg, H (1973) *The Nature of Managerial Work*, New York: Harper & Row.

Monks, J (1989) 'Trade Union Role in Communications', in Wilkinson, T (ed.), *The Communications Challenge*, London: IPM.

Naoi, A and Schooler, C (1985) 'Occupational Conditions and Psychological Functioning in Japan', *American Journal of Sociology*, 90 (4): 729–52 (quoted in Briggs, 1991).

Oliver, N and Lowe, J (1991) 'UK Computer Industry: American, British and Japanese Contrasts in Human Resource Management', *Personnel Review*, 20 (2).

Pace, W and Boren, R (1973) *The Human Transaction*, Glenview, IL: Scott Foresman.

Pascale, R and Athos, A (1982) *The Art of Japanese Management*, London: Allen Lane.

Pease, A (1984) *Body Language*, London: Sheldon Press.

Poole, M (1986) *Towards a New Industrial Democracy: Workers' Participation in Industry*, London: Routledge & Kegan Paul.

Price, R (1989) 'The Decline and Fall of the Status Divide?', in Sisson, K (ed.), *Personnel Management in Britain*, Oxford: Blackwell.

Price Waterhouse Cranfield Project on International Strategic Human Resource Management (1990) *Report*, London: Price Waterhouse.

Price Waterhouse Cranfield Project on International Strategic Human Resource Management (1991) *Report*, Cranfield: Cranfield School of Management.

Price Waterhouse Cranfield Project on International Strategic Human Resource Management (1995) *Report*, Cranfield: Cranfield School of Management.

Putnam, L and Jones, T (1982) 'Reciprocity in Negotiations: An Analysis of Bargaining Interaction, *Communication Monographs*, 49, pp 171–91.

Ramsay, H (1977) 'Cycles of Control', *Sociology*, 11: 481–506.

Ramsay, H (1992a) 'Commitment and Involvement', in Towers, B (ed.), *The Handbook of Human Resource Management*, Oxford: Blackwell.

Ramsay, H (1992b) 'Swedish and Japanese Work Methods – Comparisons and Contrasts', *European Participation Monitor*, 3 (1).

Russell, P (2001) 'In-Box Clever', *People Management*, 5 April: 38–9.

Schramm, W (1954) 'How Communication Works', in Schramm, W (ed.), *The Process and Effects of Mass Communication*, Urbana, IL: University of Illinois Press.

Sewell, G and Wilkinson, B (1992) 'Empowerment or Emasculation? Shopfloor Surveillance in a Total Quality Organisation', in Blyton, P and Turnbull, P (eds), *Reassessing Human Resource Management*, London: Sage.

Shannon, C and Weaver, W (1949) *The Mathematical Theory of Communication*, Urbana, IL: University of Illinois Press.

Smith, V (1990) *Managing in the Corporate Interest: Control and Resistance in an American Bank*, Oxford: University of California Press.

Townley, B (1989) 'Employee Communication Programmes', in Sisson, K (ed.), *Personnel Management in Britian*, Oxford: Blackwell.

Triandis, H C (1977) *Interpersonal Behaviour*, Monterey, CA: Cole (reported in Ronen, S (1986) *Comparative and Multinational Management*, New York: John Wiley).

Trompenaars, F (1993) *Riding the Waves of Culture*, London: Nicholas Brealey.

Wickens, P (1987) *The Road to Nissan: Flexibility, Quality and Teamwork*. Basingstoke: Macmillan.

Wilkinson, T (ed.) (1989) *The Communications Challenge: Personnel and PR Perspectives*, London: Institute of Personnel Management.

Wilkinson, A, Marchington, M, Ackers, P and Goodman, J (1992) 'Total Quality Management and Employee Involvement', *Human Resource Management Journal*, 2 (4), Summer.

WEBSITES

http://www.iftdo.org
International Federation of Training and Development
Organisations (IFTDO).

http://www.cipd.co.uk
Chartered Institute of Personnel and Development (CIPD).

http://www.eapm.org
European Association for Personnel Management (EAPM).

http://www.warwick-consulting.co.uk/training/
communication/stratcom.htm
Strategic communications.

http://www.hodu.com
Effective communication.

http://www.escape.ca/~rbacal/files/communication.htm
Learn to communicate more effectively.

CHAPTER 11

Human resources management

ROGER BENNETT, HELEN DAVIES AND LINDA GUNNELL

Outcomes

Having read this chapter, you will be able to:

- understand and explain the difference between personnel management and human resources management

- recognise good practice in the fields of recruitment, selection and appraisal

- appreciate the importance of human resources planning for the efficient management of enterprises

- identify key legal requirements in relation to equal opportunities

- assess the training needs of a business or large department

- analyse the significance of current trends in the techniques for managing human resources

NATURE OF HUMAN RESOURCES MANAGEMENT

Human resources management concerns the human side of enterprises and the factors that determine workers' relationships with their employing organisations. It is a wide-ranging subject that covers, among other things: management/worker communications; elements of work psychology; employee relations, training and motivation; organisation of the physical and social conditions of work; and (of course) personnel management.

Everyone who has control over others shares in human resources management. Accordingly, HRM is not a function that the individual manager can leave to specialists, although HRM professionals do play a vital role.

Human resources management and personnel management

On the ground, the terms 'personnel management' and 'HRM' are often used interchangeably by organisations. However, the term when first introduced was used, and is so used here, to indicate a *strategic* dimension, involving the total deployment of all the human resources available to the firm (Guest, 1987; Legge, 1989; Ferris and Buckley, 1996). Human resources management encompasses:

- **The aggregate size of the organisation's labour force** in the context of an overall corporate plan (how many divisions and subsidiaries the company is to have, design of the organisation, etc.).

- **How much to spend on training the workforce**, given strategic decisions on target quality levels, product prices, volume of production and so on.

- **The desirability of establishing relations with trade unions** from the viewpoint of the effective management control of the entire organisation.

- **Human asset accounting**, i.e. the systematic measurement and analysis of the costs and *financial* benefits of alternative personnel policies (e.g. the monetary consequences of staff development exercises, the effects of various salary structures, etc.) and the valuation of the human worth of the enterprise's employees.

The strategic approach to HRM involves the integration of personnel and other HRM considerations into the firm's overall corporate planning and strategy formulation procedures (Stroh and Caliguiri, 1998). It is proactive, seeking constantly to discover new ways of utilising the labour force in a more productive manner, thus giving the business a competitive edge. Practical manifestations of the adoption of a strategic approach to HRM might include:

- incorporation of a brief summary of the firm's basic HRM policy into its mission statement;

- explicit consideration of the consequences for employees of each of the firm's strategies and major new projects;

- designing organisation structures to suit the needs of employees rather than conditioning the latter to fit in with the existing form of organisation;

- having the head of HRM on the firm's board of directors.

More than ever before, human resource managers are expected to contribute to productivity and quality improvement, the stimulation of creative thinking, leadership and the development of corporate skills.

While some would argue that personnel management when practised effectively would have included all the above, there has been a new emphasis on the following since the term 'HRM' came into use:

1 HRM is concerned with the wider implications of the management of change and not just with the effects of change on working practices. It seeks proactively to encourage flexible attitudes and the acceptance of new methods.

2 Aspects of HRM constitute major inputs into organisational development exercises.

3 'Personnel management' has often been (necessarily) reactive and diagnostic. It *responded* to changes in employment law, labour market conditions, trade union actions, government codes of practice and other environmental influences. HRM, conversely, is *prescriptive* and concerned with strategies, the initiation of new activities and the development of fresh ideas.

4 HRM determines general policies for employment relationships within the enterprise. Thus, it needs to establish within the organisation a *culture* that is conducive to employee commitment and co-operation. Personnel management, on the other hand, has been criticised for being primarily concerned with imposing *compliance* with company rules and procedures among employees, rather than with loyalty and commitment to the firm.

5 'Personnel management' has often had short-term perspectives; HRM has long-term perspectives, seeking to *integrate* all the human aspects of the organisation into a coherent whole and to establish high-level employee goals.

6 The HRM approach emphasises the need:
   - for direct communication with employees rather than their collective representation;
   - to develop an organisational culture conducive to the adoption of flexible working methods;
   - to enhance employees' long-term capabilities, not just their competence at current duties.

Human resources management and competitive advantage

Research (Pettigrew and Whipp, 1991; Patterson *et al.*, 1997) has shown that the management of people makes a difference to company performance. The 1997 study confirmed that:

■ The more satisfied workers are with their jobs, the better the company is likely to perform in terms of subsequent profitability and particularly productivity.

■ Organisational culture significantly affects company performance. A culture of concern for employee welfare is by far and away one of the most striking predictors of increased performance.

■ The practices which seem to be the most important in affecting performance are job design (in terms of flexibility, job responsibility, variety and use of formal teams) and the acquisition and development of skills (selection, induction, training and appraisal).

■ HRM practices are more influential in how successful a company will be than either investment in research and development, the sophistication of the technology used, an emphasis on quality or even the use of competitive strategies.

HUMAN RESOURCES PLANNING

Definition of human resources planning

Human resources planning (HRP) is the comparison of an organisation's existing labour resources with forecast labour demand, and hence the scheduling of activities for acquiring, training, redeploying and possibly discarding labour. It seeks to ensure that an adequate supply of labour is available precisely when required. Specific human resource planning duties include:

- estimation of labour turnover for each grade of employee and the examination of the effects of high or low turnover rates on the organisation's performance;
- analysis of the consequences of changes in working practices and hours;
- predicting future labour shortages;
- devising schemes for handling the human problems arising from labour deficits or surpluses;
- introduction of early retirement and other natural wastage procedures;
- analysis of the skills, educational backgrounds, experience, capacities and potentials of employees.

Effective HRP should result in the right people doing the right things in the right place at precisely the right time. The process of human resources planning is illustrated in Figure 11.1.

HRP should help management in making decisions concerning recruitment, the avoidance of redundancies, training and staff development, and the estimation of the costs of employing labour. Sometimes redundancies can be avoided through the preparation of '**skills inventories**' (i.e. detailed listings of all the competencies, work experiences and qualifications of current employees – even those characteristics not relevant to present occupations). The purpose of a skills inventory is to inform management of all the jobs that existing employees might be capable of undertaking.

Benefits of human resources planning

In preparing a human resources plan, management can co-ordinate and integrate all the organisation's HRM activities, avoiding duplication of effort and eliminating unnecessary waste (Schuler and Walker, 1990). Specific advantages to HRP include the following:

1 The organisation will be ready to adapt future HRM activities to meet changing circumstances.

2 Careful consideration of likely future events might lead to the discovery of better means for managing human resources. Foreseeable pitfalls might be avoided.

3 Measures to influence future events can be initiated by the organisation itself.

4 Decisions concerning future HRM activities can be taken in advance, unhurriedly, using all the data available and considering all available options. This avoids decision making in crisis situations with management unable to study all relevant issues judiciously and at length.

Figure 11.1 The human resources planning process

5 Planning forces the organisation to assess critically the feasibility of its HRM objectives.

6 Labour shortfalls and surpluses may be avoided.

7 It helps the firm create and develop employee training and management succession programmes.

8 Some of the problems of managing change may be foreseen and their consequences mitigated. Consultations with affected groups and individuals can occur at an early stage in the change process.

9 Management is compelled to assess critically the strengths and weaknesses of its labour force and personnel policies.

10 Duplication of effort among employees can be avoided; co-ordination and integration of workers' efforts is improved.

PLANNING PROCEDURES

Principles of effective human resources planning (HRP)

Certain fundamental principles should always be applied when preparing a human resources plan, as follows:

- The plan should be as detailed as expenditure constraints allow.
- Plans should not extend too far into the future – accurate prediction of the distant future is simply impossible.
- *All* alternative courses of action should be considered.
- Side effects and implications of the actions envisaged should be examined.
- Instructions to individuals and departments must be incorporated into the plan.
- Plans should be concise and easy to understand.

As the plan is executed its effectiveness in achieving stated objectives should be monitored. Differences between actual and desired positions must be quickly identified and remedial measures introduced.

Labour turnover analysis

Employees may be categorised according to age, length of service, occupation, educational background, job experience and promotion potential. *Labour turnover* is commonly measured by the ratio of the number of workers who left the firm during a certain period (normally six months or a year) to the average number of workers employed during the same period. If this is relatively constant over time, the organisation can predict the recruitment needed to keep all existing posts occupied. The problem is that if just one or two posts are filled and vacated many times during a particular period, the index becomes artificially high. For instance, if a single job is filled ten times in a year, the effect on the index is identical to that of ten people leaving different jobs during that year. To overcome (partially) this problem the 'labour stability index' can be used to show the extent to which employees with longer service are leaving the organisation:

$$\frac{\text{Number of employees with more than one year's service}}{\text{Total number of people employed one year ago}}$$

Note that this index does not reveal the average length of service of employees, which should be computed separately for each category of staff.

Another useful exercise is to compute the percentages of a group of employees – all of whom are hired on the same date – who are still with the firm after certain periods. Thus for example, 10 per cent might have left by the end of one year, 25 per cent after two years, 70 per cent after five, and so on. The firm can then predict how long, on average, it takes for, say, half of all workers recruited on a particular date to leave the firm. The exercise can be repeated for various occupational groups.

High labour turnover may be due to low pay, inadequate holiday entitlement, long working hours or other conditions of employment regarded by workers as unsatisfactory. Other causes include:

- **excessively monotonous work**
- **absence of promotion prospects**

- **bad recruitment and staff induction procedures**
- **ineffective grievance procedures**
- **poor communications within the organisation.**

High labour turnover is undesirable for several reasons. Recruitment and training costs increase, new entrants are relatively unproductive during the early stages of their service, and additional demands are placed on the remaining staff. Morale is typically lower in organisations with high labour turnover. Note, however, that certain categories of employee exhibit, on average, exceptionally high labour turnover rates – notably young workers and those engaged in boring and repetitive duties. Also, workers are more likely to quit their jobs in rapidly expanding industries.

Steps in the HRP process

In drafting a human resources plan the organisation must consider the demand for labour, its potential supply (with corrections for its present misuse, over-use or under-use) and the external environment. By studying the interaction of all these factors, it can then produce a plan showing how many and what kinds of employee are expected to be required in the future. The main points to be considered are as follows:

The creation of an HRP group, including the managers in charge of the main functions within the organisation.

The statement of human resources objectives in the light of the organisation's objectives by considering:

- capital equipment plans;
- reorganisation, e.g. centralisation or decentralisation;
- changes in products or in output;
- marketing plans;
- financial limitations.

The present utilisation of human resources, in particular:

- numbers of employees in various categories;
- estimation of labour turnover for each grade of employee and the analysis of the effects of high or low turnover rates on the organisation's performance;
- amount of overtime worked;
- amount of short time;
- appraisal of performance and potential of present employees;
- general level of payment compared with that in other organisations.

Note that, for all the above, accurate and complete personnel records are essential.

The external environment of the organisation:

- recruitment position;
- population trends;
- local housing and transport plans;
- national agreements dealing with conditions of work;
- government policies on education, retirement, regional subsidies, etc.

The potential supply of labour, in particular:

- effects of local emigration and immigration;
- effects of recruitment or redundancy by local firms;
- possibility of employing categories not now employed, e.g. part-time workers;
- changes in productivity, working hours and/or practices.

FORECASTING AND THE HUMAN RESOURCES AUDIT

Human resources plans are predetermined responses to anticipated future events (Greenberg and Baron, 1997). It is axiomatic that possible future events must be predicted, so mechanisms for forecasting the future need to be devised. The demand for labour is a 'derived demand', depending as it does on the number and types of people needed to produce and distribute goods. Factors influencing the demand for a particular company's products include the rate of growth of total consumer spending, the intensity of competition (including competition from imported goods), changes in tastes and fashion, and possibly seasonal variations in levels of purchases. All these factors affect the volumes and characteristics of a firm's production and hence the labour it needs to employ. Unfortunately, accurate forecasting of such variables is notoriously difficult, for several reasons, as outlined below:

- Many variables (tax levels, business laws, interest rates, consumer incomes, etc.) are determined by government and are thus beyond the organisation's control.
- Consumer tastes can change quickly and unpredictably.
- New technical inventions may occur.
- Competitors might alter their behaviour; fresh competition could emerge.
- Past events upon which forecasts are based might not occur in the future.
- Existing suppliers, distribution options, harmonious industrial relations, etc., could suddenly disappear.
- Technical difficulties (unreliable data, incorrect choice of statistical forecasting technique, etc.) might arise.

The longer the period of the forecast, the greater the likelihood of serious error. It is wise, therefore, to generate several different forecasts, with a greater amount of detail the shorter the timespan involved, and each forecast assuming a different scenario of events. The accuracy of predictions should be monitored by comparing them with events as they occur, and sources of error (inadequate or incorrect data, faulty forecasting techniques, poor judgements by forecasters, etc.) should be identified. It is useful to know whether forecasts are on average persistently overestimating or underestimating actual performance.

The human resources audit and the final HR plan

Alongside its forecasts of the demands for various categories of labour, management needs to set out all its available information on the organisation's existing personnel, taken perhaps from a skills inventory (*see* p 309 above) plus appraisal reports on the quality of employees' work. Analysis of this information might be set out in a separate document, the 'human resources audit', which lists the abilities, performance records and apparent potential of each of the organisation's departments and its employees. The aim of the exercise is to match the organisation's present and future human resources against current and forecast requirements, thus enabling it to produce the final human resources plan showing in detail, by function, occupation and locations, how many employees it is *practicable* to employ at various stages in the future (Graham and Bennett, 1998). The following should appear in it:

- jobs which will appear, disappear or change;
- to what extent redeployment or retraining is possible;
- necessary changes at supervisory and management levels;
- training needs;
- recruitment, redundancy or retirement programmes;
- industrial relations implications;
- arrangements for feedback in case modifications in the plan or company objectives are necessary;
- details of arrangements for handling any human problems arising from labour deficits or surpluses (e.g. early retirement or other natural wastage procedures).

Short-term plans

Many organisations do not have the financial or managerial resources to forecast long-term HRP variables, or they feel that the nature of their business makes it impossible to look ahead for more than one year. Hence they might prepare short-term plans covering just the next 12 months. A short-term human resources plan is comparatively easy to put together because an organisation will usually make a production or marketing plan for a year ahead involving budgets, orders for new materials and components, and sales quotas. From this can be derived the amount of **direct labour** in terms of labour-hours required in future, and then, by dividing into this figure the number of available working hours, the number of workers can be obtained. Overtime and the average level of sickness absence and machine breakdowns must be taken into account when available working hours are calculated.

The amount of **indirect labour** may be estimated partly by fixed commitments and partly as a rule of thumb percentage of indirect to direct labour. From the total labour requirements a recruitment or redundancy plan can be derived, but the period is usually too short for any worthwhile training plan to be made.

An advantage of the short-term plan is the ease with which the forecast can be compared with the labour that was actually required, and any discrepancies analysed.

RECRUITMENT

Recruitment is the first stage in the process of filling a vacancy. It involves the examination of the requirements for filling the vacancy (particularly in relation to job and person specifications); consideration of the sources of suitable candidates; drafting job advertisements and selecting media suitable to carry them; assessing appropriate salary levels for new employees; and arranging interviews and other aspects of 'selection', the second stage in the staffing process (Cherrington, 1995). Selection requires the assessment of candidates by various means and the choice of successful candidate. It is considered further in the section on selection and induction below.

Recruitment and selection procedures should be constantly evaluated for their:

- cost effectiveness (i.e. could you get results as good while spending less money on the process?); and

- validity (i.e. reliably attracting and selecting the most suitable candidates).

The recruitment process

The department in which the recruit will work must draft or revise a comprehensive job specification for the vacant position, outlining its major and minor responsibilities; the skills, experience and qualifications needed; grade and level of pay; starting date; whether temporary or permanent; and particulars of any special conditions (shift-work, for example) attached to the job. Then the vacancy is advertised in suitable media and/or recruitment agencies are approached.

External recruitment is expensive. It involves advertising, agency fees, distribution of application forms, preparation of shortlists, writing for references, interviewing, payment of travelling expenses, etc. If the candidate appointed is unsuitable or leaves within a short period, then the entire procedure has to be repeated. The advantages of filling the vacancy internally rather than externally are:

- better motivation of employees because their capabilities are considered and opportunities for promotion are offered;

- better utilisation of employees because the organisation can often make better use of their abilities in a different job;

- greater reliability as compared with external recruitment because a present employee is known more thoroughly than an external candidate;

- that a present employee is more likely to stay with the organisation than an external candidate.

However, it should be noted that some organisations have a policy of always advertising externally, as internal recruitment methods tend to reproduce the broad social characteristics of the current workforce, thereby continuing to exclude under-represented groups, such as women or ethnic minorities.

Job advertisements

It has been estimated that about 10 per cent of all press advertising expenditure is devoted to situations vacant advertising. There is no doubt that much of this huge sum is wasted, chiefly because so little research has been carried out, compared with research in the field of product advertising. Many employers have been able to reduce their job advertising costs with no adverse effect on the quality or quantity of candidate response by experimenting with styles of advertisements, media and wording, and keeping careful records of the number of replies received to each advertisement and the candidate who was eventually selected. The only reliable guidance about advertising comes from the person who receives and analyses the replies, i.e. the employer. Newspapers and advertising agencies, which often claim to advise on the style and size of advertisements, are not usually in a position to know and evaluate the response.

Job advertisements should aim at procuring a small number of well-qualified candidates quickly and as cheaply as possible. Note the high cost of placing job advertisements in newspapers. A single advertisement covering 140 mm × 2 columns (approximately one-eighth of a page) in one issue of a quality daily newspaper can cost £4000 or more, depending on the newspaper's circulation and the page position of the advertisement. Even a small advertisement in a regional newspaper can cost £700 or more. An advertisement which produces hundreds of replies is a disadvantage to the organisation because the employer will then be faced with the lengthy and expensive task of sorting out a few candidates for interview.

The advertisement can become the first stage in selection by describing the job and qualifications required so comprehensively that borderline candidates will be deterred from applying and good candidates encouraged.

Headhunting

Very senior managers are sometimes recruited by a process known as 'executive search' or '**headhunting**'. Its advocates believe that the best candidates are not those who reply to advertisements or look for new jobs in other ways, but those who are successful in their present jobs and are not thinking of moving elsewhere.

On receipt of a commission from a client, the headhunter will search for potential candidates:

■ in competing businesses (possibly obtaining their names from company reports, brochures, etc.);

■ in the membership lists of professional bodies, trade association yearbooks, newspaper and magazine reports that mention successful managers in the relevant industry; and

■ through confidential headhunting networks.

Selected individuals are then approached discreetly and, following a discussion regarding the job and its remuneration, one or two of them are introduced to the client firm.

Advantages of headhunting are as follows:

■ Headhunters should possess expert knowledge of the salary levels and fringe benefits necessary to attract good-calibre candidates. Also, they will analyse the vacancy and offer an opinion about the type of person required, will conduct initial screening, administer psychometric tests, etc. This saves the client many administrative costs and advertising expenses.

■ Possibly, top managers who are already in employment will not bother to read job advertisements, newspapers and other conventional media and hence cannot be reached by these means.

■ Senior managers who are prepared to consider a move sometimes make this known to leading headhunters, even though they would not openly apply to competing companies.

■ If a targeted candidate does not want the job, he or she may suggest someone else who is equally suitable and who may in fact be interested.

■ Recruiting firms are assured that candidates presented to them will almost certainly be well equipped for the vacant position.

■ The anonymity of the recruiting organisation is preserved until the final stages in the procedure.

Criticisms of executive search include the following:

■ Headhunting is highly disruptive to successful businesses, which stand to lose expensively trained senior managers.

■ It can be used to avoid equal opportunities laws on recruitment and selection.

■ A headhunted individual might subsequently be enticed by other headhunters to leave his or her new firm after a short period. To avoid this, some companies attach 'golden handcuffs' to senior management positions, i.e. they pay large cash bonuses which are only available to executives who stay with the firm a certain number of years.

■ Arguably, headhunters rely too heavily on existing networks and trade contacts, creating thereby a glorified 'old boy system' which ignores good people from other sources.

■ Headhunters' fees are far higher than for conventional employment agencies (up to 50 per cent of the recruited individual's initial salary in some instances).

■ The headhunter might acquire confidential information about the client company which could then be passed on to competing firms.

■ Headhunters are not subject to the same long-term accountability as personnel managers employed within the business. Also they lack detailed knowledge of the client organisation's culture and operations.

EQUAL OPPORTUNITIES

The Sex Discrimination Act 1975 sought to ensure that men and women and married persons be treated equally in employment situations. Thus, employers are not allowed to discriminate against either sex in:

■ **selection procedures**

■ **terms on which employment is offered**

■ **access to opportunities for training or promotion**

■ **fringe benefits**

■ **deciding which workers shall be made redundant.**

Sex discrimination can be direct or indirect. The former means treating people unfavourably simply because of their sex, for example segregating women employees into separate departments and paying them lower wages. Indirect discrimination occurs when an employer applies a test or condition that puts one of the sexes at an unfair advantage. An example here would be a condition that all job applicants be over six feet three inches tall for work where the employee's height is not important. However, jobs where sex is a 'genuine occupational qualification' are exempt. Examples would be actors playing male or female roles, jobs in single-sex schools, hospitals or other institutions; and jobs where decency or privacy require employment of a particular sex.

While the law recognises discrimination in the form of sexual harassment, the courts have relied on European law to provide guidelines for what actually constitutes harassment. The 'Recommendation on the Protection of the Dignity of Women and Men at Work' (European Commission, 1991) carries a code of practice which defines sexual harassment as 'unwanted conduct of a sexual nature, or other conduct based on sex affecting the physical, verbal or non-verbal conduct'. (An aggrieved employee may also take action under the Protection from Harassment Act of 1997. This Act was aimed at stalking but applies also to bullying and harassment in the workplace.)

The Sex Discrimination Act makes it unlawful to discriminate against a person because he or she is married.

There is no ceiling on the amount of compensation that can be awarded to a person whom a tribunal considers has been directly or indirectly but intentionally discriminated against unlawfully.

The Race Relations Act 1976 offers similar rights to 'racial groups', defined by colour, race, nationality or ethnic or national origins. A racial or ethnic group has been defined by the House of Lords as being identifiable by things such as a long-shared history, a common religion, a common language, a common geographical origin, a cultural tradition of its own, including family and workplace customs. As with the Sex Discrimination Act, there are exemptions.

Equal pay

The Equal Pay Act 1970 amended by the Equal Pay (Amendment) Regulations 1983 requires that men and women receive equal pay for work of equal value. All the terms and conditions of a woman's (or a man's) contract of employment must not be less favourable than that which would be issued to a member of the opposite sex. It is illegal to lay down separate rates of pay for men and women.

In 1996 the Equal Opportunities Commission published a code of practice on equal pay containing practical guidance to businesses concerning the elimination of pay discrimination between men and women. The code has sections covering, *inter alia*, the meaning of pay, implications of the law for employers, pay systems, the identification of discrimination, and job evaluation and grading, plus a model equal pay policy. The code is admissible in evidence before an employment tribunal in any proceedings under the Sex Discrimination Act 1975 and the Equal Pay Act 1970.

Since 1 January 1984, any person has been able to claim equal pay relative to a member of the opposite sex employed by the same firm who does work of *equal value*, as determined by a job evaluation study. Hence, a woman, say, need not identify a man who is doing identical work for the firm on higher wages; she merely has to demonstrate that her job is *worth* the same in terms of its 'demands'. Such demands might relate to the effort, skill, responsibility assumed, working conditions or decision-taking capacities required for effective performance.

Disabled workers

The Disability Discrimination Act 1995 and the **Disability Discrimination (Exception for Small Employers) Order 1998** introduced new rights for disabled people in the areas of employment, education, public transport and access to goods, facilities and services. A 'National Disability Council' was established to advise the government on eliminating discrimination against disabled people, and a code of practice was published containing a wide range of examples to illustrate how employers and others can comply with the Act. The code is not legally binding of *itself*, but is admissible as evidence in courts and industrial tribunals in order to establish whether discrimination has occurred. 'Disability' is defined as 'a physical or mental impairment which has a substantial and long-term adverse effect on a person's ability to carry out normal day-to-day activities'. Hence, a severe disfigurement represents a 'disability' (though not if it results from tattooing or body piercing), as does anything likely to restrict an individual's mobility, manual dexterity, physical co-ordination, speech, hearing or eyesight, or perception of danger, or his or her capacities to learn or understand or to lift or carry everyday objects. However, addictions and anti-social behaviour do not entitle people to protection under the Act. Hay fever is also excluded (unless it aggravates another condition), together with behavioural tendencies towards theft, setting fires or exhibitionism. Specific provisions of the legislation are as follows.

- **It is unlawful for an employer with 15 or more workers to treat disabled people less favourably than others unless there are justifiable reasons.** Employers have to make 'reasonable adjustments' to working arrangements or environments where that would overcome the practical problems created by an individual's disability.

- **No service-providing firm of any size may discriminate against the disabled, who have a legal *right* to be served.** Thus, for example, a hotelier who pretends that all rooms are fully booked in order to refuse a booking from a mentally ill person is breaking the law.

- **People letting or selling land or property must not discriminate against disabled persons.**

- **Colleges of further education are required to publish 'Disability Statements' to inform students about the arrangements they have made to help them to gain access to college facilities.**

- **A disabled person who feels that he or she has been unfairly discriminated against in employment or when applying for a job has a right of redress through an employment tribunal.**

- **New buses, taxis, trains and trams must satisfy minimum standards for access by disabled people.**

Job applicants with criminal records

A person with a criminal conviction is not necessarily obliged to disclose this to a recruiting company, provided the conviction has been 'spent', i.e. a certain period has elapsed since the time of the offence.

The **Rehabilitation of Offenders Act 1974** contains a table of the time intervals that must pass by before a conviction becomes spent. For example, sentences of imprisonment are spent after seven years if the sentence was for less than six months, or after 10 years for sentences of between six and 30 months. Fines become spent after various periods according to the level of fine imposed. A probation order is spent after 12 months. The periods are halved if the person involved was under 17 years of age when he or she was convicted.

However, some sentences can never be spent, notably life imprisonment (which in practice can mean that only a short period is actually spent in jail) and other periods of imprisonment for more than 30 months. Also, there are exceptions to the Act whereby candidates for certain jobs do have to reveal past convictions, namely, any form of work with young people under the age of 18, lawyers, chartered accountants, nurses, vets, dentists, medical practitioners, social and health workers, firearms dealers and prison officers.

Under the Act it is unlawful for an employer to deny someone a job solely on the grounds that the applicant has a spent conviction and, if the person is asked to declare on an application form whether he or she has a criminal record or is questioned about this during an interview, the applicant is legally entitled to 'forget' about ever having been convicted. If an employee is dismissed in consequence of a spent conviction being discovered, the dismissal is regarded in law as being unfair. Indeed, the employer may not reveal that the employee possesses a spent conviction to third parties (when writing references, for example). The justification for the Act is twofold:

■ that in the absence of legislation the possession of a criminal record would effectively debar the vast majority of petty criminals from obtaining employment, hence encouraging them to commit further offences;

■ that criminal records are held only by people who have already been punished for their crimes, so that it is improper for such individuals to be punished again through not being able to get a job.

Age discrimination

At present there is no UK law forbidding ageism, which is frequently criticised as unfair on the grounds that older employees may in fact make extremely good workers. Older employees have lower-than-average absenteeism, lateness and labour turnover, and it has been demonstrated that older employees tend to be more satisfied with their jobs (possibly because their expectations are lower and because they are better adjusted to work routines than younger workers). Age-related decreases in individual productivity are likely to be very marginal and outweighed by the benefits of experience (Johnson and Neumark, 1997). Training difficulties might be due more to older people being out of practice than to lack of ability, and training programmes can be adapted to take this into account.

Specific problems confronted by older workers include:

■ early loss of employment because of age;

■ difficulties in finding fresh employment;

■ targeting of older people in company downsizing exercises;

■ what are, in effect, compulsory early retirement schemes;

■ loss of statutory protection against unfair dismissal once an employee has reached a certain age.

Note that companies which recruit large numbers of older employees might become unattractive to young people because of the consequential loss of immediate short-term promotion prospects for young workers. However, companies that target older people during downsizing exercises often find that they consequently suffer 'corporate amnesia' as the company's 'memory' disappears with those older, longer-term workers.

Equal opportunities policies

Today, many organisations have 'equal opportunities policies' in which they formally state their commitment to equal opportunity ideals. These can cover age, politics and sexual orientation, as well as sex, race and disability discrimination. The advantages to having such a policy are that:

- top management is seen to endorse equal opportunity measures, creating an example to be followed at lower levels;
- as part of its policy the organisation might critically examine the sex, ethnic, age, etc. compositions of all its departments, divisions, occupational categories and levels of worker, exposing any unfair employment practices currently operating;
- the best candidates for jobs will (or should) be recruited or promoted regardless of their sex or ethnic origin, age or sexual orientation;
- discontent among existing minority-group employees may be avoided;
- it is less likely that the organisation will break the law.

Organisations sometimes publish extensive equal opportunity policy documents in order to placate existing minority group workers and/or external bodies (local authorities, government purchasing agencies, the Equal Opportunities Commission (EOC) or Commission for Racial Equality (CRE), etc.) but in fact have no commitment to equal opportunities whatsoever. They have no procedures for *implementing* their equal opportunity policy documents. This creates disillusion and cynicism among all concerned.

Both the EOC and CRE publish codes of practice setting out the steps to be taken to eliminate unfair discrimination in recruitment and other employment matters. The codes offer practical guidance on how personnel policies and procedures should be constructed in order to avoid discrimination, and how existing employees must be instructed about preventing contravention of the Act when interviewing, dealing with subordinates, selecting staff for promotion, etc.

SELECTION AND INDUCTION

Selection is the assessment of candidates for vacant jobs and the choice of the most suitable people. It involves matching the requirements of a job with the attributes of candidates (Boerlijst and Meijboom, 1989). This is facilitated by drafting a 'person specification' defining the background, education, training, personality and other characteristics of the ideal candidate. The person described may not exist, but the process of drafting a person specification creates a standard against which candidates can be compared.

Schemes for categorising the various attributes required to perform certain types of work have existed for many years (Rodger, 1952; Fraser, 1954), usually presented in the form of a checklist describing the demands of the vacant job, as in the following example:

1 **Physical aspects of the work.** Does the job require someone with exceptional strength or fitness (heavy lifting work, for instance), or a specific physical appearance, dress, speech or manner (e.g. for a position as a salesperson or receptionist)?

2 **Need to communicate.** Some work involves regular contact with others. Workplace supervisors, salespeople, receptionists, training instructors, etc., need an external appearance, manners and communication skills that are not so important for socially isolated jobs (long-distance lorry driving, for instance). Jobs with social interaction require agreeable people who mix easily. Such jobs are unsuitable for hostile, aggressive individuals.

3 **Formal qualifications.** What is the minimum level of education and professional qualifications necessary for the job? It is important not to recruit people

who are massively overqualified for the vacancy as they might quickly become bored and underperform, or leave the company. It is also important not to specify formal qualifications which are not strictly necessary, for example a GCSE in English when all that is required is an ability to write and speak articulately.

4 **Experience needed.** Should the person selected have personal experience of specific tasks, and if so for what periods and at what levels?

5 **Specific competences.** Does the work require a person with particular abilities, such as mathematical competence, manual dexterity, or the capacities to think quickly, assimilate large quantities of information, exercise mental agility and interpret complicated issues? Employees who cannot easily withstand stress should not attempt harrowing or emotionally arduous duties.

6 **Personal ambition.** Repetitive production-line work is not intellectually stimulating; financial reward is probably the major motivating factor here. Other jobs present opportunities for creativity and self-development, and thus would be appropriate for people with drive, enthusiasm, self-direction and personal ambition.

Note that organisations which specify unsubstantiated criteria that unnecessarily discriminate against one gender or members of ethnic minorities are open to legal challenge on the ground of indirect discrimination (see pp 317 and 318).

Interviewing

The purpose of a job interview is to obtain information. Therefore, applicants should be put at ease as quickly as possible and hence into a frame of mind in which they will disclose the maximum amount of information about themselves. Uncomfortable, ill-at-ease candidates will not be as frank as those who are relaxed, confident and in full control of their responses. Accordingly, candidates should be interviewed promptly at the appointed time or, if delay is inevitable, apologies should be offered. Interruptions from telephone calls, secretaries, etc., disturb concentration and should be avoided.

The following rules should be followed when conducting interviews:

- Opening remarks should be supportive and uncontroversial.

- Questions which simply ask for repetition of information already provided on application forms should be avoided. Rather, the interviewer should seek supplementary information to probe in depth the candidate's potential.

- Detailed notetaking by interviewers is inadvisable because of its disturbing effects on the interviewee. Candidates should be assessed immediately after their interviews. Otherwise, important points in earlier interviews will be forgotten in the final end-of-session appraisal.

- Open-ended questions such as 'what made you decide to do that?' or 'why did you enjoy that type of work?' are usually more productive in obtaining information than direct queries. Generally worded questions invite the candidate to discuss feelings, opinions and perceptions of events. Simple yes/no questions will not draw out the candidate's opinions. Interviewers should not make critical or insensitive remarks during the interview.

- Interviewers should not compare candidates with themselves.

- Only job-relevant questions should be asked.

- The 'halo effect', i.e. assuming that because a candidate possesses one desirable characteristic (smart appearance or a good speaking voice, for example), then he or she must be equally good in all other areas, must not be allowed to influence the selection.
- 'Revealing' questions should not be asked. A revealing question discloses attitudes and beliefs held by the questioner. An example would be 'I like watching football, don't you?'
- Inappropriate criteria must not be applied. This could involve, for example, males who interview females associating attractive physical appearance with work ability, or appointing people the interviewer knows socially.
- Interviewers should not behave in a pompous manner. This wastes time and contributes nothing to the quality of the interview.
- Interview panels should be as small as possible. Over-large panels create unhelpful dramatic atmospheres, and panel members might ask irrelevant and disconnected questions.

Testing

At best, selection tests are a useful complement to interviews. At worst, they are confusing and irrelevant appendages to the selection process. The purpose of an interview is to obtain information. Thus, tests can be justified only to the extent that more and better information about a candidate is actually generated.

There are many serious problems involved in setting tests and correctly interpreting the results. Tests are particularly useful where interviews are not possible, as, for example, when large numbers of employees are to be engaged within a very short period, and for situations where candidates have no formal qualifications or experience of work, as in the case, for instance, of recruiting school leavers who have no academic certificates. Advocates of selection testing claim that tests remove subjectivity in selection procedures. In principle, a good test should measure objectively the subject's abilities and characteristics. Moreover, an effective test will:

- **be cost effective to administer** (note that a single test can be given to a roomful of perhaps 40 or 50 people at each sitting, and only a couple of people will be needed to organise and invigilate the test);
- **measure precisely what it is intended to measure.** An intelligence test should assess intelligence, not learned responses; aptitude tests should indicate candidates' true potentials for undertaking the jobs for which they are being considered, not other occupations;
- **give consistent results when repeated.** Only then can the results obtained from a single sitting be accepted as sufficiently reliable for appointment decisions;
- **discriminate between candidates.** Good quality applicants should, if the test is working properly, obtain high marks and poor candidates should consistently fail. If candidates pass the test but then turn out to be incompetent, the test has not achieved its purpose;
- **rank the candidates.** The best candidate should obtain the top mark, the next best should get the second highest mark and so on.
- **be relevant to the job.** The characteristics exposed by performance in the test should relate directly to the job specification for the vacant post.

Induction

Once an offer of appointment is accepted, a contract of employment exists. The letter of appointment must include details of terms and conditions attached to the work: wages, working hours, holidays, sick pay, pension schemes, company rules, safety regulations, etc. Having considered all the terms and conditions, the recruit now signs a document saying he or she understands and will abide by them. Subsequent breach of the contract will offer grounds for fair dismissal.

The high costs of recruitment will be wasted unless the new employee remains in employment and becomes productive as soon as possible. There is a high risk of the new employee leaving during the initial employment period:

> *'The induction period is activated during the pre-engagement process and is not complete until the employer and employee are reasonably satisfied with the employment relationship.'* (Pilbeam and Corbridge, 2002)

The period of transition during which an **induction** crisis may occur varies widely. If an induction crisis occurs, the effect can be that the new employees decide that their decision to take up employment with the organisation was a mistake and results in their resignation. This means that the induction process must be seen as requiring more than a one-off induction training. The induction process allows for socialisation into the organisation's culture and helps to reduce the risk of early departure.

Part of the induction is the process of introducing recruits to an organisation and explaining their role within it and usually begins with a guided tour of the building. Induction is important because impressions gained by new employees during this period can influence their perceptions of the organisation for many years to come. Good induction procedures also help employees to fit into strange and initially uncomfortable environments quickly and without fuss. Recruits should be welcomed personally by senior members of staff and then introduced to colleagues, supervisors and subordinates. Recruits may be given copies of the firm's organisation chart, and an explanation of individual positions within it. Particular aspects of specific jobs can be discussed and, if appropriate, training arrangements made. Efficiency standards, expected output quality, security arrangements and so on will be detailed.

A crucially important aspect of the induction process is that of informing recruits where to go for help if they experience problems. Entrants should know whom to approach, and the correct procedures to follow. Appropriate contacts might be supervisors, personnel officers, higher managers or trade union representatives. In any event, the recruit should know what to do if he or she:

- has a problem with money or understanding the wage system;
- has a medical problem;
- feels that working conditions are unsafe;
- does not get on with other people in the department;
- has difficulty with the work;
- is bullied or harassed;
- has a complaint;
- does not receive adequate training.

In addition to the direct induction process, other ways of aiding socialisation into the organisation include 'buddying'. The new starter is linked with a 'buddy' who is an existing employee who is already settled within the same department. Having a ready-made colleague helps the socialisation process to proceed smoothly and gives the new starter an information source at his or her own level. Employees who act as buddies will need to be volunteers, and have some training to ensure that they are clear about their role. Mentoring (*see* coaching and mentoring, p 328 below) can also be included within the induction process in addition to 'buddying'.

Exit interviews

Employees deciding to leave the organisation present an opportunity to collect information on what motivated their decision. Analysis of this information can be used to improve retention and to develop a staff retention policy.

The timing of the exit interview will depend on the organisation and can range from the point of resignation to a later time, even after departure. The interview needs to be conducted professionally and with tact. In some cases a questionnaire is sent to the leaver to collect information. The response rate of this method of collection is reduced once the employee has left the organisation.

For employees that the organisation wishes to retain, an early exit interview can highlight reasons for the decision to leave. An offer can then be designed to retain the employee.

TRAINING AND DEVELOPMENT

The purpose of training is to improve employees' performances in their current jobs and/or equip them for more demanding roles or a change in their role in the future. It is expensive: special instructors may have to be employed; external courses must be financed; internal courses require resourcing with materials, personnel and physical facilities. Moreover, there is no guarantee that trainees will actually benefit from participating in programmes. Employees are usually unproductive while undergoing training, and there are many incidental expenses (hotel accommodation, travel, meal allowances, etc.).

Putting aside questions of staff morale, it might not make economic sense to spend enormous sums on training existing employees for higher-level work if competent people can be recruited cheaply from outside. Equally pointless is the (not uncommon) practice of training far more employees in a certain type of work than there are vacancies in that area. This policy, while ensuring a ready supply of qualified internal applicants whenever needs for a particular skill arise, causes high labour turnover as workers become increasingly frustrated at not being able to perform the work for which they were trained. Indeed, 'overtraining' policies can backfire, resulting in shortages of trained internal applicants for higher-level jobs (Schuler, 1992).

Training seeks to improve and develop the knowledge, skills and/or attitudes of employees. Apart from the benefits accruing to the individual worker (greater versatility, extra skills, etc.), many advantages accrue to the organisation. Employees become more flexible, the productivity and quality of work should improve, job satisfaction might increase (with consequent reductions in absenteeism and staff turnover rates) and the organisation need not fear the consequences of new technology.

The 'learning organisation'

→ Ch. 3

The concept of the learning organisation is based on the view that if an organisation does not learn faster and keep ahead of its competitors it will not survive (*see* Chapter 3). If an organisation is considered to be a sum of its parts, including employees, the learning of these employees will enhance the organisation. The flaw in this argument is that it will only be true if the organisation values the learning and has systems that allow the learning to be shared through the organisation. This requires the organisation to nurture a culture that encourages learning, reflection and the sharing of its application of the learning within the organisation.

Encouraging learning in itself will not develop a learning organisation. Writers and researchers have presented varying views on the learning organisation:

'an organisation which facilitates the learning of all its members and continuously transforms itself'. (Pedler *et al.*, 1991)

According to Senge (1990):

'the basic meaning of a "learning organisation" is an organisation that is continually expanding its capacity to create its future.'

Links between the learning organisation and knowledge management can be drawn as they both highlight the importance to the organisation of continuous development to meet the changing needs of the external environment. The main differences are that the learning organisation focuses on the learning process and reflects on how the learning can be applied in the organisational context in the future. Double-loop learning occurs when the learning results in activities which modify and change the organisation's way of working. By contrast, in knowledge management the focus is on the availability and transference of knowledge that exists in the organisation, often centred on using computer systems for access.

Assessing training needs

Needs for employee training may arise from the introduction of new technologies, or the organisation's diversification into different fields (Bernardin and Russel, 1993). Other causes of the need for training might be poor-quality output, high accident rates, high absenteeism or staff turnover, or unfavourable performance appraisal reports submitted by managers on their subordinates. Note, however, that any one of these might be caused by factors other than inadequate training.

Like any other business process, training can be very wasteful if it is not carefully planned and supervised. Without a logical, systematic approach, some training may be given which is not necessary, and vice versa, or the extent of the training may be too small or too great. When the training is complete, **validation** will show whether it has been successful in achieving its aims and **evaluation** will attempt to measure its cost-benefit.

The systematic approach to training follows this programme:

1 The job is analysed and defined.

2 Reasonable standards of performance are established, perhaps by reference to experienced employees.

3 The employees being considered for training are studied to see if the required performance standards are being attained.

4 The difference (if any) between 2 and 3 is considered. It is often called the 'training gap', though it may be partly due to faults in the organisation, poor materials or defective equipment.

5 Training programmes are devised to meet the training needs revealed in 4.

6 Training is given and appropriate records kept.

7 The performance achieved after training is measured; if the training programme has been successful, the performance standards set in 2 should now be achieved (validation).

8 An attempt is made to calculate the cost of the training and compare it with the financial benefit gained by the improved performance of the employees. The training programme may be revised if a method can be seen of achieving the same result at lower cost (evaluation).

Evaluation of training

For manual workers the success of a training programme might be quantified in terms of better productivity, higher quality of output, less absenteeism, lower staff turnover, greater adaptability, fewer accidents and less need for close supervision. Unfortunately, improved performance in many jobs is difficult to express quantitatively in the short term. And some skills acquired on courses undertaken today might not be used until the future.

Training can improve workers' morale, create better interpersonal relationships, instil in employees a sense of loyalty to the organisation, and provide other intangible benefits (Beer *et al.*, 1985). Note, however, that it is not sufficient merely to ask workers whether they feel more efficient as a consequence of attending a course; hard, objective evidence is also required. Courses which participants have particularly enjoyed (especially residential courses) may be popular not because of their intrinsic educational value but because of their 'holiday camp' atmosphere, recreational facilities, friendships established among course members, and so on.

The following procedure should be adopted when evaluating the effectiveness of training:

■ Ask the question, 'What difference would it make to the organisation's overall performance if the training did not take place?' If the answer is 'not very much', then critically reassess the value of the training.

■ Relate the outcomes of the training to the organisation's initial training objectives. Isolate divergences and explain why they occurred.

■ Interview people on completion of a course and ask them whether it was relevant to their work, whether it taught them things they did not previously know, whether is was too easy or too difficult, how well supported the programme was in terms of course materials, instructors, facilities, etc., and how they think the knowledge gained will help their future careers. Keep a written record of the answers and repeat the interview after at least six months have elapsed since finishing the course.

Management development

Management (and staff) development seeks to improve a person's overall career prospects rather than train him or her to perform duties necessary for the present job. Hence it normally comprises a series of planned training activities and work experiences designed to improve a manager's performance and equip him or her for higher-level work. Activities might include attendance on courses, job rotation, understudying (i.e. spending a short period as a personal assistant to a more senior manager), attachments to project committees and special working parties, and the completion of longer-term academic qualifications in the management field. Programmes may cover:

- background knowledge of the organisation, its trading environment, products, production methods, markets and personnel;
- administrative procedures, the legal environment, specialist techniques;
- management methods, analytical skills, organisation, delegation and control, time management;
- interpersonal skills, communication, leadership and co-ordination;
- creative abilities, decision making and problem solving.

Note that some organisations insist that managerial ability cannot be taught, and that management training courses are therefore a waste of time. They argue that few courses contain material that is directly relevant and immediately applicable to real-life management situations, and that normal competition between managerial staff should ensure the 'survival of the fittest'.

In organisations which do train managerial staff, new approaches to training are increasingly common – they want to develop the initiative, self-reliance, leadership and interpersonal communication skills of managers as well as their technical abilities. An interesting recent development in the training field has been the increasing use of outdoor management training, which assumes the existence of direct parallels between the personal qualities necessary for successful management and those cultivated through participation in outdoor pursuits such as rock-climbing, canoeing, sailing or orienteering. The essential demands of these activities – planning, organising, team-building, dealing with uncertainty, direction and control – are the same, advocates argue, as those needed for management.

Coaching and mentoring

One-to-one coaching is increasingly being used as part of management development. The coaching can be targeted to achieve particular outcomes, and the type and skill-base of the coach can be selected according to need. The coach needs to be a specialist, having both coaching skills and the required knowledge base. Coaches can be used to consolidate learning following a training course, up-date business skills on a one-to-one basis, improve existing skills, recommend specific behaviours to develop or improve, reinforce on-the-job performance, and clarify performance goals and development needs. The coaching skills identified by Walton (1999) include: listening and understanding, observing, giving feedback, understanding people, communication (written and verbal) and influencing.

Mentoring is not the same as coaching. A mentor is usually a senior employee who advises the more junior member of staff on his or her personal and career development. It is essential that the mentor and protégé are not in a direct reporting relationship and that the relationship is quite separate from that which exists with a line manager. For a successful mentor–protégé relationship there needs to be mutual trust, regular meetings and confidentiality on both sides. The length of a mentoring relationship may have a fixed term or be open-ended. Mentoring can form part of an induction process.

PERFORMANCE MANAGEMENT AND APPRAISAL

→ Chs 9 and 14

Performance management is the integration of employee development with results-based assessment (*see* Chapters 9 and 14). It encompasses **performance appraisal**, objective-setting for individuals and departments, appropriate training programmes and performance-related pay. Appraisal of managers by their subordinates, peers and people in other departments (perhaps even customers) might also be included in the scheme (Philpott and Sheppard, 1992).

Target setting

An employee's targets could be stated in terms of achieving a certain standard (i.e. an ongoing performance criterion, such as a specified departmental staff attendance rate or the attainment of minimum quality levels) that is to be maintained indefinitely, or as an *ad hoc* goal (Fletcher and Williams, 1992). The advantages of bosses and employees jointly setting personal objectives are as follows:

■ It forces everyone in the department to think carefully about his or her role and duties, about why tasks are necessary, and how best to get things done.

■ Targets are clarified and mechanisms are created for monitoring performance.

■ Crucial elements are identified in each job. This information is useful for determining training and recruitment needs.

■ Personal achievements of employees are recognised and can be rewarded appropriately.

■ Bosses and their colleagues are obliged to communicate. In consequence, bosses can quickly identify which employees are ready for promotion and the help they will need in preparing themselves for this.

■ Performance is appraised against quantified targets, not subjective criteria.

■ There is forced co-ordination of activities – between departments, between junior and senior management, and between short-term and long-term goals.

The targets set should adhere to the following guidelines:

■ Targets should be precise, unambiguous and (if possible) expressed numerically. Targets can be expressed in quantity, lengths of time, money and/or percentages but generic objectives such as 'increase profits' or 'cut costs' are not acceptable.

■ Targets should relate to the crucial and primary elements of employees' jobs and not to trivial matters.

■ Targets should be consistent.

■ Each target should be accompanied by a statement of how it is to be achieved, by when, the resources necessary, and how and where these will be acquired.

A good way to assess the usefulness of objectives is to ask whether they pass the **SMART** test, i.e. targets need to be:

■ **Specific**

■ **Measurable**

■ **Agreed between boss and worker**

■ **Realistic**

■ **Time related.**

Both parties should share a common perspective on the situation intended to exist after the achievement of objectives and on how soon results may reasonably be expected.

Appraisal

Managers frequently make *ad hoc* judgements about employees, but are loath to discuss the grounds on which the opinions are based. Performance appraisal replaces casual assessment with formal, systematic procedures. Employees know they are being evaluated and are told the criteria that will be used in the course of the appraisal. (Indeed, knowledge that an appraisal is soon to occur could motivate an employee into increased effort aimed at enhancing the outcomes of the assessment.) Specifically, appraisal is the analysis of employees' past successes and failures, and the assessment of their suitability for promotion or further training. Its advantages include the following:

■ Boss and employee are compelled to meet and discuss common work-related problems. Appraisees become aware of what exactly is expected of them and of their status in the eyes of their line managers.

■ Appraisal monitors the feasibility of targets set by higher management, who receive valuable feedback on problems encountered when implementing policies. Thus, it creates a cheap and effective early warning system within the organisation's management information structure.

■ It enables bosses to learn about employees and the true nature of their duties. Conducting appraisals helps a manager to remain in touch with the staff in his or her department. Unknown skills and competences might be uncovered. This data can be incorporated into the firm's human resource plan and hence assist in avoiding compulsory redundancies, in career and management succession planning, and in identifying needs for employee training (Kinnie and Lowe, 1990).

A successful appraisal is one that results in:

■ reasonable targets which are mutually agreed, not arbitrarily determined;

■ recognition of the employee's achievements;

■ clear identification of obstacles to improved performance (organisational problems as well as individual difficulties);

■ enthusiastic pursuit of measurable objectives;

■ two-way communication between boss and worker.

It is important for appraisal to be seen as a staff development exercise, intended to be helpful to everyone concerned, and not as a form of restrictive control or disciplinary measure. The purpose, therefore, must be to assist both individuals and the organisation in improving their performances. Appraisal reviews are usually categorised into three types:

1 **Performance reviews**, which analyse employees' past successes and failures with a view to improving future performance.

2 **Potential reviews**, which assess subordinates' suitability for promotion and/or further training.

3 **Reward reviews**, for determining pay rises. It is a well-established principle that salary assessments should occur well after performance and potential reviews have been completed, for two reasons:

- performance reviews examine personal strengths and weaknesses in order to improve efficiency. If salary matters are discussed during these meetings, they might dominate the conversation and discourage employees from being frank about their weaknesses;

- ultimately, salary levels are determined by market forces of supply and demand for labour. Staff shortages can cause the firm to pay high wages quite independent of the objective worth of particular workers.

Self-appraisal and peer group appraisal

Appraisal might be more useful to the appraisee, and lead in the longer term to greater efficiency, if it is conducted either by the employee or by a colleague of equal occupational status. Such appraisals may analyse issues more critically than when people fear the career consequences of admitting mistakes. Appraisees state – using any of the methods previously discussed – how they regard their performance, the adequacy of the training they have received, effects of alterations in job content, perceptions of key objectives and future aspirations. They identify their own strengths and account for their failures and weaknesses, suggesting ways in which the firm might better use their talents, skills and recently acquired experiences.

There are, of course, problems with self-appraisal, including the following:

- Many people are quite incapable of analysing themselves. It is unusual for individuals to assess their own competence in other walks of life. At school, college and during the early stages of a career the individual becomes accustomed to being directed and evaluated by others. The transition of appraisee to self-assessor may require skilled and detailed guidance by someone already competent in appraisal techniques. Most appraisees in lower-level positions will have received no training in self-analysis or appraisal.

- To the extent that appraisals form a basis for future career development, appraisees may overstate their successes while ignoring their failings.

On the other hand, employees are compelled to think carefully about the adequacy of their contribution, about barriers preventing improved performance, about their future and about the quality of their relationships with others.

Problems with performance appraisal

There are a number of problems with performance appraisal, including the following:

- dangers of favouritism, bias and stereotyping by managers who conduct appraisals;

- possibilities that inconsistent criteria will be applied by different managers when assessing the calibre of subordinates (Schneier *et al.*, 1991);

- all the information relevant to a particular case may not be available;

- information may not be interpreted objectively;

- assessors may seek to evaluate every subordinate as 'fair' or 'average' for all performance categories, perhaps to avoid controversy;
- assessors may focus on specific cases of outstandingly good and bad performance while ignoring the employee's average overall ability;
- appraisal systems require appraising managers to undertake extra work, which they may be reluctant to accept. Hence the process becomes a ritualistic chore to be completed as quickly as possible in a manner that causes the least comment from those affected by the scheme.

Douglas McGregor noted the great reluctance with which many managers undertake assessment responsibilities; preferring to treat subordinates as professional colleagues rather than as inferiors upon whom they are entitled to pass judgement (McGregor, 1957). Senior managers, McGregor asserted, dislike 'playing God'. Usually they are fully cognisant of their own biases and thus rightly seek to avoid situations where prejudice could arise. Also, subordinates may bitterly resent their personal qualities being commented upon, seeing the appraisal as a patronising exercise designed to humiliate or to punish past inadequacies in their work.

Appraisal requires concentration, diligence and competence in the manager conducting the appraisal. Training in appraisal techniques is required, followed by substantial guided experience in their practical application. McGregor pointed out the facts that:

- few managers receive any instruction in appraisal methods;
- even managers who are properly trained may not possess all the information needed to undertake fair appraisals. They may be out of touch with current working practices or unfamiliar with environmental problems affecting subordinates' work.

360 degree appraisal

The 360 degree appraisal has developed to overcome some of the problems highlighted above. This method collects feedback from a variety of sources in addition to the manager, including peers, customers, suppliers, senior and junior staff. If a balanced view is taken, the resulting appraisal will be more informed than feedback from a single source. Individuals' feedback will be coloured by their personal stance, and this needs to be acknowledged.

The feedback process needs to be carefully managed. Special training is required for those involved in managing the process so that the information collected can be used to improve the overall work and behaviour.

The disadvantage of the 360 degree appraisal is that it is expensive, time-consuming and requires a high level of resourcing.

PROMOTION, TRANSFER, DEMOTION AND DISMISSAL

Promotion and demotion

Apart from improvements in pay and conditions of work, the most immediate incentives available to employees are opportunities for promotion. If the organisation has trained its staff adequately and ensured that employees' work experiences are sufficiently wide, internal promotion should be feasible. Thus, external recruitment will be necessary only for specialist positions, or when no one within the organisation possesses appropriate qualifications for a post, or the organisation needs or wants to increase the diversity of its staff at all levels. Prospects of promotion often represent significant motivators (van Ham *et al.*, 1986). Promotion methods are worthy, therefore, of serious discussion.

The criteria used in selecting individuals for promotion may be based on ability or seniority. Ability-related systems accelerate the careers of staff who are exceptionally competent, whereas seniority-based procedures have the advantage of ensuring steady progression for all employees; and knowledge that promotion is reasonably assured can improve morale throughout the organisation. Promotion follows logically from training, performance appraisal, management development and management by objectives programmes.

People can be selected for promotion directly – management simply appointing chosen employees to higher posts – or vacancies can be advertised within the firm. Direct selection is quick, inexpensive and suitable where management knows the abilities of all its subordinates. Internal advertisement is appropriate in organisations where several candidates of about the same level of ability might apply.

Unfair discrimination in promotion will upset and demotivate staff: it should be avoided at all costs. Organisations that operate in sensitive multicultural or multi-ethnic environments sometimes monitor the consequences of their promotion policies by checking whether certain groups are overrepresented among those who do not achieve promotion. Hence, if it is found that females, ethnic minorities or certain religious groups are prominent in the non-promoted category, reasons for this can be identified and remedial measures applied. Specifically, the following questions can be asked of any promotion system:

- What are the characteristics of non-promoted groups, and are there valid reasons explaining why individuals in these groups are not promoted?
- What contributions have non-promoted groups made to the work of the organisation? Have they been adequately rewarded for their contributions?
- Why do non-promoted individuals remain with the organisation?
- What help can be given to non-promoted groups in order to help them qualify for promotion? What are the obstacles confronting non-promoted categories, and how can they be removed?
- What can management itself do to improve its knowledge of the backgrounds and difficulties experienced by non-promoted groups? How does management feel about these people?

A non-discriminatory promotion policy has numerous benefits. Internal personal relationships between managers and subordinates are improved; labour turnover will fall, since able staff do not need to leave the organisation to do higher-level work. Efficiency should increase through utilisation in senior positions of the accumulated experience of long-serving employees. Additionally, there is little risk of the individuals promoted possessing unknown deficiencies, as can occur with externally recruited senior staff. On the other hand, outsiders can inject fresh ideas and apply new perspectives to existing problems – external recruits may be of much higher calibre than internal candidates.

Demotion is a move to a job within the company which is lower in importance. It is usually, though not always, accompanied by a reduction in pay. An employee may be demoted for the following reasons:

- His or her job may disappear or become less important through a departmental or company reorganisation.
- The worker may no longer be thought capable of carrying out his or her present responsibilities efficiently.

Unless the employee has requested it, demotion will probably have adverse effects.

- There will be less satisfaction of esteem and self-actualisation needs. The employee may show negative reactions to frustration.
- The employee may become a centre of discontent in the organisation.
- Other employees may lose confidence in the organisation.

An employee who resigns in consequence of a demotion may complain of unfair dismissal under a special category known as 'constructive dismissal' (see below).

Transfers

A transfer is a move to a job within the company which has approximately equal importance, status and pay. To manage human resources in a constructive way, it is sometimes necessary to transfer employees to other jobs, sometimes because of changed work requirements and sometimes because an employee is unhappy or dissatisfied in his or her present job.

In some organisations it is the custom for the least satisfactory employees to be transferred from one department to another, with the result that a transfer is regarded as discreditable, particularly if it occurs at short notice and without explanation. An unhappy employee may therefore prefer to leave rather than seek a transfer.

In other organisations transfers are used as a means of developing promising employees by giving them experience in several departments. A few organisations advertise all vacancies internally and consider applicants for whom the new job would be a transfer rather than a promotion.

Transfers can increase job satisfaction and improve utilisation under the following circumstances:

- A transfer is regarded as a re-selection.
- The need for a transfer is explained.
- Unsatisfactory employees are not dealt with by transferring them to other departments.
- Requests by employees for transfers are fully investigated.
- No employee is transferred to another district against his or her will.
- An employee transferred to another district is given financial assistance from the organisation to cover removal costs, legal fees, refurnishing, etc.

Dismissal

Dismissal means the termination of employment by:

- the employer, with or without notice; or

- the failure of the employer to renew a fixed-term contract; or
- the employee's resignation, with or without notice, when the employer behaves in a manner that demonstrates refusal to be bound by the contract of employment.

The latter is termed **constructive dismissal**. It means the employer is behaving so unreasonably that the worker has no alternative but to quit.

Normally, an employer must give the employee notice of dismissal, as stated in the worker's contract of employment. Occasionally, however, dismissal without notice is permissible. This is known as **summary dismissal** and can occur when an employee's behaviour makes impossible the fulfilment of a contract of employment. Examples are theft, persistent drunkenness, violence, abusiveness to colleagues or customers, wilful disobedience or incompetence that immediately causes damage to the employer's business.

Many countries have statutes that govern how employees may be fairly dismissed. Under the Employment Rights Act 1996, employees covered by the Act, as amended by an order made in 1989 (e.g. mostly those with at least one year's continuous service) may only be fairly dismissed for genuine redundancy or for:

- **gross misconduct**, e.g. refusal to obey reasonable instructions, dishonesty, persistent absenteeism, neglect of duties, etc.;
- **incapacity** to do the job, caused by such things as incompetence, illness (once the worker's contractual sick pay entitlement has expired), or the person not having the skills or aptitude for the work;
- **some other substantial reason**, e.g. going on strike, disruption of staff relations, or a temporary job coming to an end, provided the impermanent nature of the work was fully explained to the worker when the employment started.

'Redundancy' means that the organisation's need for employees to do work of a particular kind has ceased or diminished so that someone has to lose his or her job. The criteria used to select individuals for redundancy must by law be fair and reasonable. Workers declared redundant are entitled to redundancy payments. The redundancy process is illustrated in Figure 11.2.

'Wrongful', as opposed to 'unfair', dismissal occurs when insufficient notice is given or there has been some other breach of the employment contract. It gives rise to a civil action for damages equivalent to the actual loss incurred. Wrongful dismissal may be claimed by any dismissed worker, regardless of length of service – a worker who has been with the organisation for only a few days may be 'wrongfully' sacked.

Allegations of *wrongful* dismissal can be heard in a court or employment tribunal. A complaint for *unfair* dismissal goes to an employment tribunal, which can award compensation of up to £50000.

The ACAS code on dismissal

Disciplinary procedures should be in writing, easy to understand and made known to employees and their representatives. The UK Advisory, Conciliation and Arbitration Service (ACAS) has issued an important code of practice on these matters which tribunals expect employers to abide by. This code recognises that the maintenance of discipline is a management responsibility, but emphasises the desirability of involving workers' representatives when drafting procedures. In addition

Figure 11.2 The redundancy process

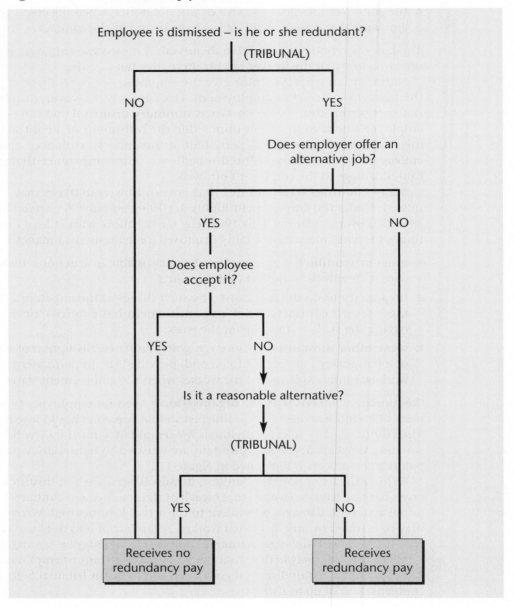

to the points outlined above, the main recommendations of the ACAS code are as follows.

1 Employers should indicate the forms of conduct that are considered unacceptable, and in what circumstances. Rules should be particular rather than universal and justified in terms of the objective requirements of a job.

2 All workers should be given a copy of the organisation's rules and have them explained orally as part of an induction programme. Employees should be informed of the consequences of breaking rules, particularly those rules which, if broken, may result in summary dismissal.

3 All disciplinary procedures should be set out in writing and provide for matters to be dealt with quickly.

4 Only senior management should have the power to dismiss.

5 The accused person should have the right to be accompanied at disciplinary hearings by a trade union representative or by a fellow employee of his or her own choice.

6 Employees should not be dismissed for a first offence (except for gross misconduct). The code distinguishes between informal oral warnings for minor infringements of rules, and formal written warnings issued following serious offences. Formal warnings should set out the nature of the breach of discipline, the likely consequences of further offences, and should state that the warning constitutes stage one of the formal procedure. If misconduct is repeated, a second and final written warning should be issued containing an unambiguous statement that a further recurrence of the offence will lead to whatever action (suspension, dismissal or some other sanction) has been determined. Assuming the errant worker's behaviour does not improve, the next step is suspension or dismissal, accompanied by a written statement of reasons for the action taken and details of the right of appeal.

7 The employer should take into account the employee's age, position, length of service and general performance, and whether domestic problems etc. make it appropriate to reduce the severity of the disciplinary action taken.

Appeals should be considered quickly and be heard by a higher level of authority than took the original disciplinary action. Wherever possible the appeal should be considered by independent people who are not the immediate superiors of the manager who decided to dismiss the worker. The procedure should spell out the actions that may be taken by those hearing the appeal, and enable any new evidence to be made known to the employee.

THE FOUR Cs MODEL OF HUMAN RESOURCES MANAGEMENT

The four Cs model – commitment, competence, congruence and cost-effectiveness – was developed by researchers at the Harvard Business School as a means of investigating HRM issues in a wider environmental context than the mundane and instrumental tasks of recruitment and selection, training, appraisal, maintenance of employee records and so on (Beer *et al.*, 1985). According to the Harvard model, HRM policies need to derive from a critical analysis of:

■ the demands of the various stakeholders in a business; and

■ a number of 'situational factors'.

Stakeholder theory

→ Chs 3 and 8

This asserts that since organisations are owned and operated by differing interest groups (stakeholders), management's main task is to balance the returns to various group interests (*see also* Chapters 3 and 8). Examples of stakeholders are shareholders, different categories of employee, customers/users of the product, creditors (including banks), unions and (possibly) local or national government. Managers therefore need to be politicians and diplomats. They must establish good relations with each group, develop persuasive skills, create alliances, represent one faction to others, etc.

Stakeholder theory implies the recognition that each interest group possesses certain basic rights. Thus, for example, management should consider workers' interests as well as those of shareholders when taking important decisions.

Stakeholders may or may not hold formal authority, although many will have invested something in the organisation, whether this be work, finance or other resources. Accordingly, every investing stakeholder will expect a reward from the enterprise and normally will wish to influence how this is determined. Management must:

- identify the stakeholders in the organisation;
- determine the minimum return each stakeholder is willing to accept;
- seek to influence stakeholders' perceptions of the organisation (e.g. by persuading shareholders that a high dividend is not in a company's best long-term interest or convincing workers that a high wage settlement is not possible during the current year);
- identify key individuals in specific stakeholder groups and establish good relations with these people.

Some stakeholders are simply groups or individuals who are affected by the organisation's activities, or who seek to represent certain 'constituencies' which cannot represent themselves, for example animals, the environment or overseas workers. Sometimes these have little influence and managers have to make moral judgements as to the responses they make to them. However, such groups can sometimes form powerful coalitions, excite the interest of the press or unsettle the organisation's staff, to the extreme detriment of the organisation!

Situational factors

These include the state of the labour market, the calibre and motivation of employees, management style (which itself depends in part on the culture of the local community), the technologies used in production and the nature of working methods (e.g. whether specialisation and the division of labour are required). Labour market situations are crucial to the analysis. The labour market comprises all the people seeking work and all the companies, government bodies and other organisations that require employees. Labour markets operate at regional, industry sector, national and (increasingly) international levels. There are sub-markets for various categories of occupation, skill, educational background and other employee characteristics and for different types of task.

Further situational factors that might be relevant are:

- form of ownership of the organisation (and hence to whom management is accountable);
- influence of trade unions and employers' associations;
- laws and business practices of the society in which the organisation operates;
- the competitive environment;
- senior management's ability to co-ordinate and control.

Stakeholder expectations and situational factors need to be taken into account when formulating human resources strategies, and will affect HRM policies concerning such matters as remuneration systems, degree of supervision of workers, use of labour-intensive rather than capital-intensive methods, etc. An increase in the intensity of business competition may cause a firm to improve labour productivity, discard employees, restructure administrative systems, and so on. A change in the age structure of the population can lead an organisation to hire more women. Rising educational standards may make it appropriate to redesign jobs in order to give workers more autonomy.

Outcomes to human resources management

According to the Harvard researchers, the effectiveness of the outcomes to human resources management should be evaluated under four headings: commitment, competence, congruence and cost-effectiveness.

1 **Commitment** concerns employees' loyalty to the organisation, personal motivation and liking for their work. The degree of employee commitment may be assessed via attitude surveys, labour turnover and absenteeism statistics, and through interviews with workers who quit their jobs.

2 **Competence** relates to employees' skills and abilities, training requirements and potential for higher-level work. These may be estimated through employee appraisal systems and the preparation of skills inventories (*see* p 309 above). HRM policies should be designed to attract, retain and motivate competent workers.

3 **Congruence** means that management and workers share the same vision of the organisation's goals and work together to attain them. In a well-managed organisation, employees at all levels of authority will share common perspectives about the factors that determine its prosperity and future prospects. Such perspectives concern the guiding principles that govern the organisation's work: how things should be done, when, by whom, and how enthusiastically.

   To some extent these perceptions may be created by management via its internal communications, style of leadership, organisation system and working methods, but they can only be sustained and brought to bear on day-to-day operations by the organisation's workers. Staff should *feel* they possess a common objective. They need to experience a sense of affinity with the organisation and *want* to pursue a common cause. Congruence is evident in the absence of grievances and conflicts within the organisation, and in harmonious industrial relations.

4 **Cost-effectiveness** concerns operational efficiency. Human resources should be used to the best advantage and in the most productive ways. Outputs must be maximised at the lowest input cost, and the organisation must be quick to respond to market opportunities and environmental change.

Problems with the four Cs approach

The Harvard model suggests that human resources policies should seek to increase the level of each of the four Cs. For example, commitment may be enhanced through improving the flow of management/worker communication, while competence can be increased through extra training. Problems with the four Cs approach are:

- how *exactly* to measure these variables;
- possible conflicts between cost-effectiveness and congruence (especially if the drive for the former generates low wages);

- the huge variety of variables potentially relevant to any given HRM situation. Often it is impossible to distinguish the key factors defining the true character of a particular state of affairs;
- the fact that sometimes a technology or set of working conditions makes it virtually impossible to increase the levels of some of the Cs. Certain jobs are inevitably dirty, boring and repetitive, yet they still have to be done.

THE MANAGEMENT OF HUMAN RESOURCES

The modern approach to the management of human resources is to emphasise co-operation rather than conflict and to integrate HRM policies into the overall corporate strategies of the organisation. This requires senior management to:

- recognise the critical importance of harmonious relations with the workforce; and
- relate HRM to the attainment of increased competitiveness, improved product quality and better customer care.

Well-constructed human resources policies are essential for the well-being of the firm, and all efforts must be made to minimise the potential for conflicts between management and workers.

Strategic human resource management

The development of human resource management as a strategic function – strategic human resource management (SHRM) – brings the function in line with the other strategic functions of the business – finance and marketing. It acknowledges the contribution of the skills and knowledge of employees to continuing business competitiveness, together with the planning for future human resource needs.

Linking human resource management to the organisation's strategy is the basis of SHRM, so that human resource management underpins the business goals and vision of the organisation. To achieve this, HRM needs to be aligned horizontally so the major components (reward, resourcing, development, retention, and employee relations) are aligned to achieve the organisation's strategy. The HR function must also be vertically integrated into the overall strategic plan.

The Balanced Scorecard

The Balanced Scorecard aims to link business areas of the organisation to its business strategy. Key measures are tracked and monitored. These measures have a direct link to the business strategy and are visible and applicable.

The key measures of the business in the main strategic areas are determined using cause-and-effect maps. Financial measures are seen as a major area to determine effective performance, but not as the sole area. Financial measures are important to shareholders, but unlike other areas of the business financial measures are short-term indicators. The Balanced Scorecard includes the monitoring of desirable long-term outcomes and performance drivers together with these short-term measures. They are used for setting targets. Having the same areas of measurement for all levels of the organisation, all employees can see how the objectives are linked to the organisation's goals.

The performance drivers selected for the Balanced Scorecard will be specific to the organisation and linked to customers, stakeholders, internal business processes and financial measures. This ensures that key business stakeholders, i.e. investors, customers and employees, are recognised.

The use of the Balanced Scorecard provides a system that helps to measure the effect of human resource management on the organisation's competitive success.

Role of the personnel department

In most (but not all) organisations human resources management is the responsibility of the personnel department. The personnel officer is often a generalist, since the variety of issues typically dealt with in a personnel department is so diverse that no one person can master all aspects of the job. Such a personnel manager requires a working rather than a detailed knowledge of:

- the organisation, its products and the industry or sector in which it operates;
- production methods and organisational structure;
- pension schemes, wage and bonus arrangements;
- law relating to employment;
- the fundamentals of management theory and practice.

The mundane tasks of writing copy for job advertisements, organising training courses, keeping personnel records, operating wages systems, looking after health and safety at work arrangements, etc,. are known collectively as the **service function** of the personnel role. Other major personnel management functions are as follows:

The control function, comprising:

- analysis of key operational indices in the personnel field: labour turnover, wage costs, absenteeism and so on;
- monitoring labour performance (staff appraisal, for example);
- recommending appropriate remedial action to line managers.

The advisory function, whereby the personnel department offers expert advice on personnel policies and procedures, for example:

- which employees are ready for promotion;
- who should attend a certain training course;
- how a grievance procedure should be operated;
- interpretation of contracts of employment, health and safety regulations, etc.

Evaluating the effectiveness of a personnel department

Effective personnel management should feed through into improved organisational performance, higher productivity among employees, better customer service and hence increased long-term sales (Burn, 1996). Measuring the value of the short-run activities of a personnel department, however, can be problematic. Specific difficulties attached to the evaluation of the personnel function are that:

- since organisations operate in widely disparate commercial environments, wide differences in labour turnover, absenteeism, etc. are to be expected among firms engaged in similar lines of work;

■ personnel management is such a wide-ranging activity that it may not be appropriate to select just a handful of variables for appraisal.

Quantitative indices of a personnel department's work may be available in relation to:

■ unit labour costs compared to those in competing companies;

■ staff turnover;

■ absenteeism rates;

■ incidence of invocation of grievance procedures;

■ the proportion of the personnel department's staff that obtain professional qualifications;

■ number of days lost through strikes;

■ how long it takes to recruit a new employee;

■ successes achieved in the implementation of equal opportunities policies.

Subjective criteria include employee motivation, team spirit and willingness to accept change; the extent to which proposals emerging from the personnel department are accepted by senior management; the quality of relationships with trade unions; the calibre of job applicants responding to job advertisements; the usefulness of documents drafted by the department (job descriptions and person specifications, for example), and so on. Staff from other parts of the firm may be questioned in order to ascertain how they rate the personnel department in terms of such matters as:

■ how promptly it responds to requests for information or advice;

■ the quality of advice given by personnel department staff;

■ politeness and approachability of the department's members;

■ individual knowledge of technical personnel matters;

■ the department's overall contributions to the work of other sections.

Senior management may evaluate a personnel department's contributions on the basis of its ability to handle satisfactorily sensitive human relations problems arising from downsizing, organisational restructuring and the implementation of change. Also the personnel/human resources officer will be expected to make meaningful contributions to top management team decisions and to assist with strategic issues such as the formulation of mission statements, the determination of corporate culture, the facilitation of technological change, and so on.

Decentralisation and devolution

Many personnel and HRM functions can be undertaken by managers in local units rather than through a central personnel department. Note that the individuals completing such duties in subsidiaries, divisions, etc. might *themselves* be personnel specialists rather than general line managers, although in practice this is rare because of the duplication of effort involved. The main problem with devolution of personnel and/or HRM work to non-specialist line managers is that they may be neither competent nor interested in personnel or HRM issues, and may not be motivated to complete HRM duties properly, so that critically important personnel tasks are neglected. Bad HRM decisions lead to a poor corporate image, higher long-term costs and loss of output due to industrial conflict. Also line managers may focus all their attention on immediately pressing personnel problems at the expense of long-term HRM planning, and it can result in HRM considerations not influencing strategic management decisions.

Effective devolution requires:

- the provision of back-up services in relation to technical problems arising from contracts of employment, legal aspects of redundancy and dismissal, union recognition, etc. An outside consultancy might assume this role;
- acceptance by everyone that line managers' workloads will have to increase following their assumption of personnel responsibilities;
- the training of line managers in HRM techniques and concepts.

EUROPEAN UNION INFLUENCES

Following the UK general election of 1997 the incoming government announced its policy of positive engagement with the European Union (EU) and, in particular, that the UK would accept the European Social Charter. The latter originated during the 1987 Belgian Presidency of the EU's Council of Ministers. It was put forward as a suggested device for ensuring that basic employment rights would not be eroded following the intense business competition expected to occur in consequence of the completion of the single internal market. Further objectives were to encourage EU governments to harmonise national employment laws and practices and to confirm the EU's commitment to an active social policy. The Social Charter was intended as a grand gesture towards the EU's labour force, representing an unequivocal statement that *people* matter as well as business competition and that the interests of employees are just as important as those of firms.

The first draft of the Charter was published by the European Commission in May 1989 with the intention that each member state would implement its requirements at the national (rather than EU) level. Action would not be taken by the EU (via Directives, Regulations, etc.), provided the Charter's basic objectives could be effectively attained by member states or bodies within them.

Contents of the Social Charter

The basic rights to be established by the Charter were as follows:

- **Fair remuneration.** This would involve the specification of rules for establishing a fair wage.
- **Health, protection and safety at the workplace.**
- **Access to vocational training throughout a person's working life, including the right to retraining.**
- **Freedom of association and collective bargaining**, i.e. to belong or not belong to a trade union and for unions to have the right to bargain with employing firms.
- **Integration into working life of disabled people** – the provision of training for the disabled, accessibility to work premises, availability of special transport and explicit consideration of disabled people during the ergonomic design of equipment.
- **Information, consultation and worker participation in company decision making**, especially in enterprises that operate in more than one EU country.

- **Freedom of occupation, residence and movement of workers**, including equal treatment as regards local taxes and social security entitlements.
- **Improvement in living and working conditions.** This embraces equality of treatment for part-time and temporary workers, controls on night working, and requirements for weekly rest periods and paid holidays.
- **Social protection**, including adequate unemployment and other social security benefits.
- **Equal treatment of men and women.**
- **Protection of young people**, with a minimum working age of 15 years (16 for full-time employment) and a ban on night work for those under 18.
- **Reasonable living standards for senior citizens**, with a specified minimum income underwritten by the state.

There has recently been a wave of laws and regulations in the UK in the spirit of some of these basic objectives and, at time of writing, there are a good deal more in the pipeline. One effect of this may be to raise the profile of HR managers within organisations, as employers seek to ensure that they keep within the new laws and regulations (many of which came into force very quickly, despite being quite complicated).

Some of the more recent acts and statutory instruments that organisations have been affected by are the following:

- Data Protection Act 1998
- Employment Relations Act 1999
- Public Interest Disclosure Act 1998
- Working Time Regulations 1998 and 1999
- Maternity and Parental Leave, etc. Regulations 1999
- National Minimum Wage Act 1999
- Part-time workers (Prevention of less favourable treatment) Regulations 2000
- The Regulation of Investigatory Powers Act 2000
- Fixed-Term Employees (Prevention of less favourable treatment) Regulations 2002
- Employment Act 2002

The Human Rights Act 1998

This statute came into force in October 2000. It incorporates the provisions of the European Convention on Human Rights into UK law. Its Articles include the right to respect for private and family life, and the right to freedom of expression. Courts and tribunals must now interpret law in a way that is compatible with the Convention. If this does not prove possible, UK law takes precedence. In fact, the British have been able to enforce their rights under the Convention since 1951, but only in the appropriate European court, in Strasbourg.

Work–life balance

During the 1990s a culture of long hours and presentism (being seen to be staying late at work) developed until it became the norm. This has resulted in an increasing tension between an employee's family commitments and work responsibilities. These changes have important considerations for the development of HR policies.

Pressures pushing for improving changes in the work–life balance include compensation payments for stress caused by work pressures, an increase in the proportion of women returning to work following maternity leave, employees' expectation of work, the need to care for elderly adults and single-parent families. Flexible working patterns were initially highlighted to give firms a flexible workforce to meet changing customer requirements in Atkinson's flexible firm model (Atkinson, 1984). Political pressure from changes in European and UK law is also causing changes in the view of work–life balance. The best work–life balance depends on the individual's needs and changes with the various life stages.

Government backing for improved work–life balance for families

The government launched an improved ACAS helpline service in January 2003. It is designed to give help and guidance on family-friendly employment rights for both employers and parents. New employment measures became law on 6 April 2003, giving parents with children under six years or disabled children under 18 years the right to request to work flexibly, and to have that request considered seriously.

Although there is no right to flexible working, a refusal may result in a claim of indirect sex discrimination, so that the employer would have to show an objective reason to justify full-time working as a requirement and the refusal to permit part-time working (Willey, 2003). Maternity leave has been increased to 26 weeks paid and 26 weeks unpaid. Paternity leave has been set at two weeks paid leave to be taken within eight weeks of the birth. Adoption leave has been set to mirror the provision of maternity leave and pay as closely as possible.

SUMMARY

- Human resources are an organisation's most important asset and the effective management of human resources is a key determinant of an organisation's success. All managers who control others are necessarily involved in human resources management and thus require at least a rudimentary understanding of what the subject is about: its problems, possibilities and prospects, and how it relates to the organisation's strategy and management overall.

- Human resources are much more difficult to manage than material resources, partly because conflict often occurs between the employer's and employees' wishes and partly because, to an increasing extent, employees try to share in making decisions about their working environment. Management must recognise workers' aspirations, and harness and develop their innate abilities for the good of the organisation. Employees will not submit passively to manipulation or dictatorial control by management but more and more expect and demand some influence in the way they are employed. Research in the behavioural sciences shows that an appropriate response by management will benefit the organisation.

- HRM is much more than the application within an organisation of a set of management techniques. It is concerned with the wider implications of the management of change and not just with the effects of change on working practices. It seeks proactively to encourage flexible attitudes and the acceptance of new methods.

Review and discussion questions

1 *What is the definition of 'human resources management'? Explain the relationships between human resources management and personnel management.*

2 *Examine the training policies of an organisation. How effective are these policies and how could they be improved?*

CASE STUDY

Work–life balance

FT

Neil Walkingshaw, a vehicle mechanic, won lots of publicity when he successfully sued his former employer for refusing to let him work part-time to look after his baby son. So rare is it for a father to win a legal battle to cut his hours that the case last November was regarded as a landmark. The tribunal found that the John Martin Group had given 'no meaningful consideration' to Mr Walkingshaw's request, even though it had agreed to four female employees working part-time after having children. He was awarded £3700 compensation for sex discrimination.

The government hopes both fathers and mothers of young and disabled children will have an easier route to flexible working from next April, when a new parental right to request a change in hours to accommodate childcare comes into force.

The flexible working provisions, part of the Employment Act, make it a legal duty for employers to consider requests seriously and to justify any refusal by explaining why a change in working arrangements would harm the business.

Pauline Matthews, a lawyer in DLA's equality and diversity group, says employers should be preparing now. 'They should be getting the procedure in order, earmarking who is going to make the decisions and how they can accommodate requests.'

Parents are likely to ask for a wide range of options, including working from home, working part-time or flexitime and compressing a five-day week into three or four days. 'It's important to get men on board,' says Ms Matthews. 'Until men start doing [childcare] it's always going to be seen as women's responsibility – going part-time and on to the "mummy track".'

About 3.8 million parents – those with children under six or disabled children under 18 – will be eligi-

ble. Small business groups have protested about the cost and effort involved in processing requests and the threat of more employment tribunal cases. The government points to lower absenteeism and savings on recruitment costs from better staff retention.

But how much difference will the new right really make? Research to be published during National Work/Life Balance Week this week shows that nearly one in three fathers works more than the 48 hours specified by the Working Time Directive, with very long hours widespread among professionals and managers.

In most dual-income families, one or both parents frequently work atypical hours – at weekends, or before 8.30am and after 5.30pm on weekdays – according to the study* by the National Centre for Social Research, published by the Joseph Rowntree Foundation.

The key to whether parents find such working arrangements benefit or damage their family life is the amount of control they have over how, when and where they work. Parents in lower socioeconomic groups, especially fathers, are more likely to feel they have no option but to work during traditional 'family times' and have no scope to negotiate greater flexibility. Atypical work and limited access to childcare often make life particularly difficult for lone parents.

So the new right, while helping many families, may not be enough to assist parents whose position in the labour market is weak, the study says. By implication, these are the employees who most need statutory help.

Putting in a request for different hours can be hazardous. A survey of people contacting the Equal Opportunities Commission in 1999 found that more than half had their requests rejected or were offered unacceptable alternatives. One in three of those refused changes was either dismissed, made redundant or forced to resign.

One employer, cited in the study by the National Centre for Social Research, introduced shift work and made employees sign an agreement saying they did not mind what hours they worked. Employees felt they had to agree, in order to keep their jobs.

Lawyers see other potential weaknesses in the new provisions. Ann Bevitt of Morrison & Foerster, the US-based international law firm, says the clear procedure for employers and employees to follow is helpful. But some women returning from maternity leave may have difficulty with the requirement that employees explain how their employer could accommodate their request. 'If for whatever reason you're less able to express yourself well, that's putting quite a burden on you at a time when you may have been off work for up to a year and the organisation may have changed.'

Employees may not have information that could help their application, such as which other colleagues want to job-share. Sympathetic employers could provide such information at the meeting they must hold with the employee within 28 days of the request's being made, which must be followed by a decision within a further fortnight.

But employers opposed to flexible working are unlikely to change without adverse publicity and financial loss – and this is more likely under the Sex Discrimination Act than under the new legislation, says Ms Bevitt.

The flexible working provisions are designed to make tribunals a last resort, if recourse to an internal appeal and external arbitration fails.

Tribunals can rule only on whether the employer has followed the procedure correctly and explained the business case to the employee, not on the merits of that case, a point that has been welcomed by the Confederation of British Industry.

James Davies, employment partner at Lewis Silkin, says merely having to be seen to consider a request will not present much of an obstacle to a reluctant employer. 'It's a misnomer to suggest it's a right [for employee] because it's a right with little sanction.'

However, Ian Taylor, employment partner at Bird & Bird, believes employers will have to think carefully about the business reasons for turning down a request.

The allowable reasons include: an additional cost burden; an inability to reorganise work among existing staff or to recruit more staff; and an adverse impact on quality or the ability to meet customer demand.

'An employee may present a complaint to the tribunal that the decision by the employer to reject the request was based on incorrect facts,' says Mr Taylor. 'As an employer, you're going to have to produce the evidence to support your decision.'

Consultation on the draft regulations, including the maximum compensation to be awarded by tribunals, ends on October 10 (www.dti.gov.uk/er/FlexConsultation.pdf), with parliamentary approval expected around the end of the year.

The government wants more than 80 per cent of requests to be agreed and will review the legislation after three years. 'This is a very significant first step,' says Julie Mellor, chair of the EOC. 'I hope they'll be able to open it to parents of school-age children in the future.'

*Happy Families? Atypical work and its influence on family life. Free summary of findings available at www.jrf.org.uk

Source: Extract from Alison Maitland (2002) 'The Future of Family Friendly Workplaces: The Work–Life Balance', *Financial Times*, 23 September, p 16.

REFERENCES AND FURTHER READING

Atkinson, J (1984) 'Manpower strategies for flexible organisations', *Personnel Management*, 16(8), 28(24): 28–31.

Becker, B E, Huselid, M A, Ulrich, D (2001) *The HR Scorecard: Linking People, Strategy, and Performance*, Boston MA: Harvard Business School Press.

Beer, M, Spector, B A, Lawrence, P R and Walton, R E (1985) *Human Resource Management*, New York: Free Press.

Bernardin, H J and Russel, J (1993) *Human Resource Management: An Experimental Approach*, Maidenhead: McGraw-Hill.

Boerlijst, G and Meijboom, G (1989) 'Matching the Individual and the Organisation', in Herriot, P. (ed.), *Assessment and Selection in Organisations: Methods and Practice for Recruitment and Appraisal*, Chichester: Wiley.

Boxall, P and Purcell, J (2003) *Strategy and Human Resource Management*, Basingstoke: Palgrave Macmillan.

Burn, D (1996) *Benchmarking the Human Resources Function*, Hutchin Technical Communication.

Cherrington, D J (1995) *The Management of Human Resources*, (4th edn), Hemel Hempstead: Prentice Hall International.

Coussey, M (2000) *Getting the Right Work–Life Balance: Implementing Family Friendly Practices*, London: Chartered Institute of Personnel and Development.

Cressey, P (1998) 'European Works Councils in Practice', *Human Resource Management Journal*, 8 (1): 67–79.

Duddington, J (2003) *Employment Law*, Harlow: Pearson Education.

▶

European Commission (1991) 'Protection of the dignity of women and men at work', Commission Recommendation 92/131/EEC of 27 November 1991, *Official Journal* 49 of 24.02.1992.

Ferris, G R and Buckley, R M (1996) *Human Resources Management: Context, Functions and Outcomes*, Hemel Hempstead: Prentice Hall.

Fletcher, C and Williams, R (1992) 'The Route to Performance Management', *Personnel Review*, 24 (10): 42–7.

Fraser, J M (1954) *A Handbook of Employment Interviewing*, London: Macdonald & Evans.

Graham, H T and Bennett, R (1998) *Human Resources Management*, (9th edn), London: FT Pitman Publishing.

Greenberg, J and Baron, R A (1997) *Behaviour in Organisations: Understanding and Managing the Human Side of Work*, Hemel Hempstead: Prentice Hall.

Guest, D (1987) 'Human Resource Management and Industrial Relations', *Journal of Management Studies*, 24 (5): 503–21.

Ham, J van, Paauwe, J and Williams, R (1986) 'Personnel Management in a Changed Environment', *Personnel Review*, 15 (3): 3–17.

Harrison, R (2002) *Learning and Development* (3rd edn), London: Chartered Institute of Personnel and Development.

Johnson, R W and Neumark, D (1997) 'Age Discrimination, Job Separations, and Employment Status of Older Workers', *Journal of Human Resources*, 32 (4): 779–811.

Kinnie, N and Lowe, D (1990) 'Performance Related Pay on the Shop Floor', *Personnel Management*, 21 (11): 45–9.

Legge, K (1989) 'Human Resource Management: A Critical Analysis', in Storey, J. (ed.), *New Perspectives on Human Resource Management*, London: Routledge.

Leopold, J (2002) *Human Resources in Organisations*, Harlow: FT Prentice Hall.

McGregor, D (1957) 'An Uneasy Look at Performance Appraisal', *Harvard Business Review*, 35 (3).

Patterson, M G, West, M A, Lawthorn R and Nickell, S (1997) *Impact of People Management Practices on Business Performance*, London: Chartered Institute of Personnel and Development.

Pedler, M, Burgoyne, J and Boydell, T (1991) *The Learning Company: A Strategy for Sustainable Development*, New York: McGraw-Hill.

Pettigrew, A and Whipp, R (1991) *Managing Change for Competitive Success*, Oxford: Blackwell.

Philpott, L and Sheppard, L (1992) 'Managing for Improved Performance', in Armstrong, M (ed.), *Strategies for Human Resource Management*, London: Kogan Page.

Pilbeam, S and Corbridge, M (2002) *People Resourcing: HRM in Practice*, (2nd edn), Harlow: FT Prentice Hall.

Plender, J (1997) 'Bullies in the Boardroom', *Financial Times*, 15 July.

Reid, M A and Barrington, H (1999) *Training Interventions: Promoting Learning Opportunities* (6th edn), London: Chartered Institute of Personnel and Development.

Rodger, A (1952) *The Seven Point Plan*, London: National Institute of Industrial Psychology.

Schneier, C E, Shaw, D G and Beatty, R W (1991) 'Performance Measurement and Management: A Tool for Strategy Execution', *Human Resource Management*, 30 (4): 279–303.

Schuler, R S (1992) 'Linking People with the Strategic Needs of Business', *Organisational Dynamics*, Summer: 18–32.

Schuler, R S and Walker, J W (1990) 'Human Resources Strategy: Focusing on Issues and Actions', *Organisational Dynamics*, Summer: 5–19.

Senge, P M (1990) *The Fifth Discipline: The Art and Practice of The Learning Organization*, New York: Doubleday.

Stroh, C K and Caliguiri, P M (1998) 'Strategic Human Resources: A New Source of Competitive Advantage in the Global Arena', *International Journal of Human Resource Management*, 9 (1): 1–17.

Walton, J (1999) *Strategic Human Resource Development*, Harlow: FT Prentice Hall.

Willey, B (2003) *Employment Law in Context: An Introduction for HR Professionals* (2nd edn), Harlow: FT Prentice Hall.

WEBSITES

http://www.hr2000.com/
HR Online. A popular and developing page which presents the services of a good range of HR consultants. Some 90 per cent is offered free.

http://www.acas.org.uk
Advisory, Conciliation and Arbitration Service (ACAS). Information and advice on employment law.

http://cre.gov.uk
The Commission for Racial Equality. Much useful information about relevant legislation, press releases, the benefits of ethnic diversity and the role of the CRE.

http://www.eoc.org.uk
The Equal Opportunities Commission. Clear explanations of relevant legislation, current issues, the role of the EOC and the latest press releases.

http://www.dti.gov.uk/er/index.htm
The Department of Trade and Industry. Information on a wide range of issues affecting people at work.

http://www.ipd.co.uk
Chartered Institute of Personnel and Development. An example of a service only available by subscription:

CHAPTER 12

The challenge of motivating others

DOMINIC COOPER

Outcomes

The objective of this chapter is to introduce the concept of motivation and explore ways to manage motivation to positively affect human performance for the good of the organisation. Having read this chapter, you will be able to understand:

- the major work motivation theories
- the psychological and situational factors that affect people's behaviour
- the characteristics common to all motivation theories
- the application of motivational concepts in the workplace
- the constraints to motivating others

INTRODUCTION

When we talk about motivation, we often mean 'why do people act in particular ways, and/or how can I get them to act in certain ways? Much evidence from the behavioural sciences indicates that ability and motivation combine to influence performance. In the behavioural sciences, motivation refers to a psychological concept that is primarily concerned with increasing the **strength** and **direction** of people's work-related behaviours to influence the quality and quantity of people's performance output.

Theories of motivation have been the subject of much debate since the early 1940s, and chronologically have broadly focused upon:

- **genetic and hereditary factors** (e.g. Maslow's hierarchy of relative prepotency);
- **people's needs, personality and interests** (e.g. McClelland's managerial needs theory);
- **organisational justice and fairness** (e.g. Adams' equity theory);
- **incentives and rewards** (e.g. Vroom's expectancy theory);
- **behavioural change** (e.g. Luthans and Kreitner's organisational behaviour management);
- **the design of people's jobs** (e.g. Hackman and Oldham's job characteristics model);
- **setting targets** (e.g. Locke and Latham's goal-setting theory);
- **role modelling and self-efficacy** (e.g. Bandura's social learning theory).

Early work on work motivation attempted to address the question: Can work motivation make a difference to work performance? By the mid-1980s development work had shifted the emphasis to a more practical viewpoint by attempting to discover *how* the various factors of the different theories affect people's motivation and subsequent task-performance. This focus on the more practical aspects led to their effectiveness being assessed on the basis of their usefulness to managers and practitioners. Such evaluations consistently rated behaviour management and goal-setting theory as the two most valid and effective work motivation theories, closely followed by expectancy theory, social learning theory and equity theory, suggesting that positive reinforcements, goals, expectancies, social learning, participation and enriched jobs are the main factors that *actually* motivate people to perform well (Pinder, 1984).

Because every employee is motivated to some end or other, it is nonsense to talk about an unmotivated person. In reality, it is often the case that employees are simply directing their energies to achieve different aims. This type of behaviour tends to puzzle managers who often ask why it is that some employees do not invest their energies in the way that is desired. Broadly speaking this is often due to unclear expectations, a failure to align employees' goals with that of the organisation, a poor history of recognising good performance and a poor supportive working environment. Often these factors combine to demotivate a previously motivated person.

Although significant levels of monetary compensation can always be used to motivate people in the short term, it must be stressed at the outset that there are no easy solutions or magic formulas that can be applied to motivate people to improve performance over the longer term. Nonetheless, the various motivational theories go a long way towards helping us understand why people behave in the way they do. Armed with such knowledge, managers should be better placed to direct employee behaviour for the good of the organisation.

One of the first things to realise is that people's motivation is dynamic: it needs constant nurturing as it can be positively or negatively affected by so many day-to-day features of organisational life. Importantly, one negative feature (e.g. a bullying manager) can outweigh ten positives features (e.g. an enriched job, etc.). Some of the factors proven to influence people's motivation are:

→ Ch. 2

- **a manager's leadership style** (*see* Chapter 2)
- **the degree of autonomy and authority allowed**
- **the degree of managerial and organisational support exhibited**
- **the amount of stress or distress experienced at work**
- **the opportunities for growth and advancement**
- **the amount of personal satisfaction people derive from their job**
- **the degree to which people are committed to their organisation or career.**

Each of these factors has been linked with specific work behaviours such as performance, absenteeism, tenure, turnover and organisational citizenship. In practice, attention to such factors is often overlooked because line managers are primarily interested in achieving short-term (e.g. monthly) production performance outcomes, set by middle or senior management. However, this can create many motivational problems that surface in substandard performance.

Influencing factors

It is well known that psychological attributes such as disposition, temperament, intelligence, abilities and skill exert large influences on people's behaviour. It is less well known that approximately 80 per cent of people's behaviour is determined entirely by situational factors. This can be illustrated by a confident, dominant person's behaviour during a selection process at an assessment centre. During leaderless group-discussion exercises, where each candidate was being assessed on his or her leadership potential, interpersonal skills, problem solving and business awareness, the person was extremely forceful to the extent that he completely dominated the proceedings. Conversely, during the selection interview the person was quiet and deferential as he deferred to the interviewer's persistent questioning. Thus, the two different situations faced by the candidate altered the way the person behaved: in the leaderless group discussion the person's disposition to dominate was allowed free rein, whereas the power relationships between the selector and candidate completely restrained the candidate's dominating behaviour. Importantly, a person's behaviour can also alter a situation. An extreme example might be that of the collapse of Barings, the British merchant bank brought about by Nick Leeson's fraudulent behaviour in the Tokyo stock markets in the mid-1990s. The types of situational factor that will influence people's behaviour in the workplace are:

- **other people**
- **the type of work a person does**
- **the presence and quality of the management control systems**
- **the effectiveness of organisational communication systems**

■ the types and effectiveness of various reward systems
■ the working environment (e.g. office or factory)
■ the size of the organisation in which they work
■ the prevailing organisational culture.

→ Chs 14
and 20

In normal circumstances, the most important situational features at work tend to be other people. This was aptly illustrated in the famous 'Hawthorne' studies conducted in the Hawthorne plant of the Western Electric Company in Chicago (Roethlisberger and Dickson, 1939) (*see also* Chapters 14 and 20). In the Bank Wiring Observation Room the work groups had established an output 'norm' averaging 6000 units per day. This 'unofficial' production norm was enforced by various methods. Workers would give each other verbal warnings or resort to physical violence to prevent 'rate-busting' (producing too much) or chiselling (producing too little). Another behavioural 'norm' was that inspectors should not be officious or pull rank on the workers. One inspector who violated this 'norm' was ostracised by all the workers and subjected to vindictive pranks until he requested a transfer to a different department. This example reinforces the point that the situation people find themselves in, their personal psychological qualities and their ongoing behaviour all interact to reciprocally determine the way that work is done. These reciprocal relationships are illustrated by the framework in Figure 12.1, which is derived from social learning theory (Bandura, 1986).

In this triadic framework, behaviour is a function of both person and situational variables. Behaviour also exerts a reciprocal influence on both situational and personal factors. The reciprocal impact of each element on the others does not always take place immediately. A change in any one element may take time to exert its reciprocal influence on the other two. For example, the impact of changing the design of a job (situational) may immediately impact people's work-related behaviour, but not positively influence their motivation for six months or more. It is unfortunate, but

Figure 12.1 Bandura's model of reciprocal determinism

Source: Bandura, Albert, *Social Foundations of Thought and Action: A Social Cognitive Theory* © 1986, pp 22–5. Adapted by permission of Prentice-Hall, Upper Saddle River, New Jersey.

true, that many good workplace improvement efforts have been abandoned because of unrealistic expectations of immediate results that did not materialise. When trying to motivate others, it is clear that a manager must take all three elements of this framework, and the time factor, into account if the effort is to be successful.

Person factors

The extent to which person or dispositional variables help to reciprocally determine behaviour in organisations can best be illustrated with the psychological concept of **job satisfaction**. Job satisfaction is an all-embracing concept that refers to job-related attitudes about various job-related characteristics, such as pay and reward policies, leadership behaviours, management styles, co-workers, etc. Attitudes about these factors are important because they are frequently seen as the precursor of employee turnover. By way of example, Jenkins (1993) studied power plant workers and found that people's disposition to self-monitor their performance predicted their intention to quit. Job satisfaction predicted the turnover of those high in self-monitoring, whereas organisational commitment predicted the turnover intentions of those low in self-monitoring behaviour. Much of the research on job satisfaction has been concerned with showing the influence of situational and dispositional factors (*see* Warr, 1996). The work of Boudreau *et al.* (2001) provides a good example of this. They examined the role of personality and cognitive ability on the job search process of almost 1900 high-level US business executives. Situational variables used in the study were organisational success (whether or not the company achieved its strategic goals), salary levels and tenure (length of time in job). They discovered that extroverted individuals (disposition) experienced greater job satisfaction. However, in companies that had been successful in reaching their strategic goals over the previous two years (situational), these same people were more likely to search for new jobs. It was also found that cognitive ability was related to both salary and greater job search, suggesting that organisations need to recognise higher intelligence through greater compensation packages and letting these people know they are highly valued if they want to keep them. The case study outlined in Exhibit 12.1 further demonstrates how dispositional and situational factors might interact to affect performance.

Other evidence to support the stability of personal qualities and their origins was provided by Arvey *et al.* (1989), who were also interested in job satisfaction. This study involved the use of 34 pairs of twins who were reared apart from an early age. The results indicated that there is a significant genetic component to job satisfaction, in so far as people inherit a tendency to view the world in an emotionally negative or positive way. Those who view the world in an emotionally negative way are less likely to be satisfied in their jobs than those who interpret events in a more positive way. This spills over into the way we view our working environment and affects our attitudes and motivation towards our job or work, and may even influence the type of work an individual seeks and finds. Evidence provided by Levin and Stokes (1989) confirms these relationships. They conducted a laboratory study with 140 subjects and a field study with 315 staff from a professional services company. In both studies, the results showed a small but significant link between negative emotions and job satisfaction. However, the presence of certain job characteristics was shown to exert the largest effects on job satisfaction, demonstrating that a motivating environment will exert much larger effects on performance than dispositional factors. This proposition

Exhibit 12.1   Interacting effects of dispositional and situational factors

Mount *et al.* (1998) investigated the relationship between people's disposition and jobs involving interpersonal interactions in the workplace. The study was based on the changing needs in the workplace where more jobs are becoming service-oriented rather than manufacturing-based, and on the drive in manufacturing towards teamworking. In both situations interpersonal skills are important to effective job performance: Service-oriented settings typically involve an employee engaging in one-on-one interactions with customers and clients. The primary interactions in manufacturing are among co-workers in co-operative team-based situations.

The investigators analysed 11 studies that made use of the Personal Characteristics Inventory (PCI), which utilises the 'big-five' factor model of personality and measures the constructs of:

- **conscientiousness** (e.g. responsible, dependable, persistent and achievement-oriented);
- **extraversion** (e.g. sociable, talkative and assertive);
- **emotional stability** (e.g. calm, secure and relaxed);
- **openness to experience** (e.g. imaginative, artistically sensitive and intellectual);
- **agreeableness** (e.g. good-natured, co-operative and trusting).

The jobs involved in the 11 studies ranged from counsellors, telemarketers and customer service representatives to teams of people involved in warehouse operations, production and delivery. The job performance of these people was rated by their own managers on two dimensions: overall job performance and the quality of interactions with others.

The initial analyses for all 11 studies indicated that the conscientiousness personality construct positively correlated with the job performance ratings in both service and manufacturing environments. This finding is consistent with much previous research that finds it a useful measure for predicitng overall job performance in a variety of settings. When the 11 studies were analysed by service orientation or team-working using the quality of interaction job ratings, it became apparent that emotional stability and agreeableness predicted job performance in teamworking. Conscientiousness and agreeableness predicted the job performance of those in service-oriented environments.

These results indicate that the type of work setting (one-on-one versus teams) interacts with people's disposition (personality) reciprocally to determine their job performance.

Source: Mount *et al.* (1998).

was confirmed in work conducted by Orpen (1994) with 135 employees from three financial services companies. He found that a lack of autonomy for highly motivated people adversely affected both job satisfaction and performance.

Situational factors

The influence of situational factors on behaviour and job-related attitudes was demonstrated by Clegg and Wall (1990) in a British electronics factory. They showed that people's mental health was directly associated with the complexity of people's jobs: simple jobs were associated with poor mental health, and highly complex jobs were associated with better mental health. Initial results suggested small differences between the two levels of mental health. The differences became much larger when dispositional factors were also considered. Those with lower levels of skill use, in a simple job, engaged in frequent daydreaming and consistently exhibited poorer levels of mental health. In contrast, those individuals who did complex jobs using a wider range of skills had much better levels of mental health. This study and others demonstrate the complexity of the interactions between person and situational factors. For example, Kohn and Schooler (1982) conducted a longitudinal study with a cohort of men to examine the relationship between a person's disposition and choice of occupation. People who could view problems from many perspectives were attracted to jobs where they could use their intellectual skills. In turn, their intellectual skills improved because of the kind of work they were doing. The more these skills improved, the more they tended to seek out even more intellectually demanding jobs. Similarly, Boswell *et al.* (2003) conducted a longitudinal study to examine the organisational and job attributes important to job choice and the impact of situational features on graduate job-seekers' decisions. They found that company culture, challenging work, compensation package and geographical location influenced both accept and reject decisions. Advancement opportunities were also important to those who accepted, but not important to those who rejected, job offers.

The above body of evidence demonstrates how person and situational variables interact to affect motivation, performance and other work-related behaviour. It makes sense, therefore, to match job demands with people's skills and abilities. The results of seven case studies (shown in Table 12.1) conducted by Caldwell and O'Reilly (1990) in a variety of organisations showed that where the person and the situation were well matched in terms of skills, abilities, job demands and so forth, motivation, performance and job satisfaction were also high. Conversely, work by Stadler (1994) and Balliod and Semner (1994) in a two-year study of turnover among computer specialists showed that where person–job fit was low, organisational commitment and job satisfaction were also low. In all instances, leaving was preceded by low job satisfaction. Only when changes in job design led to an improvement in job satisfaction did people stay with the organisation. Such findings are reinforced by work conducted in Australia, with accountants, bankers, occupational therapists and call-centre staff (BrKich *et al.*, 2002). They found that job-fit was predic-

Table 12.1 **The effects of matching people to jobs**

ORGANISATION	JOB	CORRELATIONS OF PERSON–JOB FIT WITH JOB PERFORMANCE
Consumer products	Production supervisors	0.98
Insurance company	Claims adjustment supervisors	0.60
Utility company	Senior finance managers	0.53
	Senior engineering managers	0.65
Computer manufacturers	Production supervisors	0.85
Computer distributor	Sales representatives	0.35
University	Departmental secretaries	0.53

Source: Caldwell and O'Reilly (1990). Copyright © 1990 by the American Psychological Association. Adapted with permission.

tive of both job satisfaction and organisational commitment. This body of work demonstrates that job-fit has a very strong impact on people's motivation and performance. Within everyday practical constraints, therefore, managers should do their best to ensure that the demands of a job match a person's skills and ability. Organisational change initiatives that introduce teamworking often provide such opportunities.

MOTIVATION THEORIES

In line with the triadic framework, the following addresses the major work-based motivation theories from two perspectives: from dispositional motivation theories or from situational motivation theories. Although none of them completely explains motivation, each of them serves to provide different routes to improve performance.

Dispositional motivation theories

Theories focused on dispositional factors are divided into either content or process theories. Content theories concentrate on what motivates people by attempting to develop an understanding of fundamental human needs. Conversely, process theories are more concerned with how motivation is aroused and maintained.

Content theories

Maslow's 'hierarchy of relative prepotency'

Abraham Maslow, an American organisational psychologist, attempted the first classification of human needs to explain how people's motivation changes over time. As shown in Figure 12.2, Maslow's (1942), thesis is that human needs can be classified into motivating factors that influence people's behaviour at various stages of their lives. He described this as 'a hierarchy of relative prepotency', but it is more often termed the 'hierarchy of needs'. In essence, Maslow's theory postulates that people have five basic needs and that their growth as people depends upon satisfying each of them. In order of importance these needs are:

1. To be fed, clothed and sheltered – basic physiological needs
2. To feel safe from threats – safety and security needs
3. To be accepted by other people – social needs
4. To feel valued by self and others – self-esteem needs
5. To be self-fulfilled or successful – self-actualisation needs.

Although a useful way of describing various types of motivator, the 'hierarchy of needs' theory is weak in several respects:

1. **The five needs are not uniformly motivating**. At any given moment, different people are likely to be striving to fulfil different need levels. This presents a problem for managers, in that if each worker has a different hierarchy of needs, how does a manager provide motivators for all his or her staff?
2. **The model asserts that one motive should predominate at any one moment in time.** However, humans are more complex than this. For example, people work simultaneously to attain pay and rewards (security), social contact (belonging), status (self-esteem), etc.

Figure 12.2 Maslow's hierarchy of relative prepotency

Source: Maslow (1942)

3. **The hierarchy is difficult to relate to work processes.** People do not necessarily satisfy their higher-order needs through their jobs or occupations. Many people prefer to satisfy their needs outside the workplace, for example through leisure activities.

4. **The hierarchy does not recognise situational factors.** The simplicity of the hierarchy does not reflect the reality that behaviour in the real world is shaped by situational pressures and controls that are often beyond a person's individual control.

Hierarchical need theories are flawed because they propose that everyone's needs are organised in the same order, and that everybody strives for the same fundamental goals such as self-actualisation. Everyday experience suggests that people are more varied and complex than this, and operate at many different motivational levels in these types of hierarchy. This can present many problems for employers as it is very difficult to satisfy all employees' needs simultaneously. Other problems reside in the fact that situational factors such as managerial policies and practices, an organisation's structure, the type of technology used and the external environment all influence our needs. Any motivational theory that proposes strong similarities between people can only lead to the conclusion that there is 'one best way' to manage and motivate others, which is simply not true.

Despite such problems, the theory remains popular with many human resource professionals, perhaps because the theory provides easy guidelines to follow. On this basis, managers should try to ensure that (1) pay levels are commensurate with people's experience, skills, abilities and responsibilities so that they can clothe, feed and house themselves comfortably, (2) that the workplace is safe and that there is a reasonable level of job security, (3) that opportunities for socialisation are developed (e.g. teamworking) so that people can interact with others, (4) people are recognised for their contribution to performance so that they feel valued, and (5) advancement opportunities are available to all. Importantly, each of these is known to increase people's work motivation. In practical terms, you should try to satisfy all these needs, but starting at the bottom of the hierarchy first. After all there is not much point trying to motivate people by satisfying their 'self-esteem' needs, if they have not yet satisfied the basic needs for food, clothes and housing.

Individual differences in motivational needs

Many early need theories were also flawed because they failed to take account of people's individual differences, an issue addressed by McClelland's (1961) 'managerial needs' theory. McClelland conducted research with over 500 managers from 25 different US corporations to determine just what motivates a good manager. Upon the basis of this research he argues that managers possess three basic motivational needs: achievement, affiliation and power that have been socially acquired or learnt. Unlike Maslow's hierarchy of needs, each of these three levels of needs has been demonstrably linked to both job satisfaction and competence in a number of occupations, particularly management (Medcof and Hausdorf, 1995).

Need for achievement

According to McClelland, the need for achievement (nAch), or the desire to do something better or more efficiently than it has been done before, is one of the keys to economic growth. Those who are high in nAch are people who prefer personal responsibility, positively enjoy competition, like to set, strive for and reach difficult goals, like to take calculated risks, like immediate short-term feedback on their performance and work hard until they attain excellence. Not surprisingly, in the workplace, those scoring highly on nAch are often attracted to an entrepreneurial role. McClelland suggests that people high on this motive are likely to have grown up in environments which expected competence of them, gave them independence at an early age and evaluated them highly. People low on nAch are more satisfied when jobs involve little challenge, but have a high probability of success. A great deal of work has been conducted on the achievement motivation of managers. In essence, the results show that companies whose executives have high achievement motivation produce better results. This is particularly true in an entrepreneurial rather than a bureaucratic organisation. For example, McClelland examined the motives of 51 technical entrepreneurs and calculated the growth rate of their companies in terms of the value of their sales. The growth rate of those companies led by entrepreneurs with high nAch was almost 250 per cent higher than companies led by entrepreneurs with moderate needs for achievement. Other research (Cooper *et al.* 1994) has reported that three out of four studies found a positive relationship between nAch and the success of small enterprises.

Need for affiliation

During the course of his work, McClelland found that some major figures in industry did not score highly on nAch as he had expected. He reasoned that as a large part of working life in organisations was concerned with co-ordinating the activity of others, the ability to relate to others was an important component of being a manager. He proposed that those who have this ability are high on need for affiliation (nAff), and that these people strive for approval from both their subordinates and superiors. Consequently, those high on nAff are sensitive to the needs of others. Such people are often found in people-oriented service jobs, as opposed to managerial or administrative positions (Smither and Lindgren, 1978). It has been suggested that there are two forms of nAff, one more managerially effective than the other.

The first, **affiliative assurance**, is best described as a striving for close relationships, due to the perceived security that they provide. Such a person tends to look for continual approval, and is anxious about possible rejection. In other words, these managers want to be liked. These managers will expend a lot of energy on maintaining relationships, at the expense of getting the job done. Generally speaking, those high on affiliative assurance would rather hang on to team members than see them promoted, which may result in them showing favouritism towards some.

The second, **affiliative interest**, is best described as a care and concern for the feelings of others, but not at the expense of getting the job done. It is a concern for the legitimate needs and feelings of others while remaining focused on performance delivery, which is the type of affiliation that will lead to greater organisational effectiveness.

Need for power

McClelland also discovered that a good manager was high in interpersonal skills. This was combined with a need to influence people for the good of the organisation by being in control of events, forcefully expressing opinions and being the leader. In other words, these people had a greater need for power (nPow) than the need to achieve or need to be liked. A need for power, however, has both positive and negative aspects. The positive side shows itself as an interest in persuasion and interpersonal influence. The negative side shows itself as an unsocialised concern for personal dominance at the expense of others. The aspect that dominates is determined by the degree of self-control or activity inhibition a manager possesses. Managers with a high degree of self-control will satisfy their need for power in socially acceptable ways via interpersonal influencing skills. These managers tend to be committed to organisational goals, want to serve others and, rather than dominate employees, they try to make them feel that they too have power. In contrast, managers who are more concerned with personal power show little signs of self-control and tend to exercise their power impulsively and in a haphazard manner. This inconsistency creates many difficulties for the manager's subordinates and can lead to major productivity problems.

Another important line of research arose from the work of McClelland: the leadership motive pattern. Achievement motivation is usually measured alongside the motives for power and for affiliation. McClelland noted that a certain pattern enabled people to be effective managers at the highest levels in an organisation. For senior managers, success tended to be associated with low levels of affiliation motive and a moderate to high need for power together with an ability to inhibit spontaneous impulses (i.e. good self-control). However, with lower-level managers, success was related to a combination of a high need for both power and achievement. These findings have been supported by other researchers (*see* Exhibit 12.2), who have found that those scoring high on both nPow and nAch exhibited better managerial performance and had a higher promotion rate than others. The opposite was true for those who scored low on these needs. As a whole, these findings suggest that a manager's motivating potential appears to be predictive of effective managerial behaviour, which has obvious implications for personnel selection and placement practices (*see* Cooper *et al.*, 2003).

McClelland's work is important as it recognises that people have different needs. Although his findings are extremely useful for selection purposes, in line with other need theories, McClelland does not specify the motivational links between a manager's individual needs and actual performance. Indeed, attempts to link nAch with

Exhibit 12.2 A test of McClelland's managerial needs model

Much of the early research on managerial motivation was conducted with the Thematic Apperception Test (TAT) which involves people writing stories about a series of pictures. Unfortunately, the TAT was later found to be both unreliable and invalid. Because of these problems, Stahl (1983) used the Job Choice Exercise (JCE) to re-examine McClelland's concepts of managerial motivation. The JCE requires respondents to make 24 decisions about the attractiveness of jobs in motivational terms (i.e. nPow, nAch, nAff). In seven separate distributions, the JCE was administered to a total of 1741 respondents that included managers and shopfloor workers from a variety of industries, as well as students and Air Force cadets.

Examining the data in a number of different ways, Stahl showed that respondents who scored above 3.14 on nPow and 4.64 on nAch exhibited better levels of job performance, had a higher promotion rate than others and were more likely to be managers than shopfloor workers. The opposite was found for those with lower scores for nPow and nAch.

These findings supported the work of McClelland, who had asserted that 'power is the great motivator' for senior executives. Stahl, however, found that this also held for middle and junior managers. Thus, McClelland's model of managerial needs appears to apply to all managerial levels.

performance have generally been unsuccessful. Matsui *et al.* (1982), for example, found that although nAch positively correlated with people's tendency to set goals, nAch did not actually correlate with performance. Not surprisingly, it was found that the goals themselves were related to performance. Thus, nAch appears to be indirectly related to performance, in so far as those high in nAch are likely to set goals. In turn, it is the actual goals that affect performance (*see* the section on goal setting later in the chapter). This latter finding is confirmed in more recent work, using Alderfer's (1969) ERG needs theory that explored the link between Existence, Relatedness and Growth needs, self-esteem and job performance in a South African study (Arnolds and Boshoff, 2002). This study showed that esteem and growth needs were clearly linked to performance intentions (goals). Self-esteem refers to the extent to which a person likes themselves, and views themselves as a valuable and worthy member of society. Early work (Korman, 1970, 1976) suggested that those with high levels of self-esteem will perform better than those with low self-esteem. More recent work appears to confirm this view. Using meta-analytic techniques to review the extant literature on self-esteem and performance, Judge and Bono (2001) found a significant relationship (r=0.26) between self-esteem and job performance. This relationship was tested with 124 insurance sales personnel in a field setting by Erez and Judge (2001). They found that self-esteem significantly correlated with sales volume, activity level, goal setting and goal commitment. However, the correlations were much larger for goal setting (r=0.33) and goal commitment (0.49). All self-esteem and nAch studies therefore point to the fact that those high on these attributes are more likely to set goals to increase their performance, and that it is these goals that affect performance directly, not the personal attributes *per se*. Instead, the personal attributes appear to affect the degree to which people commit themselves to goal achievement.

Such results indicate that managers should motivate others by setting a series of increasingly difficult task goals, in conjunction with the people concerned, to increase their commitment to achieving the goals. The effects of this will lead to greater performance improvements over a period of time. The more the person achieves a goal, the more the person will value themselves, which in turn will lead to higher levels of self-esteem and a higher commitment to achieving more difficult goals. The old adage 'success breeds success' is the underlying philosophy here. Other ways to increase self-esteem include managers communicating their confidence in the person's ability to achieve tasks (Rosenthal, 2002), and conducting 'self-esteem' workshops (e.g. Holstein, 1997) whereby employees learn to think positively and conduct personal SWOT analyses (*see* Chapter 4) to identify their strengths and weaknesses with a view to identifying training needs so that they can take advantage of advancement opportunities and overcome any threats to career progression. Outward Bound courses are another approach known to increase self-esteem (Clements *et al.*, 1995).

→ Ch. 4

Process theories

An alternative and complementary approach to understanding motivation lies in examining the psychological processes that are involved in motivation. Process theories recognise that people have different competing needs; that behaviour is a function of both the person and the situation; that people are decision-making organisms; and that any decisions made are based on the link between behaviour and outcomes. Thus, as Figure 12.3 makes clear, process approaches recognise that there is a direct link between effort, performance and outcomes.

In essence, the process approach to motivation proposes that people will direct their efforts towards goals that they value. However, while the existence of a valued goal is a necessary condition for action, on its own it is not a sufficient condition: people will only act if they have a reasonable expectation that their actions will lead to the desired goals and the benefits that flow from reaching the goals are of significant value.

Expectancy theory

The important role of these characteristics for motivating human behaviour was explicitly recognised by Vroom (1964) in his **expectancy model theory** of motivation. The model states that motivation (M) is a function of the expectancy (E) of reaching a certain outcome, multiplied by the value (V) of the outcome for that person:

$$\text{Motivation} = \text{Expectancy} \times \text{Value}$$

Vroom's theory predicts that outcomes which have a high expectancy of being reached (e.g. sale of five cars a week) and the rewards of which are highly valued (e.g. extra commission) will direct people to exert much greater effort in their task. Conversely, outcomes with high expectations (e.g. promotion) and neutral or even

Figure 12.3 Expectancy theory relationships

disliked values (e.g. working away from home) will reduce the amount of effort the person is prepared to invest. Similarly, outcomes with relatively low expectancies of being reached (e.g. zero accidents on a construction site) and neutral valuations (e.g. no perceived personal benefits) will not have an influence on a person's level of motivation. In a sense, therefore, Vroom's expectancy theory is hedonistic. People will only decide how much effort they are going to put into their work according to what they perceive they are going to get out of it and according to how much they value the potential outcomes.

More recent refinements (*see* Heckhausen *et al.*, 1985, for an excellent review) have extended Vroom's original theory to include an instrumentality component, based on a division of expectancy into two separate parts:

■ **the perceived probability of achieving the expected outcome**

■ **the perceived probability of actually being rewarded for achieving the expected outcome.**

Instrumentality is concerned with the latter. The heart of the issue here is the extent to which good performance is actually recognised and rewarded, and whether the rewards on offer adequately offset the costs and risks borne by an employee. For example, many MBA graduates are offered positions that attract a low salary but possess greater opportunities for more rapid advancement to the higher echelons of management. Similarly, many are offered positions with very attractive salaries, but little opportunity for advancement. A graduate fortunate to be offered both is likely to choose between the two on the basis of his or her perceptions that the likelihood of rapid advancement, with corresponding increases in compensation, is a reality. These refined versions are referred to as VIE models, where:

(a) **Expectancy (E)** concerns the perceived relationship between the amount of effort people put into their work and the levels of performance achieved. In other words: 'Do they expect greater effort to lead to better performance?' Of extreme importance here is not the actual relationship between effort and performance, but what the person believes the relationship to be. Thus the precise behaviours that constitute good levels of performance must be specified. Employees must believe they can control the quality of their job performance: if they do not, they will see no point in trying harder.

(b) **Instrumentality (I)** refers to the perceived relationship between an employee's performance and outcomes in terms of rewards and punishments. The probability of increased effort leading to increased reward (e.g. pay) will affect the amount of effort people think it worthwhile to expend in the first place, and therefore constitutes an important feedback loop. Even if the person concludes that greater effort on their part leads to better performance, this effort is unlikely to be enacted and sustained if it does not lead to some tangible reward that the person values.

(c) **Valence (V)** concerns the attractiveness of the rewards on offer. This aspect of the theory explicitly recognises that there are significant differences between people in terms of the outcomes that they find attractive. If the rewards on offer are not highly valued, people may say, 'Why bother?' The motivating potential of a reward, therefore, depends solely on the value the person places on it. If the reward (e.g. promotion) is highly valued, motivation is likely to be high. Conversely, if the reward (e.g. promotion) is not valued, motivation is likely to be low. The notion of fairness may also enter employees' minds, to the extent that they will have a view of the level and kinds of reward which ought to be available to the person for performing a particular type of work. The issue of equity (Adams, 1965) also enters into the way rewards are distributed in relation to performance and to any deprivations people may suffer in carrying out their work, such as working on a night shift. For example, when someone believes they are not receiving rewards (e.g. pay) commensurate with their experience, ability or effort, they work less hard (Hauenstein and Lord, 1989), become more selfish (Harder, 1992) and become dissatisfied with their jobs (Carr *et al.*, 1996). The important point here is that employees are unlikely to be satisfied with the rewards they receive if they are perceived as inequitable. Dissatisfaction will weaken the motivating power of any potential rewards.

Expectancy theory is useful as a means to identify what rewards are valued by employees for particular courses of action, rather than a means with which to translate motivation into performance. As such, it shows that a person's level of performance varies directly in proportion to a person's need for achievement and anticipated satisfaction with any rewards offered. Although this sounds little more than common sense, it does draw attention to certain requirements for directing motivation that are frequently neglected in practice. For example, managers should try to ensure that an employee's personal goals match those of the organisation. This might best be achieved by closer matching of the person to the job via effective personnel selection practices (*see* Cooper, *et al.*, 2003). Similarly, managers must provide feedback in one form or another (e.g. praise) to employees so that their efforts can actually be seen to be acknowledged or rewarded. Other, important implications for managers and organisations are listed in Exhibit 12.3.

Goal-setting theory

Expectancy theories have proved popular and have influenced much subsequent research into motivation in the workplace. One approach that has successfully incorporated the notions of expectancy theory and many others besides is **goal-setting theory**. This is perhaps because any and all attempts to motivate performance in the workplace inevitably include targets or goals in some form or other (e.g. vision statements, deadlines, etc.). First proposed by Ed Locke, an American psychologist, in 1968, at present goal setting is one of the most influential theories of work motivation applicable to all cultures. Hundreds of studies, conducted on over 100 different types of tasks have investigated the influence of goal setting on task performance. This body of evidence has repeatedly shown that provided a goal is concrete, related to specific task requirements and is accepted by employees, virtually any type of action that is able to be measured and controlled can be improved (Locke and Latham, 2002). Indeed, it has been stated that

> *'Goal-setting theory has demonstrated more scientific validity to date than any other theory or approach to motivation.'*   (Pinder, 1984, p 169)

Core findings

Derived from both management and academic theorising, goal setting is based on the central notion that specific, difficult goals are the immediate, though not only, precursors of human action. Reviews (e.g. Locke *et al.*, 1981) have revealed that

Exhibit 12.3 **Managerial implications of expectancy theory**

Implications for managers
- Find out what rewards employees value.
- Specify the exact behaviours that reflect good levels of performance.
- Ensure the desired levels of performance are within employees' capabilities.
- Ensure that the links between effort–performance–outcomes are clear to all employees.
- Ensure that the rewards on offer do not conflict with other rewards from different organisational sources.
- Ensure that the rewards are not seen as trivial.
- Ensure that the level of rewards actually matches levels of performance.
- Ensure the reward system is fair and equitable.

Implications for organisations
- Design pay and reward systems so that performance is rewarded, not other factors such as length of service.
- Design jobs in such a way as to provide opportunities for people to satisfy their own needs through their work.
- Allow employees to be involved in decisions affecting the type of rewards on offer.

Source: Nadler and Lawler (1979)

approximately 90 per cent of all goal setting studies have shown a beneficial effect of goal setting on performance. The core findings of this vast body of research have shown that:

- difficult goals lead to higher performance than moderate or easy goals;
- specific, difficult goals lead to higher performance than vague, broad goals or 'do your best' goals;
- feedback about goal-directed behaviour is necessary for goal-setting to work;
- people need to be committed to achieving the goals.

These core findings make clear that the main aim of any goal is to place sufficient demands upon people to motivate them to achieve higher levels of performance. However, a goal on its own is insufficient to motivate people. Any goals that are set must be both specific and difficult. In addition, people must be committed to the process and they must also be able to track their progress. Such findings are often reflected in the commonly used acronym that suggests goals should be **SMART**: Specific, Measurable, Attainable, Realistic and Time-bound. By their very nature, specific, difficult, but attainable goals affect performance by:

- presenting challenges that cause people to focus their attention and actions on the task requirements;
- mobilising people's effort;
- boosting people's commitment to try harder and persevere until the goals are achieved;
- motivating people to search for the optimum performance strategy.

Specific goals

Specific goals remove any doubt about what is expected, enabling people to focus their attention solely on the activities specified. A goal-setting study conducted in a British manufacturing organisation demonstrated this effect (Cooper, *et al.*, 1994). In an attempt to reduce accident rates, goals were set for specific unsafe behaviours in each of 14 departments. The results, illustrated in Figure 12.4, showed considerable reductions in accidents related to unsafe behaviours for which goals had been set. Conversely, accidents related to other safety behaviours, for which no goals had been set, either continued at their previous rate or increased. Similar results were found in the UK construction industry (Duff *et al.*, 1993). Improvements in safety performance were found for scaffolding, access to heights and housekeeping categories for which goals had been set, whereas no appreciable improvement was found in a personal protective equipment category for which no goals were set. Any specific goal can be viewed as an overarching goal that can be broken down into various sub-goals that will help people to meet that overarching goal. For example, to attain the goal of obtaining a degree in management (overarching goal) requires a student to attain various specific sub-goals such as find the appropriate business school, apply, be accepted, register, attend lectures, study, take exams, etc. Attainment of each specific sub-goal eventually leads to attainment of the overarching goal. Breaking down overarching goals into sub-goals is thought to significantly improve goal attainment (Klawsky, 1990) and people's self-esteem (Erez and Judge, 2001).

In practice, managers often set goals that are too broad (e.g. an accounts manager may set a productivity improvement goal of 10 per cent for the processing of orders and invoices). Unfortunately, broad goals allow people to interpret the effectiveness of their performance against a variety of performance indicators. Greater productivity improvements would be found for goals that specified exactly the performance to be improved. For example, reducing invoice 'receipt to payment' processing time

Figure 12.4 The effects of specific goals on accident rates

Source: Cooper, *et al.* (1994).

from 45 days to 28 days is a much more specific productivity goal. As such, clerks can only compare their performance to the amount of time taken. Interestingly, most people are reassured by, and more satisfied from, having a clear appreciation of what is expected of them, rather than a vague approximation.

Measurable goals

Feedback on goal achievement is only possible if progress is measured in some way (Locke and Latham, 2002; Stajkovic and Luthans, 2003). This is a further reason for goals to be specific as it helps to clarify the appropriate measurement metrics that will help to direct people's behaviour to achieve the desired goal and hold them accountable for doing so. Importantly, performance measurement should focus on the behaviours involved in the *processes* for goal achievement as well as overall outcomes (i.e. goal attainment). Monitoring process goals affects behaviour because people's attention and actions are focused on their achievement. As Deming (1986) stated, 'what gets measured gets done'. In turn outcome goals will naturally be achieved. In many organisations, composite performance metrics often centre on **quality** (e.g. number of defects per unit), **speed** (e.g. response time for customer queries), **dependability** (e.g. percentage of orders delivered on time), **flexibility** (e.g. range of services offered) and **cost** (e.g. operational efficiency). In companies

→ Ch. 7

→ Ch. 13

utilising total quality management (*see* Chapter 7), each of these is usually broken down into its constituent parts so that each part can be measured perhaps with statistical process control (*see* Chapter 13) techniques. In principle, people's behaviour in one form or another will underpin each one of these constituencies. These behaviours form the basis for specific *process* goals. A dependability example could be client managers collecting more information over the telephone from customers during a service callout, so that service engineers could more accurately diagnosis a problem and arrive at a client's premises with the correct parts. The process measure might be the number of times full information was recorded. In turn, reducing engineers' time to rectify problems would be a natural outcome. Monitoring of such process goals therefore facilitates overall goal achievement due to the provision of feedback at frequent intervals so that performance can be adjusted if necessary.

Feedback is usually defined as 'information about the effectiveness of particular work behaviours' and is thought to fulfil several functions. For example, it is directive, by clarifying specific behaviours that ought to be performed; it is motivational, as it stimulates greater effort; and it is error correcting, as it provides information about the extent of errors being made. Research has shown that feedback by itself can lead to higher levels of performance (e.g. Pritchard *et al.*, 1988). However, in combination, goals and feedback are far more powerful than either one alone (Balcazar *et al.*, 1986). Goals inspire individuals to achieve particular levels of performance, while feedback allows the person to track how well he or she is doing in relation to the goal so that, if necessary, adjustments in effort can be made. Feedback can be verbal, non-verbal, numerical, graphical or written, but best increases performance when it is positive and informational, as opposed to negative and controlling (Zhou, 1998). Feedback is important not just because it is the only variable that directly affects work performance (Roe *et al.*, 2000), but the lack of effective feedback also affects people's intention to quit their companies (Joinson, 2001), i.e. their motivation.

Attainable and realistic goals

The amount of effort and energy directed towards goal achievement depends upon how challenging the goal is believed to be. In general, assuming the goals are accepted, the more of a challenge the goal represents, the more effort people will be prepared to employ. When people rise to a challenge, they tend to be much more determined and try harder, by drawing upon more of their skills, abilities and experiences until the goal is reached. In turn, this boosts people's confidence in their abilities, causing them to set even higher goals, again reflecting the old adage that 'success breeds success'. People will be reluctant to try to reach a goal that they think is unrealistic or impossible to achieve. Again demonstrating the effects of dispositional factors, Ladd *et al.* (1997) found that optimists tend to set higher goals than pessimists, as do those scoring high on the personality factors of conscientiousness and extroversion (Judge and Illies, 2002). Impossibly difficult goals are demotivating. They lower people's goal commitment to such an extent that the goals are rejected out of hand, and people will not even try to reach them. This raises the question of when is a goal sufficiently challenging, but not beyond the capabilities of those concerned? The answer to this question depends on whether or not the goals are related to individual or group performance. If the goal is related to individual performance, goal difficulty is usually determined by comparing the output (e.g. productivity) of a few high-performing people with that achieved by the majority. The average output of the high performers is then used as the difficulty level of the goal, as it is challenging to the majority but still achievable. If a goal is to be set for a workgroup, it will be necessary to establish the average levels of current output for the group as a whole over a relatively small period of time, to provide an average baseline figure. This baseline figure is then used as the basis for discussions about the degree to which performance improvements are possible, while also providing a benchmark with which to compare future performance.

Time-bound goals

Goals that are time bound, which create deadlines, are more motivating as they set a specific timeframe for completion. Creating a deadline is simply the setting of a further specific goal for goal achievement. Most organisations will set long-term strategic goals, medium-term tactical goals and short-term operational goals. Weldon and Yun (2000) showed that groups that set both short-term and long-term goals also set more difficult goals and performed better than those who only set long-term goals. Thus, the creation of explicit timeframes helps to determine (1) goal difficulty, (2) which goals are which, (3) the order in which they are required to be achieved, and (4) the priority to be given to each. In practice, creating timeframes also highlights the importance of ensuring that the strategic, tactical and operational goals are in alignment with each other and any goal conflicts are minimised (Cooper, 1998).

Contingent factors

Although a goal should be SMART, Locke and Latham (1990) have identified various characteristics that are known to affect goal-directed performance that include:

■ **People's skills, abilities and knowledge.** An individual's or work group's ability to perform a task will obviously limit the extent to which a task goal will be reached. Ability is normally judged by how well someone has done on the same or similar tasks in the past. In general, people with high levels of ability tend to achieve difficult goals, whereas those with less ability tend to struggle, although this will be related to the complexity of the task.

- **Self-confidence.** People's confidence in their own abilities to perform a task will influence their choice of how difficult a goal should be, and the amount of effort they will spend in trying to reach a goal. Someone who is very sure, and has every confidence in his or her own task abilities is more likely to set a challenging goal, and be more committed to reaching it, than someone who is uncertain.

- **Task complexity.** Research findings indicate that specific, challenging goals produce better performance improvements on simple rather than complex tasks, although improvements can be expected for both types of task (Wood *et al.*, 1987). This is because when people work on simple tasks, their efforts lead directly to improved task performance. Conversely, complex tasks involve decisions about when, where and how to allocate effort for maximum effect. This means that any effort used has indirect effects upon performance. Managerial and supervisory functions are deemed to be complex tasks because they include multiple demands upon the individual from various organisational sources. Therefore, the complexity of the managerial function also inevitably incorporates competing goals, of which one will be reached at the expense of the others at a particular moment in time.

- **Goal choice.** The choice of how difficult a goal should be will be influenced by what the individual or work group would ideally like to achieve, what they expect to achieve and what is believed to be the minimum that should be achieved. A goal determined by ideals is more than likely to be based upon wishful thinking than reality and represents what could happen if everything went right. This type of goal is typically reflected through mission or vision statements issued by boardroom executives (e.g. that safety is a top priority; that the company has set a goal of zero accidents and that all employees should behave safely and follow company safety policies). A goal based on expectations is typically based on a realistic assessment of what can be accomplished in the light of past experience. Success or failure in attaining previous goals, the likelihood of adequate resources, the expected amount of managerial support and the importance of the goal are all primary factors likely to influence assessments when choosing the difficulty level of a goal. A goal based on the minimum that should be achieved reflects the minimum levels of performance with which people will be satisfied. Assessments of goal-difficulty levels based on minimum requirements perhaps reflect the fact that organisations typically have multiple goals. Very often, however, these organisational goals are in conflict with one another, the case of productivity versus safety being a familiar one. Organisations faced with conflicting goals, typically, trade off goals so that one goal will be reached at the expense of another. Choosing the goal-difficulty level based on minimum requirements is often seen to be a compromise that leads to the satisfaction of several conflicting goals. Indeed, a goal based upon the minimum required is the typical choice, rather than the expected or ideal goal.

- **Goal commitment.** Challenging goals only lead to higher performance when people are committed to them. Commitment refers to the degree to which the person is attached to the goal, considers it significant or important, and is determined to reach it, even in the face of setbacks and obstacles. Acceptance of and commitment to goals are crucial factors in performance in that, as commitment declines, performance also declines (Erez and Zidon, 1984). Factors which have been found to enhance commitment fall into two broad categories: those which convince people that achieving the goal is possible, and those which convince people that achieving the goal is important. Managers can play an important role in facilitating commitment to goals by persuading employees that the desired goals are both achievable and important. In addition, they should provide visible ongoing support. If they don't, the importance of the goal could be undermined, resulting in goal rejection. Commitment to a challenging goal could also be considerably improved by allowing employees to participate in the goal-setting process. For many people, a goal set and delegated by others serves as a disincentive, which may lead to people rejecting it. Some have consistently argued that provided a goal is sufficiently difficult, delegated goals are as effective as participatively set goals for inducing high commitment and high performance (Locke *et al.*, 1988). In the UK construction industry, Cooper *et al.* (1992) demonstrated that on those sites where operatives participated in the goal-setting process there was much greater improvement in safety performance than on those sites where goals were delegated (assigned) to operatives. Similarly, a meta-analysis of the extant goal-setting literature revealed the potency of participative goals, rather than delegated goals, for improving a variety of task performances (Cooper, 1992). Recent meta-analyses confirm that participation in goal setting positively influences goal commitment (Klein *et al.*, 1999).

Thus, the message from goal-setting theory is simple. A specific, challenging goal has maximum effect when an individual has confidence in his or her ability to perform the task, is committed to the goal, the task is simple, and accurate feedback is made available so that the person can track his or her progress in relation to the goal. As these kinds of contingent factor make clear, goal-setting theory explicitly recognises the influence of person and situational variables. The reciprocal relationships between important goal-setting characteristics are illustrated in Figure 12.5, which indicates how each characteristic might interact with and affect other goal characteristics. For example, productivity goals will be affected by the person's commitment to improving productivity, whether or not the productivity goals conflict with other organisational goals (e.g. productivity versus safety), and whether or not management is committed enough to provide the necessary support and resources for people to reach the goals.

➔ Ch. 5

More recent organisational applications of goal setting have developed the notion of **STRETCH** targets (Hamel and Prahalad, 1993), whereby completely unreasonable targets of such difficulty are set that they appear absolutely impossible to achieve (*see also* Chapter 5). The purpose of STRETCH is to revolutionise completely the way things are currently done. 'Thinking out of the box', or 'Pushing the envelope' are commonly heard phrases that encapsulates the thinking behind STRETCH targets. At first glance the notion of a STRETCH target appears diametrically opposed to the tenets of goal-setting theory, whereby a goal that is unattainable will reduce commitment and be rejected (Locke and Latham, 2002). Thompson *et al.* (1997) cite four successful case studies that used STRETCH targets to promote innovation, asset utilisation, reduced cycle times and performance improvements in the USA in their exploration of goal-setting theory. In essence, they concluded that the tenets of goal-setting theory are correct and that it is situational factors that underpin the success of STRETCH in conjunction with a specific goal. STRETCH targets motivate if the organisation (1) empowers the workforce, (2) allows them to operate autonomously, (3) modifies the work environment with structural changes to facilitate goal achievement, and (4)

Figure 12.5 **Reciprocally determined model of goal setting**

develops a culture of support and encouragement. Thus, changing jaded management practices and structural constraints determine the success of STRETCH targets as they provide the conditions with which to rejuvenate demotivated workers. This finding provides powerful evidence for the effectiveness of situational motivation theories.

SITUATIONAL MOTIVATION THEORIES

Extreme examples of the effects of situational influences can be found in the work of behavioural psychologists, who essentially take the view that situations condition people's behaviour. This approach proposes that because behaviour is a function of its consequences, behaviour that is reinforced in some way will strengthen and continue. On the other hand, behaviour that is punished or behaviour that produces unimportant outcomes for the person will be less likely to occur. Thus, behaviourist approaches emphasise that people's behaviour is contingent upon the types of reward or punishment received.

The different types of consequences and their controlling effects on behaviour (shown in Figure 12.6) indicate that a positive reward strengthens and increases the probability of a person behaving in a particular way. In the workplace, for example, an employee praised by a manager for completing a difficult job within a certain deadline will be more likely to repeat that type of performance in the future. Conversely, if the employee received no acknowledgement of any kind, continuation of this type of good performance would be extinguished because their performance was ignored. Similarly, avoiding a negative consequence can also

Figure 12.6 Different reinforcers and their controlling effects on behaviour

Consequences		Effect on preceding behaviour
Positive reinforcement	'It's nice when it happens'	*Increase*
Negative reinforcement	'It's nice when taken away'	*Increase*
Punishment	'It's nasty when it happens'	*Decrease*
Extinction	'Nothing happens'	*Decrease*

strengthen the way people behave. For example, removing an aspect of a job that an employee dislikes (e.g. sitting on a committee) due to that person's good job performance would also reinforce that employee's behaviour. Punishing consequences, on the other hand, are purported to stop or decrease certain behaviours. For example, issuing a written warning to an employee for persistent lateness is a punisher that is meant to stop this type of behaviour. However, the influence of punishment and rewards on behaviour differs considerably. To be effective, a punisher has to fulfil two conditions: it must be given immediately, and every single time the unwanted behaviour(s) occurs. For example, one reason people continue to break the speed limit when driving is due to this lack of instant punishment every time they breach the speed limits. Similar factors operate in the workplace. If someone breaches a safety rule and behaves unsafely, more often than not the behaviour is ignored by co-workers and managers. Most people also do not get hurt every time they behave unsafely. The lack of any punishing consequence means people learn that it is all right to behave unsafely. Indeed, many people are rewarded in some way for behaving in an undesired manner, perhaps from the time saved by taking a short cut, or that their job is made easier in some way. In contrast to punishers, positive consequences (rewards) need be given only every so often. Initially, a positive consequence should be given as soon as possible after the desired behaviour. To ensure that employees are clear about the linkages between the desired behaviour(s) and the positive consequence, they should be given only when the desired behaviour has actually occurred. Once the desired behaviour starts to become established in the employee's repertoire, the frequency of reward (e.g. praise) can be reduced over a period of time. Many workplace incentive programmes do not produce the desired result simply because the linkage between the desired behaviour and incentive is not clear. Rather, the incentives are given for the outcomes of behaviour, not the actual behaviour. Recent research has shown that extremely high-performing companies habitually use praise and recognition to acknowledge desired behaviour (Townsend, 2001).

Organisational behaviour management

Focusing solely on behaviour, this approach does not make use of any underlying psychological processes such as motivation or personality. Nonetheless, it has been successfully used to influence behaviour in a variety of work settings. When used in a strategic planned way to motivate organisational behaviour, the behavioural approach outlined in the previous section is referred to as organisational behaviour management (OBM). OBM has been used to successfully improve a variety of work-related performances that includes absenteeism, productivity and quality in a variety of settings (Andrasik *et al.*, 1981; Luthans and Martinko, 1987). Several key features of OBM, which significantly add to its success as a motivational technique, include:

- its focus on current rather than past determinants of behaviour;
- its emphasis on overt behaviour change as the major criterion in evaluating its motivational effects;
- its careful choice of the specific behaviours to be targeted;
- its structured use of appropriate metrics to measure performance;
- its use of reinforcers.

At the theoretical level, behaviourist terminology describes the flow of these procedures as antecedents–behaviour–consequents (ABC model). Antecedents are described as 'controlling stimuli' that trigger or elicit observable behaviours (e.g. rules and procedures). Consequents are any events that follow as a direct result of the behaviour, and as such are described as reinforcers or punishers. For example, the ringing tone of a telephone would be described as an antecedent when it signals someone to pick up (behaviour) the handset to speak (consequent) with the caller. Speaking to the caller reinforces the behaviour of answering the phone. Although some might think that the antecedent (e.g. ringing tone) is the most important aspect of determining behaviour, it is the consequent (e.g. speaking to the caller) that has the most powerful influence. For example, if the phone rang repeatedly and there was no caller each time it was answered, it would not take long before the ringing phone was ignored. Using the ABC model, organisational behaviourists try to discover which antecedents and consequents are controlling which behaviours. When identified, these are changed, so that the target behaviours also change to what is desired (*see* Exhibit 12.4).

Antecedents

Managerial attempts to change employee behaviour often fail in practice because they focus almost exclusively on the antecedents of behaviour (e.g. rules, procedures, etc.) instead of the consequents (e.g. acknowledgment for good performance). Antecedents come *before* a behaviour. They signal what is expected of people and largely communicate what the consequence(s) of fulfilling the expectations are likely to be. Although antecedents can influence behaviour on their own, they work much better when specifically paired with a consequence (e.g. Ray *et al.*, 1997). The factors known to increase the effectiveness of antecedents include:

- **Linkage** – explicitly linking the antecedent to a consequence.
- **Timing** – the closer an antecedent is presented before the behaviour the more it will direct subsequent behaviour.
- **Specificity** – the more specific an instruction is, the more impact it will exert as it removes doubt about what is expected.
- **Importance** – the more important an antecedent is perceived to be, the more it will direct subsequent behaviour.

Exhibit 12.4 **Rearranging consequents**

A psychology student working in a drugstore to pay her way through an American college noticed that some people completed their jobs faster than others. She examined the antecedents and consequences of each person's behaviour. She believed that those people who worked faster rewarded themselves by doing a job they liked after completing a job they disliked (Situation A), and those who took longer did the nice job first, followed by the job they disliked (Situation B). To test her theory, she observed the average length of time taken to complete certain tasks. The average timings for the different types of task were as follows:

TASK	AVERAGE TIMINGS IN MINUTES	
	Situation A	*Situation B*
Restock sweet shelves	20	35
Restock cigarette shelves	5	15
Vacuum floor	5	15
Dump rubbish	5	10
Clean store	45	90
Check in deliveries	30	60
Help pharmacist	50	60
Deliver orders	50	60
Totals	210	345

The average timings for each factor were found to be very different. Those rewarding themselves with a nice job after what was seen as a nasty job took 40 per cent less time than those people doing the nice job first, followed by a nasty job. This effect is termed the 'Premack Principle', after a researcher who had observed the same phenomena in animals. Utilising this principle, it is possible for managers to identify tasks that employees see as nice or nasty, and change the situation by rescheduling work so that a nice job always follows a nasty job. In this way, a manager can easily rearrange the consequents of employees' behaviour without the use of incentives or other inducements, and increase production.

Source: O'Brien *et al.* (1982)

Increasing the managerial effectiveness of antecedents therefore requires that they are seen to be important to achieve the desired performance, specific, explicitly linked with a consequence, and presented immediately before the desired behaviour is performed.

Consequences

Consequences come *after* a behaviour. Importantly, a behaviour may have more than one consequence *to the individual*, and some consequences will exert stronger reinforcing effects than others. For example, the consequences of finishing work early to attend a football match at Wembly may result in the person attending the match (positive) and seeing their team win (positive). Conversely, they may have missed an important phone call that resulted in the loss of a sizeable sales order to another sales representative who did not leave early which resulted in the loss of sales commission (negative). To a football fanatic, attending and experiencing the excitement of the match would provide a more positive consequence for leaving work early and outweigh the negative consequence of losing sales commission. To this person, this means that the next time his or her team played at Wembly, they would most likely leave work early again. To someone who attended the match as a causal or neutral observer, the consequence of losing the sales commission would likely outweigh the consequence of watching the match and lead that person to stay at work when other matches take place. This scenario highlights that the power of a consequence to influence behaviour is entirely dependent upon whether or not the person values it (this accords with Vroom's 1964 expectancy theory). In practical terms this means that managers must not assume that other people will find a particular consequence as reinforcing as they might think. Some people find praise reinforcing, while others prefer awards, time off or money. Try to find out what each of your employees values.

Three features are known to determine the strength of a consequent (reinforcer):

- **Timing** – the sooner a consequent follows a behaviour, the more powerful it will be.

- **Consistency** – the more certain it is that a consequent will follow a behaviour, the more powerful it will be in controlling subsequent behaviour.

- **Significance** – positively valued consequents exert greater effects than negative (i.e. punishing) consequents.

This means that the more a manager can ensure that the consequents of a behaviour are received immediately, are certain to be received and seen as positive by the recipient, the more likely that behaviour will be repeated. Indeed, staff preference for immediate feedback (a positive reinforcer) was demonstrated by Reid and Parsons (1996). Consequents that are late, uncertain and negative will have little, if any, effects on behaviour. For example, an employee may never follow certain quality procedures (antecedent) because he or she is consistently (certain) rewarded by an immediate (soon) time-saving and extra production (positive) for non-compliance. To ensure employees follow the correct procedures a manager must ensure that the consequents of following the correct procedures outweigh the consequents of not doing so (*see* Cooper, 1998). Because social rewards are one of the most powerful consequents known, a manager might try to address this problem by harnessing peer pressure and giving immediate positive feedback (e.g. praise) to those who behave in the desired manner. In some cases, organisations reinforce the very behaviours they are trying to eliminate. Attempting to save money by reclaiming surpluses from annual departmental budgets and reducing the following year's budget allocation is a classic example. In these circumstances the organisation is rewarding managers who spend up to the budget limit, while simultaneously punishing thrifty managers! Allowing departmental managers to keep a certain percentage of budget savings for other work-related uses (e.g. updating computer equipment) is more likely to result in across-the-board savings. Exhibit 12.5 outlines how an intervention utilising OBM techniques reduced the number of manufacturing rejects in a multinational aluminium manufacturer.

Exhibit 12.5 Reducing production rejects with OBM techniques

A large multinational aluminum smelter was regularly experiencing a large number of rejects in baked anodes (approximately 10 per cent per week). These anodes are used in finished aluminum production. Employees had a production target in excess of 3500 baked anodes per week. Research psychologists had approached the company to conduct an OBM study and were asked to focus their efforts on the anode reject problem. Utilising applied behavioural analytic techniques, they examined employees' production-related behaviours. This evaluation suggested that this high rate of defective anodes might have been due to weak antecedents, inefficient work procedures and weak performance consequences. An OBM intervention package that included a combination of goal setting, performance feedback and tangible rewards was designed to strengthen the antecedents and consequences of employees' job performance. Successively higher targets (i.e. antecedents) were set for reductions in the number of rejects. The consequences used were performance feedback and tangible rewards for goal achievement. Compared to the pre-intervention reject rates, the anode reject rates were much lower (better performance) during the three experimental phases. The treatment phase that incorporated the most difficult goal produced the greatest reduction in the reject rate. This study further demonstrated that a treatment combination of specific goal setting, feedback and tangible rewards can 'strengthen' antecedents and performance contingencies and result in improved objective performance in a manufacturing environment.

Source: Jessup and Stahelski (1999).

Recent innovations

Primarily due to the work of Bandura (1977), more recent OBM applications have begun to incorporate the notion of social learning theory (SLT), whereby person, situational and behavioural variables interact to reciprocally determine people's behaviour. SLT incorporates many key notions, such as role modelling and self-efficacy, each of which may interact with each other.

Role modelling

There are numerous opportunities in the workplace for colleagues to observe, learn from and influence each other's behaviour at work. A powerful motivational technique for influencing behaviour, this is usually termed '**role modelling**'. Rakestraw and Weiss (1981) showed that people who watch a high-performing role model (e.g. a trainee salesperson watching a company's top salesperson) will imitate the role model's behaviour until it is thoroughly learnt. Thereafter, as the person gains experience, he or she becomes more confident and more motivated to perform at a much higher level. Ultimately, the trainee's performance will be better than the original role model (the old adage that the pupil becomes the teacher of the master illustrates the principle here). Typically we all engage in role-modelling behaviour in our first few days in a new company or workplace as we try to fit in, for example by looking at the way people dress or the timing of rest breaks. This type of behaviour is common when someone is unsure of how to behave in a certain situation. Usually in these situations we choose to model someone who is similar to us, is thought to be successful and has status. Some forward-looking companies recognise this and provide 'mentors' who take a special interest in new employees and guide them through the labyrinth of organisational life. While some research suggests that informal mentoring relationships are better than formal ones (Ragins and Cotton, 1999), it is important to ensure that the mentor–employee fit is carefully examined (Mendelson *et al.*, 1989). The better the relationship between mentors and mentees in a formal mentoring programme, the more mentees are motivated to work hard and be committed to their organisation (Orpen, 1997). In the medical field, Wright and Carrese (2002) found that the attributes required of mentors were good interpersonal skills, a positive outlook, a commitment to excellence and growth, integrity and leadership.

Self-efficacy

Self-efficacy is very close in meaning to the expectancy concept in expectancy theory, and is defined as:

> *'how well one can execute courses of action required to deal with prospective situations.'*
>
> (Bandura, 1982)

However, self-efficacy is broader in meaning as it encompasses individuals' estimates of their total capacity to perform in a given situation, and therefore reflects a person's degree of self-confidence in performing a particular task. Much research has demonstrated very strong links between self-efficacy and a wide variety of work-related performance (Robertson and Sadri, 1993; Sadri and Robertson, 1993). This has shown that the more confident people are in their abilities, the more likely they are to set high goals and be committed to them. In turn, this results in high levels of performance (e.g. Locke *et al.*, 1984). Renn and Fedor (2001) demonstrated these effects with staff from a customer call centre that provided nationwide sales and service support for several hundred automotive retail stores in the USA. About a year before the study was conducted the company had instituted a three-pronged performance improvement programme that focused upon (1) training, (2) management monitoring of employee performance which resulted in both quantity (sales per hour) and quality (20 service quality behaviours) performance ratings, and (3) the public posting of a league table containing the employees ratings (i.e. feedback). During the study, 150 employees completed a survey that asked about the employees' perceived control over events (e.g. their sales quantity and quality), their propensity to seek feedback about their ongoing performance, how often they actually sought feedback and how they used the feedback to set their own improvement goals, and their perceived self-efficacy in relation to their work. Each individual's survey responses were correlated with their managerial performance ratings. The results indicate that self-efficacy is strongly related to personal control, feedback-seeking behaviour and the setting of personal performance goals. In terms of performance, higher levels of self-efficacy were more strongly related to quantity of sales than the 20 customer service quality behaviours. In contrast to these findings, Nicholson *et al.* (2000) showed that City of London equity traders with average levels of confidence performed much better than those with very high levels of self-confidence, whose annual bonuses were approximately £100 000 lower.

Although recent innovations have included person factors, OBM basically represents the systematic and applied use of the idea that situations can determine the strength and direction of behaviour (motivation). Changes in the situation will bring about changes in behaviour. For many people, however, the most important aspect of the situation is the nature of the job they are required to do. For example, many manufacturing jobs involve closely supervised, machine-paced, repetitive tasks. Other jobs involve a great degree of autonomy and variety of work (e.g. university lecturers). The way that these types of job characteristic influence people's work-related behaviour and motivation is important. However, these issues are unlikely to be successfully addressed purely from an OBM perspective. It may also require job design changes.

Job characteristics

A large stream of research has shown that the design of jobs can have an enormous impact on motivation, behaviour, productivity and **job satisfaction** (*see* Wall and Martin, 1987) and absenteeism (Rentsch and Steel, 1998). Two main steps have been taken in moves towards optimising the redesign of jobs. The first step has been concerned with broadening the scope of people's work to introduce greater task variety. This has generally taken the form of job enlargement or job rotation. Job enlargement strategies have generally combined two or more specialised jobs so that the worker is able to use a wider range of skills. Job rotation is thought to increase task variety by moving at regular intervals between different jobs. However, research has shown that these types of job redesign are inadequate. This is partly because these aspects have only been attempted horizontally at the same organisational levels, and partly because simply adding two boring, repetitive, mundane-type jobs, or rotating people between them, is neither satisfying nor motivating. As succinctly pointed out by Herzberg *et al.* (1959):

> *'Adding one Mickey Mouse job to another Mickey Mouse job, adds up to an enlarged Mickey Mouse job.'*

This notion was supported by Campion and McClelland (1993), who showed that people's job satisfaction increases when they are allowed to make complex decisions, but decreases when more tasks of the same difficulty level are simply added to enlarge a person's job. Recognition of these types of problem led to job enrichment schemes in attempts to make jobs more challenging rather than just more of the same. Job enrichment schemes add discretion and responsibility by vertically expanding the scope of a job while also providing some degree of autonomy.

Regarded as one of the most comprehensive frameworks for job redesign, Hackman and Oldham's (1975, 1976, 1980) Job Characteristics Model (JCM) attempts to link the situational characteristics of a job with motivation. Maloney and McFillan (1995) provided a good example of this, when they called for fundamental changes in the way that the construction industry designs people's jobs to improve performance. As illustrated in Figure 12.7, the JCM suggests that five job characteristics are important as they determine various aspects of employees' attitudes and behaviour.

According to the model, a highly motivating job will be designed to incorporate a high degree of each of the following job characteristics:

- **Skill variety** – the degree to which a job provides for the use of a number of different activities and skills.
- **Task identity** – the degree to which people complete a whole piece of work, rather than part of it.
- **Task significance** – the extent to which a job exerts a substantial influence on the lives or work of others.

Figure 12.7 Job characteristics model

Source: Adapted from Hackman and Oldham (1975). Copyright © 1975 by the American Psychological Association. Adapted with permission.

- **Autonomy** – the extent of freedom and independence a job holder has to make his or her own decisions.
- **Feedback** – the extent to which the job itself provides feedback about the job holder's ongoing performance.

The theory proposes that skill variety, task identity and significance collectively influence the **experienced meaningfulness** (EM) of the work. Somebody low in EM is not likely to care much about the job, and will therefore be less likely to produce quality products or services. Similarly, autonomy is thought to affect an employee's **experienced responsibility** (ER), i.e. the extent to which the job holder feels personal responsibility for the outcomes. For example, a finance director with high ER will be concerned to deliver a quality service to suppliers by personally ensuring that his or her staff promptly process and pay invoices by the due date. Feedback is based on the notion of personal reward or reinforcement, because it provides ongoing personal knowledge of how the person is performing. As a whole, these characteristics are thought to be motivating if people feel that they have been personally responsible for producing something worthwhile that they care about. In essence, the JCM posits the notion that jobs which are more satisfying or motivating are those which are generally more productive.

However, research has shown that the model best applies to individuals who have a strong need to grow and develop through the kind of work they do. For these kinds of people, improvements in the five core job characteristics will likely lead to greater productivity. However, people low in **growth-need strength** (GNS) are much less likely to respond to such changes, perhaps because they do not feel that they can cope with more complex demands.

Figure 12.8 shows how the JCM can be used to adopt certain kinds of change principle to design jobs so as to influence each of the five core job dimensions.

Figure 12.8 Ideas for job enrichment

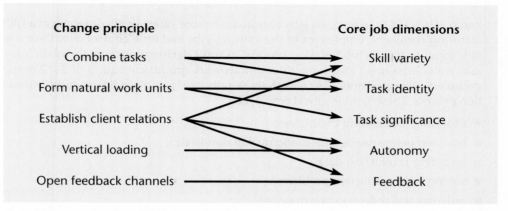

Source: Hackman and Oldham (1975). Copyright © 1975 by the American Psychological Association. Adapted with permission.

Building on earlier models of job design, Hackman and Oldham (1975) suggest that tasks can be combined to enhance both skill variety and task identity. Task identity could also be further enhanced by forming natural work groups. Modern examples of this can be found in organisations that have introduced quality circles, or interdepartmental project teams within a matrix type organisational design (*see* Robertson *et al.*, 1992). Establishing client relations addresses people's social needs and is thought to enhance skill variety and the degree of autonomy, and to provide opportunities for feedback about their performance. TQM organisations embracing the notion of internal markets provide many opportunities to establish client relations for jobs where this has previously been very difficult. Vertical loading, similar to job enrichment schemes, enhances people's autonomy as responsibility is pushed down the organisation, enabling people to make their own decisions. Indeed, this is one of the central features of TQM systems, which advocate that people should be given the responsibility and authority for identifying and solving quality problems. This reasoning is supported in a study by Kini and Hobson (2002), who found that empowerment (autonomy) of work teams positively impacted on TQM, in conjunction with clear expectations (goals) and performance monitoring (feedback).

Multiple feedback and/or communication channels assist people to monitor their performance so that they can assess how well they are doing. As such, feedback fulfils many functions, not least of which is its motivational function. An example of an application of the JCM in a British food manufacturing company is presented in Exhibit 12.6.

Work by Roe *et al.* (2000) integrated both Maslow's hierarchy of needs and Hackman and Oldham's job characteristics model into a general model of work motivation (*see* Figure 12.9). The model postulates that situational characteristics lead to critical psychological states, which induce two main motivational factors (i.e. job involvement and organisational commitment). In turn, these two factors lead to proximal motivational outcomes (i.e. effort and job satisfaction), both of which differentially affect levels of performance, stress and people's intention to leave the organisation. The model was tested with 565 Bulgarian, 614 Hungarian and 237 Dutch, blue-collar and white-collar workers. The model showed a remarkable degree of similarity across all three countries, although some differences were also observed, highlighting the importance of cultural context.

Exhibit 12.6 The effects of job redesign

Kemp *et al.* (1983) redesigned jobs to introduce more variety and autonomy in a UK food manufacturing company. Employees in the existing jobs had little control over their work, and had little input to the decision-making process, as most decisions were made by the supervisors. The jobs were redesigned into semi-autonomous work groups consisting of 8–12 employees. Each group was allocated and was collectively responsible for eight different tasks within the production process. These tasks involved employees:

- allocating jobs among themselves;
- reaching performance targets and quality standards;
- recording production data;
- solving local production problems;
- ordering and collecting raw materials;
- delivering the finished product to the stores;
- selecting and training new recruits;
- managing their day-to-day activities.

Because the redesign process abolished the supervisory function, each of the teams reported directly to first-line managers.

Changes in the attitudes and behaviours of members of the redesigned jobs over a six-month period were compared to three control groups. Experimental groups reported an enhanced degree of autonomy and greater job satisfaction. Productivity also improved. A follow-up study two years later (Wall *et al.*, 1986) confirmed these findings.

Source: Kemp et al. (1983)

In practical terms the model indicates that putting Hackman and Oldams's five job characteristics into place will lead to greater job involvement that will stimulate greater effort, better job satisfaction, higher levels of organisational commitment and performance. On the other hand, catering for Maslow's hierarchy of needs will induce organisational commitment and/or job satisfaction. The model also indicates that effort is linked to levels of arousal (i.e stress) and performance, while job satisfaction is linked to levels of arousal and an intention to leave the organisation. Thus employees who find their jobs satisfying are likely to cope positively with levels of stress, which in turn enhances their performance. Conversely, employees who are dissatisfied with their jobs are likely to experience debilitating levels of distress that increases their intention to leave. Interestingly, feedback was the only situational characteristic directly linked to performance. This suggests that the provision of feedback is an absolute requirement for motivating people to perform.

Despite the claims made about the Job Characteristics Model *per se*, not all studies have succeeded in impacting either people's motivation or performance (*see* Boonzaier *et al.*, 2001, for an excellent review of this literature). For example, Leach *et al.* (2003) showed that although empowerment can positively increase levels of job knowledge, it will not always translate into either motivation or performance. Parker and Wall (1998) state that:

'It is not possible to redesign work successfully without considering the wider context.'

Figure 12.9 General model of work motivation

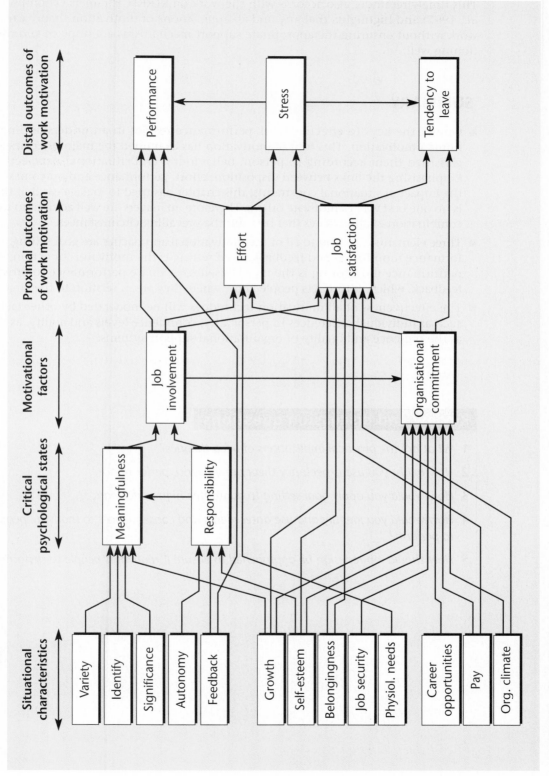

Source: after Roe, R A, Zinovieva, I L, Dienes, E and Ten Horn, L A (2000) 'A Comparison of Work Motivation in Bulgaria, Hungary and The Netherlands: test of a model', *Applied Psychology: An International Review, 49,* 658–87.

This timely reminder also accords with the work on STRETCH targets (Thompson *et al.*, 1997) and highlights that any and all applications of motivation theory cannot work without ensuring the appropriate support mechanisms are in place and functioning well.

SUMMARY

■ One of the keys to effective work performance resides in an understanding of human motivation. This tour of motivation has examined the major theories and classified them according to person, behavioural and situational perspectives. Emphasising the links between disposition, effort, performance and outcomes and the impact of situational constraints, this chapter has tried to make clear that there is no one best way to motivate others. Therefore, managers are well advised to use a combination of approaches that best suit the prevailing circumstances.

■ Three elements common to all of the motivational approaches are goal setting, performance monitoring and feedback. Goal setting is the motivator for action, and performance monitoring is the means used to evaluate performance to provide feedback, which in turn lets people know where they are in relation to the targets.

■ The effectiveness of all motivation techniques will be moderated by other factors such as individual differences in personality, confidence levels and ability, as well as the presence and quality of organisational support systems.

Review and discussion questions

1 *What are the practical implications of need theories?*

2 *How might you use expectancy theory to influence performance?*

3 *How would you apply goal setting to guarantee high performance?*

4 *How would you identify and use antecedents and consequences to motivate people to perform?*

5 *How should job redesign be approached to ensure it motivates people to perform?*

CASE STUDY

Quality Shake-up in Package Delivery Company

Started at the age of 19 by Jim E. Casey in 1907, UPS is now the world's number one package delivery company, operating in some 200 countries. Although experiencing tremendous growth since its inception, increased competition forced a shake-up in the company's strategy. In 1994, Chief Executive, Kent C. 'Oz' Nelson, began overhauling the way the world's largest package carrier did business. Comparing past practices with modern requirements, UPS stressed the goal of customer satisfaction which was to be achieved through 18 quality initiatives. The idea was to change the corporate philosophy, create new ways of thinking about the business and their customers, and align their procedures and ways of work with tomorrow's package delivery needs. UPS dedicated $550 million to team training in 1996. The objectives of the training were to:

- Build teamwork and collaboration in work with others
- Develop and understand the role trust and credibility play in personal effectiveness
- Create an environment of win–win problem solving
- Listen with skill and understanding
- Take responsibility for producing desired results
- Give and receive feedback effectively
- Confront others in a caring and constructive way
- Build self-confidence.

All management and full-time business professionals (non-management) were required to attend the three-day workshop, which concentrated on the relationships between trust and organisational performance, and how teamwork requires a win–win mindset. Portraying a previously non-existent 'soft-side', UPS aroused much employee suspicion. Many questioned UPS's commitment to this part of the change process.

An employee survey was conducted in 1995 to assess progress towards teamworking. It measured perceptions of communication efforts, leadership commitment to the change, employee understanding of the elements of the change effort, and the implementation of new goals, measurements, and reward systems. In broad brush strokes employees indicated that: (1) UPS seems to have communicated its new corporate philosophy well, but there was a large degree of ambiguity about manager's commitment, and the communication of their commitment, to the change effort; (2) there was a disconnection with the professed use of teamwork as a part of the change effort and the actual implementation of a team approach to date; (3) the reward system had not kept pace with new behavioural expectations – while goals and measures had changed employees saw little evidence that rewards had changed accordingly; (4) employees felt that the skills required for change had a high degree of variety, were relatively well defined and involved significant tasks. Conversely, ratings of the degree of autonomy and of feedback received were moderate to low.

Source: Based on Decker, K, Engleman, S, Petrucci, A and Robinson, S (1996) 'United Parcel Service and the Management of Change'. http://cbpa.louisville.edu/bruce/cases/ups/htm/ups.htm.

REFERENCES AND FURTHER READING

Adams, J S (1965) 'Inequity in Social Exchange', in Berkowitz, L (ed.), *Advances in Experimental Social Psychology* (Vol. 2), New York: Academic Press, pp 267–99.

Alderfer, C P (1969) 'An Empirical Test of a New Theory of Human Needs', *Organisational Behaviour and Human Performance*, 4: 142–75.

Andrasik, F, Heimberg, J S and McNamara, J R (1981) *Behavior Modification of Work and Work-Related Problems*, New York: Academic Press.

Arnolds, C A and Boshoff, C (2002) 'Compensation, Esteem Valence and Job Performance: An Empirical Assessment of Alderfer's ERG Theory', *International Journal of Human Resource Management*, 13 (4): 697–719.

Arvey, R D, Bouchard, T J, Segal, N L and Abraham, L N (1989) 'Job Satisfaction: Environmental and Genetic Components', *Journal of Applied Psychology*, 74: 187–92.

Balcazar, F, Hopkins, B L and Suarez, Y (1986) 'A Critical Objective Review of Performance Feedback', *Journal of Organisational Behaviour Management*, 7: 65–89.

Balliod, J and Semner, N (1994) 'Turnover and Patterns of Job Change among Computer Specialists', *Zeitschrift für Arbeits und Organisations Psychologie*, 38: 152–63. (In German.)

Bandura, A (1977) *Social Learning Theory*, Englewood Cliffs, NJ: Prentice-Hall.

Bandura, A (1982) 'Self-Efficacy Mechanism in Human Agency', *American Psychologist,* 37: 122–47.

Bandura, A (1986) *Social Foundations of Thought and Action: A Social-Cognitive Theory*, Englewood Cliffs, NJ: Prentice-Hall.

Boonzaier, B, Ficker, B and Rust, B (2001) 'A Review of Research on the Job Characteristics Model and the Attendant Job Diagnostic Survey', *South African Journal of Business Management*, 32 (1): 11–34.

Boswell, R B, Roehling, M V, Lepine, M A and Moynihan, L M (2003) 'Individual Job-Choice Decisions and the Impact of Job Attributes and Recruitment Practices: A Longitudinal Field Study', *Human Resource Management*, 42: 23–37.

Boudreau, J W, Boswell, W R, Judge, T A and Bretz Jr, R D (2001) 'Personality and Cognitive Ability as Predictors of Job Search among Employed Managers', *Personnel Psychology*, 54: 25–50.

BrKich, M, Jeffs, D and Carless, S A (2002) 'A Global Self-Report Measure of Person-Job Fit', *European Journal of Psychological Assessment*, 18: 43–51.

Caldwell, D F and O'Reilly, C A (1990) 'Measuring Person–Job Fit with a Profile-Comparison Process', *Journal of Applied Psychology*, 75: 648–57.

Campion, M A and McClelland, C L (1993) 'Follow-up and Extension of the Interdisciplinary Costs and Benefits of Enlarged Jobs', *Journal of Applied Psychology*, 78 (3): 339–51.

Carr, S C, McLoughlin, D, Hodgson, M and MacLachlan, M (1996) 'Effects of Unreasonable Pay Discrepancies for Under and Over-Payment on Double Demotivation', *Genetic, Social and General Psychology Monographs*, 122 (4): 475–94.

Clegg, C W and Wall, T D (1990) 'The Relationship between Simplified Jobs and Mental Health: A Replication Study', *Journal of Occupational Psychology*, 63: 289–96.

Clements, C, Wagner, R J and Roland, C C (1995) 'The Ins and Outs of Experiential Learning', *Training & Development*, 49: 52–6.

Cooper, A C, Gimeno-Gascon, F J and Woo, C Y (1994) 'Initial Human and Financial Capital as Predictors of New Venture Performance', *Journal of Business Venturing*, 9: 371–96.

Cooper, M D (1992) 'An Examination of Assigned and Participative Goal-setting in Relation to the Improvement of Safety in the Construction Industry'. Unpublished PhD thesis, School of Management, UMIST.

Cooper, M D (1998) *Improving Safety Culture: A Practical Guide*. Chichester: Wiley.

Cooper, M D, Phillips, R A, Sutherland, V J and Makin, P J (1994) 'Reducing Accidents Using Goal-setting and Feedback: A Field Study', *Journal of Occupational and Organisational Psychology*, 67: 219–40.

Cooper, M D, Robertson, I T, Duff, A R and Phillips, R A (1992) 'Assigned or Participative Goals: Do They Make a Difference?' British Psychological Society, Annual Occupational Psychology Conference, Liverpool, 3–5 January.

Cooper, M D, Robertson, I T and Tinline, G (2003) *Recruitment and Selection: A Framework for Action*, The Essential Business Psychology Series (C Fletcher, ed.), London: Thompson Learning.

Deming, W E (1986) *Out of the Crisis*, Cambridge, MA: MIT Press.

Dive, Brian (2002) *The Healthy Organization: A Revolutionary Approach to People and Management*, London: Kogan Page.

Duff, A R, Robertson, I T, Cooper, M D and Phillips, R A (1993) *Improving Safety on Construction Sites by Changing Personnel Behaviour*, HMSO Report Series CRR51/93, London: HMSO.

Erez, A and Judge, T A (2001) 'Relationship of Core Self-Evaluations to Goal-Setting, Motivation and Performance', *Journal of Applied Psychology*, 86: 1270–79.

Erez, M and Zidon, I (1984) 'Effect of Goal-Acceptance on the Relationship of Goal-Difficulty to Performance', *Journal of Applied Psychology*, 69: 69–78.

Hackman, J R and Oldham, G R (1975) 'Development of the Job Diagnostic Survey', *Journal of Applied Psychology*, 60: 159–70.

Hackman, J R and Oldham, G R (1976) 'Motivation Through the Design of Work: Test of a Theory', *Organisational Behaviour and Human Performance*, 16: 250–79.

Hackman, J R and Oldham, G R (1980) *Work Redesign*, New York: Addison-Wesley.

Hamel, G and Prahalad, C K (1993) 'Strategy as Stretch and Leverage', *Harvard Business Review*, March–April.

Harder, J W (1992) 'Play for Pay: Effects of Inequity in a Pay for Performance Context', *Administrative Science Quarterly*, 37: 321–35.

Hauenstein, N M A and Lord, R G (1989) 'The Effects of Final Offer Arbitration on the Performance of Major League Baseball Players: A Test of Equity Theory', *Human Performance*, 2: 147–65.

Hayes, Nicky (2001) *Managing Teams: A Strategy for Success*, London: Thompson Learning.

Heckhausen, H, Schmalt, H D and Schneider, K (1985) *Achievement Motivation in Perspective*, New York: Academic Press.

Herzberg, F, Mausner, B and Syndorman, B B (1959) *The Motivation to Work*, New York: Wiley.

Hinds, Joan-Mary (1995) *Hinds Model of Company Success: How to Overcome Boredom Through Instant Teams and Transform Your Workplace*, London: Millennium Books.

Holstein, B B (1997) *The Enchanted Self*, Amsterdam: Harwood.

Jenkins, J M (1993) 'Self-Monitoring and Turnover: The Impact of Personality on Intent to Leave', *Journal of Organizational Behavior*, 14: 83–91.

Jessup, P A and Stahelski, A J (1999) 'The Effects of a Combined Goal Setting, Feedback and Incentive Intervention on Job Performance in a Manufacturing Environment', *Journal of Organisational Behaviour Management*, 19 (3): 5–26.

Joinson, C (2001) 'Making Sure Employees Measure Up', *HR Magazine*, 46 (3): 36–41.

Judge, T A and Bono, J E (2001) 'Relationship of Core Self-Evaluation Traits – Self-esteem, Generalized Self-efficacy, Locus of Control, and Emotional Stability – with Job Satisfaction and Job Performance: A Meta-Analysis', *Journal of Applied Psychology*, 86: 80–92.

Judge, T A and Illies, R (2002) 'Relationship of Personality to Performance Motivation: A Meta-Analytic Review', *Journal of Applied Psychology*, 87: 797–807.

Kemp, N J, Wall, T D, Clegg, C W and Cordery, J L (1983) 'Autonomous Work Groups in a Greenfield Site: A Comparative Study', *Journal of Occupational Psychology*, 56: 271–88.

Kini, R B and Hobson, C J (2002) 'Motivational Theories and Successful Total Quality Initiatives', *International Journal of Management*, 19 (4): 605–13.

Klawsky, J D (1990) 'The Effects of Sub Goals on Commitment and Task Performance', *Proceedings of the 11th Annual Graduate Conference in Industrial/Organizational Psychology and Organizational Behavior*.

Klein, H J, Wesson, M J, Hollenbeck, J R and Alge, B J (1999) 'Goal-Commitment and the Goal-Setting Process: Conceptual Clarification and Empirical Synthesis', *Journal of Applied Psychology*, 84 (6): 885–96.

Kohn, M L and Schooler, C (1982) 'Job Conditions and Personality: A Longitudinal Assessment of their Reciprocal Effects', *American Journal of Sociology*, 87, 1257–86.

Korman, A K (1970) 'Towards a Hypothesis of Work Behavior', *Journal of Applied Psychology*, 54: 31–41.

Korman, A K (1976) 'Hypothesis of Work Behavior Revisited and an Extension', *Academy of Management Review*, 1, 50–63.

Ladd, D, Jagacinski, C and Stolzenberg, K (1997) 'Differences in Goal-Level Set for Optimists and Defensive Pessimists under Conditions of Encouragement', *Proceedings of the 18th Annual Graduate Conference in Industrial/Organizational Behavior*, 18: 85–6.

Leach, D J, Wall, T D and Jackson, P R (2003) 'The Effect of Empowerment on Job Knowledge: An Empirical Test Involving Operators of Complex Technology', *Journal of Occupational and Organisational Psychology*, 76: 27–52.

Levin, I and Stokes, J P (1989) 'Dispositional Approach to Job Satisfaction: Role of Negative Affectivity', *Journal of Applied Psychology*, 74: 752–8.

Locke, E A and Latham, G P (1990) *A Theory of Goal-Setting and Task Performance*, Englewood Cliffs, NJ: Prentice-Hall.

Locke, E A and Latham, G P (2002) 'Building a Practically Useful Theory of Goal-Setting and Task Motivation', *American Psychologist*, 57 (9): 705–17.

Locke, E A, Latham, G P, and Erez, M (1988) 'The determinants of goal commitment', *Academy of Management Review*, 13, 23–39.

Locke, E A, Frederick, E, Buckner, E and Bobko, P (1984) 'Effect of Self-Efficacy, Goals, and Task Strategies on Task Performance', *Journal of Applied Psychology*, 69: 241–51.

Locke, E A, Shaw, K M, Saari, L M and Latham, G P (1981) 'Goal-Setting and Task Performance: 1969–1980', *Psychological Bulletin*, 90: 125–52.

Luthans, F and Kreitner, R (1975) *Organizational Behavior Modification*, Glenview, IL: Scott, Foresman.

Luthans, F and Martinko, M (1987) 'Behavioural Approaches to Organisations', in Cooper, C L and Robertson, I T (eds), *International Review of Industrial and Organisational Psychology*, (Vol. 2), Chichester: Wiley.

McClelland, D C (1961) *The Achieving Society*, Princeton, NJ: Van Nostrand.

Maloney, W F and McFillan, J M (1995) 'Job Characteristics: Union–nonunion differences', *Journal of Construction Engineering and Management*, 121: 43–54.

Maslow, A H (1942) 'A Theory of Human Motivation', *Psychological Review*, 50: 370–96.

Matsui, T, Okada, A and Kakuyama, T (1982) 'Influence of Achievement Need on Goal-Setting, Performance and Feedback Effectiveness', *Journal of Applied Psychology*, 67: 645–8.

Medcof, J W and Hausdorf, P A (1995) 'Instruments to Measure Opportunities to Satisfy Needs, and Degree of Satisfaction of Needs, in the Workplace', *Journal of Occupational and Organisational Psychologyy*, 68: 193–208.

Mendelson, J L, Barnes, A K and Horn, G (1989) 'The Guiding Light to Corporate Culture', *Personnel Administrator*, 34 (7): 70–1.

Mount, K M, Barrick, M R and Stewart, G L (1998) 'Five-Factor Model of Personality and Performance in Jobs Involving Interpersonal Interactions', *Human Performance*, 11: 145–65.

Nadler, D A and Lawler, E E (1979) 'Motivation: A Diagnostic Approach', in Steers, R M and Porter, L W (eds), *Motivation and Work Behavior* (2nd edn), New York: McGraw-Hill.

Nicholson, N, Fenton-O'Creavy, M, Soane, E and Willman, P (2000) 'Risk and Performance among City Traders', *ESRC Risk and Human Behaviour Newsletter*, Issue 7: 2–6.

O'Brien, R M, Dickson, A M and Rosow, M P (eds) (1982) *Industrial Behavior Modification: A Learning-based Approach to Industrial Organizational Problems*, New York: Pergamon Press.

Orpen, C (1994) 'Interactive Effects of Work Motivation and Personal Control on Employee Job Performance and Satisfaction', *Journal of Social Psychology*, 134 (6): 855–6.

Orpen, C (1997) 'Interactive Effects of Communication, Quality and Job Involvement on Managerial Job Satisfaction and Work Motivation', *Journal of Psychology*, 131 (5): 519–522.

Parker, S K and Wall, T D (1998) *Job and Work Design: Organizing Work to Promote Well-being and Effectiveness.* London: Sage.

Pinder, C C (1984) *Work Motivation*, Glenview, IL: Scott, Foresman.

Pritchard, R D, Jones, S D, Roth, P L, Stuebing, K K and Ekeberg, S E (1988) 'Effects of Group Feedback, Goal-Setting, and Incentives on Organisational Productivity', *Journal of Applied Psychology*, 73: 337–58.

Ragins, B R and Cotton, J L (1999) 'Mentor Functions and Outcomes: A Comparison of Men and Women in Formal and Informal Mentoring Relationships', *Journal of Applied Psychology*, 84: 529–50.

Rakestraw, T L and Weiss, H M (1981) 'The Interaction of Social Influences and Task Experience on Goals, Performance, and Performance Satisfaction', *Organisational Behaviour and Human Performance*, 27: 326–44.

Ray, P S, Bishop, P A and Wang, M Q (1997) 'Efficacy of the Components of a Behavioral Safety Program', *International Journal of Industrial Ergonomics*, 19: 19–29.

Reid, D H and Parsons, M B (1996) 'A Comparison of Staff Acceptability of Immediate Versus Delayed Verbal Feedback in Staff Training', *Journal of Organisational Behaviour Management*, 16 (2): 35–47.

Renn, R W and Fedor, D B (2001) 'Development and Field Test of a Feedback Seeking, Self-Efficacy, and Goal-Setting Model of Work Performance', *Journal of Management*, 27: 563–83.

Rentsch, J R and Steel, R P (1998) 'Testing the Durability of Job Characteristics as Predictors of Absenteeism over a Six-Year Period', *Personnel Psychology*, 51: 165–90.

Robertson, I T and Sadri, G (1993) 'Managerial Self-Efficacy and Managerial Performance', *British Journal of Management*, 4: 37–45.

Robertson, I T, Smith, J M and Cooper, M D (1992) *Motivation: Strategies, Theory and Practice*, London: Institute of Personnel Management.

Roe, R A, Zinovieva, I L, Dienes, E and Ten Horn, L A (2000) 'A Comparison of Work Motivation in Bulgaria, Hungary, and The Netherlands: Test of a Model', *Applied Psychology: An International Review*, 49: 658–87.

Roethlisberger, F J and Dickson, W J (1939) *Management and the Worker*, Cambridge, MA: Harvard University Press.

Rosenthal, R (2002) 'Covert Communications in Classrooms, Clinics, Courtrooms and Cubicles', *American Psychologist*, 57: 839–49.

Sadri, G and Robertson, I T (1993) 'Self-Efficacy and Work-Related Behaviour: A Review and Meta-Analyses', *Applied Psychology: An International Review*, 42: 139–52.

Smither, R and Lindgren, H C (1978) 'Salary, Age, Sex, and Need for Achievement in Bank Employees', *Psychological Reports*, 42: 334.

Stadler, R (1994) 'Berufliche Veranderungen bei Computerfachleuten' ('Job Changes among Computer Specialists'), unpublished Master's thesis, University of Bern, Department of Psychology.

Stahl, M J (1983) 'Achievement, Power and Managerial Motivation: Selecting Managerial Talent with the Job Choice Exercise', *Personnel Psychology*, 36: 775–89.

Stajkovic, A D and Luthans, F (2003) 'Behavioral Management and Task Performance in Organizations: Conceptual Background, Meta-Analysis, and Test of Alternative Models', *Personnel Psychology*, 56: 155–94.

Thomas, Ken (2003) *Intrinsic Motivation at Work: Building Energy and Commitment*, New York: Berrett-Koehler Publishers Inc.

Thompson, K R, Hochwarter, W A and Mathys, N J (1997) 'Stretch Targets: What Makes Them Effective?' *The Academy of Management Executive*, 11 (3): 48–59.

Townsend, A (2001) 'Get Out of the Office', *Management OHS&E*, 5 (4): 39–40.

Vroom, V H (1964) *Work and Motivation*, New York: Wiley.

Wall, T D and Martin, R (1987) 'Job and Work Design', in Cooper, C L and Robertson, I T (eds), *International Review of Industrial and Organisational Psychology* (Vol. 2), Chichester: Wiley.

Wall, T D, Kemp, N J, Jackson, P R and Clegg, C W (1986) 'An Outcome Evaluation of Autonomous Working Groups: A Long-Term Field Experiment', *Academy of Management Journal*, 29: 280–304.

Warr, P (1996) 'Employee Well-Being', in Warr, P (ed.), *Psychology at Work* (4th edn), London: Penguin.

Weldon, E and Yun, S (2000) 'The Effects of Proximal and Distal Goals on Goal Level, Strategy Development', *The Journal of Applied Behavioral Science*; 36 (3): 336–44.

Wood, R E, Mento, A J and Locke, E A (1987) 'Task Complexity as a Moderator of Goal-Effects: A Meta-Analysis', *Journal of Applied Psychology*, 72: 416–25.

Wright, S M and Carrese, J A (2002) 'Excellence in Role Modelling: Insight and Perspectives from the Pros', *Canadian Medical Association Journal*, 167 (6): 638–43.

Zhou, J (1998) 'Feedback Valence, Feedback Style, Task Autonomy, and Achievement Orientation: Interactive Effects on Creative Performance', *Journal of Applied Psychology*, 83: 261–76.

WEBSITES

http://www.accel-team.com/motivation/index.html
Commercial website full of articles on motivation.

http://www.behavioral-safety.com
Contains practical information about OBM techniques to motivate people to comply with safety requirements.

http://www.siop.org/_vti_bin/shtml.dll/search.htm
Society of Industrial/Organizational Psychologists (USA). Type in 'Motivational Theory' as search term.

http://www.zigonperf.com
Dedicated to human resource/performance management techniques.

SECTION D

MANAGING THE ORGANISATION

What is meant by management decision making? What are the key elements in the decision-making process? What is operations management and how is it analysed? What is the transformation process within organisations? How are management, control and information related? What are the different forms of information in an organisation? How are the accounting and financial aspects of organisations controlled? Why should managers have a reasonable understanding of accounting and finance?

With increasing competition, managers have to make difficult decisions and they have to understand that there are different types of decision as well as understand the processes and techniques involved. In order to satisfy customer needs, organisations have to operate successfully, which involves harnessing and transforming resources. Organisations use different forms of information and managers have to know about the relationship between the concepts of management, control and information. They also have to grasp modern developments in information processing. All managers have to have a reasonable understanding of accounting and finance so that they appreciate the financial position of their organisations and the financial aspects of their own activities.

CHAPTER 13

Management decision making

MIK WISNIEWSKI

Outcomes

Having read this chapter, you will be able to understand:

- the different types of management decision
- the key elements of the decision-making process
- the role of models in business decision making
- some of the more common models useful to the business decision maker

INTRODUCTION

Decisions, decisions, decisions

Talk to almost any manager in any organisation and you will hear that manager comment on the increasing difficulties in taking management decisions. Decisions have to be taken more and more quickly; decisions have to be taken more and more often; and decisions have to be taken in increasingly complex and unpredictable situations.

Today's environment for an effective manager in any organisation is increasingly difficult. No matter whether the manager is involved in a private sector company, a public sector organisation or a non-profit organisation, his or her job has become increasingly difficult and complex. There are many contributory causes to this, of which Figure 13.1 illustrates some of the more obvious. All organisations must respond to a variety of strategic and operational pressures. Some of these may be internal to the organisation: the constant search for improved efficiency, for increased effectiveness and for the creation and strengthening of competitive advantage. Other factors may be largely external but generate pressure for change and decision making in their own right. These may include the following.

Figure 13.1 **Pressures for change**

Increasing competition

In the private sector competition is becoming increasingly severe. Markets that were thought secure now look vulnerable to competition from other domestic companies, from the Pacific rim economies, from the emerging market economies of what was Eastern Europe, from e-commerce. Managers must decide how best to respond to this competition: which markets to compete in (and which not to) and on what basis to compete – price, quality, customer service, availability. In the public sector competition is also increasingly becoming the norm with more internal services having to engage in competition with the private sector to win contracts. Managers in these public sector organisations must take critical decisions on when and how to compete.

Changing nature of competition

The way in which businesses compete is also changing rapidly. Organisations must constantly strive to offer 'better' products and services than their competitors. The problem, of course, is deciding what changes to the product or service will be most valued by customers. Should a company reduce its price in order to compete? Should it keep the price the same but offer extended features to the product or service? Similar problems face managers in the public sector.

Increasing focus on quality and customer satisfaction

Customers in both public and private sectors have increasingly higher expectations in terms of product and service quality. With increasing choice, customers are able to favour organisations which deliver 'quality' products and services. Managers must decide how best to respond to this pressure and how to overcome the many problems that prevent quality products and services from being delivered.

Financial environment

Financial markets today are global, with sources of investment funding and opportunities for savings and investment no longer limited to domestic financial organisations. Couple this with the fact that many capital investments for business will cost billions of pounds, and strategic alliances between different businesses – often competitors – become the norm. Consortia of organisations collaborate on ventures such as the Channel Tunnel and the development of new aerospace technology, and multi-agency initiatives are commonplace in the public sector where no one organisation has the resources to develop an initiative single-handed. Decisions are required on who to form such alliances with and the detailed nature of such co-operative ventures.

Technology

Rapid technological change creates both opportunities and problems for managers. Technology can offer the potential for improved efficiency and related cost savings and the creation of real competitive advantage. However, an organisation needs to ensure that it invests in the 'right' technology. A few years – or in some cases, months – later and the business might find its technological investment outdated and inappropriate.

Rate of change

→ Ch. 1

As if these pressures were not problem enough for a manager, the speed at which change is taking place is actually increasing (*see* Chapter 1). Changes in technology, working practices, legislation, the competitive environment and so on take place with alarming frequency. Technological products such as computers, personal CD players and mobile phones have a life span measured in months, not years, before they are overtaken by more technologically advanced products.

A simple business scenario will be used to illustrate some of the points in this chapter and the increasingly difficult task of management decision making. A company operates a number of medium-sized hotels throughout Scotland: in Glasgow, Edinburgh, Aviemore and a number of other key towns and cities. The structure of the company is typical of many. Each hotel in the group acts as a profit centre and has a manager who is responsible for the day-to-day running of that hotel, although many of the routine decisions may be delegated to other staff. The managing director (MD) of the company has the responsibility for longer-term decisions relating to the future of the business. Consider many of the factors that will influence the business environment in which the group operates. Some hotels in the group may well face increased competition from other hotels, both in Edinburgh and perhaps other parts of Scotland, for the tourist segment of the market. Customers are becoming more articulate and demanding in terms of the levels of customer service and the overall quality levels which hotels provide. Changing patterns of business and leisure both offer opportunities and create problems for the business. An increasing number of tourists visiting Scotland offer the potential for increased business, as does the increasing foreign trade in which the Scottish economy is becoming involved.

Because of the extent and rate of the change pressures discussed earlier, managers in many organisations find they have to take an increasing number of decisions: some of these are relatively minor and deal with day-to-day problems that arise. The hotel manager, for example, has to take routine decisions about the quantity of fresh food to order each day. Too much and the hotel's costs will escalate. Too little and there are obvious problems in terms of serving meals to customers. Others are more complex and may well affect the long-term future and success of the organisation. The MD may feel that, with an increasing number of foreign tourists visiting Scotland, the company should undertake an advertising campaign in selected foreign media (newspapers, magazines, TV, radio, websites) to attract customers. However, if the wrong media are used, in terms of market penetration, or the wrong countries are targeted, then the consequences could well be both adverse financial costs and lost business.

In a comparable development the consequences of these decisions take on increasing importance in terms of the future success of the organisation. Yet, at the same time as managers find themselves in a position of having to take more decisions, they also find that they have less and less time available in which to make a decision. That is, the timescale between recognising that a decision needs to be taken and having to make a decision to resolve a problem or capitalise on an opportunity is becoming ever shorter. This is illustrated in Figure 13.2. Managers are faced with taking decisions in situations of increasing complexity: there may be many different aspects to the situation that need to be carefully considered, decisions taken in one area may well have consequences for other areas of activity, there may

Figure 13.2 Decision-making pressures

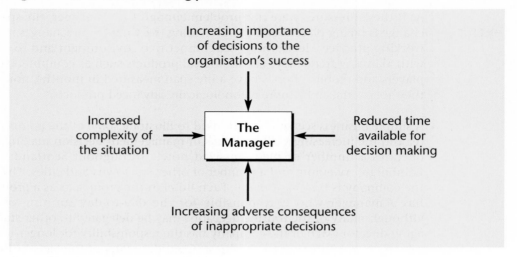

be legal implications for certain decisions, there will certainly be financial implications, and so on. Additionally, with technological change the quantity of information available to managers steadily increases, making the task of deciding what is relevant and irrelevant more difficult. In the hotel group scenario a decision as to which countries in Europe to target as part of a promotional campaign might sound relatively straightforward. However, such a decision has to be put into the context of evaluating information about population trends, income and spending patterns, leisure habits, travel patterns and the like in a number of different countries.

Decisions are also becoming increasingly important to organisational success. There are no such things as 'trivial' decisions in business any longer. Even apparently routine, day-to-day decisions may have longer-term consequences. Equally, the consequences of taking decisions which later turn out to be wrong or inappropriate become more significant. With many decisions having major financial consequences for an organisation, 'getting it wrong' might well send a company out of business. To compound these problems for the decision maker, the time available to evaluate alternatives, to research the problem and to ponder what decision should be taken is decreasing. Decisions typically must be taken in a much shorter timescale. One illustration of this relates to decisions of financial institutions in terms of buying and selling foreign currency via the financial markets. Exchange rates are particularly volatile and decisions on the part of a key decision maker as to whether to buy or sell a particular currency and which currencies to deal in need to be taken in minutes.

It is hardly surprising that considerable attention has been given both to examining the nature and methods of management decision making and to tools and techniques which can assist the manager in the decision-making process. In the rest of this chapter we shall examine some of these in more detail.

TYPES OF DECISION

It will be worthwhile at this stage considering the different types of decision that managers face. There are many different ways in which we can categorise the types of decision that managers take, and one of the more useful of these is shown in Figure 13.3. Although any such categorisation is to some extent artificial, it is possible to envisage three generic types of decision: at the operational, administrative and strategic levels. Naturally, the distinction between these types can be somewhat blurred at the edges – a series of apparently operational decisions, for example, could build into a strategic one. However, each type of decision is typically characterised by a number of features.

Operational decisions are typically routine, day-to-day decisions that will have little direct and immediate impact on the business as a whole and may well be repetitive, in the sense that such decisions have to be taken repeatedly, perhaps several times a year. Examples might be deciding how to deal with an individual customer's complaint, when to reorder office supplies and so on. Typically such decisions are governed primarily by predetermined 'rules' established by the organisation and will involve routine systems and procedures designed to help decision making. Thus there may be a formal procedure to follow in the case of a customer complaint or there may be preset guidelines as to when to reorder basic office supplies. Such decisions are typically taken by managers at the lower levels of the organisational hierarchy. Similarly, on an individual basis the consequences of wrong or poor decisions will be minor (although a series of wrong decisions can build into major consequences). Managers typically have little time available in which to reach such a decision (and this is one of the reasons why predetermined procedures are in place) and are operating in a short-term time horizon.

At the other end of the spectrum there are what can be termed *strategic* decisions, which are more concerned with the achievement of corporate aims and objectives and long-term corporate plans. **Strategic decisions** may well involve determining which products/services to offer in the future and which to discontinue, which markets the organisation will compete in, on what basis the organisation will compete, and so on. Understandably such decisions tend to be taken by the top layer of

Figure 13.3 Decision types

TIME AVAILABLE	TIME HORIZON	DECISION TYPE	MANAGEMENT LEVEL	CONSEQUENCES
Considerable	Long-term	**Strategic**	Top	Major
		Administrative		
Little	Short-term	**Operational**	Lower	Minor

management in an organisation and will benefit from lengthy consideration, simply because they have major consequences for the future success of the organisation. Unlike operational decisions, strategic decisions cannot be taken by following a set procedure or a pre-established set of rules. Typically such decisions relate to situations that are more or less unique, or one-off, or where each situation needs to be considered on an individual basis.

In between these two types of decision we have what can be termed *administrative* decisions. Such decisions are typically concerned with establishing systems for control and organisation within the business, and may well relate to the administrative decisions that follow from key strategic decisions which will help establish systems and procedures to support the operational decision-making process.

To return to the hotel scenario, strategic decisions may relate to the expansion of the chain of hotels the company owns. Clearly such a decision will be taken by senior managers in the organisation, it will have major consequences for the entire organisation (opening hotels in the wrong locations may lead to the company going out of business), and senior managers will take some considerable time (and analysis) before reaching such a decision. Such decisions will also typically be required relatively infrequently. Administrative decisions might then relate to the establishment of appropriate systems to ensure that the new hotel functions properly. Payroll and financial systems will need to be set up; supplies and logistics systems will be required, as will human resource systems and so on. Such administrative decisions are likely to be taken by middle managers in the organisation and, although they are critical to the successful running of the business, taking the wrong decision – about a particular supplier, for example – is unlikely to send the company out of business. Operational decisions will then be required by front-line managers responsible for the smooth running of the hotels on a day-to-day basis. The relevant manager – or perhaps an individual employee if operational decisions have been delegated – will have to take decisions about ensuring the hotel bar is adequately stocked. Such decisions will be taken frequently (perhaps daily) and clearly will need to be taken quickly. Such operational decisions may well be based on earlier administrative decisions. An automated stock control system, for example, may be in place to assist in such operational decisions, perhaps by producing a daily report on yesterday's sales and today's stock levels.

Clearly not all decisions fit neatly into this – or any other – classification structure. Consider, for example, an organisation which is seeking to introduce an effective equal opportunities policy. Such a decision will have to be taken by top management and will have major consequences for the organisation. However, it cannot really be called a strategic decision in the business sense of the word. It is also evident that it is not a decision for which procedures or systems can be applied. While such a classification system does not do justice to the complexity and variety of many managerial decisions, it does provide a useful framework for the different types of decision, their implications and for the roles of the different types of manager in an organisation.

THE DECISION-MAKING PROCESS

It will also be helpful at this stage to develop an overview of what can be described as the decision-making process. Consider the hotel scenario described earlier. The manager of one of the hotels in the group has received a complaint from a guest that the morning newspaper requested has not been delivered. The manager has to decide what to do. While this may seem a relatively trivial decision problem – and one which is clearly operational in terms of our earlier framework – it will serve to illustrate the various stages of the decision-making process. One immediate decision that the manager should make is to apologise to the guest and try to rectify the immediate problem. This might solve the immediate – and obvious – problem, but it is not clear what has caused the problem in the first place, nor whether the problem is likely to occur again in the future. There are various ways in which we can describe the process involved in decision making for this and any other decision situation. One of these is illustrated in Figure 13.4. (*see also* Chapter 4).

→ Ch. 4

Need for a decision

It is possible to begin at the stage described as 'need for a decision'. At some stage it will become evident to a manager that a decision is required relating to a particular situation. Such a decision might relate to a problem or crisis at the operational level as in this case, or to dealing with a key strategic threat (a competitor lowering the price of their product, for example). It might also relate at a more strategic level to the realisation that an opportunity exists (for expansion, increased market share, enhanced competitive advantage). This stage seems a very obvious one, but implies that both the organisation and manager have formal and informal monitoring systems to assess performance and standards and scan for opportunities. In the hotel scenario the manager becomes aware of the need for a decision at a relatively late stage – when the customer complains. This by itself indicates that the organisation

Figure 13.4 Decision-making process

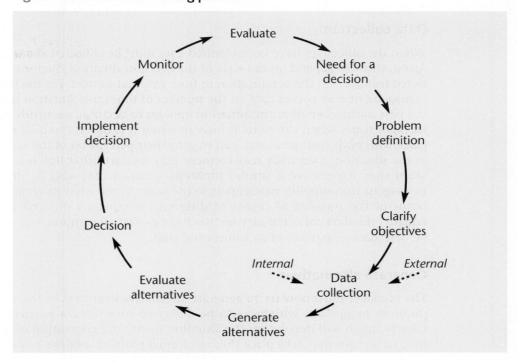

does not appear to have appropriate information systems in place to resolve such potential difficulties as they are happening or preferably before they can happen.

Problem definition

Once the decision recognition phase has occurred, then the problem definition phase is reached. The manager needs to ensure that a clear definition of the problem (or opportunity) is provided. Again, in the hotel context the problem appears to be that a customer did not receive his morning newspaper. But the manager needs to ensure a clear, concise and accurate definition of the situation is produced. Did the newspaper not arrive at all or did it arrive late? Was the wrong newspaper delivered rather than the one the customer requested? Have other customers complained of the same problem? Did this happen just today or has it happened in the past? The manager must develop an appropriate understanding of what exactly the problem is, its extent and scope.

Clarify objectives

With such a definition the manager can then develop appropriate decision objectives: what the decision (still to be taken) is intended to achieve. Clearly this in part will depend on the definition phase. A situation which has occurred only today with one customer will have very different decision objectives from one which has occurred repeatedly over the last month with a number of customers. The objectives phase is a particularly important one, however. The manager must be clear about what a particular decision, or set of related decisions, is to achieve. Without this clarification the manager will not be in a position in the future to determine whether a particular decision that was taken was effective or not.

Data collection

When the objectives have been clarified data must be collected about the problem. Again, this will depend on the scale of the decision situation. Such data may be collected from within the organisation or from external sources. For the hotel scenario, management may collect data on the number of times this situation has arisen over the past month; whether the situation appears to occur at weekends or during the week; at times when the hotel is busy or when it is quiet; discussions might take place with both customers and staff to gain their perception of the scale and extent of the situation. Externally management may contact other hotels in the group to see if they experience a similar problem. Contact may also be made with the newsagent that supplies newspapers to the hotel to see what its records indicate in terms of the number of copies of different newspapers ordered and supplied. Equally, the data collected may be 'hard' data – factual or numerical – or they may be 'soft' data – opinions of customers and staff.

Generate alternatives

The manager must now try to generate alternative decisions in the context of the problem or options which could be designed to resolve a particular problem. Clearly much will depend on the situation itself. The generation of such alternatives or options may take place through formal problem analysis using a number of techniques and decision tools (some of which are introduced later in this chapter). Other situations may call for a more 'creative' approach, particularly when the situation is unstructured.

Evaluate alternatives

Once a number of alternatives or options have been generated, then the decision maker must evaluate these. Clearly this must be done in the context of the 'clarify objectives' phase, with alternatives evaluated in the context of how far they contribute to the achievement of the declared decision objectives. Other criteria will also be used: the financial implications of each alternative, the wider organisational implications, and so on.

Decision

The critical part of this process is then reached where a decision must now be made. Of the alternatives which have been generated and then evaluated, a choice must be made as to which is most preferable and feasible.

Implement and monitor

However, decision making is about more than simply making a decision. The decision once made must be implemented and change effected in the organisation. It is tempting to conclude that the decision-making process ends here. However, the circle of the process in Figure 13.4 has yet to be closed. Some sort of monitoring system – either formal or informal – must be established to monitor the impact of the decision taken on the situation. This assists in an evaluation of the decision taken at some later date. Not only does this assist the organisation in assessing whether decisions taken to resolve particular problems have been effective, but it also helps the manager learn through experience in terms of which decisions proved effective and which did not and the reasons for this effectiveness or lack of it.

MODELS IN THE DECISION PROCESS

While a manager may encounter difficulty at any of the stages in the decision-making process, two in particular are likely to be problematic: the generation of alternatives and the evaluation of those alternatives. In either of these stages a manager may wish to apply appropriate quantitative models or techniques. A model can best be understood as a representation, or simulation, of reality. Perhaps the most familiar use of models is in the fields of science and engineering. Architects often construct a model of a new building or construction project to help visualise what it will look like and to facilitate analysis of the construction process. An engineer may build a physical model of a new piece of engineering equipment – a new aircraft type, for example, or a new model of car. Such models help in the process of trying out new ideas and assessing the impact they will have on the building or piece of equipment, without the expense and risk involved in instituting such changes on the real building or piece of equipment. Models have an equally important role to play in business. Naturally in business such models are not physical, as they are for the engineer or architect, but typically mathematical or statistical. A number of common business models will be introduced in the rest of this chapter and their potential role in the decision-making process illustrated. Similarly, we shall introduce a small number of techniques used in decision making. Naturally, we can only illustrate how models and techniques can contribute to the decision-making process. The number of models and techniques available to the manager is considerable and we are able only to introduce a few of the more basic. The list of further reading at the end of this chapter provides details of others (*see also* Chapter 6).

→ Ch. 6

THE BREAKEVEN MODEL

One of the simplest models is the **breakeven model**. Consider the following scenario. One of the hotels in the group has realised that an increasing part of its business consists of being the venue for meetings and small conferences. Typically, an outside organisation will hire a number of the larger rooms in the hotel for a meeting, seminar or training and development programme. The hotel has had an increasing number of requests from the organisers of such events to provide sophisticated on-site printing and photocopying facilities to produce course handouts for participants. Naturally, the event organisers expect to have to pay for such additional facilities, but as hotel manager you are trying to decide what to do. Clearly the option of providing such facilities is an attractive one, since it will satisfy a customer request and help contribute towards customer satisfaction and repeat business. However, there will clearly be financial consequences, and one of the key decisions would relate to how much to charge event organisers for the use of such facilities. The hotel manager has investigated the situation and collected some relevant data, and found that a local company will rent a suitable printer and photo copier to the hotel on an annual basis for £600. This company is also willing to take responsibility for the running costs of the machine (consisting of the cost of paper and toner together with routine maintenance) for £40 per 1000 copies. To assist the manager in evaluating alternatives and reaching a decision the total cost to the hotel can be broken into two elements. One is fixed or constant, the £600 rental fee, while the other varies with the number of copies produced by the machine. Referring to these as fixed cost and variable cost respectively this gives:

$$\text{Total cost} = \text{Fixed cost} + \text{Variable cost}$$
$$\text{or } TC = FC + VC$$

using FC to represent fixed cost and VC variable cost. Further, the two costs are readily quantified. FC is clearly £600, while VC will be 4p per copy (£40/1000). If the variable X is used to denote the number of copies made, then this gives:

$$TC = 600 + 0.04X$$

This equation allows the manager to determine the total cost incurred for any number of copies, X, produced by substituting a given numerical value for X in the equation and calculating the corresponding value for TC. It is often advantageous to show mathematical information graphically wherever possible (since a diagram usually conveys a much more immediate picture to a manager than does an equation). The graph corresponding to the TC equation is shown in Figure 13.5. The FC line is constant and parallel to the X axis on the graph, indicating that this cost element does not vary with the number of copies. The VC line starts from the origin (since variable costs will be zero when zero copies are produced) with a slope of 0.04

Figure 13.5 Costs

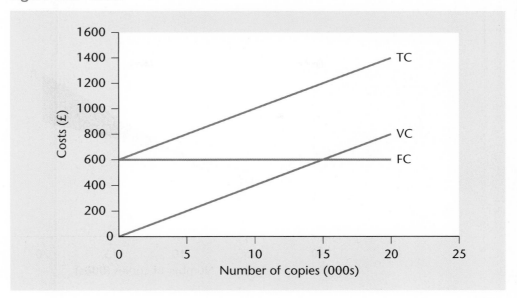

and reaches £800 when X is 20 000. The TC line, which is the combination of FC and VC, starts from 600 and has the same slope as the VC line, reaching £1400 when X is 20 000.

However, this is only one side of the situation. Clearly the hotel expects to generate revenue from the use of the equipment. Assume that the manager believes a price of 10p per copy would be acceptable to event organisers. The manager is trying to assess how this would affect the financial implications of the decision under consideration. Denoting R as revenue from copies made, the revenue equation is then:

$$R = 0.10X$$

How does this help the manager decide what the financial effects of installing the photocopier will be? Examine Figure 13.6 which shows the TC equation together with the R equation. Both the total costs and revenue implications of the decision are clearly seen, based on the information given. If the photocopier is used to produce less than 10 000 copies a year, then TC exceeds R, i.e. the total cost of providing this service exceeds the revenue that it generates. However, if the level of use exceeds 10 000 copies, the revenue exceeds costs. The figure of 10 000 copies is referred to as the breakeven point, since it indicates the level of use which generates neither a profit nor a loss and shows where costs and revenue are equal.

Clearly, this model does not indicate to the manager what the appropriate decision should be. However, it does serve its purpose in generating information about options and alternatives to be used in the decision process. The manager must now decide, based on other information, whether it is likely that usage levels will be above the breakeven figure. If the view is that they will not, then the manager has to assess whether to provide the service anyway, add to the hotel's competitive advantage and accept the extra financial consequences of this decision. One of the benefits of the model is that the manager can readily quantify what the exact financial consequences of a particular decision would be.

Figure 13.6 **Total costs and revenue**

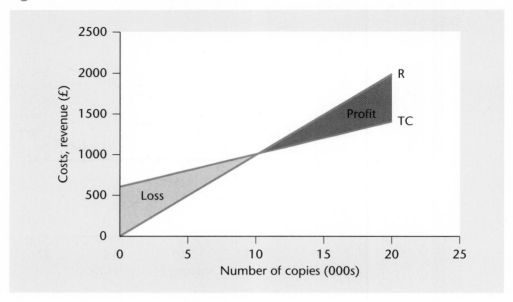

Such models can play a potentially important role in the decision-making process. This is further illustrated if the model is developed further. The graph has been used so far to determine the breakeven point. With some simple algebra this value can be determined mathematically.

$$TC = 600 + 0.04X$$
$$R = 0.1X$$

By definition the breakeven point occurs where TC = R:

$$TC = 600 + 0.04X = 0.1X = R$$
$$\text{or where } 600 + 0.04X = 0.1X$$

Rearranging gives:

$$600 = 0.1X - 0.04X \text{ or } 600 = 0.06X$$

and then:

$$X = 600/0.06 = 10\ 000$$

However, this applies only to the specific values we have for FC, VC and price charged per copy. In general:

$$TC = a + bX$$
$$R = cX$$

where a, b, c would take the appropriate numerical values. The breakeven point will then be given by:

$$X = a/(c - b)$$

This provides a general solution to the breakeven problem and the manager can generate 'what if' analyses relating to the decision situation. What if the fixed cost rises to £750? What if price charged rises to 12p per copy? What if customers are only willing to pay 8p a copy? Such analysis allows a manager to investigate other possible options in the context of the decision situation. In the first instance, for example, the new breakeven position is readily calculated as:

$$X = 750/(0.1 - 0.04) = 750/0.06 = 12\,500$$

That is, a rise in the fixed cost element would have the effect of pushing the breakeven point up by 2500 copies a year. As with all such quantitative models, the results of the analysis do not provide the manager with a decision. What they do provide is additional information about the decision situation and the various alternatives that may be under consideration. They also provide an analytical framework for the manager to evaluate such alternatives. This is illustrated further with the second model we shall examine: the **payoff table**.

PAYOFF TABLES

It will be evident that one of the key characteristics of business decision making is that it takes place under considerable uncertainty. A manager must take a decision typically with incomplete knowledge about the situation or knowing that the future outcomes of decisions taken now are uncertain. There are ways of examining these decision problems that can help clarify how decisions can be made.

This will be illustrated with a second scenario. The hotel group is considering its future direction and strategy. It has decided that there is the potential for increasing the number of business people from abroad who use the group's hotel facilities in Scotland. In particular, it feels that concentrated advertising in selected markets in Europe would increase this type of business. What the group's managing director has in mind is an advertising campaign aimed at businesses which wish to develop commercial and industrial links with companies in Scotland. What the hotel will offer to these businesses is a special 'package' deal. It will arrange air travel for foreign business people, a chauffeured executive car to collect them from the airport and take them to one of the group's hotels, and translation and interpretation facilities while they are in Scotland.

Three potential markets are currently under investigation: Scandinavia, Germany and Eastern Europe. The group has estimated that a suitable advertising campaign in each country (through TV, radio, the business press) would cost respectively:

Scandinavia	£150 000
Germany	£200 000
Eastern Europe	£300 000

The financial director has indicated that the group has financial resources to fund only one of these campaigns, and the critical decision is: which one? Naturally, the group expects a return for this expenditure through the increased business it attracts to its hotels. However, the situation is made difficult by the fact that the additional revenue generated will, in part, depend on the effectiveness of the campaign in each area. The group's marketing function has concluded that the overall effect of the campaign in each of the three areas could be classed as: low, medium or high impact. For each possibility they have quantified the financial return the group could anticipate from each area in terms of increased business. This is summarised in Table 13.1.

Table 13.1 Financial returns from the campaign (£000s)

AREA	OUTCOME		
	LOW	MEDIUM	HIGH
Scandinavia	175	225	250
Germany	150	300	350
Eastern Europe	100	250	600

So, for example, if the group decides to campaign in Germany and the campaign has a low impact, then it is expected the campaign will generate an additional £150 000 of business for the group. On the other hand, if the campaign is focused on Scandinavia and the outcome is high, then £250 000 of additional business is expected.

This scenario is typical of many situations that organisations have to face. The group is faced with a range of decision alternatives over which it has control (it can choose between them), but it also faces uncertainty in terms of the outcome of each of these alternatives. These future outcomes are referred to as 'states of nature': they are outside the direct control of the group. However, they do include all possible outcomes and only one of them can actually occur. How does the group decide what to do *now*, given that it does not know the outcome from the campaign that will be achieved in the *future*? Table 13.1 shows only one side of the situation. The cost of the campaign must also be taken into account. This can be achieved by constructing what is known as a payoff table, which shows the net effect of each possible decision and each outcome. Table 13.2 shows the results where the campaign costs for each area have been subtracted from the expected returns shown in Table 13.1.

The payoff table can now be used to consider the attractiveness of alternative decisions. Clearly the decision taken will be influenced by a number of factors other than the payoff table: how reliable the information is about the alternative decisions, how risky the various options are, how critical the decision is to the company's future, and so on. One of the key factors, however, will depend on the organisation's attitude to these future states of nature. In the absence of any other information on the likelihood of each state of nature, we can consider a number of options.

Table 13.2 Campaign payoffs (£000s)

AREA	OUTCOME		
	LOW	MEDIUM	HIGH
Scandinavia	25	75	100
Germany	−50	100	150
Eastern Europe	−200	−50	300

The maximax criterion

Assume that the hotel group's senior managers take an optimistic view of the future outcome. If this were the case, then they would choose the decision which generated the highest possible payoff, since they feel that the 'best' state of nature will occur. Such an approach is known as the **maximax criterion** since we are searching for the *max*imum of the *max*imum payoffs. In this problem the maximax decision would be to launch the campaign in Eastern Europe since this – potentially – generates the highest payoff at £300 000, compared with the best possible payoff of £150 000 for the German campaign and £100 000 for the Scandinavian. In general for this approach the maximum payoff for each decision is found and then the largest of these chosen. This approach has the advantage of focusing on the best possible outcome from the alternative decisions under consideration.

The maximin criterion

The maximax decision is based on an optimistic view of the future in terms of the states of nature that could occur. However, the group may take a different attitude and consider the worst-case scenario – a pessimistic view about future outcomes. In such a situation the **maximin criterion** can be applied: the *max*imum of the *mini*mum payoffs. The basic logic is to find the best decision given the assumption that the worst possible future outcome will occur. For each alternative decision the minimum (worst) payoff is found and then the largest of these chosen to find the most desirable decision. In this case this would lead to a decision to launch the campaign in Scandinavia since this is the largest of the minimum payoffs at £25 000 (the minimum payoffs being £25 000, –£50 000 and –£200 000 respectively). Such an approach ensures that management has taken the best decision if the worst outcome happens. However, it is also evident that the approach ignores the potentially larger payoffs from other decisions.

The minimax regret criterion

A third approach, the **minimax regret criterion**, uses the concept of opportunity loss or regret. Assume the decision is taken to launch the campaign in Scandinavia. Having committed itself to this course of action, management later observes that the impact of the campaign was high. With hindsight management realises that the decision taken was not the best given the state of nature that actually occurred (even though when it took the decision it had no way of knowing which state of nature would prevail). The optimal decision for this state of nature would have been to campaign in Eastern Europe since this has a higher payoff given this state of nature. Effectively, the group has 'lost' £200 000 by taking the decision to launch in Scandinavia. This figure is referred to as the opportunity cost – or regret – of the decision for that state of nature. The opportunity loss, or regret, associated with each possible decision and the various states of nature can be calculated using the same logic. This is summarised in Table 13.3.

Each column (state of nature) in the payoff table is considered in turn and it is determined, for that state of nature, what the optimum decision would be. So, if the campaign impact was low, the optimum decision would be to campaign in Scandinavia. If this decision had actually been taken, the 'regret' in financial terms would be zero, since it was the best decision given this state of nature. On the other

Table 13.3 **Regret (£000s)**

AREA	OUTCOME		
	LOW	MEDIUM	HIGH
Scandinavia	0	25	200
Germany	75	0	150
Eastern Europe	225	150	0

hand, if it had been decided to campaign in Germany, the regret would be £75 000, since a payoff of £25 000 could have been achieved, whereas the decision actually incurred a loss of £50 000. Similarly, if the decision had been to campaign in Eastern Europe, the regret would be £225 000. These calculations can be performed for the other two states of nature columns. This process can be repeated for each outcome in turn, producing the data in Table 13.3.

For each of the decision options the maximum of these regret values is then obtained: £200 000 for Scandinavia, £150 000 for Germany, £225 000 for Eastern Europe. Each decision is considered in turn and the maximum regret value shows the maximum opportunity cost associated with this decision on the assumption that the worst state of nature happens. Management would then wish to take the decision where this maximum regret was minimised. This would be the decision to campaign in Germany, since this has the lowest maximum regret at £150 000. The basic logic of the approach is to say: how much does the group stand to 'lose' from each decision if that decision turns out to be the wrong one? Management then chooses the decision where this potential 'loss' is minimised.

It is worth noting that in this scenario the three different approaches have led to three different decisions, with the decision taken depending on the decision maker's view of the future. One of the benefits of this approach is that it requires the decision maker to consider and justify explicitly their view of future states of nature. One of its main drawbacks is that the three states of nature have been treated as being equally likely. Management needs to be able to incorporate such likelihood information into the decision-making process, which can be achieved by introducing the concept of expected value.

EXPECTED VALUE

It is clear that management is currently assuming that the three outcomes from the campaign are equally likely. This will not necessarily be a realistic assumption. Based on further analysis, market research or simply personal intuition and experience, management might feel that some of the outcomes are more likely than others. If this is the case, and such likelihoods can be quantified, then management will clearly want to take this extra factor into account when trying to reach an appropriate decision. Assume that the group has been able to quantify such likelihoods, referred to as probabilities, as shown in Table 13.4.

Table 13.4 **Probability of outcomes**

	OUTCOME		
AREA	LOW	MEDIUM	HIGH
Scandinavia	0.2	0.4	0.4
Germany	0.2	0.4	0.4
Eastern Europe	0.5	0.2	0.3

It can be seen that the probabilities of each outcome for Scandinavia and Germany are the same, but different from those for Eastern Europe. By convention a probability is shown as a value between 0 and 1, with 0 indicating something which can never happen and 1 indicating that it is certain to happen. For example, the Low outcome has a probability of 0.2 for Scandinavia and for Germany: there is a 20 per cent chance that this is the outcome that will occur, compared with 40 per cent for Medium and 40 per cent for High. For Eastern Europe, however, the probability of Low is higher (i.e. this outcome is more likely to occur) at 50 per cent. Note that the total of the probabilities for each area individually total to 1: one of the three outcomes must occur.

Clearly management now needs to be able to use this additional information to help it reach a decision. The approach taken is to calculate the **expected value** for each of the alternative decisions. Consider the decision to campaign in Scandinavia. For this decision there are three possible states of nature, each with a payoff, and for each state of nature there is now a probability. It seems reasonable to use these probabilities to calculate a weighted average outcome for this decision. That is:

$$(£25\,000 \times 0.2) + (£75\,000 \times 0.4) + (£100\,000 \times 0.4)$$

That is, if we campaign in Scandinavia there is a 20 per cent chance of a £25 000 payoff, a 40 per cent chance of a £75 000 payoff and a 40 per cent chance of a £100 000 payoff. The calculation gives a figure of £75 000 as the expected value (EV) of this decision: the alternative payoffs weighted by the respective probabilities. Care needs to be taken in terms of what the EV represents. It is not a guaranteed payoff from this decision. Rather it is a measure taking into account both the payoffs and their likelihood. The purpose of such EVs is to facilitate comparison between alternative decisions under such conditions of uncertainty. The EVs for the three alternative decisions are:

Scandinavia	£75 000
Germany	£90 000
Eastern Europe	–£40 000

Based on this information it would be logical to recommend that the campaign is launched in Germany since it has a higher EV. Note that the option for Eastern Europe actually has a negative EV: its weighted payoff indicates a loss rather than a profit. Once again, it must be stressed that taking a decision on such a basis does not guarantee a positive payoff to the group. The state of nature that actually occurs in Germany could generate a payoff of –£50 000, £100 000 or £150 000. Overall, however, the German option is to be favoured since the weighted combination of payoffs and probabilities is higher than that for the other two options.

DECISION TREES

➔ Ch. 2

It is also possible to examine this type of decision situation by constructing a **decision tree** which shows the relationship over time between decisions, outcomes, payoffs and probabilities (*see also* Chapter 2). The tree diagram for this problem is shown in Figure 13.7. The tree starts on the left. The box symbol (known as a decision node) is used to denote that at this point a decision must be taken and the alternative decisions branch out from this node: to campaign in Scandinavia (S), Germany (G) or Eastern Europe (E). Each of these branches leads to an outcome node (represented by a circle) showing the states of nature: future outcomes from the decisions over which the decision maker has no control. In this example the node along each decision branch is the same: the campaign impact could turn out to be low (L), medium (M) or high (H). At the end of each branch there is a payoff: a total of nine possible payoffs of this problem. Information is then added on the payoffs, the probability of each outcome and the EVs of each decision branch. The decision maker now sees clearly the potential payoffs from each decision and state of nature combination. Also the EVs for each decision can be identified and used to assist in the decision-making process, as we have discussed.

Figure 13.7 Decision tree

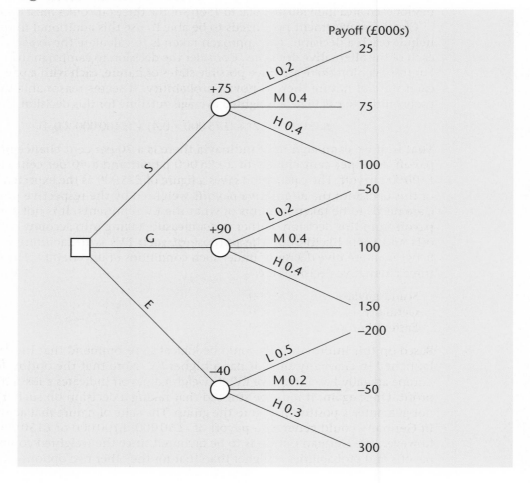

Decision trees are useful ways of showing the outcomes and potential consequences of alternative decisions. They are also particularly useful in situations where a series of decisions may need to be taken over time and where subsequent decision options may depend on future outcomes. Consider an expansion of the existing scenario. One of the members of the group's board is still not convinced that the Eastern European option should be ruled out at this stage, particularly given that potentially it offers the largest payoff of the three (at £300 000). The director believes that if the company chooses this option for its promotion campaign and if the impact of that campaign is either Low or Medium in the future (leading to a negative payoff), then there is the possibility of a supplementary advertising campaign to try to boost business further. Some additional research has been conducted into this. If, six months after the initial campaign in Eastern Europe, the impact turns out to be Low or Medium, then a supplementary campaign can be conducted at an additional cost of £100 000. If the initial impact is Low then it is felt that this additional campaign has a probability of 0.3 of increasing the payoff by £300 000. However, there is a 0.7 probability that the additional campaign will have no further impact on payoff at all. If the initial outcome is Medium then the supplementary campaign has a 0.4 probability of having a zero effect and a 0.6 probability of increasing payoff by £300 000.

Clearly the group needs to evaluate the effect of this additional option on the original decision. However, there is an additional difficulty. The finance department has indicated that it needs to know now – and not in six months' time – whether the additional £100 000 will be needed for the campaign in order to ensure that the group's cash flow is not adversely affected. In other words, the group cannot wait until it knows the outcome of the initial campaign before making a further decision. It needs to decide now what this second decision will be. It will be helpful if the additional information is summarised. For the Eastern European option we have:

Initial outcome: Low		*Initial outcome: Medium*	
Initial payoff	–£200 000	Initial payoff	–£50 000
Supplementary costs	£100 000	Supplementary costs	£100 000
Supplementary payoff:		Supplementary payoff:	
£0	(probability 0.7)	£0	(probability 0.4)
£300 000	(probability 0.3)	£300 000	(probability 0.6)

The part of the original decision tree relating to Eastern Europe has been updated to help decide what to do. Figure 13.8 shows the amended tree. The decision options relating to Scandinavia and Germany have been simplified to show only their respective EVs. If the Eastern European option is examined in detail, it can be seen how the additional information is incorporated. The initial decision is one of three: S, G, E. For the Eastern Europe decision, there are the three original initial outcomes, Low, Medium, High. For the High outcome nothing alters in terms of probability or payoff. For Low and Medium, however, a second decision node is needed to help determine whether or not to launch a supplementary campaign. These decisions are shown as Supp (supplementary campaign is launched) and No supp. For the No supp decision in both cases, the payoffs remain as they were in the original problem. For the Supp decision option, however, there is a change. If the initial impact is Low and the supplementary campaign is launched, there are two secondary outcomes: the supplementary campaign could lead to an increase in payoff or could leave the payoff unchanged. The respective probabilities and net

Figure 13.8 Amended decision tree (£000s)

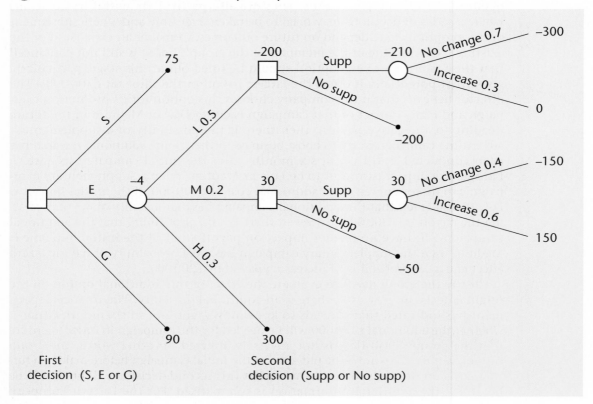

payoffs are shown. It can then be seen that the EV of launching the supplementary campaign *if* the initial impact is Low would be –£210000. This is actually a lower EV than the alternative decision of No supp. This implies that if management decides to target Eastern Europe (the initial decision) and if the campaign impact is Low, it knows *now* that a supplementary campaign is not worthwhile. In other words, management can predict now what a future decision would be relating to a particular set of outcomes based on the information given. For the initial impact of Medium a similar process takes place. It can be seen that the EV of launching the supplementary campaign is £30000 compared with the EV of not launching this campaign of –£50 000. Again, management can predict a future decision. If it decides to campaign in Eastern Europe and if the initial impact is Medium, then a supplementary campaign should be launched.

However, does this affect management's initial decision to campaign in Germany and not Eastern Europe? This can be answered by working backwards through the amended diagram. The payoffs for each of the three initial outcomes are then –£200000 (since if the initial outcome is Low the group would do nothing further), £30000 (which has changed from the original –£50000 since the group would now launch the supplementary campaign) and £300000 (which is also unchanged). Using the original probabilities the EV for the Eastern European option is now –£4000. This is still negative and would not affect the original decision to target Germany. It can also illustrate how such an approach can be used to assess in the present decisions that may have to be taken at some time in the future.

Management does not have to wait for an outcome to occur before considering and choosing between alternative decisions; with the right information management can make that decision now and be ready to implement it should that particular outcome occur.

ISHIKAWA DIAGRAMS

→ Ch. 7

The next management technique useful in decision making is descriptive rather than quantitative. This is the Ishikawa diagram – alternatively known as the cause–effect diagram or the fishbone diagram (*see also* Chapter 7). Originally developed for use in the area of quality management, organisations have found it equally useful in terms of wider problem solving and decision making. Consider the problem scenario we developed earlier, relating to customer complaints in the hotel about non-delivery of morning newspapers. An initial investigation has revealed that the problem is not a one-off: it has been happening for some time and a number of customers have experienced the problem. One of the difficulties the decision maker has in such a context is trying to determine the fundamental causes of the problem, the relative importance of each cause and possible relationships between causes. An Ishikawa diagram can help the decision maker by providing a framework to identify such causes and their relationships. The general format of the diagram is shown in Figure 13.9, although the approach is readily adapted to the exact situation under examination.

The diagram starts at the right-hand side with the observed effect. This is the issue, situation or problem that management is focusing on. The major causes, or contributory factors, relating to this effect are then identified and used to label the ends of each major branch as shown. One common approach is to consider five major factors: manpower (shortage of staff perhaps, inadequate training, poor communication between staff); materials (resources, quality of resources); machines; methods (work practices, data capture systems) and measurements. Factors which contribute to each of these major causes can then be determined and used to label sub-branches coming from each main cause branch, as in Figure 13.10.

Figure 13.9 Ishikawa diagram: effect, causes and sub-causes

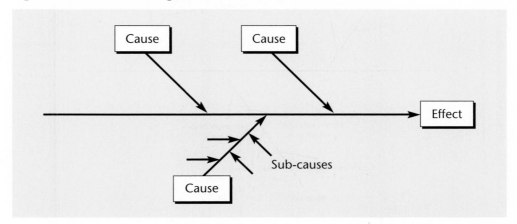

Figure 13.10 **Ishikawa diagram: the five Ms**

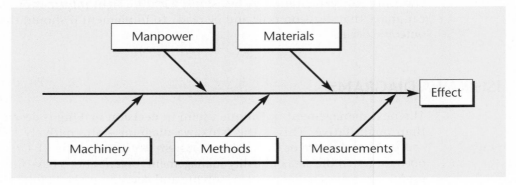

The Ishikawa diagram is a method of focusing on the major factors causing a particular effect. It seems very simple and straightforward, but is deceptively powerful when used in the right way. A team approach to identify causes is likely to be needed since most activities will involve a group of people rather than one individual. Figure 13.11 shows a completed diagram that might have been produced by the hotel manager after consultation with key members of staff.

On the manpower side, factors have been identified as: understaffing in the hotel, key staff away ill, staff having an unclear idea as to who was responsible for providing this service, new staff who had not been told it was part of their duties. On the materials side, management has identified that on occasion the wrong newspapers are delivered to the hotel and sometimes not enough newspapers are delivered. On the methods side, it can be seen that orders are often sent late to the supplying newsagent (possibly linked to some of the materials causes), the room service staff (who take orders for morning papers from customers) do not communi-

Figure 13.11 **Ishikawa diagram for hotel problem**

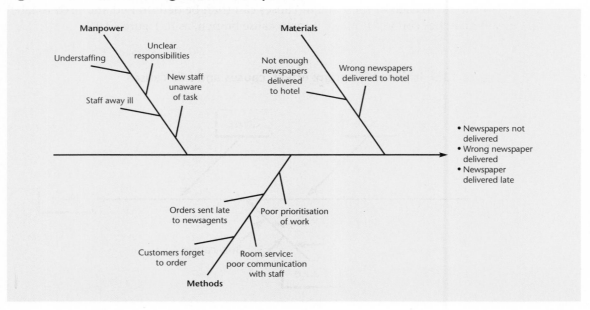

cate adequately with the staff who have to deliver the papers, occasionally the effect can be caused by customers in the hotel simply forgetting to place an order for a specific newspaper, and there can be a problem with staff prioritisation of this task with others that are expected of them (linked to one of the manpower causes). Note that the manager has decided to drop the machinery and measurement branches as redundant to this problem analysis.

What the diagram provides is a focused analysis of key factors contributing to the problem. The manager now has a clear perspective on contributing factors and can begin the process of prioritising between them and seeking solutions to them. In some cases there may be no direct solution. Understaffing, for example, may be a perennial problem if the company is exercising central control over local staff numbers. However, it is evident that improved training is needed for new staff to ensure they are aware of all their duties and it is also evident that communication needs to be improved between management, room service and staff, and also between the hotel and the supplying newsagent. Perhaps an agreement for the hotel to fax or e-mail its order last thing in the evening might help resolve some of these causes. Similarly, a new system is needed to ensure that customers are aware of their need to order before a specific time.

The diagram demonstrates the potential in terms of assisting the decision maker. Whatever the possible solutions, the diagram allows management to assess the impact each solution could be expected to have on the effect. This by itself can be a valuable conclusion to reach. Improving staff training, for example, will not solve the entire problem given that there are other factors contributing to the problem that will not be solved by this initiative. Similarly, although the diagram is readily applied to effects in the guise of problems, it can also be applied to effects which indicate 'success'. If one feature of a product or service is seen as particularly successful, this method can be a useful mechanism for identifying the key factors that have contributed to this success with a view to replicating these factors for other products/services.

FORCEFIELD ANALYSIS

The techniques and models introduced so far are focused on the stages of the decision-making process which relate to the generation of alternatives and the evaluation of those alternatives. As has already been discussed, part of the management decision-making process involves the successful implementation of the decision taken: making it work, in other words. No matter how well designed the decision, a manager may well find in practice that once implemented the decision does not have the desired or expected effect.

→ Chs 1 and 5

Naturally there may be many reasons for this, but **forcefield analysis** considers one aspect of such a situation (*see also* Chapters 1 and 5). A decision situation – where some change is seen as necessary – can be visualised as comprising two mutually opposed forces: what can be described as restraining forces which resist the change implied in some decision, and driving forces which support or encourage change. The purpose of forcefield analysis is to help the manager identify in advance of decision implementation what these critical forces are likely to be, and consider how best the restraining forces can be removed or minimised and how the driving forces can be strengthened. The approach in forcefield analysis is straightforward. Consider the decision situation shown in Figure 13.12.

Figure 13.12 **Forcefield analysis**

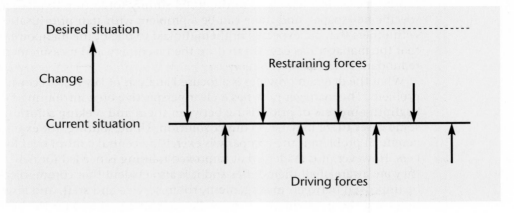

The current situation is shown as the solid line and the desired situation – after successful implementation of some decision – is shown as a dotted line. The gap between the two implies change. In the move to push towards the desired situation it is likely that a number of restraining forces will be encountered. These need to be individually identified and used to label each arrow line. A number of key driving forces can be identified in the same way. The next stage is to assess the relative strengths of each force: some will be stronger than others in either driving or restraining the change. The forcefield – and the current situation – can now be regarded as representing an equilibrium position: a position of balance. In order to push towards the desired situation, management must either strengthen the driving forces to push the situation forward or weaken the restraining forces (or, of course, do both).

Consider another hotel scenario. In one hotel in the group the main reception desk is responsible for taking telephone bookings for accommodation from customers. Typically, a customer will telephone the reception desk to make a booking, various details will then be entered into the computerised booking system and, at a later date, written confirmation sent to the customer. However, the hotel manager has recently become aware that an unacceptable number of errors occur in the input of customer details into the computerised booking system. In some cases this causes relatively minor problems – customers are greeted by the wrong name when they check into the hotel – in other cases it is more serious, with the bill sent to the wrong customer address. The manager has decided that a zero-defect target will be established: that no errors of this kind will be tolerated.

Figure 13.13 shows the results of a forcefield analysis on the situation. A number of restraining forces have been identified and the relative importance of each shown in relation to the size of the arrowed line (with longer lines implying more importance). It can be seen that the effective implementation of the zero-defect decision will be restrained by inexperienced staff, inadequate equipment (with both poor screen layouts and antiquated equipment), physical difficulties caused by the layout of the reception area, and too many distractions when staff are on the phone and keying in details. Similarly, a number of driving forces have also been identified, including managerial pressure, the corporate objective of achieving customer satisfaction, planned modification to computer software and an initiative to allow reception staff some degree of job specialisation.

Figure 13.13 Forcefield analysis for hotel problem

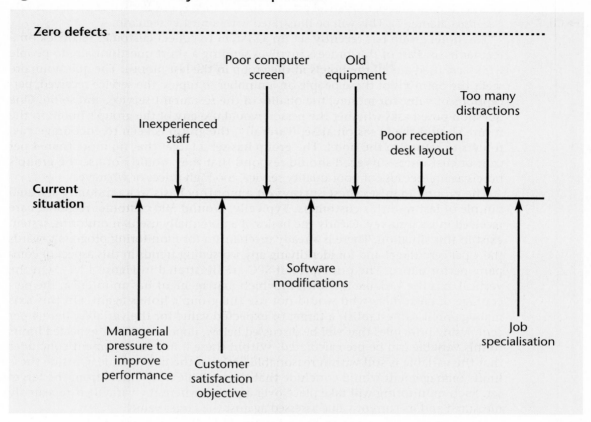

The decision maker can now use the analysis to evaluate how the restraining factors can be removed or reduced (and indeed whether this will happen with some of the initiatives under way) and how to reinforce the driving forces. For example, the manager might decide to improve communications with reception staff so that they are fully aware of the importance of achieving customer satisfaction. Involving the reception staff in an evaluation of how the physical layout could be improved might help resolve one of the restraining forces. A detailed proposal for additional capital expenditure to replace old equipment might be made to the group finance director. Whatever initiatives are taken, the forcefield analysis allows these to be focused on the key forces with a view to enhancing the successful implementation of the original decision to move towards a zero-defect situation.

STATISTICAL PROCESS CONTROL

The last technique introduced in this chapter is one which helps close the loop of the decision-making process. As discussed earlier, it is important as part of this process for an organisation to have methods and systems in place which periodically monitor and assess performance from a number of perspectives. Not only does this allow management to assess the impact of decisions that have already been taken, it provides them with a perspective on any developing situations which may

→ Ch. 7

require decisions at some stage in the future. One method that is useful in a variety of situations is that of **statistical process control** (SPC), also known as **control charts** (*see also* Chapter 7). This will be illustrated with a further scenario.

The hotel group has recently set up a system to collect customer feedback on a regular basis. Part of this process involves sending a short questionnaire to people who have used any of the hotels in the group in the last month. The questionnaire seeks the opinions of these people on a number of topics: the service received, perceptions of value for money, the quality of the restaurant service, and so on. One question posed asks whether the person would use any of the group's hotels in the future should the occasion arise. Naturally, the group is keen to encourage customers to return to the hotel. The group has set a target that no more than 4 per cent of customers surveyed should respond that they would not use the group's hotels again (because of poor-quality service, too high prices or whatever).

The group organises these surveys on a monthly basis to a randomly selected sample of last month's customers. Typically, around 500 customer responses are received in each survey. Clearly the basics of a potentially useful monitoring system exist in this situation. There is a ready mechanism for monitoring progress towards the 4 per cent target and for identifying any worsening trends in this aspect of company performance. The principles of SPC are illustrated in Figure 13.14. On the vertical axis the variable is shown in which management has an interest: the percentage of customers who would not use the group's hotels again. On this axis management can establish a target or expected value for the variable, here 4 per cent. Using principles that will be discussed below, upper and lower expected limits to this variable can be pre-calculated. Within these limits management concludes that the variable is still within reasonable limits of the target value. Outside these limits management would conclude that the variable now differs from the target set. Such monitoring will take place over a period where the variable is repeatedly measured and its current value assessed against the target value.

However, there does appear to be a slight difficulty in this process, which relates to the fact that the results in any one month will represent only a sample of

Figure 13.14 Control chart

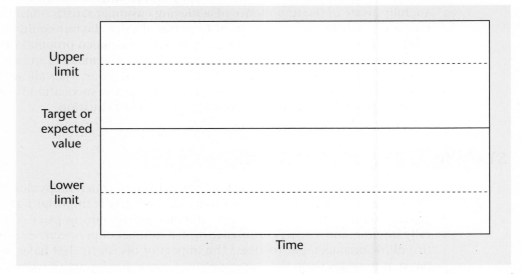

customers and not all customers. For example, suppose management finds that last month 5 per cent of customers surveyed indicated they would not use the group's hotels again. Should the group conclude that customer attitudes – and possibly hotel performance – have worsened and are unacceptably higher than the target of 4 per cent? After all, it is based on only some customers. Perhaps a different sample of 500 customer responses would indicate a different result.

This scenario illustrates what is known as '**sampling variation**', which is a common problem for any organisation engaged in market research, opinion polls or customer satisfaction surveys. Sampling variation relates to the difference in results that might be expected simply by taking different samples of customers (or whatever is being measured). The subject area itself is a very technical one and the complete technical background required cannot be provided here. However, it is possible to introduce the general principles. At the heart of SPC lies what is known as the sampling distribution. All the group's customers last month can be defined as the statistical population (perhaps several thousand), and then it becomes clear that it would be possible to take many different samples of 500 customers from this population. Each sample would provide a result in terms of the percentage who would not use the group again. Some of these sample results would be the same, some would differ (simply because there are different combinations of customers in the sample from the population).

It is possible to construct a frequency diagram showing the sample results and the frequency of these results; then, according to statistical theory, a distribution like that shown in Figure 13.15 would be obtained. This figure shows what is known as the sampling distribution, which takes a typical symmetrical shape (known as the normal distribution). In the middle of this distribution is the result that would be obtained if all customers (the population) were asked. Most sample results (even though they are based on only 500 customer responses) will be similar to the population result. Relatively few sample results would be very different from the result obtained from asking the full customer population. In fact, statistical theory allows for a further stage in predicting what these differences would be. Figure 13.16 shows the principles.

Using what is known as a standard error to measure variability, statistical theory predicts that 95 per cent of all sample results, where there is a normal distribution,

Figure 13.15 Sampling distribution: distribution of sample results

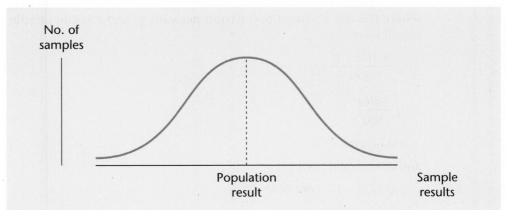

Figure 13.16 Sampling variation and standard error

will occur within 2 standard errors (SEs) of the population result, while 99.7 per cent will occur within 3 SEs. This implies that, although it is only a sample result, it is possible to quantify how close it is likely to be to the population result.

The implications are straightforward. It is possible to treat the target figure of 4 per cent as the desired population result (i.e. no more than 4 per cent of all customers saying they would not use the group's hotels again). It is possible then to compare the result from any one sample of 500 customer responses against this target figure and use the 2SE and 3SE values as a measure. Put simply, if the target is being achieved, then it can be anticipated (with 95 per cent confidence) that any sample of customer responses would be within 2SEs of 4 per cent, and with 99.7 per cent confidence that they would be within 3SEs of 4 per cent. But suppose we took a sample and found that the sample result was not within these 3SE limits? What would this imply? It would imply that the current population result was unlikely to be 4 per cent, i.e. it would imply that the target of 4 per cent set by the group is not being met.

The standard error can be calculated by using the following formula:

$$\sqrt{\frac{P(100 - P)}{n}}$$

where P is the assumed population percentage and n is the sample size. Here we would have:

$$\sqrt{\frac{4(100 - 4)}{500}}$$

$$\sqrt{\frac{4(96)}{500}}$$

= 0.876 per cent

and 2SEs would then be:

2(0.876) = 1.75 per cent

and 3SEs = 2.63 per cent.

This now provides a method for checking whether, based on a sample result of 500 customer responses, the group is meeting its target of 4 per cent or not. As long as the sample result is within 1.75 percentage points of the target (i.e. between 2.25 per cent and 5.75 per cent), it can be assumed that the target is being met. On the other hand, if the sample result is outside the 3SE limit (i.e. outside the range 1.37 per cent to 6.63 per cent), then it is possible to be 99.7 per cent confident that the target is not being achieved. If it lies between 2SEs and 3SEs away from the target, a position can be adopted of seeing this result as warning that the target might not be being met. In the terminology of SPC the 2SE limit is known as a warning limit (warning that, if the sample result has exceeded this figure, then there would be a danger of not meeting the target) and the 3SE figure as an action limit indicating that management action is needed, since, based on the sample result, the target is not being met. This can be shown in diagram form (*see* Figure 13.17).

This is a straightforward method for monitoring the target value based on samples taken every month. The sample result can be plotted on the control chart. If the result is within the warning limits, then it is possible to reach the conclusion that the target of 4 per cent is being met. If the result is outside the action limits, then it can be concluded that the target is not being met and there is a need to take action accordingly. If the result is between the warning and action limits, then it can be concluded that there are grounds for suspecting the target is not being met, although it is not possible as yet to be positive about this. It is possible, under such circumstances, to arrange for another sample to be taken. Over time there would be a plot of the sample results. Not only would it be possible to monitor each month's result against the target, it would also be possible to observe any developing trends in the sample results. Figure 13.18 shows the principles.

The results of the last six months' samples are plotted. None of them breaches the warning limits; so, on an individual basis, none of them is cause for concern. However, it should be noted that the last five months together show a definite

Figure 13.17 Control chart with action and warning limits

Figure 13.18 **Control chart for six successive samples**

upward trend in the sample results. It looks as if there is a slowly worsening attitude among samples of customers and this might be investigated before the next sample is taken.

SUMMARY

- Decision making forms an important part of any manager's workload, no matter at what level of management the individual operates and what the type or business of the organisation. Indeed, it could be argued that decision making and problem solving are at the heart of a manager's role in any organisation.

- The business environment in which such management decision making takes place is becoming increasingly complex, making the task of decision making that much more difficult. At the same time, and for many of the same reasons, the strategic and financial consequences of inappropriate decisions for an organisation are becoming greater.

- The types of decision situation faced will naturally vary considerably from one organisation to another and from one manager to another. While decision making approaches must be tailored to fit the particular circumstances, many decision situations have common aspects.

- There is no panacea that can be offered to a decision maker providing a foolproof and guaranteed method for decision making. However, adopting a logical and rational approach to a decision situation can be particularly productive. In any decision situation it will be worthwhile considering the wider decision-making process that applies and evaluating the various stages of this process that must be addressed for the particular situation under consideration. Similarly, in the task of generating potential alternative solutions for a decision situation and assessing those alternatives against the declared decision objectives, the use of a number of commonly used business models can be productive, although the output from such models must be seen as only part of the information-gathering process involved in decision making.

■ Such models are particularly valuable in decision situations where incomplete or inadequate information is available, where a number of alternatives are typically available and where uncertainty exists.

■ A number of these models have been introduced in this chapter, but it must also be said that the last two or three decades have seen a veritable explosion of such models being developed and used. The subject area known as management science has provided many of these model developments and a number of texts are detailed in the references for further reading which introduce additional models of potential use to the decision maker.

Review and discussion questions

1 *From a management perspective what is the difference between decision making and problem solving?*

2 *Consider an organisation with which you are familiar. What is the organisation's attitude to risk? How does this affect its decision-making process?*

3 *As a manager facing some decision situation which has areas of uncertainty associated with it, is it possible to quantify such areas of uncertainty?*

4 *What are the key differences between management decision making and personal decision making?*

5 *Discuss how time affects the various stages of the decision-making process.*

6 *Consider the various decision support models introduced in this chapter. What factors would discourage managers from utilising the information derived from such models in the decision-making process?*

7 *'Decision making is the most important task for any manager.' Discuss this statement.*

8 *A manager in an organisation has been offered a considerable promotion. However, the promotion would involve moving to another part of the country.*
   a *Using the decision-making process model, consider how the manager would try to reach an appropriate decision.*
   b *Draw a decision tree representing the decision situation.*
   c *Assume the manager has decided to take the promotion. Draw a forcefield diagram to assess the critical factors which will affect the 'success' of the move.*

9 *When you have read the case study on Jaguar Cars, answer the following:*
   a *What are the main strategic and operational pressures affecting Jaguar Cars over the last few years in terms of the external business environment?*
   b *What are the key strategic and operational decisions facing Jaguar?*
   c *Which of the models introduced in this chapter do you think would help Jaguar's management?*

CASE STUDY

Jaguar Cars

A Jaguar car
Instantly recognisable almost anywhere in the world.

Jaguar has had a very chequered history over the last few decades. In the early 1980s the company came close to disappearing, with reducing market share, decreasing financial viability, outdated technology and working practices, and major product quality problems. With the introduction of new management it was able – painfully – to turn itself around and achieve improvements in efficiency, quality and profitability. Towards the end of the decade a worldwide recession emerged and the company again hit problems. In 1989 the company was bought by Ford Motor Company for around US$2.5 billion, with the new owner then having to find a further $700 million to help keep the company going in the short term.

Jaguar starkly illustrates the difficulties involved in decision making in today's environment. On the face of it, the company had tremendous potential. On the other hand, it faced a number of major short-term problems. These included:

- the company was operating at a loss. It was estimated that in 1992 it actually lost $18 000 on each car sold;
- in motor-industry terms it was very small, even when compared with its competitors in the luxury car market. Mercedes Benz, for example, has annual sales almost 20 times those of Jaguar;
- it was operating at below breakeven output. Breakeven annual sales were estimated at 35 000. In 1993 Jaguar expected to produce and sell only 29 000 cars;
- worldwide there had been a dramatic collapse in the market for luxury cars;
- the company's cars had significant quality problems, particularly in relation to its major competitors, with, for example, a Jaguar car experiencing 75 per cent more defects than a Mercedes;
- many of the company's cars were relatively old models. However, the development costs of a new model were likely to run into the hundreds of millions of £s. In addition, such development would take considerable time.

The new management of Jaguar faced an array of interlinked problems as well as considerable uncertainty about markets, demand, customer loyalty and competitors' strategy. It was also constrained by the desire to keep Jaguar as a unique product and not simply another variety of Ford car. A number of decisions were taken to try to move the company forward. These included:

- immediate improvements in operating efficiency. Assembly man-hours per car, for example, were reduced by almost 40 per cent in a two-year period, with a further 50 per cent reduction planned;
- significant quality improvements, with defects down by over 70 per cent on the XJ6 model alone;
- a major cost-reduction programme leading to a reduction in the workforce of almost 50 per cent;
- the introduction of, and development of, new models, but with decisions related to different timescales. In the short term the company decided to introduce a redesigned version of the XJ6 – which was a relatively quick and low-cost option – and longer term to invest in the design and the production of a totally new car aimed at the business executive market.

The decisions faced by the company's management were clearly a mixture of the strategic and the operational. At the operational level, decisions had to be taken about how best to improve the company's immediate position. These needed to be taken quickly and needed to have an immediate impact on the company's performance. While such decisions can be taken relatively easily – relating to quality, productivity and operating costs – implementing such decisions effectively can be more problematic given issues of staff morale and uncertainty, and there is clearly considerable scope for some of the problem-solving techniques introduced in this chapter.

At the same time, a number of key strategic decisions were needed to try to ensure the company's long-term future. Such decisions related to the size of the company's customer base, the range of models available, its pricing policy and the location of its production base. Over time a series of related decisions emerged, and the sequential decision models introduced in this chapter clearly have a lot of potential in such a situation. As a short-term measure the company launched a redesigned version of the XJ6. In 1996 the company launched the XK8 sports car. The X200 executive saloon was launched in 1998 with further plans for the production of a family saloon, the X200. As with all management decision making, only time will tell whether such decisions are strategically and operationally effective. The initial signs in the twenty-first century were promising. Unit sales for Jaguar had increased to just over 90 000 by 2000 and to just over 130 000 by 2002. However, Jaguar also recorded an operating loss in 2002 of around £300 million, around 50 per cent of the total loss recorded by Ford's luxury car division (which also includes Land Rover, Aston Martin and Volvo). Clearly further strategic and operational decisions are still needed, reinforcing the point that organisations face a turbulent and ever-changing environment and that effective decision making becomes ever more difficult.

FURTHER READING

Ackoff, R L (1978) *The Art of Problem Solving*, Chichester: Wiley.

Ambrosini, V (1998) *Exploring Techniques of Analysis and Evaluation in Strategic Management*, Hemel Hempstead: Prentice Hall.

Coles, S and Rowley, J (1995) 'Revisiting Decision Trees', *Management Decisions*, 33 (8): 46–50.

Dickson, T (ed.) (1999) *Mastering Global Business*, London: FT Management.

Drucker, P (1992) *Management*, Oxford: Butterworth-Heinemann.

Dyson, R G and O'Brien F A (eds) (1998) *Strategic Development Methods and Models*, Chichester: Wiley.

Eden, C and Ackerman, F (1998) *Making Strategy*, London: Sage.

Harvard Business Review (2001) *Harvard Business Review on Decision Making*, Boston, MA: Harvard Business School Press.

Hicks, M J (1991) *Problem Solving in Business and Management*, London: Chapman & Hall.

Islei, G *et al.* (1991) 'Modelling Strategic Decision Making and Performance Measurements at ICI Pharmaceuticals', *Interfaces*, 21 (6): 4–22.

Johnson, G and Scholes, K (2002) *Exploring Corporate Strategy* (6th edn), Harlow: FT Prentice Hall.

Juran, J M and Gryna, F M (1993) *Quality Planning and Analysis* (3rd edn), New York: McGraw-Hill.

Mintzberg, H and Quinn, J B (1996) *The Strategy Process: Concepts, Contexts and Cases*, Hemel Hempstead: Prentice Hall.

Moore, P G and Thomas, H (1988) *The Anatomy of Decisions*, Harmondsworth: Penguin.

Richardson, C (1991) 'Staffing the Front Office', *Operational Research Insight*, 4 (2): 19–22.

Wisniewski, M (1996) *Foundation Quantitative Methods for Business*, London: Pitman Publishing.

Wisniewski, M (2002) *Quantitative Methods for Decision Makers* (3rd edn), Harlow: FT Prentice Hall.

Wisniewski, M and Dacre, T (1990) *Mathematical Programming: Optimization Models for Business and Management Decision Making*, Maidenhead: McGraw-Hill.

WEBSITES

Many of the topics covered in this chapter come under the broad heading of either *Management Science* or *Operational Research*. Using either of these terms as the bais for a www search will find several thousand websites detailing the use of these techniques and their development. To get you started you might want to look at the websites below:

http://www.mansci.strath.ac.uk/
University of Strathclyde Management Science Department.

http://www.orsoc.org.uk/
The UK Operational Research Society.

http://www.uk.cgey.com/services/or/index.shtml
Cap Gemini Ernst and Young's case study index of applications.

http://www.informs.org/resources
The Institute for Operations Research and Management Science.

CHAPTER 14

Operations management

RUTH BOADEN

Outcomes

Having read this chapter, you will be able to:

- describe a framework for the analysis of operations management as one of the managerial roles within an organisation. It uses the analogy of operations as a transformation process, changing inputs into outputs

- explain the past, present and future context of the transformation process within the organisation

- show how the process may be classified and explain the impact of different types of process on the role of the manager

- demonstrate how the outputs from the process may be measured and consider the relevance of new ways of measuring

- examine the impact of the external environment on operations, with particular reference to the customer and the international context

INTRODUCTION

The structure of the chapter reflects the theoretical basis around which it is built: that of **operations** being a transformation process where input resources are transformed into outputs. Following consideration of the past history and present organisational context of the process, future trends and means of classification are discussed. The role of the operations manager is also considered. Current and developing ways of measuring output are presented within the context of wider changes affecting operations. Finally, the relationship between operations and the customer is analysed, and some comment made on international trends and differences.

OPERATIONS MANAGEMENT AS A TRANSFORMATION PROCESS

Any organisation, whether it be a manufacturer, retailer, educational establishment, hospital or even government agency, exists to satisfy the needs of its customers or consumers, i.e. those who are the recipients of what is produced or the services carried out by the organisation (*see* Figure 14.1).

So within the context of an organisation, what are 'operations'? An operation may be defined as:

'a process, method or series of acts especially of a practical nature.'

In general, operations simply harness resources in order to produce something or to provide a service – they are part of every kind of organised activity within the organisation. It is argued by some authors that **operations management** is an integral part of any managerial role (*see* Exhibit 14.1).

Figure 14.1 The closed loop of customer satisfaction

Source: Production and Operations Management, 6th edition, Lockyer *et al.* (1992) Pearson Education Limited.

Exhibit 14.1 Operations

- A manufacturing company conducts operations in a mill, a foundry, or a factory.

- Banks operate from offices and branches.

- Restaurant operations take place on chopping blocks, serving tables and takeaway counters.

- Builders operate in offices where proposals are prepared and on construction sites.

- University operations take place in lecture theatres, research laboratories, seminar rooms, and on the sports field.

Source: Adapted from Schonberger and Knod (1994). Reprinted with permission of Richard D Irwin Inc., Burr Ridge, Illinois.

More specifically, 'operations' can refer to a department or functional area within an organisation where certain resources are transformed into products or services by adding value to them. 'Operations managers' therefore have to 'manage' this process in some way.

There are several definitions of operations management which highlight the key features. Schroeder (1993) defines the key terms as:

> *'Operations managers are responsible for producing the supply of goods or services in organisations. Operations managers make decisions regarding the operations function and the transformation systems used. Operations management is the study of decision making in the operations function.'*

Harris (1989) uses a simpler definition which highlights all the key features of the task:

> *'operations management is the management of a system which provides goods or services to or for a customer, and involves the design, planning and control of the system.'*

Denzler (2000) defines operations management by 'what it does':

> *'Operations management is the business function that manages that part of a business that transforms raw materials and human inputs into goods and services of higher value.'*

Many authors view operations management as a transformation process, and this helps to highlight some of the key features of the task (*see* Figure 14.2).

Examples of various operations classified in this way are shown in Table 14.1.

Figure 14.2 The transformation process

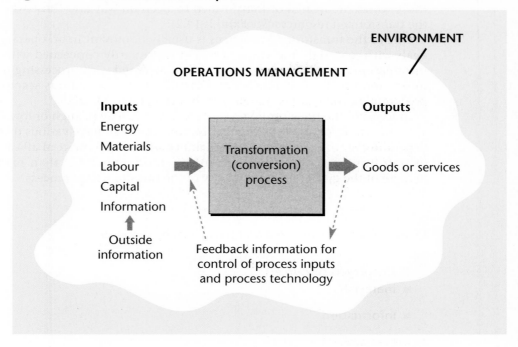

Table 14.1 Examples of operations classified as transformation processes

OPERATION	INPUTS	OUTPUTS
Bank	Cashiers, staff, computer equipment, facilities, energy	Financial services (loans, deposits)
Restaurant	Cooks, waiting staff, food, equipment, facilities, energy	Meals, entertainment, satisfied customers
Hospital	Doctors, nurses, staff, equipment, facilities, energy	Health services, healthy patients
University	Staff, equipment, facilities, energy, knowledge	Educated students, research
Airline	Planes, facilities, pilots, flight attendants, engineers, labour, energy	Transportation from one area to another

Source: Developed from Schroeder, R G (1993) *Operations Management*, 4th edn, © Copyright The McGraw-Hill Companies, Inc. 1993.

It is useful to make a distinction between **transformed** and **transforming resources**: those which are treated or transformed in a certain way and those which act upon the transformed resources (*see* Exhibit 14.2).

One of the transformed resources is usually dominant in an operation – a bank deals with materials and customers, but is primarily concerned with processing information. Manufacturing is primarily concerned with processing material, but information is also very important. Classification of operations according to their predominant transformed resource is shown in Table 14.2.

In terms of the transforming resources, facilities may be high or low tech, but are still important for any type of organisation. Staff will have various degrees of skill depending on the operation, but reliability will be important in all cases. The role of staff in service operations is relatively more important than manufacturing because of the greater labour intensity of the **transformation process**.

Exhibit 14.2 Transformed and transforming resources

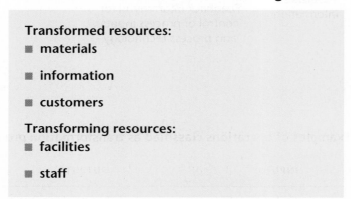

Transformed resources:
- **materials**
- **information**
- **customers**

Transforming resources:
- **facilities**
- **staff**

Source: Based on *Operations Management, 3rd edition*, Slack *et al.* (2001, p 10). Pearson Education Limited.

Table 14.2 Operations classified according to primary transformed resource

PREDOMINANTLY MATERIALS PROCESSORS	PREDOMINANTLY INFORMATION PROCESSORS	PREDOMINANTLY CUSTOMER PROCESSORS
All manufacturers	Accountant	Hairdresser
Retail operation	Market research company	Hotel
Warehouse	University research unit	Hospital
Postal service	Telecommunications company	Theatre

Source: Developed from *Operations Management, 3rd edition*, Slack *et al.* (2001). Pearson Education Limited.

THE CONTEXT OF THE TRANSFORMATION PROCESS: OPERATIONS STRATEGY

The interface between the transformation process and the environment is particularly important – both the environment within the organisation and the external environment must be considered. The relationship of operations to the environment is shown in Figure 14.3. Some of the aspects of these interfaces will be discussed in more detail when the role of the customer in operations is described.

Operations is generally considered to be a functional area, like marketing etc., rather than a basic discipline area of study, like economics, sociology, systems concepts, etc. It has traditionally been emphasised more in manufacturing because it is the major part of the organisation – in services, marketing is often considered to be more important. In terms of relationships with other functions within the organisation, the relationship between the marketing and operations functions is often considered to be the most crucial, whatever the type of organisation. Muhlemann *et al.* (1992) detail the relationship by defining a 'closed loop' which summarises all the key tasks involved in identifying and satisfying consumer needs (*see* Figure 14.4). The marketing role therefore covers stages (i) and (v) of this loop – identifying and forecasting, and distribution.

However, this approach may be criticised by those who believe that operations can offer competitive advantage to an organisation (e.g. Wheelwright and Hayes, 1985) and that customers and operations should be working more closely together.

Figure 14.3 **The relationship of operations to the environment**

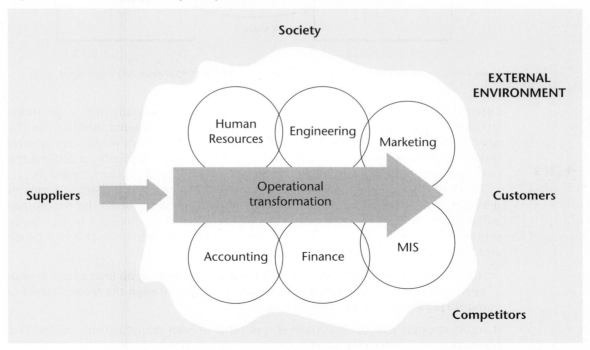

Figure 14.4 **From customer to customer – a closed loop**

Source: *Production and Operations Management, 6th edition,* Lockyer *et al.* (1992) Pearson Education Limited.

Other authors (Hill, 1993) believe that marketing strategy actually drives operations strategy, following from the premise that customer requirements should drive the operations function. This is very much in line with the recent popularity of total quality approaches, which are identified by an increasing emphasis on putting the customer first, although this may be expressed in different ways (*see* Chapter 3).

→ Ch. 3

There has been a great deal of development in the past five years in terms of developing the concept of operations strategy. This has arisen from the widespread adoption of the view that operations can offer competitive advantage to an organisation, be it manufacturing or service. One of the leading texts in the area (Slack and Lewis, 2002) defines operations strategy as:

'the total pattern of decisions which shape the long-term capabilities of any type of operation and their contribution to overall strategy, through the reconciliation of market requirements with operations resources.'

It argues strongly that the approach is applicable to both manufacturing and service organisations. It is concerned with the

'total transformation process that is the whole business.'

Slack and Lewis's model of operations strategy does not dictate the form of the operations function but proposes that giving consideration to the resources of the operation is consistent with the resource-based view of the firm that is increasingly well regarded and acts as a counter-balance to the traditionally dominant market perspective.

Another way of considering the role of operations within an organisation is to use the 'value chain' concept proposed by Porter (1985). A value chain is defined as the collection of activities used to design, produce, market, deliver and support its product. Customers, suppliers and the firm are broken down into discrete but related activities, with the value chain showing how value is created by the firm for its customers. Porter argues that competitive advantage is then gained when the value created exceeds the cost of creating it. 'Value' is what customers are willing to pay for, and is created within the firm by the activities shown in Figure 14.5 This approach links with the definition of operations management proposed by Denzler (2000), who identifies adding value as the main activity carried out by the operations function.

It can be seen that operations is considered a primary activity, and the importance of its role will be shown later in the chapter. While 'logistics' is shown separately by Porter, it actually forms part of the broad definition of operations used within this chapter. Typical functions that might be included in such a broad definition of operations management include:

- purchasing
- production
- logistics
- maintenance
- goods receiving
- dispatch.

Figure 14.5 The firm value chain

Source: Adapted and reprinted with the permission of The Free Press, a Division of Simon & Schuster, from *Competitive Advantage: Creating and Sustaining Superior Performance* by Michael E Porter. Copyright © 1985, 1998 by Michael E Porter.

THE TRANSFORMATION PROCESS

Past history

In one sense, operations management has existed as long as people have made things, although it was not recognised as such. Attention to 'production management' has been greatest in the past 200 years, and attention to operations management as a discipline only during the last 20 years or so. Operations management developed as a discipline because people realised that many different organisations were experiencing similar problems, and whether they were service, manufacturing or public sector organisations did not make a significant difference.

→ Ch. 1

It is not possible to give a strict chronological account of the way in which the area has developed, but there are a number of major theoretical and practical contributions which have affected it (*see* Exhibit 14.3). Fuller accounts can be found in Fogarty *et al.* (1989) and Evans (1997) (*see also* Chapter 1).

Division of labour

→ Ch. 9

George (1968) argues that the concept of division of labour (*see also* Chapter 9) can be traced back to the ancient Greeks (Plato's *The Republic*), where it was recognised that specialisation of labour on a single task can result in greater productivity and efficiency than assigning a number of tasks to one worker. This was also discussed by Adam Smith, author of the classic *The Wealth of Nations* (1776), who noted that

→ Ch. 20

output is increased by specialisation of labour (*see also* Chapter 20). Workers become increasingly expert at one task, there is an avoidance of lost time due to changing to other jobs, and tools and machines can be added to improve efficiency. Charles Babbage (1832) noted that specialisation of labour makes it possible to pay wages only for the specific skills required. Division of labour is now being reviewed because of its effect on worker morale, turnover, job boredom and performance, but it has been the foundation of many operations management techniques and methods of organising production systems.

Exhibit 14.3 Major contributions to the theoretical development of operations management

- The division of labour – Adam Smith and Charles Babbage
- Standardisation of parts
- The Industrial Revolution
- The scientific study of work – Frederick Taylor
- Human relations – the Hawthorne experiments
- Decision modelling
- Technology

Standardisation of parts

Manufacturing parts so that they are as interchangeable as possible is now commonplace within our society, for example light bulbs of different wattage and shape but all with the same fitting. This was not, however, the case in the past, and designing parts in this way is one of the major features of operations management which enabled increasing efficiency and specialisation of labour.

The Industrial Revolution

The Industrial Revolution took place during the late 1700s and early 1800s and was the time when machine power was substituted for human power. It was made possible by inventions such as the steam engine (invented by James Watt in 1764) and electricity. The demand for manufactured goods generated by the First World War (1914–18) aided the development of 'mass production' where very large quantities of goods were made using relatively high levels of automation. Society now appears to have shifted to a 'post-industrial' period where manufacturing is not the primary source of income for many countries, and services form the basis of the economy.

Scientific study of work

This method determines the best method of working using scientific principle: observing present work methods, developing an improved method through scientific measurement and analysis, training workers in the new method, and continuing feedback and management of the work process. Taylor (1911) was the originator of these ideas and they gained widespread acceptance, although they have been criticised for being misapplied and used by management simply to 'speed up' workers without giving full consideration to their total range of needs. The scientific method is now seen by many as a means of exploiting workers and in opposition to newer methods of working which seek to take human needs into account.

Human relations

→ Ch. 12

Motivation and the human element in the design of work are vital, and were highlighted by the Hawthorne experiments which indicated that worker motivation – along with the physical and technical environment – is crucial in improving productivity (*see* Chapter 12). The proponents of scientific management were forced as a result of these experiments to moderate their methods, which had placed an overemphasis on the technical elements of work design, and the concept of job enrichment was developed (Hackman *et al.*, 1975).

Decision models

Many of the traditional texts on production management concentrate almost entirely on the use of mathematical models to represent a production system, in order to find optimal solutions within certain constraints. Examples of these models include the economic order quantity model used for inventory management and linear programming. Such models are still an important part of operations management, but their limitations are now more clearly acknowledged, particularly in terms of their disregard for the human elements of operations, and the limited range of assumptions on which many of the models had to be based in order to make them workable.

Technology

The application of computer technology has revolutionised operations management, with computers being used for many planning and controlling tasks such as inventory management, production scheduling and costing. Computers have been used for a number of years within the manufacturing process itself, and this is still an important application. The advent of information technology in particular, where computer technology is used to store and process information, has been of particular significance within operations (Underwood, 1994). Computer technology has also had a dramatic effect on service operations, with retailing systems, office systems and even medical diagnostic systems now being widely used.

PRESENT ORGANISATIONAL CONTEXT

Operations management plays an important role in any type of organisation, but different emphasis is placed on operations in manufacturing and service organisations. The differences and similarities between these types of organisation are important for operations managers since they need to understand clearly the nature of the organisation in which they are working, and the relative importance of various aspects of operations management.

Operations can be classified in various ways. One useful classification is from Wild (1989), who identifies four different types:

- **Manufacture** – where the physical output differs from the input; there is a change in the **form** utility of resources; *making something* – examples include car manufacture, food manufacture.

- **Transport** – where the customer, or something belonging to the customer, is moved, without any change in physical resources; there is a change in **place** utility; *moving something or someone* – examples include trains, distribution companies.

- **Supply** – where the ownership of goods is changed without a change in form; there is a change in **possession** utility; *providing some physical goods* – examples include retailing, petrol stations.

- **Service** – where the customer, or something belonging to the customer, is treated in some way; there is a change in **state** utility; *something happens to someone or something* – examples include dentists, the fire service.

It is not, however, always appropriate to assign an organisation solely to one category – most organisations have aspects of all of the above to varying degrees – but it is usual to be able to assign a primary category to an organisation, and this will have implications for operations management.

It can be useful to distinguish between organisations according to the degree to which their transformation processes produce **goods**, i.e. tangible entities, or **services**, i.e. intangible entities. A good is physical in nature, and can be stored, transformed and transported. A service is produced and consumed more or less simultaneously, but cannot be stored or transported (*see* Exhibit 14.4).

Exhibit 14.4 Goods or services

Primarily goods producers:
mines, chemical factories, oil refineries, farms, with little or no customer contact and not offering services as part of their marketing package.

Mixed production organisations:
most manufacturing companies, insurance companies and fast food outlets. All offer both goods and services. Manufacturing organisations often sell warranties and provide repair and after-sales service.

Primarily service producers:
dentists, management consultants, banks, educational institutions. Any tangible good provided in connection with the service is incidental.

It can be argued that it is not appropriate to distinguish at all between manufacturing and service, but that there is simply a continuum of organisations with some having more emphasis on goods than others. However, most academics still maintain the distinction for the purposes of analysis, and the UK government continues to issue economic statistics based on these classifications.

Even within service organisations there are difficulties of classification, and the operations management implications vary. Schmenner (1986) has proposed the classification in Table 14.3 which is widely accepted. Degree of labour intensity refers to the ratio of capital to labour.

Schmenner goes on to discuss the implications of this classification for managerial roles, and the points he makes can be summarised as in Table 14.4.

The major characteristics of services and their implications for operations management can be summarised as follows:

- intangible output
- variable, non-standard output
- a service is perishable
- cannot be mass-produced
- high personal judgement used by employees
- labour intensity

Table 14.3 The service process matrix

		DEGREE OF CONSUMER/SERVICE INTERACTION AND CUSTOMISATION	
		LOW	HIGH
DEGREE OF LABOUR INTENSITY	**HIGH**	**Mass service** e.g. retailing, banking, education	**Professional service** e.g. doctors, lawyers, accountants
	LOW	**Service factory** e.g. airlines, truck transportation, hotels, leisure resorts	**Service shop** e.g. hospitals, repair services

Table 14.4 Challenges for managers in service organisations

CLASSIFICATION	CHALLENGES
Low labour intensity	Capital expenditure Technology development Managing demand to avoid peaks and promote off-peaks Scheduling service delivery
High labour intensity	Hiring staff Training staff Developing and controlling methods of working Scheduling workers Controlling a large number of dispersed locations Managing growth
Low interaction/customisation	Marketing Attention to physical surroundings Managing a rigid organisation structure
High interaction/customisation	Managing cost increases Maintaining quality Dealing with customer participation in the process Managing the advancement of staff Managing a flat organisation Gaining employee loyalty

- high customer contact
- customer participation
- decentralised facilities, near to the customer
- demand varies greatly over a short period.

Intangible output

This describes the uniqueness of services more than any other aspect. Services are not a 'thing' that is produced but an activity that is experienced in some way, either by the customer directly or as a process carried out on possessions of the customer. The physical output from the process, therefore, does not exist in a tangible state.

Variable, non-standard output

The extent of this will depend on the exact type of service provided, as shown by Schmenner (1986), and in particular the degree of labour intensity, which makes quality control difficult. Quality is difficult to predict, both for the organisation and the customer, and the reputation of the organisation is an important factor. Quality of service depends to a large extent, however, on the expectations of the consumer.

A service is perishable

A service itself is consumed instantly, for example using a hotel room or an airline seat, and cannot be stored, although consumers may enjoy the *benefit* for a long while afterwards, for example a heart transplant.

This has a major impact on capacity planning, which is a key aspect of operations management. Periods of slack demand cannot be used to build stock to meet high demand in other periods, so capacity has to be varied. The large numbers of checkouts in supermarkets, not all of which are used at slack times, is an example of this. It is, however, expensive to build in extra capacity which may only be used at certain times, and it is not possible to hire employees at very short notice to cope with extra demand, so they may have to appear as a fixed overhead rather than being varied with demand.

High customer contact

Although this varies with the nature of the service (Schmenner, 1986), in general service organisations have a higher degree of customer contact than manufacturers; nevertheless this is changing even for manufacturing organisations. The customer may not be physically in contact with the provider, especially where technology is used, for example a telephone enquiry line, but in any case employee interaction is critical. In some cases, organisations move 'messy' parts of the service process to places where they cannot be seen by the customer – sometimes referred to as backroom operations. This then allows the organisation to focus more on employee/customer interaction at the crucial point. Other organisations are proud to show all the parts of the operation to the customer, for example McDonald's restaurants, where all the kitchen operations are deliberately made visible.

Customer participation

The extent of customer participation depends on the type of service, and there may be a formal or informal relationship between the organisation and customer. It is a crucial factor in determination of quality and timeliness.

Cannot be mass-produced

This does not apply within the service factory quadrant of Schmenner's matrix, and considerable benefits have been gained by service organisations applying mass-production principles to providing a service. It is perhaps in this quadrant that operations management has had the greatest impact on service organisations. However, the customised nature of many services, such as medical treatment and legal advice, makes these types of service organisation very difficult to manage effectively.

High personal judgement used by employees

This is particularly so in professional services, for example lawyers, hairdressers, which have a reputation for being the most difficult to manage. It applies to services which cannot be mass-produced and are often relatively labour intensive.

Labour intensity

This has implications for productivity (the ratio of output to input resources): service organisations nearly always have lower overall productivity than manufacturing organisations. Where service organisations have substituted equipment for people (e.g. automatic cash dispensers in banks instead of going to the counter to obtain cash), there have been productivity improvements. People and equipment are not, however, always in opposition, and may complement each other.

Decentralised facilities, near to the customer

This is especially important where physical contact with the customer is involved, and service location is critical to revenue for many organisations. It is not possible to 'ship' services, because they have to be produced at the point of customer contact. In order to minimise variation between large numbers of locations, there is a trend towards uniformity – many high streets look the same now – where all branches appear to be very similar and common procedures are used, with central common training.

Demand varies greatly over a short period

Relative to manufacturing organisations, demand varies more often in service companies, with more of a random pattern (e.g. emergency services), and stocks cannot be made to help out. Some organisations try to alter demand (e.g. cheap off-peak offers), manage supply by building flexibility into operations (e.g. more checkouts open at busy times) or in some cases by ignoring variations (accepting that there will be longer queues at lunch time). This third option is becoming less easy to justify as consumers are offered more choice and appear to be becoming more particular about service quality. The USA is an example of a society where service quality is now a crucial determinant of market position.

CURRENT INFLUENCES

Production management was important when the Western world was an 'industrial society', but the rise of service organisations and the decline of manufacturing have caused some people to question the relevance of operations. However, there are a number of reasons why operations management is considered to be increasingly important rather than in decline.

The resurgence of interest in operations during the 1980s was fuelled by the decline in the international competitiveness of Western industry, whose markets were taken over by foreign products and competition. The rate of productivity growth was also falling behind other countries, especially those in the Far East, and this was seen as being the province (and the fault) of the operations function. Whatever the 'solution' may be to the economic problems of the West (if, indeed, there is a single solution), increased investment, more research and development, and changes in the approaches used to manage people all have to be put into action by operations managers and therefore affect the operations function.

Many of the fashionable ideas in management – total quality management (TQM), supply chain management (SCM), 'lean' thinking, business process re-engineering (BPR) – not only affect but are centred around the operations function. Many have also realised that focusing on, and improving, operations can increase efficiency (therefore reducing costs) as well as providing improved quality and service (which improves revenue). Slack and Lewis (2002) are clear that:

'"operations" is not always "operational" – operations management has an important strategic dimension.'

Some have not only seen operations as the key to future economic prosperity, but also a means of securing competitive advantage (Wheelwright and Hayes, 1985). It is clear that weak operations will affect the competitive position of the organisation, and as operations has become more closely linked to other parts of the organisation, so its role in competitive positioning has become more important. At one time a good product, superior marketing or a technology which was difficult to imitate could make up for weak operations management. The role of operations is, however, different now:

> *'Superior operations management blends with superior design, marketing, accounting, supplier relations, human resource management and business strategy as an essential component of success. Weak operations management, on the other hand, tends to coincide with many other management weaknesses.'*
>
> (Schonberger and Knod, 1994)

Current influences on operations include:

- **customer-directed operations**
- **continuous improvement and quality**
- **lean and agile production**
- **integration with other functions**
- **globalisation of operations.**

Customer-directed operations imply that operations have an external orientation so that they are well placed to meet customer requirements. However, customers may be internal as well as external to the organisation – 'customer' can mean the next process as well as the final end user of the product or recipient of the service. The trend towards subcontracting and outsourcing of services has made it it more difficult for organisations to control their external suppliers and contractors. However, the related growth of interest in supply chain management (Christopher, 1998) is a response to this influence, and is becoming increasingly important.

Continuous improvement and quality are influences that have increased in importance, not only as a result of increased emphasis on customer relationships but also because of the influence of Japanese manufacturers in the West (*see* Ishikawa, 1985). Many have described the changes in emphasis in Western organisations as a 'quality revolution' (Evans, 1997) and there is no doubt that a focus on quality is now a prerequisite for effective competitiveness in most markets. Although it originally started in the manufacturing sector, service quality is now a major focus for all organisations. This is evidenced by the inclusion in this book of → Ch. 7 a whole chapter on quality management (*see* Chapter 7) which details its influence and highlights the strategic importance of quality management.

Lean and agile production are influences that have become important as

> *'the goals of low cost and high productivity became "givens".'*   (Evans, 1997)

Lean production emphasises the reduction of waste and effective utilisation of resources in all aspects of the manufacturing process and utilises cross-functional teams, multi-skilled workers, integration of supplier relationships and communications, and flexible automation. Agile production focuses on the ability of the manufacturing process to respond quickly to changes in demand, in terms of volume and specification, and utilises lean production techniques to achieve this agility. Although the original applications were in manufacturing, the concepts are also becoming accepted in service organisations, especially those where customer 'flow' is particularly important.

Integration with other functions is to some extent a result of some of the influences already described. However, it has also developed from the recent emphasis on business process improvement (Harrington, 1991) and business process re-engineering (Hammer and Champy, 1993). Counter to this influence is the increasing trend to decentralisation, although this can be alleviated to some extent by improvements in communications technology leading to 'virtual' organisations. Improved integration can enable reductions in total cycle time and facilitate a quicker response to customers, thus improving customer service.

Globalisation of operations is inevitable as organisations compete internationally – many organisations describe themselves as competing in a global marketplace. However, the implications of such globalisation for operations has not always been simple, particularly where global companies are formed by mergers between organisations with very different operating procedures and organisational cultures. The characteristics of 'world class' manufacturers are well described by Schonberger (1996).

Within the organisation it is argued that operations has an important role, and although this may be hotly debated by other functional areas, the argument proposed by Slack (1983), and developed subsequently by him and other authors, is based on facts rather than emotion. The case can be developed as follows.

Operations . . .

- concerns the management of most of the people within the organisation, either production workers or service personnel, and often represents 70–80 per cent of the total workforce;
- has responsibility for the effective use of the organisation's assets, both fixed assets and inventory (current assets), and therefore for the management of most of the organisation's funds;
- is responsible for most of the organisation's expenditure, and has the largest budget allocation of any one function;
- is a pervasive activity (i.e. interacts with everything else);
- is the area in the organisation where many social and technological changes are taking place.

The role of an operations manager can be illustrated by the following two case studies which give accounts of what an operations manager does.

CASE STUDY 14.1

Operations management at United Biscuits

Andrew Hawley was sponsored by United Biscuits during his studies for his degree in Business, and his early work experience with the company confirmed his interest in manufacturing operations: 'Where else could you be managing 50 people from the outset, in your early twenties? The satisfaction comes from being responsible for the performance of the plant and staff, seeing immediate results and – above all – from beating targets!'

Andrew had various roles in his first five years with the company; initially he was responsible for the day-to-day supervision of a factory, then he became a deputy factory manager of a small specialised plant, before moving to headquarters, where he is now responsible for aspects of operational and strategic planning.

'It is certainly a change being in a team of just six people after helping to manage a factory and I now face a whole new set of challenges. My hands-on experience of production has been invaluable for my current position. Without it, I wouldn't be able to decide on production systems and procedures three or more years in advance of implementation. The work is very diverse. Sometimes I am working to identify potential problems so that preventive measures can be implemented, and at other times I am involved in logistics projects aimed at integrating UB

companies all over Europe, which will make enormous savings for the group. Many people have misconceptions about manufacturing and production management, they think that it is just about 'doing' and is less stimulating and intellectually demanding than other disciplines. Nothing could be further from the truth in my opinion.

'It has been my job at United Biscuits to ensure that all products leave our plant manufactured to our very demanding specifications. This involves not only responsibility for the process and the people, important though they are, but also for clear communication and involvement with all of the other business functions to ensure that the business unit is run optimally. It is especially important to understand how production must be involved with the fundamental issues of cost, service, quality and innovation and to be able to create and manage change. Managers in the manufacturing role also have an important part to play in developing the business strategy, notably in co-ordination with the Marketing Department. In a real sense, when you're involved with manufacturing, every other discipline in the company is backing you, because you are the one that is producing exactly what millions of people are buying in the shops every day. This is, after all, what the company is there for in the first place!'

Source: Slack *et al.* (1998), *Operations Management* (2nd edn), London, Financial Times Pitman Publishing. Reprinted with permission.

CASE STUDY 14.2

Operations management at a theme park

Alan Randell, the manager at Thorpe Park, Chertsey, arrives by 9 am, signs on, by radio, with Operations Control, and then calculates today's budgeted attendance – based on historic trading and present marketing initiatives. His estimate of 8000 was surpassed by the eventual attendance of 10 000. He then confirmed states of operations and ride-readiness. The maintenance staff arrive at 6.30 am and the cleaning department at 7.30 am. At 9 am, all cast

members (staff) have to be signed in and surveyed for their costume, hair length and entertainment presence. After checking with the admissions supervisor over kiosk state-of-readiness he decided to open 15 minutes early, at 9.15 am. By 9.30, there were already 436 parents and children inside.

After monitoring the turnstiles – he has entry operations responsibility as well as executive responsibility – he walks over the bridge.

▶

'I saw Harley, the costumed character. Harley gave me five. It's a case of getting and delivering a level of adrenalin, happiness and smiles. I then went to see Snoopy's aerobics show. I'm looking to maintain Snoopy for the season. Then, the duty manager briefed me on cleanliness by Octopus Garden.'

There are almost 600 'cast', with 100 having a radio, so everything that's happening in the park comes over and is known about immediately, whether it's inside No Way Out (the giant backwards turbo-booster ride in pitch blackness), over the Flying Fish by Pot Bellies or on Miss Hippo's Jungle Safari.

'Back in my office I use the computer, which tells me how many fun-seekers are in the park, what time-segment they each arrived in, how that compares with yesterday and the same day last week – or any day in the last four years – and how much each of them paid, how they paid, when they paid ...'*

Thorpe Park is dedicated to a family market and a parent-friendliness profile, so the manager constantly monitors rides and adjusts cast levels to control queue lineage and foot-flow.

'So far today I've increased to three the waterbuses from Customs House. We've also had one nosebleed, a hand hurt on a fence and someone's been sick. After lunch – with this hot bright sunshine – I will be watching closely our key rides, the smash splashers, our wet wet wets: The Depth Charge, Thunder River and Logger's Leap. They'll be the hardest hit when the restaurants and food franchises' trade levels off. And at the Fantasy Reef pool, I'll want to make sure the balance of younger children with older is acceptable, so we'll have extra monitors.'

Source: Developed from an interview by John Hind, *Observer*, 8 June 1997. Reprinted with permission.

THE PROCESS ITSELF

How can it be classified?

Operations management is about managing the transformation process, but there are a number of ways in which the process can be classified and these will affect the nature of the task. The classifications presented in this section are mainly applicable to manufacturing, but the concepts also affect service, especially when layout is considered. Process choice is important since it has implications for the way the system operates and is not quick or cheap to change.

There are five major types of process:

- project
- jobbing, unit or one-off
- batch
- line
- continuous.

These are sometimes combined into three main categories: job/project, batch/ intermittent and flow/mass. The exact terminology used will depend on the author of the book concerned, and to some extent whether the book is of US or European origin.

Project

This type of process is used to produce a one-off item, for example a new building or film, or for a one-off service, such as a consultancy assignment. There is a sequence of operations, but they are not usually repeated. The task is usually done at the customer's site (although not exclusively).

The major operations management task is to plan, sequence, co-ordinate and control the tasks leading to completion of the whole project – this is called project management. The process is usually relatively high cost with difficulty in automation because of the lack of repeatability.

Jobbing, unit or one-off

This type of process is used for one-off or small-order requirements, with the product being of a smaller nature than for a project process, for example a purpose-built piece of equipment, designer dress, handmade shoes, bespoke computer system. The product is usually made in-house and then transported to the customer, and commissioned before acceptance.

Batch

This process is used when similar items are required in larger volumes than for a jobbing process, and the products are produced in batches at intermittent intervals. The essential characteristic is that to provide another product/service the process has to be stopped and reset; the same equipment is used for a number of different products. Examples include car components, white goods, casting, a computer bureau that uses the same equipment for work from a number of different clients. General purpose equipment and highly skilled labour are used: this gives high flexibility but low efficiency, with problems in controlling inventories, schedules and quality.

This is the type of process on which most production management texts have traditionally concentrated, and for which most methods have been developed. This is realistic since the majority of production is of this type, and probably a lot of service too.

Line

In this process a linear sequence of operations is used to make the product or service, with equipment dedicated to that product or small range of products. The process is essentially repetitive where each product passes through the same sequence of operations. Examples include motor vehicle manufacturing, food preparation in McDonald's and some bank operations, for example cheque processing. The process is sometimes called 'mass' production, to distinguish it from continuous production. Line processes are very efficient but inflexible, as car makers have discovered to their cost; customers are demanding more variety in products but manufacturers have found it difficult to satisfy this demand because their processes were established for large runs of similar products. The main sources of efficiency are the substitution of capital for labour wherever possible and highly specified labour tasks with a high degree of repetition.

Continuous

This is a variation of a line process, where several basic materials are processed through successive stages into one final product. It is usually more automated and standardised than a line process. The best example is petrochemicals, but other examples include beer, paper and electricity production. The start-up cost of these processes is generally very high, so they tend to be run continuously, or as near as possible, with little or no labour intervention. This process is not used in services, because there is no labour content.

Table 14.5 Summary of process type and major operational characteristics

	JOB/PROJECT	BATCH/INTERMITTENT	MASS/LINE
Product aspects			
Product flow	None	Jumbled	Sequenced
Product variety	Very high	High	Low
Volume	Single unit	Medium	High
Labour aspects			
Skills	High	High	Low
Task type	Non-routine	Non-routine	Repetitive
Type of capital			
Investment	Low	Medium	High
Inventory	Medium	High	Low
Equipment	General purpose	General purpose	Special purpose
Operations objectives			
Flexibility	High	Medium	Low
Cost	High	Medium	Low
Quality	More variable	More variable	Consistent
Delivery	Medium	Low	High

Source: Developed from Hill (1991). Reprinted with permission.

There are many detailed accounts of the various characteristics of the different classification of operations. Table 14.5 summarises some of the key aspects as they affect the operations management task.

THE ROLE OF THE OPERATIONS MANAGER

There are many frameworks which attempt to describe what an operations manager does. The one to be presented here is based on that developed by Schroeder and has been selected because it is based around the concept that operations management is primarily a decision-making role. There are others who argue that operations is an integral part of any managerial role (e.g. Schonberger and Knod, 1994) and that to some extent, every employee is a 'manager', at least of the immediate workplace (Scott Myers, 1991), including those who actually make the product or provide the service, first-line supervisors, department heads, general managers as well as technical experts. However, a narrower definition is more common, and relates to those situated within the operations function itself. The involvement with day-to-day operations depends to a large extent on the level of the operations manager within the organisation, with lower-level managers having more detailed involvement. Job titles may include the following, and can relate to lower-level supervisory roles right up to senior management and director positions:

■ Materials manager
■ Purchasing manager
■ Inventory manager
■ Production control manager
■ Quality manager
■ Line manager
■ Planning analyst.

Operations managers make decisions in five main areas:

■ **Quality** – managing quality issues, controlling quality and improving it.
■ **Process** – selecting and designing the transformation process, selecting and using the appropriate technology, layout of facilities.
■ **Capacity** – forecasting demand, making decisions about facility location, planning at top and detailed levels, including project planning.
■ **Inventory** – planning appropriate levels of inventory and methods of control, linking inventory to production planning and scheduling.
■ **People** – managing the workforce, designing and improving jobs.

The decisions made by an operations manager are both short-, medium- and long-term and involve all aspects of a manager's role: planning, controlling, staffing, (Fogarty *et al.*, 1989). The scope of operations management decisions can be summarised in four categories (developed from Fogarty *et al.*, 1989) where the various dimensions of decision making are combined (*see* Table 14.6).

A single decision may be made using criteria from any or all of the four areas, and it should be noted that they are interrelated, so that decisions made in one area will affect other areas. An overall plan, strategy and direction are needed in order to determine the direction of the organisation. The overall goals can then be detailed to determine actions and decisions needed in each functional area, including operations management.

Fogarty says that typical operations management decisions include:

■ a plant manager deciding the number of people of different skills that will be needed to meet the schedule for the coming year;

Table 14.6 Dimensions of operations decision making

TIME PERIOD AFFECTED	RESOURCE MANAGED	DECISION AREA AFFECTED	MANAGEMENT FUNCTION
Long-range	Facilities	Capacity	Planning
Medium-range	Equipment	Materials	Execution
Short-range	Materials	Quality	Control
Present	Labour	Process	Organisation
	Information	Personnel	Staffing
	Capital		
	Energy		

- a restaurant manager deciding the number of cooks, waiters and other staff that will be needed on each shift during the coming week, and then scheduling individuals to work those shifts;
- an analyst in a bank studying the processing of customers' cancelled cheques, searching for methods of reducing bottlenecks in the operation, reducing the flowthrough time and increasing productivity;
- a manager of a goods receiving department studying methods of scheduling arrivals, assigning incoming trucks to unloading bays, unloading trucks, processing the necessary data, moving the items received to their proper location and eventually to their point of use.

The skills required for an operations manager are common with those of any manager, although there are a number of particular factors which are important. Most operations managers have a relatively high level of quantitative skill, which is useful in utilising the decision-making models which are a part of much operations management. A high level of interpersonal skill is also required, owing to the number of people involved. Many education systems in the West do not permit a wide enough range of interpersonal and behavioural skills to be developed if a high level of 'technical' education is pursued, with the result that many operations managers are criticised for being technically capable but not managerially proficient. Attempts are now being made to address this at all levels of the education system.

Some of the typical tasks undertaken by an operations manager include:

- **management of a cost centre**
- **efficiency in the short and long term**
- **management of technology**
- **control of subsystems within the whole**
- **responsibility for work and money flow**
- **managing a process characterised by tangible outputs**
- **managing complexity.**

Management of a cost centre

An operations manager is responsible for a large proportion of the organisation's assets, and therefore controls a relatively large budget. While this does not necessarily require detailed accounting skills, a good understanding of financial matters is an asset.

Efficiency in the short and long term

Day-to-day activities have to be well controlled, but an operations manager also has to have a long-term view, and must consider long-term trends too. The danger is to be only short-term oriented because that is the most pressing consideration. The operations manager's task has been described as follows:

> *'the task is problem oriented . . . pressure is also a distinctive feature.'*

Management of technology

The operations manager may have to manage technology both within the product itself and within the process. It is increasingly difficult for operations managers to keep up to date with technological advances in any detail, and so they should attempt to understand the level of technology employed and its purpose, rather than the details of individual technologies, which should be left to technical experts. Maintaining this balance and avoiding the temptation to get drawn into detailed technical issues are often difficult.

Control of subsystems within the whole

Operations managers will have a number of different groups reporting to them and may be responsible to several different functions. A balance between the potentially conflicting demands of the various groups is needed, making sure they all contribute effectively to the whole. The danger is that the performance of one subsystem will be optimised at the expense of the others.

Responsible for money and work flow

Maintaining the balance between spending money and carrying out productive work is one of the major issues for operations managers. Table 14.7 shows that money is spent until the goods have been produced, and it is only at that point that the organisation may begin to get money in (assuming a standard manufacturing process, not a project environment). In order to satisfy monthly accounting targets, operations are often put under pressure to 'get things out' at the end of the month so that money can come in, although this may not be optimal in terms of efficiency within the operations function. The link between commercial rules, negotiated by the accounting function, and the operation of the process is not always clearly defined.

Table 14.7 **Money, work and material flow**

MONEY FLOW	CURRENT ASSETS	WORK AND MATERIALS FLOW
Out	Raw materials and components	Materials/components bought from outside
Out	Work in progress (WIP)	Labour and other materials/components added
Out	Finished goods	More labour and materials/components added
In		Finished goods/services sold (cash sales)
In (eventually)		Finished goods/services sold (credit sales)
In		Payment made for credit sales

Managing a process characterised by tangible outputs

Even in the case of services, this will be true to some extent. Operations management is the management of the transformation process, which always has some form of output and which usually has at least some physical element. Because of the relative ease of measurement of the 'quality' or other features of the output, the short-term aspects of the operations management task are often given too high a priority. Coupled with the fact that operations is not always incorporated into corporate strategy, although it is argued that it should be (Skinner, 1969; Hill, 1993), there is a tendency simply to optimise the physical aspects of short-term performance.

Managing complexity

While this is true of any managerial task, the challenge for operations managers does not arise from the individual tasks involved, which of themselves can be quite tedious, but from combining the large number of these to make something which works well and is effective for the organisation as a whole. This task is well summarised by Schonberger and Knod (1994):

> *'Effective operations management blends the interests of customer, employee, and manager, along with those of the public, shareholders, and other stakeholders. Diverse resources, changing technologies, and hard-to-predict demands add to the challenge. Human ingenuity, diligence, and the right management tools, are required to blend all the interests properly.'*

A typical day in the life of an operations manager is given in the following case study.

CASE STUDY 14.3

A day in the life of an operations manager

Sue Jones is the operations manager for the UK plant of Estech Ltd – a medium-sized company that manufactures and repairs marine seismic equipment used by oil companies engaged in offshore oil exploration. The main activity is the manufacture and repair of hydrophonic cables towed by seismic survey ships. Each cable is made up of sections and costs about £500 000. Repair and technical support arrangements are vital given the hostile nature of the marine environment.

The plant is divided into two main areas, cable manufacture and repair, and technical manufacture and repair. Each area has a manager who is responsible to Sue, who currently has 40 people working for her. She is directly responsible to the managing director for all aspects of production, repairs, logistics, quality, site facilities and research and development.

8 am In the factory
The main factory starts at 7.30 am and Sue walks round the plant for half an hour talking to people, including John Butler, the filling shop supervisor. The previous day there were problems with one of the machines and Sue wants to check progress.

8.30 am Sue's office
Jim Edwards, the quality manager, appears at the office door to report that problems with the delivery of a key component have been sorted. Five minutes later it is the site facilities manager who calls. Sue operates an 'open door' policy and consciously sets this time aside for 'mopping up' problems from the previous day.

9 am Cable and repair manager's office
Sue joins the daily meeting of the production team. During the night Sue received a telephone call from

the MD who had in turn received a call from the leader of a seismic survey team on board a survey ship off the coast of Nigeria. He had damaged three of his six cables in a collision and is anxious to get the damaged sections of cable repaired. This morning's meeting has to consider the feasibility of getting the damaged sections repaired within the next two weeks as the MD promised. Sue's task is to assess the situation with all those directly involved and with them arrive at a decision.

Not only does the team have to consider what is technically possible, it has to think through the consequences of rescheduling work. Fortunately two of the jobs being done this week are routine ones put into the schedule because there was a gap between two high-priority jobs. After much discussion, the consensus is that the Nigerian job can be fitted in. Staff are going to have to reschedule their work and there will have to be some overtime, but the client is going to get what he wants.

9.45 am Sue's office
The next hour and a half are devoted to work on ongoing projects. These include negotiating the technical requirements of a major new potential customer, the development of a new product and the evaluation of a new supplier.

11 am Reception
Sue meets two visitors from a potential new customer. After a tour of the plant she joins them in a meeting with the cable repair manager and two technicians.

1 pm Canteen
Lunch and an opportunity to talk to two new members of staff about their training course.

2 pm Sue's office
She makes some phone calls and prepares some faxes, as well as holding a meeting with the management accounts manager. The board has requested that the monthly production report should be available seven days after the month end rather than 14 days as at present. The meeting is to explore what needs to be done in order to meet the request. Once this meeting is over, Sue checks her 'things to do list'. The human resource manager has requested a job specification for a new technical post which has to be ready the following day.

4 pm The factory
The job specification is still not complete. Sue is back on the shopfloor to check progress on the Nigerian job. All the schedule revisions have been sorted out and work will start in two days' time when the damaged cables arrive back in the UK.

4.15 pm Sue's office
Sue takes stock of the day. The job specification is still incomplete. She checks the 'things to do list' again. She has an appointment with the R&D manager at 5.00 pm. There are some minor administrative tasks that can be put off to the end of the day so Sue decides to finish the job specification immediately.

5 pm R&D manager's office
At the meeting Dr Broadley, the R&D manager, is anxious that a new piece of equipment be purchased to facilitate his work on an enhancement to one of the company's major products. Sue agrees to take the matter up with the MD.

5.15 pm MD's office
Sue goes to see the MD and they review the day's events, particularly their success in fitting in the repair job for Nigeria, and the R&D manager's request for new equipment. They agree to investigate this further.

5.30 pm Sue's office
Sue dictates three letters and a couple of memos for the following day, sorts out the few remaining items left on her desk ready for tomorrow, and locks up and leaves.

Source: Developed from Waters, D (1996) *Operations Management*, Reading, MA, Addison-Wesley Longman.

THE OUTPUTS

Productivity as a performance measure

Measuring performance is one of the most important aspects of operations management, and one which has received a great deal of attention during the past few years. In order to make any improvements to the functioning of the transformation process, there must be methods for measuring its current effectiveness. This section considers the 'traditional' measures of performance, and the following section discusses more recent developments.

Productivity is the broadest measure of operations management performance, but perhaps the least enlightening. All it does is to assess how resources are utilised and managed to achieve a set of desired results. Productivity is defined as the ratio of output to input:

$$\frac{\text{output}}{\text{input}} = \frac{\text{results achieved}}{\text{resources consumed}}$$

An increase in productivity can therefore result from *either* an increase in output *or* a decrease in input. However, the problems of measuring output and input in the same units, and the debate about whether the resulting ratio has any real meaning, has led to productivity being considered in relative terms, i.e. considering *changes* in the ratio, comparing results in one period with those in another. A productivity index is often used, in which one period is given a value of 100 and then subsequent periods compared to the base.

Productivity has been a popular measure for many years, primarily because it is directly linked to profit, and has therefore attracted a good deal of senior management attention. If a percentage increase in sales is compared with an equivalent percentage increase in productivity, there is a very different effect on profit (*see* Table 14.8).

While this analysis fails to indicate the relative amount of effort required to achieve the same percentage change in sales and productivity, it does demonstrate the link between productivity and profit which has for so long attracted the attention of senior managers. However, measuring productivity in services is not as simple, since the outputs are not as easy to identify and measure. Although there are techniques that can help to develop this concept within services (data envelopment analysis being one example – see Charnes *et al.*, 1978) the results of using productivity can be misleading.

Partial productivity measures relate the value of output to the value of one of the inputs:

$$\text{e.g. labour productivity} = \frac{\text{output (£ value)}}{\text{labour hours (or costs)}}$$

Table 14.8 Impact of changes in sales and productivity

	BEFORE CHANGES	AFTER 10% SALES INCREASE	AFTER 10% INCREASE IN PRODUCTIVITY
Sales	£100	£110	£100
Variable costs	£70	£77	£63
Fixed costs	£20	£20	£20
Profit	£10	£13 (+30%)	£17 (+70%)

Labour productivity has been the most common measure, especially in manufacturing, but it oversimplifies the basis on which operations should be assessed and is misleading. It was used because it is relatively easy to calculate, because labour was a significant factor of production when productivity was first conceived, and because labour cost was seen as more inherently variable than material or capital. However, the relatively low proportion of total cost represented by labour cost in most manufacturing organisations today makes this measure unrepresentative. This relative proportion of costs attributable to 'staff' in various industries is shown in Table 14.9 and it should be borne in mind that this will include indirect labour too (that allocated to overhead rather than that which varies with the volume of business being done).

An alternative measure of performance that has been developed more recently is added value:

$$\text{Added value} = \text{sales revenue} - \text{material and outside service costs}$$

$$\text{Added value index (AVI)} = \frac{\text{total employment costs}}{\text{added value}}$$

This is particularly useful for measuring managerial performance, since it is less affected by factors external to the manager's control (e.g. inflation) than is profit, and focuses on employee productivity which is a major managerial task.

NEW WAYS OF MEASUREMENT

→ Ch. 7

The limits of productivity as a measure of operations performance, coupled with the trends in organisations and the environment which have led to a greater focus on customer needs, have led to new ways of operations performance evaluation being developed (*see* Chapter 7). Productivity is no longer seen as a single measure, although it may be used in conjunction with others. It is now generally accepted that the main criteria to be used for evaluating operations management are:

- **cost** (of the transformation process);
- **quality** (of product or service);
- **delivery** (to customer), sometimes divided into delivery speed and delivery dependability;
- **flexibility** (of process).

Table 14.9 **Composition of total cost**

	STAFF	TECHNOLOGY, FACILITIES & EQUIPMENT	MATERIALS/ BOUGHT-IN SERVICES
Hospital	45%	35%	20%
Car manufacturing plant	25%	15%	60%
Bus company	52%	40%	8%
Supermarket	10%	25%	65%

Many of the trade-offs which are regarded as an inherent part of operations management are related to these factors. These factors lead to five major performance objectives (Slack *et al.*, 2001):

doing things RIGHT	→	the QUALITY **advantage**
doing things FAST	→	the SPEED **advantage**
doing things ON TIME	→	the DEPENDABILITY **advantage**
CHANGING **what you do**	→	the FLEXIBILITY **advantage**
doing things CHEAPLY	→	the COST **advantage**

An organisation may want to achieve all or one of these, although generally it is not possible to develop action plans which support all of them simultaneously.

Quality

Quality is fundamental and visible, and leads to internal benefits such as reduced cost (because less time is spent in correcting mistakes and putting confusion right) and increased dependability (because people have more time to concentrate on being good at their job, and therefore become more reliable at doing it). (*See* Exhibit 14.5.)

Speed

This is to do with how long customers have to wait to receive products or services (*see* Exhibit 14.6). Increased speed reduces inventories (stock), since less material is needed for buffering, and also reduces risks; there is less reliance on forecasting, with more opportunity to make what the customer actually wants.

Dependability

This is concerned with doing things in time for customers to receive their product or service when they were promised (*see* Exhibit 14.7). Dependability saves time: less time has to be spent on sorting out problems and therefore there is more time to spend on direct productive work. It also saves money, where other resources have

Exhibit 14.5 **What does quality mean?**

In a hospital?
- patients receive the most appropriate treatment
- treatment is carried out in the correct manner
- patients are consulted and informed
- staff are friendly and helpful

In a bus company?
- buses are clean and tidy
- buses are quiet and fume free
- timetable is accurate and easy to understand
- staff are friendly and helpful

In a car manufacturing plant?
- all parts made to specification
- all assembly to specification
- product is reliable
- product is attractive

In a supermarket?
- goods are in good condition
- store is clean and tidy
- decor is appropriate and attractive
- staff are friendly and helpful

Source: Developed from *Operations Management, 3rd edition*, Slack *et al.* (2001, Figure 2.5, p 45). Pearson Education Limited.

Exhibit 14.6 What does speed mean?

In a hospital?
- time between requiring and receiving treatment
- time for test results to be returned

In a car manufacturing plant?
- time between dealers requesting a vehicle and getting it
- time to deliver spares to service centres

In a bus company?
- time between customer setting out and reaching destination

In a supermarket?
- time taken for total transaction from selecting goods to leaving store
- availability of goods (are they on the shelf?)

Source: Developed from *Operations Management, 3rd edition*, Slack *et al.* (2001, Figure 2.6, p 47). Pearson Education Limited.

Exhibit 14.7 What does dependability mean?

In a hospital?
- proportion of appointments cancelled
- keeping to appointment times
- test results returned as promised

In a car manufacturing plant?
- on-time delivery of vehicles to dealers
- on-time delivery of spares to service centres

In a bus company?
- keeping to the published timetable at all points on the route
- availability of seats for passengers

In a supermarket?
- predictability of opening hours
- proportion of goods out of stock
- keeping to 'reasonable' queueing times
- availability of parking

Source: Developed from *Operations Management, 3rd edition*, Slack *et al.* (2001, Figure 2.7, p 50). Pearson Education Limited.

to be diverted to make up for problems, and gives stability in the operations; a level of trust is built up where things are reliable, and this will be lost when dependability is reduced.

Flexibility

This is to do with being able to change the operation in some way – what it does, how it does it or when it does it. There are four main types of flexibility:

- **Product/service** – different products or services.
- **Mix** – a wide range of products/services.
- **Volume** – different quantities of products/services
- **Delivery** – different delivery times.

Further details about flexibility can be found in Slack *et al.* (2001). Examples of flexibility in various types of operation are shown in Table 14.10.

Flexibility has a number of internal benefits. It speeds up responses, for example when emergencies arise in a hospital; it saves time in changing over from one task to another; and maintains dependability where resources can easily be swapped to other tasks in order to fulfil overall promises.

Cost

This is still the major objective for many organisations, which believe that they compete primarily on cost, although often customers do have other considerations. Cost is incurred in three main areas:

- staff costs
- technology, facilities and equipment costs
- material costs and bought-in services.

The breakdown of total cost is, however, very different in different types of organisation, as shown in Table 14.9. All the other objectives act on costs, via the internal effects described earlier, so cost improvement can be obtained from improving the other objectives.

Table 14.10 Examples of flexibility

TYPE OF FLEXIBILITY	HOSPITAL	CAR MANUFACTURING PLANT	BUS COMPANY	SUPERMARKET
Product/service	Introduction of new types of treatment	Introduction of new models	Introduction of new routes	Introduction of new goods or promotions
Mix	Range of available treatments	Range of product options	Number of locations served	Range of goods stocked
Volume	Ability to adjust number of patients treated	Ability to adjust number of vehicles manufactured	Ability to adjust frequency of services	Ability to adjust number of customers served
Delivery	Ability to reschedule appointments	Ability to reschedule manufacturing priorities	Ability to reschedule trips	Ability to obtain out-of-stock items

Source: Developed from *Operations Management, 3rd edition*, Slack *et al.* (2001, Figure 2.8, p 52). Pearson Education Limited.

Trade-off and the relative importance of performance objectives

The conventional view is that improvement in one aspect of performance can only be achieved at the expense of performance in another area:

> '*Most managers will readily admit that there are compromises or trade-offs to be made in designing an airplane or truck. In the case of an airplane, trade-offs would involve matters such as cruising speed, take-off and landing distances, initial cost, maintenance, fuel consumption, passenger comfort and cargo or passenger capacity. For instance, no one can design a 500 passenger plane that can land on an aircraft carrier and also break the sound barrier. Much the same thing is true in manufacturing.*'   (Skinner, 1969)

This has, however, been challenged by organisations which give the 'best of both worlds'. For example, quality and cost used to be seen in opposition, so that improved quality could only be had at greater cost, whereas now it is recognised that improved quality may actually reduce cost.

Constraints on improvement may be technical or attitudinal. For example, if the attitude about quality changes from: 'screen the bad products out' to 'stop the mistakes being made in the first place', then the quality/cost trade-off becomes irrelevant. This has happened in many of the 'world-class' organisations.

The long-term aim of operations managers has to be to change those things within the operation that cause performance of one aspect to deteriorate as the other improves, i.e. to change the constraints on the operation in total, rather than merely altering one aspect. Weak companies appear to embody the trade-off mentality in the way they operate, and suffer as a result. Companies attempting to improve develop immunity to some of the trade-offs, many having started with eliminating the cost/quality trade-off. 'World-class' companies aim for improvement in all areas and have largely eliminated trade-off obstacles.

The way in which the relative importance of performance objectives is determined is crucial to the link between operations objectives and overall strategy. Targets are often aggregated together or balanced with each other, perhaps using an approach such as the balanced scorecard (Kaplan and Norton, 1996). The level of aggregation of the performance targets will determine their strategic relevance as well as their ability to diagnose operations problems. This is shown in Figure 14.6 (see page 456).

THE EXTERNAL ENVIRONMENT

Operations management and the customer

→ Ch. 3

Customers are important for any organisation, and it has already been shown that interaction between the operations function and the customer has increased in the past few years, and is likely to continue to do so (*see also* Chapter 3). It is therefore important to consider the points at which the customer influences operations performance.

It has already been shown that the customer will have needs which should be met by the organisation. However, the needs of the customers themselves may have a number of components:

- a statement of recognised need
- an expectation of the way in which that need should be met
- an idea of the benefits of having that need met.

Figure 14.6 Performance targets can involve different levels of aggregation

Source: *Operations Strategy*, Slack and Lewis (2002), Figure 11.4, Pearson Education Limited.

It can therefore be seen that 'customer requirements' are not simply concerned with the product or service provided, but also the way in which the operation is carried out and the expected effect on the customer.

> *'Products are* **what** *we produce, service is* **how** *we provide them.'*   (Evans, 1997)

This is of particular importance for operations managers.

Customers have a direct influence on performance objectives through critical success factors: the key things by which the customer decides whether the organisation and its products are suitable for its needs. The link between these is shown in Exhibit 14.8.

Exhibit 14.8 Critical success factors and performance objectives

CRITICAL SUCCESS FACTORS		PERFORMANCE OBJECTIVES
If customers value these things ...		*then the operation will need to be good at these things . . .*
price	→	cost
quality	→	quality
fast delivery	→	speed
reliable delivery	→	dependability
innovative products and services	→	flexibility of product/service
wide range of products and services	→	flexibility of product/service mix
the ability to change timing or quantity of products or services	→	flexibility of volume and/or delivery

Source: Developed from *Operations Management, 3rd edition*, Slack *et al.* (2001, Figure 3.6, p 70). Pearson Education Limited.

Table 14.11 **Customer requirements**

HIGH	LOW
Quality	Costs
Flexibility: to change volume, specification, delivery	Lead times: getting shorter all the time for new products and processing ongoing demands
Levels of service	Variability: most customers prefer no variability at all

Source: Developed from Schonberger and Knod (1994). Reprinted by permission of Richard D Irwin Inc., Burr Ridge, Illinois.

While it is difficult to generalise about customer needs, it has been shown that in broad terms customers appear to have the requirements shown in Table 14.11.

These do not represent trade-offs. Most customers do not want better quality at the expense of lower costs – they want better quality *and* lower cost! They want continuous improvement in all aspects.

However, it is also important to be able to distinguish between critical success factors – not all are equally important for all customers. One way of doing this is through order-winning and order-qualifying criteria (Hill, 1993).

- **Order-winning criteria** are those things which significantly contribute to getting an order against competitors in the same market. They are the most important in terms of defining competitive position – raising performance in an order-winning factor will either result in more business or improve the chances of gaining more business.
- **Order-qualifying criteria** are the aspects of performance that have to be above a certain level in order for the product/service even to be considered by the customer. They get the product into the market or onto the customer's list.

Table 14.12 shows the characteristics of two product groups produced by the same company, the way in which they differ, and the impact this has on order-qualifying and order-winning criteria.

Another way in which the customer indirectly influences operations is through the pattern of demand which enables the organisation to decide whether to make to order or make to stock. The decision will be related to the type of process employed, but not always directly. This is a key decision for every organisation, with advantages depending on the product and the market.

A make-to-order organisation responds to a customer order before starting manufacture. However, it may manufacture kits or sub-assemblies before customer orders are received, in order to be able to deliver within an acceptable leadtime. A **make-to-stock organisation** does not assign orders to individual customers during the production process. Table 14.13 shows the impact of these two options on performance objectives and the major operations problems.

Table 14.12 Comparison of critical success factors and performance objectives

	PRODUCT GROUP 1	PRODUCT GROUP 2
Products	Standard electronic medical equipment	Electronic measuring devices
Customers	Hospitals/clinics	Other medical equipment companies
Product specification	Not high-tech, but with periodic updates	Most types are high performance
Product range	Narrow – 4 variants	Very wide with some customisation
Design changes	Infrequent	Continual
Delivery	Fast – from stock	On-time delivery important
Quality	Means reliability	Means performance
Demand	Predictable	Unpredictable
Volume per product type	High	Medium to low
Profit margins	Low to medium	Medium to very high
Critical success factors	↓	↓
Order winners	*Price*	*Product specification*
	Product reliability	*Product range*
Order qualifiers	*Delivery speed*	*On-time delivery*
	Product performance	*Delivery speed*
	Quality	*Price*
Less important	*Product range*	
	↓	↓
Internal performance objectives	*Cost*	*Product/service flexibility*
	Quality	*Mix flexibility*
		Dependability

Source: Developed from *Operations Management, 3rd edition*, Slack *et al.* (2001, Table 3.1, p 73). Pearson Education Limited.

Table 14.13 **Characteristics of make-to-stock and make-to-order environments**

CHARACTERISTICS	MAKE-TO-STOCK	MAKE-TO-ORDER
Product	Producer specified Low variety Inexpensive	Customer specified High variety Expensive
Objectives	Balance inventory, capacity and service	Manage delivery lead times and capacity
Main operations Problems	Forecasting Planning production Control of inventory	Delivery promises Delivery lead time

Source: Developed from Schroeder, R G (1993) *Operations Management*, 4th edn, © Copyright The McGraw-Hill Companies, Inc., 1993. Reproduced with permission of McGraw-Hill, Inc.

Customer interaction with the operations function will also depend on the type of process being employed. Table 14.14 shows the nature of customer and supplier relationships for different classifications of operations.

While the general principles concerning improvement of relationships with both suppliers and customers are valid for all organisations, it can be seen that operations will have a very different relationship with external agents, depending on the nature of the process employed within the organisation.

INTERNATIONAL DIFFERENCES

Operations management is the same in principle wherever it is practised. However, there are differences in emphasis in different parts of the world which are argued to have implications for differences in productivity and organisational performance,

Table 14.14 **Process characteristics, customers and suppliers**

		TYPICAL PROCESS CHARACTERISTICS		
		PROJECT	JOBBING ↔ BATCH ↔ LINE	CONTINUOUS
Customers	NATURE OF SALES	One-off tenders	One-off tenders · Defined prices with discounts	Well established
	DEGREE OF INTERACTION	Small	Small · Highly organised	Long-term and highly organised
Suppliers	RELATIONSHIPS	Variable	Informal · Formal	Long-term contracts
	DEGREE OF INTERACTION	Variable	Small · Highly organised	Highly organised

Source: Developed from Hill (1991). Reprinted with permission.

especially between the West and the Far East. There is also an ongoing debate about the extent to which the national culture affects the decision-making role of the operations manager, and the methods which may be employed.

The global nature of business is now widely accepted, and yet its implications for operations have not always been thought through. Schroeder (1993) distinguishes between three types of international firm:

- **Global** – marketing a similar product throughout the world, with a worldwide scale of operations.
- **Multinational** – marketing and producing products in various countries, suited to local tastes. It is usually organised with separate divisions or independent foreign subsidiaries in each country.
- **Export** – products are shipped to various countries from a domestic facility. It may use agents for marketing abroad.

Schroeder argues that each type of firm still has a place, since each can compete on different things. A global firm is well placed to gain economies of scale and compete primarily on price. A multinational firm can differentiate its products for the relevant local markets, as well as differentiating service, quality, responsiveness to customer demands or other factors that may have local importance.

The main issues to consider in developing an understanding of international operations strategy are as follows:

- **Location of operations to form an international network.** This is a cost issue, but also has to take into account cultural issues and legal considerations, as well as potential markets.
- **Management of the network across national boundaries.** Technology has had a beneficial effect on this but there are still issues to be considered.
- **Development of different operations practices within different countries.** This seems to be inevitable, however central the control of the organisation is. The social, political, demographic and economic environments all have a significant effect on the development of these practices.
- **Transfer of practices from one country to another.** This is a key issue for the West at present, as organisations try to implement Japanese-style practices. Many companies have found that the practices are applicable but that they need some modification. The more similar the cultural and economic context, the easier it appears to be to transfer operations practices successfully.

There is a set of common principles which appear to be followed by the leading 'world-class' manufacturers in Japan, Germany and the USA. All these principles relate to the operations function. Authors differ as to the exact wording of these principles (e.g. Schonberger, 1996) although Schroeder (1993) broadly summarises them as follows:

- **Put the customer first.** This has to be followed by everyone, not just the salesforce.
- **Be conscious of quality.** Quality has to be thought into every product and every aspect of performance has to be seen through the customer's eyes.
- **Involve employees.** This means seeking consensus and input from everyone and developing mutual trust and respect.

■ **Practise just-in-time production.** This means striving to reduce waste in all forms, including inventory, space, errors and overheads.

■ **Emphasise appropriate technology.** This includes technological innovation but also the use of technology where appropriate.

■ **Emphasise the long term.** Where the short-term interests of shareholders are promoted at the expense of long-term investment, organisations struggle on a world-class scale.

■ **Be action-oriented.** World-class companies are relatively small and decentralised, with relatively flat organisation structures.

SUMMARY

■ This chapter shows that operations management may be considered as a transformation process where inputs are transformed into outputs. This is a good basis for analysis of the influences on and functioning of operations.

■ Operations management has developed from, and been influenced by, a variety of factors from a number of academic disciplines.

■ The relationship between the operations function and other functions within the organisation depends on the type of organisation, i.e. the extent to which an organisation produces goods or services. This will also affect the nature of the operations management task, in particular the emphasis placed on various factors of operations management.

■ The major trends affecting operations include an increased emphasis on the customer, continuous improvement, involvement of everyone in the organisation, integration with other organisational functions and globalisation of organisations.

■ The operations process may be classified according to volume and type of product or service produced, and this will have an impact on the role of the manager.

■ The outputs from the process may be measured using a traditional ratio of input to output resources, but this is limited in applicability. New ways of measuring focus on the effectiveness of the five operations performance measures: quality, cost, delivery speed, delivery dependability and flexibility.

■ Customers and their requirements are increasingly important in determining how operations are managed, and it is important for the organisation to develop an understanding of the needs of the customer and the way in which customers judge the suitability of an organisation, product or service.

■ The international context has also become increasingly important, particularly with the increased market share gained by Japanese manufactured goods and merger and acquisition activity. Although it is not clear whether operations techniques are fully transferable across national boundaries, it seems that national culture may affect their implementation.

Review and discussion questions

1 *What is operations management and what is meant by the transformation process in an organisation?*

2 *How do the characteristics of services differ from those of products?*

3 *How does the operations manager carry out his or her role?*

4 *How can the performance of the transformation process be measured?*

5 *Why are both customers and the external environment important in operations management?*

CASE STUDY 14.3

DuPont

DuPont's May Plant in Camden, South Carolina, employs approximately 125 people and produces roughly 69 million pounds of textile fibre each year. The textile area includes production, shipping, inspection, and testing. Textile fibres are produced in a continuous spinning operation. After fibre is wound on a spool, it is placed on a special buggy that holds many spools. The buggies are wheeled to a test-and-inspection station. Finally, the product is grouped, packaged, and shipped. Spinning machines cannot be shut down without incurring tremendous start-up costs. Even slowing production will adversely affect product consistency and quality. Those facts complicated the job of the plant managers, who faced many problematic issues. The quality of work life for operators, supervisors and area managers was poor, with many safety problems. There were constant telephone calls from customers about delivery schedules, calls that were often unpleasant and at times confrontational. Customers' orders were not being met in a timely way. Other problems were product shortages, excessive backlogs, high inventories, and lost or misplaced yarn. Product-quality variation and production yields were unacceptable. There was ongoing pressure from the marketing group, as well as from plant executives, to stem the flow of customer complaints.

Employees, supervisors and managers were eager for change. One area supervisor had been exposed to world-class operations management principles and prompted the journey towards successfully and permanently resolving the problems. One step was to lock up many of the buggies except when needed for an emergency. With fewer buggies in operation, bottlenecks became acutely visible, and the sources of problems were more quickly identified and corrected. The result was a smoother flow of product through the facility. Jobs were simplified, and a visual control system was adopted. In the new system, buggies were placed only in small marked-off spaces, which limited the amount of inventory and flagged problems. Even forklifts had specific parking places to enable easy identification of the ones that were leaking fluid and posed a safety problem. Employees measured the time it took products to move through the facility and backlogs at each workstation, plotting the results so that deviations could be identified quickly and corrected. Extensive on-the-job education and training, supplemented by meetings and individual coaching and counseling, helped to involve all employees in the improvement efforts.

As a result of those initiatives, work-in-process inventory was reduced an astounding 96 per cent, working capital declined by $2 million; employee suggestions increased 300 per cent, and product quality improved 10 per cent. Most of the results were achieved within the first three months after implementation of the changes.

Source: Evans, J R (1997) *Production/Operations Management: Quality, Performance and Value*, St Paul, MN: West Publishing Company.

The Ritz-Carlton Hotel Company: service through people

The Ritz-Carlton Hotel Company is one example of an outstanding service company. In 1992 it became the first hospitality organisation to receive the Malcolm Baldrige National Quality Award. The hotel industry is very competitive, one in which customers place high emphasis on reliability, timely delivery and price value. The Ritz-Carlton focuses on the principal concerns of its main customers and strives to provide highly personalised, genuinely caring service. Attention to its employees, processes and use of information technology are three of the many strengths of the Ritz-Carlton that helped it to receive national recognition.

The Ritz-Carlton's company philosophy is 'Ladies and Gentlemen Serving Ladies and Gentlemen.' Its credo states, 'The genuine care and comfort of our guests is our highest mission.' The company's 'three steps of service' are (1) a warm greeting in which employees use the guest's name, (2) anticipation of and compliance with the guest's needs, and (3) a warm farewell, again using the guest's name if possible. A Ritz-Carlton employee will not point a guest in a desired direction; he or she will lead the guest to the desired destination. In attending to complaints, employees must respond within 10 minutes and follow up with a phone call within 20 minutes to make sure the customer is satisfied. The employees have the responsibility to solve problems, and they are given considerable latitude and authority in doing so to ensure total customer satisfaction. Any failure, such as not having a room ready on time, requires complimentary cocktails, an amenity sent to the room, and a letter of apology.

Employees are empowered to 'move heaven and earth to satisfy a customer', to contact other employees, to help resolve a problem swiftly, to spend up to $2000 to satisfy a guest, to decide the business terms of a sale, to become involved in setting plans for their work area, and to speak with anyone in the management hierarchy about any problem.

The company's objectives are to improve the quality of its products and services, reduce cycle time, and improve price value and customer retention. At each level of the company, teams are charged with setting objectives and devising action plans, which are reviewed by the corporate steering committee. Such an approach ensures that (1) all teams are aligned around a common vision and agreed-upon objectives, (2) all employees are encouraged to think beyond the demands of daily activities, and (3) continual communication is maintained among the diverse functions that make up the company. To provide the personalised service demanded by the company's customers, the human resource function works in close co-ordination with all other functions. All hotels have a director of human resources and a training manager, both of whom are assisted by the hotel's quality leader. Each work area has a departmental trainer who is charged with the training and certification of new employees in that unit. The Ritz-Carlton uses a highly predictive 'character trait recruiting' instrument to determine a candidate's capability to meet the requirements of each of 120 job positions. New employees receive two days' orientation by senior executives to demonstrate methods and instil the Ritz-Carlton values. Three weeks later managers monitor the effectiveness of the instruction and make necessary changes in a follow-up session. Later, new employees must pass written and skill-demonstration tests to become certified in their work areas.

Every employee receives instruction designed to make him or her a certified quality engineer capable of identifying wasteful complexity within his or her work. In all, employees receive more than 100 hours of quality education to foster premium service commitment, solve problems, set strategic quality plans, and generate new ideas. And every day, in every work area, during every shift, a quality line-up meeting of employees occurs for a briefing session.

Customised hotel products and services, such as meetings and banquet events, receive the full attention of cross-functional teams. In the process of designing and delivering customised services, all internal and external suppliers become involved as early as possible, production and delivery capabilities are verified prior to each event, samples are prepared and critiqued by event planners, and 'after-event' assessments are conducted for continuous improvement.

The Ritz-Carlton applies information technology to capture and use customer satisfaction data and other important data in real time. Its information systems enable every employee to collect and use data on a daily basis, including online guest preference information, quantity of error-free products and services, and complaints indicating opportunities for improvement. A guest-profiling system that registers the individual preferences of 240 000 guests who have stayed at least three times at any of the hotels gives front-desk employees immediate access to such information as whether a guest smokes, whether he or she prefers wine or a rose in the evening, and even which kind of pillow is preferred.

Those are only a few of the key operations management activities practised at The Ritz-Carlton. The results are impressive. Customer satisfaction is upwards of 95 per cent. Employee turnover is only 48 per cent, versus an annual industry average of more than 100 per cent. The number of employees needed per guest room during pre-opening activities of a new hotel was reduced 12 per cent. Within a three-year period, the Ritz-Carlton reduced the number of hours worked per guest room by 8 per cent. Housekeeping cost per occupied room was reduced from $7.90 at the end of 1991 to $7.30 at the beginning of 1992. The time required to clean an average room has decreased from 30 to 28.5 minutes. Even elevator waiting time has been reduced by 33 per cent. Departmental profits per available guest room are nearly five times the industry average. One lesson the hotel has learned is to never underestimate the value of even one idea or improvement effort.

Source: Evans, J R (1997) *Production/Operations Management: Quality, Performance and Value*, St Paul, MN: West Publishing Company.

REFERENCES AND FURTHER READING

Babbage, Charles (1832) *On the Economy of Machinery and Manufacturers*, London: Charles Knight.

Charnes, A, Cooper, W W and Rhodes, E (1978) 'Measuring the Efficiency of Decision Making Units', *European Journal of Operational Research* (2), 429–44.

Christopher, M (1998) *Logistics and Supply Chain Management*, London: FT Prentice Hall.

Denzler, D (2000) 'Shell One: Operations Management Circa 2000', www.clubpom.com, accessed 20 October 2000.

Evans J R (1997) *Production/Operations Management: Quality, Performance and Value*, St Paul, MN: West Publishing Company.

Fogarty, D W, Hoffmann, T R and Stonebraker, P W (1989) *Production and Operations Management*, Cincinnati, OH: South-Western Publishing.

George, C S Jr (1968) *The History of Management Thought*, Englewood Cliffs, NJ: Prentice-Hall.

Gilgeous V (1997) *Operations and the Management of Change*, Harlow: FT Prentice Hall.

Hackman, J R, Oldham G, Janson R and Purdy K (1975) 'A New Strategy for Job Enrichment', *California Management Review*, Summer, vol. 17, Issue 4: 57–71.

Hammer, M and Champy, J (1993) *Re-engineering the Corporation*, New York: Nicholas Brealey Publishing.

Harrington, H J (1991) *Business Process Improvement*, New York: McGraw-Hill.

Harris, N D (1989) *Service Operations Management*, London: Cassell.

Hill, T J (1991) *Production/Operations Management* (2nd edn), London: Prentice Hall.

Hill, T J (1993) *Manufacturing Strategy* (2nd edn), Basingstoke: Macmillan.

Ishikawa, K (1985) *What is Total Quality Control? The Japanese Way*, translated by D J Lu, Englewood Cliffs, NJ: Prentice-Hall.

Kaplan R and Norton D (1996) *The Balanced Scorecard*, Boston, MA: Harvard Business School Press.

Lockyer, K, Oakland, J, and Muhlemann, A, (1992) *Production and Operations Management* (6th edn), London: Pitman Publishing.

Murdick, R G, Rendern, B and Russell, R S (1990) *Service Operations Management*, Needham Heights, MA: Allyn & Bacon.

Porter, M E (1985) *Competitive Advantage: Creating and Sustaining Superior Performance*, New York: Free Press.

Schmenner, R W (1986) 'How Can Service Businesses Survive and Prosper?', *Sloan Management Review*, Spring: 21–32.

Schonberger, R (1996) *World Class Manufacturing: The Next Decade*, New York: Simon & Schuster.

Schonberger, R J and Knod, E M (1994) *Operations Management: Continuous Improvement* (5th edn), Burr Ridge, IL: Richard D Irwin.

Schroeder, R G (1993) *Operations Management* (4th edn), New York: McGraw-Hill.

Schroeder, R G (1999) *Operations Management: Contemporary Concepts and Cases*, London: McGraw-Hill.

Scott Myers, M (1991) *Every Employee a Manager* (3rd edn), San Diego, CA: University Associates.

Shostack, G L (1977) 'Breaking Free from Product Marketing', *Journal of Marketing*, April.

Skinner, W (1969) 'Manufacturing – The Missing Link in Corporate Strategy', *Havard Business Review*, May–June: 136–45.

Slack, N (1983) 'Operations Management and Curriculum Design', *Management Education and Development*, 14 (1): 19–32.

Slack, N (1989) 'Focus on Flexibility', in Wild, R (ed.), *International Handbook of Production/Operations Management*, London: Cassell.

Slack, N (1991) *The Manufacturing Advantage*, London: Mercury Books.

Slack, N, Chambers, S, Harland, C, Harrison, A and Johnston, R (1998) *Operations Management* (2nd edn), London: FT Pitman Publishing.

Slack, N, Chambers, S, Harland, C, Harrison, A and Johnston, R (2001) *Operations Management* (3rd edn), London: FT Prentice Hall.

Slack, N and Lewis, M (2002) *Operations Strategy*, Harlow: FT Prentice Hall.

Smith, A (1776) *An Inquiry into the Nature and Causes of the Wealth of Nations*, London: A Strahn and T Caddell.

Taylor, F W (1911) *The Principles of Scientific Management*, New York: Harper.

Underwood, L (1994) *Intelligent Manufacturing*, Wokingham: Addison-Wesley with the Economist Intelligence Unit.

Waters, D (1996) *Operations Management*, Reading, MA: Addison-Wesley Longman.

Wheelwright, S C and Hayes, R H (1985) 'Competing through Manufacturing', *Harvard Business Review*, January/February: 99–109.

Wild, R (1989) *Production and Operations Management* (4th edn), London: Cassell.

Wren, D A (1972) *The Evolution of Management Thought*, New York: Ronald Press.

WEBSITES

General resource pages

There are a number of general resource pages for operations management on the web, including:

http://www.bized.ac.uk/fme/5.htm
The Operations Management page on the Bized website (http://www.bized.ac.uk/). Bized is a unique business and economics service for students, teachers and lecturers. Studying operations management on the web can be of great value. Understanding where to access the best resources, understanding the nature of rapidly changing operations technologies and methodologies, is very important both to students and to operations practitioners. Visiting operations management websites will give a solid introduction to latest technologies to both students and executives of operations management. This site is UK-based.

http://bradley.bradley.edu/~rf/opman.html
Ross L. Fink's Operations Management Homepage. This site has a wide variety of links providing information related to various operations management topics. It is US-based and very comprehensive.

Interactive pages

Operations management lends itself well to interactive web pages and these are now exploited in a variety of ways.

http://bradley.bradley.edu/~rf/plantour.htm
Plant Tours on the Internet. The links contain interactive plant tours. These websites are developed by organisations to allow individuals an opportunity to see their operations. Most of these sites are for manufacturing facilities. However, a few are for service operations.

http://www.cbpa.drake.edu/bmeyer/POOL/index.html
Principles of Operations Online Laboratory. This site is designed as an aid to learning concepts in operations management (OM). The observatory provides video clips and image files of people at work. You can study their methods, time their operations and devise ways to improve their processes. The experiment stations contain simulations you can use online to learn about concepts in OM. The software tool chest contains computer programs and spreadsheet templates for common OM problems.

http://apps.pearsoned-ema.com:8900/public/opsmanv2/index.html
Pearson Education Operations Management Online Course Content. These materials are designed to help you learn about operations management through interactive learning materials. They are not intended to replace textbooks, journal articles or any classes that you may attend. Rather they are designed to supplement these more conventional approaches to learning about the subject. This introductory course on operations management explores various topics, including job design, TQM, JIT, operations improvement and operations strategy. As the course develops, students deal in depth with decisions in functional areas such as product and service design, and facility layout and location. They are provided with an array of examples to demonstrate quantitative techniques, and to apply the concepts to real situations through interactive exercises.

Publishers' sites

Many of the main publishers of business and management textbooks also provide pages of links to other subject resources that are useful whether or not you use the textbook that they publish. Some of the main ones include:

http://www.mhhe.com/omc/index.html
Irwin/McGraw-Hill: the Operations Management Center. A website of resources supported by the publishers Irwin/McGraw-Hill but drawing on much wider resources. Resources include Company Tours, BusinessWeek OM Articles, OM Publications On-line, OM Organizations, OM Software, OM Newsfeeds and a video library. OM Center is designed to be a fast-loading informational site, with minimal glitter and glitz that would slow it down. It is marketed as *the* source for faculty looking for pedagogical support or references and for students seeking current OM information. Links are limited only to those providing useful information. If a commercial site offers educational value, the site aims to link to it, but does not endorse products or services of any firm, except for Irwin/McGraw-Hill.

http://www.booksites.net/results_pages/cws_results/ busmang/23.htm
Pearson Education book support resources. The main page for access to the support sites for all operations/project management books published by Pearson. Students can explore a collection of resources correlated to a book's table of contents, including a study guide, multiple-choice questions and web links.

CHAPTER 15

Business and management information

MIKE HARRY

Outcomes

Having read this chapter, you will be able to:

- identify the different forms of information used in organisations and business

- establish an understanding of a systems view of the relationship between the concepts of management, control and information

- use the understanding of this relationship to identify the role of the management information system in organisation and business

- critically assess other views of information and management

- establish present and future management implications of specific forms of information and communications technology-based information systems

CASE STUDY 15.1

eEurope 2005: towards a knowledge-based Europe

eEurope is a European Union (EU) plan for guiding the process of transition to what it calls a 'truly knowledge-based economy'. The origin of the scheme is an initiative launched by the European Commission in December 1999. This aimed to speed up the adoption of information and communications technology (ICT) across Europe and to ensure that everybody in the EU would have the necessary skills to exploit the personal, social and commercial potential of ITC. A communication 'eEurope – An Information Society for All' was adopted by the EU, as setting the agenda for the eEurope initiative.

At the Lisbon Summit in March 2000, the European heads of state and government recognised that Europe must become a much more digital economy. As a result, the essential aims of eEurope were recognised and, indeed, the heads of state set a new goal for the EU – to become the most competitive knowledge-based society in the world by 2010. eEurope was also closely connected to an education strategy, which was seen as the driving force behind the EU's push to become the most competitive knowledge-based economy in the world by the 2010 deadline.

Since eEurope's original aims were to put a European stamp on the Internet and to keep Europe competitive, by late 2002 the original 1999 eEurope concept was subject to a review called eEurope 2002. This recorded the accomplishments of the eEurope scheme to date and set out further aims in a revised scheme called eEurope 2005. eEurope 2005 essentially asked the question, 'Where do we go from here?'

The original eEurope aims were to ensure that everyone in the EU – every citizen, every school, every company, every administration – had access to ICT and could exploit them as fully as possible. This would mean, for example, using the Internet for a host of everyday activities, services and products such as education, government, health, culture and entertainment. Such aims included the vision of improvement in quality of life, like 'direct and interactive online access to knowledge, education, training, government, health services, culture and entertainment, financial services and much more'. Internet access was to become a fundamental right for all citizens and responsible governments have a duty to provide it. eEurope and its component programmes (eLearning, eHealth, eGovernment and eBusiness) would focus on fully exploiting this potential for social inclusion.

However, by 2003 eEurope 2005 recognised that the potential changes in the EU itself had implications for eEurope. In May 2004, ten new countries (the Czech Republic, Estonia, Cyprus, Latvia, Lithuania, Hungary, Malta, Poland, Slovenia and Slovakia) joined the Union, adding some 75 million citizens to the existing EU of 375 million people. Social inclusion is seen by the EU as vital to the success of this major enlargement and 'digital inclusion' is regarded as an important aspect of any inclusive policy.

In eEurope 2005, the European Commission aims to distinguish between the European emphasis on digital inclusion and its approach to the information society from other regions of the world. It is no secret that the USA, for example, outperformed Europe in the initial speed with which industry and citizens took up the Internet. However, eEurope is now helping Europe catch up, channelling efforts at regional, national and European levels to ensure that the digital economy brings benefits to all European citizens and to put a European stamp on the Internet.

Source: www.europa.eu.int. Accessed on 12/09/03.

CASE STUDY 15.2

ICT in UK schools

The British Educational Communications and Technology Agency (Becta) is the UK government agency that supports the development of ICT in education. In June 2003 it announced that it had awarded three-year contracts to 28 companies to take part in the government's Laptops for Teachers initiative which commenced in June 2002. The aim of this initiative was to improve teachers' flexibility by providing them with laptops, which they could use both at home and at school. Under the initiative, local education authorities (LEAs) would purchase the laptops on behalf of their schools and the schools would allocate the laptops to teachers for their individual use. The teachers will not be required to make a financial contribution. The total cost would be £300 million over the peroid 2002–06.

In a press release Becta stated: 'The current generation of school children is growing up in a world where information and communication technology (ICT) is second nature. It is therefore crucial that we support teachers in embedding ICT in their teaching practice.' In another report published in 2003, Becta explored the relationship between primary schools' use of ICT and pupils' achievement in national tests and examinations. It found that schools with high levels of ICT outperformed those with low levels of ICT, even after allowing for socio-economic disadvantages or the effects of privileged acquisition of resources. Also, schools where ICT was used well within a subject tended to achieve better results in that subject than other schools. Likewise, schools that combined good ICT resources with very good ICT teaching gained better results than those with good ICT resources but poor ICT teaching. Thus the presence of ICT resources alone is less important than the combination of good resources and effective use.

Source: http://www.becta.co.uk. Accessed on 12/09/03.

ISSUES IN BUSINESS AND MANAGEMENT INFORMATION

The two case studies raise a number of important issues. The second case concerning the Internet and education has been chosen to raise two important issues:

- What views can be taken of the nature of information in this age of networked global information and communications technology?
- How does the view taken of information affect our view of what constitutes business and management?

The important conclusions that can be demonstrated by analysing these issues are that:

- information is a *rich* concept;
- the nature of networked information systems has changed the *concept* of business and management systems that was held before the revolution in information and communications technology (ICT).

The cases chosen for this chapter might seem different from what could have been expected under the heading of 'business' or 'management'. A case involving the problems associated with managing a large organisational computer network or database might have seemed more appropriate. Such a view would have chosen supply chain management for a large retail chain or business-to-business electronic commerce as a context for business and management information.

There is an important false assumption behind such a view, which is revealed by the eEurope initiative outlined in the opening case study. To assume that a large database is a more relevant example for the subject of information and management than, say, the recording of marks by a teacher on a laptop implies two false assumptions:

- The complexity of an organisation can be equated to its size. According to this view, the issues at a European level must be more complex than those at a personal level.
- The separation and classification of activities into different functions like education, politics, business or management is likely to remain the same after the advent of information and communications technology as it was before.

Even a simple everyday example can show that the first assumption, that equates complexity with size, is false. The plumbing system of a house takes up more space than a human being, weighs more, and contains more energy, but it is easier to make water automatically come out of a tap than to make an individual human being give out sympathy, money or secret personal information, and much less easy to get a human plumber out on Christmas Eve.

The quality that makes human beings more complex than water systems is **richness**. Richness is not determined by size but by the *variety* of components contained in a particular *whole* and the degree of *complexity* of their *interaction*. This chapter will, therefore, cover important management information issues in the context of large organisations as well as small ones.

The falseness of the second assumption is shown by the very reason that the European Commission set up the eEurope initiative. The Commission had noted that although Europe enjoyed one of the highest levels of education in the world and had the necessary investment capacity, it still lagged far behind in the use of the information and communication technology. **Boundaries** that used to be set by *physical* separation or *labels* are no longer a reliable way of looking at the world after the advent of global connection through information and communications technology. The Internet redefines boundaries. Businesses which require that both their employees and their customers have the skills to sell and buy over the Internet can no longer see education as some separate object of no interest. Similarly, an education system that hopes to produce citizens who will live in the world of global connection cannot work apart from the context and procedures of information and communications technology. The inclusion of a primary school example in our opening case studies will have achieved one of its purposes if it confirms this point.

The richness of information as a concept

To show the richness of information as a concept, this section will consider in more detail some of the different views that can be taken of it, regardless of the size of organisation involved. Whether in the whole of Europe or in a primary school, as well as many other organisations big and small, information might been seen as:

- data organised into a particular **structure**;
- the output of a **process** applied to other information or data;
- a means of **communication** between a sender and a receiver;
- a form of **knowledge**;
- a source of **clarification** and **reduction of uncertainty**;

- a possession which gives **power**;
- something of **interest**;
- **intuition**, with no obviously immediate logical source.

Examples of information as data organised into a particular **structure** can be seen in any business document. An entry like 'Quantity 10, Price £23.50' contains the same individual characters and figures as 'Quantity 23, Price £10.50', but the information represented is different in each case. The particular structure used to organise data gives it an overall meaning called 'information'. The study of the concept of a database later in this chapter will show that a major property of a **database management system** is the ability to assemble data in the particular structure required by the user to produce needed information. In the Internet context, there is a potential database of many terabytes, but how this is organised in terms of structure and connection greatly affects how far it is information, rather than confusion.

Information can also be seen as the output of a **process** applied to other information or data. The previous invoice example would also need to contain information about cost. This is easily obtained by multiplying the quantity and price, but such a trivial example is just one instance of the whole concept of data processing. From this viewpoint any information system can be seen as a kind of information factory that uses raw material called data and transforms it into produce a product called information. This chapter considers some of the different forms of transformation an information system has to carry out. The important implication for management, however, is that it is the customer who uses the product of this information factory, whether it be in paying an invoice or scanning the Internet.

Information implies **communication** between a sender and a receiver. Unread, unused or unknown information is a managerial nonsense: words have to be spoken, documents sent and electronic data transmitted. The vast potential of the information on the Internet will be of little use to the citizens of Europe if it remains undiscovered and uncommunicated. Ensuring such communication will require both information and communications technology and the human relations skills of a teacher. It is important to realise that a glance or a nod can also be the communication of information; and now that we have web cameras, the glances or nods may be electronic. This chapter will show how an information system needs to deal with the communication of both hard and soft information.

Information as a form of **knowledge** is implied by phrases like 'to know' with 'being informed'. The eEurope initiative recognises that the success of the European economy will depend on the ability of consumers and citizens to use information and communications technology. However, the technology itself can give the user some of the knowledge needed to use it. Issues like this will be explored further under intelligent and expert systems and the concept of a knowledge base.

The concept of information as a means of **clarification** and **reduction of uncertainty** follows from the view of it as a form of knowledge. A major policy measure for setting up an information economy in Europe was the establishment of a clear legal framework for electronic commerce. In particular, this needed to deal with privacy, authentication and security. It is unlikely that businesses and customers will trade over the Internet if they cannot be certain that they are protected against insecurity in its operations or fraud. The eEurope initiative to support research and development in these key areas is an attempt to reduce uncertainty.

When instigating eEurope, the European heads of state talked of creating 'the most competitive and dynamic knowledge-driven economy in the world'. They clearly saw information as a source of **power**. The strength of the European economy was no longer just seen as depending on the capacity to manufacture and sell: it should be 'knowledge-driven'. At the level of the primary school, Becta found that exploitation of information and communications technology was a major factor in empowering the success of pupils. Not surprisingly, one primary school has promoted its use of information and communications technology using the picture of an owl and the motto: 'worldwide wisdom: the Web adds power to learning'.

Information as a source of **interest** can be illustrated with the example of a parent being curious to know how far his child's school was using information and communications technology, but at that point no management activity would be involved. However, once information is also seen as a reducer of uncertainty and a source of power, it is also likely to become of interest to management. An important reason for anything but ephemeral interest in information is that we learn something from it that we can use in the future. In the example of the parent interested in managing his child's educational success, this could have been at the first stage of selecting a school on the basis of its strengths in information and communications technology. Similarly, in the wider picture, for the European Commission it was not just idle curiosity that made it interested to find that the uptake of the Internet in Europe had remained comparatively low in the late 1990s.

Information as **intuition**, with no obviously immediate logical source, can be used to question many of the views of information we have considered so far. 'Body language', 'It's not what you know but who you know', 'How come you so clever, me so rich?', are quotes and phrases from a view of management which thinks that formal views of systems ignore what really goes on in management with its human component. The enthusiasm for adapting to the world of the Internet may be shared by European Commission and Becta but, in the end, this enthusiasm cannot be based on logic alone. There is no reliable formula for predicting the future. An important ingredient of the commitment to exploiting information and communications technology is an intuitive belief that the future lies in this direction. Real management information also includes such a soft, intuitive component, and any overall view of information must take account of this.

Changing concepts of business and management systems' boundaries

Imagine the following scenes in a video. The first scene shows two Indian teams playing cricket. The camera pulls back from the cricket match to reveal that the Indian teams are playing in California, USA. The members of the teams are Indians who have moved to the USA to work as software engineers for an organisation in California.

Now for the second scene: it also shows two Indian teams playing cricket. Once again, the camera pulls back from the cricket match to reveal that the Indian teams are now playing at home in their own country. These team members also work as software engineers for an organisation in California.

What is the difference between these two scenes? The answer is quite simple: the second scene shows what is possible after the advent of the Internet. In today's globally connected world, an Indian software engineer can be as much in contact with a Californian information system as someone on a local area network. It is no longer automatically necessary for someone to be physically present in an organisation in order to be connected and part of the working system. These two illustrative scenes have their basis in fact. India, as a country with strong software engineering skills, is serving many organisations throughout the world, without its software engineers necessarily having to leave their country.

Consider two more scenes. In the first, a television news producer is assembling a news programme using a networked computer system that stores sound, pictures and videos of current news reports. The producer can use this system not only as a source of her material, she can also use its software to assemble and schedule selected material into a complete news programme. All that is now required is a newsreader and a time slot, and the news programme can go on air.

Now consider a second scene. A person who used to pay a TV licence fee now pays a subscription fee for access to the networked computer system over the Internet. He doesn't need a producer to tell him what he may see of the news; he doesn't need a newsreader to read what he can read for himself; and he doesn't need to be told what time of the day he must do it. The boundaries between the roles of news provider, editor, reader and viewer have changed and been blurred by information and communications technology. In the second scene the producer, for example, is the viewer.

Making sense of business and management information

The richness of information and the changing of roles and boundaries resulting from the new information and communications technology mean that older ways of viewing business and management information do not always work in the world of multimedia and the Internet. However, not all business and management information is on the Internet. Despite the dramatic developments in information and communications technology, much of the information used by business and management is being processed by internal computer systems and frequently uses manually produced documents.

What is needed therefore is a view of information that is relevant to *all* the different kinds of information system. Such a view ought to be able to:

■ look behind *how* management is described by titles and labels to see *what* management actually does;

■ look behind *how* information is communicated, processed or recorded to see *what* the information is, and what management uses it for.

The distinction between the 'how' and the 'what' of management and information is sometimes described as the distinction between the *physical* and the *logical*, or between the *concrete* and the *abstract*. The next section presents a relationship between:

■ **information systems**

■ **control systems**

■ **management systems**

with the aim of revealing how all forms of business and management information can be related to a common, consistent model.

INFORMATION, CONTROL AND MANAGEMENT SYSTEMS

Figure 15.1 shows the relationship between information, control and management systems. In terms of hierarchical structure, an information system can be seen as a subsystem of a control system, and a control system as a subsystem of a management system. To explain this relationship further, the meaning of the word 'system' needs exploring, followed by an explanation of the particular examples of management, control and information. For the application of systems thinking to business and management information, *see* Harry (2001).

Properties of systems

Anything called a system in this chapter will be characterised by the following features:

- **An assembly of two or more *components*.** Thus, a computer system might consist of a keyboard, screen, a tower containing the disk drives and central processor, and a printer. If an organisation like the EU is viewed as a system, it would also include human, financial, material and political components, as well as IT systems connected by networks. Components may be physical or concrete. For example, equipment is concrete; information or money is abstract.

- **The components will be *connected* together in some fixed set of relationships called a *structure*.** The components of a computer system have to be connected up correctly for it to be a system rather than a chaotic heap. Similarly, the very word 'organisation' implies appropriate forms of relationships between people, facilities, equipment and resources. The connections, like the components, may be abstract. Thus, membership of an organisation (like the EU) or the association of information with an individual (like a teacher) is a logical rather than a physical connection.

Figure 15.1 **Information, control and management systems**

■ **The components within this structure will *interact*.** Once the components of a computer system are correctly connected together, they are able to send electrical signals to each other. Once someone becomes a member of an organisation, he or she communicates with other people, uses equipment and interacts in many ways.

■ **The interaction of the components will result in the system carrying out various *transformation processes*.** A computer system will transform input data on, say, hours worked by employees, into output information such as wages to be paid. Transformations may also be concrete or abstract. Thus, building a new school computer facility physically transforms rooms and equipment into a computer lab, but when the EU Council of Ministers passes a resolution that transforms a proposal into a policy, the transformation is logical or abstract.

■ **The result of all the above properties will be that a system can be viewed as a *whole* with its own *identity* and *emergent properties*.** Once a computer system is up and working, it can do things as a whole system which are not achievable by the separate parts. What eEurope calls 'An Information Society for All' will only emerge when all the facilities and human skills come together as a result of learning and investment.

■ **The particular view of the system thus presented will be someone's concept.** A school pupil, an EU commissioner, a national politician, a schools inspector and an employer are all likely to have different views of an educational system designed to create 'an information society for all'.

These six features of any system will be referred to and developed as they apply to the particular examples of management, control and information systems, as in Figure 15.1.

Management and control

The following tentative definition of management from Harry (1990) can be used as a starting point:

> *'Management is an activity which aims to achieve something desirable to those who manage.'*

How might this apply to the Internet and education case? The EU Council of Ministers wants to create an information society for all. Becta wanted to equip teachers with laptops. Hence, both of these organisations had something desirable they aimed to achieve.

These examples of 'something desirable' can be used to establish the concept of control as an essential component of management. Control is often taken to imply a particular management style. It may be used with another concept hierarchy, to signify a rigid, authoritarian approach to management. Such a use of the two terms implies a stereotype 'boss' who 'controls' by 'giving orders'. In this chapter, control refers to a concept and not a particular management style.

This distinction between a concept of what something is and how it is done can be expressed as the difference between the whats and the hows we introduced above. *What* the EU wanted to create was an information society for all. *How* it decided to create such a thing could have involved many different methods. Thus, instead of deciding to provide all schools in the European Union with an Internet connection by the end of 2001, the EU may have thought it better to have delayed the universal installation of hardware until the advent of successful wireless technology. Instead of working through schools, it may have been more ambitious and worked through homes. It could have given remote regions or disabled people priority. Just as there can be many routes that lead to the same destination, so many different *hows* can lead to the same *what*.

The stereotyped view of control is restrictive because it fails to recognise the choice of ways of exerting control. The concept of control, therefore, needs further explanation, to show why it is the link between the concepts of information and management.

The main components of a control system

A standard model of a control system (Harry, 2001) has the following components:

- **Defined goals** – what is regarded as 'something desirable to those who manage'. Goals may be hard and soft. Becta's goal of supplying teachers with laptops can be defined in terms of specific figures for the number of teachers or the number of schools. Hard goals are those which can be assessed by objective criteria, like counting teachers or schools. However, the EU's goal of a 'truly knowledge-based economy' is not objectively definable. For such a goal, success of achievement depends on the subjective interpretation of 'truly' or 'knowledge-based'. Soft goals are those whose interpretation and definition depend on the values or world view of those concerned.

- A **transformation process** which is capable of achieving the defined goals. It may be concerned with concrete or abstract transformations. Concrete transformations are concerned with physical changes, like delivering a laptop from one place to another. Abstract transformations are concerned with conceptual changes, such as the change of ownership of the laptop. From a management viewpoint, whatever the transformation process, its output should conform as closely as possible to the system's goals.

- **Environmental disturbances**, which may interfere with the workings of a transformation process and divert it from its goals, are not part of the control system. They are, however, the reason for its existence. Changes in the number of teachers requiring laptops, or of the enthusiasm of the European public for information and communications technology, will affect what modification of inputs management will make to the particular process being controlled. More teachers might need more expenditure; less enthusiasm might require better publicity.

- A **sensor** which will enable the controller to register the outputs of the transformation process. The sensor is a concept: in practice, it can be a particular person, a group or a piece of equipment. Thus it may be an equipment supplier monitoring laptop shipments on paper, an eEurope website electronically recording the number of hits, or a teacher visually assessing pupils' skills.

- **Feedback** which communicates the values of the outputs registered by the sensor. If we seek to control, it is not sufficient to observe; the observations have to be communicated to those who need them to make control decisions. Thus, the equipment supplier having monitored laptop shipments on paper, the information has to be passed on to the person in charge of stock control. If an eEurope website has electronically recorded the number of hits, this information may be forwarded to those who have to make decisions on the basis of its success. Having visually assessed a pupils' skills, a teacher will use the results to plan future learning support.

■ A process, called the **comparator**, which compares the values of the outputs from the transformation process with the goals we wished to achieve. Thus stock levels will be compared with reorder levels to see if a new order should be placed; take-up of web access by EU citizens will be compared with eEurope plans; or pupils' skills can be compared with educational targets.

■ An **actuator/effector** which will adjust the inputs to the transformation process with the aim of bringing its outputs back towards the goals. Thus, stock may be reordered or not; eEurope plans and actions may be reviewed; or pupils may be given further help or tuition.

The terms in bold are the components of the model of a control system illustrated in Figure 15.2. This model has its origins in engineering and cybernetics, but we are interested in its role of connecting management and information systems. If we did not make the distinction between the concept and implementation of control, there would be the danger of assuming that controlling systems which included human beings were no different from controlling a central heating system or a bathroom shower. (Both of these last two examples are commonly used in textbooks to illustrate control systems.) In this chapter no such assumption is made. A stock controller at a computer equipment supplier and a teacher can both have roles as a control system's comparator and actuator, but we would not necessarily want a stock controller to teach children.

The information system as a component of the control system

An important feature of Figure 15.2 can now be noted. The loop that runs from the sensor to the actuator/effector consists of components that are all dealing with **information**. This feature represents one of the important links the control system makes between the wider management system and the information system. Looking further into the control model, we can see that three types of information are needed for any working of a control system:

■ information about the state of the process being controlled at any particular time and its behaviour over a period – this will come from the sensor monitoring the process outputs;

Figure 15.2 **Control system**

■ information about environmental disturbances;

■ information about the goals which the process being controlled should attempt to achieve.

Generally, all of the components of the control system which are concerned with the input, processing, storage and output of information can be seen as making up a subsystem of the control system itself. Since the transformation processes of this subsystem are exclusively concerned with information, it can be sensibly called an information system.

There is one important feature missing from this view. Figure 15.2 tells us nothing about where the information about goals comes from. A complete view of an information system, therefore, must also include the process of **goal setting**. Figure 15.3 shows how this can be done.

Goal setting can be explained by viewing a control system as a hierarchy. When seeking to control a process, whether it is supplying laptops to teachers or the creation of an 'information society for all', those in control must refer to goals like delivery targets or the take-up of information and communications technology by EU citizens. However, as the equipment needs of teachers and their pupil numbers can change, so can the forms of information and communications technology available and the relevant skills needed by citizens and businesses. In these circumstances, goals have to be reviewed, and sometimes changed. Thus the goals for eEurope 2005 had to be different from those of 1999, in order to take account of EU enlargement. Generally, changes in the environment of the organisation which is being managed will require modification of its goals.

This modification of goals, or goal setting, is itself a control process which seeks to control the control system modelled in Figure 15.2. The way it does it involves a simi-

Figure 15.3 **Goal setting**

lar sequence or loop from sensor to actuator, as before. Figure 15.3, therefore, shows that a complete control system is a hierarchy of two components or subsystems:

■ *Goal-seeking* control, which attempts to control a particular process, like laptop provision or citizens' exploitation of information and communications technology in the examples above;

■ *Goal-setting* control, which sets and modifies the goals used by goal-seeking control in response to changes in the environment. In the eEurope example this resulted in at least two modifications of the programme between 1999 and 2005.

Examples of goal-seeking and goal-setting functions in business organisations are shown in Figure 15.4 (Harry, 2001). The terminology used is that of Harry (2001). It is essential to see this model as *descriptive* rather than *prescriptive*. The model shows *what* the components of control are. It does not show *how* they may be implemented since that will depend on the nature of the organisation and its management.

Forms of goal setting in the control hierarchy

The need for a goal-setting control component in the whole control system adds to the role described for the information system so far. Goal-setting control requires:

■ the ability to **store** information received as feedback on the behaviour of the goal-seeking component of the control system;

■ the ability to **analyse** this information and learn from it;

■ access to information about the **values** or **world view** of management, which will enable goal setting to select goals which reflect the norms and values of management.

The ability to store information can be seen to be necessary in considering, for example, the setting of goals in the context of establishing an equipment installation budget or deciding on an educational programme. How much money is needed to equip a school? How long will it take? Which skills and subjects ought to be in a curriculum? How much time needs to be allocated to their teaching? What can be *learnt* from past experience?

The answers to questions like these enables the management of governments, organisations or schools to set their goals. Maybe last year's budget was not enough, or perhaps too much time was wasted in installing something and less ought to be allocated. Answers will only be possible if past experience is available as *stored information* available to the learning process: a record is needed of successes, mistakes and their outcome if learning is to happen.

But storage alone is not enough. Learning implies the ability to reflect and analyse the experience which is recorded. Raw data on the equipment installed over a period only becomes information after such things and actions as comparing times and costs, calculating trends, and looking at the whole picture presented by the data.

Even when data have been stored and analysed in this way, something else is needed if goals are to be set or modified. Analysis of stored data on pupil performance may tell us about such things as the effectiveness of the teaching and learning process or the popularity of information and communications technology with pupils. What it will not tell us is whether the selected syllabus is designed primarily to interest pupils, serve the needs of business, create certain attitudes in society or promote a

Figure 15.4 **Goal-seeking and goal-setting functions**

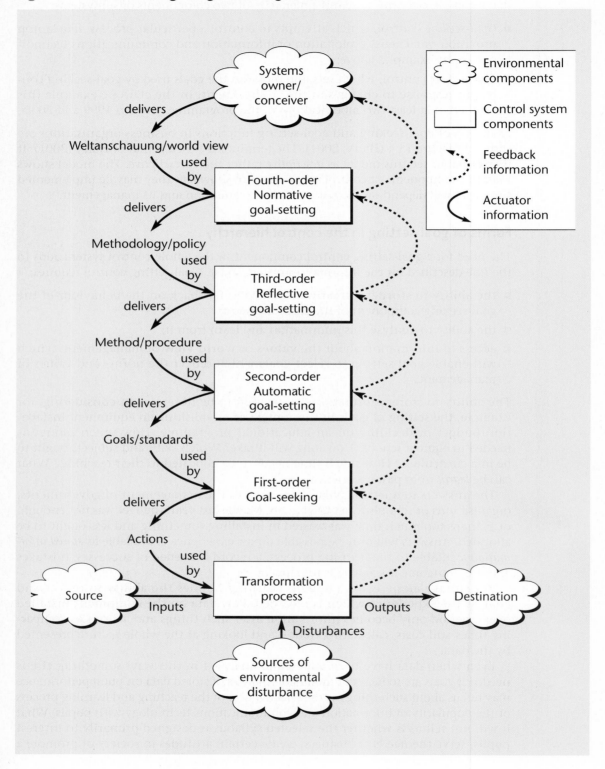

strong European economy. Such choices can only be made on the basis of a management policy, which will, in turn, reflect the values and norms which come from the *values* or *world view* of the organisation, government or school concerned.

Goal setting therefore requires the information system to deal with a mix of hard information on such things as costs or number of schools, and soft, normative information about policy or values. Whether the physical implementation of the information system in any organisation explicitly recognises the normative component or not does not prevent it from being present. Failure to recognise that all goals reflect certain values does not prevent them from doing so.

A good model of an information system should therefore explain the relationship between the different forms of information that it has to deal with, and the role that they play. Figure 15.4 represents one attempt to do this. The model distinguishes three components in the complete process of goal setting:

- **normative**
- **reflective**
- **automatic.**

It was shown above that there is a **normative** component in goal setting because goals reflect values. Whether this reflection is conscious or occurs by default, a normative component is nevertheless present in the goal-setting process. The previous example showed that goals expressed in terms of a syllabus reflected norms about pupil, society or business needs.

The **reflective** component in goal setting seeks to produce a method or procedure that can be used to set goals conforming to normative values. Thus, if the norm of 'an information society for all' means equipping schools with information and communications technology, then reflective goal setting will deliver a method for doing this. Once the method has been set, automatic testing and calculation can be used to produce a decision about how much of various types of equipment ought to be installed in each school.

From this review of information, control and management systems, the following central conclusions can be drawn:

- The information system of an organisation is more than information and communications technology and paperwork. All forms of information that are used to set goals and help management to achieve them should be considered as business and management information.

- Ignoring the existence of relevant information, on the basis that it is difficult to quantify or computerise, will merely mean that it continues to play a role in an unmanaged way. Since all forms of information interact through the control system, unmanaged information will distort the workings of the formal system.

DATA PROCESSING AND DATABASE MANAGEMENT

Designing and developing information systems

The relationships shown in Figure 15.4 have important practical implications for the design and implementation of computer-based information systems. Figure 15.4 shows the information system as a translator of management values into specific goals expressing what the organisation seeks to achieve through its operations. There is no such thing as 'the' information system. For each organisation, the particular information system that it uses, including the computer-based technological component, will reflect the values of the wider management system. This relationship may not be formalised but, as noted above, ignoring the existence of relevant information on the basis that it is difficult to quantify or computerise will merely mean that it continues to play a role in an unmanaged way. In such cases of neglect, the values will be those of accepting accident, anarchy or blind politics as a means of implementing management goals.

If the information system is consciously to reflect the values of management, it should be designed top down. The phrase 'top down' should be understood in terms of the concept of systems hierarchy. The top of this hierarchy is not senior management or the 'bosses', but the whole organisation and its needs. The phrase 'top down', therefore, refers to the concept of using the norms of the whole organisation as a basis for establishing goals and thereby defining the role of the information system in the context of Figure 15.4.

Designing the details of a computerised information system can only follow the establishment of its organisational context. In forming the eEurope programme, the EU could only decide on the design of a programme for promoting eEurope after it had decided its political position in the new world of information and communications technology and the Internet. The details of how something should be provided can only follow a decision on what values the process should reflect.

An historically mainline view like Olle *et al.* (1988), which continues to be relevant, sees four major stages in information systems development:

- **Information systems planning** – determining the information requirements of the organisation and its business objectives. Also checking any existing information strategy and objectives.
- **Business analysis** – analysing the business or organisational activities that may be covered by the information systems' development process and the properties of any existing information system.
- **Systems design** – the prescriptive or definitive activity which identifies the components of the system to be constructed and describes what they must do.
- **Construction design** – how the system design of the previous stage is to be constructed.

Approaches following a version of this sequence are top down because they first establish what the business or organisation does, then its information needs, and only finally do they do the detailed design and construction of the computer-based information system. Note also that these last two stages follow the top-down sequence of 'what they must do' preceding '*how* the system is to be constructed'.

Scheduling the information system

The discussion of sensing and feedback above showed that they were concerned with information about the behaviour of the process being controlled, and its state at any particular time. This implies that the sensor in a control system can monitor both static and dynamic properties of the process being controlled. For example, the checking of stock levels by the laptop supplier will not only reveal what is in stock at any time, but also how stock levels move over a period. The same can be said with checking the financial position of an organisation. The sensor can give the financial assets and liabilities at a particular point in time. Over a period of time it can also show their net movement. The balance sheet and the profit and loss account are thus examples of the static and dynamic properties of a controlled process.

Another feature of control is the feedback loop. This raises another important issue about sensing outputs: how frequently should the sensing and feedback take place? Our previous example of the balance sheet and profit and loss account illustrates this point. A worried shareholder might wish that accounts for shaky companies came out every month. Busy self-employed people can find that the annual task of producing formal accounts, just to satisfy government legislation, comes round frequently enough.

In practice, managing an information system must find a balance between:

- **real-time systems**, which continually sense the outputs from controlled processes, and
- **batch-processing systems**, which store the information about the outputs from a process over a period of time. Only at the end of this period will it complete the feedback, comparison and actuation loop to modify the inputs to the controlled process.

The particular way in which this balance is made will depend on costs. Figure 15.5 illustrates the principle. One set of costs is associated with the operation of the information system itself. These tend to be higher for systems which operate high-frequency or continuous feedback. The other set of costs is associated with the increase in error or bad management decisions which come with older, dated information. This tends to be associated with low update frequency, batch-processing systems. The relationship between frequency of feedback and the total costs of operating the system will have a minimum, representing the balance between the two cost types.

In practice, it is very unlikely that an exact minimum cost frequency can be calculated. It is possible, however, to use the principles illustrated in Figure 15.5 to identify which costs need to be assessed before making management judgements about the kind of information technology needed to support an information system. Some examples will illustrate this.

Figure 15.5 Costs and information systems management

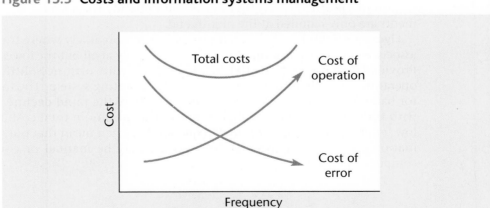

The first examples are concerned with computer-based information systems with a need for very frequent or near continuous feedback. As shown, these will be expensive to operate. Real-time systems are the extreme example of this. Every time there is any change in the business process being controlled, information about the change is immediately taken up by the computer system and then processed. Common examples of real-time systems are:

■ airline and hotel chain booking systems;

■ banking and financial trading systems;

■ large-scale electronic point of sale (EPOS) retailing/stock control systems, as part of a supply chain.

These systems all require recorded information to be up to date. A booking system that could only tell whether there were any seats on a plane flight last week would be business suicide. Similarly, records of vacancies in hotels, the price of stocks and shares, and the availability of goods from a central warehouse all require information on the state of the organisation as it is now.

Such systems are expensive to operate because the control loop joining the sensor with the rest of the information system is in continuous operation. In practice, such systems are likely to be based on a telecommunication network that can immediately transmit data on enquiries, bookings, sales, etc. to a computer system that continuously updates records. It also implies elaborate security and back-up to ensure that the system cannot be switched off by failure, as well as continually operating and paid human operators.

The expense of a real-time system is justified by the need to avoid the high cost of potential error. In Figure 15.5, organisations needing real-time systems are those whose cost of error is at high levels for all but the highest frequencies. It's hard to imagine an airline that could work with booking information that was a week out of date, or a supermarket getting by with last month's stock figures. Organisations like these need updated information every second, and this need pushes the total cost curve minimum position towards high frequencies.

Many businesses do not require such up-to-date information. The costs of information being old are not so important. If employees are paid weekly on the basis of hours worked, it doesn't matter if there is no available running total during the week. All we need is to collect the daily hours data during the week and process them as a batch. The same goes for many monthly business accounts. Documented records of sales are kept as they occur, but updating the account and issuing statements are only required at the month end.

Figure 15.5 implies that batch processing is more likely where the cost of error associated with aged information falls away rapidly at all but the lowest frequencies. Provided that we vet potential customers for creditworthiness, little is gained by operating a weekly rather than a monthly accounting system. The total cost curve for batch processing will therefore be one where the rapid decline of error costs with increased feedback frequency makes the minimum total cost correspond to low frequency feedback. This low frequency can often mean that only simple information technology is needed. The system may be manual or contracted to a computer agency.

Exploiting the information resource

One view of information considered above was of data as the structured building material of information. This stock of material can be described as a **database**. This can be managed by software to produce the information needed by the user. Such a system of controlling a database is called a **database management system** (DBMS).

To understand the relationship between the data stored and the information produced by a DBMS, consider the following:

■ What do the terms **file** and **record** mean in the context of information systems based on contemporary information and communications technology?

■ If the the two terms mean something different, how can this difference be shown to be important in terms of its implications for managing information systems?

The first question can be answered by distinguishing the *physical* and *logical* views of data and information. Recalling what we covered in our review of the properties of systems above, a logical view of information or data is concerned with what it is, and a physical view with how it is recorded, accessed or transmitted.

In everyday use, a file is seen as a source of information about a number of people or things, present as a series of records. Records and files are often seen in physical terms. Thus a file might be a box with the records as individual cards inside. In a computer system the records might be areas of magnetic patterns on a disk. However implemented, the physical view sees the connection between records in a file, and of data in the record, as physically connected on the recording.

The first computer-based systems took a physical view of records and files. The result has been that, ever since, computer-based files and records have often been subjected to the same restrictions of access as individual physical filing cabinets in separate departmental offices. Thus the sales file is seen as a set of documents for the sales department, the personnel file as a set of documents for the personnel department, and the parts file is out at the moment because the production manager has just borrowed it. And we should not assume that such backward images are not still alive. I suspect that your computer, like mine, still uses images of folders and documents to represent what are very different electronic concepts.

Modern computer-based applications of database management no longer require us to think in these terms. Instead, the data used by a DBMS can be seen as a resource that can be 'mined' by the system. Harry (2001) uses the analogy of two types of coffee machine to explain the difference. The first kind of coffee machine has separate columns containing plastic cups already filled with the ingredients. The second kind of coffee machine does not have ready mixed combinations: instead, it mixes ingredients to order.

Manual filing systems are like the first type of machine in that the data 'ingredients' are stored ready-mixed. Thus the personnel file will have all the data about name, age, address, status, tax coding, etc. arranged together to form a record on a card. For a DBMS, what is physically recorded is not data structured into records, but individual items of data. When the user asks for a record, the data items making up the record are assembled by the DBMS. This means that neither the computer nor its recording devices actually contain the records in their physical form, any more than our second type of coffee machine contains the various drinks. Instead, a database contains the potential to produce any kind of information 'drink', in the form of a record of data items assembled by the DBMS.

Figures 15.6 and 15.7 show these two views of accessing and processing data. Figure 15.7 shows that the a database system has two main components:

■ **the database**

■ **the database management system.**

The database consists of stored data and meta-data, which define the characteristics of the stored data. The database management system is the software that can assemble the data into the form required by the user, rather as the second kind of coffee machine can assemble white/black coffee with/without sugar, etc.

A DBMS makes it much easier to support the different information needs of the different functions of management, without special programming. The older, file-based view meant that data were physically stored in a way that made it easy to meet the needs of the particular department that used the file. Thus, order processing would store data about a particular customer in terms of who the customer was

Figure 15.6 File processing system

Figure 15.7 Database sysytem

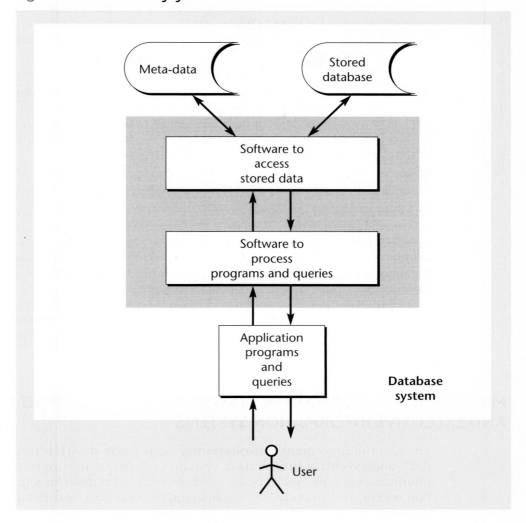

and what he/she had bought in a particular month, so that the computer program could process them to produce monthly accounts. If the marketing department wanted sales analysed by, say, classifying products sales against postcodes, the reply might have been: 'We need to write a special program.'

For current computer systems practice, this last example is misleading. It implied that the restrictions of the old, physical, file-based system are now past. In fact the managers of many current computer systems still regard a request for non-routine output as 'special' or 'difficult'. A true DBMS presents no such problem, and the 'difficulties' may well be the result of information technology specialists defending their empires.

The software used by the DBMS can take different forms depending on the type of user. There are now several common forms of high-level software which are designed to help non-technical users query and process a database. The term 'high level' can be understood as a systemic concept. High-level software communicates in terms of *whats* rather than *hows*. In particular, declarative or fourth-generation languages (4GLs) enable users to state what they want from the database using English-like statements. A near universal example of this is SQL (sometimes called 'sequel'). Various Microsoft, Oracle, and Linux database applications use SQL. Even easier forms of software use graphics on the computer screen's icons, menus or some combination of them.

The use of a DBMS has important implications for management:

- The principles for defining the contents of a database and the process of constructing it should reflect the needs of the wider management system. This means that any method for development of a database system will include initial stages that analyse the needs of the business or organisation. This confirms our statements about information systems development above.

- The management structure which controls the set-up and use of the database should reflect user need rather than computer specialist convenience.

The view of the control system in Figure 15.1 as the link between management and information shows why a database management system has more potential in management terms than the older, physical, file-based systems. It was shown that information used for goal-seeking control also needs to be stored and analysed by higher-order control to set these goals. If this process of analysis required specially developed computer programs, then all the higher-order functions of management, such as marketing, etc. as in Figure 15.4, would represent a special, expensive problem for the information system. In practice, a modern DBMS should make this concern an irrelevance: whether it does or does not is a management-information issue, not a technical issue.

MANAGEMENT INFORMATION SYSTEMS, DECISION SUPPORT SYSTEMS AND EXECUTIVE INFORMATION SYSTEMS

The terms **management information systems** (MIS), **decision support systems** (DSS) and **executive information systems** (EIS) frequently occur in books about information systems, and they are usually considered as different forms of information system. Turban *et al.* (2002) is an example of a popular text that does this. This section will consider what features are supposed to distinguish these three types of information system, and use the management, control and information systems relationship to show that they are interrelated, overlap and form component functions of the whole information system. It will also show that they are neither new concepts nor conceptually very different, as implied by Turban *et al.* (2002).

Management information systems (MIS)

The term **management information system (MIS)** is generally used to refer to the information system which deals with the control of so-called 'routine', 'structured' or 'day- to-day' operations. In many popular texts, the distinction between the MIS and DSS or EIS is made in terms of a classical view of management hierarchy. Figure 15.8 illustrates a version of this view.

Whatever its relevance or usefulness, Figure 15.8 is neither a systems view of management nor of the systems concept of hierarchy. It represents management functions in terms of who does them, or how they are carried out. It usually does

Figure 15.8 Classical view of management functions

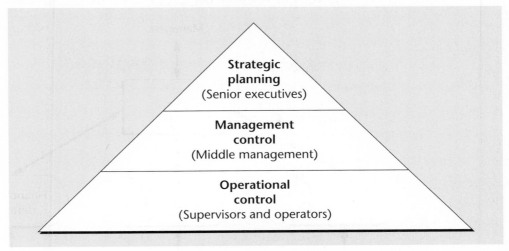

this in terms of people's job titles, like 'operator' or 'senior executive'. In contrast, the systems view considers what functions are, regardless of how they are implemented, and hierarchy as levels of conceptual aggregation.

Figure 15.9 shows a view of MIS which conforms to the classical view of management hierarchy and the role of information systems within it. Its functions may be summarised as:

- **Reporting on summaries of basic transactions and exceptions from plan.** In control systems terms: feedback on deviations from the process goals.

- **Using simple analytical tools.** This implies that the MIS will use standard programs which merely require the user to answer set questions like 'how many hours worked?' or 'what is the stock level?'

- **Solving structured, repetitive problems.** This implies that the 'lower-order' employees of the hierarchy of Figure 15.8 process information without the need to make decisions which affect management or strategic functions.

- **Producing routine reports.** In terms of control systems hierarchy, this implies batch processing of stored feedback, with the implication that this material may be used for goal setting. The term 'routine' could falsely suggest that the advent of a crisis in an organisation has never led to a special request from such 'routine' functions as sales order processing for special reports, like an immediate analysis of some defaulting customer's account. In fact, most forms of MIS take this in their stride if working with a modem database system as above.

Note also that a conventional picture of MIS like that in Figure 15.9 gives no indication of how the system might be modified or even redesigned. Conventional views of information systems would see this as the separate specialist task of some function like 'systems analysis and design', which would manage the systems development issues discussed above.

Figure 15.9 **MIS**

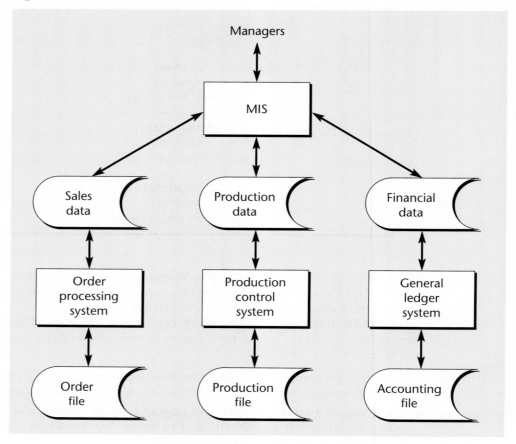

Decision support systems (DSS)

While the MIS controls routine operations using structured data processing methods, the decision support system (DSS) is seen as supporting decisions on 'less routine issues' and solving 'semi-structured' problems. The main features of DSS compared with MIS can be presented as:

- Modelling the potential effects of management decisions on the organisation in order to help select possible opportunities and find solutions to problems. This contrasts with the MIS concern with routine, structured procedures.
- Use of multi-purpose, analytical software such as spreadsheets, statistical packages and computer simulation. This contrasts with the MIS use of specific task-oriented software, such as payroll or customer accounting.
- A higher degree of interaction between the software and the user, including the exploration of 'what-if' questions and hypothesis testing.

In control systems terms, the DSS represents computer-based support for goal setting. It may be at the automatic goal-setting level in an example, like using a discounted cash flow model to investigate the effects of discount rate on project viability. It can be at a higher reflective goal-setting level, like a cost accounting analysis of the effects of different stock valuation methods. Although the feedback from using DSS would be relevant to normative goal setting, the process of deciding norms is still an exclusively human province.

Generally, the potential for DSS can be seen by referring to the goal-setting functions in Figure 15.4.

Executive information systems (EIS)

An executive information system (EIS) is seen as a supporting tool for 'senior executives', who are conceived as concentrating on the strategic planning functions of the organisation, as in Figure 15.8. Strategy is principally concerned with the future of the organisation in terms of changing markets, economies, legislation, social norms and other components of the environment. Executive information systems are seen as being more concerned with external information. Typical information accessed and processed by EIS would cover:

- **competitors**
- **business and industrial legislation**
- **regional, national and international economic statistics**
- **markets and trends.**

EIS also sees the executive working in a particular organisational context, using particular abilities and catered for by software which can provide:

- **graphics analysis and presentation** – 'the busy executive' requiring summaries of the essential features of data;
- **communications and e-mail** – 'the mobile executive' who spends much working time outside the organisation;
- **decision support** – 'a captain of industry' making decisions like other managers, hence DSS is relevant here too. Similar tools to DSS, but applied to higher-level data.

In Figure 15.4 control systems terms, EIS supports processing information about disturbances from the environment. 'Senior executives' may also form part of the role of systems owner/conceiver. The focus of a database for external information is consistent with this. A software selection linked to a supposed work and lifestyle is less convincing. What is particularly 'executive' about the need for concise graphical summary and presentation, or being mobile and needing communications software? Many sales representatives have similar needs. Perhaps the promotion of EIS owes as much to persuasive computer salesmanship?

The purpose of this criticism is to introduce an alternative holistic, systems view of information systems. This does not divide information systems into different components based on management or file labels. Instead, it looks behind the labels to see what managers actually do and, therefore, what kinds of information they use.

A systems view of information systems

In most organisations one person is unlikely to be involved in every kind of management activity. Some specialisation is usually needed. This means that everyone, not just 'managers', will only use selected information. For example, marketing is more likely to want an analysis of sales figures than an update on tax changes governing the operation of payroll. In this situation, a selected focus on particular parts of the database as an information resource makes practical sense.

There are dangers to this approach of distinguishing between MIS, DSS or EIS on the basis of job description or the software used:

■ It reverts to dividing the database so that it is not seen as an organisational resource, but the separated property of departments. Labels like 'sales data' or 'financial data' then imply that data about a sale are not also data for marketing analysis, about a change in the financial position of the organisation, about the workload placed on personnel in the order processing department and warehouse, etc., as in a systems view.

■ Such a movement away from a systems view of management fails to make the distinction between whats and hows. Hence it ignores, for example, that a salesperson who makes a delivery-date promise is making a production decision, or that an accountant who fixes a credit policy is making a public relations decision.

■ The confusion of conceptual control hierarchy with the labelled job description of Figure 15.8 confuses whats and hows. Thus 'senior executives' are those concerned with high-level, strategic thoughts and decisions about the long-term future of the company, and 'management' comprises people who worry about whether the objectives set for them by higher management are being fulfilled. Actual organisations are not like this. Lower and middle-ranking managers often worry about and contribute to strategic decisions, through meetings which feed back information into the whole management information system. Also, senior executives are often involved in actuating low-level decisions when a local crisis requires them to get involved in 'firefighting operations'.

■ The fragmentation of an information system provides no process for learning by the whole system, since this needs the integration of all it processes at all levels of control.

These conclusions are not intended to criticise MIS, DSS and EIS destructively, but to look behind the labels and focus on what they are, what they do, and their role in the whole organisation.

INTELLIGENT AND EXPERT SYSTEMS

When **expert systems** first started making the headlines, Forsyth (1989) defined an expert system as 'a piece of software that causes TV producers to lose all sense of proportion'. This section will consider how expert systems and other advanced developments work, and what they can actually do.

Artificial intelligence (AI) is the generic term used for various forms of information technology which attempt to emulate human behaviour, such as reasoning, communication or sensory perception. Important examples are:

■ **Expert systems**
■ **Fuzzy logic**
■ **Image recognition**
■ **Speech recognition**
■ **Neural networks.**

Expert systems and fuzzy logic

Virtually all of the devices which have been described as 'computers' during the last 50 years work by using a program to control the processing of data. Thus, in business, data on personnel working hours can be processed using a financial software package to produce a payroll, statistical packages can be used to analyse sales data for marketing, and so on. What all these applications do is:

■ **calculate** – the computer program subjects the input data to various calculation procedures to produce output in the form of results. Thus, in our previous examples, working hours might be used to calculate pay, or sales data to calculate a percentage.

■ **assume existence of a relevant formula** – calculations are only possible if a formula exists to govern them. Thus, a payroll calculation would need to know the formula relating to wage rates, tax and National Insurance in order to be possible.

■ **have access to correct data** – a formula can only be used to carry out a calculation if the input data are available. Also, the data need to be correct if the result is also to be correct, or else it is a case of 'garbage in, garbage out'. Thus, the reliability of a sales analysis depends on the sales data used.

There are many situations in management where it is not possible to make calculations using a known and accepted formula on reliable data. It is not automatically possible to use a formula to know the cause of failure by an industrial process or to determine how a company should respond to a lawsuit. For such situations the layman relies on the knowledge and experience of people, who are often called 'experts'. Expert systems are an attempt to apply computer systems to supporting what humans do in such situations. In contrast to the three conditions above, expert systems:

■ **diagnose** – instead of calculating a result, they consider possible answers and give judgements as to which are likely. Thus, an expert might be used to diagnose why a product failed in a market rather than calculate a percentage.

■ **do not assume the existence of a single correct formula** – there is no established theory that explains all possible market failures. Expert systems have to work in terms of the possible inferences, given the evidence available.

■ **work with fuzzy data** – diagnosis has to be carried out on the facts available, and all these may not be clear or reliable. Thus, in most marketing analysis it is not possible to have all the information about each sale, and even when people are interviewed, they don't always know or say what they mean. It is even more difficult to speculate why things did not happen.

To deal with such conditions an expert system works differently from conventional computer systems. The essence of such a computer system is a program controlling the processing of data to produce output or results, as was shown above. In an expert system, as in Figure 15.10, an **inference engine** uses the resources of a **knowledge base** to produce output in the form of diagnosis.

For a computer system to work as a component of an expert system, particular theoretical frameworks have to be used. Since computers are digital, all that they do is built on a complex combination of yes/no or 01. Human beings do not think in this way: 'Was the product successful? Well it *seemed* to be, but we're not sure if the sales were affected by the weather.' If computer-based information systems are to

Figure 15.10 Expert system

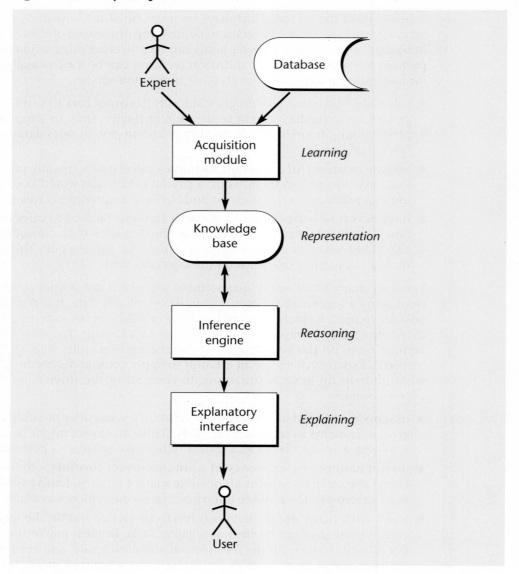

work successfully with the wider management system of which they are part, the human component must be accommodated. *Fuzzy logic* is a mathematical framework which attempts to describe the analysis and decision making that goes on when humans try to deal with concepts like 'seemed to be' or 'not quite sure'. Sometimes described as 'possibilistic logic', it was invented by Zadeh (1965). No technique can manufacture certainty out of uncertainty, or remove the judgement required when dealing with it, but fuzzy logic does provide the framework needed by any attempt at a diagnostic system.

Image and speech recognition

Image recognition refers to the many combinations of hardware and software that can enable a computer system to record and reproduce images. This is necessary if information is seen as more than just words and numbers. If the software can also identify what the image is, identify and classify its properties in relation to other images, then such a system may be described as 'intelligent'. Thus, a database of employees which can record pictures of individuals, as well as their personal details, is now quite common. An **intelligent system** goes further and can also match different photographs of that individual to the official record.

Photographs and sound recording existed well before computers. When these abilities were computerised, initial concentration was on images because the written word could substitute for the spoken word. Hence, computer-based word-processing extended the abilities of the typewriter. Like the typewriter, however, word-processing depended on the keyboard to transcribe human use of words into machine use. Given that speech is not the transmission of individual letters, and that the QWERTY keyboard was deliberately designed to be hard to use, the ability to speak directly to a computer system could enable a better integration of the machine and human components of an information system. Speech recognition is the attempt to do this.

Speech recognition can work at increasing levels of complexity. At the simplest level the computer system can recognise particular words. A more sophisticated system might distinguish between speakers of the same word. A further level comes when the system can understand the meaning of words in combination, like phrases or sentences. The highest level is where the system recognises equivalents.

An example of these distinctions would be a cash machine system which tried to work in response to a spoken request for money. The simplest system might ask how much money you wanted and could recognise individual words like 'fifty' or 'twenty-five'. The next level of complexity would be where the machine could distinguish between two people speaking the same words. The system might be more useful if it could understand combinations of words. Thus 'withdraw fifty' could be distinguished from 'have I got fifty?' At the highest level, the machine would understand that 'give me fifty', 'I'd like fifty', and 'fifty pounds please' were equivalents.

This final level of speech recognition begins to demand a machine that not only recognises speech, but starts to understand language. Even if it had not come across the particular format of a question like 'Can you give me fifty pounds please?', it would be able to communicate with the user to find out what the new request meant. To do this, the machine would have to start learning from experience. It might do this by using its recognition of a questioning tone in the voice, the use of the word 'please', and knowing what 'fifty pounds' meant, to guess at a meaning of the new phrase. The particular form of questions by the machine would then be governed by the responses of the user and what it recognised and understood. The machine would then be learning rather as humans do. Attempts at building such a machine have led to a new form of computing based on **neural networks**.

Neural networks

These represent a way of computing that tries to work in the human way just described. A conventional computer-based expert system would try to capture experience at image recognition or speech understanding by using the two components we discussed above: a list of rules or knowledge base, and ways of concluding inferences from these rules, or inference engine. When trying to recognise a face or understand language, however, there are no obvious rules that make it easier for a computer to do than a human being. Thus, how might a computer be made to understand the meaning of the word 'game'? Deciding a set of rules that was anywhere near complete would be very difficult, yet humans use words easily from childhood, and images also: I look out of the window and see six trees which I can distinguish from all the other features, including an excavator and a hen. A child could do the same, but what rules would you give to a computer to enable it to do this?

Neural networks do not work by storing up increasingly complex combinations of rules. Instead, they store the results of individual experiences in a network of interconnections which form one whole experience. Thus, a human decides that something is a tree because his senses' experience of it sufficiently matches the whole of the past experiences of trees, rather than because the brain uses a 'computer program' from its store of rules to test out the data coming from the human's senses. Every time someone has such an experience, however, the totality of the experience of a tree may be modified: like the first time a tree is seen with copper rather than green leaves.

From this survey, the following conclusions can be drawn in relation to business and management information:

- Expert systems and other forms of so-called machine intelligence are already useful for some management information systems which can work on the basis of diagnostic rules. Examples of these are in technical, legal and administrative areas where what is required can be translated into how its occurrence can be tested.

- Attempts to make machines emulate human management behaviour in dealing with more complex forms of information – like those which deal with interpretation, interest, power or intuition – may be possible using neural networks in the future, but at the moment this is still new technology whose future is unclear. Complete Integration of human and computer systems is still to come.

A CONTINUING REVOLUTION IN INFORMATION AND COMMUNICATIONS TECHNOLOGY?

Words often get devalued by frequent use. Five hundred years ago the word 'naughty' was a description that might have been given to someone who deserved to be hanged. These days, 'naughty' is used by TV adverts to cover the idea of eating chocolate in the bath. Given the continuing tendency to devalue words by exaggeration, should there be caution when the developments in information and communications technology at the start of the twenty-first century are described as a 'revolution'? The answer lies in the previous distinction of *whats* and *hows*.

When faced with something new, people often try to relate it to something that they already know, as a first step to understanding. Examples of this can be seen in the names used by previous revolutionary technologies. Many of the words used to describe the steam engine and the railway came from the pre-industrial era, such as 'carriage' or 'track'. The locomotive that pulled the carriages was thought of as an iron horse, and it is no coincidence that for nearly 100 years the iron horse continued to pull the carriages just as the horse itself had done. Only in the second half of the twentieth century did a recognition of what the motive power of a railway train does break away from how the horse did it before. The sources of motion in modern trains may be at the front, the back or underneath the vehicles they propel. They can push as well as pull, and can work as efficiently backwards as they do forwards. The danger of using old 'hows' to understand new ways of doing things is that the 'whats' are obscured and potential new 'hows' are therefore hidden also. As long as the railway locomotive was tied to the how-notions of the horse, new ways of implementing the 'what' of motive power were inhibited.

Examples of this carrying over old ideas are easy to find in information technology. One important example would be that of graphical user interfaces (GUIs), like Microsoft Windows. These aim to make computers accessible to people who are not computer specialists by presenting them with a screen made up of little symbols or so-called icons. These icons represent objects or actions which the user would like to control using the mouse as a pointing device.

GUIs seem to be very friendly and helpful, but they are a good example of the dangers as well as the advantages of carrying over old technological views into new fields. For example, to see what is recorded in a file, the user points the mouse at an icon that looks like a folder that might be used in a traditional paper-based filing cabinet system. When the button on the mouse is clicked, the contents of the file appear on the screen. If the file and its contents are no longer relevant, they are scrapped by clicking on an icon that looks like a waste-paper basket.

Although this imagery (*icon* is the Greek word for image) is helpful for a user who wants to interpret the new technology in terms of the old, it is very misleading about what actually happens. Clicking on an icon to supposedly withdraw a 'file' from the 'filing cabinet' is nonsense. Withdrawing an actual paper file from a real-life filing cabinet means that the cabinet no longer contains the file. The sort of conversation that might take place in the office would be: 'Where's the file?' 'I don't know: someone has it out at the moment.'

On a computer-based system, calling the file up on to the screen actually calls up a copy. The original information is still there, recorded on the computer disk. If the computer in question is just one of many PCs on a network, users can have a copy whenever they like, regardless of what all the other users are doing. The icon-based GUI concept of a 'file' or 'folder' in a 'filing cabinet' is therefore very misleading. Everybody who wants one can have a copy of what is in the file, and the file itself is still safely in the cabinet. In terms of an Internet connection, this has dramatic implications for the virtually costless copying and reproduction of information, impossible with physical paper documents.

It is also worth noting how misleading the images of files, folders and filing cabinets are in their implications for data security. If someone steals a folder from a filing cabinet, a quick check will show that it is missing and that theft has occurred. 'Removing' a folder from an electronic filing cabinet leaves no such gap.

To appreciate how far new technology can be a revolution therefore requires a distinction of logical and physical properties of system. In as far as new technology is used to provide new hows for old whats, the revolution is merely one of degree, like faster calculation or more efficient storage, but if new technology means new whats, it can be revolutionary indeed.

Thus, if potentially unlimited copies of a 'file' can be accessed by users on a computer network without the removal of the original data, the concept of access to information is something new compared to the old physical access to a filing cabinet. If the networking of computer systems and telecommunications means that an

Australian and a Norwegian can have the same near-instant access to that data, the concept of the location of information is completely changed. It is the breakdown of the old physical restrictions, like the location of information, that is the real revolution, not just faster ways of doing what we did before.

There are, therefore, two ways of answering the question as to whether developments in computer-based information systems amount to a revolution. If a revolution implies new ways of doing old things, then recent developments in computing do not amount to a revolution. Indeed, modern systems will still require such traditional components as printed sheets of paper, handwritten signatures and sticky labels. If, however, the whole that emerges from the combination and interaction of the new with the old is considered, the word 'revolution' is justified. The principal areas where this continues to occur are:

- **Communications** and **networking** – these are the physical means of implementing the systems principle of connecting parts into a whole, which will have its own new emergent properties. Thus, whatever the attempts by politicians to retain or remove boundaries, there is a *de facto* world information system for many types of information.
- **Multimedia integration** – the development of network integrated information and communications technology systems that cover the five human senses, thus extending information well beyond what can be expressed by printed language and numbers.
- **Intelligent learning systems** – these are likely to emerge dramatically as the Internet removes physical barriers to information, multimedia integration removes barriers between types of information, and artificial intelligence systems exploit the integration of both.

Communications and networking

It is very important to realise that all networks, including the Internet, are **systems** with all the properties that that implies. Thus the Internet, like any other system, has its abstract as well as its concrete components. People who have decided to become connected to the **Internet** find that they do not just need to buy a modem to physically connect their computer to the telephone line; connection also requires the appropriate software which is able to use the appropriate **protocols**. Thus, the 'http://www' to be found at the start of a website address is a coding to indicate that the communication is intended to make a link with information on the web rather than one of the other facilities on the Internet. Hence, connection has to be made logically as well as physically.

Like any other system also, description of the structure, processes or other properties of the Internet will be a reflection of the values and actions of the particular user concerned. The user is a component of the system who interacts with it, and it is the result of this interaction that determines the behaviour and output of the whole. Any view of the Internet that sees it as a set thing which delivers particular certainties to a passive user is a misconception.

What effects is the Internet having on business and organisational management? The following are particularly evident:

- **distortion of physical geography**
- **globalisation of information**

- reduction of systems lags
- re-evaluation of information technology
- re-thinking of conventional thinking about control.

Distortion of physical geography is the shrinking effect that the Internet has on distance. The Internet can make a manager as close to information and people halfway around the world as those in the same town. Telephones, radios and televisions have been doing this already, but telephones are mainly audio, one-to-one machines, and radios and televisions are not interactive. The Internet covers a combination of everything that these other forms of information technology can do, plus other new things such as the communication of software.

The Internet generally, and the web in particular, are leading to a **globalisation of information**. For example, someone in Britain wanted to buy a small amount of US Treasury Bills. On consulting a UK stockbroker, the person making the enquiry was informed that this is both a complex and expensive business, and that anyway it is only worth while for amounts above $35 000. However, a quick visit to the US Treasury site on the web revealed that small amounts of stock can be easily bought at little expense, and that, furthermore, an application form for the stock can be directly downloaded on to the enquirer's computer. Applying the lesson of this experience to professional, business and management activity generally implies that protecting knowledge-based competitive advantage will become more difficult in the future.

Reduction of systems lags refers to the role of the information system as a component of control as illustrated in Figure 15.8. The widespread and continuous connection that now exists between most of the major world information systems in business, economics and finance means that the world never sleeps and that much information spreading is near instantaneous. Consequently, managers as operators of control systems can pick up and respond to environmental disturbances much more quickly than in the past. Whether this leads to more or less stability in markets is a complex point that we cannot cover here, but it can be said that it leads to more extremes, in the sense that it magnifies existing tendencies.

But the most important impact of the Internet on management is likely to be the **re-evaluation of information technology**. If, as above, connection to the Internet puts the user at a terminal which has access to all the other computers and data on the Internet, then that user is effectively using a *global computer* (*see* Harry, 2001). If the wide variety of forms in which this information can be accessed is also included, such as text, live voice, audio, video, e-mail, newsgroups and software, the present forms of information technology are likely to become quickly redundant. It would be very surprising if, by 2010, televisions, computers, telephones and radios were completely separate bits of equipment as they are today. Instead, new forms of information technology (the 'hows') are likely to combine many of the logical roles (the 'whats') of existing information systems.

Re-thinking of conventional thinking about control refers to the concepts covered in the section on control in this chapter. Control is a *concept*, not a management method. The Internet is clearly under control because it works systematically and enables millions of users to interact in an orderly and controlled fashion. But who controls the Internet? The answer is that no one, single body or person controls it. Instead, control is an *emergent property* that comes from people and information and communications technology conforming to standards and protocols that bring *structure* to the system. Reference to the section above on systems concepts will recall what the terms in italics mean.

Multimedia integration

When discussing the Internet above we referred to its role in the distortion of physical geography. In fact, all forms of networking have this potential in that they remove or alter barriers. For example, two people located at two different sites, but in e-mail contact through a company area network, are more 'in contact' than two people at opposite ends of the company car park. However, separation and barriers are not just a question of distance. For people or electronic machines to communicate they must be able to use the appropriate language or protocols: they must have the appropriate *abstract* or *logical* connection, as we saw above.

Two particular ways in which this is occurring are through the development of **personal area networks** (PAN) and **wireless information devices** (WID). The idea of a personal area network is to integrate various personal electronic devices such as the mobile phone, electronic organiser, or music player. Once connected so that they can interact, these become portable networks. Any such connection is likely to be most convenient if it is wireless, and radio technologies such as WiFi and Bluetooth are perhaps the best known developments to date in this area. Besides integrating at a personal level, like sharing a headset, the wireless connection enables access to nearby fixed devices like printers. Also the connection of the mobile phone with the electronic organiser enables the PAN to be integrated with the Internet.

Emerging wireless information devices take this concept a step further by integrating the devices themselves. Thus the mobile phone and personal organiser are replaced by a single device that can perform both functions.

The key to understanding any of these developments is to remember that connections and boundaries are abstract systems concepts that may be manifested in changing technological ways. Developments in information and communications technology will continually require us to recognise what is going on behind the jargon and the labels.

Intelligent learning systems

As we saw earlier, information is a property that emerges when data items are brought together. Any arithmetic growth of available data stored leads to geometric growth of potential information since data can be combined and manipulated in just about any way needed by the user. The connection of databases over networks, whether within organisations, between organisations or over the whole Internet, means that many new forms of information are now available.

Data about, say, the sales of one particular product to one particular segment of one particular market at one particular time may reveal useful management information for that product. If, however, we consider data about many products and many market segments over time, then we are likely to learn many additional things about products and markets that only emerge in a wider strategic context. The process of discovering such emergent information by analysing large amounts of data is already established, and is sometimes called **data mining**.

The ability to deal with large amounts of data, with the hope of discovering emergent information, depends on the ability of the processes used. This becomes possible through the application of artificial intelligence based on the neural network structures we considered earlier. In particular, such abilities to learn will push information and communications technology into the higher information and control levels of decision making and goal setting of Figure 15.4. Thus it may be the information and communications technology systems that, *without prompting*, suggest desirable goals or take over high-level decisions. In this situation, as has been emphasised throughout this chapter, it is for the humans in management to decide how far such potentials for the application of information and communications technology should be realised.

SUMMARY

■ The effect of developments in modern information and communications technology on management requires a rethinking of the implications of words such as **information** and **system**, as well as the word **management** itself. New technology not only affects how management operates to achieve existing goals, it also opens up new potential for what management can hope to achieve.

■ The key to understanding the effect of information and communications technology on management is a recognition of the key role of the concept of **control** as the important connection between what management seeks to achieve, and what the information system must deliver.

■ An analysis of this requirement shows that information is more than the output of the workings of technology. A true information system also recognises the role of human beings and the organisational environment: good and bad motivation, honesty and cheating, successful and failed communication, etc. will still have the same effects as in the past, and will call for skills in human management.

■ A balanced view of the role of the information system in management must also recognise that a supposed 'revolution' resulting from information technology developments is not always as new as it might first appear. Instead, enduring principles may be interpreted in new technological ways.

Review and discussion questions

1 *This chapter discussed the richness of information as a concept. Take the list of data structure, process, communication, etc. on pp 470–1 as a starting point. Select a familiar or documented organisation. What examples can be found that illustrate the views listed? Are there other aspects of information that build on its richness as a concept?*

2 *What effects does the presence of human beings have on the concept of control when it is applied to the management of organisations?*

3 *What different uses are made of the word 'network' in different business situations?*

4 *Are senior managers or directors principally concerned with strategy, rather than operations? Choose a familiar organisation and consider how it behaves when faced with a public crisis. Discuss this issue.*

5 *What can information and communications technology do better than human beings? What can human beings do better than information and communications technology?*

▶

6 *What management functions can information and communications technology systems perform better than humans?*

7 *What do you consider to be the most important potential developments in information and communications technology in the twenty-first century? Why do you consider them to be important?*

CASE STUDY 15.3

The shape of elections to come?

The context

The Electoral Commission is a UK body responsible for the organisation of both local and national elections. For the May 2003 local elections, it carried out 59 pilot schemes across England. Over 6 million people were eligible to vote in pilot programmes which tested innovative counting and voting methods. The 2003 programme gave the chance for over 14 per cent of the English electorate to cast their vote electronically through a variety of channels – on the Internet, by telephone, via text messaging and, for the first time, through interactive digital television. Over half of the schemes also offered all-postal voting. Pilot schemes also tested new voting hours and locations.

The pilots were based on the Commission policy that voting should be made easier and more convenient for a twenty-first-century electorate. However, innovative methods made it necessary to ensure that security measures were in place that would maintain the public confidence. The current way of a voter declaring their identity should be replaced with a more secure method.

When carrying out their statutory duty to evaluate the results of the 2003 pilot programme, the Commision found that their approach had been suc-cessful in encouraging more people to vote. All-postal voting was especially successful, and the Commission recommended that all-postal elections be made available at all local government elections in Great Britain as a matter of standard practice. Traditional polling station-based voting would be provided only under exceptional circumstances, where there were compelling reasons otherwise for special groups of electors.

The issues

At first sight this looks like a leap forward from a traditional paper-based system to one which exploits information and communications technology. A closer reading however, suggests that one of the most successful ingredients of the pilot programme was a simple postal procedure.

Take a systems view and consider *what* an election is trying to do, rather than *how* it is done. List some of the potential forms of information and communications technology that may be relevant to implementing the aims of an election. What is done in other countries besides the UK? What are the advantages and disadvantages of the different forms of information and communications technology?

Source: http://www.electoralcommission.org.uk/toolkit/theme-listing.cfm/45. Accessed on 28/6/04.

REFERENCES AND FURTHER READING

Aron, D and Sampler, J R (2003) *Understanding IT: A Manager's Guide*, Harlow: FT Prentice Hall.

Forsyth, R (ed.) (1989) *Expert Systems* (2nd edn), London: Chapman Hall.

Harry, M J S (1990) *Information and Management Systems*, London: Pitman Publishing.

Harry, M J S (2001) *Business Information: A Systems Approach*, Harlow: FT Prentice Hall.

Olle, T W, Hagelstein, J, MacDonald, I G, Colette, R, Sol, H G, VanAssche, F J M and Verrijn-Stuart, A A (1988) *Information Systems Methodologies*, Wokingham: Addison-Wesley.

Schoderbeck, P P, Schoderbeck, C G and Kefalas, A G (1990) *Management Systems*, Homewood, IL: BPI Irwin.

Turban, E, McLean, E and Wetherbe, J (2002) *Information Technology for Management*, New York: Wiley.

Veryard, R (1984) *Pragmatic Data Analysis*, Oxford: Blackwell Scientific.

Winston, H W (1984) *Artificial Intelligence*, Reading, MA: Addison-Wesley.

Zadeh, L (1965) 'Fuzzy Sets', *Information and Control*, 8: 338–52.

WEBSITES

http://pespmc1.vub.ac.be/CSTHINK.html
An excellent source for books, papers and journals that give the theory, history and current sources of systems thinking and a systems approach to management.

http://cimru.nuigalway.ie/motto/links.html
A rich source of links to material on supply chain management and other forms of ICT-based business.

http://www.becta.org.uk/
Up-to-date information on the application of information and communications technology in education.

http://www.e-envoy.gov.uk/
Up-to-date information on the application of information and communications technology in government and business.

http://europa.eu.int/pol/infso/index_en.htm
The EU perspective on promoting information and communications technology in business and society.

CHAPTER 16

Managerial finance and accounting

LESLIE CHADWICK

Outcomes

The purpose of this chapter is to provide management, particularly non-financial managers/executives, with an understanding of the areas of accounting and finance so as to enable them to fulfil their strategic role more effectively. It is not the aim of the chapter to convert the reader into an accountant or to become too involved in the 'number-crunching' aspects of the subject.

It is important for management to gain a reasonable understanding of accounting and finance, which it is hoped will help them to appreciate the data which is generated and its limitations.

Having read this chapter, you will be able to:

- describe briefly the areas of activity covered by financial accounting, cost and management accounting, financial management and auditing

- illustrate how the net profit before tax is computed and appropriated, i.e. shared out

- understand balance sheet information, in particular the capital employed and what it consists of, and the employment of capital, e.g. fixed assets and working capital

- appreciate what a cash flow statement includes to help explain why cash movements have occurred

- spell out some of the ways in which 'creative accounting' can affect the reported figures in an organisation's accounts

- look at accounting ratios which cover profitability, liquidity, efficiency, capital structure and investment, and understand what they are describing and possible reasons for fluctuations

- show how to calculate particular ratios

- appreciate that there are different ways of incorporating overheads in the cost of products and services

- provide an understanding of the principles of budgetary control

- demonstrate how a cash budget is prepared, and its purpose

- explain briefly what is involved in the preparation of capital budgets for both income and expenditure

- recognise the dangers to an organisation which can result from the behavioural aspects of budgeting

- describe the duties of the external auditor relating to capital expenditure

- show how standard costing helps to control both price and quantity via variance analysis

- provide an appreciation of what financial management involves, e.g. the sources of finance, leasing, gearing, the cost of capital and capital investment appraisal

- briefly explain the following methods of capital investment appraisal: payback, average rate of return, net present value method, internal rate of return, discounted payback

INTRODUCTION

From a review of Figure 16.1, it can be observed that there are three distinct but related subject areas, which are:

- **financial accounting which incorporates financial management**
- **cost and management accounting**
- **auditing, both internal and external**

and that all three areas depend upon the same pool of data. It should be noted that the responsibility for these activities will devolve to one or a number of persons depending on the size of the organisation. For example, in a small company one qualified or semi-qualified accountant could be responsible for everything.

Figure 16.1 Accounting and finance

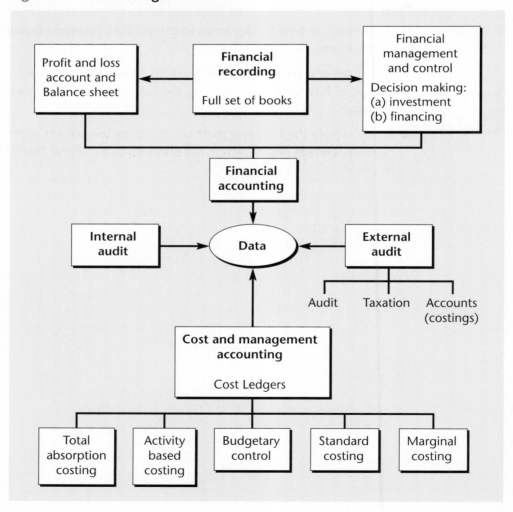

FINANCIAL ACCOUNTING

Financial accounting involves the design and management of the recording system, manual or computerised, for cash and bank balances, receipts and payments, and various assets and liabilities. In addition to the production of internal accounts, another principal output is to be found in the company's annual report and accounts, published for external reporting purposes, which includes:

- a profit and loss account
- a balance sheet
- a directors' report
- a cash flow statement
- a financial analysis consisting of appropriate ratios and statistics.

How do we compute the profit and loss?

Exhibit 16.1 shows a specimen **profit and loss account**, which may also be called an income statement, prepared for internal reporting purposes. This will be used to illustrate how certain figures have been arrived at.

The way in which the profit or loss (P&L)is computed is governed by the application of accounting concepts and accounting policies. *The figures which appear in Exhibit 16.1 will have been computed along the following lines*:

Sales

The sales figure will include all cash and credit sales for the period covered by the accounts, irrespective of whether or not the cash has been received from the sales on credit. This is known as the **realisation concept**. Any amounts which are owing from credit customers at the end of the period will be shown as 'debtors' or 'accounts receivable' in the balance sheet. Note that in the UK, for a company registered for VAT, the sales figure excludes VAT.

Cost of sales

Cost of sales is computed by adding the opening stocks to the stock purchased during the period (the purchases), and then deducting the closing stock.

The opening stock of finished products, work-in-progress, raw materials and fuels could be described as 'the previous period's deferred expense'. This is an example of the **matching concept**. The stock will be accounted for as an expense in the period in which it is sold. Until it is sold, it will be carried forward to the next accounting period as the closing stock.

The purchases figure is computed in the same way as the sales figure, i.e. it consists of all of the purchases for the accounting period, both cash and credit, even though certain of the suppliers of goods/materials on credit have not yet been paid for. Amounts which are still owing to suppliers at the end of the period will be shown as 'creditors' or 'accounts payable' in the balance sheet.

The opening and closing stocks of work-in-progress will, in addition to the material costs, include the labour cost plus a share of the overhead costs (overheads, such as rent of factory, insurance of machinery, etc.). The principle which governs

Exhibit 16.1 Le Caylar plc: profit and loss account for the year ended 30 June 20X8

20X7		Profit and Loss Account:	20X8	
£000	£000		£000	£000
	8 000	Sales		9 800
	4 420	*Less* Cost of sales		5 712
	3 580	**GROSS PROFIT**		**4 088**
	56	*Add* Other income and discounts receivable		64
	3 636			4 152
		Less Expenses (such as motor expenses, stationery, office salaries, directors' remuneration, interest on loans & debentures, bank interest and charges, and adjustment to the provision for bad and		
	1 603	doubtful debts, depreciation of fixed assets, etc.)		1 702
	2 033	**NET PROFIT BEFORE TAX**		**2 450**
		Appropriations:		
	265	*Less* Taxation		310
	1 768	*Net profit after tax*		2 140
	200	*Less* Transfers to general reserve		300
	1 568			1 840
		Less Ordinary share dividends:		
300		Interim paid	300	
900	1 200	Final proposed dividend	1 200	1 500
	368	*Retained*		**340**
		Add Profit & Loss A/c: undistributed profits		
	4 892	balance brought forward		5 260
	5 260			5 600

the way in which the stocks of finished goods and work-in-progress are valued is **consistency**. However, companies can and do change their accounting policies. If they do change them, they must **disclose** the fact in their annual report and accounts which are prepared for external reporting purposes.

Gross profit

The **gross profit** is the difference between the sales figure and the cost price of the sales. It is sometimes referred to as the 'mark up' when expressed as a percentage of sales or cost.

Other income

Other income received, such as rent received from letting some of the premises, is accounted for per period. Thus, if the accounting period is 12 months, and the property is let for the whole of that period, all the rent receivable for that period should be included even if it has not yet been received. Any amount of rent receivable owing would be carried forward as a current asset, i.e. as a rental debtor.

Discounts receivable

Discounts receivable are not discounts for bulk orders, they are discounts which are given by the suppliers of the goods and services received on credit (i.e. from creditors), for prompt payment of the amounts owing to them.

Expenses

The various expenses will be for the accounting period. Any amounts owing which are applicable to the period will be included and then shown as an accrual in the current liabilities section of the balance sheet. In the case where an expense includes an amount which has been paid in advance for the next accounting period, the amount of the prepayment will not be included as an expense for the current accounting period. It will, however, be carried forward to the next accounting period as a current asset in the balance sheet. It will then be charged as an expense in the next accounting period.

Provision for bad and doubtful debts

Provision for bad and doubtful debts is a slice of the profits which ought not/cannot be taken as profits. It represents the value of sales included in the earlier recorded sales figure which are expected to be bad or doubtful.

Depreciation

Depreciation of fixed assets, i.e. those assets such as plant and machinery, fixtures and fittings and equipment that are bought to be used in the business over several years and not for resale, are depreciated to spread their cost over the useful life of the asset concerned. They are depreciated according to the method which is stated in the company's depreciation accounting policy which, for example, could read 'plant and machinery is depreciated according to the useful life less the anticipated residual value', or 'on a straight line basis, based upon the useful life of the asset'.

Interest payments

The figure here is made up of all the interest payments for the period under review made by the company on borrowings in the form of:

- bank loans
- overdrafts
- debenture interest (*see* sources of finance for more information about debentures).

Directors' remuneration

Directors' remuneration includes all the salaries, fees, bonuses, etc. due or paid to directors for the period in question. It can be particularly interesting to note how information about this is shown in the annual reports and accounts of companies.

Net profit before tax

A more accurate description of this figure would be gross profit, plus other income less all expenses, including any adjustment to the provision for bad and doubtful debts, depreciation, interest payable (other than dividends) and directors' remuneration. A knowledge of what the net profit before tax figure represents is important and useful when looking at financial analysis regarding profitability ratios.

The profit and loss appropriation account

Appropriations in the profit and loss account show how the net profit before tax is shared between taxation, dividends for shareholders (both for ordinary shareholders and preference shareholders), transfers to reserves and 'ploughed back' as retained earnings. The retained earnings (undistributed profits) for the period will be added to the cumulative balance brought forward from the last period and shown in the balance sheet as a reserve under the heading of retained earnings, undistributed profits or profit and loss account balance. This problem of having a number of names to describe the same item happens time and time again within accounting terminology and is something that the reader should be aware of.

Materiality

Before looking at the next item on the agenda, it is important to know about another concept which on occasion may conflict with other concepts because of the way in which it is applied. It is the concept of materiality and dictates that where, for example, a fixed asset has such a low value, it may be charged to the profit and loss account as an expense of the period in which it was purchased. However, what is significant in terms of value is dependent on the judgement of whoever has to make that decision. Thus, the same expense or income item even in the same company could be treated differently by different individuals. Finally, it should be noted that the application of concepts such as materiality is affected by the taxation system, e.g. is the item a repair and renewal and chargeable as an expense in the profit and loss account, or is it a fixed asset that needs to be written off over a number of years?

What is a balance sheet?

A balance sheet is *not* an account; it is simply a statement of assets and liabilities extracted from the accounting records at a particular moment in time. It has been likened to a snapshot taken at a moment frozen in time, portraying the financial health of the organisation. This means that if another balance sheet is prepared within a few days, or a week or a month, the position could have changed dramatically. A balance sheet today, a picture of health; a balance sheet tomorrow, a picture of woe!

Assets are cash and bank balances or items which have been purchased (on cash or credit) such as machinery, stocks of raw materials and investments, or amounts owing to the company, e.g. by customers (debtors) who have been sold products or services on credit. A quick definition of assets is 'what the company owns'.

Capital and liabilities, in the form of share capital, loans and amounts owing by the company to suppliers (creditors), represent a claim on the company. In brief, capital and liabilities are 'what the company owes'.

Why is capital shown as an amount owing? The answer to this is quite logical. Capital represents an investment in the company by shareholders and loan creditors. It is, therefore, an amount which is owing by the company to them. In the event of being wound up the company, if it has sufficient funds, will repay all its debts including the share capital.

From a review of the balance sheet in Exhibit 16.2, it should be clear that the capital employed section shows where the financing has come from, e.g. share capital, reserves, etc., and the employment of capital section shows how this has been used, e.g. to buy fixed assets and current assets. It also shows, in the calculation of working capital, that current assets are partly financed by the current liabilities, e.g. creditors.

Capital employed

Share capital

- ■ Authorised share capital. The description which appears on the balance sheet is a statement included for information purposes only. The authorised share capital is the maximum amount of shares which the company can issue, as directed by its Memorandum and Articles of Association (the document which governs its constitution, e.g. it defines the rights of shareholders).

- ■ Issued ordinary share capital. The ordinary shares usually have voting rights assigned to them. They are described in a number of ways, for example:
  - £1 ordinary shares. This is their **face** or **par** value; any amount received in excess of this 'nominal' value of £1 is called the **share premium**.
  - Fully or partly paid. Where the full amount on shares has not been received, including any share premium, this is described as **calls**. The call for further cash will be made as per the terms of the share offer. The holders of ordinary shares, in addition to attracting capital gains (or losses) on their shares, will also receive a dividend.

Preference share capital

These are usually:

- ■ **fixed interest bearing in terms of their dividends**, e.g. 6 per cent preference shares;
- ■ **cumulative** (unless otherwise stated), which means that if their dividend is in arrears, it will be carried forward to be paid in the future;
- ■ **redeemable** at some future date;
- ■ **non-voting shares**, unless their dividend is in arrear.

Note that there are no preference shares in Le Caylar plc's balance sheet.

Exhibit 16.2 Le Caylar plc: balance sheet as at 30 June 20X8

20X7			20X8	
£000	£000	Authorised share capital 50m £1 ordinary shares	£000	£000
		CAPITAL EMPLOYED: *Issued share capital*		
	20 000	20m £1 ordinary shares (fully paid)		20 000
		Reserves		
2 500		Share premium	2 500	
4 400		General reserve	4 700	
5 260	12 160	P & L A/c (undistributed profits)	5 600	12 800
	32 160	*Ordinary shareholders' funds*		32 800
		Long-term debt		
4 000		Long-term loan (10%)	4 000	
nil	4 000	8% debentures	12 000	16 000
	36 160			48 800
		THE EMPLOYMENT OF CAPITAL		
	23 000	*Fixed assets* (net of depreciation)		31 000
		Working capital: (A) – (B) *Current assets*		
9 400		Stocks	12 188	
6 200		Debtors (after deducting provision for bad & doubtful debts)	8 640	
400		Prepayments	450	
2 100		Bank balances	2 600	
16		Cash in hand	22	
18 116			(A) 23 900	
		Less current liabilities (due within 12 months)		
3 556		Creditors	4 300	
235		Accrued expenses	290	
265		Taxation owing	310	
900		Proposed dividend	1 200	
4 956	13 160		(B) 6 100	17 800
	36 160			48 800

Reserves

Some of the reserves which you may come across are:

■ **Share premium account**. As indicated earlier, you may recall that this is the amount by which the share price exceeds the par value (also called **face value** or **nominal value**). For example, if ordinary shares with a par value of £1 each are issued at £2.60 each, the balance sheet will show the number of ordinary shares issued valued at £1 each as ordinary share capital, and the number of shares issued multiplied by £1.60 each as share premium in the reserves section. The uses to which the share premium may be put are restricted in the UK to those specified by company law.

■ **Capital reserve**. This may have arisen on the revaluation of freehold property or on the acquisition of a subsidiary company. (There was no capital reserve in Exhibit 16.2.)

■ **General reserve**. This is the cumulative amount of profits which have been appropriated to date (in the profit and loss appropriation account). The transfers are made at the discretion of the directors, probably because the profits represented by the transfers have been reinvested long term within the business, e.g. buying fixed assets, and cannot therefore be regarded as freely distributable as dividends to shareholders.

■ **Profit and loss account balance** (or **retained earnings** or undistributed profits) are the cumulation of all the remaining profits which have been 'ploughed back' and reinvested in the business to date. The amount which is 'ploughed back' each year is shown in the profit and loss appropriation account. It is the net profit before tax, less tax, less transfers to reserves and less dividends for the period which have been paid or proposed.

■ **Long-term debt** or **long-term liabilities**. Items which appear under this heading represent loans or debentures from banks or other financial institutions:

– **loans** may be **secured** or **unsecured** with **fixed** or **variable rates of interest**. Many types are now on the market, e.g. some loans even allow repayment holidays;

– **debentures** are a specialised type of loan (usually secured by a charge on the assets) and repayable between certain future dates. Trustees are usually appointed to protect the interests of the debenture holders.

Employment of capital

Fixed assets

Fixed assets are purchased to be used in the business and are not intended for resale, e.g. freehold land and buildings, plant, machinery, equipment, fixtures and fittings and motor vehicles. They are shown at their historic cost (or revaluation) less depreciation computed in accordance with the company's depreciation accounting policy. You may be a little confused with the way in which fixed assets appear. This should not be a problem: they tend to be shown at their original cost (or revaluation if there has been one) less the cumulative depreciation to date, i.e.:

cost of fixed asset
  less
cumulative depreciation to date
  =
net (or net book value)

Investments

This asset can be made up of the investments made by the company in the shares of other companies or government stocks. They are usually shown at their cost, with a note of their valuation at the balance sheet date. (Exhibit 16.2 did not have any investments.)

Working Capital

WC = CA – CL, meaning working capital is the difference between the current assets and the current liabilities, e.g. £17 800 in 20X8.

- Current assets are made up of:
    - **stocks** of raw materials, work-in-progress and finished goods;
    - **debtors** (amounts owing from sales of goods and/or services to customers on credit) less any provision for bad and doubtful debts, if any, to value the debtors at a more realistic figure;
    - **prepayments**, which are amounts paid for various goods and services which will benefit the next or future accounting periods, e.g. rent, insurance, advertising, etc. paid in advance;
    - **bank balances**;
    - **cash in hand** (including petty cash balances).
- Current liabilities consist of:
    - **creditors** for goods and services which have been supplied to the company on credit, i.e. amounts owing to suppliers;
    - accruals, i.e. expenses included in the profit and loss for the period, but which have not yet been paid, e.g. invoices for the servicing of company vehicles, stationery, accountancy fees, and so on;
    - **taxation**, i.e. the amount owing to the tax authorities;
    - **proposed dividends**, i.e. the dividend which has yet to be paid to the shareholders for the period in question. Where companies have already paid an 'interim dividend', this figure will represent the amount of the 'final dividend'.

There are many other items which could appear, e.g. assets such as 'patents' and 'trademarks' and liabilities such as 'convertible loan stock' (these are loans that can at some future date be converted into ordinary shares).

Cash flow statements

The format for the cash flow statement which is currently used in the UK is prescribed by a financial reporting standard (FRS 1). The cash flow statement is sometimes also described as a **funds flow statement** and gives an indication of the reasons why cash movements have happened during the accounting period under review.

A typical cash flow statement will include:

- **net cash flow from operating activities**;
- **returns on investments, and the servicing of finance**, e.g. dividends paid and received, interest paid;
- **taxation**;
- **investing activities**, e.g. the purchase and sale of fixed assets and investments;
- **financing**, e.g. funds from an issue of share capital, loans received or repaid.

Creative accounting

However, it should be appreciated that accounting is not an exact science and that it does have several limitations, some of which are as follows:

- The information included in the profit and loss account and balance sheet has been arrived at by individuals employing their own personal interpretations/ judgement of the accounting principles and concepts. They may also have been prepared with the taxation aspects in mind.

- 'Window dressing' may also have taken place to show a position which is not typical of that which existed throughout the period. For example, because of a special effort at collecting debts, the debtors figure may be much lower than the level which existed throughout the period. 'Window dressing' can and does affect the ratios which are calculated, in many instances quite significantly. Other examples of window dressing are running down stocks, changing accounting policies, revaluations, etc.

- 'Off balance sheet financing'. Many companies nowadays have many fixed assets which do not appear on their balance sheets. This is because certain fixed assets are hired, rented or leased, e.g. machinery, office equipment, etc. This makes it very difficult when it comes to inter-firm comparisons using ratio analysis.

FINANCIAL ANALYSIS

A study of the various ratios over time for one's own organisation with those of other organisations and/or industry figures can provide management with much 'food for thought'. They can help indicate areas of activity which need investigation and provoke questions.

There are many ratios, books full in fact, thus it is impossible to cover all of them here. Using Exhibits 16.1 and 16.2 of Le Caylar plc, a number of the ratios, which the non-financial manager/director/executive may find useful, are illustrated below (all amounts in £000).

Profitability

Gross profit to sales percentage

	20X7	20X8
$\dfrac{\text{Gross profit}}{\text{Sales}} \times 100$	$\dfrac{3\,580}{8\,000} \times 100$	$\dfrac{4\,088}{9\,800} \times 100$
	$= 44.75\%$	41.71%

This shows the company's average mark-up on the selling price. The reason for the fall in 20X8 could be that the margins are being cut to reach sales targets and increase market share, or that certain lines are being sold off at well below the average mark-up.

Net profit before tax to sales percentage

	20X7	20X8
$\dfrac{\text{Net profit before tax}}{\text{Sales}} \times 100$	$\dfrac{2\,033}{8\,000} \times 100$	$\dfrac{2\,450}{9\,800} \times 100$
	$= 25.41\%$	25%

One way of looking at this is to show how it explains the profit generated for each £1 of sales. Both years generate around 25p for every £1 of sales made. Movements in this percentage are caused by fluctuations in gross profit, expenses, depreciation, directors' fees, interest payments, etc. It can be said that it provides an indication of what is happening to the overheads. From these figures, it looks as though the company has managed to control its overheads more effectively. Despite a dip in the gross profit percentage, the net profit percentage is almost the same, even though the company has operated at a higher level of activity.

Net profit before interest and tax as a percentage of the capital employed (return on investment)

	20X7	20X8	
Net profit before tax	2 033	2 450	
Add Interest on loan (10%)	400	400	
Interest on debentures	–	960	(Full year assumed)
	£2 433	£3 810	

	20X7	20X8
	$\dfrac{2\,433}{36\,160} \times 100 = 6.73\%$	$\dfrac{3\,810}{48\,800} \times 100 = 7.81\%$

This is a very good measure for looking at the productivity of the capital employed. It looks at the net profit before interest and tax (NPBIT) as a percentage of the capital invested, irrespective of where that capital came from, e.g. share capital, reserves, loans, etc. It therefore gives an **overall return on the capital employed**.

Although the return is improving for Le Caylar plc, it is less than the cost of the new borrowing. The debentures are at 8 per cent. One possible explanation was that the company was fighting for survival at a time of difficult trading conditions/recession. It is to be hoped that the new investment, indicated by the increase in fixed assets, will benefit future trading periods.

The interest calculations are computed by referring to the information given in Exhibit 16.2, the balance sheet.

Liquidity

To compute some of the liquidity ratios for both years more information is needed for 20X6, which is:

	20X6
Stocks	8 600
Debtors	5 200
Creditors	2 944

Current ratio

The **current ratio** is the ratio of current assets to current liabilities, and measures the company's ability to pay its debts as the debts become due:

20X7	20X8
$\dfrac{18\,116}{4\,956} = 3.66$	$\dfrac{23\,900}{6\,100} = 3.92$

For every £1 owing, the company had £3.66 cover in 20X7 and £3.92 cover in 20X8. The increase looks as though it could be caused by the significant increases in stocks and debtors which tie up more capital. This could also provide another reason for the poor performance in the productivity of the capital employed, i.e. the return on investment.

Acid test

The acid test is computed as above, but excludes stocks as they are not classed as being as liquid as the other current assets. It may also be described as the ratio of liquid assets to current liabilities:

20X7	20X8
$\dfrac{8\,716}{4\,956} = 1.76$	$\dfrac{11\,712}{6\,100} = 1.92$

The rule of thumb for this ratio is one to one, but in practice companies do tend to manage on less. An acid test of around 0.85 is not untypical. The company had cover of £1.76 in 20X7 and £1.92 in 20X8 for every pound that is owed. In the words of the **Boston matrix**, it would no doubt be classified as a 'cash cow': not much growth in turnover but with a lot of cash. It does have a lot of capital tied up in debtors and large amounts in the bank.

Efficiency ratios

Average collection period

The average collection period shows how long it takes to collect the amounts owing from debtors. It can be computed as follows:

$$\frac{\text{Average debtors (i.e. opening plus closing debtors divided by two)}}{\text{Sales}} \times 365 \text{ days}$$

20X7	20X8
$\dfrac{5\,700}{8\,000} \times 365 = 260 \text{ days}$	$\dfrac{7\,420}{9\,800} \times 365 = 276 \text{ days}$

It would appear that the company's credit control is very poor and getting worse, and that it is allowing its debtors far too long a time in which to pay. Periods of around 45 days or 60 days are quite typical of certain industries and 90 days is not uncommon.

Again, because of adverse trading conditions and increased competition, the company may have been forced into giving more than generous credit terms.

Average credit period

The average credit period shows how long it takes to pay the suppliers of purchases on credit. This would be computed in the same way as the average collection period, if possible using the following calculation:

$$\frac{\text{Average creditors (i.e. opening plus closing creditors divided by two)}}{\text{Purchases on credit}} \times 365 \text{ days}$$

At this point it should be noted that information about the amount of sales or purchases on credit is not always available. If that is the case, just use the total sales figure or total purchases figure.

Rate of stock turnover (or 'stockturn')

Here the computation uses the 'cost of sales' if available; if not the sales figure may be used. It represents how many times the average stock held is sold in a given period and can also be converted to give the average time that it remains in stock before being sold. One way of calculating it is:

$$\frac{\text{Average stock}}{\text{Cost of sales}} \times 365$$

20X7	20X8
$\frac{9\,000}{4\,420} \times 365 = 743 \text{ days}$	$\frac{10\,794}{5\,712} \times 365 = 690 \text{ days}$

Holding stocks for long periods is expensive in terms of the amount of capital tied up, interest payments and other holding costs. The company needs to make a very careful review of its stock control area; stocks would appear to be tied up for periods which are far too long. Certain companies have been known to carry on producing stock even though their market for certain products is in decline!

Capital structure

Gearing

Gearing (also called **leverage**) is an indication of the relationship between the **long-term debt** and the equity (equity defined as ordinary share capital plus the reserves). One way of expressing this relationship is:

$$\frac{\text{Long-term debt}}{\text{Equity + Long-term debt}} \times 100$$

20X7	20X8
$\frac{4\,000}{36\,160} \times 100 = 11.06\%$	$\frac{16\,000}{48\,800} \times 100 = 32.79\%$

In 20X7 the company could be described as 'low geared', i.e. it has a low proportion of long-term debt (sometimes just called 'debt'). The debentures issued in 20X8 have caused the company to become more 'highly geared'. In times of poor trading conditions it is the more highly geared companies that are at risk of going out of business because of their obligations to make loan repayments and pay interest at regular intervals on their debentures/long-term loans. Note that what is high or low gearing will depend upon the industry/type of business concerned. Gearing has been described as 'using debt to increase the wealth of ordinary shareholders', i.e. if the project concerned generates profit, after the payment of the interest on the long-term debt, any excess belongs to the ordinary shareholders.

Investment

Earnings/shareholders' equity (return on equity)

This is computed as follows:

$$\frac{\text{Net profit after tax (less preference dividend, if any)}}{\text{Equity (i.e. the ordinary shareholders' funds)}} \times 100$$

20X7	20X8

$$\frac{1\,768}{32\,160} \times 100 = 5.50\% \qquad \frac{2\,140}{32\,800} \times 100 = 6.52\%$$

This provides an indication of the return that is being earned on behalf of the ordinary shareholders. There has been a slight improvement. It would be hoped that this will grow in the future as a result of the higher gearing and the increased investment in fixed assets.

Earnings per share (EPS)

The amount which each ordinary share is producing is calculated as follows:

$$\frac{\text{Net profit after tax (less any preference dividend, if any)}}{\text{Number of ordinary shares}}$$

20X7	20X8

$$\frac{1\,768}{20\,000}\ 8.84 \text{ pence per share} \qquad \frac{2\,140}{20\,000}\ 10.7 \text{ pence per share}$$

This would have to be compared with a 'yardstick' such as the earnings per share of the industry or various competitors.

COST AND MANAGEMENT ACCOUNTING

Cost and management accounting is involved with satisfying the information needs of management. It is there to assist management with decision making, e.g. planning the organisation's economic performance, controlling costs and improving profitability. However, it should be noted that the information provided by the management accounting function is just one component part of the decision-making jigsaw. There are other factors to take into account, e.g. non-financial factors such as the ease of maintenance, servicing arrangements, importing problems, standardisation, etc. One of the most difficult problems which the management accountant has to deal with is how to account for overheads.

Overheads comprise the indirect expenditure, i.e. expenditure which does not directly form part of the product or service.

There are three approaches which can be followed. These can be described briefly as:

- **Total absorption costing.** This method shares up the production overheads between departments/locations (cost centres), and then charges them to the products via a predetermined rate per direct labour hour or machine hour or some other basis (absorption rate/recovery rate), the aim being to recover the overhead expenditure in the product costs.

- **Activity-based costing.** This is in effect a more sophisticated total absorption costing method. The overheads are shared up according to 'cost drivers'. A cost driver is the activity which causes the cost to be incurred, for example the number of setups, the number of purchase orders, etc.

- **Marginal costing.** Only the variable overheads, those which vary directly with the production of the product, are included in the product costs. The fixed costs are not included in the product costs and are treated as 'period costs', i.e. they are written off as an expense of the period to which they belong.

The bulk of what is reviewed here regarding management accounting is budgeting, plus a little standard costing.

In order for management to control costs, budgets and standards must be set for each element of cost, i.e. materials, labour and overheads.

Standard costing and budgetary control are modern techniques which measure actual costs against predetermined standards/budgets. By analysis of the variances between actual and standard/budget, they provide managers with a means of continuous control so that they can take appropriate remedial action, as indicated in Figure 16.2. The same principle may also be applied to sales and other sources of income.

The variance reports mentioned would be designed to highlight variances which are adverse and of significant value and include an explanation as to why the variance has occurred.

BUDGETARY CONTROL

Definitions

CIMA (The Chartered Institute of Management Accountants) in the UK defines **budgetary control** and a **budget** as follows.

Budgetary control is:

> *'The establishment of budgets relating the responsibilities of executives to the requirements of a policy, and the continuous comparison of actual with budgeted results, either to secure by individual action the objective of that policy or to provide a basis for its revision.'*

Figure 16.2 The three phases of predetermined cost control system

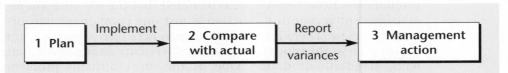

A budget is:

> *'A plan expressed in money. It is prepared and approved prior to the budget period and may show income, expenditure and the capital to be employed. May be drawn up showing incremental effects on former budgeted or actual figures, or be compiled by zero-based budgeting.'*

Some of the key words of budgeting which are included in the two definitions give a very good insight into the principles on which budgeting is founded. These are as follows.

Prepared in advance of the period

At the outset it must be appreciated that budgets are only *estimates* based on the best available information at the time of their preparation. Usually this involves updating what is known about the past, e.g. making use of the payroll analysis, the materials used analysis and the machine utilisation analysis, etc., updated by what is known about the future and involving various meetings and discussions.

To ensure that the budget is ready for implementation by the due date, a budget preparation timetable will be drawn up specifying dates for submitting drafts/revisions, meetings, etc. For all those involved there has to be effective co-ordination, co-operation and clear communication if the figures produced are to be realistic and reasonable. Usually the accountant will be responsible for co-ordinating the budget preparation process. The final budget, 'the **master budget**', is really a summary of all the other budgets and usually consists of a cash budget and a budgeted profit and loss account and balance sheet. However, it should be noted that the cost of the budgeting system should not be greater than the benefits.

Responsibilities of executives

Budgeting by its nature necessitates the authorisation and delegation of budget activities between individual managers and other personnel. This principle is known as **control by responsibility**, i.e. it makes an individual responsible for the whole or part of a particular budget, as illustrated in Table 16.1. It is designed so that the targets set can be achieved: if the machine groups achieve their targets the production department concerned achieves its target, and so on.

The setting of targets must where possible involve representation from the workforce if the relevant targets are to be fair, attainable and acceptable. Participation of managers plus workforce representatives, e.g. supervisors and trade union representatives, in

Table 16.1 **Budgeting responsibilities**

PRODUCTION BUDGET	RESPONSIBLE OFFICIAL
Company	Production director
Division	Divisional manager
Department	Departmental manager
Machine group	Supervisor or machine group leader

target setting and in the budget preparation process can make or break the budget in terms of its acceptance by the personnel involved, e.g. production workers and sales staff. 'We don't do it that way in our organisation' is not a good enough reason for not having some form of *participation*. However, to make it work does take some careful thought and it may not be as easy as it sounds.

It is also important to have knowledge of the other functional areas of the business. This should help break down barriers, overcome prejudices and lead to an appreciation of each other's point of view. Functions ideally should work together in harmony (*see* Figure 16.3), not in isolation (*see* Figure 16.4).

Requirements of a policy

Policy is the means by which objectives are achieved. Budgeting provides a formal planning framework and forces managers to plan ahead. They need therefore to have a clear understanding of what their company's objectives are, e.g. profit targets and sales targets, in order to be able to formulate the policies which they hope will achieve them. All too often certain managers follow their own personal objectives or their own perceptions of what they consider their company's objectives to be. Hence the need for clearly communicated objectives and policies. Budgeting provides a sense of direction.

Continuous comparison

The comparison of actual performance against the budget and reporting the variances at regular intervals provides an '*early warning system*' of things which are not going according to plan. Those variances which need to be looked at will be highlighted on the reports so that management can take corrective action. This highlighting of significant variances is known as '*management by exception*'. It enables managers to get to the heart of the matter and spend their valuable time and energy on those items

Figure 16.3 Working together

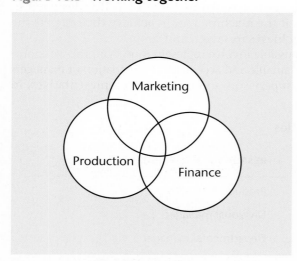

Figure 16.4 Working in isolation

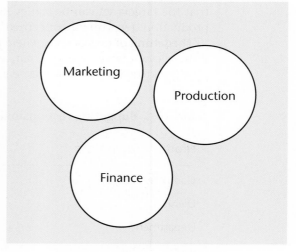

Source: *Essential Financial Accounting for Managers*, Chadwick (2001), Pearson Education Limited.

which really do need their attention. This frequent comparison system is the control element of budgeting, i.e. performance evaluation. Budgeting in effect provides a '*benchmark*' against which performance can be assessed.

Policy revision

There is always a danger of adhering to the budgets (which as mentioned earlier are only estimates) too stringently and following the perception that 'the budget should be achieved at all costs'. For control purposes the budgets used should be flexible, i.e. computed for the actual levels of activity (output) which have been achieved. Information provided by the system may lead to a revision of policy. The budget will have been computed using certain basic assumptions about the business environment; if these change, then the budgets/policies may also have to change.

Financial or quantitative statements

Budgets are interrelated, for example the sales budget determines the production requirements, the production budget dictates the amount of raw materials required and the labour budget, and so on. Thus, when the budget preparation process commences, budgets first tend to be drawn up in terms of quantity only. After a series of consultations/meetings to ensure the figures match, they are then costed. One of the prime considerations which has to be looked at before the budgeting process begins at all is the **limiting factor** (or **principal budget factor** or **key factor**). It places a constraint, i.e. a limit, on what a company can or cannot do. For example, if the limiting factor is the availability of certain raw materials, i.e. the company can only obtain a specific quantity in the forthcoming period, this in turn restricts the production of products using the material in question, which in turn limits the sales.

The limiting factor, however, is not unchangeable. Management can by its actions reduce its effect or eliminate it altogether. For example, management action where the supply of raw materials is limited could include one or more of the following:

- improve production methods to reduce waste;
- amend product designs to use less of the raw materials in question;
- use a substitute raw material;
- buy some of the components which use the raw material from external suppliers;
- search for new suppliers.

Planning

To be successful in business, planning for the future is essential. Budgeting demands that planning backed by co-ordination, co-operation and clear communication can take place at:

- **the stage of setting objectives and formulating policy**, e.g. discussions about how to achieve the objectives;
- **the budget preparation stage**, e.g. in order to keep to the budget timetable and to set sensible targets;
- **the control stage**, e.g. the way in which information is to be reported and acted upon;
- **the monitoring stage**, e.g. monitoring the environment to detect changes in basic assumptions, and reviewing and revising to cope with changing circumstances.

Cash budgets

Cash budgets (also called the **cash flow forecast**) attempt to predict what the cash and bank balances will be for a specified period, e.g. usually between three and 12 months. The movement of cash is recorded when it is expected to come in or go out. This involves taking into account the average period of credit granted to customers, i.e. debtors, or that allowed by suppliers, i.e. creditors. It does not matter about the period covered by the expenditure, e.g. rent paid or dividends paid. What does matter is the date on which the rent or dividend is expected to be paid in cash. Certain items which affect the measurement of the profit or loss in the P & L account do not affect the cash budget. For example:

- **depreciation** is a non-cash item: the money moves when the fixed asset is paid for;
- **stocks** of raw materials, work-in-progress and finished products;
- **accrued expenses**, i.e. expenses belonging to the period but still outstanding at the end of the period;
- **prepaid expenses:** any cash involved for these will all have gone through the cash budget and no adjustment will be made, as the cash has already moved;
- **provisions for bad debts** are non-cash items;
- **taxation owing** which will be paid in the future;
- **transfers to reserves:** no cash moves, it is just an appropriation of profits;
- **proposed dividends.**

The purpose of the cash budget is to:

- make sure that cash is **available as and when needed**;
- **highlight shortages** so that early action can be taken, e.g. internal action to delay certain payments, put back certain investment plans or hold discussions with the bank;
- **highlight surpluses** in order to put them to work, e.g. investing them in the short term, or switching them to a bank account which provides a better return. This activity is known as the **treasury function.**

Figure 16.5 **The cash graph**

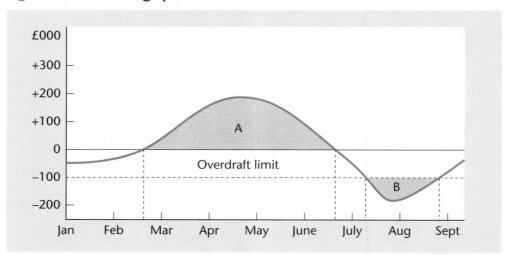

It can be observed from the cash graph in Figure 16.5 that position 'A' indicates a period of around four months when the company has surplus funds. Simply to leave it in a bank current account would be considered poor financial management, i.e. the balance could be earning a better return elsewhere. The critical position identified by area 'B' arises when the bank balance falls below the agreed overdraft limit. Because this position has been estimated and identified well before it is anticipated to happen, there should be time enough for management to decide on the appropriate form of action. It could be possible to take internal action without having to apply to the bank for a loan or an increase in the overdraft limit.

A very brief specimen layout of a cash budget is provided in Figure 16.6. The analysis provided could, however, be much more detailed.

Figure 16.6 A cash budget

		INFLOWS	OUTFLOWS					
20X7	Opening balance	Sales	Purchases	Labour costs	Overheads (rent, etc.)	Dividends and tax paid	Fixed assets	Closing balance
Jan								
Feb								
Mar								
Apr								

CAPITAL BUDGETS

The **capital budget** (*see* Figure 16.7) spells out the organisation's future requirements in terms of:

(a) **fixed assets**, e.g. buildings, plant and machinery, equipment;

(b) **working capital**, e.g. to finance an increase in the holding of raw materials;

(c) **investment in securities**, e.g. shares in UK companies;

(d) **redemption of preference shares and debentures**;

(e) **repayment of loans**;

(f) **forms of finance to be used and their timing.**

The capital budget will be subdivided into short-term and long-term plans. These plans will need to be carefully monitored and action taken to combat the effects of

Figure 16.7 Capital budgets

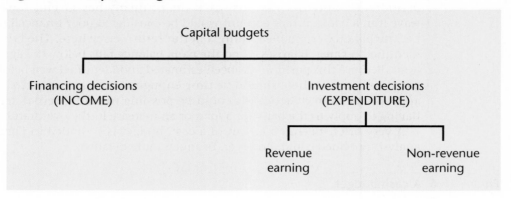

changes in the perceived environment. (Capital investment appraisal is covered later on in this chapter.)

Capital budgets: finance

The planned requirements in terms of expenditure must be financed from internal or external sources. Although the financing decision is closely related to the investment decision, it is in fact a quite independent decision. The capital budget relating to the financing requirements will be drawn up to cover:

- **the amount** required to cover the budgeted expenditure;
- **the timing** of the expenditure. In this respect, the cash budget is a very important tool as it indicates when the cash is needed;
- **the type of finance** to be used, e.g. debt, equity or internal financing such as retained earnings.

It is most important to keep a watchful eye on what is happening in the capital markets. The possibility of the refinancing of existing borrowings should not be ignored. Refinancing could well save an undertaking (be it in the public or private sector) a great deal of money. It is imperative that alternative courses of providing fixed assets are considered, such as rental, hire purchase, leasing, hiring, sale and leaseback.

Capital budgets: investment

Management has the onerous task of seeing that all the personnel who should be involved with the preparation of capital budgets are in fact actively involved.

The preparation of the capital budgets for revenue-earning and non-revenue-earning investments could well be along the following lines.

Timetable

A timetable will need to be drawn up and circulated in good time, giving dates for submission of proposals, meeting dates for consideration of proposals, and the final meeting date at which the budget should be approved.

Co-ordination

The person responsible for co-ordinating all the budgets, usually the accountant, must ensure that all personnel concerned know what is expected of them. The co-ordinator should also make sure that appropriate data and information are made available to all those who are involved in the capital budgeting preparation process. Such information may include:

- **details of environmental change** (internal and external);
- **industry figures**, e.g. performance indicators, growth in sales;
- **the revenue implications of capital expenditure**, e.g. the recurring annual costs associated with a particular fixed asset;
- **the company's policy on credit, stock and the replacement of fixed assets**;
- **grants available**, e.g from UK and EU sources;
- **taxation implications**.

In order to obtain the co-operation and participation of those involved, it is essential that there be clear and effective communication.

Assessing the needs

To a large extent, the needs in terms of plant, machinery, equipment and fixtures will be determined by the other, interrelated budgets.

Submitting proposals

Departmental managers, knowing what is required of them, will need to formulate and submit their proposals. In the case of revenue-earning capital expenditure, their needs will no doubt be based on:

- **matching** the needs of the other functional budgets;
- **replacement** of existing assets.

It is important for management to formulate a replacement policy for revenue- and non-revenue-earning capital expenditure: for instance, executive cars and IT equipment could be replaced every three years, while certain machines could be replaced every five years. A replacement schedule may be drawn up containing details of the fixed assets which are to be replaced (e.g. estimated residual values) and their proposed replacements. The policy must be flexible and reviewed at regular intervals.

For non-revenue-earning capital expenditure the managers concerned should provide those who have the final say with satisfactory justification for the expenditure. Organisations spend a great deal of money on items that are non-revenue-earning, such as fixtures and fittings and office equipment.

Search

When submissions have been received, a search should take place to reveal other alternatives which were not pointed out at the time of the original submission.

Preliminary vetting

The managers concerned will look carefully at all the proposals and obtain further information if necessary. They will then decide which proposals will go through to the next stage of the exercise. Rejecting some proposals at this stage will avoid wasting valuable time and effort later on.

Evaluation

The evaluation of the revenue-earning capital budgets will take place, using, for example, capital investment appraisal. Various factors such as price, quality, reliability will have to be taken into account when assessing alternative non-revenue-earning capital expenditures.

Presentation

The results of the evaluation will be presented to management in an appropriate format. Meetings may be arranged to discuss the proposals further with the staff concerned.

Selection

After careful consideration of the information contained in the evaluation, plus any further information, management will meet to decide and approve the capital expenditure budget. This may be subdivided into short-term, medium-term and long-term capital budgets.

Communication

The process does not end with selection. It is also important to inform the appropriate personnel of the decisions which have been reached, and to thank them for playing their part in the budgeting exercise. The budgets may be reviewed and revised several times before they are finally accepted and approved.

Capital allocation

When faced with the task of allocating **capital expenditure** between the various departments and cost centres, the following points should be taken into account:

- Is capital expenditure over the last few years a good guide to what will be expected next year? This approach tends to look backwards and not forwards and goes against the principles of sound budgeting. The information relating to past allocations is just one very small component part of the mass of information required. If historic capital expenditures were acceptable as a basis for fixing future allocations, this would encourage spending on unnecessary projects. Justification of projects is therefore of paramount importance.

- Across-the-board cuts in capital expenditure do not make any sense. This kind of compromise has the effect of cutting the essential as well as the not so essential projects.

- It is important that needs are assessed, expenditure justified and projects and alternatives considered and carefully appraised.

Zero-based budgeting

Zero-based budgeting (ZBB) has been found to be particularly useful for non-revenue-earning capital projects and for service and support areas. It forces managers to justify and rank their programmes/projects. Top management can then screen and review the proposals and after careful consideration decide which ones will go ahead. It is claimed that ZBB promotes a much more efficient allocation of the scarce resources of an organisation.

Capital expenditure: the role of audit

It is the duty of the external auditor to verify:

■ **the existence**
■ **the ownership**
■ **the basis of valuation**

of fixed assets and investments.

The external and internal (if any) auditors are particularly concerned with internal control systems governing the purchase of fixed assets. They will look most carefully to see that the purchase has been correctly authorised by the appropriate personnel. Their role also extends to preventing and/or detecting errors and fraud in this area and thereby reducing/eliminating losses.

Capital budgets: conclusions

Success in the area of capital budgets depends on a number of factors, some of the principal ones being as follows:

■ It is essential for there to be adequate and effective co-ordination, co-operation and communication between all those who are involved in the budgeting process.

■ Time should be devoted to a full and frank discussion of the proposals and alternatives.

■ The process should involve the appropriate personnel concerned.

■ Thought is needed to secure control over the capital budgets and authority should be laid down and clearly defined, for example the authority to order up to a certain value of materials and the authority to sign orders.

■ All the personnel concerned should be educated regarding the benefits of budgeting and the way in which capital budgeting decisions are made within their organisation.

■ As with other budgets, provision should be made for the monitoring and comparison of budgeted and actual results. Reasons for variances should be investigated and, where appropriate, remedial action should be taken.

■ The plans should be flexible enough to alter as changes in the environment dictate.

■ The interest of directors (and managers) in contracts should be established, recorded and taken into account.

■ The internal and external auditors have a part to play in the control of capital expenditure. Their help in devising internal control systems should not be overlooked.

■ Another approach that is worth looking at is zero-based budgeting, which challenges managers to rank and justify their proposals.

■ Behavioural factors cannot and should not be ignored.

■ It is important for the whole capital budgeting process to be planned and timetabled, so that it can be ready for implementation on time.

Behavioural factors

Behavioural aspects of budgeting can significantly influence the capital expenditure decision and budgeting in general.

Seats of power

Certain individuals and/or groups within an organisation may be able to exert considerable influence over the outcome of proposed capital expenditure. This could lead the organisation in a direction which conflicts with its corporate objectives. For example, it could destroy itself by going overboard with the development of a new product. The power referred to may be by *political access* (i.e. access to top management) or by *voting rights on committees*.

Empire builders

Empire builders within an organisation can involve it in unnecessary expenditure. Actions by such individuals and/or groups may fulfil their own personal objectives, but these may run counter to the organisation's corporate objectives. The organisation in such cases could well find itself with a high proportion of surplus assets such as plant, equipment and buildings.

Gatekeepers

Gatekeepers are personnel who sit on important information flow junctions. They are in a position to regulate the flow of information, and so are in a position to determine what various levels of management may or may not see.

Beat the system

Individuals or groups may be able to *beat the system*. They may even take a pride in doing so.

For example, a company places a limit of £10 000 on the ordering of capital equipment. Above this limit, additional authority is required. The personnel beating the system simply buy a machine for, say, £11 500 by making out two orders, one for, say, £9000 and the other for £2500. This does happen in the real world and efficient internal control systems and audit procedures are called for.

The know-all

Managers have been known to buy expensive equipment without realising that the equipment concerned would only work if certain additional equipment was also purchased. Had they discussed this with their subordinates, they might have avoided making such disastrous and expensive decisions. In one case, although the subordinates were not consulted, they knew of the decision by their know-all manager to purchase a fixed asset. They all remained silent, even though they knew there would be problems, and were pleased when things went wrong! This highlights just how important *participation* is and that meetings to discuss investments in fixed assets can save a great deal of time and money.

STANDARD COSTS

Definition

A standard cost is an estimated cost, prepared in advance of production or supply, correlating a technical specification of materials and labour to the prices and wage rates estimated for a selected period, with the addition of an apportionment of the overhead expenses estimated for the same period within a prescribed set of working conditions.

The advantages of standard costing are:

- it provides management with regular and prompt reports on matters which are not proceeding according to plan or expectations, thus enabling corrective action to be taken;
- it ensures control of all factors, whether related to expenses or output, which affect production costs;
- it looks at both price and quantity variances when it reviews performance;
- cost control is exercised in standard costing via variance analysis.

Figure 16.8 illustrates how standard costing fits into the cost control picture. The feedback loop is important and indicates that standards must also be monitored so that any necessary amendments can be made.

Calculation of the variances

The cost (total) variance is the difference between the standard cost (for the actual level of activity) and the actual cost. This can be subdivided into two subvariances, as in Figure 16.9.

Figure 16.8 Cost control using standard costing

Figure 16.9 The cost variance

Exhibit 16.3 Labour variances

	LABOUR OR WAGES VARIANCE	LABOUR RATE OR WAGE RATE VARIANCE	LABOUR EFFICIENCY VARIANCE
	£	£	£
Actual hours @ actual rate (1950 @ £8.40)	16 380	16 380	–
Standard hours @ standard rate (2000 @ £8)	16 000	–	16 000
Actual hours @ standard rate (1950 @ £8)	–	15 600	15 600
	£ 380 (A)	£ 780 (A)	£ 400 (F)

SUMMARY (PROOF)	£	
Labour rate variance	780	(A)
Labour efficiency variance	400	(F)
= Labour cost variance	£380	(A)

(A) = Adverse (F) = Favourable

The labour variances (*see* Exhibit 16.3) are the labour rate variance and the labour efficiency variance. The materials variances are the material price variance and the material usage variance. The division into both price and quantity variances is an aid to control, e.g. if the labour force is taking longer to produce products than the time allowed, this can be investigated/discussed with appropriate personnel.

It can be observed from the calculations in Exhibit 16.3 that both subvariances add back to the cost (total) variance. What really matters is the reporting side and the decision as to what form of corrective action will be taken.

FINANCIAL MANAGEMENT

Although **financial management** was shown as being part of the financial accounting side of the business in Figure 16.1, it has developed over the years into a specialist area in its own right. Whether or not the financial management function is carried out by a financial accountant or a management accountant will depend to a large extent on the size of the organisation. Financial management covers numerous areas such as sources of funds, cost of capital, capital structure, the value of companies, dividend policy, capital investment appraisal, etc. It is considered that all managers/executives should know something about capital investment appraisal. However, first there will be an attempt to provide a brief insight into some of the other areas of financial management.

Sources of finance

Managers, especially on the financial management side of an organisation, are particularly involved with the raising of capital and the management of the financial structure.

Capital can be obtained from a multitude of places. The charges for capital will reflect the timespan concerned and the risk to the institution which is providing the finance. It must be remembered that in addition to paying the interest on certain types of finance, e.g. loans and debentures, there is also an obligation to repay the capital at some future date.

Finance is always available, but at a price. Matching the life over which finance is repayable with the life of the project or investment is worth considering. There are numerous sources of finance, but internal finance, e.g. retained earnings, selling surplus assets, improved credit control, etc. must not be overlooked.

In addition, a careful watch needs to be kept on what is available through government agencies and the EU. These sources change quite frequently, hence the need for regular monitoring.

The lease or buy decision

An alternative to outright purchase of a fixed asset is leasing. It enables firms to acquire various fixed assets, such as premises, plant, machinery, fixtures, equipment and motor vehicles. With a lease, the lessor retains ownership of the asset, although at the end of certain leases ownership passes or may pass to the lessee. The lessee agrees to meet certain conditions, e.g. to pay a rental at specified intervals, to keep the asset in good condition, to carry out regular maintenance and to insure the asset.

Leasing tends to be encouraged by tax implications, high interest rates and cash shortages. It frees an undertaking from having to find a large lump sum and the costs of acquiring and servicing such a sum.

It can be said that in relation to machinery and equipment, leasing provides a *hedge against obsolescence*. Leases are negotiated for a number of years, at the end of which the asset in question may be returned and another asset leased. This enables the undertaking concerned to keep pace with developments in new technology without being burdened with machinery and equipment which are out of date.

Capital structure and gearing

The term **capital structure** is generally used to describe a concern's more permanent and/or long-term financing, e.g. ordinary shares, preference shares, long-term debt and reserves.

Gearing (known as leverage in the USA) refers to the relationship between the long-term debt (i.e. debentures and long-term loans) plus preference shares, if any, and the equity (i.e. issued and paid-up ordinary share capital plus reserves). However, certain gearing calculations include the preference shares with the equity. If the proportion of long-term debt to equity is high, the company is described as being *highly geared*. If the position is vice versa, the company is classed as *low geared*. However, to state with authority whether or not a company is high or low geared, one must look at the gearing ratios for the particular industry in which the company operates.

There is a greater possibility of increasing the return on net worth and the stake of the ordinary shareholder if the company is highly geared and trading conditions are favourable. Conversely, when trading conditions are poor, a highly geared company stands to make low returns because of the obligation to pay interest. It is this obligation to pay interest and in certain cases to repay the capital within a specified period, e.g. on a long-term loan, that increases the risk to the company. The interest (e.g. on debentures) must be paid whether or not the company makes a profit.

The cost of capital

The cost of capital cannot be ignored because all capital does have both a cost and an opportunity cost. When selecting a discount rate for capital investment appraisal purposes, many authorities favour the use of the cost of capital figure. However, there are a number of different cost of capital figures which could be used. A full discussion of this subject is outside the scope of this chapter. Investors are only likely to invest in a business if the return is commensurate with the risk involved.

CAPITAL INVESTMENT APPRAISAL

The planning, control and investment of capital projects

The planning, control and investment of capital involve attempting to answer numerous questions, many of which are open-ended, subjective and not easily defined. Some of the key questions are:

- **Which source of funds should be used for financing a particular investment?** This involves considering factors such as the cost of capital, the term (e.g. long term or short term), repayment arrangements, legal aspects, etc.
- **What is the cost of capital?** In determining this it will also be necessary to establish which cost of capital figure should be used (e.g. weighted average cost).
- **What should the expected (ROI) return on investment (return on capital employed) be?** It is very difficult to define an adequate return and the amount anticipated will vary between firms and industries. ROI is very important from the viewpoint of the providers and users of the funds.
- **In the area of capital investment appraisal, which discount rate should be used?** A number of alternatives could be selected and deemed appropriate, e.g. the cost of capital or the anticipated returns on projects commensurate with the risk involved.
- **In deciding on an investment of capital, how will the risks involved in the project be assessed and taken into account in the computations?** This very broad area is the subject of constant debate and features regularly in the financial press. Uncertainty may be handled by probability approaches to likely results, to give the best and worst and most likely outcomes.
- **Why should the company opt for a particular capital structure?** Following on from this, one could also ask: Which capital structure would be most appropriate for the company now and in the future?
- **How much working capital should a firm have?** Cash flow and profitability do not go hand in hand. It is vital to a business's long-term survival to be able to pay debts as the debts become due.

The essential elements of a system for planning and evaluating capital investments are illustrated in Figure 16.10, and are as follows:

■ **Objectives.** All projects should be in line with the objectives and/or the policy of the company concerned. In particular, the company's objectives relating to the required return on capital employed should be clearly stated.

■ **Data collection and analysis.** Data has to be collected, classified, analysed and presented in a form appropriate to the needs and understanding of the user. A key decision that has to be made is the method/s by which the investment is to be appraised (e.g. discounted cash flow).

■ **The management information system.** The provision of relevant and appropriate information to management can most certainly enhance the decision-making process. An effective management information system is, therefore, a prerequisite for efficient planning and control. The quality of the information will help determine the accuracy of forecasts relating to future performance. However, it is possible to provide management with too much information, and *information overload* tends to weigh them down. The quality of the information rather than its quantity is therefore closely linked to the quality of decision making (*see* Chapters 13 and 15).

→ Chs13 and 15

Figure 16.10 **The capital investment decision**

■ **Monitoring the external environment.** The external environment in which a firm operates is diverse and complex. It must be continuously monitored to reveal threats and opportunities which could, at a stroke, change the whole nature of the firm's activities and capital investment programme, e.g. political instability in the country of a major customer (*see* Chapter 4).

→ Ch. 4

■ **The internal environment.** A firm cannot ignore its own internal environment, the analysis of which should indicate strengths and weaknesses, e.g. in industrial relations, idle capacity, etc. The acceptance by workers of new plant or new processes can be of prime importance (*see* Chapter 9).

→ Ch. 9

■ **Evaluation.** In addition to the financial factors which have to be examined, management must also take various non-financial factors into account, e.g. availability of spare parts, flexibility, standardisation, etc.

A decision to go ahead with an investment does not end the story. The investment should be carefully monitored, and changes in the environment cannot be ignored. Companies must be able to adjust rapidly to meet changes in circumstances if they are to survive and prosper.

The real value of a business is the sum of the value of its *existing* assets plus the value of its *future* investment opportunities. Existing assets represent prior investment decisions, the consequences of which (in terms of profits and cash flows) are still with us. Future investment opportunities represent the scope a business possesses for making profitable investment decisions in the future. The investment potential will vary from firm to firm and industry to industry and will depend, to a large extent, on:

■ management's ability to generate, select and execute investment projects;

■ its capacity to raise funds to finance investments;

■ corporate strategy.

The problem of data

The key to good investment decision making rests with the quality of information on which an investment project is evaluated. The actual method of appraisal is of only secondary importance compared with the vital issue of the reliability of the underlying estimates and assumptions. At best the data is often a reasoned estimate; at worst it may be little more than a guess. It is of little benefit to introduce sophisticated appraisal techniques unless the degree of accuracy they suggest is matched by the quality of data supporting the analysis.

The methods described in this chapter all depend on the predetermination of the cash flows. Thus, one should always be aware that the cash flows used in capital investment appraisal are only estimates. The cash flows which are to be used should be relevant/incremental cash flows, i.e. if the expense or revenue arises as a direct result of the project going ahead, it is a relevant cash flow. If the expense or revenue would happen whether or not the project goes ahead, it is irrelevant, e.g. the costs of a feasibility study and certain fixed costs. As with cash budgets, depreciation is a non-cash item and so is not included in the cash flows.

EVALUATION METHODS

Methods which do not take the time value of money into account

Payback

This method calculates how long it takes the cash flows generated by a specific project to recover the initial cost of the investment. Those who use this method of evaluation prefer projects which repay the cost of the initial investment in the shortest time. In estimating cash flows, the earlier cash flows are likely to be more accurate than the later ones.

Average rate of return (unadjusted rate of return)

This return on investment method expresses the average cash flow per year as a percentage of the initial investment. Although it is simple to calculate, it must be pointed out that it does ignore the timing of the cash flows, i.e. it averages the cash flows over the life of the project, when in fact they could fluctuate quite significantly from year to year and within each individual year.

Methods which do take account of the time value of money

Both the payback and average of rate of return methods suffer because they ignore the **time value of money**. The timing of the cash flows, i.e. the year in which the money comes in or goes out, can have a dramatic impact on a project. The time value of money means that £1 tomorrow will be worth less than £1 today. Thus cash flows which are to be received in the future are not worth as much as they are now. The following methods are preferable because they do take into account the time value of money.

Net present value method

To find the **net present value** (NPV), each of the cash flows is multiplied by the appropriate discount factor using discount tables, e.g. the present value of £1 table. These are then added up and the initial investment deducted. If the resulting NPV figure is positive, the project is worthy of consideration; if the NPV is negative the project should be rejected because it is not a wealth-creating opportunity. Note that when using this method, if all the cash flows are identical, the present value of an annuity of £1 table could be used and would save calculation time. Note also, however, that the selection of the discount rate is at the discretion of the selector.

Profitability index

The **profitability index** is the present value of the cash flows divided by the initial cost of the project and is useful for comparing two dissimilar projects.

Internal rate of return (IRR) or yield method

The **internal rate of return** is the discount rate which will produce an NPV of nil, i.e. the cash flows discounted less the initial cost of the machine/equipment/project = nil. Therefore, projects with an IRR greater than the cost of capital are worthy of consideration.

Discounted payback

This method simply calculates the payback using the discounted cash flows.

Taxation aspects

Taxation allowances must be included in the cash flows for the period which benefits from those allowances. Tax payments must be included in the cash flows for the period in which they are to be paid over. Thus, care needs to be exercised in taking the tax factor into account by considering the various time lags, e.g. the tax on the income from year 1 could be paid in year 2, and so on.

Non-quantitative aspects

Frequently, the cost or benefits arising from a particular investment decision are difficult if not impossible to quantify. Yet non-quantitative aspects should not be ignored. There is a real danger of accountants being so preoccupied with the financial aspects of capital investment appraisal that they may tend to ignore other important factors. Such non-quantitative factors include:

■ **efficiency of servicing**
■ **reliability**
■ **risks associated with buying from overseas**
■ **desire for technical superiority**
■ **flexibility.**

SUMMARY

■ In financial accounting the profit and loss account and balance sheet were reviewed together with the terminology associated with them, e.g. prepayments, depreciation, assets and liabilities, and the way in which the figures are arrived at. In addition, their limitations were highlighted, e.g. the way in which 'creative accounting' can affect the figures.

■ Financial analysis was also introduced via a selected number of ratios, e.g. profitability and liquidity ratios, and some possible explanations for movements in them were provided.

■ The management accounting area covered budgetary control and an introduction to standard costing. In budgeting the key words should act as a reminder of the principles of good budgeting practice. They were:
 – preparation in advance
 – control by responsibility
 – setting targets
 – participation
 – policy, objectives and planning
 – continuous comparison and 'management by exception'
 – budgets are interrelated
 – monitoring, reviewing and revising.

■ An introduction was also provided to the way in which cash budgets are prepared and the 'treasury function', and capital budgets relating to both financing decisions and investment decisions, including zero-base budgeting (ZBB) and the role of audit. The final component of the budgeting portion of this chapter is a reminder to all management that the behavioural aspects of budgeting cannot and should not be ignored.

■ From the study of the standard costing area it should be noted that variances are caused by price movements, e.g. material prices, labour rates or quantity variances, e.g. material usage and labour efficiency.

■ In the financial management area mention was made of the sources of finance, the lease or buy decision, capital structure and gearing and the cost of capital.

■ Capital investment appraisal was discussed briefly and the influences on the capital investment decision, the methods of evaluation and the problems associated with the data used. The final section highlighted the fact that financial data is just one part of the decision-making jigsaw, and that there are a number of non-financial factors which are also worthy of consideration.

The relatively large number of review and discussion questions reflects the number of concepts and practices in this chapter. These are followed by a case study, which illustrates the problems faced by financial management.

Review and discussion questions

1 *How is the cost of sales figure arrived at?*

2 *How is the gross profit calculated?*

3 *What is the purpose of depreciation?*

4 *How is the net profit before tax arrived at?*

5 *Why can 'materiality' affect the net profit or loss figure?*

6 *What differences are there between ordinary shares and preference shares?*

7 *Explain what the reserves section of a balance sheet may consist of.*

8 *Describe how the capital invested in a company may be represented under the heading in a balance sheet of employment of capital.*

9 *At what value are fixed assets shown in a balance sheet?*

10 *How can 'creative accounting' affect the figures shown in the profit and loss account and balance sheet?*

11 *If the acid test ratio is 0.85 does the company have liquidity problems?*

12 *Explain briefly how production overheads are dealt with in total absorption costing and marginal costing.*

13 *Explain the importance to budgeting of:*
   ■ *the budget preparation timetable*
   ■ *control by responsibility*
   ■ *management by exception*
   ■ *behavioural aspects*
   ■ *participation.*

▶

14   *What is the purpose of a cash budget?*

15   *Explain what factors/considerations the capital budget relating to the financing requirements will take into account.*

16   *Explain what the capital expenditure budget will take into account during its preparation stage.*

17   *Explain briefly the importance of the following to capital expenditure budgeting:*
- *communication*
- *education*
- *authority*
- *monitoring.*

18   *How does cost control using standard costing work?*

19   *What are the dangers of high gearing?*

20   *In relation to capital investment appraisal, explain briefly the following:*
- *the 'time value of money'*
- *the external environment*
- *the net present value method*
- *non-quantitative factors.*

21   *Obtain copies of the annual published reports and accounts of three companies which operate in the same industry.*
- *(a) Compare their directors' reports and accounting policies.*
- *(b) Compare their profit and loss accounts, balance sheets and cash flows.*
- *(c) Compare their statistics, financial ratios, etc. and comment on the variations.*
- *(d) Make a list of why it is difficult to compare the three companies, e.g. consider 'off balance sheet financing' and the variations in their published statistics, etc.*
- *(e) Find out how capital investment appraisal is performed within an organisation with which you are familiar.*

22   *Discuss how three companies with identical products, identical income and identical expenditure could all end up computing different net profit before tax figures.*

23   *'A balance sheet can never show how much a company is really worth.' Discuss.*

24   *Why is it so difficult to compare the financial performance of one company with another, even in the same industry?*

25   *Discuss why participation is such an important part of the budget preparation process.*

CASE STUDY

The Queens Moat Houses creative accounting saga

The following newspaper articles help to explain just what did go wrong at Queens Moat Houses and pose quite a number of still unanswered questions, such as: why was it allowed to happen?

Catalogue of mistakes at Queens Moat

Hotel group brought to its knees by £1.2bn debt

A corporate horror story was unfolded yesterday when Queens Moat Houses published a 34-page catalogue of mistakes and mismanagement with its results for 1992.

The once high-flying hotel group formerly run by Mr John Bairstow, a typically aggressive 1980s entrepreneur, has been brought almost to its knees under nearly £1.2bn of debt.

Though some investors had become concerned by the company's rapid expansion, funded by high levels of debt and a number of rights issues, few were prepared for yesterday's revelations. One shareholder said yesterday, 'There was no way you could have discovered what was going on from previous sets of accounts.'

The revelations included alleged breaches of company law, including the unlawful payment of more than £20m in dividends; the earlier overstatement of profits; losses of more than £1bn and a £803.9m property write-down, and an apparent lack of financial controls. There were minimal reporting systems, a scarcity of management information and no monthly consolidated accounts. There was no clearly defined treasury function.

These revelations could lead to an investigation by the Department of Trade and Industry, although the company has not requested one.

Legal action against the group's former advisers and directors is under consideration by the new management team – probably over the question of the dividend payments.

The former advisers included Bird Luckin, the auditors, Charterhouse Bank, the merchant bank, Beeson

Gregory and De Zoete & Bevan, the joint stockbrokers. All either failed to return calls or refused to comment.

Mr Bairstow admitted the group had got out of control but defended himself yesterday blaming the spirit of the times. 'The sheer size of the growth in the 1980s was such that it would take care of any mistakes,' he said.

He said he was 'perplexed' by the £1.1bn difference between a property valuation by Weatherall Green and Smith at the end of 1991 and that by Jones Lang Wootton at the end of 1992.

'With so much at stake and with such a vast difference in the valuations, the issue should go to arbitration,' he said.

- DTI and Stock Exchange told of more than £20m in unlawful dividends paid in 1991, 1992 and 1993.
- 1992 pre-tax loss of £1.04bn. Exceptional losses of £939m including £803.9m write down.
- 1991 profit £90.4m pre-tax restated as £56.3m loss.
- 1993 interim loss £48.4m before tax.
- Balance sheet July 4 1993 – net debt of £1.18bn, negative net assets £435.5m.
- Legal action being considered against former advisers and directors.
- Restructuring to be finalised by January 31, 1994, at a cost of £32m.

Source: Maggie Urry and Peggy Hollinger, *Financial Times*, 30 October 1993. Reprinted with permission.

Drowning in Queens Moat

Until March this year when its shares were suspended, Queens Moat Houses appeared a respectable hotel chain with a long and successful history as a publicly-quoted company. The document released by the company's new management, however, depicts a company lacking the most basic financial controls. Some of the choicer elements include the payment of unlawful dividends over three years and the non-existence of records used to construct the 1992 interim results. Even among the many horrors unearthed by the recession, this catalogue of concerns ranks high. Despite the praiseworthy efforts of the Cadbury committee and Accounting Standards Board, many questions about corporate governance and financial reporting remain unaddressed.

The most disturbing aspect is the flimsiness of opinions expressed by the company's past advisers. It is perplexing, to say the very least, that two firms of property valuers could arrive at such different valuations of QMH's hotels in the space of a year. QMH's previous auditors and brokers deserve censure for permitting the publication of misleading accounts. The Department of Trade and Industry would appear to have much to investigate.

The new management has done its best to draw a line under past errors. But given the incomplete-

FT-SE Index: 3170 (+8.0)

Queens Moat Houses

Share price (pence)

Source: FT Graphite. Reprinted with permission.

ness of records at QMH's 200-odd subsidiaries and its remaining lease liabilities, this can only be drawn in pencil. The future strategy of the group is dictated by circumstance. There is little point in QMH's banks appointing receivers and dumping 200 properties on a glutted hotel market.

Source: *Financial Times*, 30 October 1993. Reprinted with permission.

New management puts strategy to banks
Queens Moat plans to form core hotel chain

The essence of the business strategy Queens Moat Houses has put to its bank is a plan to form a core chain of 50 UK hotels, which will be rebranded and form a base for eventual expansion.

The new management expects to be ready to launch this chain by the first quarter of 1995. The 50 hotels are expected to contribute 80 per cent of budgeted trading profits for 1994.

The new chain, a name for which has yet to be chosen, will be 'leading, three-star-plus' hotels, each with more than 100 rooms, located in or near city centres, and having a restaurant and bar.

QMH believes these can achieve 'substantial increases in both trading profits and cash flows'. The operational gearing in hotels is such that profits can

rebound sharply once occupancy and room rates are moving upwards.

The rest of the group's hotels, another 53 in the UK and 86 in continental Europe, will not be put up for sale immediately. They will run for profit with the aim of maximising their value either through eventual sales or as additional security for the group's lenders.

Hotel sales in the present climate – with large numbers of UK hotels in receivership and the market in continental Europe worsening – are unlikely on a large scale although some, such as the Dutch hotels, are up for sale.

At the same time, the financial restructurng will give the group a balance sheet more appropriate to its operations. This will involve a substantial debt for equity swap, cutting the interest charges QMH must service from its operation and giving the banks control of a majority of the equity. The exact size of the swap has yet to be decided but it is certain the existing shareholders will be substantially diluted.

Bankers who have seen the business plan say the new management team has put forward 'sensible projections' which indicate a beginning of a recovery in UK profits in 1993 and 1994, with a larger rise later on. Profits from continental Europe are still under pressure.

In the UK occupancy rates began to pick up in late May and early June, QMH said yesterday, although room rates were still under pressure. A rise in room rates is expected in 1994, however.

UK hoteliers were increasingly confident that the down-turn had ended, Mr Trevor Ward, a director of the Horwath hotels and leisure consultancy, said yesterday. The consultancy's quarterly survey in September found that nearly 80 per cent of hoteliers questioned believed recovery had started, compared with 57 per cent three months previously. Over 80 per cent, however, believed full recovery was a year or more away.

Mr Maurice Segal, chairman of Expotel, a large reservations agency, said yesterday that QMH appeared to be trading reasonably well but that room rates for the industry were still lower than last year.

The plan assumes some revival in hotel prices in the longer term, which could even repay the group's loans in full. One banker said yesterday, 'if the banks sit tight the restructuring has to be better than receivership'.

Source: Maggie Urry and Michael Skapinker, *Financial Times,* 31 October 1993. Reprinted with permission.

Valuations 'altered to inflate QMH profit'

The thorny issue of hotel valuations was put under the spotlight in the High Court yesterday as four former directors of Queens Moat Houses were accused of manipulating valuations to inflate profits artificially.

The four men, including John Bairstow, the former chairman, were all sacked in 1993 in the wake of the suspension of QMH shares, and are now suing the company for unfair dismissal.

In the run-up to the start of the trial this week, Mr Bairstow and his colleagues – Martin Marcus, David Hersey and Allan Porter – had tried to argue that a controversial £922 million property writedown instigated by current management was largely to blame for the financial mire in which QMH finds itself.

Michael Burton, QC, for QMH, continuing his opening remarks, cited valuations as one of the tools used by former directors to cover up profit shortfalls. He estimated that up to £60 million of the £90 million pre-tax profit reported in 1991 had been 'either non-existent and artificially created or, at the very least, should have been separately disclosed' as exceptional items.

He cited the example of London's Sloane Club, which was valued at £17 million when QMH acquired it in 1990 as part of Norfolk Capital Hotels. As a result, Mr Burton said, when the hotel was sold on in 1991, the company should have booked a loss on the transaction of £3 million.

'In fact, it appears that the £17 million was revalued to £15 million, then, just before the interim report at the end of June 1991, it was devalued again to £9.5 million.'

But, according to Mr Burton, that was not the end of the matter, as the directors then decided to use yet another valuation, this time the £3.8 million that the Sloane Club had originally cost Norfolk Capital in 1988. 'When it came to the end of the year they needed some more profit to be found, and squeezing as much as they could out of a pint pot, they had a rethink on the Sloane Club transaction, and at the year-end, what should have been a loss of £3 million had become a profit of £10.2 million.'

Mr Burton, who this week has outlined how sale and leaseback deals and incentive management schemes were also used to inflate profits, said that Mr Bairstow and the other three men had failed in their duty to disclose such one-off profits in the report and accounts, choosing instead to disguise them as trading profits.

The case continues.

Source: Dominic Walsh, *The Times,* 10 October 1997. Reprinted with permission.

Incentive plan 'used to falsify QMH profit'

Former directors of Queens Moat Houses used an incentive management scheme to falsify profit figures and paint a positive picture of the company's worsening financial performance, the High Court was told yesterday.

The controversial scheme, under which some hotel managers paid an agreed annual fee to QMH head office and pocketed any additional profits, is at the centre of a case for unfair dismissal brought by John Bairstow, former chairman of QMH, and three other former directors.

The four men, all of whom were sacked after trading in the company's shares was suspended in April 1993, were accused yesterday of misleading the market to expect profits of between £80 million and £85 million when they knew this could not be achieved. The accounts produced after their departure showed losses of £1.04 billion after a £922 million property writedown.

Michael Burton, QC, for QMH, said the problem with the incentive management scheme was that the annual fee paid by hotels was booked to group profits in the year the contract was signed, even though the money was normally paid in 13 monthly instalments

the following year. This 'front-loading' had led to the double-counting of profits from hotels transferring from the management to the incentive scheme.

'The mischief of that,' Mr Burton said, 'is that if you have a hotel which is in the managed sector from January through to October, and then have 12 months' worth of the next year in the form of the incentive fee, you thus get yourself 20 months' profit in one year.' He alleged that hotels were deliberately signed up to the scheme towards the year-end to bolster current-year profits.

Even when the recession had made it difficult for some managers to pay the annual fee, the company had often persuaded them to renew their contracts so the fees could again be booked to profits.

He further claimed that to avoid profits being too heavily weighted towards the second half, interim results had been boosted by the addition of a proportion of the front-loaded fee the company expected later in the year, completely falsifying the profit figure for the year.

The case continues.

Source: Dominic Walsh, *The Times*, 7 October 1997. Reprinted with permission.

Queens Moat auditing under scrutiny

The near collapse of Queens Moat Houses (QMH), the hotels group, in 1993 is to be investigated by the accountancy profession's disciplinary scheme.

Chris Dickson, the former Serious Fraud Officer lawyer who is executive counsel of the accountants' Joint Disciplinary Scheme, is to investigate both the company's controversial accounting policies and shares dealings by Martin Marcus, a qualified accountant and former deputy chairman of QMH. Mr Dickson will then decide whether the case should be heard by an independent tribunal.

'The case will revolve around the accounting policies adopted by the company and the extent to which the auditors waved them through.'

The company's then auditors, Bird Luckin, will come under scrutiny, with Maurice Hart, a partner of the firm and a non-executive director of QMH, expected to be central to the investigation.

QMH's accounting policies at the start of the 1990s have been called into question, in particular,

an incentive scheme for managers which allegedly enabled future profits to be brought forward.

Similarly, the group allegedly had not been charging depreciation on its portfolio of hotels, further inflating profits.

However, a statement from the Joint Disciplinary Scheme said the referral of the matter to it by the Institute of Chartered Accountants in England and Wales 'should not be construed as meaning that a view has been formed that a prima facie case exists against any member or member firm'.

The company is currently embroiled in a long-running trial at the High Court involving former directors. The four men, including John Bairstow, QMH's founder and former chairman, are claiming wrongful dismissal.

The hearing, which started last October, is scheduled to conclude some time next month, although a decision is not expected until much later this year.

Source: Dominic Walsh, *The Times*, 16 June 1998. Reprinted with permission.

Judge orders former QMH directors to pay back £42m

John Bairstow, the founder of Queens Moat Houses, and three other former directors face bankruptcy after the High Court ordered them to repay £28 million of unlawfully paid dividends – or £42 million after adding interest.

Mr Justice Nelson, who in July rejected their claim for wrongful dismissal, ruled that the hotel group's 1991 full-year accounts had not given a true and fair view and that there had been insufficient distributable reserves to pay a dividend to ordinary shareholders.

He added: 'None of the claimants were acting honestly or reasonably. I am not satisfied that any dividends – save for preference dividends – would have been paid if the accounts had shown a true and fair view.' Upholding QMH's counterclaim, he ordered the repayment of £27.7 million to the company plus interest of about £14 million.

The judge also found that the 1990 accounts had shown insufficient reserves and that the men were in breach of duty in paying a dividend totalling about £30 million.

However, he ruled that it would not have to be repaid as they acted 'honestly and reasonably' in authorising the payout. He deferred a decision on what proportion of QMH's legal bill of £6.5 million they will be liable for. Even so, the £42 million they must pay dwarfs the combined assets of about £3.5 million declared to the court. Mr Bairstow, who has built a personal fortune of about £3 million, will be forced to sell his Essex mansion and other properties.

Speaking outside the court, a surprisingly sanguine Mr Bairstow said the ruling called into question the whole issue of directors' responsibilities and the role of advisers in signing off accounts. 'What it amounts to is that the director of a public company cannot rely on external accountancy advice, auditors' certificates or other professional advice, because ultimately they will themselves be held liable for any subsequent problems.'

Mr Bairstow, who has yet to decide whether to apply for leave to appeal, added: 'The only beneficiaries from what happened were the shareholders, who got a dividend which would have otherwise gone to the banks under the financial restructuring undertaken by the new management.'

Mr Bairstow – together with Martin Marcus, deputy chairman, David Hersey, finance director, and Allan Porter, deputy finance director – were sacked in the wake of the suspension of trading in QMH shares in March 1993. The subsequent restructuring resulted in a £922 million writedown of assets and a resultant £1 billion loss.

In his damning judgment in July, Mr Justice Nelson found that the four had attempted to prop up the company through 'dubious transactions, doubtful accounting policies, the creation of artificial profit . . . and the making of false statements to analysts.'

Source: Dominic Walsh, *The Times*, 24 September 1999. Reprinted with permission.

JDS takes Luckin case

The English ICA has transferred its investigation into the role played by auditor Bird Luckin in the £1bn losses suffered by hotels group Queens Moat Houses to the senior accountancy watchdog, the Joint Disciplinary Scheme.

The investigation, which has faced increasing criticism for a series of delays since the company nearly crashed in 1992, will be taken up by JDS head Chris Dickson.

Fifteen-partner firm Bird Luckin was sacked by Queens Moat in June 1993, after the troubled company had been forced to reveal large-scale accounting irregularities that led to the suspension of its shares on

the Stock Exchange and property writedowns worth more than £800m.

Since then, the institute has waited for the results of a major Department of Trade and Industry investigation, led by Binder Hamlyn senior partner Adrian Burn and barrister Patrick Phillips, before launching its own probe.

Binder Hamlyn has run up bills of more than £2.5m since taking on the investigation. A report has yet to be published.

Chris Dickson said a prima facie case has yet to be established in the case against any members, but he would be looking into the 'discovery of serious accounting issues in relation to Queens Moat Houses plc group which led to prior year-end adjustments in financial statements for the year ending 31 December 1992'. He added he would also be questioning a member of the institute who was a director of the company about his sharedealings at the time.

Four chartered accountants sat on the company's board: Martin Marcus, deputy chairman and joint managing director; finance director David Hersey; deputy FD Allan Porter; and Maurice Hart, an ex-senior partner of Bird Luckin.

Source: Phillip Inman, *Accountancy Age*, 15 October 1998. Reprinted with permission.

REFERENCES AND FURTHER READING

Attrill, P and McLaney, E (2001) *Accounting and Finance for Non-specialists*, Harlow: FT Prentice Hall.

Chadwick, L (2000) *Management Accounting: Elements of Business*, 2nd edn, London: Thomson Learning.

Chadwick, L (2001a) *Essential Financial Accounting for Managers*, Harlow: FT Times Prentice Hall.

Chadwick, L (2001b) *Essential Management Accounting For Managers*, Harlow: FT Prentice Hall.

Chadwick, L (2002) *Essential Accounting and Finance for Managers*, Harlow: FT Prentice Hall.

Drury, C (1998) *Management Accounting for Business Decisions*, London: Thomson Learning.

Dyson, J R (2004) *Accounting for Non-Accounting Students*, Harlow: FT Prentice Hall.

Hussey, J and Hussey, R (1998) *Business Accounting*, Basingstoke: Macmillan Business.

WEBSITES

www.itbp.com
For the virtual school of accounting.

www.ft.com
For the *Financial Times* website.

www.thisismoney.co.uk
For sources of finance.

www.drury-online.com
The leading author in Europe on management accounting.

www.pearsoneduc.com and **www.booksites.net**
To help search for other textbooks on various subjects.

In addition, why not look at the websites of a number of companies?

SECTION E

MANAGEMENT ISSUES

What is meant by business ethics? What are the ethical responsibilities of corporations? What internal and external factors influence a corporation's ethical stance and internal values? What is meant by 'environmental issues' in relation to organisations? What pressures do these issues place on industry? What constitutes an environmentally friendly product or operation? What management strategies can improve an organisation's environmental performance? What differences are there between the management of business operations in a domestic setting and in a multinational setting? What strategies enable foreign organisations to maximise their advantages in foreign markets? How do multinational organisations operate? What skills are required in management? How do management careers develop? How far have present ideas on management built on those of the past? How do managers deal with change?

It can be argued that all corporate decisions are linked to a set of business ethics and that the structures and procedures which define the ethos of an organisation can predict the prospects for corporate performance. Corporations have ethical responsibilities and they have internal values which are influenced by both external and internal factors. There has been a growth in public interest and awareness of environmental issues and this places pressures on industry. Different industrial sectors have varied effects on the environment. Management strategies can improve an organisation's environmental performance. Management in a multinational setting differs from business operations in a domestic setting. There are management strategies which enable foreign organisations to maximise their advantages in foreign markets. Management careers evolve through a series of stages within which managers need to acquire a range of skills. Present management practices have built to some extent on past experience while managers today need constantly to adapt to changing circumstances.

CHAPTER 17

Business ethics and corporate social responsibility

RICHARD WELFORD AND PETER A. STRACHAN

Outcomes

Having read this chapter, you will be able to:

- argue that all corporate decisions are linked to a set of business ethics

- analyse how far the structures and procedures which define the ethos of an organisation can predict the prospects for corporate performance

- understand the importance of public interest and the relationship of an organisation with stakeholders

- explain the ethical responsibilities of corporations

- outline the internal and external factors which influence a corporation's ethical stance and internal values

INTRODUCTION

Corporate social responsibility (CSR) is now on the global policy agenda, with the last 20 years having seen great strides forward in CSR. Domestically and internationally governmental, business and other organisations are getting involved with CSR initiatives. At the European and UK domestic levels, the European Commission in 2002 adopted a new strategy on CSR, and in the same year the UK government published its second national CSR report. The UK government has now also appointed a minister for CSR. Internationally, organisations such as the United Nations, the International Labour Organisation (ILO), and the Organisation for Economic Co-operation and Development (OECD) have also taken the lead. Initiatives such as the UN Global Compact, the ILO Declaration on Fundamental Principles and Rights at Work and the Tripartite Declaration of Principles Concerning Multinational Enterprises and Social Policy, and the OECD voluntary guidelines for multinational enterprises now dominate the corporate agenda, thus making CSR important for organisations of all kinds, large and small alike (Hopkins, 2003).

Although CSR remains a relatively new line of study among business students, its roots undoubtedly go back to some of the key philosophical debates over ethics, values, equity and equality (Smith, 2003). The emergence of business ethics and responsible action on the corporate agenda is, however, more a function of the growing awareness of the social, political and environmental impact of the modern industrial enterprise. Many of the shifts in political attitudes towards firms, for example, reflect serious abuse by specific companies and specific business leaders. The misappropriation of pension funds, repression of workers in the Third World, environmental incidents, and even the bribery and corruption associated with deals to gain large government contracts are all issues which have hit the headlines over the last few years.

The starting point in this chapter is to argue that all corporate decisions are linked to a set of business ethics, and that by considering the structures and procedures which define the ethics of an organisation we ought to be able to say something about the prospects and preconditions for corporate performance. However, the systematic treatment of business ethics has been neglected in most advanced economies. Within the social sciences we have seen the study of political economy, for example, replaced by economic science and positive economics, and this has placed an emphasis on theories of optimisation rather than wider corporate and social responsibility at the firm level. Western economies, in particular, have developed along particular paths, with an emphasis on industrial growth, efficiency (defined in narrow monetary terms) and performance (usually defined by profits and increases in share prices). The politics associated with Thatcherism and Reaganomics led to the common cry that 'there is no alternative' and to the development of a narrow, profit-centred corporate ethic.

There are those who suggest, however, that social responsibility and environmental considerations can no longer be ignored in the context of an ethical (and indeed efficient) approach to doing business. Hartley (1993), for example, suggests that the interests of a firm are actually best served by scrupulous attention to the public interest and by seeking a trusting relationship with the various stakeholders with which a firm is involved. In the process, society is also best served because the firm is forced to consider a whole range of competing objectives and to move away from activities which are derived from short-term performance indicators. These various stakeholders which the firm must consider are its customers, suppliers, employees, shareholders, the financial institutions, local communities and government. The stakeholder concept stresses the idea that a company has responsibilities to all these groups (even though they will have unequal amounts of power) and will be involved in balancing the often competing demands put upon it. A company's ethical stance will therefore be influenced both by internal values and by pressures exerted on it from external sources. Such pressures have grown as stakeholders have become more interested in the activities of business and as information availability and communications technology have increased.

BUSINESS ETHICS

The starting point must, therefore, be to provide some sort of definition of business ethics. This is difficult because it will depend on both the values of individuals working in the organisation and particularly on the culture created by the individual ethics of senior management, and on any codes of conduct which formally exist within the organisation or standards adopted from external agencies. We do not observe one single ethical code in all parts of society, but different codes in different places and at different times, and this is replicated within any organisation. We can, however, distinguish between 'personal value systems', which individuals will bring to the workplace, and a 'formal business code', which may exist in some businesses through an explicit set of rules (Burke *et al.*, 1993). Perhaps more importantly, we ought to think about the 'actual value system', which is the moral climate experienced by staff in their daily business lives and which will determine the behaviour of the organisation as a whole, and a 'necessary value system', which is the minimum level of ethics (often equated with legal requirements) that has to exist for the organisation to survive.

In a pluralistic society, social, cultural and organisational power structures will tend to interact with these value systems. Such interaction may bring about a consensus or norm in certain areas of business activity, but it may also result in conflict where the ultimate outcome will depend crucially on the balance of power. One of the phenomena we have seen in the last few years is a shift of some of that power towards the consumer and the general public, and this has renewed the interest in business ethics and corporate responsibility.

Ethics tend also to be culturally specific. In some societies what may be considered as unethical by others may be considered as completely normal. Take the case of child labour for example. In the West we view the idea of 14-year-olds working full time as intolerable, but in many parts of Asia there is no choice between work and education. If 14-year-olds do not work, they are left to beg on the streets.

Another issue which causes problems for those advocating stronger codes of business ethics is that not all desirable ethics are mutually consistent. In those circumstances, judgements have to be made based on valuing different ethical actions. This too is a significant source of conflict. Again, outcomes will be determined by power structures and dominant ideologies will tend to arise. Such ideologies are nevertheless often a product of compromise and may not necessarily be first best solutions.

The study of business ethics is not new. In the nineteenth century, utilitarian reformers highlighted the need for ethical principles to be part of the free enterprise system. Currently, the literature on business ethics and on ethics generally is vital and growing. A key issue, however, is that there are many dilemmas where major principles, held to be moral imperatives, can in some circumstances be incompatible. There must, therefore, exist some sort of hierarchy which places more emphasis on one principle than another. What we are clearly observing today is the movement of social and environmental considerations up that hierarchy, for example.

Ultimately, it is organisation which dictates the hierarchy of different principles. The various levels of organisation, from whole economic and political systems via institutions and organisations to individual relationships, suggest particular hierarchies of principles (Donaldson, 1989). These hierarchies obviously shift over time and between different economic and political systems. They can be influenced, although that, in turn, will depend on power relationships. Many principles of business ethics might be considered somewhat abstract. A key issue, therefore, is how commonly accepted principles (such as improved environmental performance at the organisation level) can be translated into practice. This has to be done via codes (legal and self-regulating), education, communication and information, but these vehicles for change are themselves open to manipulation by those with power and the best principles are not always translated into best practice.

When ethical outcomes are discussed, words such as 'moral', 'ethical', 'good', 'efficient', 'rational', 'effective', 'fair', 'best' and 'improved' all come to mean different things in different circumstances. The meanings, connotations and overtones of words and phrases are often deployed in the conflicts and struggles for supremacy. The language of management is rich in emotive and ideological content, and therefore what organisations and managers say they are doing must be treated with healthy scepticism. What they are actually doing, assessed against clearly defined principles and measures, is much more important. Hence, in communicating their message about corporate social responsibility, organisations must be open and honest and not be tempted along the road of self-gratification and overstatement which is so often observed.

According to Donaldson (1989), there has been a relative neglect of the systematic handling of values in business which has been self-conscious. The consequences of the neglect can be seen both in anxiety about industrial performance in the West and a rise of concern about moral or ethical issues. A patchy awareness of the problem is to be seen in the sporadic (and at times piecemeal) nature of attempts by governments to regulate industry. This is well illustrated by the uneven growth in environmental legislation in the West and the continued growth of ad hoc codes of conduct in this area.

All organisations operate an ethical code, whether they know it or not. This may not be at all times consistent, but it is based on codes of conduct embedded in company culture and through the actions and decisions of senior management. Those codes will also be influenced by society's norms and, in the business world, by institutions and practices which stress the need to create wealth measured in quantitative financial terms. For any business which wishes to survive or avoid hostile takeover, the system necessarily pushes profits to the top of the corporate agenda and pushes other issues down the agenda.

Moreover, there is no business practice, action or statement that cannot have an ethical dimension. Businesses serve a variety of purposes for different stakeholders. Therefore, we might argue that as a necessary condition, business activities are justifiable only in so far as they can be shown to meet the legitimate requirements of stakeholders. However, these requirements can be, and often are, in conflict and can change over time. In identifying requirements and reconciling them, we have major problems. Moreover, we have suggested that the principles, ideals and moral values on which stakeholders' requirements are based can be, in themselves, contradictory. The traditional way of resolving these issues is for the organisation to assume primacy over individuals, allowing it to pursue objectives dictated by senior management subject to financial constraints imposed by owners and lenders. Thus, organisations often adopt their own identity and culture and often exist outside the democratic framework. But we must realise that business ought to be a means and not an end, and it is a means for satisfying the requirements of all who have a legitimate claim.

It might be argued that any philosophy or course of action that doesn't take the public interest into consideration is intolerable in today's society (Hartley, 1993). Today's firms face more critical scrutiny from stakeholders and operate in a setting which is becoming more regulatory and litigious. The notion of public trust is also becoming more important. A clear measure of how far we have come towards a more responsive and responsible business climate is indicated by the fact that if a firm violates public trust, then it is likely to be surpassed by its competitors, who will be eager to please customers by addressing their wants more accurately. Moreover, while the overwhelming majority of business dealings are non-controversial, any abuses increasingly receive considerable publicity, harming the image of business. Once a company's image has been damaged, it often takes a long time to reverse that damage.

In order to remain economically active, organisations need to learn from their mistakes or from those of other organisations. They need to take care to avoid situations and actions that might harm their relationship with their various stakeholders. In the worst of all cases, where an organisation faces a catastrophe, suddenly and without warning, its whole market image and business strategy can be destroyed. Examples of such events are increasingly commonplace. For example, in the case of Union Carbide, when one of its chemical plants in Bhopal, India leaked 40 tons of toxic chemicals, the event had (and continues to have) a profound effect on the reputation of that company. Although the company quickly rushed aid to the victims, it was bitterly condemned for complacency and the loose controls that permitted the accident to happen in the first place.

Environmental considerations are only one of many issues which might be included under the umbrella of business ethics. They nevertheless constitute an issue which has grown in importance. As a result of the many accidents and growing environmental damage caused by organisations, there have been increasing demands from consumers for firms to operate more ethically in this area. The consumer movement has fundamentally shaped and contributed to the significant increase in legislation and regulation at all levels of government. This has been aimed at preventing abuses in the marketplace and in the environment and, therefore, environmental management strategies are increasingly commonplace in leading organisations around the world. To date, however, environmental considerations have not been given enough attention within the framework of business ethics, because dominant ideologies are being shaped more by short-term financial considerations than by the need to do business in a sustainable way. However, we must recognise that there will be spatial differences in ideologies and ethics, and before we proceed we ought to examine international and cross-cultural issues.

INTERNATIONAL AND CULTURAL DIFFERENCES

Ethics might be viewed as a subset of culture, and where cultural differences exist across borders there are likely to be differences in ethics which are culturally defined. 'Culture difference' is a term frequently used to explain behavioural and other differences when doing business in foreign countries. However, it is a concept which has received scant attention and although most people would have ideas about the generic implications of different cultures, whether or not they really understand the specific features is more questionable.

Kroeber and Kluckhohn (1952) provide the following definition of culture:

> *'Culture consists of patterns, explicit and implicit, of and for behaviour acquired and transmitted by symbols, constituting the distinctive achievement of human groups, including their embodiments in artifacts: the essential core of culture consists of traditional (i.e. historically derived and selected) ideas and especially their attached values; culture systems may, on the one hand, be considered as products of action, on the other as conditioning elements of further action.'*

This somewhat complex definition brings with it a number of important distinguishable factors:

- Culture is not innate, but learned. In other words, people are not born with an understanding of culture. It is something acquired through the socialisation process.
- It is shared, communicated and transmitted by members of a social set and defines the boundaries between different groups. This point is linked with the first, since it is through reinforcement within a social group that culture is learned.
- Various elements of culture are interrelated. Attitudes and beliefs may, in turn, be related to religious and/or ethical ideologies, and ethics and ideologies may be adopted which match attitudes and beliefs resulting from experience and socialisation.

Corporate social responsibility and business ethics are very much interrelated and the behaviour of the organisation with respect to these issues will be dependent on shared cultures within social groups, the organisation of the business (which itself will tend to have a corporate culture) and countries (or regions). We must also recognise, however, that culture changes over time; this explains some of the swings towards and away from issues of corporate responsibility which we have seen over the past four decades. Such change can be gradual or extremely swift. Changes in the treatment of and attitudes towards women and their abilities in the workplace is something which we have seen develop gradually. However, we have seen rapid changes in attitudes surrounding sexuality as a result of HIV and a rapid awareness of the problems caused by global warming following obvious changes in the world's climate.

Differing ethics across national boundaries will be fundamentally related to values and attitudes. Values are often considered to be the standards by which things may be judged and serve to shape people's (and organisations') beliefs and attitudes (Welford *et al.*, 2001). This is probably the most elusive element of culture, as values and attitudes only become apparent through communication and interaction. Ethics, which will be part of these values, will therefore often have to be discovered, and where there are additional barriers to understanding (e.g. different languages, legal frameworks and customs) such discovery is very difficult. However, not to attempt to identify the values and ethics of a business means that a trading partner may well find itself in trouble if such values and ethics are not congruent.

Culture, therefore, helps us to define not only individual attitudes and behaviours (including those of managers), but also business norms. It is difficult to isolate the business culture in a country from that appertaining to the people and their society. Both feed off each other and similar patterns can be observed between the systems and networks at both an individual and commercial level. However, we must remember that ethics and attitudes held by an organisation will not simply be the sum of all individual ethics within it. That would be to ignore the differing amounts of power which various stakeholders have to influence corporate culture. Equally, the politics and economic policies of a country cannot really be isolated from the framework within which the organisation operates, and organisations often find it useful to change their corporate priorities (and thus their ethics) when political power shifts externally.

Conducting international trade therefore requires organisations to manage across cultures, within a wider array of ethical considerations and where the notion of corporate responsibility may be very different indeed. Mole (1990) defines culture as 'the way we do things round here', recognising that people and organisations in different countries, as a result of their specific cultural backgrounds, behave differently, and that to analyse the situation any further is extremely difficult. Therefore, operating across borders requires respect and a basic understanding of political, economic, legal, professional and ethical norms. At the management level, business cultures and those pertaining to the individual interact to dictate the behaviour of managers within the work organisation. Failure to adapt approaches to the nuances of behaviour and attitudes in different countries can cause expensive mistakes.

As business becomes increasingly internationalised, there is an increasing likelihood of encountering business partners from very different cultures, who subscribe to radically different ethical systems. The fact that there are different management cultures with different value systems means that there are no easy solutions to ethical dilemmas in international business. Many would argue that the simplest and most practical approach to ethical problems is to adopt moral relativism. In its simplest form, this means adopting local values and ethics when doing business in any particular location. This may be acceptable when it is the Western business executive who must be prepared to forgo alcohol in countries where it is shunned. However, it might also mean going along with the practice of bribery in countries where this is the norm, indeed it could even be argued that bribery is not so insidious in these countries as it is in the West, since it is regarded as quite a normal way to supplement rather low wages.

However, there is a serious problem with adopting a stance based on cultural relativism. If it is desirable for Westerners abroad to adopt the prevailing norms in the countries in which they do business, then the same might have to apply in the reverse situation. In other words, immigrant workers, for example, would be expected to adopt Western norms of behaviour, dress and customs. There would be no room for the Jewish sabbath or regular prayer breaks for Muslims. But such a stance would run counter to ideals of religious (and other) freedoms which are inherently bound up with respecting the individual (Chryssides and Kaler, 1993).

CODES OF CONDUCT AND STANDARDS

Although there has been an increasing amount of regulation covering a range of social and environmental issues, there is still more emphasis put on market-based and voluntary measures. Coupled with this, previous deregulation measures, introduced by more right-wing governments to appease industry, have continued to result in more emphasis being put on voluntary codes of conduct and standards. The design and definition of voluntary codes and standards are, therefore, important to consider.

Codes of conduct defined within an organisation or imported from elsewhere in the form of standards are usually associated with practical sets of rules and guidelines. They tend to be expressions of mixtures of technical, prudential and moral imperatives. They influence behaviour and therefore ethical outcomes. However, standards which are externally driven are typically expressed in a form that is well protected from discussion, expressing aims in a matter-of-fact language (Donaldson, 1989). In turn, therefore, a standard carries with it a dominant ideology which, because it is standardised, has a multiplier effect and increasing weight if the standard becomes a norm.

The adoption of codes of conduct and standards within any organisation necessarily raises a number of questions. The most obvious one concerns the type of subculture which a code brings with it. Does it represent a piecemeal attempt to placate demands from pressure groups and consumers, or is it a more serious attempt at ethical behaviour, for example? We ought also to ask how effective the codes are in promoting what they stand for. Taken together these questions provide a measure of the extent to which the standards are genuine and operational, rather than cynical and self-deluding.

Codes of conduct which become accepted across firms in an industry or even across industries are very powerful, and we often see them written into contracts between organisations. We might be inclined to think that a code promoting some sort of social commitment or environmental improvement is a huge step forward, and that organisations which follow others in adopting such standards should be congratulated. But rather more analysis of the content and purpose of such a code is necessary before we can reach an answer to that question. Without suggesting that codes may be bad, we must nevertheless consider whether, in fact, some codes push employees and customers into a set of values which verge on indoctrination. Stakeholders in those sorts of situation come to possess what Marxists see as false consciousness. In addition, the fact that a code of conduct is widely accepted does not guarantee that the values within it are not restricted or inconsistent.

There is very little research on the generation, operation, monitoring and amendment of codes of conduct. However, it is argued forcefully by Donaldson (1989) that because codes tend to be expressions of mixtures of technical, prudential and moral imperatives, and because they tend to vary in the extent to which they are or can be enforced, they cannot be regarded as the major vehicles for identifying and encouraging the practices which will raise the level of values in business and industry. Moreover, codes and standards are defined outside the normal democratic framework which determines laws. They are constructed by agencies (often professional bodies or representatives of senior management in industry) with their own motivations, values and interests. On this subject Donaldson and Waller (1980) point to a statement of Bernard Shaw when he asserted that professions can be conspiracies against the laity, and their codes, it may be added, are widely held to be primarily aimed at the protection of the members of the profession, rather than the public. Much the same accusation might be levelled against industry standards. Moreover, the matter of the development of codes and standards is bound up with the matter of enforcement. Codes which are not enforced or fail to deliver their expected outcomes, for whatever reason, might be thought of as little more than cynical expressions of pious hopes.

Much of what has been discussed here can be illustrated by reference to the Responsible Care Programme, which in itself provides a standard for firms operating in the chemical industry to adopt. It is a voluntary code where performance is measured in terms of continuous improvement. Responsible Care is unique to the chemical industry and originated in Canada in 1984. Launched in 1989 in the UK by the Chemical Industries Association (CIA), the cornerstone of the system is commitment. Chief executives of member companies are invited to sign a set of guiding principles pledging their company to make health, safety and environmental performance an integral part of overall business policy. Adherence to the principles and objectives of Responsible Care is a condition of membership of the CIA. All employees and company contractors have to be made aware of these principles. The guiding principles also require companies to:

- **conform to statutory regulations**
- **operate to the best practices of the industry**
- **assess the actual and potential health, safety and environmental impacts of their activities and products**
- **work closely with the authorities and the community in achieving the required levels of performance**
- **be open about activities and give relevant information to interested parties.**

A company operating the Responsible Care Programme is required to have a clear corporate policy and the communication of this is seen as vital. The key principle being used in the Responsible Care Programme is self-assessment. However, the CIA does assess the effectiveness of the programme across all firms by collecting indicators of performance from them. Companies are encouraged to submit six classes of data to the association. Individual company data are not published, but a national aggregate figure is published annually. This shows industry trends and enables individual companies to assess their own placing accordingly. The six indicators of performance are:

- **environmental protection spending;**
- **safety and health** (lost time, accidents for employees and contractors);
- **waste and emissions:**
  - discharges of 'red list' substances;
  - waste disposal;
  - an environmental index of five key discharges by site;
- **distribution** (all incidents);
- **energy consumption** (total on-site);
- **all complaints.**

A key element of the Responsible Care system is the sharing of information and participation of employees and the local community. Local Responsible Care 'cells' operate for the exchange of information and experience between firms. Employee involvement is also welcomed, and the CIA has established training programmes which set targets for appraisal. Firms are encouraged to have community liaison groups and initiatives recognising the continuing need to forge improved relationships with the public.

However, in its 1993 report on the Responsible Care Programme (ENDS, 1993), the CIA was implicitly forced to admit that the programme was not functioning in accordance with its aims. The main reason for this is that sites claiming to adhere to the Responsible Care standard were simply not adhering to its principles. Over the three-year reporting period, only 57 per cent of firms made returns for all three years, and only 74 per cent made any returns at all. Even more importantly, the third indicator of performance deals with waste and emissions, where firms are supposed to report an environmental index by site designed to give a composite picture of gaseous, liquid and solid releases. Only one-third of the total firms supposed to be operating Responsible Care reported this data in full, and of those which reported the index, over 30 per cent reported a worsening environmental impact. In 1997, although these statistics showed some improvement, it was still the case that many companies claiming to operate a Responsible Care Programme were still not adhering to all its principles.

Codes of conduct are, therefore, nothing if they are not adhered to, and voluntary approaches often slip down a list of priorities when other pressing issues arise. While some chemical companies are clearly committed to improving their health, safety and environmental performance, it seems that not all are adhering to the spirit of Responsible Care. Indeed, while some make efforts to follow the guidelines of the programme, many more treat Responsible Care as a smokescreen. Many of those managers in the chemical industry who appear confident of their procedures to improve environmental performance are certainly either suffering from the false consciousness which was suggested earlier, or are making much more cynical attempts to hide their environmental impact in an attempt to hang on to market share and profitability.

THE CONTRIBUTION OF ETHICS TO MANAGEMENT STRATEGIES

Ethics refer to standards of right conduct. Unfortunately, there is often incomplete agreement as to what constitutes ethical behaviour. In the case of illegal and exploitative activities, there is not much dispute. But many practices fall into a grey area, where opinions may differ as to what is ethical and what is unethical and unacceptable. One possible example of environmental strategies which fall into that grey area relates to the eco-labelling of products and claims associated with the environmental friendliness of a product. There are examples of firms using tactics to persuade people to buy, often misleading customers into thinking they are getting a product which will not harm the environment, and exaggerating advertising claims. Unfortunately, some business organisations have decided to 'walk on the edge' of ethical practices (Hartley, 1993). This is a dangerous strategy because the dividing line will be different for everybody. Moreover, what society once tolerated as acceptable behaviour is rapidly becoming unacceptable, and organisations which choose to position themselves so close to criticism will end up battling with time. To a large extent business ethics are firmly on the agenda in the mid-2000s. Society expects, and is now demanding, much more ethical conduct, whereas it had previously regarded questionable practices with apathy or ignorance.

It is now no longer justifiable to see business ethics as directly connected with the law and 'necessary value systems' are inappropriate. The relationship between ethical conduct and the law is sometimes confusing. Naïve businesses might rationalise that actions within the law are, therefore, ethical and perfectly justifiable. But an 'if it's legal, it's ethical' attitude disregards the fact that the law codifies only that part of ethics which society feels so strongly about that it is willing to support it with physical force (Westing, 1968).

Many organisations assume that the more strictly one interprets ethical behaviour, the more profits suffer. Certainly, the muted sales efforts that may result from toning down product claims or refusing to buy raw materials which result in the exploitation of indigenous populations may hurt profits. Yet, a strong argument can also be made that scrupulously honest and ethical behaviour is better for business and for profits. Well-satisfied customers tend to bring repeat business, and so it is desirable to develop trusting relationships not only with customers but also personnel, suppliers and the other stakeholders with which an organisation deals. Ethical conduct is not incompatible with profitability, but it does change time scales. It is more compatible with maximising profits in the long run, even though in the shorter term disregard of these ethical principles may yield more profits.

It is perhaps useful at this point to turn to some particular areas where the issue of corporate responsibility is seen as being important. Let us consider the following four issues:

- **profits and growth**
- **the dominance of competition**
- **expediency and indifference**
- **dominant ideology and business strategy.**

Profits and growth

In most organisations, career development and higher salaries depend on achieving greater sales and profits. This is true not only for individual employees and executives but for departments, divisions and the entire organisation. The value that stockholders and investors, creditors and suppliers place on a company depends to a large extent on growth. In turn, the dominant measure of growth is increasing sales and profits. The better the growth rate, the more money is available for further expansion by investors and creditors at attractive rates. Suppliers and customers are more eager to do business. Top-quality personnel and executives are also more easily attracted.

In particular, the dominant drive would seem to be towards profits and profit maximisation. This is justified by economists such as Friedman (1963), who argues that:

> *'few trends could so thoroughly undermine the very foundations of our free society as the acceptance by corporate officials of no social responsibility other than to make as much money for their stockholders as possible.'*

Friedman's view and that of many others simply neglects the responsibility that all actors in society have to benefit society in terms which are wider than the narrowly based performance measures which he adopts.

The emphasis on quantitative measures of performance and on growth, in particular, has some potential negative consequences. It tends to push social issues down the corporate agenda. An emphasis on growth becomes all pervading, and social and environmental objectives (which may or may not exist) are compromised. Moreover, with a dominant growth strategy, people are not measured on the basis of their moral contribution to the business enterprise. Hence, they become caught up in a system which is characterised by an ethic foreign to, and often lower than, the ethics of human beings (Holloway and Hancock, 1968). That tends to devalue the role of the worker and of those involved further down the supply chain. It is little wonder, therefore, when it comes to the consideration of the effect that the production and processing of raw materials might have on indigenous Third World populations, that very little weight is attached to the needs and aspirations of these peoples.

According to Bloom *et al.* (1994), in a wide-ranging survey of European directors, companies are perceived, by their leaders, as always needing to act within a social as well as an economic context because of the range of stakeholder pressures. All shareholders, suppliers, employees, clients, creditors, local communities, etc. have legitimate interests in the future of the company, and this influences decision making and planning. As a result, many directors implicitly wish to take a longer-term perspective on their activities but are hindered from doing so because of the shorter-term demands of shareholders and stock markets.

Many senior managers come to realise, however, that profit maximisation measures are not the only measure of success in a company, and nor should they be the central aim or starting point of business strategy. Profit comes as the product of success, and success, in turn, depends on creating an organisation where all the interlocking elements work well together and function appropriately. For example, paying workers the lowest possible wage, making them work in poor conditions and treating them in a patronising way are more likely to lead to conflict than to co-operation. Such conflict will lower productivity and profits. Moreover, a strategy producing maximum profit today may not be consistent with maximum profit tomorrow. That will depend on the investment strategy of a company and that, in turn, requires managers to create a durable company which can survive competing pressures from all its stakeholders.

Because of the nature of capital markets, however, Bloom *et al.* (1994) report that many British directors are caught in a trap. In the UK about 80 per cent of company shares are quoted on the stock market, compared with under 50 per cent in Germany and less than 20 per cent in Italy. Because of pressure for dividends from shareholders and the threat of hostile takeover if profits (and therefore share prices) fall, managers do not have the breadth of movement to think about longer-term issues. Shareholders have a very important role to play in allowing companies to operate on the social dimension. They are just one stakeholder, but their ownership of shares and, therefore, the ownership of part of the company, often means that their position is firmly at the top of the pile of stakeholders. This, perhaps, requires us to think carefully about what ownership really means. Shareholders provide money to companies for reasons which they choose, but they can get out of their commitment to the company a lot more quickly and easily than an employee or a supplier can. Some see shareholding as rather more analogous with horseracing than anything else. When you back a horse in a race, you put money on that horse hoping for some sort of return if it does well. But you do not own a bit of the horse. If you did own the horse, it would require much more of a commitment than simply providing the money and sitting back. If the horse was flogged and abused in order to win a race, then the owner would be accountable for its ill-treatment. In the corporate sense, therefore, we must not only consider the rights of ownership but also the responsibilities and obligations of ownership, which are often forgotten.

That is not, however, to devalue economic performance. Often economic performance, motivation and commitment are the basis of a company's capacity to perform in a social dimension. For larger companies the need to operate on a social scale is increased because of the magnitude of their decisions. Whereas small firms will have little impact on social structures around them, a large firm deciding to lay off large parts of its workforce, for example, will have a much bigger influence. Moreover, companies operating on an international scale (particularly those which are essentially transnational) will have an enormous social impact. They will have a complicated network of stakeholders to deal with, including governments, international agencies, workers and customers with very different cultures and often powerful pressure groups.

The dominance of competition

An intensely competitive environment, especially if coupled with a firm's inability to differentiate products substantially or to cement segments of the market, will tend to motivate unethical behaviour (Hartley, 1993). The actions of one or a few firms in a fiercely competitive industry may generate a follow-the-leader situation, requiring the more ethical competitors to choose lower profits or lower ethics. Moreover, in a fiercely competitive environment, the objective of the business organisation is dominated by the need to increase market share, to stay one step ahead of competitors, and therefore to adopt isolationist and independent strategies. To succeed in the marketplace, businesses feel the need to cut costs, to downgrade other objectives which might be perceived as expensive, and to cut corners where possible.

That is not to suggest that competition is bad, but that its dominance does mitigate against the opportunities which can be brought about through co-operation. Moreover, wider social issues are often overlooked because they are perceived as adding to costs with any benefits being somewhat intangible. The blind belief that competition is always in some way superior to other models means that alternative arrangements, such as co-operative strategies, public sector monopolies, not-for-profit organisations and local purchase and trading schemes, are often devalued. Yet, these alternatives often provide for outcomes which may be ethically, socially and environmentally superior.

Expediency and indifference

The attitude of expediency and indifference to customers' best interests accounts for both complacency and unethical practices. These attitudes, whether permeating an entire firm or affecting only a few individuals, are hardly conducive to repeat business and customer loyalty. They are more prevalent in firms with many small customers and in those firms where repeat business is relatively unimportant. To take an example, such attitudes also have an impact on environmental issues. They tend to mean that corners are cut and due care is not taken to protect the environment. They tend to increase the unnecessary use of resources and generate excessive waste, and to mitigate against the adoption of systems and procedures which can prevent accidents and environmental damage. Moreover, indifference and apathy tend to mitigate against accepting the responsibility which every individual and every organisation has in protecting the environment now and into the future.

Welford (1994) demonstrates that in the context of environmental issues, managers often have higher environmental ethics for themselves and their families than they do within the workplace. Whereas they are often complacent within the workforce, they see environmental improvement more generally as important to their own quality of life. This clear contradiction represents a 'free-rider problem'. While they want to see environmental improvement, they are unwilling to adjust their own behaviour in their workplace to achieve that, relying only on other people to make the changes required to improve overall environmental performance. Such indifference to the real importance of everyone working together is explained by an unwillingness to spend the time and effort considering what improvements managers might make themselves. Other priorities (often associated with profitability) are allowed to provide the excuse for inaction.

Dominant ideology and business strategy

Significant evidence exists that management trends which become popular exert a strong influence on the ongoing techniques of corporate management. New concepts which are successfully implemented in certain organisations become accepted, become dominant and even when they are inappropriate become the norm (Mintzberg, 1979). DiMaggio and Powell (1983) offer three explanations for this phenomenon. First, organisations will submit to both formal and informal pressures from other organisations on which they depend. Secondly, when faced with uncertainty, organisations may model themselves on organisations which have seemed to be successful and adopt the sorts of technique which they see being introduced. Thirdly, normative pressures, which stem from a degree of professionalism among management, can cause the adoption of 'fashionable' management techniques. Universities, training institutions, standard setters and professional associations are all vehicles for the development of normative rules. These are precisely the trends we are seeing in contemporary approaches to corporate responsibility, which are often piecemeal and sporadic. This piecemeal approach is becoming the accepted ideology because it is being adopted by leading firms, espoused by academics and legitimised by standard setters and policy makers.

The attitudes, values and actions of senior management will tend to form the culture in any organisation. In particular, the chief executive will tend to be very important in influencing the behaviour of the next tier of executives, and down the line to the shopfloor employees. We know that senior managers will tend to have a contagious influence, and too often they will have a vested interest more associated in short-term performance than in acting ethically. Acting ethically and in a socially responsible manner, therefore, often requires culture change from the top down, but if the chief executive is not keen to drive such change, then we must ask ourselves who will.

Related to the top executive's influence over a company are the often mechanistic management systems and structures which so often exist in the most inflexible organisations. These are in place because they are easy to control, but such structures will often stifle creativity. Moreover, any discussion relating to values will be second to structure, and this will too often define the firm's immediate interests as regards short-term performance. Customer and employee safety, integrity and environmental protection will be secondary considerations.

While senior management itself may not be directly involved in unethical practices, it often promotes such behaviour by strongly insisting on short-term profit maximisation and performance goals. When these goals are difficult to achieve and not achieving them can be met with severe penalties, the climate is set for undesirable conduct: deceptive advertising, overselling, adulterated products, inappropriate waste management practices, negligence towards environmental standards and other unethical behaviour. A clear alternative to the mechanistic, management-dominated approach is to encourage the participation of the workforce and make them feel valued. This, in turn, encourages commitment to the organisation and better work practices, and avoids problems associated with apathy and indifference (Welford, 1992).

STRUCTURAL BARRIERS TO ETHICAL BUSINESS AND CORPORATE SOCIAL RESPONSIBILITY

The very nature of the contemporary capitalist structure which stresses competition, the maximisation of profits and the reduction of costs acts as a fundamental barrier to the adoption of ethical practices in business. In many markets, particularly where oligopolistic structures exist, we often see strategies which are based on tacit collusion, where firms will follow dominant market leaders. It is often perceived that unless such a strategy is adopted, firms will be at a competitive disadvantage and their viability may even be threatened. Therefore, what becomes accepted business practice, by dominant companies, tends to permeate a whole industry, so that the dominant ideologies associated with the most profitable companies perpetuate themselves and set the tone for business strategies. In these circumstances it is market share and financial performance which come to dominate other measures of the success of the company.

On the other hand, in times when demand falls or when any organisation finds itself in a very competitive situation, financial indicators remain dominant and cost cutting often prevails. However, we know that in two major catastrophes, Bhopal and the Alaskan oil spill, cost cutting severely affected safety measures and contributed greatly to the gravity of the problem and the consequent handling of it (Hartley, 1993). Whatever the market structure, therefore, success is measured first and foremost on principles of financial management and wider ethical considerations are sidelined. The overemphasis on money, dictated by the economic system, therefore represents a barrier to the adoption of real corporate responsibility.

According to Donaldson (1989), however, the most serious barriers to improvement are not in the nature of people or business and industry, but are attitudinal. There is, therefore, a need to change attitudes via a change in the culture of an organisation. Central here is a commitment towards improved ethics. Many studies have demonstrated the ease with which the commitment of employees can be gained through methods associated with behavioural science (Luthans, 1985). While such techniques are sometimes criticised as being potentially manipulative, we must recognise that they hold great potential for increasing ethical behaviour. We are, however, not seeking a 'bolt-on' morality (so common with codes of conduct and standards), but a genuine attempt at introducing real ethical improvements.

This inevitably leads us on to considering whether current bureaucratic structures in society and industry are conducive to the introduction of systems which promote ethical behaviour. The stunted development of any consideration of alternative forms of bureaucracy provides us with a major challenge for the future.

There is a need for more innovation and imagination on the part of management. Co-operative and participative forms of industrial organisation have, for example, often been seen as appropriate only to alternative small artisan operations, or have been a last-resort attempt at rescuing businesses which are due to close for commercial reasons. Ethical concerns challenge us to look more closely at developments associated with industrial democracy and alternative industrial arrangements. The bureaucratic habits of hierarchy and the narrow distribution of power may not, in the end, be conducive to a sustainable future.

OPERATIONAL BARRIERS TO ETHICAL BUSINESS AND CORPORATE SOCIAL RESPONSIBILITY

Businesses are also prevented from acting in a more responsible way by ideologies relating to product responsibility, promotional activities and international trade which are based on custom and practice rather than any real evaluation of ethical considerations. There is an accepted code of conduct in each of these areas which, once again, stresses short-term performance, perceives change as being costly, and fundamentally devalues the rights of individual human beings. It is worth examining each of these issues in turn.

Product responsibility

The traditional view of a product is that once it is sold the responsibility for its safe use and disposal passes to the consumer. That cut-off point means that firms often do not consider the wider impacts caused by the use and disposal of their product. More forward-looking companies are now accepting that the product which they produce is fundamentally their responsibility from cradle to grave, and the most advanced companies have introduced product stewardship procedures to ensure that a product is used correctly and disposed of in an environmentally friendly way. However, this approach is yet to be found throughout industry, where the dominant ideology seems to stress the idea that property rights imply responsibility, so that as soon as such rights are transferred through the sale of the product, the company no longer has a duty of care against environmental damage.

Promotional activities

Promotional activities are designed to increase sales and are judged on the basis of so doing. Too many experiences of marketing strategies, to date, have been associated with exaggeration and deception. There is often a temptation in marketing departments to overemphasise a product's attributes. Unfortunately, moderation is not always practised. Mild exaggerations often multiply and become outright deception. With many products, false claims can be recognised by customers, who refuse to buy the product again. But where such claims cannot be easily substantiated, false claims are harder to detect. Nevertheless, pressure groups and competitors are always willing to expose unreasonable claims and that damages not only product sales but also the reputation of the firm. Advertising statements, if well presented and attractive, should induce customers to purchase the product, but if the expectations generated by advertisements are not realised, there will be no repeat business. Repeat business is the very thing most firms seek – a continuity of business, which means loyal and satisfied customers.

International trade

Many companies today do business worldwide and source their raw materials from a range of countries. Although this presents great opportunities, it also poses some problems, some ethical dilemmas and many opportunities for abuse. Unethical practices have a critical effect on the image of companies at home and abroad. Union Carbide's acceptance of lower operating standards in its Third World operations led to the Bhopal accident. The lesson to be learned is that standards and controls must be even more rigidly applied in countries where workers and managers may be less competent than they are in more economically and educationally advanced countries. A major ethical question also revolves around the sourcing of raw materials from parts of the world where indigenous populations are adversely affected. The drive for low-cost inputs leads to the exploitation of such people and the abuse of their land, and attacks their fundamental right to lead their lives as they would wish.

CORPORATE SOCIAL RESPONSIBILITY AND INDUSTRIAL DEMOCRACY

So, it is commonly claimed that there is an inevitable trade-off between profit and ethics or morals, and that the ultimate constraint to improved ethical behaviour is the need to show an acceptable rate of return on investment. The counter-claim is that behaving responsibly is good business and that taking an honest and ethical approach to industrial activities will lead to satisfied customers and repeat business. The problem with both of these arguments is twofold. First, they implicitly assume that we can measure ethics and thereby characterise the 'ethical firm' or provide lists of good or bad practices. The notion of the ethical firm is not only difficult to describe but attempting to do so is also fruitless. Secondly, both arguments implicitly assume an underlying business structure where the primary outcome is profitability, even though alternative models might be more applicable.

There is a need to look towards alternative ideas and alternative structures. Many of these actually require quite marginal changes but can bring about much improved outcomes. For example, there are key procedures associated with reforms in the workplace which firms can adopt that will push them along the path of more ethical behaviour. This revolves around issues of industrial democracy, respecting the values of everybody associated with an organisation and allowing diversity to exist. More open procedures and less hierarchical bureaucracy in decision making could be developed within organisations. This, in turn, needs to be linked to an ethical awareness-raising campaign both within and external to the firm, helping to raise the overall ethical profile.

The debate surrounding bureaucracy is too wide to go through here, but one of the most important points, and of direct relevance to the contemporary business scenario, is expounded by Argyris (1964). Argyris argues that firms typically place individuals in positions of passivity and dependency that are at odds with the needs of mature individuals. Bennis (1972) and Burns and Stalker (1963) go further in suggesting that bureaucracies are too inflexible to be able to adapt to changes in increasingly volatile and discriminating markets (*see also* Chapter 3). Traditional

→ Ch. 3

bureaucracies reserve decision making to the top of the organisation and decisions are subsequently handed down. Because of the narrow constituency involved in the decision-making process, they may not only be sub-optimal decisions but may be severely at odds with the values of a workforce. Bureaucracies hold within themselves methods of controlling and channelling information. Those with power in the bureaucracy will go to great lengths to ensure conformity to internal codes, and they have a great range of sanctions available to them for persuasion and enforcement. We have already argued that such codes may be at odds with more ethical behaviour. Flatter hierarchies, participative decision making and increased self-determination by workers seem to be initial obvious steps to be taken to begin to resolve such problems.

If increased industrial democracy better enables firms to act in ethical ways, and if the many advocates of participative arrangements (e.g. Welford, 1989) are right in suggesting that participation improves productivity and performance, then we need to consider why we have seen no manifestation of this form of industrial organisation. Any movement towards some form of corporate democracy is taking place slowly and in a piecemeal fashion, but it might be accelerated if legislation which more freely permits different styles of participation and democratic processes were to be introduced, thus doing away with the restrictive structure of authority and responsibility required by law which often inhibits moves in this direction.

SUMMARY

- CSR is now on the global policy agenda, with the impact of recent initiatives being that companies are increasingly being faced with the challenge of integrating ethical considerations into their production and marketing plans. There is always an incentive, however, for profit-maximising companies seeking short-term rewards to opt out of their ethical obligations towards corporate social responsibility. What is required, therefore, is a thorough re-examination of business ethics within any organisation and a change in ideology towards an acceptance by industry of its moral and social responsibilities.

- Perhaps one of the most important lessons which business organisations are beginning to learn relates to the desirability of seeking an honest and trusting relationship with customers (as well as with their other stakeholders). Such an ethical relationship requires concern for customer satisfaction, widely defined, and fair dealings. Objectives should be written in ethical terms and stress loyalty and repeat business. Such a philosophy and attitude must permeate an organisation. It can easily be short-circuited if a general climate of opportunism and severe financial performance pressures prevail.

- An honest and trusting relationship should not be sought with consumers or final users alone. It should characterise the relationship between sales representatives and their clients, which suggests no exaggeration or misrepresentation, greater efforts at understanding customers' needs and better servicing. It may even mean forgoing a sales opportunity when a customer's best interest may be better served by another product or at another time. The trusting relationship suggests repudiating any adversarial stance with employees, with suppliers and, beyond this, with all the communities in which a firm does business. Firms need to throw away ideologies based on financial performance alone and consider their corporate relationship with society. Such a relationship requires sound ethical conduct. It should foster a good reputation and public image.

■ It has been argued that the competitive nature of markets is often a barrier to responsible corporate performance and creates isolationist strategies. Unethical and unilateral actions may result in an initial competitive advantage, but may hurt a firm's overall image and reputation in the longer term. To have a coherent social strategy, firms need a consistent set of business ethics and need to measure their performance using a range of longer-term indicators. The notion of stakeholder accountability also reminds us that it is really not possible to separate ethical considerations from other issues such as the treatment of women and minority groups, the treatment of animals and the protection of indigenous populations. A set of ethics alone will not necessarily lead to better business practices, however. What we also require is a fundamental re-examination of dominant ideologies in the business world and culture change which is capable of challenging accepted wisdoms.

■ The rise of organised pressure groups and interest groups makes it doubly important that managers consider the arguments of all stakeholders in a decision's outcome. Since these groups publicly promote their causes in a single-minded way and do not, therefore, have the competing objectives so often faced by management, they have an advantage over the traditional company in the strong message which they can convey. Decisions taken in isolation by an elite group are therefore far more likely to result in sub-optimal outcomes.

■ The main thrust of the argument in this chapter, however, is that the major issues and arguments surrounding business ethics and corporate social responsibility are not so much substantive but more associated with procedures and received 'wisdom' associated with structures and hierarchies. It has been argued that these barriers to improved ethics can be removed through the removal of such traditional structures. We need to think carefully about putting a new emphasis on stakeholder accountability and a move towards new democratic forms of organisation within the workplace. There is nothing in the nature of people or businesses which makes adjustment towards ethical behaviour impossible. Vested interests held by those in power do have to be addressed, however, and this is one of the major challenges which we must overcome.

Review and discussion questions

1 *What is the link between corporate responsibility and business ethics?*

2 *Is it enough for business ethics to be defined so as to meet the legitimate needs of stakeholders?*

3 *How do differences in cultures often found in different countries make the role of the manager more difficult?*

4 *Do you consider that codes of conduct and standards simplify ethical dilemmas or simply reinforce accepted ideology (which may actually be unethical)?*

5 *What do you consider are the biggest barriers to improving corporate responsibility?*

6 *Is it always unethical to offer bribes when doing business internationally?*

CASE STUDY 17.1

Shell to face shareholder vote on ethics

Shell Transport & Trading, the UK arm of the Anglo-Dutch oil group, is facing a potentially embarrassing battle with some institutional shareholders over a resolution they have put down for the annual meeting in May. A group of shareholders holding just under 1 per cent of the company is calling on it to improve accountability by establishing new procedures for dealing with environmental and human rights issues. Pirc, the corporate governance consultant advising the shareholders, says the Shell resolution is the first of its kind in the UK. In the US, public companies regularly face resolutions from shareholders about environmental and social concerns.

The Shell shareholder group includes 18 public and private pension funds, five religious institutions, an academic fund, and individuals from a pressure group called the Ecumenical Committee on Corporate Responsibility. They say Shell's reputation has been damaged by controversies such as the aborted plan to sink the Brent Spar oil storage rig at sea and its environmental and human rights record in Nigeria. Their statement supporting the resolution says: 'Shareholders have a responsibility as owners to ensure that companies have structures and policies in place to enable them to operate to the highest standards, and that companies should

disclose to shareholders progress made in achieving improvements in performance. We believe that this resolution will help Shell accomplish these goals.'

In particular, the group wants a named member of Shell's committee of managing directors to take charge of environmental and corporate responsibility policies. It also wants Shell to agree to an external audit of these policies, and to publish a report to shareholders before the end of this year on its operations in Nigeria, which have been the focus of pressure group campaigning for several years.

Shell has denied allegations from pressure groups that it has contributed to pollution of the environment in the Niger Delta region and has assisted the Nigerian government's alleged persecution of the region's Ogoni tribe. Shell Transport & Trading, a UK quoted company, and Royal Dutch Petroleum, quoted in The Netherlands, own the Royal Dutch/Shell group on a 40:60 basis. The company confirmed that the resolution had been lodged and that shareholders would be voting on it at the annual general meeting. 'We are considering our response to it at the moment,' the company said, adding that the issues in the resolution were being covered by a company review of its Statement of General Business Principles, which deals with environmental issues.

Source: *Financial Times*, 24 February 1997. Reprinted with permission.

CASE STUDY 17.2

The UK Government's CSR strategy and web-based activity

The UK Government CSR strategy

The UK Government has provided a commitment to encourage the development of CSR and the following provides a summary of the national vision, strategy, and priorities and keynote action areas, as outlined in the UK Government's Department of Trade and Industry, *Business and Society: Corporate Social Responsibility Report 2002*. This report can be downloaded from http://www.societyandbusiness.gov.uk,

which is the UK Government's corporate social responsibility website.

Vision

The UK Government's vision for corporate social responsibility is: to see private, voluntary and public sector organisations in the UK take account of their economic, social and environmental impacts, and take complementary action to address key challenges based on their core competences – locally, regionally, nationally and internationally.

Strategy

The UK Government's strategy for advancing its vision is to:

- Promote activities that bring economic, social and environmental benefits;
- Work in partnership with a range of organisations, including the private sector, community bodies, unions, consumers and other stakeholders;
- Encourage innovative approaches and good practice in CSR;
- Define minimum levels of performance; and
- Encourage awareness, trust and healthy public dialogue on CSR.

The UK Government's CSR strategy is tied to its strategy for sustainable development, with its aims of social progress, protection of the environment, prudent use of natural resources, and economic growth and employment.

Priorities and keynote actions

The UK strategy addresses five priority issues and identifies key action points in each area, with these being to:

- Raise the profile and highlight the importance of CSR
  Action: The Government states that it will take full account of opportunities to increase the adoption and reporting of CSR (see http://defra.gov.uk *for the New General Guidelines on Environment Reporting) as part of a continuing review of intelligent regulation and fiscal incentives.*
- Make responsible behaviour considerations integral to the decision-making processes of organisations
  Action: The Government states that it will take steps to establish CSR within the mainstream decision-making of organisations, with a strong focus on the following areas: the environment, neighbourhood renewal, adult basic skills and international developments (see, http://www.societyandbusiness.gov.uk *for further details).*
- Assist the involvement of small and medium-sized enterprises (SMEs) in CSR initiatives

Action: The Government states that it will create a step change in the consistency and quality of CSR guidance to SMEs by stimulating a joint approach among their key advisory organizations (see http://www.societyandbusiness.gov.uk *for further details).*

- Promote greater transparency in CSR reporting and awareness
  Action: The Government states that it will consult widely with all stakeholders to ensure that greater transparency and clarity is brought to the current confusing set of reporting models and codes of practice (see for example, http://unglobalcompact.org, http://ilo.org, http://ftse4good.com *and* http://oecd.org *for a range of such initiatives).*
- Promote and facilitate good practice in CSR internationally as well as domestically
  Action: The Government states that it will support the development of the Ethical Trading Initiative (see http://ethicaltrade.org *for further details) and other international, as well as national, work on best practice.*

These keynote policies are supported by steps to improve the impact and example of the Government's own activities, including consideration, within the policy and legal framework, of departmental and public procurement practices.

Web-based activity instructions

Please ensure that you read the case above and consult the UK Government CSR website (http://www.societyandbusiness.gov.uk) before completing the activity. Consulting the additional web links provided should also assist you.

The task

Drawing on the UK Government strategy for CSR:

- consider how the UK Government defines CSR;
- outline further the UK Government's vision and strategy for CSR; and
- discuss the difficulties that the UK Government might encounter when implementing its strategy and in particular the priority/keynote action areas identified.

Source: Department of Trade and Industry, (2002). *Business and Society: Corporate Social Responsibility Report 2002*, London: DTI.

REFERENCES AND FURTHER READING

Argyris, C (1964) *Integrating the Individual and the Organization*, New York: John Wiley.

Bennis, W (1972) 'A Funny Thing Happened on the Way to the Future', in Thomas, J and Bennis, W (eds) *The Management of Change and Conflict*, Harmondsworth: Penguin Books.

Bloom, H, Calori, R and de Woot, P (1994) *Euromanagement: A New Style for the Global Market*, London: Kogan Page.

Burke, T, Maddock, S and Rose, A (1993) *How Ethical is British Business?*, Research Working Paper, Series 2, No. 1, University of Westminster.

Burns, T and Stalker, G (1963) *The Management of Innovation*, London: Tavistock Press.

Chryssides, G D and Kaler, J H (1993) *An Introduction to Business Ethics*, London: Chapman & Hall.

Department of Trade and Industry (DTI) (2002) *Business and Society: Corporate Social Responsibility Report 2002*, London: DTI.

DiMaggio, P J and Powell, W (1983) 'The Iron Cage Revisited: Institutional Isomorphism and Collective Rationality in Organisational Fields', *American Sociological Review*, 48: 147–60.

Donaldson, J (1989) *Key Issues in Business Ethics*, San Diego, CA: Academic Press.

Donaldson, J and Waller, M (1980) 'Ethics and Organisation', *Journal of Management Studies*, 17 (1).

ENDS (1993) 'Jury Still Out on Responsible Care', *Industry Report No 55*, ENDS 222, July.

Friedman, M (1963) *Capitalism and Freedom*, Chicago, IL: Phoenix Books, University of Chicago Press.

Hartley, R F (1993) *Business Ethics: Violations of the Public Trust*, New York: John Wiley.

Holloway, R J and Hancock, R S (1968) *Marketing in a Changing Environment*, New York: John Wiley.

Hopkins, M (2003) *The Planetary Bargain: Corporate Social Responsibility Matters*, London: Earthscan.

Kroeber, L and Kluckhohn, L (1952) *Culture*, New York: Vintage Books.

Luthans, F (1985) *Organizational Behaviour* (4th edn), New York: McGraw-Hill.

Mintzberg, H (1979) *The Structuring of Organizations*, New York: Prentice-Hall.

Mole, J (1990) *Mind your Manners: Culture Clash in the Single European Market*, London: The Industrial Society.

Smith, C (2003) 'Corporate Social Responsibility: Whether or How?', *California Management Review*, 45 (4).

Welford, R J (1989) 'Growth and the Performance Participation Nexus: The Case of UK Producer Cooperatives', *Economic Analysis and Workers' Management*, 23.

Welford, R J (1992) 'Linking Quality and the Environment: A Strategy for the Implementation of Environmental Management Systems', *Business Strategy and the Environment*, 1 (1).

Welford, R J (1994) 'Barriers to the Improvement of Environmental Performance', in Welford, R J (ed.), *Cases in Environmental Management and Business Strategy*, London: Pitman Publishing.

Welford, R J, Prescott, K and Mercado, S (2001) *European Business: An Issue Based Approach*, Harlow: FT Prentice Hall.

Westing, J H (1968) 'Some Thoughts on the Nature of Ethics in Marketing', in Mayer, R (ed.), *Marketing Systems*, 1967 Winter Conference Proceedings, Chicago, IL: Marketing Association.

Zadek, S (2001) *The Civil Corporation: The New Economy of Corporate Citizenship*, London: Earthscan and the New Economics Foundation.

WEBSITES

http://defra.gov.uk
This is the website of the UK Government Department of Environment, Food and Rural Affairs. Of particular interest are the new General Guidelines on Environment Reporting, developed in partnership with the Department of Trade and Industry (DTI) and the Confederation of British Industry (CBI). These guidelines explain in a comprehensive way the basics of how to produce an environment report and suggest contents and key indicators to report against.

http://ethicaltrade.org
This is the website of the Ethical Trading Initiative (ETI) which was set up in 1998. Corporate members of the ETI include major high street names, with a combined annual turnover estimated to be almost £100 billion, with these businesses addressing supply chain issues such as working hours and the 'living wage', rights-based and related issues.

http://europa.eu.int
This website will provide access to the European Union's corporate social responsibility Green Paper, which was published in July 2001, the consultation documents and the 250 responses received.

http://ilo.org
This website will provide access to the 1988 Declaration on Fundamental Principles and Rights at Work of the International Labour Organisation (ILO). This establishes internationally agreed core labour standards and provides commitments to eliminating the worst forms of child labour, slavery and forced labour, and to uphold workers freedom

of association and the right to work free of discrimination. This website will also provide access to the ILO Tripartite Declaration of Principles Concerning Multinational Enterprises and Social Policy (1977, amended 2000). This sets out guidelines for action by governments, multinational enterprises and workers' and employers' organisations.

http://ftse4good.com

This is the website of the FTSE4Good which was introduced by the FTSE in May 2001. Of particular interest are the four socially responsible investment (SRI) indices covering UK, European, US and global companies. These are used to list companies which demonstrate responsible behaviour on human rights, the environment and society. An independent committee of 14 international experts undertakes a review of the indices every six months, with the scheme being supported by UNICEF.

http://oecd.org

This is the website of the Organisation for Economic Co-operation and Development (OECD). Of particular interest are the voluntary guidelines for multinational enterprises which set out government expectations of business behaviour globally in areas such as environment, labour and disclosure. Although voluntary, they do contain a mechanism whereby concerns about the activities of multinationals can be brought to the attention of signatory governments.

http://www.societyandbusiness.gov.uk

This is the UK Government's corporate social responsibility website. Of particular interest is the Department of Trade and Industry, *Business and Society: Corporate Social Responsibility Report 2002*.

http://unglobalcompact.org

This is the website of the UN Global Compact, which was launched in July 2000. This encourages companies to build human rights, labour and environmental principles into their business strategies for the developing world. Many leading companies, such as Shell, BP, Rio Tinto, BG Group and Unilever, have signed up to the Compact.

CHAPTER 18

Environmental issues and corporate environmental management

RICHARD WELFORD AND PETER A. STRACHAN

Outcomes

Having read this chapter, you will be able to:

- explain why there has been a growth in public and corporate environmental awareness in recent years

- explain the strategic and functional issues which environmental issues place on business

- discuss a range of management strategies to improve a company's environmental performance

- outline the components of the environmental management systems ISO 14001 and the Eco-Management and Audit Scheme (EMAS) Regulation

- discuss the concept of product stewardship and the EU's eco-labelling Regulation

INTRODUCTION

Over the last 40 years there has been a growing interest in the environment or, more specifically, in the damage being done to the environment worldwide. In Europe the process of integration has brought the transnational nature of the environmental problem to the forefront of the social, political and corporate agenda. Environmental problems and issues such as the hole in the ozone layer, climate change and global warming are the result of not one country's action but that of many. Acid rain, which is polluting rivers and lakes and damaging forests, often emanates from one country and is deposited in another.

The effects of different industrial sectors on the environment vary enormously. At one end of the spectrum we might put multinational oil companies, whose very business is environmentally damaging, and at the other end we might put retailers and the service sector, who have less of a direct impact on the environment, although, in most cases, they could still make environmental improvements through recycling and improved transportation policies. There is still much confusion for both consumers and companies about what constitutes an environmentally friendly product or operation, and the 'green revolution' to date has provided few answers, although many misrepresentations, particularly in the area of product marketing, have been exposed.

At the root of some of the environmental problems we face is the growth in consumerism and materialism. The notion that 'the consumer is king' may drive the market mechanism, but the overemphasis placed on the satisfaction of customers' wants in the developed economies of the world has had a profound effect on our planet's ability to sustain life and on biodiversity. It is generally accepted that the world cannot go on using the resources of the planet at the present rate, but there is a 'free-rider problem' at work. Everyone thinks that something should be done, but many people just assume that everyone else will do it, and since their individual impact is minute, it will not matter to the environment.

Everything that consumers, companies and other institutions do will have some impact on the environment, but the emphasis in this chapter is placed on the strategies that organisations can follow to improve their environmental performance. Even substances which, in their final form, are environmentally benign may have been unfriendly in their manufacture, especially if that manufacture was energy greedy. They may have been produced using non-renewable resources and may also pose problems after they have been used and come to be disposed of. If we take what is commonly called a cradle-to-the-grave view of products, where we examine their environmental impact through their life cycle from raw material usage to disposal, then there are few, if any, products which will not have some negative impact on the environment. The key question is, therefore, not how we completely eliminate environmental damage, but how we reduce it over time, and how we achieve a state of balance such that the amount of environmental damage done is repairable and therefore sustainable.

Industry, particularly in the developed world, must increasingly take into account the costs of the effects of its operations on the environment, rather than regarding the planet as a free resource. In the past, few companies have counted the costs of the pollution which they discharged into the atmosphere, and the debate has now turned to legislation aimed at forcing companies to comply with certain standards and taxing firms which pollute. The so-called 'polluter pays' principle is now central to legislation in the developed countries. The implication here is clearly that prices will rise for consumers as organisations experience increased costs associated with environmental improvements. Less energy consumption and more efficient use of resources are obvious targets for improvement and should not conflict with industry's aims, since their attainment can actually reduce costs. Many materials are already recycled and a thriving, and at times profitable, recycling industry has been established across Europe.

Many of the products now considered to be environmentally hazardous were at the time of their discovery regarded as an invaluable resource. The best example of this has been the use of chlorofluorocarbons in refrigerators, which have since been found to be a major ozone-depleting agent. Predicting a product's long-term impact on the environment is a difficult process and, until recently, has rarely been done. This will change as firms are forced to consider cradle-to-grave management of their products and as we increasingly give the benefit of doubt to the welfare of the planet. Moreover, industry has a responsibility to ensure that its products are less harmful to the environment and there is a need to push along a very steep environmental learning curve.

Many governments across Europe have been implementing increasingly stringent environmental legislation. At the level of the European Union there has been an emphasis on the provision of information about products and processes to the public. However, a common problem is that the statutory bodies which do exist with responsibility for monitoring the environmental performance of organisations have limited resources and powers in most cases. Organisations themselves have often, in the past, been shown to be ignorant of current environmental legislation, particularly with regard to EU environmental directives and legislation on issues such as waste disposal, air pollution and water quality. However, such ignorance is not an excuse for non-compliance. Moreover, non-compliance which can be attributed to negligence cannot only result in fines but also occasionally in imprisonment for company directors.

In the USA the Environmental Protection Agency (EPA) is an independent environmental body with significant power. In 1980 the US Congress passed the Comprehensive Environmental Response, Compensation and Liability Act, better known as Superfund. Under the provisions of the Act, companies must report potentially toxic spills and releases greater than a clearly defined minimum. Violations of this are criminal offences with penalties of up to one year in jail and a significant fine. Superfund also deals with uncontrolled hazardous waste sites, where previous or present owners and operators of a site must help pay for whatever remedial action is necessary. If the previous firm has gone out of business, the EPA has often managed to obtain funds from companies which sent the waste there for treatment or disposal in the first instance. In the UK, by contrast, local authority regulators and pollution inspectors all adopt an approach of constructive engagement with companies rather than fining them in the first instance for pollution violations.

The rapid growth of public environmental awareness in recent years has placed new pressures on industry. These pressures can take many forms as individuals collectively exercise their environmental conscience as customers, employees, investors, voters, neighbours and fellow citizens. However, whether it is due to intellectual fatigue with environmental issues, a lack of conviction that an individual's own actions will have an impact or a reluctance to reduce private consumption for public welfare, many individuals seemingly prefer to pass their responsibilities on to those parties that they feel can make a significant impact. The two major parties that the public perceive can make a difference are government and industry. Given the public's inherent reluctance to reduce its own levels of consumption, it is apparent that government and industry must respond in order to protect the environment effectively.

USING THE PRICE MECHANISM TO ALLEVIATE POLLUTION

The use of the market mechanism to distribute goods and services in the West, with its consequent stress on property rights, has contributed to the environmental degradation which we have experienced. Much of the environment (particularly the air and atmosphere) is treated as a free good since no individual owns it and there are no assigned property rights to it. Firms and consumers have therefore made excessive use of environmental resources both as an input and as a source of output (or sink). This is illustrated in Figure 18.1.

Suppose that a firm produces a good and in the process of doing so it pollutes the air around it. Traditionally, and ignoring legislation which might or might not exist, the firm can do this freely since no one owns the air. Assume that the demand for the product is D_1 and the production and marketing costs of the firm imply that it is willing to sell along a supply curve given by S_1. Essentially, S_1 is drawn based on only the private costs of the firm, that is, those which it must pay in a monetary form, but the pollution imposed on the local community imposes a cost on them and on society as a whole. If the firm was required to internalise those costs, either by paying a tax to pollute based on an estimate of the social cost that that pollution imposed (the tax might subsequently be used to clean up the pollution), or by the use of legislation banning the pollution, meaning that the firm would have to invest in a new non-polluting process, then its own costs would rise. The firm's willingness to supply at any particular price would be reduced and S_1 would shift backwards to S_2. The equilibrium in the market would shift from P_1q_1 to P_2q_2. Thus, less of the good would be produced and at a higher price.

Figure 18.1 Using the market mechanism to deal with environmental damage

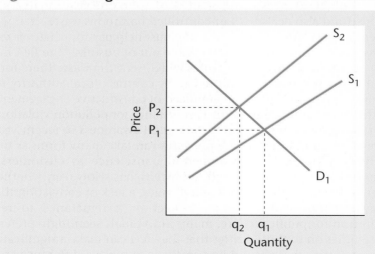

The premise on which most developed countries' environmental legislation has largely been based is the 'polluter pays' principle. In other words, this is a notion that public money should not be used in clearing up or avoiding pollution but, as described above, the polluters themselves should face those costs. From a welfare point of view, the difference between a firm compensating a local community for the pollution it creates and the community paying the firm not to pollute is purely distributional, but from an ethical perspective, it is often argued that the 'polluter pays' principle is superior.

We might extend the sort of analysis described by Figure 18.1 to the economy as a whole. Since most processes will impose at least some negative impact on the environment, the fact that the environment has not been properly costed and treated as a free good over time has meant that we have produced too many goods. Moreover, we might hypothesise that mass-production techniques which have enabled firms to produce more and more goods and to charge lower prices have been particularly damaging.

SUSTAINABLE DEVELOPMENT

The belief which lies behind the concept of sustainable development is that there is a trade-off between continuous economic growth and the sustainability of the environment. Over time growth causes pollution and atmospheric damage. The concept of sustainable development stresses the interdependence between economic growth and environmental quality. It is possible to make development and environmental protection compatible by following sustainable strategies and by not developing the particular areas of economic activity that are most damaging to the environment.

The Brundtland Report (World Commission on Environment and Development, 1987), commissioned by the United Nations to examine long-term environmental strategies, argued that economic development and environmental protection could be made compatible, but that this would require quite radical changes in economic practices throughout the world. They defined sustainable development as:

> *'development that meets the needs of the present without compromising the ability of future generations to meet their own needs.'*

In other words, mass consumption is not possible indefinitely, and if society today acts as if all non-renewable resources are plentiful, eventually there will be nothing left for the future. More importantly than that, however, mass consumption may cause such irreparable damage that humans may not even be able to live on the planet in the future.

The challenge that faces the economic system is how to continue to fulfil its vital role within modern society while working towards sustainability. Complying with the principles of sustainability cannot be achieved overnight. However, both for entire economies and for individual businesses, there is hope that it can be achieved within the time scales which appear to be necessary if environmental catastrophe is to be avoided.

According to Welford (1993), sustainable development is made up of three closely connected issues and associated conditions:

■ **Environment.** The environment must be valued as an integral part of the economic process and not treated as a free good. The environmental stock has to be protected, which implies minimal use of non-renewable resources and minimal emission of pollutants. The ecosystem has to be protected so the loss of plant and animal species has to be avoided.

- **Equity.** One of the biggest threats facing the world is that the developing countries want to grow rapidly to achieve the same standards of living as those in the West. That in itself would cause a major environmental disaster if it were modelled on the same sort of growth as experienced in post-war Europe. Therefore, there needs to be a greater degree of equity and the key issue of poverty has to be addressed, but it seems hypocritical for the West to tell the Third World that it cannot attain the same standards of living and consumption.

- **Futurity.** Sustainable development requires that society, businesses and individuals operate on a different time scale than currently operates in the economy. While companies commonly operate under competitive pressures to achieve short-term gains, long-term environmental protection is often compromised. To ensure that longer-term, intergenerational considerations are observed, longer planning horizons need to be adopted and business policy needs to be proactive rather than reactive.

The Brundtland Report concludes that these three conditions are not being met. The industrialised world has already used much of the planet's ecological capital and many of the development paths of the industrialised nations are clearly unsustainable. Non-renewable resources are being depleted, while renewable resources such as soil, water and the atmosphere are being degraded. This has been caused by economic development, but in time will undermine the very foundations of that development.

Like the Brundtland Report, more recent initiatives by the United Nations, including the Earth Summit held in Rio in 1992 and the World Summit on Sustainable Development (Rio+10) held in Johannesburg in 2002, call for development which is environmentally and socially sustainable rather than the current situation of unplanned, undifferentiated growth. This means reconsidering the current measures of growth, such as gross national product (GNP), which fail to take account of environmental debits such as pollution or the depletion of the natural capital stock. While concern about the depletion of materials and energy resources has diminished since the 1970s, there is nevertheless concern surrounding the environment's capacity to act as a sink for waste. For example, bringing developing countries' energy use up to the level of the developing world's would mean an increase in consumption by a factor of five. Using present energy-generation methods, the planet could not cope with the impact of sulphur dioxide and carbon dioxide emissions and the consequential acidification and global warming of the environment.

One major obstacle preventing sustainability from being achieved is the overall level of consumption. However, Western consumers are apparently reluctant to reduce significantly their own levels of consumption. While governments are increasingly adopting economic instruments such as taxes, subsidies and product-labelling schemes to reduce and channel consumption towards more environmentally friendly alternatives, industry itself must be encouraged further to increase environmental efficiency.

Sustainability challenges industry to produce higher levels of output while using lower levels of input and generating less waste. The problem that remains is that while relative environmental impact per unit of output has fallen, increases in the absolute level of output, and hence environmental impact, have more than offset any gains in relative environmental efficiency. However, if we examine the ways in which environmental efficiency has been improved, then we can begin to understand some of the key practical elements with which sustainability may be better promoted.

CORPORATE RESPONSES TO SUSTAINABLE DEVELOPMENT

Organisations are faced with a challenge of integrating environmental considerations into their production and marketing plans. There is always an incentive, however, for profit-maximising firms seeking short-term rewards to opt out and become a free-rider (assuming that everyone else will be environmentally conscious such that their own pollution will become negligible). However, European Union environmental legislation is increasingly plugging the gaps which allow this to happen, and firms attempting to hide their illegal pollution are now subject to severe penalties. In many cases individual company directors can also be prosecuted and imprisoned for negligence which leads to environmental damage. Even before then, businesses should recognise that it is not only ethical to be environmentally friendly, but with the growth of consumer awareness in the environmental area, it will also be good business.

Organisations clearly have a role to play in the development of substitutes for non-renewable resources and innovations which reduce waste and use energy more efficiently. They also have a role in processing those materials in a way which brings about environmental improvements. For many products (e.g. cars and washing machines), the major area of environmental damage occurs in their usage. Organisations often have the opportunity of reducing this damage at the design stage, and when new products are being developed there is a whole new opportunity for considering both the use and disposal of the product.

Given the internal and external demands to improve the environmental performance of organisations, those that achieve high standards of environmental performance will benefit in a number of ways. In order to realise this competitive advantage, organisations must seek to develop management strategies which will improve their environmental performance and address the environmental demands placed on them by government, the EU and stakeholders. By incorporating the increasingly important environmental dimension into the decision-making processes of the organisation, managers can seek to reduce costs and exploit the opportunities offered by increased public environmental concern within a dynamic marketplace. Such a strategy must be proactive and honest. It may also involve a degree of education and campaigning, such as that undertaken by The Body Shop, but more than anything, it must be ethical.

The general principles of such a strategy are embodied within the International Chamber of Commerce (ICC)/World Business Council for Sustainable Development (WBCSD) Business Charter for Sustainable Development. The key elements to this strategy are embodied in 16 'Principles for Environmental Management'. Organisations are encouraged to endorse the following aims:

1 **Corporate priority** – to recognise environmental management as among the highest corporate priorities and as a key determinant to sustainable development; to establish policies, programmes and practices for conducting operations in an environmentally sound manner.

2 **Integrated management** – to integrate these policies, programmes and practices fully into each business as an essential element of management in all its functions.

3 **Process of improvement** – to continue to improve corporate policies, programmes and environmental performance, taking into account technical developments, scientific understanding, consumer needs and community expectations, with legal regulations as a starting point; and to apply the same environmental criteria internationally.

4 **Employee education** – to educate, train and motivate employees to conduct their activities in an environmentally responsible manner.

5 **Prior assessment** – to assess environmental impacts before starting a new activity or project and before decommissioning a facility or leaving a site.

6 **Products and services** – to develop and provide products and services that have no undue environmental impact and are safe in their intended use, that are efficient in their consumption of energy and natural resources, and that can be recycled, re-used or disposed of safely.

7 **Customer advice** – to advise, and where relevant educate, customers, distributors and the public in the safe use, transportation, storage and disposal of products provided; and to apply similar considerations to the provision of services.

8 **Facilities and operations** – to develop, design and operate facilities and conduct activities taking into consideration the efficient use of energy and raw materials, the sustainable use of renewable resources, the minimisation of adverse environmental impact and waste generation, and the safe and responsible disposal of residual wastes.

9 **Research** – to conduct or support research on the environmental impacts of raw materials, products, processes, emissions and wastes associated with the enterprise and on the means of minimising such adverse impacts.

10 **Precautionary approach** – to modify the manufacture, marketing or use of products or services to the conduct of activities, consistent with scientific and technical understanding, to prevent serious or irreversible environmental degradation.

11 **Contractors and suppliers** – to promote the adoption of these principles by contractors acting on behalf of the enterprise, encouraging and, where appropriate, requiring improvements in their practices to make them consistent with those of the enterprise; and to encourage the wider adoption of these principles by suppliers.

12 **Emergency preparedness** – to develop and maintain, where appropriate hazards exist, emergency preparedness plans in conjunction with the emergency services, relevant authorities and the local community, recognising potential cross-boundary impacts.

13 **Transfer of technology** – to contribute to the transfer of environmentally sound technology and management methods throughout the industrial and public sectors.

14 **Contributing to the common effort** – to contribute to the development of public policy and to business, governmental and intergovernmental programmes and educational initiatives that will enhance environmental awareness and protection.

15 **Openness to concerns** – to foster openness and dialogue with employees and the public, anticipating and responding to their concerns about the potential hazards and impacts of operations, products, wastes or services, including those of transboundary or global significance.

16 **Compliance and reporting** – to measure environmental performance; to conduct regular environmental audits and assessments of compliance with company requirements and these principles; and periodically to provide appropriate information to the board of directors, shareholders, employees, the authorities and the public.

This Business Charter for Sustainable Development is one of the most widely supported business and environment charters, with over 1500 signatories worldwide, including leading companies such as Shell, BOC, British Airways, ICI, British Gas, Samsung, General Motors and Ford. Many of these companies have implemented the Charter's recommendations within existing environmental initiatives and management systems.

THE EUROPEAN INTEGRATION PROCESS AND CORPORATE ENVIRONMENTAL MANAGEMENT

The original Treaty of Rome was concerned with stimulating economic growth and contained no specific reference to the environment. Since then, however, EU environmental policy has developed in line with general concern in Europe and the deteriorating environmental position in which Europe finds itself. By 2003, over 300 pieces of environmental legislation had been passed covering pollution of the air and water, noise pollution, chemicals, waste, environmental impact assessment, the prevention of industrial accidents and wildlife protection. Exhibit 18.1 outlines the principal EU landmarks up to 2003.

However, few member states have been able to enforce EU legislation fully. Denmark is probably the only country with a consistently good record and the southern European countries have consistently bad records. Once again, this highlights the emphasis often given to economic growth rather than environmental

Exhibit 18.1 Examples of important EU landmarks

1967	First Environmental Directive, on classification, packaging and labelling of dangerous substances (67/548)
1970	Directive establishing framework for measures to combat air pollution from motor vehicles (70/220)
1973	Launch of first European environment action programme 1973–76
1979	Birds Directive, on the protection of birds and their habitats (79/409)
1980	Directive laying down minimum standards for drinking water (80/778)
1985	Directive on Environmental Impact Assessment (85/337)
1990	Directives to limit the use and release of genetically modified organisms (GMOs) (90/219 and 90/220)
1991	Maastricht Treaty Article 6 lays down that all EU policies and activities must integrate environmental protection
1992	Habitats Directive, on the conservation of natural habitats and wild flora and fauna (92/43)
1994	European Environment Agency established
1999	Start of Green Week, the annual EU environmental conferences
2000	Framework Directive for European policy on water (2000/60)
2001	Launch of the Sixth Environmental Action Programme 2001–10: Environment 2010, Our Future, Our Choice
2002	Ratification of the Kyoto Protocol on Climate Change

Source: EC (2002, p 8)

protection, with the primary aim of countries such as Spain and Portugal being the attainment of similar living standards to the rest of the Union.

The Single European Act gave environmental policy a boost, stating that there is not only a need for such legislation but that the laws should meet three key objectives:

■ **preservation, protection and improvement of the quality of the environment**

■ **protection of human health**

■ **prudent and rational use of natural resources.**

These objectives must be met by applying four principles:

■ **prevention of harm to the environment**

■ **control of pollution at source**

■ **the polluter should pay**

■ **integration of environmental considerations into other European Union policies** (all EU policies are now required to take the environment into account).

The Internal Market Programme has added a new note of urgency to environmental problems. The relationship between economic growth and the environment has returned to centre stage. Clearly, there exists a major opportunity with industrial and legislative restructuring to put into place the appropriate financial and regulatory mechanisms that would make the internal market environmentally sustainable. The extent to which this happens will be seen over time, but the Single European Act also provides the necessary constitutional basis for a forceful environmental response. Perhaps the strongest part of this is the requirement that policy makers should make environmental considerations a component of all the European Union's other policies.

In 2001, the European Union introduced its Sixth Environmental Action Programme, setting out priorities for action, practical objectives and the means to achieve them in the areas of climate change, nature and biodiversity, environment and health and quality of life, and natural resources and waste. The Sixth Environmental Action Programme provides the environmental component of the European Union's strategy for sustainable development until 2010, with the objectives being set out in Exhibit 18.2.

Exhibit 18.2 Objectives of the EU's Sixth Environmental Action Programme

1 To stabilize the atmospheric concentrations of greenhouse gases at a level that will not cause unnatural variations of the earth's climate.

2 To protect and restore the functioning of natural systems and halt the loss of biodiversity in the European Union and globally. To protect soils against erosion and pollution.

3 To achieve a quality of the environment where the levels of man-made contaminants, including different types of radiation, do not give rise to significant impacts or risks to human health.

4 To ensure the consumption of renewable and non-renewable resources does not exceed the carrying capacity of the environment. To achieve a de-coupling of resource use from economic growth through significantly improved resource efficiency, dematerialization of the economy, and waste prevention.

Source: EC (2001, pp 4–5)

The First Environmental Action Programme launched in 1973 set out a number of principles which have formed the basis of environmental action in the EU ever since, with these remaining important when examining the strategic aims of EU environmental policy more broadly. The aims are set out in Exhibit 18.3.

The main activities of the EU in the environmental policy arena, until 1987, were centred on the application of nearly 200 command and control directives in areas as diverse as lead in petrol and aircraft noise. More recently, realising that environmental policy is of little use unless enforced, EU environmental policy has given increased emphasis to the improved enforcement of existing legislation, with this being an important component of the Sixth Environmental Action Programme. Emphasis has also shifted from the use of traditional command-and-control instruments in environmental policy to the application of economic market-based instruments such as the proposed carbon tax, and voluntary initiatives such as the eco-labelling and eco-management and audit schemes (*see* below). The aim of such measures is to encourage change in all sectors of industry and society in a more general way than can be achieved through the use of tightly defined legislative instruments. Economic instruments and voluntary measures are seen as complementing rather than substituting for the more traditional application of command-and-control measures.

The EU view of the future of environmental policy and its interface with industrial development is clear. With over 400 million inhabitants, the European Union is the largest trading bloc in the world, and so is in a critical position to take the

Exhibit 18.3 The EU's environmental principles

1 Prevention is better than cure.
2 Environmental effects should be taken into account at the earliest possible stage in decision making.
3 Exploitation of nature and natural resources which causes significant damage to the ecological balance must be avoided. The natural environment can only absorb pollution to a limited extent. Nature is an asset which may be used but not abused.
4 Scientific knowledge should be improved to enable action to be taken.
5 The 'polluter pays' principle: the polluter should pay for preventing and eliminating environmental nuisance.
6 Activities in one member state should not cause environmental deterioration in another.
7 Environmental policies of member states must take account of the interests of developing countries.
8 The EU and member states should act together in international organisations and in promoting international environmental policy.
9 Education of citizens is necessary as the protection of the environment is a matter for everyone.
10 The principle of action at the appropriate level: for each type of pollution it is necessary to establish the level of action which is best suited for achieving the protection required, be it local, regional, national, EU-wide or international.
11 National environmental policies must be co-ordinated within the EU without impinging on progress at the national level. It is intended that implementation of the action programme and gathering of environmental information by the proposed European Environment Agency will secure this.

Source: Official Journal of the European Communities: C112 20.12.73

lead in moving towards sustainability. The Commission accepts that tighter environmental policy will have an impact on the costs of industry. However, a high level of environmental protection has increasingly become not only a policy objective of its own, but also a precondition of industrial expansion. In this respect, a new impetus towards a better integration of policies aiming at consolidating industrial competitiveness and at achieving a high level of protection of the environment is necessary in order to make the two objectives fully mutually supportive.

These views are given more substance within the Sixth Environmental Action Programme, and a number of specific measures relating to industry are included. Perhaps most importantly, the commitment of the EU to strengthen environmental policy is underlined. The EU shares the view that urgent action is needed for environmental protection, and that many of the great environmental struggles will be won or lost in the next ten years. Further, it states that achieving sustainability will demand practical and political commitment over an extended period and that the EU, as the largest trading bloc in the world, must exercise its responsibility and commit itself to that goal.

For industries and companies that are facing a rising tide of environmental legislation, it is essential that attempts are made to find out about and then positively address the legislative pressures which they are under. However, the Sixth Environmental Action Programme primarily focuses on the improved enforcement of existing legislation as a key objective rather than the adoption of new legislation. To some extent this should allow industry to take stock of the rapid increase in environmental legislation that has taken place in recent years and to focus on achieving compliance with existing legislation. Despite the stated objective to concentrate on the effective implementation of existing policy, there are many pieces of environmental legislation in the EU policy pipeline which are awaiting final adoption. Many of these measures have fundamental implications for business, and it therefore remains essential to track forthcoming legislation.

Furthermore, the Sixth Environmental Action Programme reiterates the aspiration that environmental policy should be fully incorporated into all other European Union policies (sometimes known as 'mainstreaming'). Therefore, while it may become easier to track the development of policies which are explicitly environmental, it will become more difficult to monitor the development of environmental policy throughout the activities of the Commission as a whole. The European Environment Agency now collects data and monitors compliance throughout the European Union and disseminates information to all interested parties. It is being proactive in encouraging all firms (including smaller enterprises) to take environmental issues more seriously.

The strategic significance of the EU's views cannot be overstated. By taking a long-term, EU-wide perspective and accepting that industrial competitiveness is enhanced by tight environmental legislation, the policy framework within which all European organisations must participate will reflect these views. Some organisations, some regions and some nations will benefit. If the views of the EU are correct, the economic prospects of the European Union as a whole will benefit and the environment will certainly benefit. However, at the organisation level, realising these benefits will not be automatic, and strategic planning and proactive responses to the changing policy climate are imperative if success is to be secured. Information must be gathered, its implications assessed and the necessary action taken in a systematic and integrated way.

Tackling environmental problems always requires a concerted and co-operative effort, and in the EU success will depend on the extent to which member states are politically committed to the environmental philosophy and the extent to which they are willing to co-operate. The balancing of the economic growth/environment trade-off is likely to determine the Europe-wide success of any policies, but there also need to be concerted and co-operative political motivations. There will be those who will argue that the attainment of an effective and concerted environmental policy in Europe will require political and economic union. However, since the EU and national governments legislate over environmental protection and police offenders, significant environmental improvement will only be attained with the co-operation and commitment of producers. There is therefore a need for firms to institute environmental management practices and it is to this issue that the rest of the chapter is devoted.

CORPORATE ENVIRONMENTAL MANAGEMENT STRATEGIES

Most companies have realised that environmental issues need to be addressed for a number of reasons, including consumer pressure, potential cost savings, legislation and ethics. Larger companies are, in turn, putting pressure on supply chains, insisting that their smaller suppliers also respond to environmental issues. There is, therefore, growing interest in the area of corporate environmental management. Environmental considerations are likely to be a source of quite profound changes in business practices. With this in mind, there are a number of important questions which organisations should ask themselves:

■ Is the organisation meeting its existing environmental commitments?

■ Is the organisation adhering to environmental legislation, and what will be the impact on it as environmental legislation becomes more stringent?

■ Is concern for the environment integral to each of the organisation's operations?

■ Do managers and workers see environmental improvement as a goal and in what ways are personnel being encouraged to be more involved?

■ Does the organisation have the capacity to evaluate the environmental impact of its processes and products, including packaging and distribution channels?

■ Are there new product opportunities which the organisation could exploit which would have less negative environmental impact?

■ How vulnerable is the organisation to environmental changes such as climate change?

■ What financial and organisational constraints are there which might prevent environmental improvement from taking place?

■ How are the organisation's competitors placed in terms of environmental accountability, and can the environmental performance of the organisation be turned to a competitive advantage?

■ Does the organisation have a systematic approach to management which can be used to integrate environmental issues?

The answers to these questions provide the organisation with the basis of a strategic plan for the environment. An environmental policy can be developed from these questions and it can be circulated to the organisation's personnel, suppliers and vendors, and the public. The environmental policy sets out the context for future action. There is no single model and the policy will reflect an organisation's structure, location, industrial sector and business culture. If such a document is published, then it is important that it is adhered to, thereby providing an all-important environmental ethos around which the organisation must operate.

All aspects of an organisation's operations, from accounting and purchasing, to product design, manufacture, sales, marketing, distribution and the use and disposal of the product, will have an impact on the environment and the environmental policy should reflect a recognition of this. The policy needs to be comprehensive and detailed, but it should not contain statements or targets which the organisation cannot hope to achieve. This will do more harm than good if exposed. The content of any policy will vary and be influenced by the activities of the particular organisation. However, there are some general principles which can be applied to the content of the policy statement:

- Adopt and aim to apply the principles of 'sustainable development', which meet the needs of the present without compromising the abilities of future generations to meet their own needs.
- Strive to adopt the highest available environmental standards in all site locations and all countries, and meet or exceed all applicable regulations.
- Adopt a total 'cradle-to-grave' environmental assessment and accept responsibility for all products and services, the raw materials used and the disposal of the product after use.
- Aim to minimise the use of all materials, supplies and energy, and wherever possible use renewable or recyclable materials and components.
- Minimise waste produced in all parts of the business, aim for waste-free processes, and where waste is produced avoid the use of terminal waste treatment, dealing with it, as far as possible, at source.
- Render any unavoidable wastes harmless and dispose of them in a way which has the least impact on the environment.
- Expect high environmental standards from all parties involved in the business, including suppliers, contractors and vendors, and put pressure on these groups to improve their environmental performance in line with your own.
- Be committed to improving relations with the local community and the public at large and where necessary introduce education and liaison programmes.
- Adopt an environmentally sound transport strategy and assess the general infrastructure of the organisation.
- Assess, on a continuous basis, the environmental impact of all operations and procedures via an environmental audit.
- Assist in developing solutions to environmental problems and support the development of external environmental initiatives.
- Preserve nature, protect ecological habitats and create conservation schemes.
- Accept strict liability for environmental damage, not blaming others for environmental damage, accidents and incidents.

Environmental policies should identify key performance areas and form a sound basis for setting corporate objectives. They need to be detailed enough to demonstrate that the organisation's commitment goes beyond lip-service. A clearly defined environmental policy should be implementable, practical and relate to the areas in which the organisation wishes to improve its environmental performance. In particular, when designing an environmental policy, the organisation needs to think hard about how it is going to quantify its objectives and measure its environmental performance.

For a policy to be implemented, personnel with special responsibilities for environmental performance will have to be found. Many organisations in Europe have discovered that the best way to achieve this, in the short run, is to appoint a main board environment director. This person will be there to champion the environment and will need some very important personal skills as well as legitimacy. Such legitimacy is often achieved by the publication of the organisation's environmental policy.

There are three very clear roles which an environmental director can take on:

1 **Taking a strategic view** – promoting minimal environmental impact from products and processes and developing an integrated and comprehensive approach.

2 **Raising the profile of the environment** – co-ordinating educational effort within the organisation, developing partnerships with customers, other organisations (particularly suppliers), environmental pressure groups, legislators, the EU and national government.

3 **Putting policy into practice** – the establishment of monitoring systems and environmental audits, the establishment of environmental improvement plans, involving all personnel and making them accountable and responsible for the environmental performance of their business, and taking anticipatory action which is central to good environmental performance.

The initial stage in the implementation of an environmental approach at organisation level must be for the organisation to establish exactly how well or how badly it is performing environmentally. Moxen and Strachan (1998) indicate that an increasingly common way of achieving this is to undertake an environmental audit, with this often being the first step in 'greening' an organisation.

ENVIRONMENTAL AUDITING

The first **environmental audits** can be traced back to the USA, where corporations adopted this methodology during the 1970s in response to their domestic liability laws. Such audits are now common among European businesses. Many banks and other financial institutions are insisting on companies undertaking environmental audits in order to reduce future environmental liabilities (Welford, 1998). Environmental audits are usually carried out by teams which include lawyers, economists, engineers, scientists and environmental generalists drawn from industry, government and consultancy.

Environmental auditing is a check both on the environmental performance of an organisation and on the performance of the management system (see below) which should be designed to bring about improvements in that performance. In the first instance, the organisation needs to establish a baseline against which to measure future audits, commonly referred to as the environmental review. The environmental review follows many of the procedures of an audit, as laid out below. However, strictly speaking, an audit measures the attainment or non-attainment of some target objectives, whereas the environmental review simply provides an initial assessment of the environmental performance of the organisation.

The environmental audit consists of a regular, independent, systematic, documented and objective evaluation of the environmental performance of an organisation. It should measure how well organisations, management and equipment are performing with the aim of helping management to safeguard the environment. It also provides management information which can be used in the control of environmental practices and in assessing compliance with organisation policies, which include meeting regulatory requirements. It should be stressed, however, that within the task of environmental management there is a role for everyone in the organisation.

The overall aim of environmental auditing is to help safeguard the environment and minimise the risks to human health. Although auditing alone cannot achieve that, it is a powerful managerial tool. The key objectives of the environmental audit are:

■ to determine the extent to which environmental management systems in an organisation are performing adequately;

■ to verify compliance with local, national and European environmental and health and safety legislation;

■ to verify compliance with an organisation's own stated corporate policy;

■ to develop and promulgate internal procedures needed to achieve the organisation's environmental objectives;

■ to minimise human exposure to risks from the environment and ensure adequate health and safety provision;

■ to identify and assess risk resulting from environmental failure;

■ to assess the impact on the local environment of a particular plant or process by means of air, water and soil sampling;

■ to advise an organisation on environmental improvements it can make.

There are a number of benefits to organisations in undertaking an environmental audit. These include assurances that legislation is being adhered to and the consequent prevention of fines and litigation, an improved public image, which can be built into a public relations campaign, a reduction in costs (particularly in the area of energy usage and waste minimisation), an improvement in environmental awareness at all levels of the organisation, and an improvement in overall quality. On the other hand, there are some potential disbenefits of the audit. These include the initial costs of the audit and the cost of compliance with it, and the temporary disruption of plant operations. It is also vital that management sees that the recommendations of the environmental auditor are adhered to, otherwise an audit report could be incriminating in a court case or insurance claim.

All environmental audits involve gathering information, analysing that information, making objective judgements based on evidence and a knowledge of the industry and of relevant environmental legislation and standards. There is also the need to report the results of the audit to senior management with recommendations and possible strategies for the implementation of the findings. This all requires considerable preparatory work as well as follow-up time in order that the findings are accurate and comprehensive. Ideally, therefore, there need to be three clear stages to an audit (see Figure 18.2).

Figure 18.2 Stages of an environmental audit

Pre-audit stage	Audit stage	Post-audit stage
1 Plan scope of audit	5 Inspect records	10 Evaluate findings
2 Select audit team	6 Examine organisation policy	11 Report findings
3 Industry analysis	7 Examine lines of management	12 Prepare action plan
4 Involve the workforce	8 Interview selected staff	
	9 Physical inspection	

Environmental audit stages

The first, pre-audit stage, will aim to minimise the time spent at the site and to maximise the audit team's productivity. It will involve:

1 Planning the nature and scope of the audit and providing a framework for setting goals and objectives, developing strategies for their achievement and specifying accountability for accomplishing the work and scheduling the audit process.

2 Selecting members of the audit team and allocating resources to the strategies and policies determined in the previous step. The audit team will consist of people chosen for their expertise, not only in environmental matters but also having knowledge of the industry in which the organisation operates. An assignment of audit responsibilities should be made according to the competencies and experience of the team.

3 Getting to know the industry and organisation to be audited. A useful strategy here is to use pre-survey questionnaires submitted to management in order for the audit team to familiarise themselves with the type of installation, the site and the location. It will also focus the minds of management on what will be required of them during the audit.

4 Questionnaires may also be sent to a representative sample of the workforce (to be filled out in confidence), asking about key issues such as communications, planning, health and safety, and working conditions.

The second stage is the on-site audit itself. This will include:

5 An inspection of records kept by the organisation, certificates of compliance, discharge consents, waste licences, etc.

6 Examination of inspection and maintenance programmes and the organisation's own policy on what to do in the event of spills and other accidents. Auditors will have to assess the soundness of the facility's internal controls and assess the risks associated with the failure of those controls. Such controls will include management procedures and the equipment and engineering controls that affect environmental performance.

7 Examining lines of management and responsibility, competence of personnel and systems of authorisation. There needs to be a working understanding of the facility's internal management system and of its effectiveness.

8 A confidential interview of selected staff at all levels of operation with a view to collecting information, particularly in the area of the effectiveness of systems and waste management.

9 A physical inspection of the plant, working practices, office management systems and surrounding areas, including a check on safety equipment, verifying the organisation's own sampling and monitoring procedures, investigating energy management systems and, where necessary, taking samples of waste, liquids, soil, air and noise.

The final stage of the audit will involve:

10 Confirming that there is sufficient evidence on which to base and justify a set of findings and evaluating the audit information and observations. Such evaluation will involve the audit team meeting to discuss all facets of the environmental audit.

11 Reporting the audit findings in written form and in discussion with the management of the audited organisation. This entails a formal review of the audit findings to avoid misinterpretation, and discussion about how to improve the environmental performance of the organisation based on the audit report. Management is thus provided with information about compliance status and recommendations regarding action which should be taken.

12 It will often result in the development of an action plan to address deficiencies. It will include assigning responsibilities for corrective action, determining potential solutions and establishing timetables. Recommendations for the next audit may also be made.

The environmental audit is more likely to be successful if the general ethos of the organisation is supportive to the success of the programme and the welfare of the organisation. To this extent it is useful to consider some key characteristics which will provide the foundation for a successful programme. These factors will include:

■ comprehensive support for the programme throughout management and particularly by senior management;

■ acceptance that an auditing programme is for the benefit of management rather than a tool of individual performance assessment and is a function which, in time, will improve management effectiveness;

■ the recognition that useful information will come out of the audit programme and that information needs to be shared and acted upon;

- the commitment to considering the comments and suggestions at each level of the organisation's management and workforce and encouraging responsible participation;

- a commitment to establishing systems for managing and following up on results;

- clearly defined roles and responsibilities and clear operational systems;

- the recognition of an integrated approach where the auditing system is linked to a wider management system.

Much stress needs to be placed on the idea that audits should be seen by management as a positive help rather than a threatening or hostile exercise (Welford, 1992). The organisation must create a culture, led by its top team, which recognises the positive benefits of the audit and sees it as good day-to-day management practice. Management must feel that it owns the audit and even though some external expertise may be used, the audit is an activity which is promoted and driven internally rather than externally.

In The Netherlands the concept of environmental auditing has been known since 1984, although Dutch subsidiaries of American-owned firms had used the technique before then. The Confederation of Dutch Industries promotes environmental management within organisations, encouraging interaction between government and industry and providing guidelines. Environmental auditing in The Netherlands is largely confined to the largest of industries, but the Dutch expect that good practice by large, successful firms will be emulated by small and medium-sized organisations.

In Norway, factories are required to establish and maintain an internal environmental control system, supervised by a government agency. Environmental auditing is not legally required but a number of organisations practise environmental auditing on a voluntary basis. Within the Norwegian company Norsk Hydro every major installation is audited once every two years, the audit lasting between three and five days in each case.

In the UK, the Confederation of British Industries (CBI) has published a set of environmental auditing guidelines. These stress the practicalities of undertaking an environmental audit and stress the need to implement audit recommendations and continue monitoring processes.

The number of companies operating audit programmes in Europe has grown significantly in the last ten years, with this trend likely to continue whether or not the EU implements environmental auditing legislation in the future. Demands from groups such as environmentalists or local communities will lead to pressure on organisations not only to undertake environmental audits but also to disclose the results of those audits. The increase in auditing activity is also likely to lead to more standardisation of auditing practice and environmental standards. However, without the development of an overall integrated environmental management system, environmental auditing will be a mere palliative.

THE EU ECO-MANAGEMENT AND AUDIT SCHEME

While the primary stance of the Environment Directorate of the EU has always been to encourage organisations to improve standards of environmental performance without waiting for regulation, there is nevertheless a growing amount of European environmental legislation and directives. Moreover, the EU has been keen to establish common environmental standards and systems for environmental reporting. One such system is embedded in the eco-management and audit scheme Regulation.

At the end of 1991 the European Commission approved a proposal for a Council Regulation to establish a European Union eco-management and audit scheme (EMAS) which would be open for voluntary participation by industrial companies. The Regulation was published in March 1992. The EMAS provides a framework for companies to think ahead, assess their own environmental impacts and commit themselves to a policy of reducing them. It also encourages firms to keep the public informed by regularly making statements and reporting progress. At the present time EMAS is voluntary and administered by individual member states, but many expect the system to become compulsory for larger firms in time and the Council has retained the right to introduce compulsory registration. Member states themselves also have the right to adopt a compulsory registration system for certain industrial categories if they feel this is beneficial.

The objective of the scheme is to promote improvements in the environmental performance of industry by encouraging companies to:

- establish and implement environmental protection schemes;
- carry out regular, systematic and objective evaluations of the environmental performance of these systems;
- provide information about environmental performance to the public.

The purpose of the scheme is not to confirm compliance with legislative requirements (although this must be achieved), nor is it aimed at awarding best practice or performance. The scheme aims to recognise efforts to improve environmental performance over time, given a baseline established by an environmental review of the organisation. The scheme highlights the need for a continuous cycle of improvement.

In order to join EMAS, a company has to adopt and adhere to the cycle depicted in Figure 18.3. Essentially this requires the company to:

- define an environmental policy, based on an overall review of the environmental impacts of its activities;
- set targets for achievement within a set time;
- put into place plans and systems to achieve these targets and include provisions for the constant monitoring of these;
- periodically audit to assess progress;
- report the audit findings to the public and have these findings verified by a third party;
- set new targets for further progress and repeat the procedure.

There is a need to establish systems based on the environmental review which:

- assess and manage the environmental impact of activities;
- manage the use of energy, raw materials and water;
- minimise waste;
- consider the selection and design of products and processes;
- prevent accidents;
- include staff in consultation and provide motivation and training;
- inform and involve the public.

Figure 18.3 The European EMAS cycle

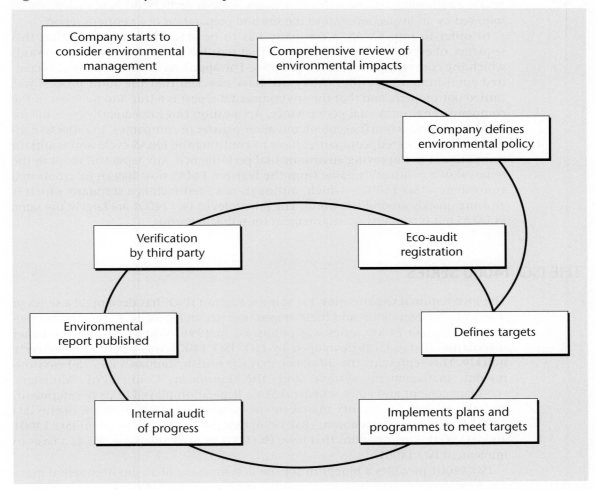

Essentially, the audit assesses this system and evaluates performance in relation to the environmental review and the operation of the system as defined and documented. The results of the audit have to be considered by senior management and any necessary revisions to the company policy, objectives, targets, action plans and systems made.

All of these steps can be internal to the company if there is sufficient expertise available to perform the various tasks adequately. Indeed, the intention of EMAS is that the discipline of having to follow these steps should help the company better manage its own environmental performance. However, there are also important external aspects to the scheme.

EMAS requires that an external environmental statement is prepared based on the findings of the audit or initial review. Validation of this statement must be made by external accredited environmental verifiers. The validation will confirm that the statement has covered all of the environmental issues relevant to the site in enough detail and that the information presented is reliable. The validation process involves the examination of relevant documentation, including information about the site, its activities, a description of the environmental management system, and details and findings of the environmental review or audit. This would normally be followed by an inspection visit to the site and preparation of a verifier's report.

In order to join EMAS, a company has to be able to demonstrate that this sequence of events has taken place, and that sensible targets have been set towards which the company should make progress. The approved independent and accredited environmental verifier (AEV) will have checked that the audit process was carried out properly and that the environmental report is a true and fair view of the company's environmental performance. Application can subsequently be made for inclusion in the eco-management and audit register of companies. In order to continue to be registered, companies have to continue the EMAS cycle and maintain commitment to improving environmental performance. Any lapse will result in the removal of a company's name from the register. EMAS now has an international equivalent – ISO 14001 – which, although not identical, is a standard which is growing quickly around the world. The principles of ISO 14001 are largely the same as EMAS but it contains no requirement for public reporting.

THE ISO 14000 SERIES

The International Organisation for Standardisation (ISO) has developed a series of 'Global Green Standards' and these are summarised in Figure 18.4. The first component of the ISO 14000 series was published in 1996. When compared to other international standards developed by ISO, ISO 14001 was published relatively quickly. This represents the influence that the British Standards BS 7750 environmental management system and the European Council of Ministers' eco-management and audit scheme (EMAS) Regulation played in its development, and also that of the quality management system ISO 9001. Annex B of the ISO 14001 Specification Document (BSI 1996) describes the links between ISO 14001 and ISO 9001. Organisations that have ISO 9001 in place often use this as a basis to implement ISO 14001.

ISO 14001 provides a blueprint for the development of an environmental management system, with its overall aim being to support environmental protection and prevention of pollution in harmony with socio-economic needs. Those organisations that wish to demonstrate continual improvements in environmental performance are recommended to certify their environmental management systems to ISO 14001. ISO 14001 consists of five core components, with Strachan *et al.* (2003) noting that these represent the main steps to implementing this strategic environmental management system:

1 **The Environmental Policy.** Senior management must produce an environmental policy statement. This needs to set out an organisation's intentions in relation to its environmental aspects and must contain a commitment to continual improvement, the prevention of pollution and compliance with relevant environmental legislation. The policy statement must be appropriate for the nature, scale and environmental aspects of the organisation, set a framework for objectives and targets, be documented and be made available to the general public.

2 **Planning.** An organisation must then set itself appropriate objectives and targets in relation to the environmental policy and devise an appropriate action plan to meet them. During the planning stage an organisation must identify what ISO

Figure 18.4 The structure of the ISO 14000 series

Evaluation and auditing tools	Management system standards	Product-oriented support tools
Auditing guidelines ISO 14010 ISO 14011 ISO 14012 Environmental performance evaluation guidelines ISO 14031	EMS specification ISO 14001 EMS guide ISO 14004	Life-cycle assessment ISO 14040 ISO 14041 ISO 14042 Environmental labelling ISO 14020 ISO 14041 ISO 14042

Terms and definitions
ISO 14050

To be used by other standard writers ← Environmental aspects of product standards
Guide 64

Source: BSI (1996)

14001 refers to as environmental aspects, with this defined as: 'elements of an organisations' activities, products or services that can interact with the environment'. An organisation is recommended to undertake an environmental review to establish its aspects, with other issues included in the planning component of ISO 14001 being: legal and other requirements, objectives and targets and the environmental management programme.

3 **Implementation and Operation.** An organisation must then establish the various elements necessary for the implementation and operation of the plan. ISO 14001 offers a blueprint to do this, and when implementing ISO 14001 an organisation must consider the following issues: structure and operation; training, awareness and competence; documentation and control; operational control; and emergency preparedness and response.

4 **Checking and Corrective Action.** Having implemented the management system, an organisation must then check to ensure that it has been successful in meeting its environmental objectives and targets. If these have not been met, then corrective action is needed. The management system must be periodically audited.

5 **The Management Review.** Senior management must periodically review the management system to ensure its continuing effectiveness and suitability. Changes must be made to reflect the changing context of the organisation and the commitment to continual improvement made in the environmental policy statement.

The components of ISO 14001 and their sub-elements are brought together and are shown as a model in Figure 18.5. Since the launch of ISO 14001 approximately 20 000 companies around the world have implemented the initiative, with another reported 80 000 now in the process of doing so. Those companies which have implemented ISO 14001 have done so for a number of reasons. Some of the external drivers and benefits are: third party assurance and recognition; market access; regulatory relief; improved investor confidence; and enhanced public image and community relations. The internal drivers and benefits are: reduced incidents and liability; cost savings and improved efficiency; and improved business performance. However, many commentators, such as Strachan *et al.* (2003), have voiced their concerns over the difficulty and cost of introducing ISO 14001, and have indicated that ISO 14001 requirements are too sophisticated and do not add value in small and medium-sized enterprises.

PRODUCT STEWARDSHIP AND ECO-LABELLING

Product design managers are increasingly examining ways in which the total life cycle of a product can be managed to ensure that potential environmental damage is minimised. In other words, they are looking to create an enclosed resource loop where waste is recycled and even the product itself is recycled at the end of its use. Natural ecosystems operate in a similar fashion so that the waste from one process feeds into another as a nutrient. Traditional environmentally damaging production and consumption work more in a linear way, such that inputs and outputs are not connected and possible environmental improvements are missed. One alternative is cradle-to-grave management where organisations have to recognise their wider responsibility and manage the entire life cycle of their products.

Many organisations are recognising their responsibility in this area in terms of what has been termed 'product stewardship'. This involves:

- examining the design of a product and considering how efficient it is;
- considering the energy sources, raw materials and components used in the product and deciding whether they might be replaced by alternatives which are more environmentally friendly;
- examining the production process itself and considering whether a more energy-efficient and less polluting process innovation might be found;
- re-examining the disposal of the product and the waste from its production in terms of recycling and returning the used materials to the production cycle after use;
- reconsidering the after-sales service and packaging of the product and ensuring that adequate information is provided for its safe and energy-efficient use and environmentally friendly disposal of waste caused by consumption of the product.

It is relatively easy for organisations to target their internal systems and make changes to improve the environment. The part of cradle-to-grave management which is probably hardest to achieve is the return of materials from the consumer-waste stream. For example, only 2 per cent of consumer-used plastic is recycled in the EU, owing to a lack of an effective collection infrastructure combined with underdeveloped markets for recycled plastics. One solution is for companies to take action and to construct their own recycling infrastructure. Many environmentalists would like to see the re-introduction of deposits on glass bottles, for example.

Figure 18.5 The five steps of ISO 14001

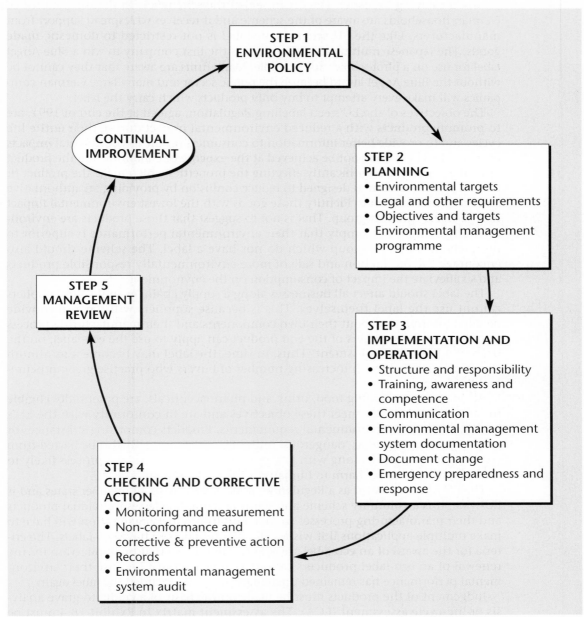

Source: Welford (1998)

Over time, eco-labelling schemes have been devised in a number of countries in an attempt to promote the use of production methods which are less harmful to the environment. The first such scheme was introduced in the Federal Republic of Germany in 1978. Canada, Japan and Norway established their own schemes in 1989. The schemes were also introduced to prevent spurious environmental claims. Germany's Blue Angel eco-labelling scheme is probably the world's best established programme. Launched in 1978 by the German government, it now has almost 4000 products carrying the label. The organisers of the scheme claim that 80 per cent of German households are aware of the scheme and it receives widespread support from manufacturers. Like the EU scheme, the label is not restricted to domestic-made goods. The Japanese multinational Konica was the first company to win a Blue Angel label for use on a photocopier, for example. Many firms are aware that they cannot be without the Blue Angel award because the public sector and many large German companies will make every attempt to buy only products which carry the label.

The objectives of the EU's eco-labelling Regulation, agreed at the end of 1991, are to promote products with a reduced environmental impact during their entire life cycles and to provide better information to consumers on the environmental impacts of products. These must not be achieved at the expense of compromising the product or workers' safety, or significantly affecting the properties which make the product fit for use. The EU scheme is designed to reduce confusion by providing an authoritative and independent label to identify those goods with the lowest environmental impact in a particular product group. That is not to suggest that those products are environmentally benign, but simply that their environmental performance is superior to products in the same group which do not have a label. The scheme should also encourage the production and sale of more environmentally responsible products and so alleviate the impact of consumption on the environment.

The label should affect all businesses along a supply chain, even if some suppliers cannot use the label themselves. This is because suppliers will have to provide detailed information about their own components and their manufacturing process in order that the suppliers of the end product can apply to use the eco-label, on the basis of a life-cycle assessment. Thus, in time, the label may become a minimum standard, specified by an increasing number of buyers who practise green procurement policies.

All products, excluding food, drink and pharmaceuticals, are potentially eligible for an eco-label if they meet these objectives and are in conformity with the EU's health, safety and environmental requirements. Products comprising substances or preparations classified as 'dangerous' under EU legislation will also be barred from receiving an eco-label, along with any product manufactured by a process likely to cause significant direct harm to humans or the environment.

The EU scheme, issued as a Regulation, applies directly to all member states and is EU-wide. It is a voluntary scheme and self-financing. It assesses individual products and their manufacturing processes so that a multi-product organisation will have to make multiple applications if it wishes all of its products to have eco-labels. The criteria for the award of an eco-label are ever tightening, so that on application for the renewal of an eco-label producers cannot assume that just because their environmental performance has remained unchanged it will be awarded the label again.

Judgement of the products must be made on the basis of a cradle-to-grave analysis or life-cycle assessment (LCA). The assessment matrix in Exhibit 18.4 must be used in setting criteria for the award of an eco-label. This will require account to be taken, where relevant, of a product group's soil, water, air and noise pollution impacts, waste generation, energy and resource consumption and effects on eco-systems. These impacts must be assessed in the pre-production, production, distribution, use and disposal stages. The criteria established for the award of an eco-label within a product group must be precise, clear and objective so that they can be applied consistently by the national bodies which award the eco-labels.

National competent bodies, which are independent and neutral, award the eco-labels for products. They are made up of representatives from industry, government,

Exhibit 18.4   EU eco-labelling scheme indicative assessment matrix

Environmental fields	Product life cycle				
	Pre-production	Production	Distribution	Utilisation	Disposal
Waste relevance					
Soil pollution and degradation					
Water contamination					
Air contamination					
Noise					
Consumption of energy					
Consumption of natural resources					
Effects on ecosystems					

environmental pressure groups and consumer groups, and the body has to reflect the full range of social interests. These bodies act as a kind of jury and assess the environmental performance of the product by reference to the agreed general principles and specific environmental criteria for each product group.

The use of an eco-label is not necessarily open to any product. The first step is to get a particular product group accepted as suitable for the award of a label. It may be the case that a particularly polluting group of products (e.g. cars) will not be open to such an award. Requests for the establishment of new product groups may come from consumers or industry itself and are addressed to the competent body in the member state. The competent body, if it so wishes, can ask the Commission to submit a proposal to its regulatory committee. In any event, the Commission will consult with interest groups and take advice from a range of sources. If it is decided that a particular product group will be open to the award of an eco-label, then this will be announced in the *Official Journal of the European Communities*. This process is outlined in Figure 18.6.

Following applications from manufacturers or importers of a particular product for the award of an eco-label, the national competent body has to notify the Commission of its decision relating to the award of an eco-label, enclosing full and summary results of the assessment. The Commission will then notify other member states and they usually have 30 days to make reasoned objections to the recommendations. If there are no objections, the award proceeds and a contract to use the label for a specified period is drawn up. Lists of products able to use the eco-label are published. In the case of any objections and disagreement, the Commission, acting through its advisory or regulatory body of national experts, will make the final decision. This procedure is summarised in Figure 18.7. Companies applying for an eco-label have to pay a fee to cover administration costs and a fee is also charged for the use of the label if

Figure 18.6 Selection of new product groups

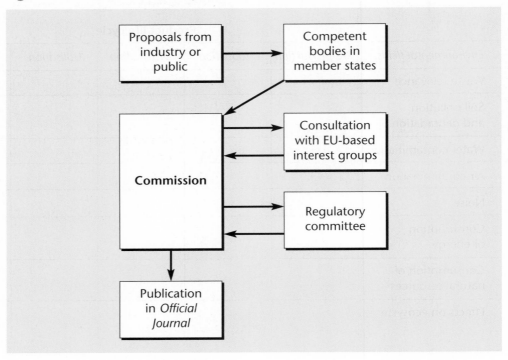

Figure 18.7 Award of an eco-label to individual products

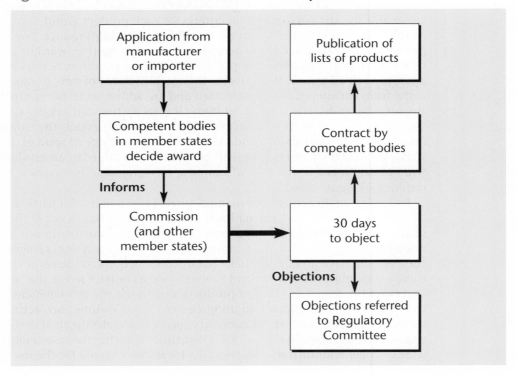

awarded. Companies which succeed with their applications can only use the eco-label in advertising the specific products for which it was awarded.

SUMMARY

■ Governments will increasingly seek to make the polluter pay, and one consequence of this is that some industries and products may simply disappear. Ultimately, however, the success of environmental improvement will be determined largely by the responsiveness of business.

■ That is not to suggest that legislation is a bad thing. Indeed, it can act as the impetus to an organisation thinking about instituting proper environmental management. In addition, increasing legislation and government expenditure to increase environmentally related expenditure might be seen as a win–win situation. It stimulates the economy without leading to the pollution problems often associated with growth. Moreover, a shift in expenditure from the military to promoting security on the environmental front is possible.

■ The environmental revolution has been gathering momentum and speed since the 1960s and developed rapidly in the 1980s and 1990s. Environmental considerations are likely to form an integral part of commercial normality and, indeed, competitiveness in the twenty-first century. Definitions of business success are likely to include the assumption of zero negative impact on the environment at the very least.

■ A competitive advantage can be achieved not merely by keeping abreast of environmental developments, but also by initiating change within an organisation and responding with new environmentally friendly products and production processes.

■ Indeed, growing consumer awareness and environmental pressure groups are likely to ensure that organisations which do not take action on the environmental front will lose market share. With increased competition as a result of European integration, environmental management will provide organisations with a competitive edge.

Review and discussion questions

1 *In general, how can an organisation turn an expensive environmental management policy into a competitive advantage?*

2 *How would economic theory suggest that a pollution problem is tackled?*

3 *Is a sustainable development model of economic development possible?*

4 *In what ways does European integration help to control pollution? What sorts of step are being taken in the EU?*

5 *How can industry be encouraged to institute environmental management systems?*

6 *To what extent will new EU voluntary standards become the norm for European business?*

CASE STUDY

The Body Shop International

Background

The Body Shop was founded in March 1976 when Anita Roddick opened her first shop in Brighton. Before 1976, working for the United Nations, she had travelled around the world and met people from a number of different cultures. Observing how people treated their skin and hair, she learned that certain things cleansed, polished and protected the skin without having to be formulated into a cream or shampoo. When she started The Body Shop, Anita Roddick aimed to utilise these raw ingredients such as plants, herbs and roots in products which would be acceptable to consumers. Only six years later she was described by the International Chamber of Commerce as 'the inventor of sustainable retailing' (Williams and Goliike, 1982).

The first shop was basic and at first sold only 15 lines. They were packed in different sizes to fill up the shelves and to give the customer an opportunity to try a product without buying a large bottle. A refill service operated which allowed customers to refill their empty bottles instead of throwing them away. Although this was clearly an environmentally friendly strategy, it was also initially implemented to cut down the costs of packaging.

Today, The Body Shop's principal activities are to formulate and retail products which are primarily associated with cleansing, polishing and protecting the skin and hair. The underlying aims are to conduct that business ethically, with a minimum of hype, and to promote health rather than glamour. Naturally based, close-to-source ingredients are used wherever possible and ingredients and final products are not tested on animals (Wheeler, 1992). Packaging is kept to a minimum and refill services are offered in all shops. Packaging, in the form of plastic bottles, can be returned to shops and is recycled into accessories.

The Body Shop's full range now contains over 300 products. The organisation trades in over 40 countries and employs around 6000 people, either directly or in franchises. Senior management in the organisation is committed to the encouragement of positive change. The aim is to establish a new work ethic that will enable business to thrive without causing adverse damage to the environment, at both the local and global level. There is an emphasis placed on not selling products which have an adverse effect on sustainability, i.e. those which consume a disproportionate amount of energy during manufacture or disposal, generate excessive wastes, use ingredients from threatened habitats, which are obtained by cruelty, or which adversely affect other countries, especially the developing countries.

Environmental strategies are at the centre of The Body Shop's approach to business. Moreover, the organisation has been so successful in raising the profile of the environment both within and external to the business that it is endlessly cited as being the leading business, worldwide, in this field. Even though the organisation itself would argue that there is still more to be achieved, this case study examines the practices and systems which have enabled The Body Shop to reach this leading position.

Commitment and policy

One of the most apparent characteristics of The Body Shop is its commitment to environmental and social excellence. This is often attributed to Anita Roddick herself. While many of the principles are hers, the truth is that commitment exists not only at board level but throughout the whole organisation. Everybody is encouraged to contribute to environmental improvement. The ultimate aim of The Body Shop is to include environmental issues in every area of its operations but, at the same time, the organisation rejects environmental opportunism which has often paralleled the green marketing strategies of more cynical firms.

At first, The Body Shop did not commit itself to a formal strategy or programme of environmental improvements. Action was taken when environmental problems were identified. This approach tended to increase employee involvement and reduce bureaucracy. However, with the continued growth of the organisation, it has been necessary to move to a more systematic approach, setting targets and planning for environmental improvement.

The overriding factor for The Body Shop is the perception of a moral obligation to drive towards sustainability in business (Roddick, 1991). It is impossible to measure progress towards this ideal without a detailed policy statement followed by a systematic process of data gathering and public reporting. Hence, auditing activities are considered absolutely essential to the company's long-term mission to become a truly sustainable operation. In other words, it aims to replace as many of the planet's resources as are utilised. That fundamental aim translates into a wish to play a full part in handing on a safer and more equitable world to future generations. The fundamental basis of this goal is a commitment to the broader concept of sustainable development. It is the strong belief of The Body Shop that the moral burden of achieving sustainability in business should become the principal driving force behind business in the future.

Social and environmental auditing

The only real way to achieve environmental improvement is to take a systematic approach to achieving its aims through an appropriate management structure and periodically to assess or audit progress, measuring the extent to which targets and basic objectives are being met. For that reason social and environmental auditing has a very high profile at The Body Shop. It involves all staff and managers in continuous data collection, frequent reviews of priorities and targets (on a department-by-department basis) and an annual process of public reporting of results.

In parallel with the necessity for environmental auditing, there is a need to put in place management systems capable of achieving targets and adhering to environmental policy. The Body Shop maintains a very decentralised system of corporate environmental management. A corporate team of social and environmental audit specialists acts as a central resource for networks of environmental 'advisers' and co-ordinators in headquarters departments, subsidiaries, retail outlets and international markets. Advisers and co-ordinators are usually part-time, fulfilling their role in social and environmental communications and auditing alongside normal duties.

The Body Shop carries out its environmental auditing in line with the EU eco-management and audit scheme, publishing social, environmental and fair trade reports which lay out its annual report to the public on its environmental and social performance.

In 1996 The Body Shop carried out and published its first full social audit of its activities. The approach was to assess the environmental, social and animal protection performance of the company, by reference to the opinions and perceptions of a range of stakeholders. This move widened the environmental auditing methodology previously adopted by The Body Shop and included a range of social issues. This is fully consistent with the moves towards incorporating wider aspects of sustainable development into the organisation and is now being replicated by a number of other companies. Although there have been many changes at The Body Shop in terms of reorganisation, social and environmental issues continue to differentiate the company from many of its competitors, and are often seen as a source of competitive advantage.

REFERENCES AND FURTHER READING

BSI (British Standards Institution) (1996) *Environmental Management Systems Handbook: A Guide to the BS EN ISO 14000 series*, London: BSI.

EC (2001) *Communication from the Commission to the Council, the European Parliament, the Economic and Social Committee and the Committee of the Regions, On the Sixth Environment Action Programme of the European Community, 'Environment 2010: Our Future, Our Choice' – The Sixth Environment Action Programme, Proposal for a Decision of the European Parliament and of the Council Laying down the Community Environment Action Programme 2001–2010, Brussels, 24.1.2001 COM (2001) 31 Final*, Brussels: European Commission.

EC (2002) *Choices for a Greener Future: The European Union and the Environment*, Brussels: European Commission Directorate-General for Press and Communications

Hopkins, M (2003) *The Planetary Bargain: Corporate Social Responsibility Matters*, London: Earthscan

Jordan, A, Wurzel, R K W and Zito, A R (2003) 'New Instruments of Environmental Governance?: National Experiences and Prospects', *Environmental Politics*, 12 (1), Spring.

Moxen, J and Strachan, P A (1998) *Managing Green Teams: Environmental Change in Organisations and Networks*, Sheffield: Greenleaf Publishing.

Roddick, A (1991) 'In Search of the Sustainable Business', *Ecodecision*, 7.

Strachan, P A, Haque, M, McCulloch, A and Moxen, J (1997) 'The Eco-Management and Audit Scheme: Recent Experiences of UK Participating Organisations', *European Environment*, 7 (25): 25–33.

Strachan, P A, Sinclair, I and Lal, D (2003) 'Managing ISO 14001 Implementation in the United Kingdom Continental Shelf (UKCS)', *Corporate Social Responsibility and Environmental Management*, 10: 50–63.

Welford, R J (1992) 'A Guide to Environmental Auditing', Supplement to *European Environment*, 8 (4).

Welford, R J (1993) 'Breaking the Link between Quality and the Environment', *Business Strategy and the Environment*, 2 (4).

Welford, R J (1998) *Corporate Environmental Management 1: Systems and Strategies*, London: Earthscan.

Welford, R J, Prescott, K and Mercado, S (2001) *European Business*, Harlow: FT Prentice Hall.

Wheeler, D (1992) 'Environmental Management as an Opportunity for Sustainability in Business – Economic Forces as a Constraint', *Business Strategy and the Environment*, 1 (4): 37–40.

Williams, J O and Goliike, U (1982) *From Ideas to Action, Business and Sustainable Development*, ICC Report on the Greening of Enterprise, London: International Chamber of Commerce.

World Commission on Environment and Development (1987), *The Brundtland Report*, or *Our Common Future*, Oxford: Oxford University Press.

WEBSITES

http://www.corporateresponsibilitygroup.com/what/core.htm
This is the website of the Corporate Responsibility Group. It includes 50 of the UK's leading companies which are committed to a responsible approach to business practice.

http://www.emas.org.uk
This is the website of the UK EMAS body, which provides information about EMAS.

http://www.europa.eu.int
This is the website of the European Union, which provides information about the EU's sustainable development strategy.

http://www.iso.ch
This is the website of the International Organisation for Standardisation, which provides information about the ISO 14000 series.

http://www.sustainable-development.gov.uk
This is the website of the UK Government, which provides information about the UK Government's sustainable development strategy.

CHAPTER 19

Globalisation and multinational management

KATE PRESCOTT AND DAVID EDELSHAIN

Outcomes

Having read this chapter, you will be able to:

■ understand the differences between the management of business operations in a domestic setting and in a multinational and global setting

■ explain the problems faced by organisations in foreign markets

■ analyse the management strategies which enable foreign organisations to maximise their advantages in foreign markets

■ compare the wide range of management practices in multinational organisations

■ understand the complex task of multinational management

INTRODUCTION

An obvious question to ask in relation to multinational management is: How does it differ from management of business operations in a domestic setting? There are four key issues which must be addressed in order to provide an answer:

1 Understanding and reacting to change in the global environment.

2 Cross-cultural management.

3 Managing flexibly and creatively in today's dynamic business setting.

4 Drawing on the knowledge and skills of the worldwide management arena in order to develop 'best practice'.

This chapter seeks to address the implications of all four factors in order to provide an understanding of the complex task of multinational management. In addition, since one of the most significant changes in international business in recent years has been the rise in the incidence of international activity by small enterprises, discussion throughout the chapter will not be restricted to the challenges of multinational enterprises (MNEs). The managerial demands on small and medium-sized enterprises (SMEs) will also be discussed.

The process of international management does not take place in a vacuum; success depends on adapting to the diverse environments in which businesses operate. For managers this is a highly complex task, not least because human beings, by their very nature, often feel uncomfortable or dislocated when operating outside their own cultural domain.

Setting a context

The challenge of international management is fitting strategic development to a continually evolving marketplace. Before embarking on a discussion of what this means in practice, it is useful to establish some parameters and terminology which explain different stages of development and current trends in the strategic activities of international operators.

There are four basic strategies which firms may employ to enter and compete in the foreign market. The choice of type depends critically on the extent to which firms wish to focus on cost reduction or local responsiveness. The choice must also depend on the linkages between the different constituent businesses and products a firm may have as many international firms are multi-business and multi-product (*see* Calori *et al.*, 2000). The four strategic options are international strategy, multidomestic strategy, global strategy and transnational strategy.

International strategy

Here firms transfer skills and advantages, usually developed domestically, to overseas markets where there is the potential to secure differential advantage. Product development tends to be centralised, and tight control and co-ordination come from the centre. In foreign markets, firms typically establish sales and marketing activities, and sometimes production.

This strategy is useful where firms are attempting to exploit their core competence internationally without pressures for local responsiveness and cost reduction, an example being McDonald's. For them, the focus is on exploiting their brand and image. Customisation of products is less important (although elements of the product range are adapted from market to market) and duplication of business in different centres is not damaging to profitability as economies of scale are not critical to success.

Multidomestic strategy

With a multidomestic strategy, the focus is on maximising local responsiveness. Unlike international firms, these organisations extensively customise both their product and marketing strategy to suit the local needs of the market. This usually means not only local production and sales and marketing, but also local product development and R&D centres designed to support market-specific rather than international activity. A structure of this type typically gives rise to a high cost base, although this can be compensated for by adding value to local products through targeted differentiation and marketing.

A major problem facing multidomestic firms is control. With different divisions pursuing their own objectives, this can mean the creation of decentralised federations through which it is difficult to transfer skills and information.

Global strategy

A global strategy is one in which firms exploit experience curve effects and economies of scale. Production, marketing and product development activities are concentrated in a smaller number of advantageous locations (e.g. low-cost production centres or regionally based marketing centres). The extent of customisation tends to be limited, as this raises costs through duplication. Instead, firms exploit cost advantages, often competing aggressively on price.

This strategy is inappropriate where the demands for local responsiveness are high. Today, this option is therefore only really available to firms where there is an option to develop a common worldwide product, often only the preserve of industrial goods companies. For many consumer goods companies, there remains continued pressure to adapt to local market conditions, customising products and strategies.

Transnational strategy

For two decades now, the highly competitive nature of world markets has meant that firms have been exploring strategies which allow them to reap the benefits of both cost minimisation and local responsiveness and to exploit competences which are developed in all business centres worldwide (Hedlund, 1986). While this is obviously the ideal, it is a far from straightforward approach to international development: rationalising the demands for cost minimisation (which dictate more centralised business operations and larger-scale operating units) with those for local responsiveness (which dictate customisation and duplication) is a highly complex task and one which demands a high level of flexibility.

The only way of achieving such a complex mix is to split businesses into a series of constituent functions which are variously centralised and decentralised. For example, a firm may choose to concentrate its R&D and production operations in a small number of regional sites (maybe one in the Americas, one in Europe and one in Asia Pacific) while at the same time dispersing sales and marketing activity to each target market to ensure maximum local responsiveness.

Some of the first moves made in this direction were by the Japanese in the early 1980s. Multinational giants such as Honda and Canon fostered the idea of the four headquarters system. This involved establishing their major regional research, production and marketing centres in the three main areas of the global triad (America,

Europe and Asia Pacific), each responsible for adapting business to regional needs. These were then supported by an all-embracing corporate headquarters which co-ordinated the transfer of competences and skills between regions as well as establishing global policy and corporate identity. Within each region, local adaptation is also made possible by the establishment of market-based sales and marketing centres. Today, there is evidence of transnational strategy (or at least elements of such an approach) across a wide range of producers, including Nestlé, Unilever, Caterpillar and Ford.

These four different approaches to international expansion incorporate a number of key issues which will be revisited later in the chapter:

- managing the diversity of global regions and markets;
- selecting appropriate strategies which take into consideration market and product characteristics (these include market entry strategies as well as those concerned with internalisation versus externalisation of business operations);
- centralisation versus decentralisation; standardisation versus adaptation;
- establishing strategies and structures which are flexible and responsive to change;
- learning and developing systems for best practice.

On the first of these issues, it is important to understand how international managers are reacting to change in the global environment, managing across different international cultures and coping with commonality and diversity between markets.

THE CHANGING GLOBAL ENVIRONMENT

Regionalisation

'Regionalisation' has become an increasingly important feature of the global business environment since the Second World War, although the constructs on which regional integration are based (principally free trade) are far from new. Adam Smith, writing in the eighteenth century, noted that the greatest economic benefits accrue from free trade, the 'invisible hand' of government trade policy serving only to distort the process of industrial specialisation which allows countries to utilise their resources to best effect. In 1947, as countries moved to forge greater global co-operation in an effort to put the adverse experiences of the Second World War behind them, the General Agreement on Tariffs and Trade (GATT) was formed with the intention of reducing/removing tariffs and quotas between countries on a unilateral basis.

GATT and free trade

Through 11 multilateral rounds on tariff negotiation, the achievements of GATT had been considerable, extending in the Uruguay round to concerns of trade in services on a global basis. However, many critics now argue that the role of its successor, the World Trade Organisation (WTO) – has been undermined. In particular, they note that, as international business flows in the modern world have grown more complex, trade policies and protectionist measures have become more concerned with non-tariff barriers which are less easy to detect and far harder to control.

Trading blocs

Compounding the problems of GATT and now the WTO has been the development of regional trading blocs, the single European market being the most publicised and far-reaching. Although the more recent signing of the North American Free Trade Agreement (NAFTA), including the USA, Canada and Mexico, and ongoing talks concerning greater unification of Asia Pacific countries, demonstrate the importance of regionalisation in the global 'triad' (the three leading regions of the developed world), the most notable feature of trading blocs is that they promote free trade on the 'inside' (between participating member states), although external protectionism can be (and often is) a central tenet of supporting government policy. It is only necessary to look to the accusations by the Japanese and Americans of the Europeans creating an impenetrable 'fortress', or the efforts of the USA to reduce Japan's trade surplus with the USA and the concomitant threat of increased protectionism, to understand that many of the trade deals currently being forged are between the triad members – the Americas, the Asia Pacific region and Europe. This has led to a re-emergence of 'bilateral bargaining' in trade negotiations, for example in relation to steel and bananas, which GATT was so anxious to eradicate in the post-war era (Welford and Prescott, 1996).

The desire for countries to affiliate themselves in large economic groupings stems from the belief that large, unrestricted markets lead to intensified competition and thus provide an impetus for improved efficiency. While the term 'efficiency' is often used loosely, here it specifically refers to both static effects (those arising from immediate cost-saving strategies) and dynamic effects (those accruing from better innovation and product development). From the perspective of the European Union, poor economic performance over the last quarter century has been seen to stem from the inability of firms to operate freely on a pan-European scale, restricting competition and efficiency, and thus putting European firms at a disadvantage vis-à-vis their global rivals, from America and Japan in particular.

Protectionism

The magnitude of change within the single European market inevitably raised concern among American and Japanese industrialists, not least because the external trade measures being proposed smacked of renewed protectionism through such means as anti-dumping measures (penalties against firms adjudged to be selling goods in export markets 'below cost' or the selling price in the domestic market); rules of origin (which dictate that the country of origin must be the country where the last major transformation took place, effectively eliminating firms moving goods through countries with unrestricted trade links with the target market); local content rules (which stipulate that, in certain industries, goods sold locally have to contain a certain proportion of components produced in the target market); and voluntary agreements (which act in the same way as quotas, although they are set by the exporting rather than the importing nation, usually on the basis of goodwill).

However, rather than restricting global competition, these measures have, arguably, compounded competition as firms have sought to bypass the non-tariff barriers through foreign direct investment (FDI). This latter point gives credence to the belief that the scope of GATT was not sufficient to control 'trade' on a global scale. Whereas in the early stages of global development firms tended primarily to consider exporting as the available route for foreign market development, in more recent times firms have extended their world activities through a variety of strategic methods. Unsurprisingly, then, the remit of the WTO has been extended beyond just trade agreements and into the realms of global business flows.

The managerial challenge

The questions being asked of managers operating in countries within trading blocs appear clear: embrace the advantages being offered by free trade and extend business activities throughout the internal free market. However, this belies the fact that in many industries, particularly since the advent of electronic commerce, the marketplace has become more global than regional. Concentrating on the extended domestic market (the artificially created internal market) overshadows the importance of establishing a strong global presence. This wider thinking can still be summed up in the words of one UK manager who was asked about his attitude towards the European single market:

> *'We should not get together in an incestuous huddle and ignore the opportunities provided by the rest of the world.'*
> (Buckley *et al.*,1992)

Relying solely on the advantages of regionalisation and attempting to avoid the hurdles of renewed global protectionism are likely to produce few rewards. Managers have to be aware that to be successful globally means taking advantage of the benefits stemming from regionalisation (the impetus for efficiency and technological development) and harnessing the benefits to exploit wider global markets.

This is as applicable to small firms as to their larger counterparts. Taking the example of the UK, managers are well advised first to consider expansion into markets which are 'close to home'. In a geographic sense, this would mean markets such as Belgium, The Netherlands, France and Germany. However, as the experience of many small firms has demonstrated, while such countries are 'close' in spatial terms to the UK, culturally they are far more distant than the USA, Canada, South Africa and Australia, where old colonial links mean a great deal of cultural similarity and a far more familiar operating environment. Consequently, 'cultural or psychic distance' may persuade firms to look beyond the extended European market at an early stage in their internationalisation.

Technological development

Change and demands on product development

While it was once possible for firms to develop a new technology, protect it with patents and exploit the monopoly advantages of the uniqueness of the products developed from the technology, in today's dynamic global environment this is no longer the case. Indeed, Porter (1990) argued long ago that firms attempting to follow this strategy are likely to lag behind in terms of world development as they rest on their laurels from past technological development rather than attempting to produce a continuous stream of new products.

Part of the reasoning behind Porter's argument stems from the rapid rate of change in technology in the modern world and thus the shortening of technological life cycles. This has two important implications: first, product development processes need to be improved to speed up the introduction of new products into the market; secondly, in order that such a rapid introduction of new products can be managed efficiently, managers must adopt new production techniques so that major plant refitting does not become commonplace.

The car industry provides a good example of these management demands in practice. Japanese car manufacturers, whose encroachment on the global car industry was dramatic to say the least, concerned themselves with just these challenges. They developed design techniques which allowed them to introduce new models at a more rapid rate than their Western counterparts (under 43 months in 1990 compared with 62 and 58 months for their American and European volume competitors respectively (*see* Clark and Fujimoto, quoted in Grant, 2002)), and introduced flexible working practices which permitted a large number of models to be produced at the same time. Much of this is still achieved via manufacturing modularisation, which means that most of the components which go to make up a Japanese car are in-sourced from external suppliers:

> *'Modular manufacturing involves designing and assembling the entire car as a series of sub-assemblies or modules. New modules can be developed directly to replace an existing one, allowing cars to be changed easily.'*   (*The Economist*, 29 July 1989)

In this way the Japanese are able to combine the benefits of rapid new technology introduction and production efficiency (through scale economies).

Technology as a facilitator

So far, it has been suggested that technology change is a 'hurdle' which managers must overcome to keep abreast of the competition. Technology change has also, however, served to facilitate internationalisation of firms by making communication, information handling and distribution easier and more efficient (Hill, 1997).

The introduction of the microprocessor, electronic commerce, satellite and cable technology has speeded up global communication and made it possible for very large volumes of information to be gathered and transmitted. Containerised shipping and air-freight have also had a profound effect in terms of physical product distribution, commercial jet travel 'shrinking the globe' in terms of ease of travel to far-flung destinations (Dicken, 1992).

Such changes have all reduced the real costs of communication and transportation, which means that it is now possible to co-ordinate and manage a global organisation with subsidiaries based in the far-flung corners of the world. No longer do various subsidiaries operate as discrete, stand-alone entities divided from their parent company by geographical distance. They may now form an integral whole, joined by modern communication and systems designed to share and develop information on a global basis.

On the one hand, such developments have served to facilitate global business developments; on the other, they have posed serious challenges in terms of effective management and business development. They have raised the importance of integration and co-ordination, but have often resulted in 'information overload' at a head office level, to the extent that many managers have recognised that, in order to avoid the organisation becoming a bureaucratic monolith beset by problems of red tape and X-inefficiency (so often associated with large organisations), new management and organisational structures are essential to combat the information challenges of the modern era. These will be discussed in more detail later in the chapter.

Research and development

Research and development (R&D) tend to be treated as a single term when, in reality, these constitute two separate managerial functions. *Research* refers to the creation of new technologies or product innovations, whereas *development* relates to the process of turning the technologies into products for the marketplace. The importance of this distinction can be clearly seen when considering the success of leading-edge Japanese firms in the global marketplace. In the early post-Second World War years of Japan's economic development, the country was concerned with licensing Western technologies as a way of improving the country's technological base. However, rather than simply replicating the technology and selling it back to the West, the Japanese focused on the process of 'development', refining and improving the technologies to better 'fit' market demands. Nevertheless, more recently, Japanese firms, which have been supported by government programmes and have extended their activities into the area of primary research, have arguably failed to realise the potential to improve their technological position in world marketplaces in the way their American counterparts have. What seems essential, though, is that research activities take place in conjunction with global market considerations and that technologies are tailored to meet market demand.

In line with the above, new product ideas and technologies have generally emanated from those countries with the strongest demand conditions and the largest consumer markets. In the post-war period this meant that many major product developments originated in the USA. With the rise of the Asia Pacific region and recovery of West European markets after the war, this became no longer the case. In 1990, for example, Japan spent 3 per cent of GDP on R&D, Germany 2.7 per cent and the USA 1.8 per cent, though this percentage increased in the 1990s concomitant with America's unequivocal reassertion of technological leadership. Nevertheless, in 2000, gross expenditure on R & D as a percentage of GDP was 2.7 per cent in the USA compared to 2.9 per cent in Japan and 2.5 per cent in Germany. Other countries too have been developing strong research centres in certain industries, which means that developments can now emerge from any number of world markets. For this reason many firms have recognised the importance of internationalising their R&D activities, setting up facilities in centres of global excellence and using local market demand conditions as the impetus for new ideas. This trend will be fully explored later.

Managerial challenges

For MNEs with 'deep-pocket advantages' (i.e. extensive resources for investment), the message is clear. Invest in programmes for continual product development and especially in improvement (*see* Porter *et al.*, 2000) and manufacturing/business systems that facilitate international business activity and flexibility. This does not mean a 'scattergun' approach to investment, but requires careful decision making about the most appropriate areas for investment at any one time. Modern technologies, which are highly complex, require significant amounts of money for research and development. Choosing the direction of research is therefore critical and can be something of a lottery. Governments in many of the developed markets of the world have reacted to this problem and have highlighted key areas of technological development which they consider to be the important growth areas into the new millennium. The main areas highlighted by American, Japanese and European governments are outlined in Table 19.1.

Encouragement of development in these critical areas is also backed by government research funding. In the EU, this includes ESPRIT (European Strategic Programme for Research and Development in Information Technology), RACE (Research and Development in Advanced Communication Technology for Europe),

Table 19.1 **Emerging areas of technology**

JAPAN	USA	EC
Software engineering	Automation	Information technology
New materials	Computing	New materials
Biotechnology	Advanced materials	Biotechnology
Biomaterials	Medical technology	Energy
	Thin layer technology	

Source: European Commission (1988)

BRITE (Basic Research in Industrial Technology for Europe) and EURAM (European Research in Advanced Materials). Many of the grants targeted through these programmes are available to firms prepared to engage in joint activities with competitors. They are, therefore, not only designed to promote new technologies, but also technology transfer for the improvement of the wider European technology base. Managers are well advised to be aware of potential grants and be prepared to liaise with other industry players while nevertheless shielding their unique advantages from them.

For smaller firms, with fewer resources to dedicate to technological development, the challenges are more severe. Failure to keep abreast of technology may ultimately result in their demise, but investment in R&D may be considered too high risk. Nevertheless, as there is no documented proof that large firms are more successful innovators than small firms, there is no size limit on firms allowed to bid for government support. Alternatively, small firms may be best served by concentrating their efforts on product development, refining technologies for specific market niches or licensing in technologies with market potential.

Political change

The opening up of communist countries to Western businesses and the adoption of capitalist principles by many previously centrally planned economies has, albeit haltingly, extended business opportunities on a global scale. The initial rush for developed country multinationals to establish a presence in the newly emerging markets, be it via joint venture or foreign direct investment, has met with mixed fortune and has led to greater caution and tempered optimism. China, India, the Czech Republic, former East Germany, Brazil and a whole host of other 'best' emerging markets have become the focus for international operators seeking long-term growth and development.

Although many of these regions are far from ensuring long-term political stability, as the Asian financial crisis that began in 1997 has illustrated only too well, their growing liberalisation, deregulation and genuine openness to companies from developed countries (and their technologies) have changed the orientation of many businesses. Even where corporate governance needs substantial upgrading and opportunities may not turn out to result in short-term profit, the search for first-mover advantages and the belief that countries such as these will offer up vast consumer markets in the future make them attractive to today's investors.

Management challenges

Entering these new countries and servicing the needs of customers pose a number of serious challenges to international firms:

■ Dealing with new cultures, some of which are still dominated by communist ideals and work practices that can make the establishment of efficient business systems difficult. Employees who fail to understand the importance of productivity, partner companies for whom the concept of marketing is alien, bureaucratic rules, black-market economies, cronyism and corruption all need to be understood and catered for.

■ Co-operative business solutions are often the only means of entry, either to reduce risk or to secure access where governments place restrictions on foreign ownership. Hence some companies need to develop new internal skills to manage co-operative rather than competitive business operations.

■ Changing the balance of world business operations. Emerging markets in the East (particularly India and China), with their large populations and extensive natural resources, mean a further shift in economic activity towards the Asia Pacific region, despite the greater uncertainties of doing business there. This will inevitably change the balance of world business and force companies to reassess their own international balance and coverage.

International money markets

The achievement of monetary union in 'Euroland' in the single European market in 1999, although beset by problems as a result of national sovereign concerns, has received a lot of support from European managers. The main reason for this is that a common currency in Europe has allowed firms to plan with greater certainty, as European business transactions have largely been removed from the uncertainties of exchange rate fluctuations.

In recent years, flexible exchange rates have come to characterise international business transactions. This means that the value of any currency for international traders is the price at which the currency is traded in the open market. Consequently, international business traders are subject to sometimes dramatic changes in domestic and foreign economic conditions which have an important impact on the price competitiveness of goods traded abroad. With exchange rate fluctuations difficult to predict, there is always the risk that between agreement of terms for exporting contracts and final payment, exchange rate movements eradicate profits. Nevertheless, exchange rate movements can confer as many advantages as they can pain. Multinationals, paradoxically exposed to a greater mix of currencies of input or supply and of output or demand, are much less at risk. They find that often as a result of globalisation pressures, they are much more naturally hedged than the simple exporter or importer, whose reliance on operational techniques and financial instruments may still leave their currency imbalances unsolved (*see* Edelshain, 1995).

Such is the case for small firms, usually dealing in fewer overseas markets and thus spreading their risk more thinly, for whom adverse movements in exchange rates can be critical. Recurring risks can only be minimised at the cost of taking out 'insurance'; forward exchange protection provided by banks (at a price) can only eliminate each transaction risk to ensure that the final payment matches the agreed price at the time the contract was signed. Risk to its future business, its economic exposure, remains. For larger firms, establishing overseas facilities may prove a more favourable alternative. This means that activities are undertaken in the foreign country (and currency), and cash flow and profits may only be converted into the domestic currency when exchange rates are favourable.

A fixed exchange rate (sought through the European Exchange Rate Mechanism) and the single European currency eradicate most (but not all, as there is still exposure to non-euro competitors) such problems for European business operations in Euroland, further facilitating the potential to operate unhindered in a wider European market. Many economists believed that European firms would only reap the full benefits of economic union once the single currency had been fully established, putting them on a par with their American and Japanese counterparts, who are able to conduct business in large domestic markets in a single currency. However, a proviso must be that the euro replaces the US dollar as the currency of many current European business transactions and it is still uncertain whether these benefits have yet been captured.

CROSS-CULTURAL MANAGEMENT

The terms 'culture' and 'cultural difference' are used liberally by international managers, although the reality of what these concepts mean in practice is likely to be far less widely understood (Figure 19.1 shows the main elements of culture). As soon as any organisation begins to sell its products and services outside its own domestic market, indeed to set up an operation in a local market to do so, it will be exposed to

Figure 19.1 Elements of culture

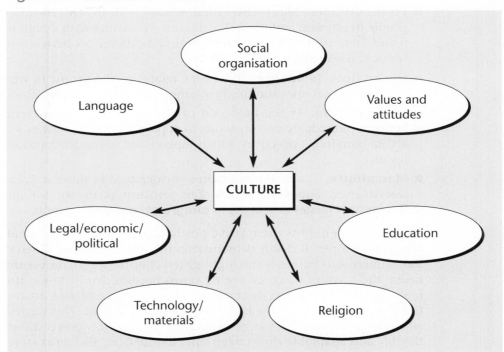

a different cultural environment with its own distinct norms and behaviours. Ultimately, cultural sensitivity can mean the difference between success and failure. Ricks and Mahajan's (1984) analysis of 'blunders' in international marketing examines a number of cases where firms (even leading multinational players) have failed to understand fully local market nuances, with disastrous results. For example, General Motors' promotional campaign in Belgium centred on a slogan of 'Body by Fischer', which in translation read 'Corpse by Fischer'; the same company launched a brand of car in Puerto Rico called the 'Nova', which in the local language sounded like 'no va' – it does not go; Goodyear Tyre and Rubber Company made illegal claims of superiority about its products in West Germany, because it did not take account of local legal requirements; and General Mills allegedly targeted its advertising in the UK at children, which was considered unethical. Mistakes of this kind can prove costly and may also damage the reputation of the firm in the marketplace. As damaging can be an ethnocentric approach to the way one's staff in foreign branches and subsidiaries are managed. Perlmutter (1969) has highlighted the danger of doing everything the way it is done in the home or head office country, as distinct from the way they do it locally or anywhere else in the world where they may do it better still. Remembering that we employ self-reference criteria in evaluating other cultures, taking cultural management seriously is, therefore, a prerequisite to doing business abroad if a firm wants to ensure long-term growth and survival.

Defining and categorising culture

One of the most notable studies of the relationship between national cultures and values in the workplace was undertaken by Geert Hofstede between 1967 and 1973. Based on research of 116 000 business personnel from over 17 countries, he identified 11 clusters of countries along his four original key dimensions (Hofstede, 1983):

- **Power distance.** This focuses on how society deals with inequalities between people in physical and educational terms – countries with a high score (between 0 and 100) are those which feature broad differences between individuals in terms of power and wealth.
- **Uncertainty avoidance.** This index relates to the extent to which countries establish formal rules and fixed patterns of life (such as career structures).
- **Individualism.** At the high end of the scale are those societies where ties between individuals are very loose, as opposed to those societies where individuals are born into 'collectives' which support and foster development in return for loyalty.
- **Masculinity.** The more 'masculine' a society, the more it values outcomes, assertiveness and materialism. Less concern is shown for quality of life. 'Femininity' relates to process, to caring and concern for people.

Figure 19.2 highlights the relative positions on a four-dimensional matrix for a range of countries. It clearly demonstrates that there are broad differences along the four dimensions between the highlighted countries, differences that need to be taken into account when managing across borders. For instance, the UK displays low scores for both power distance and uncertainty avoidance, an average score on the masculinity index and a high score for individualism. This suggests a society in which negotiation figures large in decision making (low power distance), rules are flexible and adaptable (low uncertainty avoidance), and great store is placed on

Figure 19.2 **Cross-cultural comparisons**

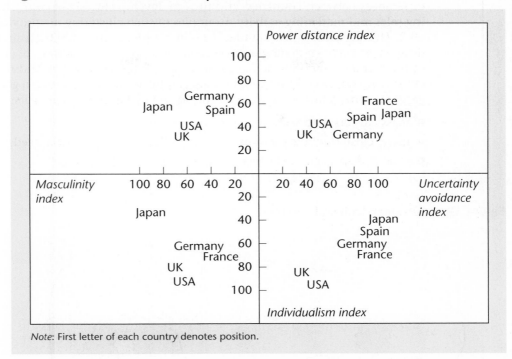

Note: First letter of each country denotes position.

personal development, and success and entrepreneurship (high individualism and medium masculinity). This compares with a country like France, where society is based on a pyramidal hierarchy held together by tight rules and unity of command, or Germany, where personal command is largely unnecessary as rules settle everything.

More recently, Hofstede has also added a fifth dimension to his research: **time-frame**. Here he distinguishes between long-term and short-term orientation of business. **Long-term orientation** relates to such values as thrift and perseverance, while **short-term values** include respect for personal tradition, social obligations and 'saving face'. Generally, East Asian cultures show the most long-term orientation, while European and American cultures figure quite low in the rankings.

Research, by those like Hofstede (1983) and Trompenaars (1993), has provided managers with insights into different business behaviours and practices around the world, preparing them for the challenges of management in terms of:

- understanding business practices and ways of viewing business development;
- understanding business structures and organisation from a cultural perspective;
- understanding what motivates people in terms of their career and personal aspirations.

It may be argued, however, that Hofstede's five dimensions provide an oversimplistic view of cultural difference between the markets of the world and fail to give much insight into the workings of society as a whole. Here, other alternatives need to be considered. The model depicted in Figure 19.1, which suggests a number of cultural elements for analysis, provides an alternative that extends understanding beyond the business world to customers and markets.

Cultural analysis of this nature allows managers to identify commonalities and differences between countries, and thus to develop clusters of countries for targeting sales and marketing activity. Examples of such clustering are provided in Figure 19.3. This is based on work undertaken by Vandermerwe (1993) on similarities and differences between demographics, economic variables and lifestyle characteristics of the member states of the European Union. Interestingly, her findings show that clusters are not necessarily based on geographic boundaries. She also goes on to suggest that other 'clusters' need to be considered by European managers:

- mass clusters with common consumer needs;
- niche clusters where consumers have similar but not identical needs;
- local and specialised clusters.

Figure 19.3 European 'cultural clusters'

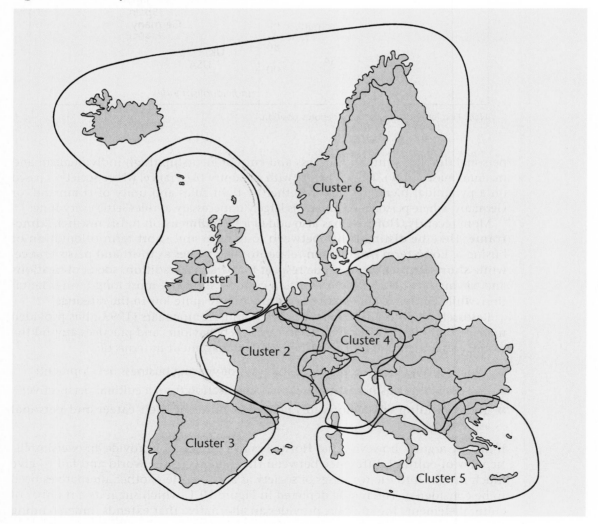

Source: Vandermerwe (1993)

The management challenge, then, is not simply to be aware of the individual cultural elements of each society, but in understanding and managing the extent and nature of diversity between different cultures.

Managing diversity

Nations and societies are not the same: each has features which make it unique and distinct from both immediate and distant neighbours. This diversity poses a serious challenge to international managers, who not only have to understand different needs, wants, business and buyer behaviours in different clusters, but also have to integrate this diversity into an holistic strategy.

It has been argued (Bloom *et al.*, 1994) that Europeans are better than their international counterparts at dealing with diversity. Because business in Europe has been developed across a wide array of diverse national cultures, mechanisms for integrating diversity have been central to competitive success. This compares with the Japanese, who developed their businesses in a highly homogeneous market, and with the Americans who have sought to integrate diverse cultures into a uniquely identifiable and all-embracing 'American' norm. As a result, it is not surprising that American and Japanese management models typically highlight diversity as a problem, while Europeans consider it a way of life.

This kind of thinking has led to distinct differences in approach to international strategic development across the world. Porter (1991), perhaps idealistically, suggested:

> *'One of the things that Europe 1992 integration will do is hasten the process by which larger European companies move from confederations of subsidiaries to become truly integrated, world-wide competitors. For each product line, there will be a clear home base, with some or many outside the home country. European companies have tended to do well in businesses that are essentially a collection of national markets but not so well in the truly global arena.'*

In other words, Europeans' tendency to deal with diversity by focusing on differentiation and local market adaptation, while attractive in the past, is less desirable in the European (and global) markets of today, where greater commonality between regions and potential for more standardisation and integration of business practices are not only possible, but desirable.

Brian Goldthorp, Director of Personnel at Trafalgar House, confirms this line of thinking:

> *'But the reverse side of the coin is that when we look at parts of the world where these pressures of diversity are not as overwhelming as they are in Europe, we continue to concentrate on dealing with differentiation, so Europeans are less successful there. American and Japanese corporations show the reciprocal traits. They are enormously good where there are products and strategies of an undifferentiated kind.'*

(Bloom, *et al.*, p 41)

Aside from advantages of local responsiveness, other benefits accrue from a differentiated approach to strategic management across cultures: an ability to work successfully in other cultures and adapt to the nuances and norms of different societies. Japanese managers often find this difficult as a result of their 'sheltered' development in a homogeneous society. The literature is now awash with examples of the serious problems experienced by Japanese companies attempting to introduce Japanese management practices into the West. Their approach is to persuade people that the

Japanese way is the best, even if some of the practices run counter to local cultural norms and practices. Americans, on the other hand, tend to be more dogmatic: they impose structures and rules, and demand change from local employees.

The message seems to be that managers need to extend their 'toolkit'. They need to be made aware of the different strategic options available to them so they can devise the most appropriate fit between strategy and diverse market structure. This may mean shifting towards a more transnational strategy: balancing differentiation (local adaptation) and standardisation (centralisation into larger units), simply looking for parts of the business where change of this kind is appropriate, or consolidating the chosen approach (global or multidomestic) to suit the needs of the product market.

Cultural change

All of the above takes place against a backdrop of change. Culture, whether national or business-based, is a dynamic phenomenon: norms and practices are continually adjusting and changing. However, there is little agreement on whether such change is bringing markets closer together, or breaking them apart into smaller niche segments.

Some industry observers argue that culture is becoming increasingly homogeneous on a global scale. Certain global products have become widely accepted, partly because they appeal to large, cultural subgroups which show a degree of standardisation on a global scale. Coca-Cola, Levi jeans and Reebock training shoes, McDonald's hamburgers and Swatch watches have broad appeal to the youth 'sub-culture'. Products of this kind suggest that there is scope for global standardisation, although in all these cases the way in which the product is managed at a local level shows a degree of differentiation on a market-by-market basis as a result of local country cultural conditions. Such adaptation may include:

- product/servicing adaptation to cater for different needs and wants and competitor activity;
- adaptation of promotion and advertising such that the message is relevant to local customers and meets with local legislation and standards;
- adaptation of channel decisions due to different buying behaviour;
- adaptation of recruitment policies in line with local educational systems and standards;
- adaptation of pay and remuneration to ensure staff motivation;
- adaptation of price to fit with local conditions.

Others point to the way in which cultural groups are becoming more distinct from each other:

> '*In Coca-Cola we're seeing a dichotomy taking place in business today. Some of the customers of the Coca-Cola system in Europe, such as large international companies, are becoming more European. Many of them want one programme for Europe.*
>
> *On the other hand, the consumer is becoming more local, in our view. We are advertising Coca-Cola in Barcelona today in two languages – Spanish and Catalan. It is a recent phenomenon and we see it taking place in Scotland, Wales, the French regions, the German Länder ... People are becoming more culturally attuned with their localities and marketeers have to recognise it and be prepared to deal with it.*'

(Ralph Cooper, President of Coca-Cola's European Community Group,
Bloom *et al.*, 1994: 50)

It is clear that Levitt's (1983) prediction that intensified competition and techno-logical development would lead companies to operate globally, ignoring 'superficial' national differences, is unlikely ever to apply to all firms in all indus-tries across the world. This is particularly so when growing consumer wealth allows consumers to be more discriminating.

While we may be seeing the emergence of a 'global village' in terms of our aware-ness of our neighbours, this does not automatically suggest that neighbours will seek to become like each other. With evidence apparently to prove both sides of the debate, the only conclusion can be: 'it depends'. While, from a management point of view, this is far from satisfying, as it provides few guidelines and prescriptions, it is important to consider the strategic management challenge as one which incorpo-rates a review of individual markets, products and timeframes (Halliburton and Hünerberg, 1987).

MATCHING STRATEGIES TO THE INTERNATIONAL ENVIRONMENT

International firms have at their disposal a wide range of strategic options from which to draw. At a generic level, firms may choose between exporting, licensing and other contractual arrangements and foreign direct investment, although at an operational level each of these alternatives offers up a wide range of strategic alter-natives. It is beyond the scope of this chapter to explore fully the nature of these alternatives but see Dunning (1988), who does so. What is important, however, is understanding some of the key differences and managerial considerations.

Understanding decision-making criteria

To return to the argument outlined above, the dynamic and diverse global business environment of today makes it difficult to prescribe generic solutions to manage-ment challenges. Much depends on the nature of the market, the product and the firm itself. Failure to make pragmatic decisions about the best 'fit' of strategy to market conditions is likely to result in managers missing the best opportunities for exploiting their advantages in foreign markets. This involves managers considering a wide array of both internal and external factors and choosing the most appropri-ate strategy in each instance.

External factors include:

- **host market factors** – size, growth, competitive conditions, distribution, infra-structure;
- **host market environment** – political, economic and socio-cultural conditions;
- **host market production factors** – availability, quality and costs of inputs;
- **domestic market factors** – competitive conditions, growth, government policies and internal factors.

Internal factors include:

- **product factors** – product technology, differentiation, service provision and potential for global standardisation;
- **company resources** – management, capital and technology, and overall commit-ment to international business.

Assessing the most appropriate means of entering and servicing the market along each of these dimensions is likely to result in a number of different options being appropriate for a variety of reasons. Managers therefore have to decide on a final strategy based on (a) their overall objectives for growth and development, and (b) the weighting of factors in their own industry's competitive development.

For instance, the company has to decide on both the long-term and short-term objectives for entering a particular market. If, for instance, the company's objective is merely to sell off excess capacity in overseas markets, it is unlikely that foreign investment will prove attractive. If, on the other hand, the company is looking to establish a committed presence in the market, it may wish to invest significant resources in establishing a strong market presence. In terms of weighting factors, in some industries certain factors emerge as being more critical than others. Take, for example, the retail financial service industry: with many markets being mature and in a state of overcapacity, foreign direct investment, attractive in terms of local presence and closeness to customers, is both expensive and limited in its potential to secure significant market penetration. Gaining access to established distribution networks through alliances (or possibly takeover of existing organisations) is the priority, and thus distribution conditions should be highly weighted in making the final decision.

It is clear from this very brief overview that the decision-making challenge facing international managers, with regard to market entry, is highly complex, requiring high levels of research and detailed analysis. This is explored more fully in Grant (2002). More often than not, however, firms base their decisions on imperfect information, as information is either too expensive to gather or not available, or decisions need to be made quickly if firms are to take advantage of available opportunities. For many managers, then, the reality of international decision making is strategic adjustment, considering changes in operational modes, which mean either shifts between generic modes of market servicing or inter-mode shifts, such as from exporting via a sales representative to exporting via a wholly owned subsidiary. These decisions are usually made in line with the ongoing experience of the firm, the learning curve, wherein additional knowledge about the market and the product's experience in that market gives better information on which to base strategic decisions.

Consequently, foreign market servicing decisions are dynamic. Continual assessment and reassessment is essential if firms are to adjust to changes in both internal and external conditions.

Exploiting compensating advantages

Firms entering foreign markets are often at a disadvantage *vis-à-vis* indigenous companies as a result of their lack of understanding of the local market. The pioneering work of Hymer (1960), which is often considered to be the foundation of current international business theory, proposed that market entrants require some form of compensating advantage to compete successfully with local firms, which possess innate strengths. Such advantage may include proprietary technology (raising the emphasis of technology development and management), preferential access to capital, superior marketing skills, absolute cost advantages, economies of scale, or product differentiation.

Firms exporting to the foreign market are usually at a disadvantage compared to local organisations because of their distance from the market. This has two effects: it makes it difficult to monitor market conditions; but, perhaps more importantly, it also raises doubts in the mind of the consumer about the firm's ability to deliver on time and to provide appropriate service and back-up. Local agents and distributors can act as a surrogate presence in the market, alleviating these problems, although the question for consumers remains: Why should I buy from a foreign firm if a local organisation can equally satisfy my needs? Managers must therefore concern themselves with positioning the product (through differentiation) and promoting it in such a way that there are perceived advantages in purchasing a foreign alternative.

Firms undertaking licensing and other contractual arrangements avoid the problems of 'foreignness', because local firms act as representatives in the local market. Indeed, as products are produced locally, consumers may be unaware of the fact that the technology or brand belongs to a foreign firm. The main concern with licensing (and joint ventures) is that the agreement will give rise to a competitor. Because the company is imparting knowledge and/or expertise to a third party, there is the possibility that the company's comparative advantage will be eroded through transfer and this will subsequently be used against it on termination of the contract. Patents and trademarks may provide a degree of protection. Alternatively, firms may consider providing partners with a 'secret ingredient' supplied to the third party through a tied purchase agreement, where the licensee or joint venture partner is contracted to obtain certain components from the licensor. Some anti-trust authorities, however, rule against such agreements as they see them as being anti-competitive.

Within licensing and other contractual arrangements, therefore, the key managerial decision is not so much what returns will be produced in the short term, but the long-term implications of technology transfer. If the firm's compensating advantage is its proprietary technology, sharing technological information should usually be avoided.

Foreign direct investment gives firms the ability to establish a local persona and compete on a more equal level with indigenous firms. Indeed, many of the long-established multinational enterprises in global markets have carved out a global rather than a home-country persona which gives them complete acceptability in foreign markets.

The issue of government procurement requires some attention in relation to foreign direct investment. In some industries, governments are the major purchasers of goods and services (e.g. the defence industry and pharmaceuticals). There is a natural tendency for governments to purchase goods and services from local firms to the exclusion of foreign organisations, regardless of price and quality differentials, because of the benefits of lower transport and trading costs, better after-sales service and quicker delivery. There are also social benefits in terms of supporting employment, assisting ailing industries, bolstering new emerging sectors and ensuring profits are earned locally. Firms operating in these industries, therefore, have little choice but to locate activities in the target market. Failure to do so is likely to result in their exclusion from public procurement contracts and an inability to penetrate the market.

Internalisation versus externalisation

Taking the three generic modes, it is possible to suggest that exporting and foreign direct investment differ from licensing in that production is internalised, i.e. carried out by the firm itself. In the case of licensing and other contractual relationships, however, production (and possibly other complementary functions) are 'externalised' and are carried out by a third party. In many ways this is an oversimplistic way of categorising strategies, as it only relates to the nature of the production process and ignores other business functions such as sales and marketing and distribution. Taking this wider perspective, it is possible to suggest various forms of exporting via intermediaries which also include elements of externalisation, and licensing which involves the supply of critical components to the licensee firm and involves a degree of internalisation. What is important, therefore, is not an attempt to categorise various strategic alternatives, but an understanding of the managerial challenge in terms of balancing advantages from internalisation and externalisation (i.e. weighing up relative costs of administration against those of conducting transactions, in undertaking business activities within the firm or relying on third parties conducting various value chain activities).

Critical to the management consideration in this respect is the concept of control. Internalisation of activities implies full control over business functions. This is often believed to be a source of advantage as it gives managers free choice over strategies and operational decision making, which can be hard to achieve when working with a third party. Nevertheless, firms have to trade-off the additional costs incurred in gaining control, both in terms of ownership of business facilities and the ongoing costs associated with day-to-day management of a full range of business functions, against the benefits of ownership.

This assumes that success is critically dependent on control, which may not always be the case. Take the example of a firm exporting via a host country distributor. In an effort to ensure that the foreign intermediary maximises business on the exporter's behalf, the firm may set targets and quotas, offer rewards for meeting specified sales volumes, or impose sanctions if targets are not met. In this way, the firm may seek to 'control' the intermediary. Alternatively, the firm may choose to co-operate with the intermediary, providing additional support, such as sales and service training, and providing targeted promotional literature.

Research by the Industrial Marketing and Purchasing Group (Valla, 1986) underlines that for more than two decades the idea that co-operation in such circumstances is preferable to control has been recognised. Here, better results stem from investing more human resources into the operation, basing staff from the supplier organisation in the target market to assist the intermediary, demonstrating positive commitment and encouraging the agent to work harder on the principal's behalf. Similarly, encouraging personnel to become involved with their counterparts in the customer organisation at various functional levels strengthens the bond between supplier and final customer, and raises the level of trust and understanding. Here, bilateral relations between supplier and intermediary are extended to 'tripartite' relations, where the manufacturer is also in direct contact with the final customer, working in conjunction with the intermediary.

The success of Japanese firms in the car industry provides a further example of co-operation rather than control. Rather than integrate backwards and 'internalise' component manufacture, Japanese firms prefer to establish close working relationships with their suppliers, a co-operative solution rather than an attempt to derive full control. The success of this kind of practice has led Western car manufacturers to follow suit, the industry now being characterised by car assemblers (the leading manufacturers) extending their power through close business linkages rather than ownership of diverse business functions.

What ownership does afford, however, and the focus of Japanese foreign direct investment in the USA in setting up or acquiring distribution companies underlines this, is internalisation of information and more direct lines of communication between the market and the decision-making locus of the organisation. In this respect, intermediaries may be seen as either facilitators or bottlenecks for information gathering. Where working relationships are good, the third-party organisation is more likely to collect and pass on critical information, although there is a limit to the amount of time and attention it is able or prepared to dedicate to such a function for one manufacturer, which may only contribute a small part to its total business portfolio. This has led, in many instances, to firms establishing sales and marketing offices in foreign markets, not only for the purpose of handling contracts in the overseas market, but in order to have an operation 'on the ground' that is able to monitor changes in market conditions and demand patterns. This points to the splitting up, in locational terms, of various business functions in the value chain.

Centralisation versus decentralisation

It is also possible to distinguish between the three generic modes of foreign market servicing in terms of the location of business activities. With manufacture, licensing and foreign direct investment involve manufacturing in the host country, while exporting involves manufacturing in the domestic market or another manufacturing base outside the target market. Once again, however, this oversimplification ignores the tendency for firms to internationalise different parts of the business rather than all elements of the value chain.

The critical managerial decision here is between centralisation and decentralisation. Centralisation assumes that advantages accrue from conducting business in large-scale centres where economies of scale can be achieved in a variety of business functions. Decentralisation, on the other hand, assumes that greater advantages arise from conducting business in the host market, where adaptation to the local environment and greater decision-making flexibility through local autonomy permit a higher degree of local sensitivity.

Within the European Union, many of the cost-saving benefits ascribed to unification are seen to come from economies of scale, which suggests centralisation is the key challenge. This need not, however, mean single-site production locations. Plant economies can be achieved through specialisation, individual manufacturing units concentrating on single products, or on a narrow range of the company's portfolio, which allows the removal of effort duplication and thus greater plant efficiency. McCains, the Canadian frozen food manufacturer, has followed this approach in its European operations, and the UK pharmaceutical firm, Glaxo, has taken advantage of the liberalisation of the American market through the NAFTA agreement to reorganise production in its Mexican, American and Canadian plants on a product-specific basis.

A trend may, however, be observed in terms of decentralisation of sales and marketing activities. While cost-saving and plant economies may be attractive in production, closeness to the market and local responsiveness dominate in sales and distribution. Management can no longer consider the business as an amalgam of functions. These need to be unbundled and decisions made separately concerning their centralisation or decentralisation, if a balance is to be struck between the advantages offered by both approaches.

This means looking beyond simple taxonomies and classifications, and finding creative solutions to problems. Take the case of Lucas Girling, part of the Lucas Engineering Group, manufacturing motor braking systems. As closeness to customers is paramount (because of the co-operative alliances established in the car industry), the company has little choice but to manufacture in close proximity to the major car assemblers. At face value, this dilutes the potential for economies of scale, necessitating the establishment of many global production centres, with a degree of duplication of effort. However, through the adoption of 'flexible specialisation' and computer-aided manufacturing, its plants are small (employing between 40 and 50 employees) and capable of batch-sized production. Thus, even with decentralisation, it is able to achieve adaptability and efficiency.

Standardisation versus adaptation

Standardisation of products also gives the potential for economies of scale. However, global standardisation is not possible for many products, as they need to be adapted to cater for local market conditions and, in particular, for that country's cultural nuances. Where product adaptation is necessary, the attraction of centralised production diminishes, as the downtime in production required to change machinery over from one product to another can be outweighed by the benefits of establishing dedicated manufacturing facilities in the target market.

The decision to standardise or adapt involves a trade-off between the costs and benefits to the firm. In essence, managers have to decide whether the cost savings from producing on a large-scale basis outweigh the profits resulting from local market adaptation (which may involve the establishment of local manufacturing plants). This decision is determined by a number of factors:

- **the nature of the product** – it is generally agreed that industrial products are easier to standardise than consumer products, the latter being greatly influenced by cultural tastes;
- **legal requirements** – product, packaging and labelling standards which often differ markedly on a country-by-country basis;
- **physical conditions** – such as climate, living conditions and income;
- **competition** – which will dictate market positioning and differentiation.

What also emerges is that the standardisation versus adaptation issue impinges on the decision to centralise or decentralise manufacturing and, taken together, these two issues combine to explain the overall strategic orientation discussed above: international, multidomestic, multinational and transnational.

Business organisation

Business organisation is seldom something which is planned: typically it evolves as a firm grows and diversifies. Structures emerge out of strategic decisions regarding the nature of products and services, and the geographic coverage of the firm in the international marketplace. Through this evolutionary process, there are four different 'ideal' types of organisational structure the firm may employ: an international division structure, a product division structure, a geographic division structure and a matrix structure. Each of these is depicted in Figure 19.4.

International division structure

Small firms expanding abroad for the first time, as Swedish research (Johanson and Vahine, 1977) has uniquely confirmed, tend to establish an export office or an

Figure 19.4 (a) Product division structure with separate international division (b) Global product division structure (c) Global geographic division structure (d) Simplified global matrix structure

international division, staffed, in the first instance, by a small number of personnel, responsible for all international business dealings (i.e. all products in all markets). As the scale and scope of international activity grows, the export focus of this division may change to one that supports international production effort. This production may be organised on a country-by-country basis (a full range of the portfolio being produced in each target market) or a product basis (different products being produced in different centres). But, whilst Davis (1992) reported that 60 per cent of all firms that have internationalised have first adopted this structure other research has consistently failed to identify any one pattern of internationalisation.

There are some problems associated with this kind of structure. First, it creates conflict between national and international decision making. It is not uncommon for the international division to have less say in corporate policy making, even when it contributes more to the overall business, simply because it was 'added-on' at a later stage in the company's development. Secondly, it is difficult for the head of the international division to rationalise the demands of different countries and/or products. Thirdly, it does not provide opportunities for co-ordination between domestic and international activities. This can make global product development difficult to achieve and global production planning, based on experience curve and locational economies, hard to manage. As a result of these limitations, firms expanding internationally often shift to one of the international organisation structures outlined below.

Product division structure

This is usually a structure adopted by companies that have a diverse product portfolio. The headquarters is responsible for supporting and managing each product on a worldwide basis in terms of design, value adding, sales and promotion. The great advantage of this kind of structure is that it allows a company to focus on global efficiencies within disparate product divisions, locating production in low-cost centres and generating efficiency through product focus. The main disadvantage of such an option is that it can hamper the ability of the company to be responsive at a national level.

Geographic division structure

The focus here is on adapting to differences between countries and geographic regions. Different divisions are set up in geographic centres and decision making is regionally rather than internationally centralised. This structure tends to be used where companies have a low degree of diversification but are intent on maximising advantages from local adaptation. Geographic areas are often self-contained, with their own R&D, production, and sales and marketing. The main advantage of this approach is the ability to maximise local responsiveness, although this may be traded-off against a higher cost structure, as duplication is commonplace.

Global matrix structure

The above description suggests that a geographic division structure better suits a multidomestic focus, while a global product division structure is appropriate for firms pursuing global or international strategies. But what is appropriate for firms attempting to pursue a transnational strategy? The global matrix structure offers the potential to derive the benefits from both the geographic and product division structures outlined above. The theory suggests that decision making is organised along two dimensions – product and market – based on a process of co-operation, consultation and compromise.

While, in theory at least, the matrix structure looks to offer distinct advantages, in practice these advantages are far from easy to realise. Consensus decision making is hard to achieve, particularly as there is inherent conflict between local adaptation and the generation of scale economies. Attempts to reach consensus can severely slow down the decision-making process and limit the degree to which the firm is responsive to the dynamics of the market.

As a result, 'matrix' organisations of the 1990s have emerged from attempts to evolve flexibility rather than from wholesale adoption of new structures. The matrix structure involves the establishment of networks, the splitting up of businesses into constituent functions (production versus marketing versus R&D) and the establishment of inter-function/inter-country project groups.

Research on managing the multinational enterprise points to the development of global 'heterarchies' characterised by multiple centres of control (functional, geographic or product-based) co-ordinated through normative means:

> *'Corporate culture, management ethics, style and similar concepts become critical in understanding why a heterarchy does not break down into anarchy.'*

> (Hedlund and Rolander, 1990 pp 25–6)

A multinational company might, therefore, have various 'headquarters' around the world: an administrative HQ in its domestic market; a financial centre in London; an R&D centre in Germany (a centre of excellence for technological development); and manufacturing headquarters in the three triad regions – the Americas, Asia Pacific and Europe. Certain Japanese multinationals, such as Canon and Honda, have developed what has been termed 'the four headquarters system', which involves establishing regional headquarters in Japan, Asia, the USA and Europe. The aim is to satisfy local requirements while at the same time exploiting the strengths of being a worldwide producer.

The main advantage of the heterarchy is its flexibility. It allows managers to concentrate on different functional areas of the business independently (and perhaps at different times) and permits a high degree of diversity in strategic development, giving subsidiaries scope to develop local business operations in a way which is appropriate to local conditions. Flexibility also extends to the development of co-operative agreements with other organisations which may be decided at a functional rather than corporate level. The obvious question, though, is how does this highly diverse and geographically dispersed organisation integrate? The answer lies in the sharing of information between the various parts, now possible with modern technology, which means that experiences of one division in one part of the world can be shared and drawn on by divisions elsewhere. The domestic head office therefore becomes a conduit for information transfer and a co-ordinating mechanism for the company's objectives and overall direction. No longer is it a decision-making machine; it is a facilitator for a global business network.

Organising for technological development

With technology change featuring so largely in the emerging global business environment, the challenge of managing technological development deserves some comment. Up until relatively recently, many multinational companies took the decision to centralise their global R&D activities for a variety of reasons. First, there was the need to control the development of new technologies on which the company's future competitiveness might rest. Secondly, there were economies of scale in R&D where very large amounts of resources can be concentrated into single centres with no duplication of effort. Finally, there was the fear that foreign research departments might be a source of leakage of ideas and knowledge.

Changes in the global environment and the carving up of the world market into three leading global centres, many yielding 'centres of excellence' in research in particular industries, has changed the thinking of technology managers in many multinationals. Decentralisation of R&D functions has begun to feature in the strategies of global firms as they seek to derive maximum advantage from a global organisation. The following outline of various types of R&D organisational development, derived by Bartlett and Ghoshal (1990), explains this thinking:

- **Centre for global.** This is the approach typically followed by multinationals (outlined above). While there are advantages in terms of control and scale economies, this approach runs the risk of being insensitive to local market demands in the leading markets of the world.

- **Local for local.** This approach suggests conducting research in all target markets in order that the technologies which are developed match local market demands. While beneficial in terms of local adaptation, the approach implicitly involves duplication of effort and a tendency for subsidiaries to 'reinvent the wheel' in an attempt to maintain the local autonomy.

- **Locally leveraged.** Under this arrangement managers can take the most creative and innovative developments from the various subsidiaries and share them with other subsidiaries worldwide. The main disadvantage here is that there are frequently impediments to transferring products from one market to another – particularly cultural differences and local market demand conditions.

- **Globally linked.** The final approach (promoted by Bartlett and Goshal as the optimum solution to the technology development challenge) involves the establishment of flexible linkages between research teams from various global centres. Structures of this kind allow companies to exploit synergies in technology development at the same time as exploiting local leverage advantages. The major drawbacks to this approach are the cost of co-ordination and the complexities of managing the linkages on an ongoing basis.

None of the approaches, therefore, emerges as adeptly suited to the changing global environment. Each has its advantages and disadvantages. This points to managers developing flexible systems which allow them to maximise a variety of advantages from the different approaches, while at the same time minimising the costs and managerial complexities. This may mean having major centres for R&D in a number of key global locations, with a series of local R&D support offices acting more as idea-generating centres than capital-intensive research laboratories.

International strategic development of small firms

The literature on business start-up has typically suggested that companies should concentrate their activities on securing a defensible domestic position before exploring international opportunities. The belief is that small firms should start in a national region, roll out to the national market, and then cherry-pick opportunities in the international arena, but how appropriate is such a prescription for a small firm in the twenty-first century which has developed an innovative technology and whose marketplace is a niche which extends beyond national borders?

Today, many global industries sport the features of a global oligopoly: at one end of the scale, a small number of large multinationals (often no more than one from each developed nation) competing globally on differentiation rather than price and, at the other, a large number of small, specialist niche players satisfying the needs of small customer groups. With intense competition, these niches are tending to get smaller and smaller, and firms are therefore forced to target their activities more closely towards ever more specialised customer groups. This often means that national marketplaces are not of a sufficient scale to support the activities of small, specialist firms, which are therefore forced to internationalise, often early on in their development cycle.

These firms, lacking the financial resources to consider large-scale investment, are forced to explore creative solutions to their international expansion and development. This often leads them to work co-operatively, either with distributors or partner-manufacturers, or to establish small-scale offices (often staffed by only one person) in key markets where it is essential to have eyes and ears to the ground.

While many of the problems of standardisation versus adaptation, internalisation versus externalisation and co-ordination remain the same for small organisations, they face a series of other challenges:

- cash flow management, which has implications if adding resources to support international expansion;
- financial management and the high risk of non-payment – whereas large firms can cross-subsidise, small firms are vulnerable and so have to seek protection through the purchase of, often expensive, insurance products;
- strategic vision and international capabilities – with a small workforce, much depends on the vision and ability of the chief executive.

It is arguable, therefore, that small-firm managers need to be better prepared than their large-firm counterparts. For them, survival may rest on their successfully exploiting opportunities in a diverse array of markets worldwide, which stretches their resources and demands very high levels of cultural sensitivity and diversity integration.

Business co-operation

One of the issues highlighted above was the importance of flexibility in strategy development. Firms need to be able to react quickly to changes in the marketplace and emerging trends in business development. It is possible to argue here that firms with extensive fixed assets may find themselves at a disadvantage. Take, for example, a firm that has integrated backwards and internalised its sources of supply. Although this means guaranteed inputs into the production process, it limits the extent to which the organisation can shop around for the cheapest components and materials, or those incorporating the latest technological breakthroughs. In other words, it limits the extent to which the firm can react to developments in the market. The alternative position, buying on the open market, may, however, be equally unsatisfactory: there is no control over the flow of supply or the price of the inputs. The solution being sought by many firms is to consider co-operation rather than internalisation. Similar trends are also being witnessed further down the channel when working with distributors and retailers.

Co-operation is not, however, restricted to relationships within the organisation's value chain. More and more organisations are combining their resources to solve common strategic problems, be it in the area of product development and R&D or production, business development or marketing. Such relationships with other organisations not only mean sharing knowledge and skills, but also the ability to switch allegiances and the nature of alliances when market conditions change.

Technological collaboration

The recent trend towards greater co-operation in business may be partly adduced to rapid changes in technological developments, as outlined above. With shortening technology life cycles, and, therefore, the marketable 'life' of products, managers are increasingly looking to lower costs of R&D and to ensure rapid returns on their investment in the marketplace. The latter is often achieved through rapid internationalisation of new product developments, whereas the former is increasingly causing firms to share the costs and risks of technological development with other competitors in the industry. This trend has been further reinforced by the rising costs of R&D, which in some developed markets have outpaced rates of inflation by as much as 10 per cent. In some sectors, therefore, even the largest multinational enterprises are finding it difficult to fund major research initiatives on their own. This is spawning a large number of industry linkages and co-operative arrangements for the development of new primary technologies.

At face value, this may appear to be tantamount to 'collusion', diluting the impact of free trade and restricting competition. However, the position in the value chain of many of these collaborative linkages suggests otherwise. As the research process is distinct from the marketing of products, firms may collaborate on upstream activities but compete aggressively in the marketplace. A further feature of such collaboration is the setting of industry standards. In the consumer electronics industry, for example, firms will not have forgotten the case of the video cassette recorder, where the VHS technology introduced by Matsushita 'cannibalised' the Betamax technology and led to Matsushita controlling approximately 45 per cent of the world VCR market in 1983. With this in mind, Philips entered into an alliance with Matsushita in 1992 to manufacture and market the digital compact cassette (DCC) which Philips had developed. It hoped that the global power of the joint company would eliminate market competition provided by Sony's 'mini-compact disc' technology, the sharing of the risk and the pooling of global resources, giving it extensive global spread through which such an international standard could be set.

Collaboration and market entry

Linkages between firms are not, however, restricted to technology development. Intensified competition brought about by free trade initiatives means that many mature, developed markets can be difficult to enter. Strategic alliances between firms can serve as a useful means of securing market access as well as bypassing the cultural difficulties of being a foreign firm operating on alien soil. Furthermore, entering into an alliance with a partner in this way can be an effective way of side-stepping head-to-head competition. It also provides firms with an important means of learning about the foreign market. The significance of the learning curve in international business activity cannot be overstated. When operating in a foreign market for the first time, foreign firms are often at a disadvantage *vis-à-vis* local indigenous firms as a result of their lack of understanding about local cultures and business practices. By entering into an alliance with a local player, there is a form of 'quasi-internalisation' of market knowledge and development, critical information being passed from the local organisation to the international entrant.

Many Western firms have used the joint venture route as an important means of securing a strong foothold in the Japanese market. Typically Japan is seen as a 'black box' to Western managers, its culture and business practices differing markedly from those pertaining to Western nations. Lowering the risk of failure through joint ventures and using the strategy as a pre-emptive stage in developing wholly owned manufacturing facilities in the Japanese market has been a popular development route for Western firms attempting to consolidate their activities in Japan.

Collaboration and vertical integration

Alliances have also become popular between manufacturers and their suppliers. This may arguably result from the well-publicised success of Japanese firms, which have developed very strong co-operative links with their suppliers, although the rapid technology change must also play a part. In order to ensure that suppliers and manufacturers are continuing to move in the same direction, joint research programmes can facilitate component development and ensure an automatic 'match' between the demands of the producer and the products of the supplier. Once again, the car industry provides a good example of this in practice. Component suppliers are no longer seen as being separate from the automobile production process; they are involved throughout the research, development and commercialisation process in order that the elements of the final vehicle fit the standards and specifications outlined by the car designers and manufacturers.

Industry networks

Emerging from the various forms of co-operation and alliance are a number of complex industry networks where firms are linked together through both formal and informal contracts. Figure 19.5 outlines the nature and scope of such a complex network in the information technology sector. It clearly shows that there are very few firms in the industry which remain insular as regards the process of co-operation. The number of alliances between firms also gives rise to the notion that many of them are 'project based', i.e. entered into in order to develop a solution to a specific problem. This contradicts the traditional view of joint ventures which implies long-term commitment and co-operation, and highlights the changing nature of modern-day alliances, which tend to be more fluid and flexible. The main implication here is that firms which remain on the outside are likely to be left out of the technological changes, market developments and vertical business agreements which are now characteristic of many industrial sectors. They are thus likely to fall behind their competitors and find it difficult to stay abreast of the dynamic changes taking place. Failure to embrace the challenges posed by industrial co-operation may therefore cost companies dearly.

Figure 19.5 Alliances in the information technology sector 1985–89

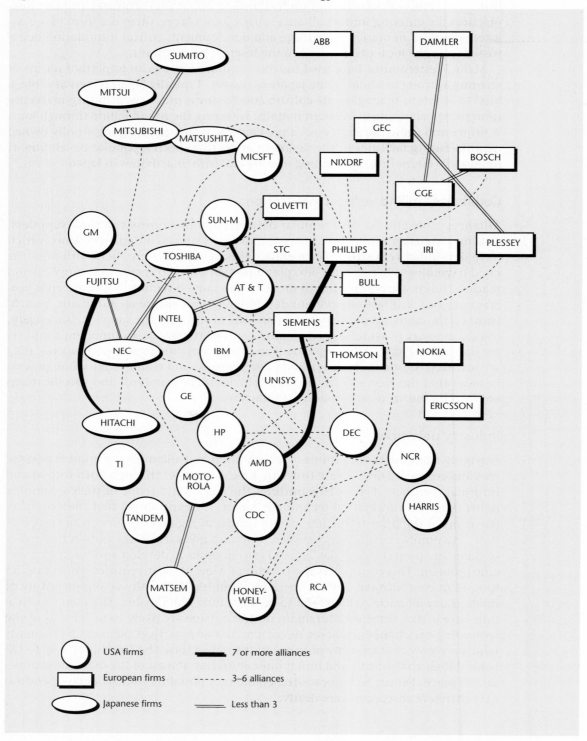

Source: Freeman and Hagerdoorn (1992). Reprinted by kind permission of the authors.

Managerial challenges

Joint ventures may prove as attractive to small firms as to their larger rivals. However, the risk for small firms is being taken over by the more powerful partner. Small organisations dealing in innovative products are a rich source of new technology introduction for larger firms, joint ventures serving as a pre-emptive stage in acquiring the technology (and the firm).

For all firms, successful joint ventures usually necessitate a shift in company 'culture'. Companies generally grow on the basis of their ability to compete and to develop strategies allowing them to gain a strong market position at the expense of leading rivals. However, as the global market environment is becoming increasingly competitive in terms of market entry and development as well as technological innovation, success in some business sectors is becoming more and more reliant on striking a balance between competition and co-operation, rather than simple organic expansion. Nevertheless, it must be stressed that joint ventures are not a 'quick fix' for firms attempting to develop their international activities. While many firms have found that entering markets through established distribution networks of competitor firms can provide rapid access to markets and easy assimilation of cultural differences, the longevity of joint ventures is thrown into question by the documented high failure rates resulting from the difficulties of managing joint operations on an ongoing basis (Doz *et al.*, 1990). Conflict between partners is common in joint alliances due to a number of factors:

- the ongoing desire to sub-optimise – this can result in a failure to share information or overpricing for managerial/component inputs;
- resource imbalances resulting in a failure by one party to dedicate managerial time or finance to the activity;
- exchange rate fluctuations resulting in lowering of expected returns for one party;
- conflicting strategic objectives and hidden agendas – all too often firms enter into joint ventures for reasons which they do not publicise to their partner; this inevitably results in a lack of trust and in failure of the venture;
- the relative strategic importance of the venture leading to conflict over control of the operation.

It is clear, then, that failure to embrace the challenges posed by co-operation will ultimately result in the demise of the venture. Indeed, some industry observers now suggest that project-based alliances are preferable to the pursuit of long-term business alliances, which tend to be fraught with problems, not least because flexibility can be hard to achieve, since it means constantly re-evaluating expectations and outcomes:

> *'Purely contractual agreements offer little flexibility, unless they are constantly renegotiated, a cumbersome and often irritating process. Contracts, though, by limiting the partners' commitment, can be terminated at a relatively low cost. Flexibility may thus be achieved through belonging to a network of companies, engaging in flexible short-term contracts, provided these companies know each other well enough to limit transaction costs.'* (Doz *et al.*, 1990, pp 140–1)

The trend in business seems to be so much in this direction that Handy (1994, pp 38–9) has concluded:

> *'When intelligence is the primary asset, the organisation becomes more like a collection of project groups, some fairly permanent, some temporary, some in alliance with other parties.'*

BEST PRACTICE MANAGEMENT

Boyacigiller and Adler (1995) point to an interesting limitation in the understanding of multinational management: management, as an academic subject, is biased towards the cultural understanding of the American way of doing things. In the English-speaking world a strong focus on the largest English-speaking community is unsurprising, and likewise the ignorance of all that is not translated into English. The economic power of the USA through the 1950s and 1960s led to the development of models and theories that can be considered peculiarly American in nature. As international activity spread to the multinational enterprises of Europe and Japan, new and equally culturally bound and self-referring theories of business developed.

It is only in the last decade or so that theorists and businesses alike have begun to learn and make the effort to learn from their international neighbours that there are many ways of doing business and the key is not to try to persuade the world that a particular way is best, but rather that an amalgam of different elements, together delivering 'best practice', may or even must be the ultimate goal.

In the West in the early 1980s interest in Japanese management practices grew rapidly, the key question asked being: What makes the Japanese so successful? This led to an exploration of the various facets of Japanese management and questions regarding the transferability of these facets to non-Japanese business. In many ways, this hunger for knowledge was unremarkable. In 1987 Japan produced over 10 per cent of world GDP, compared with a figure of only 2 per cent 20 years earlier. Japan's share of world exports has risen from 7 per cent in 1962 to 16 per cent in 1990, and in 1989 the outflow of Japanese foreign direct investment (FDI) totalled US$67.5 billion (up from an average of US$3.6 billion throughout the 1970s). The question for Western firms was to what extent could this formula be copied or, indeed, should it be copied as a means of attaining global success? From the perspective of the early twenty-first century, now that the Japanese bubble has burst and America has shown that in technology, particularly in services that for decades have been more important than manufacturing, this attention to Japan seems misplaced, but it is only with the benefit of hindsight that this is obvious. Academics and managers alike failed to see that the Japanese excelled only in manufacturing and only in specific sectors, but they provided important lessons even so.

Japanese management practices

'We are going to win and the industrial West is going to lose out: there's nothing much you can do about it, because the reasons for failure are within yourself ... for you, the essence of management is getting the ideas out of the heads of the bosses into the hands of labour ... for us, the core of management is precisely the act of mobilising and pulling together the intellectual resources of all employees ... only by drawing the combined brainpower of all employees can a firm face up to the turbulence and constraints of today's environment.' (Konosuke Matsushita, *The Economist*, 6 March 1993)

This quotation from a top Japanese executive demonstrates that Japan's success in the 1980s may partly have been attributable to a totally different managerial ethos, an integral part of the local business culture. This immediately cast doubt over the ability of Western firms simply to replicate Japanese working practices in Western organisations. Nevertheless, it was possible to distinguish between the 'hard' production techniques that could be copied relatively easily, and the 'soft', more intangible cultural framework in which the Japanese economy operated.

Production techniques utilised so successfully in Japan are ironically not unique. Many of them were introduced into Japan with US aid packages and technology transfer deals after the Second World War, particularly the quality control philosophy and associated business methodologies. They were implemented enthusiastically by Japanese managers after being adapted to suit the Japanese cultural preference for group and teamworking – the concept of *wa* which is about belonging, co-operation, harmony and achievement.

Oliver and Wilkinson (1992) identify four groups of factors characteristic of Japanese industry:

1 **Manufacturing methods** (including total quality control, quality circles, in-process controls such as statistical process control, just-in-time delivery and management systems and continuous improvement – *kaizen*).

2 **Organisational structures and systems** (including management accounting, which does not simply inform but forces improvements, research and development, led by powerful *susha* – project leaders) and flatter organisational structures.

3 **Personnel practices** (including lifetime employment, longer working hours and commitment to consultation and improvement).

4 **Wider social, political and economic conditions** (incorporating enterprise unions, buyer–seller relationships, government support and economic structures, including an integral banking system).

Manufacturing methods

The first of these areas constitutes the most tangible elements of the Japanese business system. The practices focus on quality and efficiency and, as such, have the potential to enhance competitiveness. It is these, more than the other factors highlighted, which have been transferred to the West. Table 19.2 outlines the nature and scope of the most commonly utilised business practices.

Organisation structures and systems

The main distinguishing feature of Japanese organisations is their flat structure, which promotes a 'hands-on' management ethos and management by consensus. This 'bottom-up' approach to management reflects the belief that workers have the potential to improve the quality of their work. This consensus mentality and team approach to business is reflected in narrow salary differentials between the top and bottom of the organisation.

Nevertheless, while teams are used to solve problems and aid company efficiency, this is not at the expense of personal leadership and individual champions of industry. Many leading Japanese companies have attained their position in world markets as a result of strong leadership.

Management accounting procedures also differ radically from those typically found in Western organisations. They are extremely product-focused and involve activity-based costing programmes rather than the 'cost plus' variant. This gives organisations greater flexibility to adapt to changes in the business environment and reflects a market-driven rather than profit-driven view of organisational development. This approach is part of the reason why Japanese firms have tended to have a longer-term view of business development, planning being based on the development of market share rather than on quick returns on capital, which can often preclude new investment and development.

Table 19.2 Japanese manufacturing techniques

MANUFACTURING TECHNIQUE	OVERVIEW
Total quality control	The de-specialising of the business function. Responsibility for quality remains in its 'natural' place, namely where production is performed. It incorporates all business functions with the aim being customer satisfaction, both internal to the organisation (downstream business units) and external to the company (intermediaries and final customers).
Quality circles	These are small groups, usually between five and ten people, who meet voluntarily to try to find ways to improve quality and productivity. Members are trained in statistical analysis and problem-solving techniques.
Statistical process control (SPC)	This system is used to assist in the control of production processes in order to achieve less variation in output and to ensure quality. SPC involves operators periodically sampling their own production, not with a view to accepting or rejecting it, but in order to produce a chart of how the process itself is behaving. In addition to reducing scrap and reworking costs, minimising variation in components can significantly improve product performance.
Just-in-time (JIT) production	'The JIT idea is simple: produce and deliver finished goods in time to be sold, sub-assemblies just in time to be assembled into finished goods, fabricated parts just in time to go into the sub-assemblies and purchase materials just in time to be transformed into fabricated parts' (Schonberger, 1982). The system requires predictable and planned demand, or production flexibility, to cater for changes in demand.
Kanban production system	This system involves containers for holding stock and cards for initiating production. This means that the amount of stock in the system can be varied by altering the number of cards in the system. In this way materials are pulled through the production process according to the demand for final assembly rather than pushed through by an inflexible production plan.
Flexible working	In Japanese firms this includes teamworking (or cellular manufacturing). This is facilitated by multi-skilled workers, who can be rotated between jobs. The system simplifies workflow, allowing workers to be moved to alleviate bottlenecks and ensure a continuous flow of production.

However, tendencies to overemphasise the long termism of the Japanese economy were soon realised:

> *'A far-sighted Japan and a myopic America make a tidy contrast, but one with little basis in fact. By and large, Japanese managers are at least as much obsessed with short-term results as their American counterparts ... They have arrived where they are today not by rigidly adhering to predetermined long-range strategies, but by paying scrupulous attention to performance on a monthly or even weekly basis – performance measured not against a three- or five-year plan, but against budget, against return on sales, against competitor performance.'* (Ohmae, 1982)

It is therefore the difference in approach to measuring profits rather than profit concerns themselves which distinguish between Japanese and Western firms. Whereas Western firms tend to concentrate on return on investment (ROI), Japanese organisations concentrate on return on sales (ROS).

A final area of interest is the links developed between manufacturing companies and their suppliers. As outlined earlier in the chapter, co-operation, either formal (through joint development agreements) or informal (through shared communication and assistance), can be regarded as quasi-internalisation of up-stream business functions. The Japanese have developed very sophisticated mechanisms for co-operating with contractors and suppliers, to the extent that they have even supported FDI programmes for their 'partner' organisations to service their business needs in overseas markets.

In the last few years and particularly since the onset of the Asian financial crisis as Japan has increasingly stagnated, America's telecommunications and technology revolution attention has reverted to American management practices. In particular, the USA is now seen as the leading provider of services, the sector that long ago eclipsed manufacturing and contributes almost three-quarters of GNP in all developed economies. Moreover, a growing proportion of all trade is now in services, ironically particularly in those very financial services of banking and insurance so troublesome for the Japanese.

Personnel practices

Japanese personnel practices are very suited to manufacturing organisation. They rely on co-operation, not mere compliance. The concept of 'collectivism' starts in the family and extends to the business organisation, where mutual dependence and loyalty are central features. Within such groups there is a strict hierarchy, based on seniority, where those lower down the organisation (or family) have a duty to their elders, which must be repaid through diligence and loyalty. Seniority is also the basis for promotion.

Loyalty gives rise to a sense of belonging, and concern over the future welfare of the group, which results in a committed and motivated workforce, working for the good of the company (group) rather than the individual. Loyalty also leads to lifetime employment, as workers and managers feel tied to common goals rather than individual development and career progression.

The best Japanese companies are highly dependent on the contribution of their skilled, flexible workforce. Core workers are protected and nurtured because they are viewed as a critical resource. They face tough selection and induction procedures and ongoing training, but in return they enjoy secure contracts and attractive remuneration packages. Nevertheless, profit-linked bonus schemes can result in broad differentials in pay between boom and slump periods.

The question arises as to how far such practices are helpful in developing services, in focusing on the individual consumer and in tailoring business to the uniqueness of services, when services lack the homogeneity of products and where production and consumption are seen to be simultaneous.

Wider social, political and economic considerations

The term 'Japan Inc' was coined in response to the coherence and interrelatedness of Japan's economic effort. Western organisations, which for many years believed that

Japan was closed to Western business, have used this term to describe the highly protectionist nature of the Japanese economy, wherein the Ministry of Trade and Industry (MITI) has carved out comfortable cartel-like markets devoid of the threat of Western competition. The reality, however, is far more complex.

First, it is important to allay the myth that the Japanese market is devoid of competition. Domestic competition among Japanese firms is highly aggressive and, while many industries are characteristically oligopolistic in nature (tending to lead to oligopolistic-style strategies), this has more to do with the *keiretsu* **groups**, which are broad-based conglomerates stemming from the activities of large and wealthy industrial families. Companies within these groups are highly interrelated through a complex array of cross-shareholdings and directorships. Each *keiretsu* involves a number of disparate industries, including manufacturing organisations, banking institutions, trading companies and service firms. There is, therefore, great potential for synergy within *keiretsu* groups, as skills and resources can be drawn from a wide pool of industrial and commercial activity. The 22 existing groups account for a substantial proportion of the economy, are extremely influential and constitute the international face of Japan.

However, this is not the full picture. Outside the *keiretsu* groups, the economy boasts a very high proportion of small firms and family firms that make up half of the employment in Japan. They enjoy long-term relationships with the *keiretsu* groups, although, significantly, they are vulnerable and tend to suffer in periods of economic downturn. As these firms are subcontractors and suppliers to the major economic groups, they are a significant feature of the total Japanese business system. For example, in the late 1980s Toyota manufactured approximately 4.5 million cars and employed 65 000 workers. General Motors, on the other hand, needed 750 000 employees to produce 8 million cars. The difference may be explained by the value of the car produced by the suppliers – one-quarter for General Motors but one-half for Toyota.

A key feature of the *keiretsu* group is the integral nature of the banking sector. With banks being part of the conglomerate, they are tied into the successes and the failure of the group. So Japanese firms tend to enjoy more favourable banking rates than their economic counterparts overseas though this has tied them in with the fortune of the banks. In addition, the *keiretsu* groups have strong links with powerful state bureaucracies which involve joint decision making and consultation. This gives the main economic groups a leading voice in industrial policy and development, which ensures political policy takes into account the needs of industry and commerce, but also any reluctance to tackle unpalatable problems like those of massive unperforming loans.

Western business practices

Table 19.3 provides a summary of key Japanese principles and a comparison with Western business practices. For the sake of convenience, this comparison treats 'Western business practice' as a single common entity. It has already been suggested in this chapter, however, that there are distinct differences in culture between the developed markets of the West. How, then, can such an agglomerative analysis provide a useful foundation for understanding business practices? The answer to this lies in the focus of analysis. What is being discussed here is corporate culture and business practice, which shows a higher degree of commonality between Western nations than social and economic culture. Nevertheless, differences between nations do exist and where these are deemed important they are given due regard.

Table 19.3 Japanese-style versus Western-style management

JAPANESE STYLE	WESTERN STYLE
Organisational principles	
1 The firm viewed as a collective body; total devotion of the individual to the firm, i.e. joining the firm, not hiring by contract.	1 Functionalist organisation of individuals as specialists.
2 Human-centred, not functionalist-centred organisation.	2 Co-operative work system based on division of labour; subdivision and standardisation of jobs.
3 Stress on co-operative teamwork.	3 Pyramid-shaped bureaucracy.
4 Indeterminate job description and job standing (authority and responsibility); generalist-oriented.	4 Clearly defined job description and job standing (authority and responsibility).
5 Japanese-style adaptation of modern bureaucracy.	5 Employment of contract ('give and take' commercial exchange).
Decision making and communication	
1 Collective decision making (bottom-up consensus-type decision making as seen in the *ringi* system).	1 Top-down decision making and one-way orders (no consideration given to opinions at the lower echelons).
2 Verbal and non-verbal communication (*nemawashi* or behind-the-scenes manoeuvres; information transmitted by implicit understanding, gut decision).	2 Autocratic authority at the top; expanded power of the bureaucracy.
3 Collective work performance system (common-room system; total membership participation and planning).	3 Individual responsibility and competition (fair-play principles).
4 Exemption from responsibility (seat of authority is obscure; no one takes responsibility).	4 Strong owner consciousness (the company president is also a hired hand).
5 Separation of ownership and management (no real power in officers' meetings and general stockholders' meetings).	5 Local armament by lawyers (legal specialists).
6 'Japan Inc' (collusive relationships of government, business and labour).	
Personnel system/labour management	
1 Life-long employment (no layoffs but there is flexibility by means of part-time and temporary employees).	1 Employment of people only at times when needed; layoffs in bad times.
2 Seniority-based promotion system (evaluations for promotions are quite comprehensive; they stress not just work results but incentive and effort, as well as reflecting capability).	2 Wages and job compensation according to competency (efficiency system) with no relationship to age and seniority.
3 Seniority wage system (stress is placed not just on compensation for labour but on overall exhibition of ability); stress on fringe and welfare benefits.	3 Seniority system at times of promotion and layoffs.

▶

4 Extensive employee training and education.	4 Labour unions are functionally organised by craft and job type; unions safeguard the individual's life and rights.
5 Enterprise labour unions; co-operation between labour and management.	5 Much tension in labour–management relations.

Human relations and values

1 Groupism (the group comes first; value placed on the group; the individual is devoted heart and soul to the group) and mutual dependence.	1 Individualism (ultimate value placed on the individual; devotion and loyalty to the group are weak).
2 Concurrence of the firm's goal and the individual's life goal (devotion to the group; prestige, sense of security; morale pursuant to participation; co-prosperity idea; love of company spirit).	2 To the individual the firm is nothing more than a means to obtain wages and to the firm the individual is like a piece of machinery, a tool.
3 Stress on harmony in human relations (emphasis on feelings and motives, warm human relations, mutual consent of all members and linking of hearts).	3 Human relations in the workplace are simply artificial relations for work purposes; relations cease outside of the company.
4 Egalitarianism in substance (little chance for class discrimination; small earning differentials).	4 Egalitarian in form (strong class consciousness, competition for equal opportunity).
5 Strong desire for the elevation of quality and efficiency.	5 Purpose of life resides in the family and leisure; strong community consciousness.

Source: Based on Mirza (1984).

Individualism

The benefits of individualism have been well proven in Western organisations. The notion of entrepreneurial spirit is not only welcomed, it is actively encouraged, as the tendency for individuals to compete against each other frequently gives rise to the development of new ideas. In the commercial organisation this means new products and technologies. This supports the notion that individualism promotes benefits for society.

Nevertheless, individualism has its drawbacks. First, it tends to promote mobility between organisations, as employees attempt to build impressive work records and move up the management ladder at a faster rate than their peers. This produces managers with broad general management experience but limited knowledge and understanding of the workings of an individual company. Nevertheless, mobility can mean that Western managers are exposed to a wide array of differing business practices as they move between organisations. This mirrors the situation in Japan, to some extent, although here mobility tends to be controlled within organisations by senior managers rather than at the personal level.

Secondly, it dilutes continuity in management, with new personnel frequently replacing old and constantly moving business departments in a different direction. This can be unsettling to the workforce and overall morale, with concomitant adverse effects on productivity.

Finally, individualism may make it difficult to build co-operation, both within and outside the company. With co-operation between business departments and between organisations becoming an increasingly important feature of global business activity, there is a case for concern regarding Western managers' ability to adapt from a competitive to a co-operative mentality.

Given the above, it is not difficult to see why there has been a renewed interest in the development of teamworking. Management education increasingly stresses the importance of the ability of managers to work closely together and to recognise that bringing to bear multiple perspectives on issues at hand is a powerful tool. In an international context where cultural differences need to be recognised and accounted for, bringing together parties from different cultures is even more important, but easier in societies where heterogeneity rather than homogeneity is the tradition.

Communication and employee involvement

Traditionally, employee involvement in Western business management has been somewhat limited, with organisations demonstrating classic hierarchical structures, decisions being made at a senior level and executed by the workforce. Interestingly, the Social Chapter of the single European market initiative attempts to redress this balance and create a more harmonious relationship between managers and workers. The UK has been vehement in its criticism of this proposal, partly because it is seen as rejuvenation of union activity through the 'back door'. The Conservative government of the 1980s worked hard to dilute the power of UK trade unions in an effort to eradicate union interference in working practices, which frequently led to industrial action and lost output. Their criticisms, however, appear to have missed the point. Employee involvement is not so much about empowering the workforce to take action against management as to provide an environment in which employees are encouraged to take a greater interest in the long-term success of the organisation.

Germany provides a direct corollary to the UK case. It has broadly adopted the concept of 'co-determination' where, in companies of more than 2000 employees, the law dictates that 50 per cent of representation on supervisory boards must come from employees other than management. In the early stages of introduction there was a great deal of management scepticism, not least because worker representatives have to be given access to full company information, including objectives and strategic direction. An indirect benefit of worker participation is its ability to protect firms from hostile takeovers.

In the USA, slow take-up of employee involvement programmes is partly due to union resistance. Rather than favour teamwork programmes, certain unions have seen them as a covert means of 'union-busting' by changing the nature of employee interaction. Interestingly, the programmes of employee involvement being implemented in the USA are beginning to diverge from those in Japan:

> *'In American-style teamwork, for example, workers not only gain a more direct voice in shop floor operations – as in Japan. They also take over managerial duties, such as work and vacation scheduling, ordering materials, and hiring new members.'*
>
> (*Business Week*, 10 July 1989)

In essence, American systems are building on Japanese principles in such a way that they fit with local cultural conditions. By empowering employees in this way, companies are combining the benefits of co-operation and teamwork with individualism and entrepreneurship.

Training and development

As the demands on firms are changing and increasingly requiring more flexible manufacturing and work practices, teamwork, as already noted, and multi-skilling are essential if firms are to remain competitive. This means training the workforce in a variety of skills so that it can react quickly to changes in models and production runs as in service requirements. Harnessing the knowledge and expertise of in-house managers can reduce the cost of such training considerably. SP Tyres in Birmingham, a company which has introduced teamwork and flexible manufacturing, has an extensive and very cost-effective training programme:

> *'This is because most of it is done relatively inexpensively in-house by multidisciplinary teams, led by senior managers. These teams take responsibility for training other members of staff, often in areas outside their occupational expertise.'*
>
> (*Financial Times*, 3 January 1990)

Wider education and training issues are also of relevance. Japan's managerial educational system stresses life-long learning programmes which provide for ongoing training once and usually only once individuals have left the formal education system. In the West, it is the German education system which is held up as an example of good practice. A key feature of the system is the close relationship between business organisations and educational institutions, and the high propensity of organisations to make in-house provision for training their employees. This runs the gamut from the extensive apprenticeship system to management training programmes, supported by university and polytechnic staff but conducted in the workplace. The main benefit of such industry/education co-operation is that it allows individuals to be trained in the necessary skills for their career/job role as well as meeting the skills training needs of the organisation, while also creating company loyalty. Moves in other countries to encourage greater co-operation between industry and education are testament to the benefits that can be derived. Failure of managers to consider the educational needs of their workforce is likely to result in long-term problems for the organisation, as the skills required of workers are continually changing in response to developments in technology and global economic conditions.

Western short-termism

In the late 1980s and early 1990s before the USA managerially eclipsed Japan, Western short-termism, though sometimes denied, had often been accused of being the root cause of failings in Western relative competitiveness. A study on the competitiveness of British industry (Buckley, *et al.*, 1992) concluded that the short-term mentality of many British businesses restricted investment and development in such a way that full exploitation of advantages was not possible. The UK stock market was frequently cited as a major contributory factor in this short-term mentality, with companies being constantly judged on their share performance rather than on their long-term potential. The other major contributory factor is obviously Western business culture, which, as outlined above, tends to measure company performance in terms of ROI rather than on more market and growth-led dimensions, but, while there is some truth in these allegations (which continue, despite the revival in Western competitiveness), aspiration to be long-termist may, in an increasingly unpredictable world, be equally unwise.

In many ways the plethora of articles on 'Japanese success' have been misleading. Many implicitly assumed that everything about Japanese management was better than anything the West could offer. This belied the fact that America continued to boast a larger number of multinational companies and the UK remained the second-largest foreign direct investor in the world economy.

Nevertheless, it is said that the Japanese have never been too proud to learn from their Western counterparts (and this needs to continue to be true if Japan is to return to growth), and this is perhaps the key lesson, not the idea that Japanese management practices are inherently 'better'. Japanese management has been a continually developing phenomenon which has often drawn on Western input. Peters and Waterman's *In Search of Excellence* (1982) described the practices employed by the most successful US corporations and sold 50 000 copies within two days of the Japanese translation being published, and Ohmae (1982) reported Japanese managers remarking on similarities between their companies and the 'excellent' ones in the USA.

The message for firms, therefore, is to pursue good business practice, regardless of its source. The Japanese never did have and do not now have a monopoly over 'best practice' and, while they have developed successful mechanisms for manufacturing management, each firm has to adopt policies which fit with all of its national, industry and corporate culture.

It should be stressed that no country's business system can be replicated in another country. Subtle ambiguities of culture and different ways of thinking (which mean many things cannot be precisely defined) and acceptance of constant dynamism, as distinct from seeking an end to a process, underpin the concept of constant improvement (Fry, 1991). Rather, any country's success should act as a catalyst to other nations to pursue the development of 'lean organisations' with the capability for global competitiveness.

Perhaps all firms should take a lead from companies such as IBM which, for many years, pursued strategies which have sometimes been labelled 'Japanese'. The 'IBM way' was described by Bassett (1986) as 'exactly the opposite of the Japanese method', as the company culture was based on individualism rather than collectivism. Nevertheless, efficiency and quality are key elements of company strategy and there are perhaps grounds to suggest:

> *'Japanese and American management is 95 per cent the same and differs in all-important respects.'*   (Takeo Fujisawa, co-founder of the Honda Motor Company)

Differences lie in approach rather than practice.

That said, responsiveness to changes in the environment remain key. International operators seem no less immune to bubbles, financial crises and busts than their domestic counterparts. Developed country authorities cannot be expected always to ignore the hollowing out of their manufacturing any more than can their developing country equivalents accept the obstacles their own businesses face in penetrating developed markets. Indeed, none can ignore major developments such as EU enlargement and the impact of 'terrorist activity'.

SUMMARY

- This chapter has outlined many of the complexities of multinational management, which essentially centre on managing organisations in a diverse and dynamic global environment.

- Readers should now understand something of the importance of managing in an ever-changing global environment, be aware of the decision-making challenges facing managers with regard to developing strategies which cater both for environmental change and cultural diversity, and have some knowledge of varying business practices employed by firms around the globe – practices which are now converging and merging to make international firms more efficient and effective in their global operations.

- It should be apparent that management of multinational and international firms requires continual change and adaptation. The economic world is not static and thus, in order to remain competitive, managers must constantly look for new strategies and business practices that allow such changes to be turned into opportunities rather than threats. Resting on the laurels of past business success or simply attempting to capitalise on monopolistic technologies is not sufficient to carry firms into the future.

- Innovating organisational structures and strategies are just as important as developing new products and technologies, such that the 'winners' in the new global order will be those firms adept at managing change, rather than those intent on managing fixed resources.

Review and discussion questions

1 *With environmental change serving as a key exogenous factor in organisational decision making, how can managers develop business systems which allow them to prepare for, and adapt to, such change?*

2 *How may managers ensure that they do not lose their competitive advantage by deciding to 'externalise' key parts of the value chain?*

3 *The literature on international business is awash with examples of failed joint ventures between firms. How, then, can the increased trend towards joint venture activity be justified?*

4 *Consider why firms are beginning to reject hierarchical organisational structures in favour of flatter, functional-centred business systems?*

5 *To what extent can any country's management practices be transferred to multinational firms?*

6 *Are management practices employed in particular parts of the world intrinsically 'superior' or 'inferior' to those employed elsewhere?*

CASE STUDY

On *The Globalization of Business*

It is widely recognized that over the last quarter of the twentieth century, some major changes have occurred in the character of contemporary capitalism, as the political-economic order established in the wake of World War Two came under increasing pressure, leading in turn to questions about the viability and morality of the post-Enlightenment project of modernity. This was registered in phases such as 'the crisis of Fordism' and 'the crisis of the welfare state'. The references to crisis raised disturbing questions as to the sustainability of existing arrangements (even more so as recognition of the ecological limits to mass production and consumption lifestyles began to emerge) and about what might replace them, ushering in an era of 'post-isms' (post-Fordism, post-colonialism, post-modernism, for example). Furthermore, they also raised questions as to the adequacy of existing forms of knowledge and ways of understanding political, economic and social life, generating further 'post-isms' (post-positivism, post-structuralism and so on).

Over the same 25 years, and linked to the explosion of post-isms, there was a growing recognition within the social sciences of the importance of spatiality to cultural, economic, political and social life. The difference that place and space make became of central concern across much of the social sciences. This reflected a growing assertion that the spatial was too important to be left to geography, the 'traditional' disciplinary locus of concerns with questions to do with the production and meanings of space and territory. The net result was a remarkably vibrant and productive cross-disciplinary debate on the centrality of the spatiality of social life, especially within Europe. There had previously been recognition that spatial variation was important (at scales ranging from the micro to macro), but there had also been a strong tendency to conceptualize space as a preformed container into which these various processes were then poured and sedimented. Now, however, there was an increasing recognition of the importance of the social production of place and space and of varied spatial scales as integral to the constitution of economies and societies, drawing on long-established work, primarily in human geography. As part of this, there were growing claims as to the significance of both supra-national and sub-national spatial scales and interest in

the complex ways in which the sub-national and supra-national became combined with the national in complex multi-scalar architectures of economies and societies and systems of governance and regulation.

A strong strand running through all this is a debate that revolved around concepts such as 'globalization', 'Europeanization' (especially as this relates to the formation, widening and deepening of the European Union) and 'transnationalization'. Such concepts are intended to register recognition that a formerly international political economy, constructed around the building blocks of national economies, polities and societies, and multinational forms of corporate organization, is being transformed to create new, qualitatively different forms of supra-national organization. Of these new concepts, however, it is fair to say that 'globalization' has generated the most heat, if not always corresponding light, as it has become a site of fierce theoretical and political disagreement and debate. 'Globalization' is a strongly contested concept, with no consensus as to its meaning and significance (or even as to its spelling), not least because analytical and theoretical concerns are often elided (deliberately or inadvertently) with political and normative claims.

Proponents of 'globalization' often disagree amongst themselves as to its meaning and most significant aspects, while others simply challenge the validity and utility of the concept. Few would now subscribe to the simplistic view that 'globalization' implied global homogenization (of cultures, markets, production structures, fashions and tastes) as an almost automatic consequence of the annihilation of space by time due to technological innovations in transport and ICT. Recognition of this, however, simply raises a more difficult question: how best to conceptualize and comprehend the more complex and multi-scalar geographies of a globalizing world? While 'the national' is no longer unquestioningly prioritized, and almost automatically accorded methodological and onto logical pre-eminence, there are various responses to this. Some argue, for example, that 'the national' remains the critical spatial scale in understanding contemporary political-economies, albeit in transformed relations with social actors constituted at other spatial scales. Others emphasize the centrality of sub-national spatial scales, such as the urban and regional, as the central nodes within an emergent global economy. Indeed, the most sophisticated theorizations are those that focus upon the multi-scalar organization of contemporary political economies, and seek to establish empirically which scales and processes are dominant in a given conjuncture via careful, theoretically informed empirical analysis rather than seeking theoretically and/or politically to pre-empt the answer to this question.

Source: Extract from Ray Hudson (2002), 'On the Globalization of Business', *British Journal of Management*, December, Vol. 13, No. 4, pp 362–6.

REFERENCES AND FURTHER READING

Bartlett, C A and Ghoshal, S (1990) 'Managing Innovation in the Transnational Corporation', in Bartlett, C A, Doz, Y and Hedlund, G (eds), *Managing the Global Firm*, London: Routledge.

Bartlett, C A, Doz, Y and Hedlund, G (1990) *Managing the Global Firm*, London: Routledge.

Bassett, P (1986) *Strike Free: New Industrial Relations in Britain*, Basingstoke: Macmillan.

Beamish, P W J, Killing, P, Lecraw, D J and Crookell, H (1991) *International Management: Text and Cases*, Homewood, IL: Irwin.

Bloom, H, Calori, R and de Woot, P (1994) *Euromanagement: A New Style for the Global Market*, London: Kogan Page.

Boyacigiller, N A and Adler, N J (1995) 'The Parochial Dinosaur: Organisational Science in a Global Context', in Jackson, T (ed.), *Cross Cultural Management*, Oxford: Butterworth-Heinemann.

Buckley, P J, Pass, C and Prescott, K (1992) *Servicing International Markets: Competitive Strategies of Firms*, Oxford: Blackwell.

Calori, R, Atamer, T and Numes, P (2000) *The Dynamics of International Competition – From Practice to Theory*, London: Sage.

Davis, S M (1992) 'Managing and Organising Multinational Corporations, 1979', reprinted in Bartlett, C A and Ghoshal, S (eds), *Transnational Management*, Homewood, IL: Irwin.

Dicken, P (1992) *Global Shift: The Internationalisation of Economic Activity* (2nd edn), London: Paul Chapman.

Doz, Y, Prahalad, C K and Hamel, G (1990) 'Control, Change and Flexibility: The Dilemma of International Collaboration', in Bartlett, C A, Doz, Y and Hedlund, G (eds), *Managing the Global Firm*, London: Routledge.

Dunning, J H (1988) *Explaining International Production*, London: George Allen & Unwin.

The Economist (1993) 'The Japanese Economy – From Miracle to Mid-life Crisis', 6 March.

Edelshain, D J (1995) 'British Corporate Currency Exposure and Foreign Exchange Risk Management', unpublished PhD thesis, London Business School.

Fry, E (1991) 'Subtlety and the Art of Japanese Management', *Business Credit*, October.

Graham, J (1988) 'Japanisation as Mythology', *Industrial Relations Journal*, 19 (1).

Grant, R M (2002) *Contemporary Strategy Analysis*, 4th edition, Oxford: Blackwell.

Halliburton, C and Hünerberg, R (1987) 'The Globalisation Dispute in Marketing', *European Journal of Marketing*, 5 (4): 243–9.

Handy, C (1994) *The Empty Raincoat: Making Sense of the Future*, London: Arrow.

Hedlund, G (1986) 'The Hypermodern MNC – A Heterarchy?', *Human Resource Management*, 25 (1), Spring.

Hedlund, G and Rolander, D (1990) 'Action in Heterarchies: New Approaches to Managing the MNC', in Bartlett, C A, Doz, Y and Hedlund, G (eds), *Managing the Global Firm*, London: Routledge.

Hill, C W L (1997) *International Business: Competing in the Global Marketplace*, Homewood, IL: Irwin.

Hofstede, G (1983) 'The Cultural Relativity of Organisational Practices and Theories', *Journal of International Business Studies*, Fall: 75–89.

Hymer, S (1960) 'The International Operations of National Firms: A Study of Direct Investment', doctoral dissertation, Massachusetts Institute of Technology, Boston.

Johanson, J and Vahine, J (1977) 'International processes of the firm: a model of knowledge development and increasing foreign market commitment', *Journal of International Business Studies*, 8: 23–31.

Levitt, T (1983) 'The Globalisation of Markets', *Harvard Business Review*, May/June: 92–102.

Mirza, H (1984) 'Can – Should – Japanese Management Practices be Exported Overseas?', *The Business Graduate*, January.

Ohmae, K (1982) *The Mind of the Strategist: Art of Japanese Business*, Harmondsworth: Penguin.

Oliver, A and Wilkinson, S (1992) *The Japanisation of British Industry: New Developments in the 1990s* (2nd edn), Oxford: Blackwell.

Perlmutter, H V (1969) 'The Tortuous Evolution of the Multinational Corporation', *Columbia Journal of World Business*, 29 (1): 85–99.

Peters, T and Waterman, R (1982) *In Search of Excellence*, New York: Harper & Row.

Porter, M E (1990) *Competitive Advantage of Nations*, London: Macmillan.

Porter, M E (1991) 'Towards a Dynamic Theory of Strategy', *Strategic Management Journal*, 12 (2): 95–112.

Porter, M E, Takeuchi, H and Sakakibara, M (2000) *Can Japan Compete?*, Basingstoke: Macmillan.

Ricks, D A and Mahajan, A (1984) 'Blunders in International Marketing', *Long Range Planning*, February: 78–85.

Schonberger, R (1982) *Japanese Manufacturing Techniques*, New York: Free Press.

Trompenaars, F (1993) *Riding the Waves of Culture: Understanding Cultural Diversity in Business*, London: Nicholas Brealey Publishing.

Valla, J P (1986) 'Industrial Firms in European Markets: The French Approach to Europe', in Turnbull, P W and Valla, J P (eds), *Strategies for International Industrial Marketing*, New York: Croom Helm.

Vandermerwe, S (1993) 'A Framework for Constructing Euronetworks', *European Management Journal*, 11 (1), March.

Vernon, R and Wells, L T Jr (1991) *The Manager in the International Economy* (6th edn), Upper Saddle River, NJ: Prentice-Hall.

Welford, R and Prescott, K (1996) *European Business: An Issue Based Approach*, London: Pitman Publishing.

Young, S, Hamill, J, Wheeler, C and Davies, R (1989) *International Market Entry and Development: Strategies and Management*, Hemel Hempstead: Harvester

WEBSITES

http://internationalecon.com/
Straightforward explanations of international trade.

http://www.ilo.org/
The website of the International Labour Organisation, which provides comprehensive information on international business.

http://www.odci.gov/cia/publications/factbook/
The *World Factbook* provides information about countries.

http://libweb.uncc.edu/ref-bus/vibehome.htm
Virtual International Business and Economic Sources provides links to internet sources on international business.

http://www.internationalist.com/business/
The Center for International Business provides information about international business.

CHAPTER 20

Management in perspective

TIM HANNAGAN

Outcomes

Having read this chapter, you will be able to:

- discuss the universality of the role of managers

- summarise the skills required in management

- analyse the development of careers in management

- compare and contrast management theories

- explain the results of flatter management structures as organisations face the challenges of their business environment

- discuss management ideas in the context of the need for managers to take advantage of changing circumstances

THE MANAGEMENT ROLE

The management role is as old as history, although it only became the subject of serious study in the late nineteenth century. The organisation of the building of the pyramids in the years before 2000 BC, the exploits of generals such as Alexander the Great around 300 BC, and the development of great civilisations and empires all over the world through history required management at all levels. The extent to which management is universal and involves generic skills is a point of argument and discussion. Is managing a commercial organisation that different from managing one in the public sector? Is managing a football team very different from managing a hospital or university? There is no doubting the views of Socrates, who suggested by his usual method of asking questions that successful businesspeople and generals perform much the same functions (Exhibit 20.1).

Socrates went further to argue that 'the management of private concerns differs only in point of number from that of public affairs. In other respects they are much alike, and particularly in this, that neither can be carried on without men, and the men employed in private and public transactions are the same.'

Exhibit 20.1 Socrates

NICOMACHIDES: Isn't it like the Athenians? They have not chosen me after all the hard work I have done since I was called up, in the command of company or regiment, though I have been so often wounded in action. They have chosen Antisthenes, who has never served in a marching regiment nor distinguished himself in the cavalry and understands nothing but money making.

SOCRATES: Isn't that a recommendation? Suppose he proves capable of supplying the men's needs?

NICOMACHIDES: Why, merchants also are capable of making money, but that doesn't make them fit to command any army.

SOCRATES: But Antisthenes also is eager for victory, and that is a good point in a general. Whenever he has been a choir-master, you know, his choir has always won.

NICOMACHIDES: No doubt, but there is no analogy between the handling of a choir and of an army.

SOCRATES: But you see, though Antisthenes knows nothing about music or choir training, he showed himself capable of finding the best experts in those activities. And therefore if he finds out and prefers the best men in warfare as in choir training, it is likely he will be victorious in that too; and probably he will be more ready to spend money on winning a battle with the whole state than on winning a choral competition with his tribe.

NICOMACHIDES: Do you mean, Socrates, that the man who succeeds with a chorus will also succeed with an army?

SOCRATES: I mean that, whatever a man controls, if he knows what he wants and can get it he will be a good controller, whether he controls a chorus, an estate, a city or an army.

NICOMACHIDES: I would never have thought to hear you say that a good business man would make a good general.

SOCRATES: For the good business man, through his knowledge that nothing profits or pays like a victory in the field, and nothing is so utterly unprofitable and entails such heavy loss as a defeat, will be eager to seek and avoid what leads to defeat, prompt to engage the enemy if he sees he is strong enough to win; and above all, will avoid an engagement when he is not ready.

Source: Adapted from Adair (1989)

The management role has always involved decision making, choice, supervision and control, and has always been much more than a purely operational function. In the future as in the past it will include the need to forecast and plan, to organise, to command and co-ordinate. The role does not mean following instructions without question or carrying out routine tasks as is the case in an operational job; it does mean taking decisions between different courses of action. A manager has been described as a person who decides what needs to be done and who arranges for someone to do it, and clearly a managerial job offers opportunities for making choices in what is done, how it is done and when it is done. All of this is within the context of an organisation, its corporate and ethical structure and its external environment.

It is possible to 'measure' a management job by the length of time the manager is left to work on his or her own before the work is checked for quality. This 'time–space discretion' may be a few hours for a supervisor or foreman, to a few days for junior and middle managers, to weeks or months for senior managers. Generally speaking, the more choices a manager has, the further up the management hierarchy he or she has climbed. A junior manager has a limited area of choice and limited means to manoeuvre, but the management function can be said to have clearly entered a job at the moment when a significant amount of decision making and choice enters the role.

Promotion in an organisation normally means an increase in the management function, so that decision making and choice become an increasing part of the job. The move from 'player' to 'manager' requires a considerable adjustment, one which people find difficult to make. The brilliant salesperson, for example, may not be a good sales manager: his or her expertise is in the process of selling and not in the organising, controlling and decision making required to be a manager. At the next stage, top managers are concerned much more with planning and organising and will spend relatively little time supervising, while middle managers may spend fairly even amounts of time on planning, organising, directing and controlling. Again, the change in role will involve an adjustment which may be hard to make.

The so-called 'Peter principle' can come into play as people are promoted. This suggests that people tend to be promoted to their level of incompetence, that is, just above the point at which they can cope, to a point where they can no longer cope. Luckily this is not always the case, but it is essential for managers to discover the level at which they are confident in their ability and can be a success. This is not an easy process, because ambition and higher salaries will encourage managers to seek promotion perhaps to a point where they are no longer successful. At the same time, senior managers may promote more junior managers because of their performance at that level.

Organisations have introduced training and development programmes to prepare managers for more senior levels and to attempt to assess their suitability for promotion. The armed services have had this procedure in place for many years in order to decide who should become an officer and then be promoted at every level. This type of process establishes a structured management career, which is reflected in many large companies but is becoming rarer as managers take more responsibility for their own development.

MANAGEMENT SKILLS

Managers need a diversity of skills because of the complexity of the job, including conceptual skills which involve planning and thinking, and the ability to see the organisation as a whole and the relationship of its various parts. They need to understand how their particular role fits into the total organisation. As managers are promoted, the ability to think strategically becomes more important. For example, the software company Microsoft reflects and is perhaps dependent on the strategic decisions of Bill Gates, the founder and chairman. He is able to spread his ideas throughout the whole giant organisation via e-mail. This includes the decision to move into the superhighway of communication and information technology. The senior vice-president for US sales and marketing has been quoted as saying:

> *'Each part of the company has a life of its own, but Bill is the glue that holds it all together.'*
>
> (Schlewder, 1990)

As managers are promoted into more senior positions, they must develop conceptual and strategic skills or their performance will be poor and they will effectively have reached their level of incompetence.

Managers are responsible for organising and controlling people, so that the ability to work with people is an essential skill. People management skills are demonstrated by the way a manager is able to motivate, co-ordinate and communicate with other people. This not only involves distributing work and resolving conflicts, but also coaching and encouraging people. Managers have to relate to a wide range of people, employers, colleagues, more senior managers, customers, suppliers, members of the community. They need to have social skills to enable them to be comfortable in a range of situations, to represent the organisation confidently and to focus people's efforts on the objectives of the organisation, and to encourage teamwork and a high level of motivation in order to provide for the needs of customers.

Technical skill is the understanding of proficiency in the performance of specific tasks, whether they are concerned with product engineering, marketing or finance. These skills include specialised knowledge, analytic ability and competence in processes and procedures applied to solving problems. Such skills are more important for junior and middle managers than for senior management, where human and conceptual skills are more important. However, most managers have to prove themselves in a technical area before they are given the opportunity to exhibit their conceptual and human skills.

MANAGEMENT CAREERS

Management careers tend to evolve through a series of stages. These can either be seen as a fairly straightforward move from exploration, through establishment and maintenance to decline, or as a more complex process of transition which occurs every five or seven years. Individual careers do not, of course, necessarily follow either of these patterns exactly, but these patterns do help in understanding where managers are in their careers and what shape the future may be.

The first stage is one of exploration, which occurs at the beginning of a career and is characterised by self-analysis and the exploration of the different types of available jobs. This is a stage which most people experience in their late teens and into their 20s. They may hold part-time jobs while at school or college which help them understand about work and the type of job they may want or want to avoid if possible. The first full-time job is often not the one people settle into these days (in contrast to the pre-1940s) and there may be some experimentation with various jobs before a career begins to be established.

A career can be seen as a sequence of work experiences which accumulate over a person's working life more or less successfully. The second stage is when the career path is established. This is typically when people are aged between the middle 20s and middle 30s. Jobs may now establish a pattern where the experiences of the exploration stage are put into practice and each job is sought as a progression on the previous one. Promotion is sought in the same company or in different companies and a career pattern begins to develop.

The third stage in career evolution is the maintenance stage, where the established career pattern is maintained and nurtured. The manager's career may stabilise at this stage, grow or even stagnate. It is particularly at this point that careers may reach a plateau where there is little further development. The last stage is the decline stage which usually occurs near retirement, when people may not be able to maintain prior performance levels because of a loss of interest or difficulty in keeping their job skills up to date. The maintenance stage may occur at any age from the mid-30s or 40s onwards, while decline may set in during the 40s, 50s or not until the 60s.

The career plateau occurs when a person becomes stuck in a particular job where the likelihood of promotion or major development is very low. It may arise because of a level of ability or bad luck or poor assessment by superiors, but most people will experience it in one way or another. There is a tendency for there to be far more candidates for higher-level positions than there are positions available, so that as managers rise up the hierarchical pyramid, even highly successful managers eventually reach a career plateau. This is at least the case in terms of promotion and with flatter organisations the number of promotional steps has declined in most organisations. At the same time, companies can no longer afford to keep large numbers of 'plateaued' managers, with the consequence that redundancy and early retirement become a feature of management careers (*see* Figure 20.1).

In practice, managers may reach their career plateau at any time because a promotion may prove to be the last at junior, middle or senior management level. Pay levels may reflect this situation as well, so that real pay reaches a maximum as the plateau is reached. It is important for managers to recognise that they have reached this stage and to make the most of it. The plateau can be made much more interesting if sideways moves and changes in job roles are possible, or fresh opportunities may open up by changing jobs or taking on new developments.

The Levinson model of career evolution (Levinson *et al.*, 1978) suggests that adult life involves a series of transitions in a fairly predictable sequence every five to seven years (*see* Exhibit 20.2).

The plateau in their career which managers may reach in their 40s or 50s can lead to the mid-life crisis or the age 50 transition, and perhaps a relatively early decline. Some managers move from one job to another in an attempt to find an area of growth, while others attempt to maintain their interest in a role in which they have become expert. They have to accept that younger managers may overtake them and that they are not going to reach the top of their career path. Levinson's model may act as a guide to pitfalls and opportunities ahead, and to some extent

Figure 20.1 Career stages

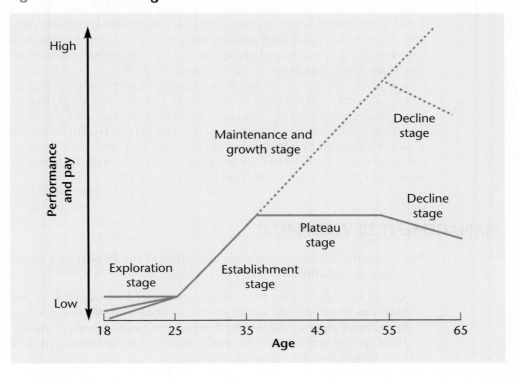

Exhibit 20.2 Levinson model of career evolution

- **Age 17–22**   **Early adult transition** – assertion of independence, breaking away from family ties. Those who prolong parental ties may underperform in their careers

- **Age 22–28**   **Entering the adult world** – a preoccupation with entering the adult world, education completed and career selection begins

- **Age 28–33**   **Age 30 transition** – review of career and life progress and feeling of last chance to change career

- **Age 33–40**   **Settling down** – job and career advancement takes precedence

- **Age 40–45**   **Mid-life transition** – another period of review, possible mid-life crisis

- **Age 45–50**   **Entering middle adulthood** – consolidation of period of review, with a possible sense of fulfilment

- **Age 50–55**   **Age 50 transition** – possible crisis or review of previous periods of transition

- **Age 55–60**   **Combination of middle adulthood** – relatively stable, with preparation for retirement

- **Age 60–65**   **Late adult transition** – retirement with review and reflection on career

- **Age 65+**   **Late adulthood** – evaluation and summing up

Source: Levinson *et al.* (1978). Reprinted by permission of Sterling Lord Literistic, Inc. Copyright 1975 by Daniel Levinson.

these stages are 'proved' by the exceptional cases which are highlighted in pop music and film careers. A pop group may compress all these stages into a few short years so that they reach the top of the charts and their highest pay levels in their 20s. They then reach a brief plateau and a quick decline from which they may never recover. The more talented groups 're-create' themselves for new audiences every few years, while others move into different areas of the entertainment industry.

It is obviously necessary for all managers to analyse their career aims and objectives, to be clear about their own abilities and shortcomings, to be realistic about the opportunities that are available and accept the fact that no one is as interested in an individual's career as that particular person can be. For an ambitious manager, a career needs to be planned so that the correct steps can be taken at the right moments, but these plans are unlikely to succeed without a realistic analysis of what opportunities exist and what talents are on offer.

MANAGEMENT DEVELOPMENT

The Institute of Management has reported on the importance of managers to the economy of a country:

'One of the most important resources possessed by a nation is its managerial skills. Ideas can be turned into wealth when combined with effective management. The ability to create more wealth is vital if the growing expectations of society are to be met. Those services which spend the wealth must also be well managed to ensure the maximum benefit from the resources available.'

The Institute has found that over 10 per cent of the working population are in managerial roles in Great Britain and this proportion is growing as more people are required to manage other people, physical resources, financial resources and information, ideas and knowledge. As compared with other industrial countries, such as France, Germany, Japan and the USA, the UK was found to have limited systems for management development and these countries were thought to have superior methods which matched their educational patterns and their particular culture.

The largest companies, such as Shell and ICI, have recognised the need for management development for a long time, but there remains a difference between the demand for management development by employers and the demand by individuals. From the employers' point of view, their interest is in managers obtaining skills rather than qualifications. Some employers have been found to be opposed to qualifications because they made managers potentially more mobile. Individuals, on the other hand, want to obtain qualifications as well as skills in order to build up their curriculum vitae and to increase their opportunities in the job market. Employers have tended to emphasise job experience and innate ability as the most important factors contributing to creating an effective manager, although training would help. Education and management training has also been recognised to play an important part in broadening a manager's perspective, especially in a situation in which many managers obtain much of their experience within a single function. They may be experts in managing areas of production, or sales or finance, but may have very little knowledge across these functional borders. This not only limits the number of potential senior managers with a width of experience, but can also encourage a blinkered perspective amongst managers, so that, for example, they know about production but little about the finances that provide investment and facilities.

The idea that management might become a 'profession' similar to medicine or the law has been floated at times without much support from major companies. The possibility that their managers could accumulate qualifications which might not be closely related to their actual work has sometimes been felt to be a distraction from their main occupation, so that while MBAs and other management qualifications have expanded in availability and in the number of managers obtaining them, they are often studied as a result of individual initiative rather than organisational support. In support of the Charter Group Initiative in the 1980s and 1990s, the President of the Board of Trade threw out a challenge to companies:

> *'I want to find one hundred leading companies to start the crusade. And then one hundred more. Give us the benefit of your experience. I would like Chief Executives to make the following pledge: that their company recognises the professionalism and enterprise of their managers at all levels as a key to their business success. That they will develop the talents of their managers as an essential part of their business strategy.'*

In practice, a survey of 258 chief executives, carried out for the *Sunday Times* (Smith, 1997), found that British managers did not have the skills to obtain the full potential from their businesses. This survey suggested that they lacked the vision and were too concerned with cost-cutting to build their businesses. The majority of the chief executives thought that the business, social and economic environment in Great Britain had created a culture in which cost-cutting was the driving force for managers instead of the development of the skills to manage growth and innovation. They believed that leadership and a strategic vision were by far the most important skills, while, in practice, managers were better versed in technical and financial skills.

Surveys have shown that employers tend to encourage their employees to undertake courses that do not lead to qualifications, but are directly related to their work, while individuals want 'portable credentials' which recognise not only formal management education and training, but also accumulated managerial experience. From 1995 onwards, when they were introduced, National Vocational Qualifications in management have assessed prior experience and learning and provided for progressive levels of qualifications. This process has drawn in business and professional qualifications in order to provide an assessment framework that enables both recognition and progression to take place.

Also in the 1990s there was the development of the government-supported National Education and Training Targets to provide both a focus on and objectives for foundation and lifetime learning targets. The White Paper 'Learning to Succeed' was followed by the establishment of the Learning and Skills Council in 2001 in order to encourage lifelong learning and the development of a highly skilled labour force in the UK. This was a further development in the lifelong learning initiative introduced in 1998 in an attempt to develop a 'learning society' and to encourage 'learning organisations'. It can be argued that management development has always reflected the needs of organisations rather than those of individuals. Past theories about management, such as scientific management and administrative management, were based on what were perceived to be the needs of the time.

Some views about organisational theory have taken the long view that people were equipped for one way of life through most of human evolution and relatively recently have had to try to adapt to another way of life. The idea of the 'hunter-gatherer' that was predominant over millions of years has given way to city-dwelling organisation people over the last few hundred years. This has led to a collision directly between people's natural instincts and a rational business model and, as a result, there are leadership failures, strategic errors and discriminatory practices. The question then arises of how far it is possible to manage with the grain of human nature rather than against it, especially by exploiting the opportunities offered by the innovations of the new economy. For example, power hierarchies and competition can be seen to be male-oriented developments, while in modern management what is required is teamwork, communication skills and problem-solving. Leadership is linked to rewards and may be the only way of obtaining status and recognition, so that managers may have these motivations rather than a desire to have responsibility for people. As organisations become more flexible, what is required is the emergence of leaders who really want to manage other people, rather than management decision making confused by over-confidence in the ability to control complex situations in the face of uncertainty and difficulty, because this may result in unreasonable risk-taking leading to ill-considered strategic decisions (Nicholson, 2000).

The various theories of management have been particularly important since the Industrial Revolution because this produced the need for a systematic approach to management as a result of the development of new machinery and the concentration of great quantities of raw materials and large numbers of workers in one place. Workshops and then factories produced goods in large quantities which had to be distributed widely, while the move from a self-sufficient economy to one based on the division of labour created a need for organisation and control. The development of economic theories based on the factors of production developed by Adam Smith in *The Wealth of Nations* (1776) emphasised the relationship between separate elements in the production of goods and services.

Management as a science

The science of management is based today on the view that 'what can't be measured isn't worth doing'. This is a view supported by Professor Sir Roland Smith, but even this apparently 'up-to-date' theory has been described by John Harvey-Jones as out of date (*see* Chapter 1). This is partly because of the echoes thrown forward from the 1960s when there was a management view that everything could be measured and that success would follow improvements in systems of measurement, particularly accountancy. The modern version of this theory has been greatly encouraged by developments in information technology which has vastly increased the potential for measurement. Although all managers have to accept the need for business accounts and the application of statistics in making decisions, at the same time managers must consider the derivation and accuracy of the numbers presented to them. At times it may be sensible to override all the facts and figures that are available; for example, Sony produced the Walkman against the evidence of market research which suggested that the product would not be successful. This example does not invalidate market research, but puts it in its place as one of a number of factors in the management decision-making process.

→ Ch. 1

Managers have to operate in the situation in which they find themselves:

> *'The difficulty is that there can never be any single correct solution to any management problem, or any all-embracing system which will carry one through a particular situation or period of time.'*
> (Harvey-Jones, 1993)

The fact is that over the years management styles and fashions change and business environments alter. As a subject of study and analysis management can be seen as a mongrel form of social science, borrowing as necessary from other social sciences, and because it is concerned with people and their behaviour there is an element of unpredictability about the whole process.

Scientific management developed at the end of the nineteenth century when skilled workers were in short supply in the USA, and in order to meet demand, productivity needed to be expanded by increasing the efficiency of the workers who were available. In order to do this, Frederick W Taylor (1856–1915) developed a body of principles which came to be known as 'Taylorism'. He based his managerial system on production-line time studies. He analysed each job by breaking it down into its component parts and then designed the quickest and best methods of operation for each part. By doing this he was able to establish how much workers should be able to do with the equipment and materials available, and how far pay could be related to levels of productivity.

This process developed into a 'differential rate system' based on greater pay for greater productivity which in turn, it was argued, would lead to greater profits. The higher payments would continue, Taylor thought, because they were 'scientifically correct' rates set at a level that was best for the company and the worker. Increased profits would encourage companies to expand and ensure continued employment for those workers able to meet the required productivity standards. Those who did not meet these standards would easily find work, in his opinion, because of the shortage of skilled workers. This process is what might be referred to now as a form of performance-related pay, and it is interesting to note that Taylor decided to put his ideas into effect as a private consultant as early as 1893.

One well-documented example of his work as a consultant management engineer was with the Simonds Rolling Machine Company. In one operation, 120 women inspected bicycle ball-bearings. Taylor's approach was to study and time the movements of the best workers; he then trained the rest of the workers in the methods of their more effective colleagues and transferred or laid off the poorest performers. He introduced rest periods during the working day and a differential pay rate system. The results were increases in productivity, quality, earnings and morale and a fall in costs (*see* Exhibit 20.3).

The problem with Taylor's approach was that it did lead to lay-offs, and there was the fear that increased productivity would mean that the available work would be completed even sooner, causing more lay-offs. By 1912 opposition to Taylorism led to strikes and to hostile members of Congress asking for explanations of his ideas and methods. Taylor stated that his philosophy rested on a few basic principles:

- **The development of a true science of management, so that the best method for performing each task could be determined**
- **The scientific selection of workers so that each worker would be given responsibility for the task for which he or she was best suited**

Exhibit 20.3 **The Taylor process**

- **Monitor, study, time the best workers**
- **Train the other workers to the same standard**
- **Introduce changes such as differential pay rates in order to increase productivity**

■ **The scientific education and development of the worker**

■ **Intimate, friendly co-operation between management and labourer.**

Taylor's views are summarised in his book *Scientific Management* (1947). He believed that for these principles to succeed there needed to be a change in working attitudes and practices, 'a complete mental revolution' on the part of management and employees. He felt that the concentration of effort should not be on profit, but that both management and labour should concentrate on increased production, which he believed would mean that profits would rise to an extent where management and labour would no longer have to compete for them.

This need for change was at the heart of the problem with the Taylor approach, because changing attitudes is notoriously harder than changing practices; although the new technology was adopted by management, Taylor's philosophy was not. Increases in productivity in fact often led to lay-offs or changes in pay rates that left workers producing more output for the same income. The proponents of scientific management did not sufficiently take into account the actual needs of people at work. They assumed that the prime motivation for work was pay, and that provided there was an increase in their pay workers would be happy. In fact, modern views suggest that workers wanted then, as they do now, to have satisfaction in their work, to have good working conditions and to feel they have a say in matters which directly affect them. As summarised in Table 20.1, modern management practices are based on consulting people and giving them responsibility for their work, while scientific management was based on telling people how to increase their earnings, training them and then expecting them to go ahead and do it.

Contributors to scientific management extended Taylor's work. For example, Henry L Gantt (1861–1919) reconsidered and developed his incentive system and produced the 'Gantt' chart to record a worker's progress. Frank B Gilbreth (1868–1925) extended Taylor's research on time and motion problems, and his wife Lillian M Gilbreth (1878–1972) focused on the scientific selection, training and placing of employees to provide the precursor to present-day human resource management. Lillian Gilbreth, in particular, developed as well as extended scientific management. However, the basic theory remained the concept of the division of labour and the belief that, by specialising in certain tasks, a team of people can out-produce the same number of people each performing all the tasks. The highly productive modern assembly line is a direct descendant of these ideas. The ideas of

Table 20.1 'Taylorism'

ARGUMENTS FOR:	PROBLEMS WITH:
Use of technology	Attitudes
Productivity increases	Lay-offs
Motivation: pay	Motivation: satisfaction, working conditions, control
Telling employees	Consulting employees
Long-term benefits	Focus on work design Training

efficiency propounded by scientific management, such as time and motion studies, promoted awareness of the equipment and physical movement involved in a task, while the emphasis on the training of workers recognised the importance of ability and its development in increasing productivity. The focus on work design has encouraged managers to have a fresh look at the way a job is done and has pointed the way towards the idea of the professional manager.

Administrative management

Of course, Frederick Taylor was concerned largely with the detail of organisational functions and how they could be managed to provide benefits for the whole company. Other contemporary ideas were based on the whole organisation and the influence of the management of this on company functions and effectiveness.

In classical organisation theory it was believed that managerial practice fell into certain patterns that could be identified and analysed. Henri Fayol (1841–1925), for example, was a contemporary of Taylor, but was interested in the management of large groups of people rather than organisational functions. Fayol believed that 'with scientific forecasting and proper methods of management, satisfactory results were inevitable'. He insisted that management was a skill like any other so that managers were not born, but made. Once the underlying principles were understood and a general theory of management formulated, management could be taught. This was a major change in views of leadership as well as management and forms the basis of many modern attitudes.

Fayol divided business operations into units which he described as technical, commercial, financial, security, accounting and managerial, all of which were closely dependent on one another. His primary focus was on the management of the operational areas which he defined in terms of five functions:

- **planning** – a course of action for the organisation to meet its goals;
- **organising** – to ensure the availability and co-ordination of the material and human resources of the organisation to put the plans into effect;
- **commanding** – to provide direction to employees;
- **co-ordinating** – to ensure that the resources and activities of the organisation work together to achieve the desired goals;
- **controlling** – to monitor the plans and ensure they are being achieved.

Compared with Taylor, Fayol had a comprehensive view of management very similar to modern ideas. This comprehensive view was being developed at much the same time by Max Weber (1864–1920) in Germany. His ideas were based on the structure of the organisation, or the 'bureaucracy', which was characterised by:

- **a clear definition of authority and responsibility**
- **a chain of command**
- **selection based on qualifications, training and examination**
- **appointed officials working for fixed salaries**
- **strict rules, disciplines and controls.**

Weber wanted to depersonalise management in order to promote a uniformity which would provide for the fair and equal treatment of all workers. His 'bureaucracy' was designed to provide stability and certainty in an organisation and his model of management has contributed to organisational thinking over the last 100 years, particularly in large national and multinational companies.

The Hawthorne effect

In the late 1920s and early 1930s, American researchers such as Elton Mayo (1880–1949) emphasised the concept of 'social man' to complement the classical concept of 'rational man'. Although it was recognised that personal economic needs remained an important source of motivation, it was emphasised that social needs, such as job satisfaction and work group pressures, were also very important. These social factors placed a heavy emphasis on management style, on how managers operated as well as what they did. Elton Mayo was involved in the famous 'Hawthorne experiments' which were an important study in human behaviour at work and are still influential today. They were a series of experiments carried out mainly at Weston Electric's Hawthorne plant near Chicago. The early studies were carried out by company engineers in collaboration with the National Academy of Sciences, with problems posed by this initial research then investigated by a team of researchers led by Elton Mayo, F J Roethlisberger and W J Dickson of Harvard in the period between 1927 and 1932.

The research was to examine the effects of changes in lighting on the productivity of workers. These were divided into two groups so that the control group could be exposed to a consistently well-lit workplace, while the experimental group worked under varied lighting conditions. The results of the experiment were ambiguous because although the productivity improved when the test group's lighting conditions were improved, the increases were erratic. There was also a tendency for productivity to continue to increase when lighting conditions were made worse. To add to the confusion, the control group's productivity also rose as the test group's lighting conditions were changed, even though there was no change in their lighting. Similar results were achieved in a new set of experiments which varied wages, rest periods and the length of working days and weeks for the test group. Mayo and his associates decided that financial and other incentives and changes were not causing productivity improvements. They believed that a complex chain of attitudes was involved in the productivity increases, with the main factor arising from the situation that the groups had been singled out for special attention, so that a group pride developed which motivated them to better performance (*see also* Chapter 12).

→ Ch. 12

The phenomenon known as the 'Hawthorne effect' suggests that employees work harder when they believe management is concerned about their welfare and when managers pay special attention to them. It was also concluded that the social environment of workers and their informal work groups had a positive influence on productivity. Many employees found their work dull and meaningless, but their social links with co-workers imparted some meaning to their working lives. This reinforced Mayo's concept of the 'social man' motivated by social needs and responding more to work group pressures than to management control. The Hawthorne experiments have exerted a profound influence on the way managers approach their jobs in that they have focused attention on the development of people-management skills. In terms of motivation, follow-up experiments only served to illustrate the complexity of the issue. Attention is now given to working conditions and to motivation, and while the experiments did not solve any problems, they did highlight relatively neglected areas where management could have an important influence.

Behavioural theory: the organisation of people

Some of the classical theories of management appear inappropriate for consideration today, but they developed when organisations were relatively stable and existed in relatively predictable environments. As working situations have changed and become more unsettled, classical theories have become less relevant but have still left their mark on management thinking. The administrative approach shifted the emphasis of management thought towards considering the organisation as a whole. This was followed by more people-oriented ideas and a human relations approach which is more in tune with present-day ideas on styles of management.

Early contributors to this included Mary Parker Follett (1868–1933), who asserted that the hierarchical distinction between managers and subordinates was artificial and obscured a natural partnership between labour and management. In her view they shared a common purpose as members of the same organisation, and she stressed the interdependence among their activities and functions. She considered that leadership should not be based on authority but on the superior knowledge and ability of the manager.

Other managers, such as Chester I Barnard (1886–1961), carried these ideas further. He became president of New Jersey Bell in 1927 and through his experience as a manager and his reading he developed the view that an organisation could operate efficiently only when its goals and the aims of the individuals working for it were kept in balance. He put an emphasis on both the individual worker as the strategic factor in organisations and the importance of individuals working in groups. This was a clear statement of the behavioural view that 'the organisation is people'.

While management theories and styles have altered over the years, the basic management problems have remained the same. One of these is to increase productivity in order to increase output and to compete successfully. The scientific management approach was to consider this mainly as an engineering problem, while the behavioural management approach considered it to be concerned more with people. The latter rediscovered the views of Robert Owen who in the early 1800s managed several cotton mills in New Lanark in Scotland. In the new factories that had developed as a result of the Industrial Revolution, working conditions for employees were very poor and Owen saw the manager's role as one of reform. He built better housing for his workers, opened schools for their children and reduced the number of hours in the standard working day. He believed that by improving conditions there would be increased productivity and profits, so that while other managers concentrated on technical improvements he stressed that the manager's best investment was in the workers. In fact, his methods did work in that his factories were profitable, but it took a long time for people to apply these ideas more generally.

Responsive management

In order to create more responsive organisations, many companies have shed management layers and created a 'flat' or 'flatter' organisation. The objective has been to create a leaner, more flexible organisation which could cope with the challenges of change and increased competition. These changes have brought new problems, with companies feeling that they face a range of increasing challenges:

■ **the rate of change is speeding up**
■ **customers are becoming more demanding**

■ **more markets are becoming global**

■ **environmental and social pressures are increasing.**

Many companies have been turning to the flat organisation as an alternative to the conventional hierarchical structure in an attempt to maximise the use of staff. The philosophy of the flat organisation is based on breaking down the tiers of the hierarchy and ensuring that more staff have a broader base of skills, eliminating the need for many specialisms. Rewards are based on outcomes and value added, rather than work.

The Institute of Management reports have revealed a gap between the perceptions which senior managers had of how their staff coped with the changes and the reality of those trying to implement them. Middle and junior managers felt that they were receiving conflicting signals, for example by being under pressure both to improve customer satisfaction and to achieve staff reductions and cost savings. At the same time, managers were being asked to do more with less. When a layer of management is taken out, previous workloads and responsibilities are often simply passed on to those who remain without a systematic reassessment of priorities and resources. It was found that extra training was seldom provided so that managers were expected to work harder without being equipped to work smarter.

At the same time, many organisations were found to be clinging to traditional boundaries and practices, despite the awareness of the need to change. For example, a survey showed that 90 per cent of managers agreed that issues and problems no longer correspond with traditional functional boundaries, while 73 per cent thought that functional specialists and departments must be maintained. There was a wide recognition that managers required new skills, although little help was provided for them to acquire these. In fact, 95 per cent of respondents agreed that 'managers need to be equipped with new skills', and 97 per cent 'that management development will become increasingly important'. Figure 20.2 shows the changes that managers thought were important to enable their organisations to respond better to challenges in the business environment.

In most areas managers believed that their organisations ought to have been doing more than they were in terms of teamwork, networking, flexibility and ensuring the interdependence of both functions and organisations. Only in creating slimmer and flatter organisations was there a view that the organisation might do a little less. At the same time, the qualities managers were felt to need supported and were complementary to these views. It was considered that future managers should possess:

■ **a broad perspective on the organisation's goals**

■ **flexibility**

■ **adaptability**

■ **the ability to communicate**

■ **an understanding of the business environment**

■ **a balanced perspective.**

Nine out of ten of the respondents believed that managers would need to be:

■ **able to assume greater responsibility**

■ **able to contribute to teams**

■ **aware of ethics and values**

■ **able to handle uncertainty and surprise.**

Figure 20.2 Changes which allow organisations to respond better to challenges in the business environment

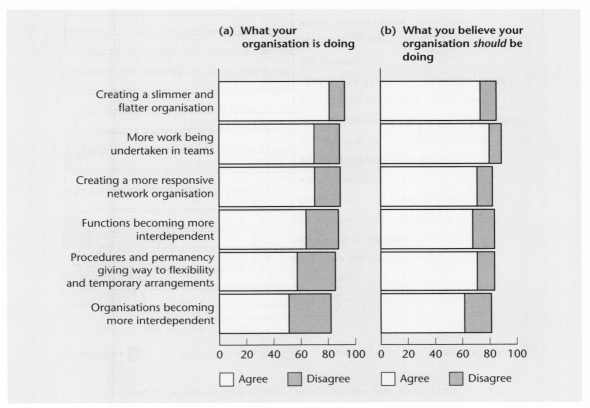

Source: Coulson and Coe (1991). Reproduced with permission of the Chartered Management Institute (formerly the Institute of Management).

As Figure 20.3 shows, there was strong agreement about the importance of qualities such as good communications skills, flexibility and adaptability, whereas tolerance of ambiguity and specialist expertise were felt to be less important.

The survey exposed contradictions in the views of respondents about flatter and leaner organisations. While most respondents thought that they should be moving to a flexible network organisation with a breaking down of functional barriers, only 10 per cent thought that the multi-skilling implied by this process was very important. While two-thirds of respondents felt that developing human potential was very important to managing change, only one-quarter were committed to ongoing learning as a very important management quality. In fact, it can be argued that what is required to promote success is a highly skilled and adaptable workforce, whose skills are continually updated in order to respond to the even faster pace of change.

Similar problems were exposed in terms of teamworking skills and the importance of vision and mission to an organisation. More work was seen to be in teams, but the ability to work in teams was seen as very important by only 36 per cent of respondents. More training and support were needed in this area, as they were in terms of vision and mission, where to be effective the mission had to be compelling, shared and realistic. As organisations flatten their hierarchical pyramids, the report identified that managers were not necessarily being equipped with the skills to work in the new managerial environment.

Figure 20.3 **Importance of particular management qualities**

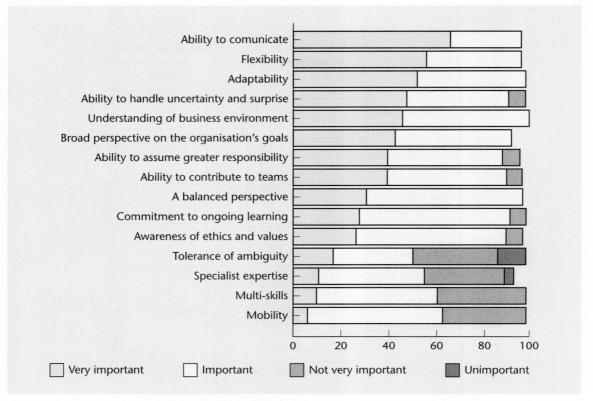

Source: Coulson and Coe (1991). Reproduced with permission of the Chartered Management Institute (formerly the Institute of Management).

MANAGEMENT IDEAS

Management ideas and techniques come in and out of fashion, and writers such as Pascale (1991) have agreed that management ideas have acquired the 'velocity of fads' in the post-1945 period. This has been attributed to the rise of so-called professional management, based on the premise that a set of generic concepts underpinned management everywhere. At the same time, there was the view that there were instant solutions to management problems and these have been packaged in the form of conferences and workshops, books and software offering a mass market of managerial techniques. In these there is the suggestion that a day spent on 'time management' will completely alter the ability of a manager to organise working time and improve productivity; the attendance at a conference on 'selling techniques' with 2000 other potential super salespeople will enable managers to sell 'ice-cream to Eskimos'; listening to cassette tapes and following the instructions of computer discs will increase 'brain power' sufficiently to enable managers greatly to increase their potential advancement.

> *'Today the bewildering array of fads pose more serious diversions and distractions from the complex task of running a company. Too many modern managers are like compulsive dieters, trying the latest craze for a few days, then moving relentlessly on.'*
> (Byrne, 1986)

The search for panaceas to management problems may arise from increasing competition or from individual needs. Competition may encourage the adoption of new ideas before they are well tested. Organisations may be forced by a fear of competition to experiment with a variety of solutions in order to obtain a competitive advantage. This is obviously likely to be particularly the case in periods of recession, but may occur at any time in a particular sector. The 'solutions' may be imitated quite widely and even institutionalised through government support. Support for quality management, for example, has moved through quality circles, team building, the Management Charter, Investors in People, benchmarking and so on.

Management programmes to do with people – 'putting people first', 'participatory management', 'customer service through staff development' – whether customers or employees, have been constantly replenished and refurbished. Peters and Waterman found that excellent companies changed service-incentive programmes at least once a year in order to keep them fresh. The companies did not expect their programmes to last long:

'No one device . . . even in the best institutions – is likely to be effective indefinitely.'
(Peters and Waterman, 1982)

Individuals may view a new idea as a method of enhancing their careers. A new idea needs a 'champion' who promotes its adoption within a company and this enables an individual to be a star. For a time the champion becomes an expert to whom other managers have to turn for understanding of the new technique or system. The introduction of a new technique can provide a defence against the accusation that management is not up to date and trying every available method of meeting competition. Also, new ideas may be seen as offering relatively quick solutions to different problems. As managers are promoted from their specialist function, they may look for 'quick-fix' ideas and techniques as a way of exerting an immediate influence.

The whole process can be seen as a superficial approach to deep-seated problems. While it may be sensible to look for up-to-date ideas as hooks on which to hang long-term solutions, it may not be sensible to believe that most problems can be easily solved. A study of the management of change shows that while people's behaviour may be altered fairly quickly, for a time at least, changing their attitudes will take much longer. For example, a customer-care programme can encourage employees to smile and to answer consumer questions promptly and positively, but if attitudes have not changed this may be a thin veneer which disappears once things begin to go wrong. This does not mean that the programme should not be introduced, but it does mean that it needs to be considered as a long-term programme.

'A review of the more popular "new" management ideas of the 1980s shows that many of them represent new wine in old bottles. The total number of bottles remain the same, but each is refilled with new contents.'   (Huczynski, 1993)

Huczynski argues that a management idea which addresses an individual's own needs is likely to have the greatest impact. This suggests that management ideas should be packaged on this basis. For example, quality management was popular in the 1980s, packaged in terms of the idea of quality circles because it integrated elements of group leadership, teamworking, problem solving, delegating and so on (*see* Table 20.2).

A further perspective on management ideas can be obtained by comparing short courses, such as those on time management, against MBA-type programmes. The former type of course may be perceived as too relevant, while the latter may be

Table 20.2 Management ideas classified by personal impact

INNER SELF	OUTER SELF	INTERPERSON	GROUP	ORGANISATION
Self-confidence	Rapid reading	Delegating Communicating		
Stress management	Writing skills	Appraising	Group leadership	Quality management
Learning styles	Assertiveness Problem solving Decision making Goal setting	Motivating Interpersonal skills Negotiating	Running meetings Team working	Searching for excellence Customer care Managing change

Most impact ⟵━━━━━━━━━━━━⟶ *Least impact*

Source: Based on Huczynski (1993). Reprinted with permission.

perceived as threatening because MBA-type programmes are based on research and the objective assessment of management performance. This could expose managerial weaknesses and undermine a manager's positive image. In practice, organisations which provide short courses often focus on individual managers and emphasise success in order to promote a feeling of well-being. The development of this positive feeling may be more important than the actual content of the course.

It can be argued that the whole search for management principles is not designed to maximise profit but to legitimise the manager's role. Mant (1979) argues that managerial literature went beyond the description and categorisation of management tasks and engaged in manufacturing:

> '*a mythology about executive work, sedulously nourished by the management consultants, business school professors and so on. Executives like the myth and are prepared to pay good money to have it reinforced.*'

The myth concerned rational, scientific decision making and relied on creating a theory of management which underpinned the practice of management. In fact, of course, there are a number of theories of management, some of which contradict each other. These can be summarised in a slightly different form which suggests that there are four main views of management (based on Watson, 1986):

- **Management as science** – successful managers are those who have learned the appropriate body of knowledge and have developed an ability to apply acquired skills and technique. This view has been supported by scientific management and classical administrative theory.

- **Management as art** – successful managers are those born with appropriate intuition, intelligence and personality which they develop through the practice of leadership. Leadership skill can be developed although not taught.

- **Management as politics** – successful managers are those who can work out the unwritten laws of life in the organisational jungle and are able to play the game so that they win. Managers are involved in power struggles and in competition for scarce resources with fellow managers.

■ **Management as magic** – successful managers are those who recognise that nobody really knows what is going on and who persuade others of their own powers by calling up the appropriate gods and by engaging in the expected rituals. Charismatic leadership can be seen in this context.

Experienced managers know that successfully playing the role may involve all four of these approaches. Intuition will play a part, as will information, persuasion, charisma and personality. Intelligence is important and communication as well as an understanding of other people, the games they play and their attitudes and prejudices. It helps to acquire skills in running meetings, in negotiating, in finance and personnel policies, and it is important to be aware of techniques of selling and marketing for creating popular products and services. Successful managers learn from successes and failures and never stop learning, and see themselves as serving others, supporting them as well as leading them in order to achieve certain objectives.

In an article in 1994 Sir Geoffrey Chandler argued that:

'Drivers have licences, doctors seven years' training and the Hippocratic Oath, businessmen the seat of their pants. And pants can be very successful. The history of business and industry is starred with self-made figures whose lack of formal education, abundant determination and acute intuition are part of the folklore.'

The article continues by pointing out that driving and medicine are of course dangerous to others, while business too can make or break the lives of individuals and communities. Yet, the UK tends to allow the management of business to be amateur without universal standards of competence and training. In France, Germany and Japan, on the other hand, there are much higher levels of qualification and training of both management and workforce. In the USA the belief in self-development has gone hand in hand with a belief in education as a route to success. The Wharton School of Business was founded in 1881, Harvard in 1908, while the London Business School opened in 1965.

'Just as a driving licence doesn't make a good driver, so an MBA doesn't make a good manager.'
(Sir Geoffrey Chandler, 1994)

In response to industrial and commercial globalisation, and competition from other countries, the 'lifelong learning' initiative was introduced in the UK in 1998 in another attempt to improve education and training. The objectives included the expansion of further and higher education numbers by half a million by the year 2002, launch of a University of Industry (UFI) by 1999 and establishment of Individual Learning Accounts. The ILAs have the aim of widening participation in education and training, while the UFI was designed as an open-all-hours one-stop shop for training based on a freephone service giving information and advice on a range of lifelong learning courses at convenient places near where people live. The UFI has been described as the first college to be built in cyberspace!

Analysis needs to be balanced by intuition and by an understanding of people. A manager does not need to have heard of Theory X and Theory Y to know that people respond better to persuasion and encouragement than coercion, but if a manager does not have this intuitive understanding, training in the theories of management and in the practical experiences of managers can lead to a rational understanding of the most successful methods.

With organisational restructuring, the career expectations of managers have changed dramatically. The connection between how well a manager performs and job security has been shaken. There has been a shift from managers being secure in their jobs if they did not make mistakes, to job security based on performance measurement, to losing a job irrespective of performance because of organisational requirements. In the past, middle managers in particular were reasonably paid, had job security and could expect a slow but steady rise in pay even if they had reached their career plateau. This is no longer the case. Faith in the orderly, single-company career path has been lost.

Managers have now to take control of their own careers to an extent unknown in the past. They have to become entrepreneurial about their own careers, and entrepreneurial managers have to create a product or service of value. Instead of seeing career development as moving up a hierarchy, entrepreneurial managers see progress in their careers as the territory grows below them, as the demand for their services grows, as their pay increases. These managers may become traditional entrepreneurs in developing their own business or modern entrepreneurs developing their own 'consultancy' based on their skills and ideas, but they all have to make sure that they obtain the training and experiences they need in order to remain 'employable' and 'in demand':

> *'Hereafter, the employee will assume full responsibility for his own career – for keeping his qualifications up-to-date, for getting himself moved to the next position at the right time, for putting away funds for retirement, and, most daunting of all, for achieving job satisfaction. The company, while making no promises, will endeavour to provide a conducive environment, economic exigencies permitting.'*   (Kiechael, 1987)

In many cases, managers have been able to move out of companies and then be re-employed by them as independent advisers or consultants. These developments are threatening for many people but hold out considerable benefits for those managers able to take advantage of the situation. 'The future ain't what it used to be', and the economic environment, international competition and the global environment have all changed. The major challenge from a management perspective is to create a situation where managers welcome change and are in a position to take advantage of it.

MANAGEMENT CONCEPTS AND PRACTICES

In facing the challenges to management, **leadership** plays an essential part because it is through this quality that the strands of an organisation can be drawn together for a productive outcome. Leadership creates the climate of an organisation and affects its culture and it has been suggested that this is a result of 'emotional intelligence', that is the ability of leaders to manage themselves and their relationships with others efficiently. This is as a result of **self-awareness**, **self-management**, **social awareness** and **social skill**.

Self-awareness is felt to include emotional awareness, which is the ability of leaders to understand their emotions and to recognise the impact of them in work situations. It also includes a realistic self-evaluation of strengths and weaknesses and self-confidence. Self-management includes such matters as self-control, a consistent display of honesty and integrity, facing up to responsibilities, skill at adjusting to changing situations and overcoming obstacles, and a drive to meet internal standards of excellence and to seize opportunities. Social awareness includes empathy with other people and their feelings, taking an active interest in their concerns, while navigating the politics of working life and recognising the needs of customers. Social skills involve taking charge of situations, inspiring and persuading people, helping to develop others, listening and communicating, helping to resolve conflicts and competence at promoting co-operation and building teams.

Managers with a strong 'emotional intelligence' are able to provide leadership and meet the challenges presented by changing circumstances. Research into the appointment of company chief executives (Bennis and O'Toole, 2000) argues that many are appointed on the basis of their past record rather than on their leadership qualities. They may have had financial successes or have been excellent deputies, but if they are to lead an organisation they require other qualities. They need to inspire confidence, to be able to delegate, to develop leadership qualities in others, to energise others and to communicate well. Social awareness in a manager helps in the focus on customers and the understanding required in order to provide consumer benefits. Managers can help their organisations to recognise and seize opportunities by inspiring and supporting innovation. A marketing culture can be an integrating force in a company encouraging an outward-looking approach which builds on the skills and competencies of the organisation.

Strategic thinking and implementation promotes a sustainable competitive advantage by providing a structure which develops people and helps to produce a climate in the organisation which encourages quality and achievement. Human resource management can support these approaches underpinned by the financial strength of the organisation, the information flows and the production process. Management is not an exact science, but nor is it a complete mystery, and managers can develop and be developed so that they lead effectively. The goal is to create managers who can transform bold strategic, financial or organisational objectives into reality.

SUMMARY

- This chapter places management and careers in management in context. It discusses how far it is possible to see management as a transferable skill which can be applied with success to a variety of circumstances, so that a manager has the ability to manage any type of organisation.

- The career paths of managers can be viewed in different ways, but tend to follow a fairly distinct pattern from an exploratory stage through to retirement.

- In many countries the role of the manager has to a greater or lesser extent been affected by company re-engineering and the move to 'flatter organisations'.

- Management ideas can be considered in terms of organisational as well as personal needs, and the management role can be seen as constantly evolving in response to change.

Review and discussion questions

1 *Is it possible for a manager to manage any type of organisation successfully, or is it necessary to have knowledge and experience of the area to be managed?*

2 *What are the most important skills a manager requires?*

3 *Do management careers follow a pattern because of organisational, individual or other factors?*

4 *What qualities are required for managers to cope with the development of flatter organisations?*

5 *Are past theories of management of any assistance to managers in the twenty-first century?*

6 *Of what use are management ideas and concepts in the practice of management?*

CASE STUDY

Loss of faith in managers

When we asked 140 MBA students at the London Business School to describe their career ambitions, only six aspired to management positions in established corporations. Most hoped to derive professional satisfaction by constantly broadening and deepening their personal portfolio of skills, and by contributing to society in meaningful ways. As managers in established companies, they felt, they could neither develop personally nor contribute to social and economic progress.

It is easy for corporate executives to write these students off as arrogant or naïve. Easy but dangerous. Managers must confront the reality that the best and the brightest from other professional schools, universities and technical programmes are not joining established companies. This inability to attract and retain talented young people is only one symptom of a more profound challenge to managers of large corporations – society has lost faith in them.

The evidence of lost faith is overwhelming. Corporate executives fare poorly in polls of public trust. We admire football players for their multi-million pound contracts, but vilify managers who prosper from performance-based incentives. The best selling Dilbert series argues that management positions exist as places where the least competent employees can do the least harm.

This crisis of faith in management has serious implications, not only for business, but for society as a whole. Unless the tide is turned, firms will not replenish their management ranks with talented young people; executives will find themselves increasingly hemmed in by regulations designed to limit their influence; and managers will lose faith in themselves. These trends could hobble the large businesses that now represent society's main engine of economic progress.

From its beginnings in the nineteenth century, management has stood out as the ungainly stepchild among the professions. The goal of law is justice, the goal of medicine health. Management, in contrast, lacks a clear idea. Professionals in other fields may fall short of their lofty goals, but at least they have ideals to fall short of. Some argue that managers create wealth for society, but this goal too easily blurs into personal greed, so losing social legitimacy and inspirational power. Moreover, few managers of large companies are seen to be generating new economic value. In contrast to entrepreneurs who are lionised for creating wealth and institutions *de novo*, managers of ongoing concerns are viewed as mere rentiers, living off their companies' past legacy like dissolute heirs squandering the family fortune.

Bill Gates becomes a cult hero by creating Microsoft, while Michael Eisner wins at best grudging recognition for transforming Disney from a tired theme park in the US to a global creative power-house. The spate of recent restructuring, layoffs and divestment has further eroded confidence in managers. Through repeated bouts of restructuring many managers have elevated efficiency to the corporation's highest goal. While they are a necessary means, operational efficiencies rarely succeed as a goal to attract, impassion and retain motivated employees.

Moreover, employees in contracting companies see few attractive opportunities for professional development. Nor, in an age of layoffs and downsizing, do employees trust companies to manage their careers for them.

The first step in reversing this growing crisis of faith is to recognise that corporations and their managers act as the primary engine of social and economic progress. Progress requires innovative combinations of resources, technologies and knowledge to create new products and services. Innovation requires human will and creativity to impose change on the world. While individual entrepreneurs often provide the initial creative spark, large organisations are generally necessary to stoke the flame. Apple computers started in a garage, but the Macintosh was produced by an established company, as were the Walkman, synthetic fabrics and AZT. Placing societal progress at the heart of the company's vision and purpose is not a public relations gimmick. Rather the ideal of progress underpins the success of the companies we most admire. The precise vision of progress varies across companies, with different companies aspiring to change the world through technological innovation (Honda, Merck, Sony, 3M), social activism (The Body Shop, Ben & Jerry's) and empowering the underdog (Mary Kay Cosmetics, Ikea, Wal-Mart). These visions of progress infuse organisations with a sense of purpose that allows them to attract, motivate and retain committed employees.

Inertia is the enemy of progress. Past insights ossify into clichés, processes lapse into routines and commitments become ties that bind companies to the same course of action. Perhaps the most vital and fulfilling element of a manager's job is to prevent inertia. To seize the promise of the future, managers must constantly overcome the burdens of the past.

A manager's role, therefore, is not to toil long and hard to make the inevitable happen. His or her job is to make happen what otherwise would not happen.

Source: *Financial Times*, 6 June 1997. Reprinted with permission.

REFERENCES AND FURTHER READING

Adair, John (1989) *Leaders*, Guildford: Talbot Adair Press.

Barnard, Chester (1938) *The Functions of the Executive*, Cambridge, MA: Harvard University Press.

Bartlett, Christopher A and Ghoshal, Sumartra (2000) 'Going Global, Lessons from Late Movers', *Harvard Business Review*, March/April.

Bennis, W and O'Toole, J (2000) 'Don't Hire the Wrong CEO', *Harvard Business Review*, May/June.

Byrne, J A (1986) 'Business Fads: What's In and What's Out', *Business Week*, 20 January.

Chandler, Sir Geoffrey (1994) 'The Business of Book-Learning', *Management Today*, November.

Confederation of British Industry (1992) *World Class Targets*, London: CBI.

Constable, J and McCormick, R (1987) *The Making of British Managers*, London: British Institute of Management and Confederation of British Industry.

Coulson, Colin and Coe, Trudy (1991) *The Flatter Organisation: Philosophy and Practice*, Corby: Institute of Management.

Drucker, Peter F (1998) *Managing in a Time of Great Change*, New York: Plume.

Fahey, Liam and Randall, Robert M (1998) *Learning from the Future: Competitive Foresight Scenarios*, New York: John Wiley.

Further Education Unit (1994) *Tackling Targets*, London: FEU.

Garvin, David A (1993) 'Building a Learning Organization', *Harvard Business Review*, July/August.

Hamel, Gary and Prahalad C K (1994) *Competing for the Future*, Boston, MA: Harvard Business School Press.

Handy, Charles (1987) *The Making of Managers*, London: Manpower Services Commission, National Economic Development Council, British Institute of Management.

Harvey-Jones, John (1993) *Managing to Survive*, London: Heinemann.

Hesselbein, F, Goldsmith, M and Beckhard, R F (2000) *The Organization of the Future*, San Francisco, CA: Jossey-Bass.

Huczynski, Andrzej A (1993) *Management Gurus*, London and New York: Routledge.

Imai Masaaki (1997) *Kaizen: The Key to Japan's Competitive Success*, Maidenhead: McGraw-Hill.

Kiechael III, Walter (1987) 'Your New Employment Contract', *Fortune*, 6 July.

Levinson, Daniel J, Darrow, Charlotte N, Klein, Edward B, Levinson, Maria H and McKee, Braxton (1978) *The Seasons of a Man's Life*, New York: Knopf.

Mant, Alistair (1979) *The Rise and Fall of the British Manager*, London: Pan.

Mayo, Elton (1953) *The Human Problems of an Industrial Civilization*, New York: Macmillan.

Mullin, Rick (1996) 'Knowledge Management: A Cultural Revolution', *Journal of Business Strategy*, September/October

Nicholson, Nigel (2000) *Managing the Human Animal*, London: Texere.

Nonaka, Ikujiro and Tegeuchi, Hirotaka (1995) *The Knowledge-Creating Company*, Oxford: Oxford University Press.

O'Dell, Carla and Grayson, C Jackson (1998) *If Only We Knew What We Know: The Transfer of Internal Knowledge and Best Practice*, New York: Free Press.

Parker Follett, Mary (1941) *Collected Works*, New York: Harper and Brothers.

Pascale, Richard Tanner (1991) *Managing on the Edge*, Harmondsworth: Penguin.

Peters, T and Waterman, R (1982) *In Search of Excellence*, New York: Harper & Row.

Pirie, Dr Madson (1994) *20-20 Vision: Targets for Britain's Future*, London: Adam Smith Institute.

Prahalad, C K and Hamel, Gary (1990) 'The Core Competence of the Corporation', *Harvard Business Review*, May/June.

Ringland, Gill (1998) *Scenario Planning: Managing for the Future*, New York: John Wiley.

Schlewder, Brenton (1990) 'How Bill Gates Keeps the Magic Going', *Fortune*, 18 June.

Schwartz, Peter (1996) *The Art of the Long View: Planning for the Future in an Uncertain World*, New York: Doubleday.

Senge, Peter M (1994) *The Fifth Discipline: The Art and Practice of the Learning Organization*, New York: Doubleday.

Smith, Adam (1776) *An Inquiry into the Nature and Causes of the Wealth of Nations*, London: A Strahn and T Caddell.

Smith, David (1997) 'Managers Lack Proper Skills', *Sunday Times*, 14 September.

Sumantra, Ghoshal and Sull, Donald (1997) *Financial Times*, 6 June.

Taylor, Frederick W (1947) *Scientific Management*, New York: Harper & Brothers.

Watson, T J (1986) *Management Organisation and Employment*, London: Routledge.

WEBSITES

http://www.inst-mgt.org.uk
The website of the Institute of Management, providing information about its services and publications.

http://www.ifslearning.com
Information about the *Financial World* publication.

GLOSSARY

Accruals Amounts which are owing at the year (period) end, e.g. vehicle repairs, or light and heating not yet paid for.

Activity-based costing Overheads are shared out according to cost drivers, a cost driver being the activity that causes a cost to be incurred.

Ansoff matrix An analysis to provide managers with an indication of the type of policy they should follow for new or existing products or services, with respect to market penetration, product development, market extension and diversification.

Appropriations (profit and loss account) Sharing out the net profit before tax between the stakeholders which are: taxation, dividends paid and proposed, transfers to reserves, and retained earnings.

Artificial intelligence Any form of information technology which attempts to emulate human behaviour, such as reasoning, communication or sensory perception.

Attitude survey A survey, usually conducted by questionnaire, to elicit employees' opinions about issues to do with their work and the organisation.

Audit The prevention and detection of errors and fraud, by using the verification of assets and liabilities, checking on the delegated authority, obtaining explanations, checking documents and systems of internal control, and reporting, e.g. the statutory Auditors' Report of a company.

Authorised share capital *See* Share capital.

Authoritarian management A management style which is task oriented and stresses the quality of the decision over the wishes of subordinates.

Balance sheet A statement of assets and liabilities extracted from an organisation's accounting records as at a particular moment in time.

Behavioural aspects of budgeting The way in which budgets affect people, e.g. in terms of motivation, the achievement of targets, participation etc.

Benchmarking An objective measure of performance, i.e. a measure which can be used for comparability purposes.

Boston matrix A classification of products or services into categories – stars, problem children, cash cows, dogs – to indicate performance and prospects with respect to market share and market growth rate. It can also be amended to illustrate the financial life cycle of a company.

Breakeven model A model for analysing costs and revenue associated with some decision problem. Breakeven in marginal costing takes place when the contribution is equal to the fixed costs.

Budget A plan expressed in money, showing expected future income, expenditure and the capital to be employed.

Budgetary control The establishment of budgets, and the frequent and continuous comparison of actual results with budget targets.

Business ethics A set of moral principles or values in business activity and business organisations, which interact with society and vary from organisation to organisation, country to country, over time, etc.

Capital budgets Budgets for the finance required for projects, expansion etc.

Capital expenditure The amount spent on fixed assets e.g. buildings and equipment.

Capital investment appraisal A review of capital projects using one or a number of methods, e.g. the payback method and the net present value method, but also taking into account other information.

Capital reserve *See* Reserves.

Capital structure The mix of financing which is used by companies, and which has an impact on gearing.

Cash budget Also known as a cash flow forecast, it attempts to predict what the cash and bank balances will be for a specific period, usually for between 3 and 12 months.

Cash cow A company's product or service that has a high market share and low market growth in a reasonably stable market (*see also* Boston matrix).

Cash flow statements The historic statement showing where the cash has come from and gone to over the financial period (do not confuse this with the cash budget/cash flow forecast).

Cause–effect diagram *See* Ishikawa diagram.

Chaos theory A situation in which broad patterns are predictable but detailed features within these broad patterns are completely unknown.

Charismatic leadership The style of leadership which relies on personal vision and energy to inspire followers.

Coercive power The power that results from the ability to punish people who do not behave as required.

Communications (in organisations) The provision and passing of information and instructions which enable an organisation to function efficiently and employees to be properly informed about developments. It covers information of all kinds, the channels along which it passes and the means of passing it. It also takes into account formal and informal mechanisms and processes that operate between employers, managers and employees.

Competitive advantage The significant advantages that an organisation possesses over its competitors, which allow an organisation to add more value than its rivals in the same market.

Competitive forces strategy A strategy of competitive advantage through differentiation, cost leadership or a combined strategy concentrated on a narrow target market, developed in the 1980s by Michael Porter, based on the idea of five competitive forces in an organisation's environment (threats from new market entrants and substitute products, bargaining power of buyers and suppliers, and rivalry among competitors).

Connection power The power that results from personal and professional access to key people.

Control chart A graph used to monitor whether a process is under control by showing the variation from the average level of performance.

Core competencies The distinctive group of skills and technologies that enables an organisation to provide particular benefits to customers and deliver competitive advantage.

Corporate social responsibility (CRS) Is concerned with business ethics, organisational values, corporate equity and equality.

Cost control systems Systems such as budgeting and standard costing which involve: setting targets, comparing them with the actual performance and reporting the variances to management.

Cost and management accounting The costing of products and services, and the provision of information for planning, control and decision-making purposes.

Cost of capital There are various ways of calculating this. It is made up of all the costs of the permanent and long-term capital, e.g. ordinary shares, retained earnings, debentures.

Cost of sales Sales revenue less the direct cost of the product or service. There are a number of possible combinations.

Country club management A management style based on a belief that the most important leadership activity is to secure the voluntary cooperation of group members in order to obtain high levels of productivity.

Creative accounting Using accounting concepts, policies etc. to paint a picture of the financial situation which is different from that which really exists; it may also be referred to as 'window dressing'.

Culture *See* Organisational culture.

Current assets Stocks of raw materials etc., debtors, prepayments, short-term investments, cash and bank balances shown in the balance sheet.

Current liabilities Debts due to be paid within the next 12 months, e.g. creditors, accruals, proposed dividends, taxation owing.

Current ratio The ratio of current assets to current liabilities.

Customer benefits Customers are not so much looking for particular products and services; they are looking for the benefits that these may be able to provide.

Customer pyramid An inverted pyramid hierarchy in which customers are at the top and management is at the base, management's role being to devolve power and decision making to self-managed teams at the point of production or customer service, with the aim of providing the best quality or service and gaining competitive advantage.

Customers Whoever receives benefits from an organisation's products and services.

Decision tree A diagram used to represent a decision-making situation. The diagram shows all the information relating to the situation: the alternative decisions that can be taken, the outcomes from each decision, the probabilities of each outcome and the financial consequences of each outcome.

Delayering The removal of layers of management and administration in an organisation's structure.

Delegation The act by which a person or group of persons possessing authority transfers part of that authority to a subordinate person or group.

Delphi technique A qualitative forecasting technique where panels of experts are asked their opinions of a new product/service, and then the average of these groups of opinions is used as a base for arriving at a judgement of the future of the product/service.

Departmentalisation The grouping of jobs, tasks, processes and resources into logical units for performance of an operation.

Depreciation Spreading the cost of a fixed asset such as machinery, fixtures and fittings over its useful life.

Directors' remuneration All the salaries, fees, bonuses, etc. due or paid to a company's directors for the period in question.

Directors' report Their report to shareholders in their company's annual published report and accounts.

Discounts receivable Discounts received from suppliers for prompt payment of their account.

Dividends A reward for shareholders for investing/risking their money in a company.

Division of work The breaking down of tasks into component parts so that individuals are responsible for an activity or limited set of activities instead of the whole task.

Downsizing Reducing the size of the workforce of an organisation without necessarily reducing the output.

Efficiency ratios These look at the way in which the assets are being managed including working capital management.

Emergent strategy A strategy where the financial objective is unclear and its elements develop as the strategy proceeds.

Empowerment The devolution of power and decision making to those lower down in the organisation.

Environmental audit A check on the environmental performance of an organisation and on the performance of the management system.

Equal opportunities Everybody should be treated equally in employment situations, whether they are men, women, married or single, of different ethnic or religious backgrounds, or different sexual orientations.

Expectancy theory Motivation is a function of the expectancy of reaching a certain outcome, multiplied by the value of the outcome for that person.

Expected value For a decision problem, the weighted average payoff or outcome. The weights are the probabilities associated with the outcomes.

Expert power The power that comes from the superior expertise that a leader has or is believed to have.

Expert systems An attempt to apply computer systems to support what people do in arriving at a solution to a problem.

Federal organisation This consists of a variety of individual organisations or groups of organisations allied together by a common approach and mutual interest, which can provide a way for relatively small organisations based on core workers to obtain the advantages of large companies.

Financial analysis Tends to use ratio analysis to compare financial performance internally and externally.

Financial management Looks in particular at financing decisions and investing decisions, and covers working capital management, the valuation of companies, dividend policy and take-overs and mergers etc.

Fishbone diagram *See* Ishikawa diagram.

Fixed assets Assets purchased to be used in the business and which are not intended for resale, e.g. freehold land and buildings, plant, machinery, equipment, fixtures and fittings, motor vehicles.

Flatter management This aims to reduce the layers of control and of approval, and veto over decision making, to speed up decision making and push the point of decision nearer to the point of action.

Forcefield analysis A technique to identify the 'forces' which apply to some change situation. Restraining forces are those likely to prevent the change from being implemented successfully. Driving forces are those that will help in pushing the change through.

Forcefield theory In any organisation there are forces for change and forces resisting change.

Four Cs model The effectiveness of outcomes to human resource management can be evaluated under four headings: commitment, competence, congruence and cost-effectiveness.

Four Ps *See 'P'.*

Gatekeepers A person or persons who is/are responsible for an important information junction, e.g. they can control the flow of information which reaches top management.

Gearing The proportion of debt (i.e. long-term liabilities and preference shares) to debt plus equity (equity being ordinary share capital plus reserves).

General reserve *See Reserves.*

Globalisation The process whereby an organisation's operations span the world and the strategic position of competitors in national markets is influenced by their overall global positions.

Goal-setting theory A theory of motivation that predicts the intensity and direction of effort on task performance. The theory argues that specific, difficult goals are better than vague or 'do your best' goals. Important moderating factors are feedback about progress towards goal achievement, and a person's commitment to achieving a goal.

Goods Tangible entities that are the output from the transformation process.

Gross profit This is the difference between the sales figure and the cost price of the sales, sometimes referred to as the 'mark-up' when expressed as a percentage of sales or cost.

Halo effect An assumption that because a candidate has a desirable characteristic (e.g. smart appearance) he or she must be equally good in all other areas.

Hawthorne effect Employees work harder when they believe management is concerned about their welfare and when managers pay special attention to them.

Headhunting Contacting and actively recruiting personnel from another organisation.

Hierarchy of relative prepotency The classification of human needs by motivating factors, as proposed in 1942 by Abraham Maslow, an American organisational psychologist.

Hierarchical pyramid The hierarchical pyramid positions the most numerous and, in management terms, the most junior people at the bottom of the pyramid and the least numerous, and most senior, people or items at the top.

Horizontal integration When an organisation acquires its competitors or forms a close association with another organisation at the same stage of production or in the same competitive area.

Human resource management Concerns the human side of enterprises and the factors that determine workers' relationships with their employing organisations.

Impoverished management This does not provide leadership in a positive sense but believes in a laissez-faire approach, relying on previous practice to keep the organisation going.

Individualism index A culture index by Geert Hofstede defined as the relationship between the individual and the group to which he or she belongs, or the preference for living and working in collectivist or individual ways.

Induction The process of introducing recruits to an organisation and explaining their role within it.

Information power The power that results from personal and professional access to key information.

Intelligent systems *See Artificial intelligence.*

Intended strategy A strategy consisting of a set of actions planned to achieve well-defined organisational goals.

Interest payments Payments to the providers of loans, debentures and overdrafts.

Internal rate of return The rate which gives a net present value equal to the initial investment, i.e. a net present value of nil.

Internet An international network of computer services providing a range of communication (such as e-mail) and information (such as the World Wide Web) systems.

Interviewing A conversation with a purpose.

Intranet An internal organisational version of the Internet protected by passwords and restricted to employees and customers. Parts of it may be limited to one group or another. It usually contains various communications to employees, such as the company strategy, vision and values as well as bulletins and other useful information. It can also contain interactive packages, training programmes, employee selection programmes and an internal e-mail facility. It is increasingly being used by organisations as a virtual meeting medium, replacing teleconferencing.

Investments Money lent by individuals or organisations to a company, usually as quoted or unquoted shares or loans.

Ishikawa diagram A brainstorming technique used to identify the factors contributing to, or causing, some quality or performance problem, often referred to as a 'fishbone' diagram because of the completed shape of the diagram.

Issued ordinary share capital *See* Share capital.

Japan Inc A team coined in response to the coherence and interrelatedness of Japan's economic effort.

Job satisfaction A psychological label that refers to a job holder's perceptions about, and satisfaction with, job-related characteristics such as pay and reward policies, promotion prospects, management styles, leadership behaviours, resource allocation, etc.

Joint consultative committee (JCC) A body made up of employee representatives and management, which meets regularly to discuss issues of common interest.

Just-in-time production A technique concerned with improving production efficiency and reducing waste, by minimising storage through careful planning and purchasing to meet the exact requirements of the customer, internal or external.

Just-in-time systems Systems that ensure stock is delivered from suppliers only when it is required so that stock is not stored and held in reserve.

Kaizen The process of continuous improvement in production.

***Kanban* production system** A system of production where containers hold stock for initiating production, so that the amount of stock in the system can be varied by altering the number of cards in the system. Thus, materials are pulled through the production process according to the demand for final assembly, rather than pushed through by an inflexible production plan. From the Japanese, *kanban*, meaning card.

***Keiretsu* groups** Broad-based Japanese conglomerates stemming from the activities of large and wealthy industrial families, and having a high degree of synergy as skills and resources are drawn from a wide pool of industrial and commercial activity.

Key success factors Those resources, skills and competencies of an organisation in an industry that are essential to deliver success in the market.

Knowledge management The retention, exploitation and sharing of knowledge in an organisation that will deliver sustainable advantage.

Leadership The process of motivating other people to act in particular ways in order to achieve specific goals.

Learning organisations Organisations skilled in continually seeking knowledge deficiencies, acquiring knowledge and modifying their behaviour to reflect this new knowledge.

Legitimate power The power that comes from the socially accepted duty for people to obey the leader.

Leverage The term used in the USA for 'gearing'.

Leveraging The exploitation by an organisation of its existing resources to their fullest extent.

Life-cycle analysis Products and services, after they are introduced, tend to pass through periods of growth, relative stability and then decline.

Liquidity ratios Ratios which look at a company's/organisation's ability to pay its debts as the debts become due.

Long-term debt Long-term loans and debentures (debentures are a special type of long-term loan, the holders being protected by a Deed of Trust).

Make-to-stock organisation An organisation that responds to a customer order before starting manufacture.

Management The process of planning, organising, leading and controlling people so that there is a productive outcome to work.

Management accounting The more modern pre-determined cost and management accounting systems such as budgeting and standard costing.

Management by objectives (MBO) Describes a set of procedures that begins with objective setting and continues through performance review.

Management by walking about (MBWA) Management by observation.

Management information systems (MIS) The information system which deals with the control of so-called 'routine', 'structured' or 'day-to-day' operations.

Marginal costing A system which separates fixed and variable costs. Only the variable costs – those that vary directly with the production of the product – are included in the product costs.

Market The group of actual or potential customers who are ready, willing and able to purchase a commodity or service.

Market extension This occurs when an offer is introduced into a market segment other than the one in which it is currently positioned.

Market penetration This involves either increasing sales to existing users or finding new customers in the same market.

Market positioning This is often seen in terms of market share as a precursor to profits (*see also* Positioning).

Market research The planned, systematic collection, collation and analysis of data designed to help the management of an organisation to reach decisions about its operation and to monitor the results of these decisions.

Market segmentation The identification of specific parts of a market and the development of different market offerings that will be attractive to these segments.

Marketing The management process responsible for identifying, anticipating and satisfying customer requirements profitably.

Marketing audit A formal review of everything that has affected or may affect the organisation's marketing environment, internal marketing system and specific marketing activities.

Marketing mix The appropriate combination, in particular circumstances, of product, price, place and promotion (and people, process and physical evidence).

Marketing orientation In which the marketing function is at the centre of the structures of an organisation, integrating the work of all the other functions.

Masculinity index A culture index by Geert Hofstede defined as pertaining to societies in which social gender roles are clearly distinct, i.e. men are supposed to be assertive, tough and focused on material success. Femininity pertains to societies in which women are supposed to be more modest, tender and concerned with the quality of life.

Maslow's hierarchy *See* Hierarchy of relative prepotency.

Materiality Whether or not an amount of income or expenditure is of a significant value, e.g. in making the decision to treat an item as revenue or capital expenditure in the accounts.

Maximax criterion A method of choosing between decision alternatives where the preferred decision is the one generating the maximum possible payoff.

Maximin criterion A method of choosing between decision alternatives where the preferred decision is the one that maximises the minimum payoff.

Middle-of-the-road management A style of management which believes in compromise, so that decisions are taken only if endorsed by subordinates.

Minimax regret criterion A method of choosing between decision alternatives where the preferred decision is the one that minimises the maximum regret.

Mission statement The encapsulation in a single short statement by an organisation giving the purpose of its activity.

Model A simplified representation of reality created for the purpose of explanation.

Net present value The present value of the cash flows less the initial cost of the investment/ project being evaluated.

Net profit before tax Gross profit, plus other income, less all expenses, including any adjustment to the provision for bad and doubtful debts, depreciation, interest payable (other than dividends) and directors' remuneration.

Networking Interacting for mutual benefit, usually on an informal basis, with individuals and groups internal and external to the organisation.

'O' (six) of markets Occupants, objects, occasions, organisations, objectives, operations.

Open and closed systems These reflect the extent to which an organisation interacts with its environment.

Operation A process, method or series of acts, especially of a practical nature.

Operations management The process of transforming an organisation's resources from one state, such as raw materials, to another, such as a finished product. Other definitions include: (a) the study of decision making in the operations function; (b) the management of a system that provides goods or services to or for a customer, and involves the design, planning and control of the system; (c) the business function that manages that part of a business that transforms raw materials and human inputs into goods and services of higher value.

Operations managers Those responsible for producing the supply of goods or services in the organisation. They make decisions regarding the operations function and the transformation processes used.

Ordinary shares *See* Share capital, ordinary shares.

Organisational behaviour modification Is used to improve work-related performance such as productivity quality and absenteeism.

Organisational culture The generally accepted beliefs and assumptions that have evolved over time and which represent the organisation's collective experience, also influenced by the wider cultural, political, economic and environmental context in which the organisation operates.

Organisational development A management-supported, long-term effort to improve an organisation.

Outsourcing The decision by an organisation to buy in products or services from outside, rather than supply them from within the organisation. The practice of handing over the management and operation of certain functions to a third party.

'P' (four or seven) in the marketing mix Product, price, place, promotion; and people, process and physical evidence.

Participatory theory of leadership The involvement of employees in solving organisational problems.

Particularism A cultural dimension which prevails in a culture where unique circumstances and relationships are more important considerations in determining what is right and good than abstract rules. It is the opposite cultural dimension to universalism (*see* Universalism)).

Path-goal theory of leadership Attempts to predict how different types of rewards and leadership styles affect the performance of subordinates.

Payback The time taken for an investment/project to repay its original cost.

Payoff table A table showing the payoffs, or outcomes, for a decision problem.

Peer group appraisal Work performance assessment by a colleague of equal occupational status to the employee being assessed.

Performance appraisal Establishes objectives for an individual or a group and judges performance on how well they have been achieved.

Performance management Systems designed to establish individual objectives which assist the achievement of corporate objectives and monitor progress on accomplishing them.

PERT (program evaluation review technique) Helps managers to schedule large-scale projects.

PESTLE factors The political, economic, social and technological aspects of an organisation's environment.

Place Where the final exchange takes place between the seller and the purchaser.

Positioning (organisational) Where the organisation sees itself and its products and services in the market.

Power distance index (PDI) A culture index by Geert Hofstede defined as the extent to which the less powerful members of institutions and organisations within a country expect and accept that power is distributed unequally.

Privateness The degree to which an organisation depends on direct charges to consumers and direct market dealing rather than taxed funds.

Productivity The most common measure of operations management performance, defined as the ratio of output to input: output means results achieved; input means resources consumed.

Products Tangible objects whose sale involves a change of ownership.

Product/service portfolio The products and services that an organisation decides to offer to customers.

Profit and loss account The account in which the profit or loss for the period is computed and shared out between the various stakeholders.

Profitability index The present value of the cash flows divided by the cost of the original investment.

Profitability ratios These look at the return on capital employed and the productivity of the capital employed.

Provision for bad and doubtful debts An amount which is charged in the profit and loss account and then deducted from debtors in the balance sheet to give debts recoverable a more realistic value.

Publicness How far an organisation is in the public sector, reflected by the degree to which it depends on taxed funds.

Quality An attribute of a product or service which ensures that it is attractive in the eyes of the customer.

Quality circle A group of people that meets regularly to identify and solve its own work-related problems and implement its own solutions with management approval.

QUEST analysis Quality in Every Single Task: everybody in an organisation is a 'customer' and 'supplier' and receives products and services from colleagues within the organisation.

Ratio analysis Used to assess and compare financial performance by companies. (*See also* Profitability ratios, Liquidity ratios, Efficiency ratios and Capital structure).

Re-engineering Instead of trying to improve co-ordination between departments organised into vertical functions, the organisation is structured into a collection of horizontal processes, each of which takes orders and delivers a product or a service.

Referent power The power that comes to someone who is a role model for others.

Regression analysis Designed to estimate one variable on the basis of one or more other variables.

Regret The loss due to not making the best decision.

Reserves Ploughed back profits which have been retained and reinvested in the business.

> **Capital reserve** Not available for distribution as dividend, e.g. share premium, revaluation reserve.

> **General reserve** Available for distribution as dividend.

Retained earnings The amount ploughed back into the business after the deduction of all other appropriations, e.g. taxation, dividends, transfers to general reserve.

Reward power The power that results from the ability to reward required behaviour.

Risk analysis The analysis of a situation where there are several possible outcomes and the probability of their occurrence is unknown; the uncertainty that arises when a particular action may lead to one of several outcomes.

Sampling A sample is anything less than a full survey of a 'population'.

Sampling variation Relates to the difference in results that might be expected by taking different samples of whatever is being measured.

SARAH The change process in terms of Shock, Anger, Rejection, Acceptance and Help.

Scientific management An analytic approach to problems of organisation emphasising the codification of routine tasks, based on the work of Frederick Winslow Taylor (*see also* Taylorism). He believed managers must accept full responsibility for planning, organising and supervising work, based on the reduction of people's tasks into rules, laws and formulae.

Self-fulfilling prophecy A prophecy where people believe that something will happen, they act on this view and their actions mean that it does happen.

Services Intangible processes that do not result in a change of ownership; intangible entities that are the output from the transformation process.

Seven Ps *See* 'P'.

Shamrock organisation A form of organisation composed of three interlocking leaves in the sense of three distinct groups of workers.

Share capital Consists of ordinary shares and preference shares:

> **Authorised share capital** The maximum number of shares that a company can issue.

> **Issued share capital** The number of shares which have been issued by a company.

> **Ordinary shares** The owners of these shares have voting rights and receive dividends.

> **Preference shares** Usually fixed interest and no voting rights.

Share premium account When shares become fully paid, this account represents the difference between the total amount received for the shares and the face (or par) value of those shares.

Six Os *See* 'O'.

SMART objectives Objectives which are Specific about what is to be accomplished, Measurable differences, Attainable target, Results oriented and Time limits established.

SOHO 'Small office, home office' market.

Span of management The number of people or units for whom a manager is responsible.

Spectacles Social, Political, Economic, Cultural, Technological, Aesthetic, Customers, Legal, Environmental and Sectoral factors in an organisation's environment.

Stakeholders People or groups who have an interest in an organisation, e.g. in the private sector the shareholders, the tax authorities, the directors, the employers, the providers of finance, the creditors etc., and in the public sector, the government, taxpayers, the 'public', employees and employers etc.

Standard costing A pre-determined system which uses standard quantities of labour, materials etc. at standard rates/prices, and compares these at regular intervals with actual performance.

States of nature Uncontrollable future events that determine the outcome of a decision.

Statistical process control (SPC) A technique for statistical monitoring of a process.

STEP factors Social, Technological, Economic and Political factors in an organisation's environment (*see also* Spectacles).

Strategic analysis The complexity arising out of ambiguous and non-routine situations with organisation-wide rather than operationally-specific implications.

Strategic business plan This outlines the process of allocating resources in an organisation in order to achieve its strategic objectives.

Strategic change The implementation of new strategies that involve substantive changes beyond the normal routines of the organisation.

Strategic decisions These decisions are concerned with achieving an advantage for an organisation in the long term.

Strategic drift When the actual strategy of an organisation drifts further and further away from the strategy needed for success.

Strategic fit The matching of the activities and resources of an organisation to the environment in which it operates.

Strategic leadership Motivating people to move in a particular direction in order to achieve particular objectives.

Strategic management The decisions and actions used to formulate and implement strategies that will provide a competitively superior fit between the organisation and its environment to enable it to achieve organisational objectives.

Strategic marketing This involves moving the organisation from its present position to a more competitive one where it has a competitive advantage.

Strategic plan Provides an idea of an organisation's overall direction, the way it is planning to develop if it is able to control matters, its overall purpose and objectives.

Strategic planning A formal planning system for the development and implementation of the strategies related to the mission and objectives of the organisation.

Strategy A sense of purpose, looking ahead, planning, positioning, fit, leverage and stretching.

STRETCH When resources are used in challenging ways to build up a number of core competencies.

Suggestion scheme Schemes whereby employees are encouraged to make suggestions or put forward ideas to improve workplace efficiency and organisational effectiveness. Many organisations that operate such schemes give rewards for the best suggestions.

Sustainable competitive advantage An advantage over competitors that cannot be easily eliminated.

SWOT analysis Highlights the internal Strengths and Weaknesses of an organisation from the customers' point of view as they relate to external Opportunities and Threats.

Synergy One plus one = three, e.g. joining two companies together could bring about greater efficiency.

Systems approach Managers should focus on the role that each part of an organisation plays in the whole organisation, rather than dealing separately with each part.

Taguchi method Helps to quantify the loss due to lack of quality of a performance characteristic, with the objective of identifying the real cause of the problem.

Taylorism The division of work into measurable parts so that standards of work performance can be defined (named after F W Taylor, 1856–1915).

Team briefing Regular meeting of groups of between four and 15 people based round a common production or service area. Meetings are usually led by a manager or supervisor and last for no more than 30 minutes, during which information is imparted, often with time left for questions from employees.

Team management A style where there is a belief that tasks need to be carefully explained and decisions agreed with subordinates to achieve a high level of commitment.

Teleconferencing A system whereby meetings, lectures, presentations and similar events are performed between individuals and groups in different geographical locations via television satellite links. Because of expense many organisations are turning to the Intranet for similar functions.

Theory X Managers who tend to believe that people have an inherent dislike of work, regarding it as necessary for survival and avoiding it whenever possible.

Theory Y Managers who believe that people see work as a natural phenomenon, that they accept responsibility and, in fact, seek it.

Three other Ps *See 'P'.*

Total absorption costing A costing system which charges all of the production overheads, and possibly other overheads, to the cost of the product/service.

Total quality management An intensive, long-term effort to transform all parts of the organisation in order to produce the best product and service possible to meet customer needs.

Tough-guy culture An organisation made up of individuals (entreprenuers) who are prepared to take high risks and quick feedback.

Trait theories Based on the personal characteristics of leaders.

Transactional leadership The leader determines what subordinates need to do in order to achieve their own and organisational objectives, and then classifies these requirements and helps subordinates to become confident of reaching their objectives.

Transformation process The activity that changes inputs into outputs. This is the most commonly used theoretical model of operations management.

Transformational leadership The leader, using his/her personal vision and energy, inspires people to do better than they would have expected by raising motivation and the importance of the value of people's tasks within the organisation.

Transformed resources The things that are themselves changed during the transformation process: normally classified into materials, information and customers.

Transforming resources The resources that act on the transformed resources to carry out the transformation process: normally classified into facilities and staff.

Treasury function The function responsible for investing surplus cash short term, e.g. for 24 hours or one week or one month.

Triple I organisation Based on Intelligence, Information and Ideas which form the intellectual capital represented by the core workers.

Uncertainty avoidance index (UAI) A culture index by Geert Hofstede defined as involving the creation of rules and structures to eliminate ambiguity in organisations, and support beliefs promising certainty and protecting conformity. This means that human beings try in various ways to avoid uncertainty in their lives by controlling their environment through rules and regulations.

Undistributed profits Those profits which have been ploughed back and reinvested in the business.

Universalism A cultural dimension whereby people believe that what is true and good can be discovered, defined and applied everywhere. It is the opposite cultural dimension to particularism (*see* Particularism).

Valence In expectancy theory of motivation, the perceived attractiveness or the value a person places on the rewards on offer for pursuing a particular course of action.

Variance analysis The frequent comparison of budgets and/or standards with actual performance, and the reporting of the variances to management.

Vertical integration The acquisition by an organisation of another that is further back in the stages of production or further forward (such as an organisation acquiring its raw material suppliers or its distributors).

Vision statement *See* Mission statement.

Window dressing *See* Creative accounting.

Working capital Current assets less current liabilities.

Works councils Committees made up either solely of workers or of joint representatives of workers, management and shareholders, which meet, usually at company level, to discuss a variety of issues relating to workforce matters and sometimes general, wider-ranging organisational issues. They are usually supported by legislation, which compels organisations to set them up.

X theory *See* Theory X.

Y theory *See* Theory Y.

Zero-based budgeting A system where managers are forced to justify and prioritise their requirements.

Zero defects An error-free approach to quality control, 'doing it right first time'.

INDEX